Dictionary of Literary Biography

Documentary Series

donald, edited by Matthew J. Bruccoli and Richard Layman (1989)

7 *Modern American Poets: James Dickey, Robert Frost, Marianne Moore*, edited by Karen L. Rood (1989)

8 *The Black Aesthetic Movement*, edited by Jeffrey Louis Decker (1991)

9 *American Writers of the Vietnam War: W. D. Ehrhart, Larry Heinemann, Tim O'Brien, Walter McDonald, John M.*

Del Vecchio, edited by Ronald Baughman (1991)

10 *The Bloomsbury Group*, edited by Edward L. Bishop (1992)

11 *American Proletarian Culture: The Twenties and The Thirties*, edited by Jon Christian Suggs (1993)

12 *Southern Women Writers: Flannery O'Connor, Katherine Anne Porter, Eudora Welty*, edited by Mary Ann Wimsatt and Karen L. Rood (1994)

13 *The House of Scribner, 1846-1904*, edited by John Delaney (1996)

14 *Four Women Writers for Children, 1868-1918*, edited by Caroline C. Hunt (1996)

15 *American Expatriate Writers: Paris in the Twenties*, edited by Matthew J. Bruccoli and Robert W. Trogdon (1997)

16 *The House of Scribner, 1905-1930*, edited by John Delaney (1997)

Yearbooks

1980 edited by Karen L. Rood, Jean W. Ross, and Richard Ziegfeld (1981)

1981 edited by Karen L. Rood, Jean W. Ross, and Richard Ziegfeld (1982)

1982 edited by Richard Ziegfeld; associate editors: Jean W. Ross and Lynne C. Zeigler (1983)

1983 edited by Mary Bruccoli and Jean W. Ross; associate editor: Richard Ziegfeld (1984)

1984 edited by Jean W. Ross (1985)

1985 edited by Jean W. Ross (1986)

1986 edited by J. M. Brook (1987)

1987 edited by J. M. Brook (1988)

1988 edited by J. M. Brook (1989)

1989 edited by J. M. Brook (1990)

1990 edited by James W. Hipp (1991)

1991 edited by James W. Hipp (1992)

1992 edited by James W. Hipp (1993)

1993 edited by James W. Hipp, contributing editor George Garrett (1994)

1994 edited by James W. Hipp, contributing editor George Garrett (1995)

1995 edited by James W. Hipp, contributing editor George Garrett (1996)

1996 edited by Samuel W. Bruce and L. Kay Webster, contributing editor George Garrett (1997)

Concise Series

Concise Dictionary of American Literary Biography, 6 volumes (1988-1989): *The New Consciousness, 1941-1968; Colonization to the American Renaissance, 1640-1865; Realism, Naturalism, and Local Color, 1865-1917; The Twenties, 1917-1929; The Age of Maturity, 1929-1941; Broadening Views, 1968-1988.*

Concise Dictionary of British Literary Biography, 8 volumes (1991-1992): *Writers of the Middle Ages and Renaissance Before 1660; Writers of the Restoration and Eighteenth Century, 1660-1789; Writers of the Romantic Period, 1789-1832; Victorian Writers, 1832-1890; Late Victorian and Edwardian Writers, 1890-1914; Modern Writers, 1914-1945; Writers After World War II, 1945-1960; Contemporary Writers, 1960 to Present.*

American Literary Journalists, 1945–1995
1945–1995
First Series

American Literary Journalists, 1945–1995
First Series

Edited by
Arthur J. Kaul
University of Southern Mississippi

A Bruccoli Clark Layman Book
Gale Research
Detroit, Washington, D.C., London

Printed in the United States of America

Published simultaneously in the United Kingdom
by Gale Research International Limited
(An affiliated company of Gale Research)

The paper used in this publication meets the minimum requirements
of American National Standard for Information Sciences–Permanence
Paper for Printed Library Materials, ANSI Z39.48-1984. ∞ ™

Library of Congress Cataloging-in-Publication Data

American literary journalists, 1945–1995 / edited by Arthur J. Kaul.
    p. cm.–(Dictionary of literary biography; v. 185)
"A Bruccoli Clark Layman book."
Includes bibliographical references and index.
ISBN 0-7876-1119-0 (alk. paper)
1. American prose literature–20th century–Bio-bibliography–Dictionaries. 2. Journalism–United States–Bio-bibliography–Dictionaries. 3. Authors, American–20th century–Biography–Dictionaries. 4. Journalists–United States–Biography–Dictionaries. I. Kaul, Arthur J. (Arthur Jesse), 1945- .
II. Series.
PS369.A45 1998
818'.54090809–dc21
                                                                97-40240
                                                                CIP

10 9 8 7 6 5 4 3 2 1

Dedicated to the late Rev. Dr. Arthur O. Kaul, pastor and publicist, and the late Dr. James E. Murphy, mentor and scholar, who understood the art and power of language

Contents

Plan of the Series

. . . Almost the most prodigious asset of a country, and perhaps its most precious possession, is its native literary product — when that product is fine and noble and enduring.

Mark Twain*

The advisory board, the editors, and the publisher of the *Dictionary of Literary Biography* are joined in endorsing Mark Twain's declaration. The literature of a nation provides an inexhaustible resource of permanent worth. We intend to make literature and its creators better understood and more accessible to students and the reading public, while satisfying the standards of teachers and scholars.

To meet these requirements, *literary biography* has been construed in terms of the author's achievement. The most important thing about a writer is his writing. Accordingly, the entries in *DLB* are career biographies, tracing the development of the author's canon and the evolution of his reputation.

The purpose of *DLB* is not only to provide reliable information in a convenient format but also to place the figures in the larger perspective of literary history and to offer appraisals of their accomplishments by qualified scholars.

The publication plan for *DLB* resulted from two years of preparation. The project was proposed to Bruccoli Clark by Frederick C. Ruffner, president of the Gale Research Company, in November 1975. After specimen entries were prepared and typeset, an advisory board was formed to refine the entry format and develop the series rationale. In meetings held during 1976, the publisher, series editors, and advisory board approved the scheme for a comprehensive biographical dictionary of persons who contributed to North American literature. Editorial work on the first volume began in January 1977, and it was published in 1978. In order to make *DLB* more than a reference tool and to compile volumes that individually have claim to status as literary history, it was decided to organize volumes by

From an unpublished section of Mark Twain's autobiography, copyright by the Mark Twain Company

topic, period, or genre. Each of these freestanding volumes provides a biographical-bibliographical guide and overview for a particular area of literature. We are convinced that this organization—as opposed to a single alphabet method—constitutes a valuable innovation in the presentation of reference material. The volume plan necessarily requires many decisions for the placement and treatment of authors who might properly be included in two or three volumes. In some instances a major figure will be included in separate volumes, but with different entries emphasizing the aspect of his career appropriate to each volume. Ernest Hemingway, for example, is represented in *American Writers in Paris, 1920–1939* by an entry focusing on his expatriate apprenticeship; he is also in *American Novelists, 1910–1945* with an entry surveying his entire career, as well as in *American Short-Story Writers, 1910–1945, Second Series* with an entry concentrating on his short stories. Each volume includes a cumulative index of the subject authors and articles. Comprehensive indexes to the entire series are planned.

The series has been further augmented by the *DLB Yearbooks* (since 1981) which update published entries and add new entries to keep the *DLB* current with contemporary activity. There have also been *DLB Documentary Series* volumes which provide biographical and critical source materials for figures whose work is judged to have particular interest for students. One of these companion volumes is entirely devoted to Tennessee Williams.

We define literature as the *intellectual commerce of a nation:* not merely as belles lettres but as that ample and complex process by which ideas are generated, shaped, and transmitted. *DLB* entries are not limited to "creative writers" but extend to other figures who in their time and in their way influenced the mind of a people. Thus the series encompasses historians, journalists, publishers, book collectors, and screenwriters. By this means readers of *DLB* may be aided to perceive literature not as cult scripture in the keeping of intellectual high priests but firmly positioned at the center of a nation's life.

DLB includes the major writers appropriate to each volume and those standing in the ranks behind them. Scholarly and critical counsel has been sought in deciding which minor figures to include and how full their entries should be. Wherever possible, useful references are made to figures who do not warrant separate entries.

Each *DLB* volume has an expert volume editor responsible for planning the volume, selecting the figures for inclusion, and assigning the entries. Volume editors are also responsible for preparing, where appropriate, appendices surveying the major periodicals and literary and intellectual movements for their volumes, as well as lists of further readings. Work on the series as a whole is coordinated at the Bruccoli Clark Layman editorial center in Columbia, South Carolina, where the editorial staff is responsible for accuracy and utility of the published volumes.

One feature that distinguishes *DLB* is the illustration policy—its concern with the iconography of literature. Just as an author is influenced by his sur-roundings, so is the reader's understanding of the author enhanced by a knowledge of his environment. Therefore *DLB* volumes include not only drawings, paintings, and photographs of authors, often depicting them at various stages in their careers, but also illustrations of their families and places where they lived. Title pages are regularly reproduced in facsimile along with dust jackets for modern authors. The dust jackets are a special feature of *DLB* because they often document better than anything else the way in which an author's work was perceived in its own time. Specimens of the writers' manuscripts and letters are included when feasible.

Samuel Johnson rightly decreed that "The chief glory of every people arises from its authors." The purpose of the *Dictionary of Literary Biography* is to compile literary history in the surest way available to us—by accurate and comprehensive treatment of the lives and work of those who contributed to it.

The DLB Advisory Board

Introduction

On 6 August 1945 an atomic bomb obliterated the Japanese city of Hiroshima and forever altered human consciousness. A year later John Hersey's "Hiroshima" exploded in the pages of *The New Yorker,* launching the post–World War II era of literary journalism that began to flourish as a result of shifting critical and aesthetic sensibilities. In the ensuing half century this new genre gained practitioners, prestige, and prizes and may now be recognized as a defining achievement of late-twentieth-century American literature.

This volume of the *Dictionary of Literary Biography,* the first of two devoted to American literary journalists, focuses on thirty-six practitioners whose writings appeared from 1945 to 1995, including those who marched awkwardly and imprecisely under the 1960s banner of the New Journalism. In the past fifty years literary journalists and novelists-turned-journalists have produced masterful nonfiction writing of enduring aesthetic, cultural, and political significance; they have, in fact, reshaped the contours of contemporary American letters.

In the 1970s Tom Wolfe's youthful braggadocio promoted the notion that literary journalism would, as he predicted in *The New Journalism* (1973), "wipe out the novel as literature's main event." While reports of the novel's demise were exaggerated, literary journalism has unmistakably challenged fiction's privileged status in modern American literature. "In the last 15 years there has been a rather appalling decline in fiction," novelist Thomas Fleming lamented in *The New York Review of Books* (21 July 1968), "and a steady rise in the popularity and sales of nonfiction. . . . the man who can sell a dozen short stories a year is either a miracle worker or his name is John O'Hara." Indeed, the fact that John O'Hara introduced his stepson, C. D. B. Bryan, to *The New Yorker,* where Bryan began his career in literary journalism, symbolizes the generational shift that was producing a new literary genre.

For decades American mass-circulation magazines were a leading source for popular fiction. Then the spectacular rise of television in the 1950s challenged the narrative dominance of the national-circulation magazines, threatening their existence. Magazines either shifted gears into new editorial directions to recapture their shrinking readership or went out of business. The demise of *Collier's* in 1957 and of the venerable *Saturday Evening Post* in 1969 testified to the radical impact of television and the increasing displacement of fiction from magazines into the new medium of television.

Esquire magazine emerged as a paradigm of the mass-circulation periodical that successfully redefined its identity in order to reposition itself in the media marketplace. In the growing prosperity of the early postwar years it faced competition not only from television but also from the new magazines, including *Playboy* and its imitators, that competed for the attention of the swelling ranks of "baby boomers." Arnold Gingrich, editor of *Esquire* since the magazine's founding in 1933, recognized his distance from the emerging youth culture and recruited junior editors more attuned to the generation coming of age in the late 1950s and 1960s. The savvy founding editor, then in his late fifties, gave his young turks the freedom to redesign the magazine and its contents so that *Esquire* would appeal to the new and affluent youth culture.

These young editors at *Esquire* toned down the saucy pinup image that had defined the magazine since its inception, distancing it from the skin magazine rivals that imitated the well-established *Esquire* editorial formula and pushed it to salacious new depths. With a less risqué image and a renewed emphasis on youthful sophistication, *Esquire* began to capitalize on its traditional literary strengths. Younger contemporary fiction writers (for example, Philip Roth and J. D. Salinger) joined the magazine's already distinguished list from the earlier generation that included Ernest Hemingway and F. Scott Fitzgerald. In the 1960s groundbreaking examples of what came to be known as New Journalism filled the pages of *Esquire,* pushing the magazine in a distinctly new direction that helped elevate the new style of journalism to the literary status of fiction. Gay Talese's celebrity profiles of Joe Louis, Joshua Logan, and Frank Sinatra joined Tom Wolfe's reportage about custom cars, which was avidly read by California teens. By the end of the decade John Sacks and Michael Herr were providing *Esquire* with electrifying, fiercely realistic accounts of the Vietnam War.

Several other publications seized the opportunity to publish significant works of literary journalism in the 1960s and 1970s. *The New Yorker,* already renowned for publishing the literary journalism of Joseph Mitchell and John Hersey, began featuring such writers as Truman Capote and John McPhee. Under the editorship of a youthful Willie Morris, *Harper's* became a venue for the literary journalism of Norman Mailer. The Sunday magazine of the failed *New York Herald Tribune* became a model of the new independent city magazine that emerged in the 1960s, with *Esquire* editorial alumnus Clay Felker at the helm, giving Jimmy Breslin and Tom Wolfe another outlet. *Rolling Stone* publisher Jann Wenner expanded the scope of his narrowly focused rock music publication into the realm of youth politics by adding Joe Eszterhas and Hunter S. Thompson to the masthead.

Critics, scholars, and practitioners of literary journalism have grappled with ways to define this emerging form of expression that revitalized post–World War II American writing as it appeared primarily in magazines. In *The New Journalism* Tom Wolfe argues that four principal devices characterize the form: scene-by-scene construction that places characters in dramatic settings; extensive, fully developed, and realistic dialogue—not the snippets and sound bites of quotation found in conventional reportage; third-person point of view that gives readers the sense of being inside a character; and the deployment of symbolic details that disclose people's "status life." According to Wolfe, the use of these literary techniques produced a style of journalism that rivaled realistic fiction and allowed its reportage to "read like a novel." And besides, it was all true, based on the saturation reporting of real characters, events, places, and lifestyles.

Norman Sims broadened the repertoire of defining devices in *The Literary Journalists* (1984). Based on his interviews with writers who have achieved distinction as literary journalists, Sims extends the list of characteristics to include emphases on immersion reporting, accuracy and attention to detail, narrative voice, story structure, responsibility to sources, and symbolic representation. More recently, in *Literary Journalism* (1995), Sims adds the writers' "personal involvement with their materials" and "artistic creativity" to the list. Describing the form as "an innovative genre that is still developing," he cautions that "literary journalism resists narrow definitions."

The resistance of the genre to narrow definitions stems, in part, from its affinities to other literary forms stretching back to the personal essay of Michel de Montaigne in the late sixteenth century and the travel writing of James Boswell in the eighteenth century. With the literary history of reporting still to be written, the debate over the origins of the form remains contentiously unsettled. In his essay "Breakable Rules for Literary Journalists," published in *Literary Journalism,* Mark Kramer declares: "Literary journalism has established an encampment ringed by overlapping cousin-genres—travel writing, memoir, ethnographic and historical essays, some fiction and even ambiguous semi-fiction stemming from real events—all tempting fields just beyond rickety fences."

Nevertheless, literary journalism has matured to the point that it has developed its own set of conventions "to keep things square with readers," Kramer observes, with a prohibitive list of thou-shall-not commandments that includes no composite scenes, no misstated chronology, no invented quotes, and no attribution of thoughts to sources unless the sources have said they had had those very thoughts. "It is not accidental," observes Kramer, "that the rise of literary journalism has been accompanied by authors' nearly universal adherence to these conventions, which produce trustworthy, in-the-know texts and reliable company for readers."

The rise of literary journalism in the post–World War II era has also been accompanied by American culture's fascination with emotion, intimacy, and personality, a style of postmodern romanticism that counters the bureaucratic routines of everyday life and its muted corporate voices. Literary journalists often write with a subjective narrative voice that can be frank, humorous, informal, ironic, intimate, even apocalyptic and confessional. Indeed, "the defining mark of literary journalism is the personality of the writer," declares Kramer, "the individual and intimate voice of a whole candid person not representing, defending, or speaking on behalf of any institution, not a newspaper, corporation, government, ideology, field of study, chamber of commerce or travel destination. The genre's power is the strength of this voice."

The extensive debate and discourse about the defining aesthetic techniques of literary journalism has obscured the cultural and political dynamics of the genre. In "The Politics of the New Journalism," published in *Literary Journalism in the Twentieth Century* (1990), John J. Pauly argues that the New Journalism of the 1960s was a staging area where "vexing conflicts over cultural style" were condensed, intensified, and contested. "The very term *New Journalism* proved singularly effective at calling out opponents into symbolic combat," he writes, "for its old-new distinction joined, by chains of implication, several other contested oppositions—adult-child, objective-subjective, reason-emotion, fact-fiction, corporate-personal." The New Journalism published in *Esquire, Harper's, New York, The New Yorker,* and *Rolling Stone,* offered "a double dare to the establishments of Journalism and Literature," challenging the representational authority of both "Journalism's empire of facts" and "Literature's garden of imagination."

The conflict over cultural style, in terms of New Journalism, also represented generational conflicts bound up in the politics of youth. The New Journalists collected in Tom Wolfe's groundbreaking anthology were quite young, Pauly points out, ranging in age from twenty-one to forty-two in 1965, when Capote's self-styled "nonfiction novel" *In Cold Blood* set off a rancorous public debate about the blurring of conventional boundaries between fact and ficion, objectivity and subjectivity. As Pauly observes, "A whole generation of nonfiction writers came of age in the mid-1960s."

Many of the writers profiled in this volume of the *Dictionary of Literary Biography* represent the legacy of the tumultuous 1960s, and their narrative voices often speak the language of that decade's contested cultural terrain. Mailer's entire corpus of literary journalism may be read as an extended discourse on the politics of existential engagement with cultural identity. Bryan's *Friendly Fire* (1976) serves as a propaganda tract against the government's conduct of the Vietnam War; Herr's *Dispatches* (1973) contests the politics of America's collective memory of the Vietnam War. Hunter S. Thompson's *Fear and Loathing: On the Campaign Trail '72* (1973), a deliberate effort to mobilize the newly enfranchised eighteen-year-old youth vote to thwart Richard Nixon's reelection to the presidency, followed *Fear and Loathing in Las Vegas: A Savage Journey to the Heart of the American Dream* (1973), a chronicle of his generation's failure to seize the political and cultural moment of the 1960s to redeem the American Dream.

In the 1990s literary journalism has become so well established that scholars devote their careers to it and students study it in graduate seminars and writing workshops. Theses, dissertations, and books are written about its practitioners, practices, and themes. Literary journalists, meanwhile, have achieved a notoriety and status in the literary hierarchy hardly imaginable a half century ago, winning major journalism and literary prizes. Their books have earned huge royalties after weeks and even months on the nation's best-seller lists, with lucrative spin-offs into film and television.

A telling testimony to the power of literary journalism is its insinuation into newspaper feature writing in the past decade. Across the country newspaper editors in the 1990s called for renewed emphasis on compelling writing and storytelling that has an emotional impact on readers. Storytelling techniques that Tom Wolfe described two decades ago once earned him a reputation for being the "Great Satan of journalism schools." Today those techniques are taught in journalism feature-writing classes, and students are encouraged to emulate the works that successfully embrace them.

It is interesting to note that in recent years practitioners of literary journalism have teamed up with academics to produce anthologies and primers to further the cause and appreciation of the genre. For example, Mark Kramer wrote a set piece for Sims's second anthology, *Literary Journalism* (1995), and Talese wrote an autobiographical essay, "Origins of a Nonfiction Writer," for the collection he co-authored with Barbara Lounsberry, *The Literature of Reality* (1996).

Finally, it is hoped that in the growing literature devoted to the form, this volume of the *Dictionary of Literary Biography* will help to underscore the significant and remarkable place that literary journalism has achieved in American literature in the past fifty years.

–Arthur J. Kaul

Acknowledgments

This book was produced by Bruccoli Clark Layman, Inc. Karen L. Rood is senior editor for the *Dictionary of Literary Biography* series. Kenneth Graham was the in-house editor.

Administrative support was provided by Ann M. Cheschi and Brenda A. Gillie.

Bookkeeper is Joyce Fowler.

Copyediting supervisor is Jeff Miller. The copyediting staff includes Phyllis A. Avant, Patricia Coate, Christine Copeland, Thom Harman, and William L. Thomas Jr. Freelance copyeditor is Rebecca Mayo.

Editorial associate is L. Kay Webster.

Layout and graphics staff includes Marie L. Parker and Janet E. Hill.

Office manager is Kathy Lawler Merlette.

Photography editors are Margaret Meriwether and Paul Talbot. Photographic copy work was performed by Joseph M. Bruccoli.

Production manager is Samuel W. Bruce.

Software specialist is Marie L. Parker.

Systems manager is Chris Elmore.

Typesetting supervisor is Kathleen M. Flanagan. The typesetting staff includes Judith E. McCray, Pamela D. Norton, and Patricia Flanagan Salisbury. Freelance typesetters include Melody W. Clegg and Delores Plastow.

Walter W. Ross, Steven Gross, and Mark McEwan did library research. They were assisted by the following librarians at the Thomas Cooper Library of the University of South Carolina: Linda Holderfield and the interlibrary-loan staff; reference-department head Virginia Weathers; reference librarians Marilee Birchfield, Stefanie Buck, Stefanie DuBose, Rebecca Feind, Karen Joseph, Donna Lehman, Charlene Loope, Anthony McKissick, Jean Rhyne, and Kwamine Simpson; circulation-department head Caroline Taylor; and acquisitions-searching supervisor David Haggard.

Dictionary of Literary Biography® • Volume One Hundred Eighty-Five

American Literary Journalists, 1945–1995
First Series

Dictionary of Literary Biography

Roger Angell
(19 September 1920 –)

Howard Good
State University of New York at New Paltz

See also the Angell entry in *DLB 171: Twentieth-Century American Sportswriters.*

BOOKS: *The Stone Arbor and Other Stories* (Boston: Little, Brown, 1960);
A Day in the Life of Roger Angell (New York: Viking, 1970; revised edition, New York: Penguin, 1990);
The Summer Game (New York: Viking, 1972);
Five Seasons: A Baseball Companion (New York: Simon & Schuster, 1977);
Late Innings: A New Baseball Companion (New York: Simon & Schuster, 1982);
Season Ticket: A Baseball Companion (Boston: Houghton Mifflin, 1988);
Once More Around the Park: A Baseball Reader (New York: Ballantine, 1991).

OTHER: "Early Innings," in *Birth of a Fan,* edited by Ron Fimrite (New York: Macmillan, 1993; Oxford: Macmillan, 1993), pp. 1–25.

SELECTED PERIODICAL PUBLICATIONS–UNCOLLECTED: "Homeric Tales," *New Yorker* (27 May 1991);
"Early Innings," *New Yorker* (24 February 1992);
"Oh, What a Lovely War," *New Yorker* (22 November 1993);
"Hardball," *New Yorker* (17 October 1994);
"Called Strike," *New Yorker* (22 May 1995): 46–53;
"One Game's the Thing," *New Yorker* (27 November 1995);
"Conic Projection," *New Yorker* (27 May 1996);
"One for the Good Guys," *New Yorker* (25 November 1996).

Roger Angell (photograph by Janet Malcolm)

Roger Angell may be the best baseball writer of his era. For more than thirty years, and in five books, he has expressed a youthful enthusiasm for the American game in mature prose. He has managed to make rooting for the Los Angeles Dodgers or the Chicago White Sox or even the last-place New York Mets seem intellectually respectable. When not writing about baseball Angell is likely to be writing about other, more recognized arts. He recently published in *The New Yorker* an admiring profile of eighty-seven-year-old author-illustrator William Steig as well as a lyrical little essay on time and the river in Mark Twain's *Huckleberry Finn* (1885). But whatever the subject, his prose always possesses the hyperclarity of a ball game played under the lights. He might have been speaking of himself when he said in the Steig profile, "Good writers and painters . . . compliment their audiences by expecting only the best of them; the responding thrill of understanding is what art is all about."

Born in New York City on 19 September 1920, Angell is one of two children of Katharine Sergeant Angell, an editor at *The New Yorker,* and Ernest Angell, a Wall Street lawyer. After his parents divorced, he lived with his father, who regularly took him and his younger sister to the Polo Grounds and Yankee Stadium. Among his earliest baseball memories is seeing Babe Ruth and Lou Gehrig bop back-to-back home runs.

As Angell writes in *The New Yorker* in "Early Innings" (24 February 1992), the late 1920s to the mid 1930s were difficult times in the United States, which was suffering through the Great Depression, but great times for a young baseball fan in New York. Between them the Giants and Yankees won eight pennants in the 1930s and even played against each other in the World Series in 1936 and 1937. Angell followed it all in the sports pages of the four newspapers that arrived at his house every day. He read John Drebinger, James P. Dawson, Roscoe McGowen, and John Kieran in the *The New York Times;* Rud Rennie and Richard Vidmer in the *New York Herald Tribune;* Dan Daniel, Joe Williams, and Tom Meany in the *New York World Telegram;* and Frank Graham in the *New York Sun.* "I became an addicted reader at a precocious age," Angell told *Newsweek* in 1988. By the time he turned twelve, his favorite authors included Arthur Conan Doyle and Charles Dickens. However, if his style was influenced by anyone, it was E. B. White, the acclaimed essayist and children's author—and also Angell's stepfather. "[White] suffered when writing," Angell said, "but made it look easy."

Angell graduated from the Pomfret School in Connecticut in 1938 and from Harvard in 1942. He wrote for and edited an Air Force magazine in the Pacific Theater during World War II and *Holiday* magazine from 1947 to 1956. Since 1956 he has been a fiction editor and general contributor at *The New Yorker.*

In 1962 William Shawn, editor of *The New Yorker,* suggested that Angell try writing some sort of baseball piece. Shawn was not a baseball fan himself—Angell actually had to explain to him one day what a double play was—but that did not matter. Shawn had found the right combination of subject and writer. Angell visited the spring training camps in Florida and published "The Old Folks Behind Home" (April 1962) on his return from the "sun-warmed, sleepy exhibition celebrating the juvenescence of the year and the senescence of the fans." Thereafter, no baseball season was complete without his scouting reports.

All Angell's baseball books are collections of pieces that originally appeared in *The New Yorker. The Summer Game* (1972) covers nine seasons, 1962 to 1971, and was greeted with wild cheers, like a clutch hit or a spectacular running catch. "Page for page," Ted Solotaroff declared in *The New York Times Book Review,* "'The Summer Game' contains not only the classiest but also the most resourceful baseball writing I have ever read." Arthur Cooper of *Newsweek* called it a "splendid book" and added, "Roger Angell . . . writes the way someone named Angell should." Larry Merchant, a sportswriter for *The New York Post,* agreed. "Angell," he said, "is the clear-eyed poet laureate of baseball." It might be expected that long, detailed pieces on players, games, pennant races, and World Series of the 1960s and early 1970s would appear dated when read two and three decades later, but such an expectation would fail to reckon with two things: Angell's ecstatic prose and the special place of baseball in American culture. Perhaps baseball is no longer the "national pastime," but it still has a strong hold on America's affections. If anything, the years have enriched the value and interest of Angell's *The Summer Game.* Out of its pages rise legendary figures—Duke Snider, Sandy Koufax, Mickey Mantle, and Willie Mays—miraculously restored to the reader. Gil Hodges, big and strong as ever, steps to the plate. "The bat is held in the left hand while he fiddles with his eyelashes with his right hand, then settles his helmet, then tucks up his right pants leg, then sweeps the hand the full length of the bat, like a duelist wiping blood off a sword, and then at last he faces the pitcher," Angell writes in "The Old Folks Behind Home."

Baseball, the late Bill Veeck said, should be savored. Writing for *The New Yorker,* "a leisurely and most generous weekly magazine," Angell has been able to savor the sport, concentrating on aspects of the game that newspaper reporters generally have neither the time nor the space to explore. As Angell notes in the preface to *The Summer Game,* he has tried to give the "feel of things," to explain baseball as it happens to him, "at a distance and in retrospect." It happens to him humorously, . . . elegantly. In fact, "elegant" is

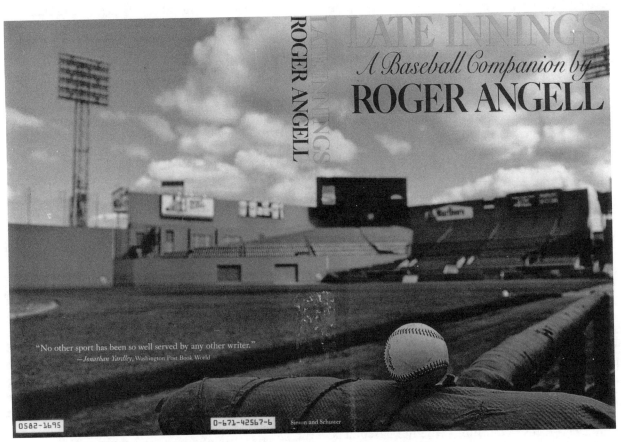

Dust jacket for Angell's third collection of baseball essays

his pet adjective for describing baseball, which may seem strange to anyone who has seen players caught on camera picking their noses. But Angell is able at times to report from an "interior stadium"—the title, incidentally, of a piece for which he won the E. P. Dutton Company's Best Sports Stories award in 1972—wherein the knickered ghosts of summers past appear in extraordinary combinations: "Ruth bats against Sandy Koufax or Sam McDowell . . . Hubbell pitches to Ted Williams, and the Kid, grinding the bat in his fist, twitches and blocks his hips with the pitch; he holds off but still follows the ball, leaning over and studying it like some curator as it leaps just under his hands."

Angell's readers are not typical baseball fans any more than he is a typical baseball writer. Sometimes he shares his reader mail, and it tends to come from a professor of Byzantine history, or a physicist at Cal Tech, or a medical journal editor, or a Greenwich Village art critic. "I was born in 1952," confides one correspondent, a woman graduate student. "I remember listening to the Yankees . . . on a little yellow transistor radio on an island in Lake Champlain, where we spent our summers." His highly literate readership brings

to mind the old joke about baseball and intellectuals: it is the only game slow enough for them to understand.

The joke contains a certain amount of truth. Baseball is a game of frequent pauses, of graceful intermittences, the pace of play regulated by outs and innings rather than by the minutes left on the clock. "It's not much like the swirl and blur of hockey and basketball," Angell says in the preface to *Once More Around the Park: A Baseball Reader* (1991), "or the highway crashes of the NFL." There is time while the batter digs in at the plate to analyze managerial strategies, time while the umpire checks the ball for scuffs to soak up atmosphere, time while the pitcher and catcher consult on the mound to look ahead or reflect back. Of all professional sports, baseball is the most unhurried and subtle and hence the most writable.

Then again, baseball over the past three decades has chaotically confirmed what Angell has called its "Age of Alteration." Franchises have migrated; fourteen new teams have been added; and the World Series has been diminished by a vastly expanded postseason. Grass has been replaced by carpet, legendary ballparks by entertainment complexes, and beanball wars by labor disputes. The American League has adopted the designated hitter rule, and both leagues have abolished the traditional Sunday doubleheader.

Angell is not as alienated by such changes as he might be. To be sure, he resents that baseball has been goosed up to make it more appealing to the casual fan. He also has had his fill of egocentric players and arrogant owners squabbling over money, like partners in a bad marriage. Yet he never quite loses his enthusiasm for baseball, though enthusiasm does become harder to sustain—or, at least, justify—with each successive book.

Five Seasons (1977), Angell's second collection of baseball pieces, spans the years 1972 to 1976, a hectic half decade that saw a players' strike, a spring training lockout, the advent of free agency, and the inflation of players' salaries. He reacts to the various upheavals with predictable gloom, complaining that they have "caused the once elegant estate of baseball more and more to resemble a littered, slovenly Oz." In several pieces—"Starting to Belong," "The Companions of the Game," "In the Counting House," "Cast a Cold Eye"—he even questions whether baseball is worth following anymore. "A typical modern ball team," he wrote in "The Companions of the Game," " is operated coldly and from a distance, just like any other conglomerate subentity with interesting tax-depletion built-ins and excellent PR overtones."

Ultimately in the pieces, however, Angell shakes off his doubts and forebodings, grabs his car keys and notebook, and heads to the ballpark. Down on the field, familiar figures move in familiar sunlit patterns; it is still the same old beautiful game. Indeed, the rituals of spring training and the thrills of pennant races and the mannerisms of players seem all the sweeter now because they seem threatened by commercial bastardization.

To sustain the fan state of mind has required that Angell look beyond the fact that baseball is an enormous and cold-blooded corporate enterprise. "The ability to find beauty and involvement in artificial commercial constructions," he writes in a 1964 piece, "Two Strikes on the Image," "is essential to most of us in the modern world. . . ." In the mid 1970s, confronted by a Fortune 500 version of baseball, he restates the point at greater length and with a greater sense of urgency in "Agincourt and After" (November 1975):

It is foolish and childish, on the face of it, to affiliate ourselves with anything so insignificant and patently contrived and commercially exploitative as a professional sports team, and the amused superiority and icy scorn that the non-fan directs at the sports nut . . . is understandable and almost unanswerable. Almost. What is left out of the calculation . . . is the business of caring—caring deeply and passionately, really caring . . . which is a capacity or an emotion that has almost gone out of our lives. And so it seems possible that we have come to a time when it no longer matters so much what the caring is about . . . as long as the feeling itself can be saved.

The forms of Angell's caring emerges most distinctly in *Five Seasons* in his sometimes surreal, sometimes homey, and always precise images of players in action. He describes Louis Tiant of the Boston Red Sox "wheeling and rotating on the mound like a figure in a Bavarian clock tower"; Joe Morgan of the Cincinnati Reds "waiting at the plate for a pitch, pumping his left elbow like a rooster wing"; and Bernie Carbo of the Oakland A's "flailing at one inside fastball like someone fighting off a wasp with a croquet mallet." Despite—or perhaps because of—his disgust with the business side of baseball, Angell writes about what happens on the field with exuberance. His analogies, full of humor and surprise, have the effect of rescuing the game from rank commercialism and returning it to its original purpose: fun.

Critics seem to have competed in coming up with superlatives for *Five Seasons*. Jonathan Yardley of the *Washington Post* pronounced it "one of the two best baseball books we have," the other being Angell's own *The Summer Game*. Donald Hall, after calling Angell in *National Review* baseball's "most articulate fan," continued by saying that the pleasure of reading Angell's prose is, "like the pleasure of watching effortless fielding around second base." Edward Hoagland simply said in *Harper's*, "The book is irresistible."

With the publication of *Late Innings: A New Baseball Companion* (1982), his third collection of baseball pieces, Angell received more plaudits from critics. " . . . Angell is back," Art Hill noted in *Sports Illustrated*, "and the stuff is as good as ever." But for at least one critic, Jonathan Yardley, "good as ever" meant the same as ever—meant that Angell was in a rut. "He has, perhaps, stayed too long at the fair," Yardley suggested, "especially in his by-now-traditional spring-training and post-season pieces, he too often seems to be going through the motions."

There is perhaps some justification for Yardley's point. Since *The Summer Game*, Angell has been in danger of plagiarizing himself. His subsequent collections feature dyspeptic rumblings about club owners and big salaries and baseball as a business; memories of the players and ballparks of his youth; angst-ridden asides on the conflicts and pressures of belonging to the family of fans; and a sometimes predictable, *New Yorker*-style humor.

On the other hand, there have been several subtle changes in Angell's writing over the years. First, he has acquired access to baseball figures who once seemed as remote and unapproachable as gods. Where he used to describe baseball from the perspective of someone perched in the bleachers, he now describes while sitting in the press box or hanging around the batting cage. In *Season Ticket: A Baseball Companion* (1988), his fourth collection, he makes frequent reference to his insider status: "Carlton Fisk told me . . . "; "Keith Hernandez told me . . . "; "Roger Craig told me . . . "; and so on.

Angell has also devoted increasing attention to exactly how players do what they do—snap off a curveball, turn a double play, lay down a sacrifice bunt. This focus on craft—the "fundamentals," in baseball parlance—has been his way of combating his own disillusionment with the game at a time when it has been seduced by money and adulterated by gimmicks. "Almost everything in baseball looks easy," he writes in "One Hard Way to Make a Living," but really learning the game . . . can take a lifetime, even if you keep notes." He interviews hitters about hitting in "One Hard Way to Make a Living" (1981), catchers about catching in "In the Fire" (1984), infielders about fielding in "Taking Infield" (1985), and pitchers about pitching in "The Arms Talks" (1987). Unlike his other pieces, these are more instruction manuals than narratives, and though they probably will not teach the reader to hit, catch, or throw a major-league curve, they will teach one to appreciate the skill of men who can.

A certain somberness has crept into Angell's prose. The title of his 1982 collection, *Late Innings,* suggests a loss of confidence in the future—"a humdrum, twilight quality to all the doings of middle life, however successful." In *Season Ticket,* written between 1983 and 1987 when he was in his mid sixties, there is a rather subdued tone to some of the writing. Not too surprisingly, men who dominated baseball for a generation—players Johnny Bench, Reggie Jackson, and Carl Yastrzemski and manager Earl Weaver—meet the "little death" of retirement within the first hundred pages.

Angell's latest collection, *Once More Around the Park* (1991), brings together pieces from his four previous collections. The baseball writing he has done since then has sometimes sounded heavy-hearted. "Baseball becomes feasible from time to time, not much more," he writes in "Early Innings," "and we fans must make prodigious efforts to rearrange our profoundly ironic contemporary psyches in order to allow its old pleasures to reach us."

The 254-day players' strike that snatched away the 1994 pennant race and wiped out the World Series for the first time in ninety years served only to further alienate Angell's affections. But he still is not ready to renounce baseball. On the contrary, he offers a plan for repairing its shattered image. "We can go to a game," he proposes shortly after the start of the 1995 season, adding:

> Then we can go to another, maybe with friends. We won't stay home and catch the game on television again—where Don Mattingly shares time with Larry King, and the difficult two-out-and-one-on threat in the sixth is suspended by our click-click to old bits of 'NYPD Blue.' We won't balk at the price. . . . We'll *go*. Then, along about the All-Star Game break, we might even take a chance and hurry back to the same park in the hope of picking up a pair of tickets at the window, just before game time. Anybody who follows this plan—I semi-guarantee this—will stop thinking that he can play ball as well as or better than the guys on the field and won't care by as much as an old peanut shell whether he is helping the plutocrat owners. He will be a fan again, and—for this season, at least—the proprietor of our amazing game.

Is such loyalty wasted on baseball? Perhaps the best way to answer this is to point out that no other sport has inspired so much writing. The literature of baseball is vast—some three hundred baseball books were published in 1990 alone—and proves that the game stimulates memory and imagination. There have been baseball essays, baseball memoirs, baseball short stories, and baseball novels. There have even been baseball poems. "I dreamed of Ted Williams / leaning at night against the Eiffel Tower, weeping," begins "Dreams of a Baseball Star" by Beat poet Gregory Corso.

Angell belongs on any list of the "all-time greatest" baseball writers. He has avoided the cardinal sin of sportswriting (and sports movies)—the tendency to represent the games people play, or pay others to play for them, as a character test. His writing embodies the most endearing qualities of baseball itself: a complex harmony of parts; a leisurely, meditative pace; and a capacity to startle and delight.

References:

Ira Berkow, *Red: A Biography of Red Smith* (New York: McGraw-Hill, 1987);

Tristram Potter Coffin, *The Old Ball Game: Baseball in Folklore and Fiction* (New York: Herder & Herder, 1971);

Brendan Gill, *Here At* The New Yorker (New York: Random House, 1975);

Howard Good, *Diamonds in the Dark: America, Baseball, and the Movies* (Metuchen, N.J.: Scarecrow, 1997);

George Grella, "Baseball and the American Dream," *Massachusetts Review,* 16 (Summer 1975): 550–557;

Allen Guttman, *A Whole New Ball Game* (Chapel Hill: University of North Carolina Press, 1988);

Ring Lardner, *Some Champions,* edited by Matthew J. Bruccoli and Richard Layman (New York: Scribners, 1976);

Christopher Lehmann-Haupt, *Me and DiMaggio: A Baseball Fan Goes in Search of His Gods* (New York: Simon & Schuster, 1986);

Wilfred Sheed, "Reds," *New York Review of Books,* 29 (23 September 1982): 45–48;

Leverett Y. Smith Jr., *The American Dream and the National Game* (Bowling Green, Ohio: Popular Press, 1975).

Bill Barich
(23 August 1943 –   )

Edd Applegate
Middle Tennessee State University

BOOKS: *Laughing in the Hills* (New York: Viking, 1980);
Traveling Light (New York: Viking, 1984);
Hard to Be Good (New York: Farrar, Straus & Giroux, 1987);
Big Dreams: Into the Heart of California (New York: Pantheon, 1994);
Carson Valley (New York: Pantheon, 1997).

SELECTED PERIODICAL PUBLICATIONS–
UNCOLLECTED: "Our Far-Flung Correspondents: Feather River Country," *New Yorker* (26 August 1985): 66–73;
"A Reporter at Large: The Jimtown Store," *New Yorker* (11 November 1985): 114, 116–118, 120–122, 124–130, 133–135;
"The Sporting Scene: Dreaming," *New Yorker* (7 April 1986): 80–88;
"A Reporter at Large: The Crazy Life," *New Yorker* (3 November 1986): 97–98, 100, 102–105, 108, 110–122, 124–130;
"The Sporting Scene: Chasers," *New Yorker* (23 March 1987): 78–83;
"Profiles: Board-and-Care," *New Yorker* (12 October 1987): 51–52, 57–58, 60–62, 75–76, 79–80, 84–85, 87–90;
"Annals of Sport: In Prime Time," *New Yorker* (29 August 1988): 68–75;
"A Reporter at Large: Ulster Spring," *New Yorker* (21 November 1988): 94, 101–116, 121–124, 126, 129–132;
"Annals of Sport: Pride of the Sunset," *New Yorker* (7 May 1990): 92–96, 99–101;
"A Reporter at Large: La Frontera," *New Yorker* (17 December 1990): 72–79, 82, 85–92;
"Annals of Sport: Going to the Moon," *New Yorker* (22 July 1991): 74–79;
"Onward and Upward with the Arts: Still Truckin'," *New Yorker* (11 October 1993): 96–102;
"Singin' the Blue," *Sports Illustrated* (9 December 1996): 70–86;
"The Poet's Masterpiece: A Profile of Gary Sny-

Bill Barich (photograph by Barbara Hall)

der," *San Francisco Focus* (February 1997): 44–47, 102.

Bill Barich has written many articles and several books of nonfiction based on his personal experiences and observations. His powerful reporting skills, evident throughout his work, show most clearly when he documents his most personal passions–from observing horses racing at a track to characterizing the varied, colorful individuals who inhabit the state of California–as he does in his book *Big Dreams: Into the Heart of California* (1994). Most of Barich's articles have been written for *The New Yorker* magazine. His writing often presents in dramatic form his ceaseless search for some kind of meaning in what often appears to him a cruel and often absurd world.

Barich was born in Winona, Minnesota, on 23 August 1943 to Russell and Lois Barich. The oldest of three children, Barich moved with his parents to Westbury, New York, in 1950. He grew up in the 1950s "in a suburb of ordinary tract houses," as he says in an article in the *San Francisco Examiner* (20 November 1994), ate TV dinners in the evening, and, like millions of other young Americans, watched television. As a youngster he was interested primarily in baseball and rock and roll. "Whenever I wasn't out on a diamond," he recalled, "I could be found tunneling through the bins of 45s at Modell's, a bargain basement store." Barich fondly remembered that on his thirteenth Christmas he received a Zenith hi-fi record player and two albums—one by Frankie Lymon and the Teenagers and the other by Elvis Presley.

In the 1960s Barich's father became the president of Ace Books, a paperback publishing company in New York. Every summer he gathered the family at a lake in Minnesota where they spent their vacations fishing for bass and perch. Barich's father introduced him to fishing during one of these early occasions, and Barich was immediately intrigued by the experience. In high school he played on the basketball and baseball teams; later he attended Colgate University, where he majored in the humanities. During his junior year Barich lived in Florence, Italy, and studied the Italian Renaissance. Joe Flaherty wrote in *The New York Times Book Review* (15 June 1980) that Barich "came to know the galleries of the Uffizi by heart, the statuary and cafes, and fell in love with the Humanist philosophers who had formed ranks around the Medici."

Barich graduated from Colgate in 1965. He aspired to be a film director and briefly attended graduate school in Boston, leaving in February 1966 to be a Peace Corps teacher in Eastern Nigeria (later Biafra). Upon his return he was hired to teach seventh grade in a boarding school in New Jersey. By 1969 Barich, dissatisfied with teaching, left New Jersey and moved to San Francisco, where he worked as a stockboy for a book distributor. Although he advanced within the company, his desire to write eventually surfaced in 1972, a year after he met his wife, Diana. During this time he turned out one novel after another, and all were rejected by publishers. By 1978 he and his wife had suffered miserably—both their mothers had died of cancer; Diana had suffered two miscarriages and had been misdiagnosed as having a brain tumor; Barich was unemployed and consequently almost out of money; and they were living in a battered rented mobile home about seventy miles north of San Francisco. Barich told his wife that he was going to Golden Gate Fields, a horse track about sixty miles away. He announced that he was going to get a room at a motel near the track so he could stay and gather information about horse racing, a subject that he knew something about. Barich became obsessed with a favorite pastime of the Florentines, horse racing, while his mother lay dying, because it seemed to provide a spark of life in a difficult time.

Barich visited Golden Gate Fields, located on San Francisco Bay, for at least ten weeks and became fascinated by what he saw—from the jockeys in their brightly colored clothes to the fast-running thoroughbreds. What he observed, what he learned about horses and racing from trainers and jockeys, and what he learned from bettors filled page after page in his journal. Barich learned much from his study of racing, especially when the horse he bet on won. In *People Weekly* (11 August 1980) Barich says, "It's a crazy, electric moment. Your consciousness is totally obliterated." His notes, together with memories of his mother and his time in Florence, were weaved into a remarkable book titled *Laughing in the Hills* (1980). The book was noticed by Robert Bingham and William Shawn, the editors of *The New Yorker*. Shawn desired to purchase the first serial rights, so he called Barich and made an offer. Barich agreed to the terms, and excerpts from the book appeared in the magazine. Reviews of the book showed up in many newspapers and magazines. In *The New York Times Book Review* Joe Flaherty wrote:

> Under the guise of "a race track book" (though he handles that admirably), Mr. Barich offers a touching portrait of a young man in trouble. He interrupts his narrative, constantly and audaciously, and segues into the history of the horse and of Albany, Calif., examines the theories of thoroughbred breeding, attempts to cross-pollinate 15th-century philosophy and contemporary life and applies the logic of philosophy to the magic of plunging—Damon Runyon and the Renaissance.

Some reviewers both praised and criticized Barich's writing. Roger Sale, for instance, claimed in the *New York Review of Books* (5 March 1980) that Barich's "prose suffers from defects" associated with *The New Yorker*. Sale wrote, "When Barich calls nature 'hydrogen intertwined with embryos and tumors,' I see only showiness; and his description of Sunday afternoons in the East Bay is worse." Sale's review, however, ended on a positive note: "*Laughing in the Hills* can be placed alongside Andrew Beyer's *My $50,000 Year at the Races* and James Guetti's novel, *Action,* as being among the books honorably describing a fascinating subculture." Sale also admitted that Barich's book belongs alongside Robert Pirsig's *Zen and the Art of Motorcycle Maintenance*

(1974) and Frederick Exley's *A Fan's Notes* (1968) because the book's structure, like these, fused several nonfiction genres into a kind of autobiography and because the book was an "inflated gospel of defeat." Gary L. Fisketjon, in *Esquire* (May 1980), wrote: "One of Barich's considerable achievements in this moving, graceful, and spirited work is his ability to sort out loose ends—without chest thumping or brainstorming. Instead of dogging the meaning of it all, he experienced a great deal with humor and sensitivity, every so often cashing in a ticket to boot."

Barich's book is part documentary and part autobiography. He discusses what he has learned about horse racing and concurrently attempts to make sense of what appears to him a senseless world. The reader realizes that Barich is actually mourning the death of his mother. In *Literary Nonfiction: Theory, Criticism, Pedagogy* (1989) Mark Allister notes about Barich's book that "The intentional weaving of the mourning process into the documentary creates autobiography." The book begins when Barich learns about his mother's illness and flies to New York to see her. The cancer has ravaged her body, and she appears to be years older than she actually is. Later he flies back to California, where he slips into sadness; the reader then learns about other relatives becoming ill. Other problems rise and multiply, and Barich eases his despair by going to the race track and by writing. According to Allister, "*Laughing in the Hills* exemplifies a situation in which the patient becomes, in a figurative sense, his own analyst through the act of writing." Barich tried to find comfort by learning about horse racing and by reading about the Renaissance. However, the healing process does not begin until he focuses on the thoroughbreds, the horses themselves, and then writes about the experience. Through winning and losing Barich begins to feel restored. Finally, reflecting on his mother's suffering, he becomes capable of distinguishing two processes that before had seemed one and the same. He writes, "In my mind the dying and the cancer had become separated, almost discrete, the one a natural process of organic decay, the other a cultural hastening of that process."

Over the next year Barich traveled through the northwestern United States, particularly Oregon, and contributed articles to *The New Yorker*. He and his wife then put their furniture in storage, packed their Datsun (Nissan), and headed east. As he wrote in the preface to *Traveling Light* (1984), "Over the next year or so, we had three different addresses. We lived on eastern Long Island; in London; and in the Arcetri district, above Florence. There were side trips to upstate New York; to the English countryside; and to Rome, Venice, and Ravenna." These travels provided further material for pieces for *The New Yorker*.

Traveling Light contains most of his articles for *The New Yorker* during this period. John Skow wrote in *Time* (6 February 1984) that "Barich is especially good at the travel writer's peculiar con—getting the reader to enjoy his enjoyment—in a couple of pieces he wrote about spending several months in Florence. He is so deft at this that even a long list of pasta types . . . seems to be infused with joy." The book contains ten essays about friends, fishing, horse racing, family, art, and history. He captured everyday conversation extremely well, as the following excerpt from "O'Neill among the Weakfish" illustrates:

> In a drenched, despondent condition, I reported to O'Neill. He gave me coffee and sold me an emergency poncho that folds up to the size of a dime and fits in your trouser pocket.
>
> "You was wasting your time," he said. "Nobody the hell's ever caught a weakie off that beach."
>
> "Why not?"
>
> "Because that's how God made it, is why not."
>
> Another pantheist.
>
> "Anyhow, the fish is more offshore now," O'Neill said. "What you really need is to get yourself a boat."
>
> "I'll bet you sell boats."
>
> O'Neill shrugged. "There's outfits that'll rent you one," he said.

Barich interests the reader by the subject he presents and by the style he chooses and causes the reader to desire more. Skow wrote, "Take more trips . . . for those of us whose luggage has grown too heavy to lug." Barich allows the reader to experience what he experiences, to see what he sees, to taste what he tastes, and to hear what he hears. The personal style of reporting, unlike straight reporting in which the reporter is prohibited from getting involved, is the reason.

In 1987 his collection of seven stories, *Hard to Be Good,* was published to mixed reviews. Ed McClanahan in the *St. Petersburg Times* (29 November 1987) wrote appreciatively:

> Barich's tone is always carefully modulated, his prose is crisp and purposeful, and his narratives seem, at least on the surface, altogether straightforward. Yet a beguiling strangeness pervades these stories, a sense that almost anything can happen, which keeps the reader on alert, expecting the unexpected.

Dust jacket for Barich's 1994 book, based on his interviews with Californians and his study of the history of the state

Russell Banks, however, claimed that Barich's characters were not memorable. In *The New York Times Book Review* (13 December 1987) he wrote: "They all give in too easily, almost with relief. So that, in the end, it's difficult to care whether they relinquish anger or nurse it, struggle to become a novelist or settle for being a technical writer, seduce an older woman or give up the chase." All but one of the stories had been published earlier in magazines.

In 1994 Barich returned to a subject he knew: California. *Big Dreams: Into the Heart of California* is a well-written attempt to paint a picture of the state. Barich journeyed from northern to southern California and provided historical details as well as descriptions of those he met along the way. In *Time* (4 July 1994) Skow wrote:

Barich starts at the Oregon border and works his way south through the failed fishing and lumber towns of the north coast. What he finds there, and virtually everyplace else in the great coastal kingdom—on through Yuba City, Copperopolis, San Jose, Fresno, Bakersfield, Los Angeles, the Salton Sea, San Isidro—is the hunkered down, fearful middle-aged and the resentful, nihilistic youth who see no future and no present worth the trouble.

Barich traveled the minor and major highways and visited Indian reservations, San Francisco, the San Joaquin Valley farming communities, Los Angeles, Disneyland, and Venice. He searched the areas that attracted illegal immigrants. His style of writing was clear and full of energy. M. Dion Thompson wrote in the *Baltimore Sun* (15 May 1994): "At times the writing is perfect, the imagery and insights pure, true." Todd Gitlin, in the *San Francisco Chronicle* (15 May 1994), observed: "Barich is a discreet and subtle writer (sometimes too quiet), his prose style appropriate to his modesty and the magnitude of his task. He doesn't indulge in the whiz-bang breathlessness that affects many a day tripper zooming through California in search of an angle and illustrative sound bites. He takes his time."

Barich's personal style of writing accurately describes his surroundings, and one learns in the following excerpt from chapter 1, "Away," that the writer is preparing to cross California's state line:

On the Chetco River in Brookings, with a light fog burning off and a smell of sun-warmed bay leaves rising, I stood knee-deep in the stream casting flies to invisible steelhead, the big, sea-run rainbow trout that return to their natal waters to spawn. The stream had a flat, neutral color from the rocks and pebbles lining its bed, and I looked across it to a ridge where some silvery-green Douglas firs arched toward the sky.

No fish, the meditative motion of casting, the sun roaring in my bones. Happiness, for a moment.

Tomorrow, I thought. Tomorrow I'll cross the border.

Barich included brief biographies of John Muir, among other early explorers, to provide a backdrop against which he painted portraits of other Californians. In "Far North," the second chapter in part 2, he describes young men searching for their place in society:

Throughout the long day I felt the forlornness of Crescent City. Young men cruised absently around the harbor in their trucks, smoking dope and popping the tops on half-quart beers. They were tough kids raised to work in mills or on boats, and they wouldn't stoop to being waiters or clerks—they weren't servants. They'd been cheated of a future, really, so they behaved recklessly and acted out their anger, getting into fights and copping DUIs.

In his 7 August 1994 review in the *Los Angeles Times* Page Stegner wrote, "Piece by piece these portraits, sketches, anecdotes and vignettes add up to an extraordinary profile of the Californian and his habitat." Walter Kirn wrote that "One thing *Big Dreams* does well is spread out one's mental map of California to something like its actual size and shape. Barich reminds us how much of his state is not Los Angeles, and how much of the part that's not Los Angeles is not the Bay Area, either."

Barich tried to explain and capture California's appeal in his impressive prose style, but the size and complexity of the state were sometimes overwhelming, and, despite the general praise for the book, some reviewers felt that Barich's depictions of some of the characters he met should have been more vivid.

In 1997 Barich's first novel, *Carson Valley,* was published to favorable reviews. The novel, which is set in the wine country of California, is about Anna Torelli, a recently divorced woman who has returned to California to care for her ailing mother and her aging father. Although she had no intentions of becoming romantically involved with anyone, she is soon attracted to Arthur Atwater, the grandson of one of her father's best friends. Barich, having lived in the area about which he writes, knows the characters and landscape well, and he provides readers with a realistic romantic novel. In *The New York Times* (3 March 1997) Linda Gray Sexton wrote that, in addition to the realism of *Carson Valley,* "there is also a sense of magic. Mr. Barich pulls in fate and luck with an elegant sleight of hand that guides his characters to their difficult destinies."

References:

Mark Allister, "Writing Documentary as a Therapeutic Act: Bill Barich's *Laughing in the Hills,*" in *Literary Nonfiction: Theory, Criticism, Pedagogy,* edited by Chris Anderson (Carbondale: Southern Illinois University Press, 1989);

Norman Sims, ed., *The Literary Journalists* (New York: Ballantine, 1984), pp. 321–339.

Jimmy Breslin
(17 October 1929 -)

Michael J. Dillon
State University of New York at New Paltz

BOOKS: *Sunny Jim: The Life of America's Most Beloved Horseman, James Fitzsimmons* (Garden
City, N.Y.: Doubleday, 1962);

Can't Anybody Here Play This Game? (Garden City,
N.Y.: Doubleday, 1963; revised edition,
New York: Ballantine, 1970);

The World of Jimmy Breslin, annotated by James G.
Bellows and Richard C. Wald (New York:
Viking, 1967);

The Gang That Couldn't Shoot Straight (New York:
Viking, 1969);

World Without End, Amen (New York: Viking,
1973);

*How the Good Guys Finally Won: Notes from an Im-
peachment Summer* (New York: Viking, 1975);

.44, by Breslin and Dick Schapp (New York: Viking Press, 1978);

Forsaking All Others, by Breslin with the coopera-
tion of Team C Homicide (New York: Simon
& Schuster, 1982);

The World According to Breslin, annotated by Michael J. O'Neill and William Brink (New
York: Ticknor & Fields, 1984);

Table Money (New York: Ticknor & Fields, 1986);

He Got Hungry and Forgot His Manners (New York:
Ticknor & Fields, 1988);

Damon Runyon: A Life (New York: Bantam Doubleday, 1991);

I Want To Thank My Brain For Remembering Me (Boston: Little, Brown, 1996).

Jimmy Breslin's influence on the current generation of New York City columnists is as pronounced as was Ernest Hemingway's on Breslin's
generation. In any city newspaper—especially the
tabloids—one finds echoes of Breslin's spare, muscular prose, vibrant with machismo yet suffused
with tenderness, full of irony and humor yet bri-
dling with outrage, fiercely proletarian yet decidedly literary. That is Breslin's legacy some thirty
years after reviving Roaring Twenties newspaper
prose and emerging as a progenitor of the "New

Jimmy Breslin (The New York Times)

Journalism" at the ill-fated *New York Herald Tribune.*

Breslin's style, which combines old-fashioned street reporting with the vernacular of the
city's working class, is distinct, but rather than an
inventor of a new journalism he is more properly
seen—as he himself has declared—as the reviver of
an older journalistic tradition, albeit one to which
he has brought a modern sensibility.

Despite the fact that Breslin worked alongside many in the vanguard of the New Journalism
at the *New York Herald Tribune,* whose writers dis-
dained the cold, distant, "objective" style of reporting in favor of the more personal and vivid
techniques of fiction, Breslin found his models in
the generation of columnists that preceded his on
New York's raucous daily papers.

14

Unlike, say, Tom Wolfe—a contemporary at the *New York Herald Tribune*—Breslin's prose style in the 1960s did not run to Kandy-Kolored Tangerine-Flake dreaming excess. Instead, there are echoes of older times in his voice: echoes of Jacob Riis, Lincoln Steffens, Damon Runyon, and Jimmy Cannon. The voice is tough and raspy, all–New York, equally at home in conversation with mobsters or politicians, of whom Breslin might say it is hard to tell the difference. It is a fiercely provincial voice, Gotham *uber alles,* and yet Breslin has never failed to perceive the larger social, political, and cultural currents that shape the life of the city.

Breslin has carefully crafted both a persona and a unique literary voice as a columnist, but he also represents a confluence of diverse literary and cultural movements that came of age—or at least came back into fashion—during the 1960s, movements in which, at one time or another, the journalist was seen primarily as a voice of conscience, a participant in the events that were reported, a social critic, an interpreter, or a celebrity. Breslin has won most major journalistic awards—including the Pulitzer Prize in 1986 while at the *New York Daily News*—and has dabbled both in radical Greenwich Village and traditional Democratic Party politics. Scandal and criticism, however, have increasingly become a part of his legacy. His journalistic accomplishments notwithstanding, Breslin is the Ty Cobb of American Journalism, brilliant but tempermental, charging with spikes high at stories, rivals, and critics, and creating his own rules as he goes along: the passion for justice he exudes in his columns is surpassed only by his passion for applause and self-congratulation. He has been accused of inventing facts for his columns, using his editorial influence to settle personal scores, and bigotry; the man who championed civil rights in the 1960s was suspended briefly from *Newsday* in 1988 for making racial slurs against an Asian American colleague who dared to criticize one of his columns.

Jimmy Breslin was born on 17 October 1929 in Jamaica, Queens, to James Earl Breslin and the former Francis Curtin. Breslin was born on the eve of the Great Depression, and his family struggled like other working families in Queens amid the disastrous circumstances of hard times. Breslin's father, an alcoholic piano player, abandoned the family when Jimmy was six years old. His mother, also an alcoholic, was prone to tantrums and incapable of showing warmth to Breslin or his younger sister, Diedre. Still, his upbringing was not as dire or hardscrabble as he later portrayed it in columns and books. Nor was Breslin a literary savant, a "primitive," as one early editor called him; his mother was an English teacher who drilled her son on the importance of the precise use of language. Breslin exhibited an early interest in journalism, publishing a neighborhood paper, the *Daily Flash,* with his friend Al Henson, who later became a noted performance artist.

Breslin attended parochial schools and then enrolled at Long Island University, quitting after three years without earning a degree; he had already begun working as a sportswriter for the Long Island *Daily Press,* covering scholastic sports and sandlot football. In the mid 1950s Breslin joined the Hearst-owned *New York Journal American,* and, frustrated by the low pay and lack of creativity daily journalism offered, he began to freelance extensively. Many of his early magazine pieces appeared in *The Saturday Evening Post.* These early pieces, although concise and competent, did little to foreshadow the personal or stylistic flair that led to his emergence as a prominent New Journalist in the 1960s. A 1958 piece on Baltimore Colts quarterback Johnny Unitas, for example, was full of the heroic clichés and adoring prose that characterized much of the sportswriting of that era.

Breslin married Rosemary Dattolico in 1954, and the couple had six children. As a young freelancer working for mainstream magazines, Breslin had little opportunity to experiment, and with a large family to support he wisely stuck to the formats of the magazines in which his stories were published. A turning point for Breslin came with the publication in 1963 of *Can't Anybody Here Play This Game?,* a humorous and well-crafted book about the first season of the inept but lovable New York Mets baseball team. It was this work that gave Breslin the opportunity to use real people, such as manager Casey Stengel and the comically incompetent player Marv Throneberry, to draw rich characters. The book also brought Breslin to the attention of the *New York Herald Tribune,* whose editors, in a desperate attempt to save the foundering newspaper, were creating a new look and style for the paper that broke with staid newspaper conventions and gave readers a lively, interpretive view of their world. The paper, though short-lived in this incarnation, proved to be an incubator of the New Journalism and greatly influenced the look and tone of newspapers for years.

According to Richard Kugler, a contemporary of Breslin's and the author of *The Paper: The Life and Death of the* New York Herald Tribune (1986), editor Jim Bellows and publisher Jock Whitney, impressed by Breslin's book about the Mets, "summoned the author, drank with him, and decided they had a genuine primitive on their hands, a rowdy noble savage." Breslin knew what the vast working-class readership of New York was thinking, and he could give voice to their un-

Mayoral candidate Norman Mailer and his running mate, Breslin, in New York City during their 1969 Democratic primary campaign (Wide World Photos)

articulated fears and longings. "Beyond his gritty prose and high bravado," writes Kugler, "Jimmy Breslin loved New York—all of it, especially the outer boroughs that Manhattanites scorned—with a chauvinism that prompted him once to dismiss Los Angeles as 'two Newarks back to back.'"

Breslin was thirty-three when he was hired by the *New York Herald Tribune* at a then-princely $20,000 per year plus $200 per week in expenses, and in Kluger's estimation it was Breslin's work that contributed most to the identity of the newspaper as both literary innovator and urban survivor: " it was Breslin, the fat, fierce self-absorbed swaggerer from the rough Ozone Park section of Queens, who more than any other writer on the staff came to represent the social journalism, with its intensity of feeling and social ironies, that the *Herald Tribune* was exploring at the end of its life."

The creation of the New Journalism at the *New York Herald Tribune* was by design and both influenced and reflected an American literary upheaval that was erasing the line between fact and fiction. From the autobiographical novels of Jack Kerouac

and Norman Mailer to the sensational non-fiction novel *In Cold Blood* (1965) by Truman Capote, the stuff of real life was increasingly displacing traditional fiction as the paramount form of literature. The style of the New Journalists is often referred to as "novelistic" and with good reason: as Tom Wolfe points out in *The New Journalism* (1973), many star writers of the *New York Herald Tribune* wanted to be novelists. Wolfe also remembers that while Breslin was either lauded or dismissed for his style—he was called both "a cop who writes" and "Runyon on Welfare"—it was his tireless reporting that made that style work. "Breslin worked like a Turk," according to Wolfe. "He would be out all day covering a story, come back in at 4 p.m. or so and sit down at a desk in the middle of the city room. It was quite a show. He was a good-looking Irishman with a lot of black hair and a wrestler's gut. . . . I've never seen a man who could write so well against a daily deadline."

Breslin, however, who was honing a larger-than-life persona in his column and the newsroom that would soon make him renowned throughout the city, knew that his writing, while superb, was anything but "new." "The story could be entertaining," Breslin later explained. "It was nothing new. Capote had written the book *In Cold Blood,* but I was copying Westbrook Pegler. I was copying what he was doing in 1934."

Yet Breslin's work was much more than imitation. His neighborhood wiseguy persona allowed him to be personal and populist at the same time, and tight deadlines, rather than inhibiting his creativity, seemed to enhance it: the more urgent the story, the better the column. Instead of pontificating on the day's events, as political columnists did, Breslin waded into breaking stories to capture the larger truth that lurked behind the facts. "I never thought about how to do a column," Breslin wrote in *The World According to Breslin* (1984). "It just came naturally, I guess. It had to spin right out of the news."

The characters in Breslin's *New York Herald Tribune* pieces at worst hung out at dark little bars in Queens and at best owned modest homes and lived at the periphery of the city's powerful institutions—legal and otherwise. Through their eyes and his own carefully crafted Everyman persona Breslin told the stories of cops, workers, and minor thugs. Peering from the outside in, he could savagely ridicule the city's "swells," its politicians, executives, and crime bosses. His labeling of onetime friend Governor Hugh Carey as "Society Carey" helped destroy Carey politically.

Some of Breslin's best and most enduring pieces for the newspaper arose from the assassination of President John F. Kennedy. These pieces showed that Breslin's appeal was more than literary; what gave them their vitality was Breslin's reportorial instincts, which might be summarized as find out where all of the other reporters are and then go someplace else. With the news staff of the *New York Herald Tribune* covering the obvious angles of the killing, Breslin was free to probe the edges of the story, and there he found the doctor who had operated on Kennedy. Breslin, of course, saw the doctor not simply as a source of information for a news report but as a compelling character in a drama. Using the omniscient voice and copious use of detail, he re-created the last moments of Kennedy from Dr. Malcolm Perry's point of view in a chillingly emotional deadline piece titled "A Death in Emergency Room One."

This is how Breslin set the scene in the operating room:

> Malcolm Perry unbuttoned his dark blue glen-plaid jacket and threw it onto the floor. He held out his hands while the nurse helped him put on the gloves. The

President, Perry thought. He's bigger than I thought he was. He noticed the tall, dark-haired girl in the plum dress that had her husband's blood all over the front of the skirt. She was standing out of the way, over against the grey tile wall. Her face was tearless and it was set, and it was to stay that way because Jacqueline Kennedy, with a terrible discipline, was not going to take her eyes from her husband's face.

As is characteristic of all of Breslin's work, the Kennedy pieces took liberties with the facts but spoke to the truth with what one editor called "an odd mixture of restraint and emotionalism that manages to capture the mood of sorrow in its varying shades." Dr. Perry later pointed out that Breslin's authoritative descriptions of the surgical procedures performed on the president were inaccurate—after all, while the piece made it seem that Breslin had been in the operating room, he had not been—but concluded that "the major focus was correct."

In the wake of Kennedy's murder Breslin continued to seek out the unexpected angle. His attention shifted to the man who would dig Kennedy's grave, and in topic and style Breslin managed to project his populist sensibility onto the tragedy. The piece opened with Arlington National Cemetery gravedigger Clifton Pollard waking up, enjoying a breakfast of ham and eggs prepared by his wife, Nettie, and receiving a call he knew would come. Using his hallmarks of omniscience, detail, and understatement, Breslin set up the reader in the first two paragraphs with mundane details and then grabbed him by the throat: "He hung up the phone, finished breakfast, and left his apartment so he could spend Sunday digging a grave for John Fitzgerald Kennedy." The story has since become a legend in newsrooms everywhere, and many a city editor has sternly directed a cub reporter to "bring back a gravedigger piece"—that is, a piece that captures the human dimension of the news.

Breslin's populist touch was again called upon as Winston Churchill lay dying in 1965. His coverage of the great man's passing showed both his formidable gifts for capturing and evoking emotion and the intellectual limitations of Breslin's working-class romanticism. His Churchill columns were full of cockney pub dwellers and a real sense of the loss felt by Britain's commoners at the loss of Churchill, but in the main it largely took for truth the myth of the man, and any ironies and ambiguities that existed in the political relationship between the high-born and conservative Churchill and the working-class worshipers Breslin found and interviewed were absent from the pieces he filed.

In the end Breslin's pieces on Churchill were compelling, emotional, and marvelously literary; they were also marred by Breslin's parroting of clichéd history. Thus, at heart the pieces sounded like dialogues from the patriotic war movies of Breslin's youth; in one, Breslin writes: "Sir Winston Spencer Churchill, who saved his nation; saved, perhaps, the entire English-speaking world, stepped into history with its scrolls and statues, and he will be the last who ever will do it as he did because the world never again can survive the things that had to be done in the years he lived." Without so much as a dollop of irony or a hint of connection, Breslin later romanticized the struggle of Belfast's Roman Catholics to throw off the imperial yolk of Churchill's Britain.

Breslin's view of class divisions in his own country, in contrast, was stark and unflinching. He covered civil rights marches in the South and later explored simmering tensions in Harlem, actually moving into an apartment there briefly. His was some of the first in-depth and sympathetic reporting in the city's mainstream press on Harlem and the problems of blacks in the city; the sympathy he demonstrated eventually cost him some support among his white blue-collar readers, who saw blacks as a threat to their jobs and a menace to their safety.

When the *New York Herald Tribune* folded in 1966, Breslin continued to freelance and began work on a novel, *The Gang That Couldn't Shoot Straight* (1969), a satire on the mafia whose strong sales upon its completion allowed Breslin more financial breathing room. He also remained a city voice, writing columns for *New York Magazine,* which had spun off from the *New York Herald Tribune,* and the *New York Post*. Politically, Breslin was drifting farther to the Left, a move that gave him great appeal with some of the city's elite liberals but ultimately strained his credibility with his constituency of working-class readers.

In 1969, when Norman Mailer ran for mayor of New York City, he chose Breslin as his running mate. Mailer believed that he could capture the votes of the city's liberal intellectuals while Breslin might rally his blue-collar readers from the outer boroughs behind the ticket. The campaign was a disaster. Few of Mailer's intellectual friends were impressed by Breslin, and the working class whom Breslin supposedly spoke for wanted nothing to do with radical politics. When Breslin appeared at an Irish rugby match to make a speech during the campaign, he was booed and threatened. In the aftermath of the campaign he described his disillusionment with his so-called people: "I think that was the hardest part of the campaign to accept," he told an interviewer, "the fact that, yes, politics is a business where imbeciles thrive because of the total indifference of the people." After the election debacle Breslin returned to traditional Democratic Party politics and served as a delegate to the 1972 and 1976 national party conventions.

Breslin's reputation among working-class readers suffered from other contradictions between his Everyman image and his growing wealth and celebrity—and from changes in the newspaper industry. During the newspaper strike of 1966, for instance, Breslin announced that he was fed up with blue-collar employees who controlled the city's newspaper unions, and he proposed a separate union for "creative" employees. When critics pointed out that such a union flew in the face of Breslin's advocacy of working people and could help reverse the gains they had made when they battled to unionize the industry in the 1930s, Breslin declared, "we know nothing of the past."

Breslin railed against the unions in his columns, mocking members of the printers' union as "the people who have taught New York how to read misspelled words." But in many ways his rage was justified and was not really driven by arrogance or elitism, as some critics charged. After all, many newspapers had disappeared in New York during the previous two decades, victims of the growth of television, declining advertising revenues, and outmoded production techniques. The unions' resistance to modernization and automation hindered some newspapers at a time when they desperately needed to compete more efficiently, and strikes led to the demise of others, including the *New York Herald Tribune,* which died in 1966 after a desperate and unsuccessful merger with the *New York World-Telegram and Sun* and the *New York Journal-American.*

At the *New York Herald Tribune* and later as a freelancer and regular contributor to New York newspapers and national magazines, Breslin's growing prominence brought more diverse assignments, often far from New York. Politically, he continued to drift toward the Left, moving farther away from his provincial and sometimes xenophopic blue-collar readers. In 1965 he toured Vietnam at the same time as *The New York Times* political columnist James Reston. While Reston talked policy with the brass, Breslin told the story of the war from the point of view of the soldiers on the ground. "Lodge and Rush are not my set," he told *Newsweek* in a 1969 interview. "I regard the whole joint like the sixteenth precinct in Manhattan. I don't get involved with anybody but the arresting officer and the desk sergeant. It's like a crime story." Breslin's columns from Vietnam were stark and evenhanded, but he told the magazine that no matter how deserving the soldiers were of public support, the war was wrong. "This is all so worthless," he said. "All you get is an empty feeling. Win, lose or draw the whole country ain't worth one kid."

In 1976 Breslin again established a permanent address at a city newspaper, signing on with the *New York Daily News*. As Breslin's work evolved and his fame spread, his favorite subject became Breslin. He had always drawn on his upbringing, his adventures in the city, his marriage, and his children (much to their chagrin) for his columns, but by the 1980s Breslin increasingly created situations in which he could perform. The results of his self-referential, celebrity-tinged columns ranged from the vainglorious to the hilarious, as when he cruised to France to challenge the French president to a duel over supersonic Concord flights above his beloved Queens neighborhoods.

Labor troubles also dogged Breslin at the *New York Daily News,* and in 1976, even though he was no longer in the union, he asked the newspaper to withhold his column during a strike. In a searching and eloquent column titled "Strike in My Business," which was not published by the *New York Daily News* but was distributed nationally under the terms of Breslin's syndication contract, Breslin explained his changing views of labor unions and acknowledged that his status as a journalistic star made his Everyman persona harder and harder to maintain. Watching a newspaper guild member and a replacement driver do battle at the picket line, Breslin wrote that he could not decide whom to root for. He also admitted that the decision not to run his column was made to protect his reputation as a friend of the workingman:

> My column did not appear in the News, then, because of a great principle. I have done so well writing about the working guy that nothing should be done to distort that image. . . . Of course the decision will cost me money. But it will not cost me everything. And I give it up for self-advertisement, not lifelong belief. I have changed: too many years, too many strikes, I find, have turned me around inside.

By the 1980s he had also left his beloved Queens for a swank address in midtown Manhattan. Other changes marked this period for Breslin, including the death of his wife, Rosemary, in 1981 and his marriage to Ronnie Eldridge, a political activist, in 1982.

Breslin's foreign and national assignments gave him national exposure, but his tales of New York—"urban parables," one contemporary called them—have always been his forte. Breslin's identity and persona were shaped by his heritage as a descendant of European immigrants who passed through Ellis Island during the great waves of immigration at the turn of the century, but he has never overlooked more recent arrivals from the American South, from Latin America, from Asia. Moreover, as he has chronicled the reshaping of city life by these new residents, he has defended them against prejudice.

When *The New York Times,* which Breslin derisively refers to as "the commuter paper," ran a sympathetic article on the fears of white commuters who unhappily took the subway through the city's minority neighborhoods, Breslin denounced the commuters as "suburban riff-raff" and provided an insightful critique of the city's inherent class inequalities:

> We have had enough of these cheap looters who ride in here from Connecticut and Westchester each day, grab money they never would earn in the places they live, and then, without a trace of class, wring their hands over the condition of the city, its transit system, and the people of the city who ride on it.

In another column Breslin considered the changing racial landscape of the city and predicted its continued decay. The blame for the chaos and division in the city, he wrote, rested largely with the whites who had abandoned it out of fear and prejudice:

> Williamsburg now is Puerto Rican, black and white. Most of the whites are Jewish. It is a marvelous example of how the poor are left in the cities to fight among themselves while those with enough money move to the suburbs and watch the fight on the evening news.

Breslin's stint at the *New York Daily News* ran the gamut from the brilliant, such as a taut piece on the killing of John Lennon filed two hours after Lennon's death to make deadline, to the notorious, as when Breslin printed letters sent to him by "Son of Sam," the serial killer who terrorized New York City in the late 1970s. *The New Yorker* accused Breslin of sensationalism when he printed a letter from the killer in 1977 but failed to report that Breslin had turned the letter over to the police as soon as he received it and published it at their urging because they hoped it might help them establish a line of communication with the person known as Son of Sam. Breslin was furious at the criticism, but according to an editor, he also "reveled in the attention he was getting" as Son of Sam's confidant.

Breslin capped his career at the *New York Daily News* with a Pulitzer Prize for commentary in 1986

Dust jacket for Breslin's 1975 book on the Watergate scandal

for a series of columns, some of which exposed how policemen tortured suspects with stun guns, others of which chronicled the ravages of AIDS and attacked the veracity of subway-mugging-victim-turned-vigilante, Bernard Goetz. The stun gun columns also won the George Polk Award.

In 1988 Breslin was lured by a $500,000-per-year contract to the Times Mirror Company's *New York Newsday,* another worthy but doomed aspirant to daily success in the New York market, which purchased Breslin's services to give the new offering instant New York authenticity. Like the *New York Herald Tribune,* however, *New York Newsday* could not make money—it closed in July 1995, with many awards but too few readers despite a lineup of editorial talent that included Breslin, Murray Kempton, and Mike Lupica.

Despite the triumph of his Pulitzer Prize and the lucrative *Newsday* contract, scandal and censure overshadowed Breslin's work during his seven years at the newspaper. Breslin, venerated as one of the last of the old-time newsmen, discovered that his old-fashioned sensibilities were a liability with younger colleagues, readers, and even

his traditional allies on the Left. No longer could his roguish charm extricate him from the problems he caused with his intemperate pen and tongue.

Breslin did much to undermine and tarnish his reputation as a champion of those on the city's margins—especially immigrants and poor ethnic groups—with an abusive and racist outburst he directed at a young female *Newsday* colleague, Mary Ji Yeon Yuh, who dared to send Breslin an electronic message chiding him for the sexist tone of some of his columns. Breslin stewed over the matter for a few days and complained to editors before erupting in the newsroom. Breslin called Yeon Yuh a "slant-eyed cunt." "She's a little dog, just a little cur, a cur running along the street. She's a yellow cur. Let's make it racial," Breslin declared.

Breslin's tantrum was not news to old friends and enemies—they had seen such displays countless times in bars and newsrooms. But this time the antics of the private Breslin became public because younger colleagues, forty-seven of whom signed a petition demanding his suspension, refused to obey the code of silence of the newsroom—a sacrosanct rule for those of Breslin's generation—and leaked details of his outburst to rival papers. Breslin received a two-week suspension for his outburst.

Columnists Murray Kempton and Robert Reno came to Breslin's defense, with Reno lamenting that "a great voice has been stilled, an original mind has been pastured for two weeks." Breslin himself showed no contrition and called radio shock jock Howard Stern to defend himself on the air. The suspension was but a small part of the fallout from the attack, for Breslin's traditional allies on the Left began to attack him in the wake of the incident. After a similar incident two years earlier in which he denounced Lansford Wilson's *Burn This* as "a fag play written for fags," Breslin made it clear that he was not concerned by what old friends on the Left thought of him. "Lots of people find me offensive," he said. "Everyone knows I'm abusive; everyone knows I stand up when it counts. So I don't care."

Breslin has also been dogged throughout his career by allegations that he makes up facts, sources, and dialogue for his columns. Breslin has certainly created convincing parodies of criminal types, such as burglar Sam Silverware, pickpocket Larry Light Fingers, arsonist Marvin the Torch, and "Un Occhio," Breslin's fictional "boss of bosses" of New York's underworld; his portrait of the crime committed was so convincing that the Arizona State Police asked the newspaper for more details about him so they could issue an All Points Bulletin. Such invention is hardly pernicious and in fact is an accepted tradition in column writing. But the charges of faking stories go beyond these caricatures. For instance, Breslin reported from Three Mile Island that the "evil" steam from the cooling towers of the nuclear plant was laced with deadly radiation when in fact there was no such steam. "That was wrong," Breslin told *Newsweek* in 1986, "but the absolute truth of the column was overwhelming."

Just as the imaginary steam added to the drama of the article, so the poignant quotes from the characters that populate his columns have led critics to charge that Breslin puts literary considerations over accuracy and truth. As reporter Jonathan Alter pointed out in *Newsweek* (12 May 1986): "for years Breslin's fabled ear for dialogue has struck people as a bit too good, too epigramatic for the way people really speak between quotation marks."

Even though Breslin filed a column three times a week almost nonstop for more than thirty years and produced frequent freelance pieces, he has also managed a prodigious output of fiction. His novels, which, like his columns, have typically focused on the bumbling thugs, hardcase survivors, and desperate characters of New York, have been well received by critics and readers. In some of his novels, moreover, Breslin has provided poignant and even harsh portraits of himself, betraying a self-doubt that rarely permeates his columns. Danny Cahill, his thinly disguised alter ego in *.44* (1978), a fictionalized treatment of the Son of Sam serial murder case written in collaboration with Dick Schapp, is a celebrated columnist whose professional success cannot quell his insecurities:

> All day long, and particularly at night over a drink, Danny Cahill told everyone who would listen, himself first, how good he was. But each morning when he woke up, his first thoughts were how long it would take him to write his column for the New York Dispatch, four to five hours on a typewriter, and how hard it was to think of words and put them in a line. "If you're so good," Cahill always asked himself in the mornings, "then why does it take you so long to do?" The answer was obvious: He was not as good as he boasted.

The character of Cahill, who exalts in his "instinct for the essence of a story and his gift for getting people to sound in print the way they sounded in person," also reveals just how contrived the public character of Breslin might be:

> Cahill did not like to admit that he had attended college for a year . . . or that his mother was a high school English teacher. He insisted that he had no knowledge of grammar—"I ain't very smart"—and he made certain that all of his writing sounded as if it were coming out of the side of his mouth.

Breslin has also published several nonfiction books. In addition to two collections of his newspaper columns and his book on the New York Mets, he has published a book on Watergate, *How the Good Guys Finally Won: Notes from an Impeachment Summer* (1975), and, in 1991, an acclaimed biography, *Damon Runyon: A Life*. The Runyon book is as much about Breslin as it was about Runyon, and in it Breslin deservedly enshrines himself in the pantheon of great New York newspaper figures. In the book's first chapter Breslin makes it clear that he is Runyon's heir, the new reigning king of the New York chroniclers:

> I am going to tell you a story about a guy, Damon Runyon, and newspapers and a city and deliver . . . a lot of it straight from memory, and I am about the

only one who can do it because of the life I've lived. I must have heard a thousand conversations about the man and his time from all parts of town because I spent so much of my life, too much of it, in bars and police stations, in racetrack receiving barns, fight gyms and political clubhouses. I don't think that anybody working in New York today has been in more places or heard more, or has so many street memories[.]

Breslin is indeed a direct descendant of Runyon and other New York writers, such as O. Henry, who have used short pieces, be they fiction or nonfiction, to chronicle and make into myth the life of New York City. The contradictions between his staunch support of the city's poor and blue-collar citizens and his occasional outbursts of intolerance and illogic notwithstanding, Breslin remains a compelling influence both on the city in which he lives and on journalism in general.

References:

Alexander Cockburn, "The Liberal Imagination," *Nation,* 4 June 1990, pp. 776–777;

Richard Kluger, *The Paper: The Life and Death of the New York Herald Tribune* (New York: Knopf, 1986);

James Ledbetter, "Breslin Agonistes," *Village Voice,* 22 May 1990, p. 31;

Peter Manso, ed., *Running Against the Machine: The Mailer-Breslin Campaign* (Garden City, N.Y.: Doubleday, 1969);

Nicolous Mills, *The New Journalism: A Historical Anthology* (New York: McGraw-Hill, 1974);

Tom Wolfe, *The New Journalism* (New York: Harper & Row, 1973), pp. 10–16.

C. D. B. Bryan

(22 April 1936 -)

R. Thomas Berner
Pennsylvania State University

BOOKS: *P. S. Wilkinson* (New York: Harper & Row, 1965; London: Longmans, 1965);

The Great Dethriffe (New York: Dutton, 1970; London: W. H. Allen, 1972);

Friendly Fire (New York: Putnam, 1976);

The National Air and Space Museum (New York: Abrams, 1980);

Beautiful Women, Ugly Scenes (Garden City, N.Y.: Doubleday, 1983);

The National Geographic Society: 100 Years of Adventure and Discovery (New York: Abrams, 1987);

In the Eye of Desert Storm (New York: Abrams, 1991);

Close Encounters of the Fourth Kind: Alien Abduction, UFOs, and the Conference at M.I.T. (New York: Knopf, 1995).

SELECTED PERIODICAL PUBLICATIONS—UNCOLLECTED: "Jack & Jackie: A Perfect Day for Honeyfitz," *Monocle* (June 1962);

"The Veterans' Ordeal," *New Republic,* 188 (27 June 1983): 26–33;

"Barely Suppressed Screams: Getting a Bead on Vietnam War Literature," *Harper's,* 268 (June 1984): 66–72;

"Flaunting It," *Esquire,* 103 (June 1985): 283–297;

"My John O'Hara," *Esquire,* 104 (July 1985): 100–105;

"Say Goodbye to Camelot: Marilyn Monroe and the Kennedys," *Rolling Stone* (5 December 1985): 36–41, 74–76, 80;

"A Lesson in Tragedy," *New York Times Magazine,* 135 (23 February 1986): 32–37;

"Operation Desert Norm: Getting to Know the General," *New Republic,* 204 (11 March 1991): 20–27.

C. D. B. Bryan has written books of fiction and nonfiction but is best known for *Friendly Fire* (1976), his nonfiction book about a patriotic Iowa family that sours on the Vietnam War and the United States government after their son is killed by gunfire from U.S. troops. Some critics rated *Friendly Fire* one of the best works of nonfiction published in

1976, and Walter Clemons in *Newsweek* called it one of the three best books on the Vietnam War. Tom Shales, the television critic for the *Washington Post,* said of *Friendly Fire,* "There have been significant books about Vietnam—perhaps none more brilliant and troubling than Bryan's."

Courtlandt Dixon Barnes Bryan was born on 22 April 1936 in New York City, the son of Joseph III and Katharine Barnes Bryan. After his parents divorced his mother married the novelist John O'Hara. Bryan received a bachelor of arts degree from Yale University in 1958, then served as an intelligence officer in Korea in the U.S. Army. (It was O'Hara who, liking some short stories his stepson had written, introduced him to his editor at *The New Yorker.* Bryan's first story was published in June 1962.) Bryan was first married to Phoebe Miller (they divorced in September 1966), then to Judith Snyder (they divorced in 1978), then to Monique Widmer. He has three children: Saint George III, Lansing Becket, and Amanda Barnes.

Bryan's first book was a novel, *P. S. Wilkinson* (1965), which was called "entertainment of a high order" by David Dempsey, writing in the *Saturday Review* on 6 February 1965. Dempsey noted the similarities between the main character, P. S. Wilkinson, and the author—the use of initials, military service, education at Yale—to suggest that the novel is autobiographical. In *The New York Times* (21 October 1970) John Leonard saw similarities in Bryan's first two novels and called the second one, *The Great Dethriffe* (1970), "a rewriting of *The Great Gatsby* with a Gatsby who got what he wanted and couldn't abide it." A reviewer in the *New Republic* said the novel is "remarkable for its grace and depth of perception."

Friendly Fire, published in 1976, recounts the reaction of Peg and Gene Mullen to the death of their son Michael Eugene under conditions that make the couple suspicious. Bryan's story traces their lives, with some flashbacks to provide an ancestral context, from the time their son leaves for Vietnam in September 1969 until April 1972, when

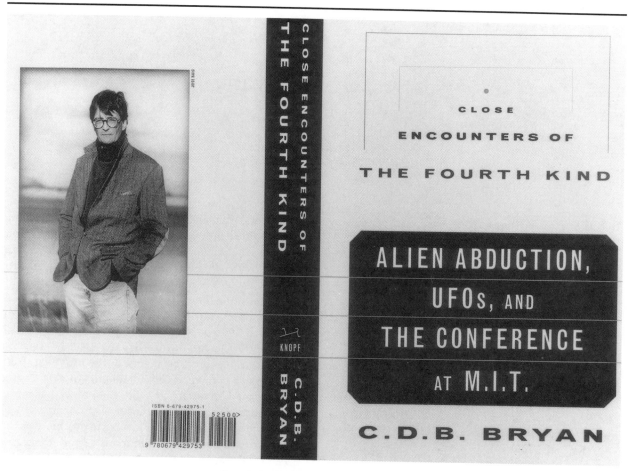

Dust jacket for Bryan's most recent book

Bryan sits down with the couple at their kitchen table and tells them what he has learned about the death of their son. "I drove out to Iowa like a white knight thinking that I could set this family at ease now," Bryan said later. "I could tell them, 'This is the truth of how your boy died.' I told them, and they didn't believe it."

Given their background, Peg and Gene Mullen appeared to be predisposed to the philosophy of "my country, right or wrong," not to becoming antiwar protesters. Bryan says that he "believed Iowa to be at least ten years behind the tensions, the conflicts, the polarizations of a California or a New York. I was wrong, of course." So middle American are Peg and Gene Mullen that Bryan originally titled the book "Heartland." In reviewing the made-for-television movie based on the book, Shales refers to "a Norman Rockwell painting . . . slashed to ribbons" and to the Mullens as "an ideal American family." Their doubt begins when their questions about the death of their son by "friendly fire"—in this event, artillery fire by U.S. troops—cannot be answered to their satisfaction: the answers they receive appear evasive

when in fact they are bureaucratic. The Mullens seek to learn the truth, and it is their attempt that Bryan sets down.

When ABC-TV's Sunday night movie-of-the-week version of *Friendly Fire* aired in 1979, drawing a viewing audience of sixty-four million, the book had sold only 17,500 copies in cloth. "I always had hope that it would be a television show," Bryan commented in an interview with Eric James Schroeder. "That was how I knew people would be moved by the story. . . . People would sit down with their beers and slog through it, and bit by bit they would see what had happened. . . . That's what I wanted. So I admit there was that real political propaganda intent behind it."

Bryan first learned of the situation while he was visiting the author Vance Bourjaily at the University of Iowa. Peg Mullen had recently placed an advertisement in the *Des Moines Register,* paid for out of the money the army sent to bury their son. The advertisement showed 714 crosses, which the copy said represented the "714 Iowans who have died in Vietnam." Bryan decided to do a magazine article and received clearance from William Shawn, then the editor of *The New Yorker*. Bryan expected he would finish with a six-thousand-word article.

Bryan told Schroeder that the book "was born out of a sense of frustration about the war." After seeing what *The New York Times* reporter Seymour Hersh had done reporting on the My Lai massacre, Bryan thought to himself, "Boy, I can really bring the Army to its knees." But it did not work out quite that way. In the June 1976 issue of *The Atlantic Monthly* Amanda Heller observed that Bryan "soon found himself recording not the neat political morality play he thought he had discovered but a frantic and unsettling psychodrama." According to Heller, "The Mullens' obsession is not a pretty one, and Bryan does little to soften it in this overstuffed, melodramatic account, full of unlikely third-person omniscience. But Peg and Gene Mullen were casualties of the Vietnam War as surely as their son was."

Friendly Fire is divided into three parts. The first two-thirds of the book records the Mullens' increasingly obsessive search for truth. In chapter 20 (out of twenty-five chapters), Bryan appears, starting the second part. The third part of the book, presented not as a chapter but as a sidebar, is Bryan's reconstruction of the mission on which Michael Mullen died. When Bryan appears in *Friendly Fire* he issues this disclaimer: "I never wanted to be in this book. I had intended to be a journalist: unbiased, dispassionate, receptive to all sides." Instead, he admits, he adopted the technique of the novelist, not the journalist, and it led him to participate. His experience invites comparison with Joe McGinniss's in *Fatal Vision* (1983), a controversial book in which McGinniss begins believing that an army doctor is innocent of the murder of his wife and two daughters but ends up deciding that the doctor is guilty. Bryan himself makes the comparison. "Suddenly you become a character in the story. . . . By the time of the Bryan character's appearance, I think that the reader wants to know what the hell is going on."

That Bryan himself becomes a character is not particularly surprising. Several reviewers noted the autobiographical nature of his first novel, *P. S. Wilkinson*. After *Friendly Fire* Bryan published a novel, *Beautiful Women, Ugly Scenes* (1983), that he wanted to seem to be nonfiction. Furthermore, he wrote *Close Encounters of the Fourth Kind: Alien Abduction, UFOs, and the Conference at M.I.T.* (1995) in the first person. Rather than make a sharp distinction between Bryan's works of fiction and his nonfiction, perhaps they should be seen as part of a continuum to which neither categorization is precisely suited.

Friendly Fire is a narrative reconstruction of events, which is not atypical of many journalistic accounts. In the first sentence of the book, in an author's note, Bryan explains:

> All material in this book not derived from my own first hand observation of the events is taken from historical texts, public or official records, original correspondence, journals kept by a participant or extended interviews with those persons directly involved. All interviews with the major participants were tape recorded. Transcripts of these interviews were then submitted to those individuals to provide them an opportunity to make corrections. In those few instances of disparate recollections or failing memory, I have had to rely upon the majority opinion and my own judgment in determining what actually took place.

Bryan tape-recorded his many interviews and turned a year's worth of tapes over to Fay Kanin, who wrote the television movie of *Friendly Fire*. In the author's note to his book Bryan explains how he confirmed the accuracy of various conversations that he himself did not hear. He says he felt comfortable reconstructing dialogue because he relied on third parties to corroborate conversations that Peg and Gene had. Notes by Peg Mullen and "the consistency of details as recalled" were also useful to Bryan.

In his introduction to *The Literary Journalists* (1984) Norman Sims observes that, in standard journalism, journalists stay outside their sources, as it were, waiting for scraps of information. Literary journalism is different. "Rather than hanging around the edges of powerful institutions," Sims writes, "literary journalists attempt to penetrate the cultures that make institutions work." That attempt clearly defines one aspect of *Friendly Fire* in which Bryan uses the Mullens' story as a way of looking at how government—more specifically, the Pentagon—operates. It is an outside-in view rather than an inside-out view. The governed look at the governors. The writer's intention also counts. In addition to adopting the techniques of the novelist rather than the journalist, Bryan felt the need to render not the selective direct quotations typically used in journalism but dialogue and conversations, to show people interacting. For this Bryan salutes the influence of his late stepfather, the novelist John O'Hara. "I don't think anybody has put conversations on a page as well as O'Hara. . . . O'Hara, I think, helped me know what to say."

Bryan also intentionally gives the story away immediately. By the end of the opening chapter the reader knows that the Mullens' son Michael had been killed in Vietnam and that "one year after that,

My John O'Hara

The writer my mother married, and the man I loved, was neither a drunk nor a brawler, but a shy, generous soul

BY C.D.B. BRYAN

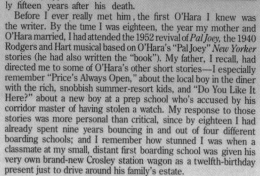

When I think about my stepfather, John O'Hara—and I find myself thinking about him a lot these days—I think about the three "John O'Haras" I knew when he was alive and the fourth "John O'Hara" I was aware of but never adequately appreciated until nearly fifteen years after his death.

Before I ever really met him, the first O'Hara I knew was the writer. By the time I was eighteen, the year my mother and O'Hara married, I had attended the 1952 revival of *Pal Joey*, the 1940 Rodgers and Hart musical based on O'Hara's "Pal Joey" *New Yorker* stories (he had also written the "book"). My father, I recall, had directed me to some of O'Hara's other short stories—I especially remember "Price's Always Open," about the local boy in the diner with the rich, snobbish summer-resort kids, and "Do You Like It Here?" about a new boy at a prep school who's accused by his corridor master of having stolen a watch. My response to those stories was more personal than critical, since by eighteen I had already spent nine years bouncing in and out of four different boarding schools; and I remember how stunned I was when a classmate at my small, distant first boarding school was given his very own brand-new Crosley station wagon as a twelfth-birthday present just to drive around his family's estate.

C.D.B. BRYAN's *book* Beautiful Women; Ugly Scenes *is published in paperback by Dell. He is a frequent contributor to Esquire.*

First page for Bryan's 1985 memoir of his stepfather, published in Esquire

his mother was under surveillance by the FBI"–two of the major facts about the incident. Bryan sees the story as not about Michael Mullen's death but about what happened to his parents after his death and the impact of the war on the United States. But, Bryan writes:

> Nobody would want to read that book, so the way to handle it was to create the sense that it was a mystery. How did Michael die? And it isn't until you're about two-thirds of the way through *Friendly Fire* that you realize this isn't what the book's about at all. But by that time you're hooked. The characters, Peg and Gene, are so strong that you have to find out what happened to them, so you have to keep reading it.

Nearly a decade after *Friendly Fire* was published Bryan wrote in the June 1984 issue of *Harper's* magazine:

> Vietnam literature is concerned with something more than form. What all the novels, memoirs, collections, journalistic treatments and nonfiction accounts set out to do is not merely get at the absurd or capture the ambiguities; they aim to make sense of the experience, to contain the war within some comprehensible, graspable context, to give geographical and historical coordinates to the landscape it occupies in the author's mind. The books attempt to say, this is what it was like. This is what happened. This is what I saw. This is for the record.

After establishing the scope of the book in chapter 1, Bryan then sets out to tell the story. The approach mimics *In Cold Blood* (1966) by Truman Capote, in which the murder of the four members of the Clutter family is revealed on the third page, although the reader does not learn their names at that time. As one reads on to learn what the story is about, only after the killers are captured and tried does the reader learn the details of how the murders were carried out. "Capote had the same sort of problems with sources that I had," Bryan said nearly two decades later. "He has a scene where the two boys, the murderers, are together in a car. Rather than blend the two accounts, he did one person's recollections in one chapter and then in the following chapter did the other's. And for me as well that was the only way to do it." In both books, and in many others, the writer gives his form to the material. In doing that, Bryan imposes a theme. He goes beyond the facts of the situation to provide the feeling those facts evoke.

A major theme in *Friendly Fire* is the obsessiveness–especially of Peg Mullen–to learn what actually happened to her son Michael. In showing the Mullens' increasing doubt about how their son died and their growing impatience with what they perceive to be the unresponsiveness of various government officials, Bryan tells how Peg and Gene Mullen refuse to be reconciled to the ambiguities of Michael's death and how this changes them. In a related theme Bryan changes both in his attitude regarding the circumstances of Michael's death and his feelings toward Peg and Gene. Bryan shows the change in the Mullens and gradually reveals the change in himself. Christopher Lehmann-Haupt in *The New York Times* (May 1976) praised Bryan for carefully interweaving two opposing points of view chronologically and in such a way that "gradually weans us from one attitude to the other by showing us how the Mullens grew increasingly obsessed with their antiwar mission and how they eventually lost touch with reality."

Bryan's feeling that he had somehow violated his intention to be a journalist is false; he did behave as a journalist by seeking out the many sides of a dispute. "He tended himself to be more tolerant, to see both sides," according to Robert Sherrill in the *New York Times Book Review* (9 May 1976). Lehmann-Haupt commended Bryan for dealing with two points of view "with the utmost sensitivity and precision."

Bryan the journalist appears when he enters the story and attempts to resolve the issue of how Michael Mullen died. As he says both in the author's note at the book's beginning and in chapter 25, where he tells the Mullens what he believes is the truth, Bryan interviewed as many of the soldiers as possible and even read the transcript of a court-martial for one of them, a court-martial unrelated to Michael's death. Bryan interviewed Michael's battalion commander, his company commander, the senior medic, the assistant machine gunner (one of Michael's friends), the court-martialed soldier, and a rifleman who lost his leg in the explosion from the same shell that killed Michael. "Each separately confirmed the details of the incident which had brought about Michael's death," Bryan writes. "Each of them had been on that hill that night; each of them furthered my conviction that Schwarzkopf [the battalion commander] had told the Mullens the truth. I felt, therefore, that I had come to the end of the story."

One of the jolting aspects of *Friendly Fire* is the appearance of Bryan in the story. He changes from Bryan the author to Bryan the investigator or from Bryan the narrator to Bryan the character as he attempts to learn how Michael died. The story line changes from the third person and voice of Peg and Gene Mullen to the first person of Bryan and the mixed voice of Bryan and the Mullens. But once the jolt is over the reader begins to appreciate what Bryan has done. He does not let the story rest until he searches out his best notion of the truth. This is the method of a good journalist. Bryan uses the opening two-thirds of the book as a device to get the reader to the last third. As noted, he admits that he structured the story as a mystery in order to hook the reader.

The mixed voice employed in *Friendly Fire* is also pointed out in the reviews. For example, while Sherrill sees the journalist in Bryan, he also notes the change that occurred in Bryan's attitude toward the Mullens. "Suddenly, he became fed up with them." A disinterested journalist would not behave that way. Whereas Sherrill is mostly favorable toward Bryan, Diane Johnson, writing in the *New York Review of Books* (5 August 1976), is less satisfied. She read Bryan's book in its original three-part serialization in *The New Yorker*. When Bryan enters the story, Johnson writes: "It was as if the Sinister Force had come in and finished Bryan's book for him in the night. Qualified, now, was the generous sympathetic tone. A note of condescension had crept into his voice when he came to explain to the Mullens the 'truth' of what he had discovered about Michael's death." Sherrill suggests that the typography of *The New Yorker* and the serialization of the story diminished it. "This is one tale," he writes, "that should not be chopped into pieces separated by week intervals." Jane Howard, writing in the *Washington Post* "Book World" (2 May 1976) has a different view. She writes that the series took her from weeping to cheering–cheering because *Friendly Fire* "is a work of passionate energy."

In raising questions about Bryan's methods, Johnson says she feels that readers will find themselves dissatisfied, even though they will accept Bryan's conclusions. "The problem," she writes:

> may lie in part in the nature of New Journalistic accounts, in which truth is attested to, verified by third parties, taken from tapes, and so on, but dramatized like fiction. The reader experiences such accounts as both truth and fiction, that is, as adequate accounts of the real world, but also as having certain formal qualities we expect in art. If we complain that somehow coherence, integrity, unity have been violated in the work, the journalist can protest, like the student in a beginning creative writing class, "but that's the way it really happened," and to a certain extent we have indeed contracted to believe him.

Sherrill and Johnson challenge Bryan's conclusion that he had done the maximum a person could to learn the truth. Sherrill is dismayed that Bryan changed heroes, from the Mullens to Michael Mullen's battalion commander, and Johnson wonders if Bryan pursued every document he could and points out the self-interest of some of those interviewed. But by Bryan's own account, he had interviewed various people present during the night of Michael's death and had received separate confirmation of the events of that night. Perhaps Bryan might be criticized for not seeking yet one more document. But given that Sherrill and Johnson are both skeptical of Bryan's government sources to begin with, one wonders how another official document would assuage their doubts.

Friendly Fire tells how a couple comes to terms with the horrible death of their son in Vietnam and how the writer who chose to tell their story comes to terms with the material. In the *Harper's* article Bryan describes what the "necessary book" about Vietnam would be:

> I think it would have to be a Mystery, a Political Expose, a Horror Story, a War Novel, a Tragedy; it would have to be a fantastical, hallucinogenic, nightmarish black comedy born of rage and despair and betrayal and, yes, love. It would not be available at bookstores. Instead, it would be helicopter-assaulted onto readers' front lawns; it would come videotaped, computerized, and Dolby-stereoed, with acetate overlays and a warning that eight or so years after being exposed to it, the reader stood a good chance of getting cancer.

Some of the characters in *Friendly Fire* reappear. Battalion commander Schwarzkopf becomes Gen. H. Norman Schwarzkopf and in 1990 directs a war in the Persian Gulf called Desert Storm. After Schwarzkopf retires, Bryan is among those considered to ghostwrite the general's memoirs. Bryan does not do it but does contribute to a book of photographs about the war.

Friendly Fire was written as a "matter of record," Bryan said in an interview published in 1992. "I wanted a record somewhere in the Library of Congress of what the government had done to these people. . . . Throughout the book is an underlying sense of outrage. I thought, 'God damn it! they can't do this to this country. Somebody's got to do something about it.' Writing the book seemed to be the only way I could do anything."

References:

R. Thomas Berner, "C. D. B. Bryan," in *A Sourcebook of American Literary Journalism,* edited by Thomas B. Connery (Westport, Conn.: Greenwood Press, 1992);

Eric James Schroeder, *Vietnam, We've All Been There: Interviews with American Writers* (Westport, Conn.: Praeger, 1992);

Norman Sims, Introduction to *The Literary Journalists,* edited by Sims (New York: Ballantine, 1984), p. 3.

Truman Capote

(30 September 1924 – 25 August 1984)

Lloyd Chiasson
Nicholls State University

See also the Capote entry in *DLB 2: American Novelists Since World War II.*

BOOKS: *Other Voices, Other Rooms* (New York: Random House, 1948; London: Heinemann, 1948);

A Tree of Night and Other Stories (New York: Random House, 1949; London: Heinemann, 1950);

Local Color (New York: Random House, 1950; London: Heinemann, 1950);

The Grass Harp (New York: Random House, 1951; London: Heinemann, 1952);

The Grass Harp: A Play (New York: Random House, 1952; London: Heinemann, 1952);

The Muses Are Heard (New York: Random House, 1956; London: Heinemann, 1957);

Breakfast at Tiffany's (New York: Random House, 1958; London: Hamish Hamilton, 1958);

Observations (New York: Simon & Schuster, 1959; London: Weidenfeld & Nicolson, 1959);

Selected Writings (New York: Random House, 1963; London: Hamish Hamilton, 1963);

In Cold Blood: A True Account of a Multiple Murder and Its Consequences (New York: Random House, 1965; London: Hamish Hamilton, 1966);

A Christmas Memory (New York: Random House, 1966);

The Thanksgiving Visitor (New York: Random House, 1967; London: Hamish Hamilton, 1969);

House of Flowers (New York: Random House, 1968);

Trilogy: An Experiment in Multimedia, by Capote and Eleanor and Frank Perry (New York: Macmillan, 1969);

The Dogs Bark: Public People and Private Places (New York: Random House, 1973; London: Weidenfeld & Nicolson, 1974);

Music for Chameleons: New Writing (New York: Random House, 1980; London: Hamish Hamilton, 1981);

Answered Prayers (London: Hamish Hamilton, 1986; New York: Random House, 1987).

Truman Capote (International Portrait Gallery, Gale Research)

PLAY PRODUCTIONS: *The Grass Harp,* New York, 27 March 1952;

House of Flowers, New York, 1968.

MOTION PICTURE: *Beat the Devil,* screenplay by Capote, United Artists, 1954.

At the heart of Truman Capote's writing was his dedication to, and fascination with, the importance of style. In seeking to elevate the art of storytelling Capote forged together various techniques, and, at least for the second half of his career, he embarked on a fusion of journalistic, cinematic, conversational, and literary writing styles. The result, according to Capote, was the creation of a new art form, something he called the nonfiction novel.

Capote's storytelling techniques nurtured, fostered, and almost welcomed controversy. Critiques of his work were often as varied as Capote's literary devices. Although the body of his work is generally held in high regard, Capote was criticized in the early part of his career for being no more than a short-story writer and was often classified as a southern Gothic romanticist. Later he was criticized for not meeting his early "promise," and, finally, debate swirled around Capote because of his most famous work, *In Cold Blood* (1965). The literary brouhaha surrounding that work was simple and has proven enduring. It focused on the question: can reportage in any form be considered art?

As he writes in *The Dogs Bark: Public People and Private Places* (1973), the writers "who had been most valuable to me were, in no particular order, James, Twain, Poe, Cather, Hawthorne, Sarah Orne Jewett . . . Flaubert, Jane Austen, Dickens, Proust, Chekhov, Katherine Mansfield, E. M. Forster, Turgenev, De Maupassant, and Emily Brontë."

Born Truman Streckfus Persons in New Orleans on 30 September 1924, the son of Archuylus (Archie) Persons and Lillie May Persons Capote, Capote died in Los Angeles on 25 August 1984 of complications from liver disease. Between these two events Truman Capote managed to construct one of the most intriguing and highly visible literary careers in the twentieth century.

Capote's childhood was a particularly lonely one. By the time he was four years old his parents were divorced, and he was shuffled from relative to relative; the happiest part of his youth was undoubtedly spent with his elderly, unmarried cousins in Monroeville, Alabama. Here he met one of his lifelong friends, Harper Lee, to whom he would dedicate *In Cold Blood*. When Lee wrote *To Kill a Mockingbird* (1960), she patterned the character Dill after her childhood friend, whom she remembered as lonely and dreamy. Of Dill she writes that "Beautiful things floated around in his dreamy head. . . . he preferred his own twilight world, a world where babies slept, waiting to be gathered like morning lilies."

At the age of ten Capote submitted a short story to a Mobile newspaper sponsoring a children's writing contest. He won and in the process provoked a vigorous response in little Monroeville, not unlike those his stories in later years provoked. The winning story, "Old Mr. Busybody," was clearly based on several persons living in Monroeville, a point that few townspeople missed and a technique that Capote often employed throughout his career.

Although Capote admitted that after winning the award he wanted to become a writer, his goals were not set until he was in his teens. By then he had developed his style, although that style underwent major changes throughout his career. All his life Capote seems to have sought more from his writing, and over time he demonstrated a willingness to reinvent his writing style(s). This, of course, ultimately led to the development of what he considered a new art form, but it also may have been at the heart of his artistic crisis later in his career.

In 1939 Truman, at age fifteen, joined his mother and her second husband, Joseph Capote, in New York. Although Truman took his stepfather's surname, his personal life remained unstable. His relationship with his mother was emotionally debilitating and remained so throughout his life. Capote attended several boarding schools in New York and then a high school in Connecticut before dropping out when he was seventeen. He began work at *The New Yorker* as a copyboy.

Given the mood and tone of his early works, it is clear that Capote was influenced by the writings of Edgar Allan Poe, but his constant experimentation with technique makes it difficult to classify his works as belonging to any one school. Capote biographer William Nance refers to Capote's earliest works as "The Dark Stories," tales "dominated by fear" that sometimes intermingle the real with fantasy. These tales include "A Tree of Night" (1943), "Miriam" (1944), "The Headless Hawk" (1946), "Shut a Final Door" (1947), and "Master Misery" (1948).

In 1948 Capote's first novel, *Other Voices, Other Rooms,* established him as a bright new talent. Like the stories before it, the novel is a dark and dreamlike tale, a romance with symbolism and imagery. It is the story of leaving childhood—some would say losing childhood—and the protagonist's search for love. The book had strong autobiographical elements, a point to which Capote later agreed.

As with almost everything Capote wrote, reviewers of *Other Voices, Other Rooms* clashed sharply about the value of the young author's latest work. Although the majority of reviews were favorable, Capote was criticized for his choice of subject matter and a tendency to overwrite, what the *Times Literary Supplement* reviewer termed Capote's willingness to "mystify for the sake of mystification."

In his early writing the images of two different types of people clearly emerge from his characteriza-

Capote during his trip to the Soviet Union in 1955 with the troupe of
Porgy and Bess

tions: the eccentric and the normal. Capote seems to find no place for what lies between the offbeat and the norm, a point that initially led to disagreement about his writing. In addition, critics seemed determined to evaluate him as a southern writer in the tradition of "Gothic romance," a narrow and unjust labeling of the young author.

Just twenty-three years old at this juncture, Capote was suddenly a celebrated person, primarily because of his writing but also because of the subject of his book (homosexuality) and to some degree because of a photograph of a lounging, languid Capote on the book's dust jacket. As Capote explains in *Conversations with Capote* (1985) by Lawrence Grobel: "It [*Other Voices, Other Rooms*] was . . . a best-seller. But oddly, the photograph of me on the book aroused a great deal of controversy . . . it's just me lying on the sofa looking at the camera. But I guess it assumes . . . I'm more or less beckoning someone to climb on top of me."

In part because of his effete and unusual persona, his proclivity for renowned friends, and his willingness to promote both himself and his work, Capote seemed at times as much a celebrity as an author. He seemed also either to attract or be attracted to well-known people, all of which heightened his fame as a celebrity, perhaps at the cost of muddying his reputation as a writer. At first it was his lavish lifestyle and the people with whom he surrounded himself that attracted attention. Later it was his exposure in film (*Murder by Death,* 1976) and his many television appearances, in which he often discussed his views about the criminal justice system. In any case Capote's nonliterary celebrity may have resulted in some critical resentment against him and translated into negative reviews for his writing.

In 1949 *A Tree of Night and Other Stories* proved to be consistent with his earlier fiction. This collection of short stories focuses either on the darker side of life, a psychic world, the supernatural, or a combination of each. As Mark Schorer explains, Capote's stories are "about people who are alone and without love, who are alone because they are without love, and who, in their isolated, alienated condition, come upon sinister, usually grotesque, often disgusting creatures with whom they are imprisoned and whom they are unable to. . . elude" because these creatures are themselves, and in learning this, perhaps then "they are free to love."

Two stories in *Tree of Night*, "Jug of Silver" and "Children on Their Birthdays," display a definite shift in Capote's writing, however. Both stories are bright, first-person narratives that sometimes present the characters in a comedic fashion, offering a glimpse of a new Capote, or at least another aspect of the old Capote.

About the same time *Tree of Night* was published, Capote left for Europe and traveled extensively across the Continent, writing travel essays and portraits. This shift from fiction proved important because Capote refined the technical skills of observation, interviewing, and detail needed to produce what he considered significant works of nonfiction. The result was *Local Color* (1950), a collection of travel articles about New Orleans, New York, Brooklyn, Hollywood, Europe, Ischia, Spain, and Tangier that often displays Capote's flair for lyrical writing with precision in both detail and dialogue.

In 1951, while in Sicily, he wrote *The Grass Harp*, and a year later he adapted it into a Broadway play. *The Grass Harp* is reminiscent of "Children on Their Birthdays" because of the first-person narration, and, as Nance observes in *The Worlds of Truman Capote* (1970), the story "gives the impression of being set in the world of real people, thus firmly establishing a movement from the subjective (such as in *Other Voices, Other Rooms*) toward the objective."

Capote also adapted a story by O. Henry into a Broadway play, *House of Flowers*. Like his adaptation of *The Grass Harp*, it was not a financial success. Capote was dissatisfied with his efforts in playwriting, but in 1954 he branched out once again, this time by writing the screenplay for *Beat the Devil*, a movie directed by John Huston. It became a cult classic, probably because, as John Barry Ryan put it, Capote "was making a movie for his own amusement." Starring Humphrey Bogart, Jennifer Jones, Robert Morley, Gina Lollobrigida, and Peter Lorre, it was originally intended to be a mystery similar to *The Maltese Falcon* (1941). Working on a tight deadline, however, Capote turned it into a mystery-comedy. With offbeat dialogue and a plot that seemed to go in opposite directions all at once and yet magically come together, Capote's screenplay was a creative if not a financial success.

In the winter of 1955 Capote accompanied the company of *Porgy and Bess* as it toured Russia. The result was an article in *The New Yorker*, "The Muses Are Heard," which was later published in book form. Capote's interest in nonfiction as literature is not only evident in this work, but its critical success almost certainly started his thinking that a more expansive work with the proper subject could be highly successful. As he did for his later nonfiction, Capote took copious notes. *The Muses Are Heard* (1956), however, is different from *In Cold Blood* in that Capote takes facts and makes them read like fiction. *The Muses Are Heard* proved pivotal in Capote's career. In the preface to *Music for Chameleons: New Writing* he writes:

> that book was an important event for me: while writing it, I realized I just might have found a solution to what had always been my greatest creative quandary. . . . For several years I had been increasingly drawn toward journalism as an art form in itself. I had two reasons. First, it didn't seem to me that anything truly innovative had occurred in prose writing, or writing generally, since the 1920s; second, journalism as art was almost virgin terrain, for the simple reason that very few literary artists ever wrote narrative journalism and when they did, it took the form of travel essays or autobiography. *The Muses Are Heard* had set me to thinking on different lines altogether: I wanted to produce a journalistic novel, something on a large scale that would have the credibility of fact, the immediacy of film, the depth and freedom of prose, and the precision of poetry.

In 1956, the same year he published *The Muses Are Heard*, Capote wrote a nonfiction short story, "A Christmas Memory," which was published a decade later as a book. This was one of his favorite pieces, probably because it was about his relationship with his beloved Sook Faulk, the cousin primarily responsible for raising him. As the narrator, Capote describes with pristine clarity his memory of her:

> I am seven; she is sixty something. We are cousins, very distant ones, and we have lived together—well, as long as I can remember. . . . We are each other's best friend. She calls me Buddy, in memory of a boy who was formerly her best friend. The other Buddy died in the 1880's when she was still a child. She is still a child.

Capote's next work resulted from a bet with editors at *The New Yorker* that he could turn "even" a journalistic piece into literature. An interview in 1957 with Marlon Brando at the time the movie *Sayonara* was being filmed offered the author the opportunity to prove his point. The result was "The Duke in His Domain," a profile piece that is part travel sketch, part flashback, and part descriptive narrative. This nonfiction article, as Capote later related, "turned out quite successfully. Of course I won the bet."

In 1958 *Esquire* published *Breakfast at Tiffany's.* Published in book form with three short stories, this novel introduced Capote's best-known character, Holly Golightly. It also produced some of the best reviews for any of Capote's work to that point. Stanley Kaufman wrote that from her first appearance "Holly leaps to life. Her dialogue has the perfection of pieces of mosaic fitting neatly and unassailably in place.... His fiction is strongest, most vital, when it resembles his best nonfiction."

Many critics also felt that Capote had displayed a level of maturity missing in his earlier fiction. In *Breakfast at Tiffany's* Capote's characters are more likable, more realistic, and fashioned with a humorous pen. More important, Capote had been criticized in earlier works for prose that at times seemed contrived. For the most part, *Breakfast at Tiffany's* escaped this criticism and had the critic for the *Times Literary Supplement,* as well as others, placing Capote "among the leading American writers of the day." After publication of *Breakfast at Tiffany's* even Norman Mailer felt a need to comment about the highs and lows of Capote's writing:

> Truman Capote I do not know well, but I like him. He is tart as a grand aunt, but in his way he is a ballsy little guy, and he is the most perfect writer of my generation. He writes the best sentences word for word, rhythm upon rhythm. I would not have changed two words in *Breakfast at Tiffany's,* which will become a small classic. Capote has still given no evidence that he is serious about the deep resources of the novel, and his short stories are too often saccharine. At his worst he has less to say than any good writer I know.

In late 1959 Capote came upon the idea for his best-known book. While reading *The New York Times* he ran across an article about a brutal murder in Kansas. For the next six years Capote wandered the plains of Kansas as he researched the story of the murder of the Clutter family. The result was *In Cold Blood,* a blending of journalistic style and fictional technique that captured Capote's desire to outline the events with the fuller description and dialogue given to novelists. Anxious to prove that "journalism is the most underestimated, the least explored of literary mediums," Capote hoped that *In Cold Blood* contained "the credibility of fact, the immediacy of film, the depth and freedom of prose and the precision of poetry."

From the outset the book was highly successful–it was on *The New York Times* best-seller list for more than a year–and critically acclaimed. However, in due time a literary uproar ensued. The debate was more like a groundswell than an eruption. Critics and supporters had ample time to line up and digest Capote's latest work because in 1965 it was serialized in four consecutive issues of *The New Yorker* prior to its publication as a book. The author called it the "nonfiction novel"; others labeled it a type of "new journalism." Supporters said it was a literary masterpiece that heralded a new genre. Critics said it was nothing new at all.

Although the narrative is brilliant, the characters vivid, and the reporting full of depth, it is doubtful that Capote offered up anything new as far as writing techniques. But while the medium remained the same, the source changed. Instead of fiction, Capote used fact; rather than the imagined, he portrayed a reality so cold and ruthless that it seemed as though it only could have come from the imagination.

Avoiding conventional forms of journalism, Capote presented facts with an array of literary devices. He told the story chronologically, reconstructing the story in dramatic scenes, thereby achieving a scenic depiction rather than a historical summary. He recorded dialogue in full rather than in the bits and pieces common to reportage and historiography. He depicted mannerisms, gestures, styles, and manner of dress to portray characters in rich detail. He employed point of view, which new journalism critic John Hollowell writes "generates sympathy for the killers [Perry Smith and Dick Hickok] by narrating their stories from the viewpoints of comforting women close to them." Capote extended these techniques to interior monologue by reporting events as his characters were thinking about them. For example, in describing the night of the murders, Capote reports Smith's impressions:

> And I thought, Why don't I walk off? Walk to the highway, hitch a ride. I sure Jesus didn't want to go back in that house. And yet–How can I explain this? It was like I wasn't part of it. More as though I was reading a story. And I had to know what was going to happen. The end.

As the story unravels, the effect is dramatic, perhaps because it is untainted with subjective musings by the author. The story begins with the mix of scenes between the major characters and between the two aspects of American life that Capote portrays and explores. Although the biographical portraits of the two murderers certainly do not dominate the narrative, they are lengthy compared to those of the Clutters.

This, of course, may have fit perfectly into Capote's structure in telling the story, but some critics felt it displayed a lack of balance that revealed Capote's deeper fascination with the social misfits rather than ordinary members of normal society.

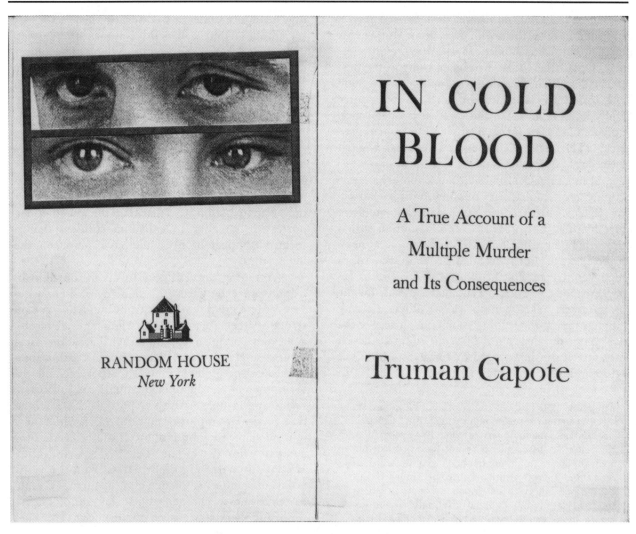

Title page spread for Capote's best-known work

Capote's expert handling of the horrific meeting of the "haves" and "have nots" can hardly be criticized, however. He relentlessly builds suspense by shunning a purely chronological retelling of the tragic story. He avoids an early description of the murders by jumping to the following morning. Instead of providing details about the deaths, Capote relates the attitudes of those who knew the Clutters. The effect is powerful yet quiet and frighteningly human. For example, Capote records a conversation between the local postmistress, Myrtle Clare, and a mail messenger, Sadie "Mother" Truitt, the morning following the murders:

> In fact, on that Sunday morning Mrs. Clare had just poured herself a cup of coffee from a freshly brewed pot when Mother Truitt returned.
>
> "Myrt!" she said, but could say no more until she had caught her breath. "Myrt, there's two ambulances gone to the Clutters."

Her daughter said, "Where's the ten-thirty-two?"

"Ambulances. Gone to the Clutters'."

"Well, what about it? It's only Bonnie. Having one of her spells. Where's the ten-thirty-two?"

Mother Truitt subsided; as usual, Myrt knew the answer, was enjoying the last word. Then a thought occurred to her. "But Myrt, if it's only Bonnie, why would there be two ambulances?"

Capote also focuses the reader's attention on the irony of a visit to an insurance office by Mr. Clutter just hours before his death. "'Yes, yes,' said Mr. Clutter as though conversing with himself. 'I've plenty to be grateful for—wonderful things in my life.'"

Not until Dick and Perry have been captured does Capote, through Perry's confession, describe the murders. Only then does it become clear that the tragedy need not have occurred, that fate, in the form of Hickok and Smith, had indiscriminately descended upon the Clutter family. Whatever the reasons—discord between the fugitives, Perry's hatred for his father, or the cold practicality of leaving no witnesses—the crime was senseless. As Perry so coldly relates in his confession: "I didn't want to harm the man (Herbert Clutter). I thought he was a very nice gentleman. Soft-spoken. I thought so right up to the moment I cut his throat."

The success of the book, coupled with the vast amount of publicity it received, seemed to many to herald new horizons for journalists and journalism while challenging the traditional role of fiction. More than one critic said Capote had written a factual story fictionally, apparently meaning that Capote fictionalized some of the facts of the story. The author adamantly denied this, remaining steadfast in his claim to have created a new writing form, a claim that ruffled feathers in the literary community. At the heart of the debate was the nature of reportage. Since the earliest newspapers in the 1600s, journalists usually have had to rely on "sources" for information. The problem was obvious: sources are often self-serving, and stories are often distorted representations of reality because of it. The question then becomes: How can the reporter report the reality of an issue without being intensely involved? Capote's answer was simple: the reporter cannot.

Capote became, in fact, intensely involved. With extraordinary stamina and patience he researched, interviewed, collected, and stored information about the Clutter murders, about the police investigation, about the arrest and charges, about the conviction of the men who perpetrated an act so senseless as to be inexplicable. Of course, that is what *In Cold Blood* is: an explanation. It explains how four deaths—six if the executions of Smith and Hickock are counted—resulted when the distant poles of society violently meet. Industrious, honest, and God-fearing, the Clutters are an American family that represents what are considered America's core traditions. Both Smith and Hickok are removed from this rubric. They are the misplaced and forgotten, and, interestingly, they are the force that drives *In Cold Blood* and what makes it so powerful. Capote tells about the crime, relates the characters, and gives the characters' insights to both, but the story is about the *why*, not the how or the what. This seems essentially the story behind the new journalism and the nonfiction novel.

Critics of Capote's nonfiction novel said that the use of literary devices—sketches, dialogue, and in-depth reportage akin to that of *In Cold Blood*—had a long journalistic tradition, particularly by journal-

ists turned novelists such as Stephen Crane and Mark Twain. "Realistic" novels—stories that fictionalize real events, persons, or issues, novels such as *Sister Carrie* (1900) or *The Red Badge of Courage* (1895)—were compared to *In Cold Blood*. The story was also compared to Theodore Dreiser's *An American Tragedy* (1925) and Ernest Hemingway's *Green Hills of Africa* (1935), but the work it may have most closely resembled is Frank Norris's muckraking classic, *The Octopus* (1901). Like *In Cold Blood*, this early-twentieth-century novel is based upon factual events, and the author uses similar techniques as he juxtaposes characters and settings. According to detractors of *In Cold Blood*, many of these books were superior to Capote's because they contained the imagination necessary for fiction.

To Capote, criticism that in-depth reportage represented what Normal Mailer termed "a failure of imagination" was short-sighted. Capote explained that he had to transcribe verbatim long quotes and have a perfect eye for visual detail, understand the subtleties dealing with real people, and yet somehow maintain an objective approach. According to Capote, these were all elements of reporting and writing that good fiction writers had to master. He writes:

> the reporter must be able to empathize with personalities outside his usual imaginative range, mentalities unlike his own, kinds of people he would never have written about had he not been forced by encountering them inside the journalistic situation. . . . It seems to me that most contemporary novelists. . . are too subjective, mesmerized by private demons. . . . If I were naming names, I'd name myself among others. At any rate, I did at one time feel an artistic need to escape my self-created world. I wanted to exchange it, creatively speaking, for the everyday objective world we all inhabit.

To some, *In Cold Blood* was reportage, perhaps great reportage, but it was nothing new, and it certainly was not literature. Capote even drew criticism for employing the journalistic concept of objectivity. Some critics believed that in removing himself so completely from the story Capote provided only facts and no voice *about* the horrible acts he outlined. James Gindlin wrote:

> *In Cold Blood* . . . seems a substitute for the novelist's concerns. In attempting to stick so literally to the story and in placing his authorial stance so completely within his characters, Capote evades the responsibility of an author to understand and comment upon his characters through some kind of complex perspective that is not necessarily theirs.

Capote believed that, from a technical viewpoint, this was one of the most difficult aspects of writing the book. "Ordinarily, the reporter has to use himself as a character, an eyewitness observer, in order to retain credibility. But I felt that it was essential to the seemingly detached tone of the book that the author should be absent. Actually, in all my reportage, I had tried to keep myself as invisible as possible."

In retrospect, criticism of Capote's supposedly objective approach bears close scrutiny since the author *subjectively* chose the Clutter murders as the story; he also chose the people to be interviewed, what to record of those interviewed, what to leave in and to leave out about those interviews, what scenes to write and how to order them, how the book begins, how it ends, who would be emphasized, and who would not. In short, Capote chose which facts to include, and in doing so he created the distinctive point of view of *In Cold Blood*.

At times it appeared nothing about *In Cold Blood* would escape criticism. Even when Capote's writing was complimented, other aspects of the book, including the publicity, were criticized. Hilton Kramer wrote in *The New Leader,* "It is not enough, apparently, for this book to be very good; it must be thought great. It is not enough that it has something to tell us about our own time, but must be promoted as if it were a work for all time."

Others suggested that *In Cold Blood* was more research than writing. Capote disagreed. "Several critics complained that 'nonfiction novel' was a catch phrase, a hoax, and that there was nothing really original or new about what I had done. But there were those who felt differently, other writers who realized the value of my experiment and moved swiftly to put it to their own use."

Interestingly, journalists such as Tom Wolfe, Jimmy Breslin, Gail Sheehy, Robert Daley, David Halberstam, and Larry L. King did put it to use, and some (Wolfe, for example) can claim some fame along with Capote as one of the fathers of the new journalism, an honor Capote quickly discarded after publication of *In Cold Blood*. "James Breslin and Tom Wolfe, and that crowd," said Capote in an interview with George Plimpton, "they have nothing to do with creative journalism—in the sense that I use the term—because neither of them nor any of that school of reporting, have the proper fictional technical equipment. It's useless for a writer whose talent is essentially journalistic to attempt creative reportage, because it simply would not work."

Capote believed that the new journalists could not write a nonfiction novel because the writer had to be in control of various fictive techniques as well

as being "a very good fiction writer." Of course, many new journalists would have disagreed with his assessment of their literary talents. What is interesting about Capote's position is that he placed himself squarely in agreement and then disagreed with his critics. Capote agreed that there was a distinct difference between fiction and nonfiction techniques and seems to have believed that the difference between writing literature and reportage was too large a gap to bridge for all but the most gifted.

Criticism of nonfiction fiction centers around what literature is and is not and what each writer, critic, and reader considers it to be. Basically, the definitional problem is ideological in nature. At the heart of the debate are values, and one could argue that whether something is literary or not is not as much a trait of the text itself as it is a way of reading the text. Chris Anderson writes that "the problem with nonfiction is that it's a negative term for something positive, implying that somehow nonfiction is less than fiction."

It was even difficult to name this new genre, if in fact it was new or a genre. As practitioners, critics, and proponents struggled to name this new style, there was no shortage of labels: nonfiction fiction, new journalism, nonfiction novel, literature of fact, creative journalism, even parajournalism. Whatever the name, Capote's style combined autobiography, confession, novel, and journalism into a narrative that led to questions about the differences between fiction and nonfiction; definitions about what comprises a novel, what a novel is, and what it is not; and the difference between literature and journalism.

This leads to the heart of what supporters of nonfiction argued: the novel as a form is either dead or dying. Although this claim may be wildly inaccurate, some valid questions were raised at the time. Was there still a place for realistic fiction? In a world that increasingly produced the unbelievable, why write fiction when reality could be immensely more interesting and exotic? Philip Howard Jr., in his 1971 master's thesis, "The New Journalism: A Nonfiction Concept of Writing," argues that:

> fiction writers tell us about a reality that has far outraced them at their own game. They cannot compete with the authorship afforded the reporter with each new hour. A good novel today is only a diminished echo compared to a piece of well written new journalism.

The question after *In Cold Blood* was what would follow. Quantitatively, the answer is very little. In 1973 Capote's *The Dogs Bark,* a collection of previously published material, was published. *Music for Chameleons* (1980) represented fresh new work by Capote, offering a calliope of forms that included short stories, a novella ("Handcarved Coffins"), and a series of conversational portraits, one even with himself. A continuation of his exploration of uniting literary devices with reportage, *Music for Chameleons* perhaps revealed more about Capote than any other work. His conversational portraits are written in first person, with dialogue between himself and the interviewees, and indicate Capote's lifelong fascination with celebrities (Marilyn Monroe), social misfits (Robert Beausoleil), and offbeat characters (Big Junebug Johnson).

These portraits are written much as Capote would begin a play, placing the characters in the scene, providing any necessary background necessary for context, and using colorful dialogue (even Capote's harshest critics appreciated his virtuosity in handling dialogue) such as the following from "Hidden Gardens":

Big Junebug Johnson (eyes rotating): Oh, honey, don't let me commence. . . .

TC: Just how long you been Mrs. O'Reilly?

Big Junebug Johnson: Three years next July. Actually, I didn't have much choice. I was real confused. He's a lot younger than me, maybe twenty years. And good-looking, my goodness. Catnip to the ladies.

In "Then It All Came Down," an interview with Bobby Beausoleil, notorious for his involvement with Charles Manson, Capote writes:

TC: Listen to me, Bobby. And answer carefully. Suppose, when you get out of here, somebody came to you—let's say Charlie—and asked you to commit an act of violence, kill a man, would you do it?

RB (after lighting another cigarette, after smoking it half through): I might. It depends. I never meant to . . . to . . . hurt Gary Hinman. But one thing happened. And another. And then it all came down.

TC: And it was all good.

RB: It was all good.

The novella in *Music for Chameleons,* perhaps the book's most intriguing piece, is a return to nonfiction fiction, but this time Capote places himself in the story. "Hardcarved Coffins: A Nonfiction Account of an American Crime" represents another attempt by Capote to intermingle reportage and extended dialogue to tell a story and illustrates his willingness to experiment with styles. As Capote explained:

I set myself center stage, and reconstructed, in a severe, minimal manner, commonplace conversations with everyday people . . . after writing hundreds of pages of this simple-minded sort of thing, I eventually developed a style. I had found a framework into which I could assimilate everything I knew about writing.

However, if some critics were hostile to Capote's lack of documentation in *In Cold Blood,* "Handcarved Coffins" contained even less. Although highly detailed, the larger facts are omitted. For example:

March, 1975.

A small town in a small Western state. A focus for the many large farms and cattle-raising ranches surrounding it, the town, with a population of less than ten thousand, supports twelve churches and two restaurants. A movie house, though it has not shown a movie in ten years, still stands stark and cheerless on Main Street. There once was a hotel, too; but that also has been closed, and nowadays the only place a traveler can find shelter is the Prairie Motel.

From 1968 to 1972 Capote had selected, rewritten, and indexed his letters, other people's letters, and his diaries and journals (which contain detailed accounts of hundreds of scenes and conversation) for the years 1943 through 1965 to use in a variation on the nonfiction novel. According to Capote, he wrote the different chapters of *Answered Prayers* (1986) out of sequence. "I was able to do this because the plot—or rather plots—was true, and all the characters were real: it wasn't difficult to keep it all in mind, for I hadn't invented anything."

Following the publication of *In Cold Blood,* Capote's health began to deteriorate, and professionally he seems to have gone through an artistic crisis. This crisis, related to a form of overwriting that he termed "dense," can be tied directly to his health problems with alcohol and drugs. It sharply curtailed work on his eagerly awaited *Answered Prayers.* Although neither Capote nor his editor knew it at the time, the four chapters published by *Esquire* in 1975 and 1976 represented the final published work of *Answered Prayers.* (Although the book, minus the chapter "Mojave," was published by Random House in 1987, editor Joseph Fox explains that Capote may have written other chapters titled "A Severe Insult to the Brain" and "Father Flanagan's All-Night Nigger-Queen Kosher Café" but then destroyed them. Fox adds that friends of Capote claim to have read them or had had them read aloud by Capote.) For various reasons Capote was not satis-

The last photograph of Capote, 23 August 1984 (photograph by Joanne Carson)

fied with his writing at this time. As he explained: "I was not using everything I knew about writing—all I'd learned from film scripts, plays, reportage, poetry, the short story, novellas, the novel. A writer ought to have all his colors . . . But how?"

Unfortunately, Capote's promise of producing a book that would turn gossip into an art form failed to bear fruit, although it was clear that he intended this work to be his best. "*Answered Prayers* is not intended as any ordinary roman à clef, a form where facts are disguised as fiction," Capote wrote. "My intentions are the reverse: to remove disguises, not manufacture them." The degree to which Capote achieved his goal certainly caused consternation among some of his principals. His portraits were often of real people, or thinly disguised at best. The following excerpt from *Answered Prayers,* aptly titled "Unspoiled Monsters," tells of Denham Fouts's background:

Denny . . . was a legend well-known to me, a myth entitled: Best-Kept Boy in the World. When Denny was sixteen, he was living in a Florida crossroads cracker town. . . . Rescue . . . arrived one day in the fattish form

of a millionaire driving a brand-new built-to-order 1936 Duesenberg convertible. . . . [H]e had been married twice, but his preference was Ganymedes between the ages of fourteen and seventeen. When he saw Denny, it must have been as though a collector of antique porcelain had strayed into a junkshop and discovered a Meissen "white swan" service: the shock! the greedy chill! he bought doughnuts, invited Denny for a spin in the Duesenberg, even offered him command of the wheel; and that night without having returned home for even a change of underwear, Denny was a hundred miles away in Miami. A month later his grieving parents, who had despaired after sending searching parties through the local swamps, received a letter postmarked Paris, France. The letter became the first entry in a many-volumed scrapbook: The Universal Travels of Our Son Denham Fouts.

With Capote's death, the promise of *Answered Prayers* could not be fulfilled. Whether he destroyed other chapters, never wrote them, or filed them away is not known. As Joseph M. Fox wrote in the editor's note to *Answered Prayers,* "There is only one person who knows the truth, and he is dead. God bless him."

An evaluation of Capote's work is somewhat daunting. His career was multidimensional. In the early years he wrote fiction and later turned to fact; at first he wrote dark, mystical, and unreal tales; later he wrote stories about real people in real situations. Capote seemed fascinated with the distant poles of behavior, emotion, and action rather than the gray area of life that comprises the bulk of everyday living. There are also clear biographical elements that run throughout his writing and across his career. Capote obviously drew upon his childhood and early experiences for *Other Voices, Other Rooms* and *A Grass Harp. Breakfast at Tiffany's* could have included some of his New York friends. *A Christmas Memory* (1966) and *The Thanksgiving Visitor* (1967) are specifically about his childhood. *Music for Chameleons* and *Answered Prayers* relate tales of people, places, and conversations from New Orleans to Paris.

After *In Cold Blood* Capote was best known as a master of the short story. In fact, most of his work is generally short. His work is also characterized by its subject matter. Capote wrote more about people and places than about issues and ideas. In one sense this brought more attention to the writer, as can be seen in his unwillingness to "taint" *In Cold Blood* with moralistic judgments.

Honesty, sprinkled liberally with ego, is consistent with the Capote persona. As he writes in the preface of *Music for Chameleons,* "one day I started writing, not knowing that I had chained myself for life to a noble but merciless master. When God hands you a gift, he also hands you a whip; and the whip is intended solely for self-flagellation." In *Music for Chameleons* Capote shares more of himself with the reader in one paragraph than most writers ever do: "I'm an alcoholic. I'm a drug addict. I'm homosexual. I'm a genius. Of course, I could be all four of these dubious things and still be a saint. But I sure ain't no saint yet, nawsuh." Capote was fun-loving, flamboyant, uninhibited, witty, charming, and at times, perhaps because of his unstable childhood, insecure. A description by Humphrey Bogart when *Beat the Devil* was being filmed perhaps best captures the spirit of Capote, particularly before his health began to fail: "At first you can't believe him, he's so odd, and then you want to carry him around with you always."

Capote felt strongly about taking chances, about "risking" six years in Kansas, and about being at the forefront of a new literary form. "Writers, at least those who take genuine risks, who are willing to bite the bullet and walk the plank, have a lot in common with another breed of lonely men—the guys who make a living shooting pool and dealing cards."

Whether Capote created a new art form as he claimed seems of little importance in retrospect. Although critics waged war over the labeling of *In Cold Blood,* its legacy can be found in the blurring of what was once a clear dividing line between literature and journalism. Neither the new journalism nor the nonfiction novel has died, and the successes of writers such as Norman Mailer and Tom Wolfe, as well as Capote himself, provide evidence that the "literature of fact" continues to intrigue and challenge readers.

Biographies:

William Nance, *The Worlds of Truman Capote* (New York: Stein & Day, 1970);

Helen S. Garson, *Truman Capote* (New York: Ungar, 1980);

Gerald Clarke, *Capote* (New York: Simon & Schuster, 1988).

References:

Chris Anderson, ed., *Literary Nonfiction, Theory, Criticism, Pedagogy* (Carbondale & Edwardsville: Southern Illinois University Press, 1989);

Edward J. Epstein, *Between Fact and Fiction: The Problem of Journalism* (New York: Vintage Books, 1975);

Lawrence Grobel, *Conversation with Capote* (New York: New American Library, 1985);

John Hollowell, *Fact & Fiction, The New Journalism and the Nonfiction Novel* (Chapel Hill: University of North Carolina Press, 1977);

Philip Howard Jr., "The New Journalism: A Nonfiction Concept of Writing," master's thesis, University of Utah, 1971;

Ronald Weber, ed., *The Reporter as Artist: A Look at the New Journalism Controversy* (New York: Hastings House, 1974);

Tom Wolfe, *The New Journalism* (New York: Harper & Row, 1973).

Francis X. Clines
(7 February 1938 –   )

David R. Davies
University of Southern Mississippi

BOOK: *About New York* (New York: McGraw-Hill, 1980).

Well known for his foreign correspondence from London and Moscow, *New York Times* reporter Francis X. Clines established his reputation as a literary journalist in the late 1970s as the author of a long-running column, "About New York." In the course of three years Clines reinvigorated the column with vivid prose that captured the colorful and varied life of city-dwellers, the poor and the rich, the forgotten and the influential. The best of his "About New York" columns were collected in 1980 in the book *About New York.*

Clines, a native New Yorker who has spent his entire professional career at *The New York Times,* was born 7 February 1938 of second- and third-generation Irish stock, the son of Francis A. Clines, an accountant, and Mary Ellen Lenihan Clines. Clines was reared in Brooklyn, but his mother had been born in Hell's Kitchen, the working-class Irish ghetto on Manhattan's West Side. After high school Clines attended Fordham University briefly, but, finding his college experience unrewarding, he dropped out with the intention of getting drafted into the army and seeing the world. He was drafted in December 1956, but he spent both years of his army enlistment at nearby Fort Dix, New Jersey. He and his wife, Kathleen Conniff, had four children.

After mustering out of the army in 1958, Clines worked briefly at an aeronautical company, where the work bored him. Because he had enjoyed writing in high school, he began looking for work as a copyboy at New York's daily newspapers. The newspapers were not hiring, but Clines was persistent, overcoming his reserved nature and continually pestering a woman in the personnel office of *The New York Times'* about a job. "I knew that it was my only shot," Clines recalled in an unpublished interview on 8 August 1996. "I must have known that I had better push this one." The woman, who had been impressed with the essay Clines had written on his application for employment, finally relented and

Francis X. Clines

found Clines a position, and he was hired as a copyboy in the editorial writing department in December 1958.

In this era *New York Times* copyboys could gradually work their way up to become full-time reporters, and Clines began a long apprenticeship. From copyboy he moved up to cub reporter, working during a lengthy probationary period in a host of entry-level jobs–night rewrite, night police, even radio script writing at *The New York Times* radio station, WQXR. "It was a while, and then I finally passed," Clines recalled. Once hired as a full-time reporter, he began a series of reporting jobs, each one moving him a little farther up the reporting hierarchy. He started his reporting career by covering real estate news. Becoming a suburban reporter in 1965, he covered Suffolk County and eastern Long Island, working alone in the town of Riverhead far from the main *New York Times* office and getting, as he joked later, a taste of the life of a foreign correspondent.

Called in from the suburbs in 1968, Clines returned to Manhattan and for two years worked on the welfare-poverty beat in New York City. In 1970 he began a seven-year hitch in the statehouse bureau of the *Times* in Albany, becoming grounded in the nuances of political reporting, a job that Clines calls "the potter's wheel of the business." No matter what job reporters ultimately get, Clines said, "You always wind up having to go back to basic political reporting." In Albany, Clines tried to have fun with his writing, he recalled later, and he quickly earned a reputation as a good writer who injected personality and color into his political articles. During his final two years in Albany, Clines was bureau chief. He left the statehouse bureau in 1976 to return to New York City, where he worked in the City Hall bureau of the *Times*.

Later in 1976 *Times* editors were searching for someone to take over the "About New York" column. A *Times* editor, Sydney Schanberg, suggested Clines because of his colorful political articles. "His idea, which seemed odd to a number of people, I suspect, was that I try it," Clines recalled. Executive editor Abe Rosenthal gave the go-ahead, and Clines took over the column that was twenty-five years old in August 1976. From its inauguration in the early 1950s the column had been intended as a forum for colorful descriptive writing that would brighten the pages of the often-staid *Times*. The first "About New York" columnist had been Meyer Berger, the legendary *Times* reporter whose wide-ranging curiosity and detailed reporting were perfectly suited for the column. Berger's bright writing style set the tone for the three-times-a-week essay and set an example for successors as the column changed hands over the years. Clines, an eighteen-year veteran of the *Times* when he began writing "About New York," had always been a fan of Berger's style and had once met him during Berger's last years.

Clines approached the column first and foremost as a reporter. "The way I operate," Clines said, "I'm rooted in reporting, and then writing. If I have some interesting stuff out of the reporting, then that turns on the writing a bit. I don't like situations where I have to resort to writing when you don't have enough." Overemphasizing writing at the expense of careful reporting, Clines believed, would have been a mistake, one often committed by other "About New York" columnists over the years.

"They didn't go out and get enough information to stir the writing from within, and, of course, that's the key to it, I think, or to any story, and particularly to a column."

For Clines, the purpose of "About New York" was to re-create for his readers, in about nine hundred words, a moment and a place in time. He wanted, he said, to take a snapshot of reality in the column. Early in his "About New York" years, as Clines was preparing a piece on New York's Greenwood Cemetery, he ran across an unsigned *New York Times* essay written years earlier that perfectly captured the atmosphere of the magnificent old cemetery. "It was just brilliantly done, and I could stretch back because of its honesty and beautiful writing to that time," Clines recalled. "And so, when I went around to do the Greenwood Cemetery piece that I wanted to do, I had a wonderful connection to past reality. I remember reading that and thinking, 'I would like to have one of the stories I write found that way.' Because the best thing is capturing reality, capturing it honestly and not performing while you do it, just getting it right and clicking into the reader's mind." For Clines, that column served as a model for what he wanted to do—re-create the past in narratives that would stand in sharp contrast to the analytical prose that predominates in day-to-day news articles in the *Times* and other daily newspapers.

New York, of course, offered ample situations for Clines to re-create. Clines strove above all for wide variety in topic selection; he wanted to be unpredictable. "Honest curiosity is that way, I think," Clines said. "And in New York City, my God, I really didn't want to get into a rut. I feared that, actually. And so, I would force myself into areas that I might not otherwise get into, which was fun. I was forced to range in the city." His range was wide indeed. One day he would write about the Gotham Hotel barbershop and the patrons' discussions about changing hairstyles; then a column would describe the owners of a model ship shop; then Clines would report on a preschool class for disadvantaged children on the Lower East Side. The column varied from nuts-and-bolts reporting of city programs to descriptions of personalities to explorations of weighty civic issues. The columns were occasionally examinations of offbeat news items—the Good Humor Corporation's decision to liquidate its ice-cream trucks, for example. But most often the column reflected snapshots of the city's day-to-day life in all its variety—workers at their jobs, men and women at leisure, civic disputes, scenes of city life, and assorted tales of the down-and-out and up-and-coming.

Dust jacket for the collection of Clines's columns from The New York Times

"I would try to put myself in narrative situations," Clines recalled. This firsthand observation was the root of his "personal narrative authority," according to him: "What I mean is, the best story possible is the one you witness and retell, and then, the next best is talking to someone who actually saw what you're writing about." Accordingly, Clines's best device for pursuing a column, he said, is to invent an excuse to inject himself into a story, as when he visited a tunnel booth under the Hudson River, or when he visited the Bronx Zoo after closing time. "If I could get to these things, I'd be OK," Clines recalled. "I mean I would still have a lot of work to do, and then the writing after the reporting, but that was my comfort, my device."

"About New York" not only reflects Clines's narrative authority but also consistently reflects his working-class origins. Clines endeavored to write about middle- and lower-income people and to choose topics representing all New York City boroughs, not just Manhattan. The privileged and the affluent already had ample access to the newspapers, he believed. "In terms of New York City and in terms of *The New York Times,* I am from steerage,"

Clines said. "I mean I'm an Irish-Catholic college dropout from the outer boroughs. I'm from nowhere, so this was an opportunity to educate, I thought, the people who ran the paper about the rest of the city. It was a little conceit in my head, but I would always gravitate toward the non-celebrity and the humbler neighborhood and that sort of thing. And I really felt that it was a good idea because I was providing a richer mix for the newspaper."

Another feature of Clines's "About New York" columns is his striking and descriptive turns of phrase, evident in column after column no matter what the subject. Clines's writing is always rich in description and varied in language even while reflecting the facts and figures of nuts-and-bolts reporting. The writing is rarely overdone, however, and always serves to draw attention to the subject and not to Clines. "The day was the kind when the sun starts to stand up to the tired winter cold and bring color back to town," he writes of a March morning. A blind street singer warbles "like a plump urban robin." As deli countermen rapidly throw together sandwiches, customers watch closely with "a close, truth-in-bologna eyeballing as the sandwiches are flicked into being." A scientist stands in her laboratory and "seems like a finely wrought antimacassar glinting in the dimness of a shuttered mansion." Clines visits a morgue that "is a place of cold steel, pallid tile, and supine flesh," where "death is perversely vivid in surreal colors and odors."

Clines's columns were sometimes profiles of the varied lives of workers in New York City, profiles that include some of his best work. In "Oh-all Right!" (16 January 1979) Clines profiles one Herbert Jacobs, a nimble fifty-three-year-old who parks and moves his customers' cars all day long in an eight-block area of the Upper West Side, his job for twenty-five years. The constant movement of the cars is required by New York City's arcane parking regulations, which prohibit cars from remaining on one side of the street for more than a few hours at a time. Clines follows Jacob—everyone calls him Jacob—through a wintry day at work as he moves cars, hails his customers, and explains his secrets. Typical of Clines's work, the piece is a detached descriptive narrative of one man's toil, and Jacob is treated with dignity and respect. The car mover is described down to his calloused hands, all-season knickers, three stocking hats, ten undershirts, three sweaters, and multiple pairs of long johns. Throughout, Clines is only an observer, not a participant, and he injects little of himself or his own opinions into the piece. The story instead belongs to Jacob, a joyful man who proclaims throughout, "Everythin's gonna be oh-all right!"

In "Virtuoso" (22 February 1977) Clines describes Jacques Francais, a restorer and broker of rare violins and other stringed instruments, in the vivid detail that again demonstrates his subtle skill in turning a phrase. Clines observes as Francais welcomes customers into his thirteenth-floor office on West Fifty-seventh Street, a wide-open room "highlighted by the earthy and caramel tones of violins and cellos grouped in the shadows like dinner guests mellowed by brandy." He describes the intricate work of Francais, a descendant of eighteenth-century French violin makers, as the craftsman meets patrons who bring him violins to repair. Many bring him ancient instruments long forgotten in attics or basements, all the while hoping they have uncovered a Stradivarius. Most often their hopes are dashed. "Here is a combination of hearth and shop," Clines writes, "with a dozen fresh roses on the monsieur's desk and customers arriving like rich and wretched law clients, carrying their hopes and broken loves to him in velvet-lined cases and in sacks of chamois and of mundane plastic." The rare violins that do find their way into Francais's able hands are re-paired and stored on wooden shelves inside a steel safe. "Atop this wealth of wood," Clines writes, "rests a bust of Beethoven, who seems appropriately transfixed by a swoon of genius."

For another work-related column, "Openers" (9 April 1977), Clines finds himself in the locker room at Yankee Stadium early in a new baseball season. Clines is there not to describe the New York Yankees baseball players but the 250 vendors who sell beer and snacks to fans. The vendors range from Ken Spinner, a career hawker at thirty-seven who is "a kind of Satchel Paige of hawking who began at Ebbets Field with 15-cent frosticks," to fourteen-year-old Mary Nestor, whose youthful talents far outpace her rookie status. "Mary showed a beautiful move in the opening game," Clines writes with admiration, "keeping her back to the field and going to her nickel and dime pockets cleanly to continue making change at the moment Jim Wynn hit the first Yankee homer and her clientele jumped up and burst into screams." The vendor "lineup" includes medical students and hustlers, baseball lovers and entrepreneurs, and Clines lets several tell their stories in their own words. The vendors are overseen by field manager Sal Luigi, who exhorts them "in the honest, now antediluvian accent" of old Ebbets Field to go forth and make money: "O.K., guys, let's stay together," Luigi declares. "This is a family deal. Yiz wanna make a buck?—I'll see yiz make a buck. Let's get to our areas and keep the stuff moving!"

Some of Clines's columns deal with the peculiarities of New York City politics, reflecting his longtime experience covering the statehouse and citywide welfare issues. Here his features focus more on the personalities of politicians than on the political machinations of insiders. A 1977 profile of then-mayor Abraham D. Beame, titled "Tough Talk," focuses on the mayor's reticence and youthful rumbles with neighborhood gangs during his boyhood on the Lower East Side. In "The Good Life" (24 March 1977) Clines profiles a member of the city's Commission on Human Rights who is the first publicly identified homosexual to be appointed to a city commission. It is a sympathetic portrayal that focuses as much on the subject's ordinariness as on his declared homosexuality. "People don't realize it's fun being gay," the commissioner exuberantly declares to Clines. "I am conventional. I believe in the system. Most gay people are conventional." In "So What Do You Think?" (7 May 1977) Clines interviews teenage applicants for a competitive summer jobs program after revelations that plum jobs were being reserved for politically connected applicants. The young job-seekers, all from poor families, are both discouraged and cynical. "I want to know who's behind all this," one applicant declares. "I don't trust government one bit," declares another.

Clines's best essays are those in which he succeeds in his stated goal of capturing a moment in time. One of the most provocative is "The Battle of Lexington" (9 June 1977), in which Clines spends a Friday night watching the prostitutes on Twenty-third Street and Lexington Avenue as they solicit men in passing cars. At each red light the prostitutes materialize beyond each windshield "like a fantasized hood ornament," dressed in "the garish, dated skimpiness of hot pants" that is their uniform. Pimps preside over their domain from a neighborhood coffee shop. A balding man watches the scene from his third-story apartment. The police swoop in, but only briefly, and the prostitutes quickly return to working the street. "This," Clines writes, "was the ultimate convolution of the American drive-in experience of uniformed smiling waitresses gathered in a mercantile chorus of you-deserve-to-have-a-nice-day-sugar—a nightlong commercial of offerings to a glaring, humming chrome-plated line of lechery." Some prostitutes remain at daybreak, their diminishing numbers now watched by army reservists gathering at the armory down the street. The piece ends as a well-dressed pimp brushes by an army officer, "two men of natty rank passing in a dawn of shifting bodies." Clines draws the scene crisply but without comment; the reader is left to judge it on his or her own.

Similarly, in "Rolling into the Dusk" (16 November 1976) Clines succeeds in re-creating a reality of a different sort, the exhilarating love of street hockey that sustains a group of fourteen- and fifteen-year-olds on West Forty-ninth Street. "Even between the strolling hookers on Eighth Avenue and the Tenth Avenue variety who cater at corners to slow-driving motorists on carnal prowl," Clines observes, "childhood can be a meadow, an asphalt meadow." Watching fourteen-year-old Brian Mullen and his friends as they throw themselves into roller hockey, Clines observes, "is a restorative without equal for anyone wondering lately whether humanity has packaged and peddled itself into a fatally indentured circus." Clines follows Brian as he scrimmages and swaps skating stories with his friends on the street. Brian is a rising star on the tenement hockey circuit, destined like his two older brothers to find a place on a college ice hockey team. But the essay is less about Brian than the passion for sports that consumes the youth of his and so many other working-class neighborhoods. "While all about us there is the depressing TV-induced threat of children wasting away as mere sports spectators,"

Clines writes, "Brian and his friends are living the real life of childhood."

Clines's columns are not always so serious; sometimes he simply has fun, and he is occasionally whimsical. In "It Floats" (15 September 1979) Clines spends a day on the west coast of Staten Island at the Port Ivory factory, watching and listening as workers manufacture Ivory Soap, and he endeavors to learn why, just why, it floats. The occasion is the one hundredth anniversary of the soap, and Clines explains not only why it floats but the origin of its slogan, "99 44/100 percent pure," which Clines declares is "surely one of the tightest and best American slogans since 'Jesus Saves.'" Clines delights in the twists and turns in the history of Ivory, named decades ago in Harley Procter's moment of inspiration as he read the Forty-fifth Psalm. The company, Clines exults, has "enough success to warrant a Broadway musical entitled 'Harley!' with a frothy psalm scene featuring a line of dancers in ivory-clad derbies doing the Fosse float." Clines even asks the workers what they think about smelling like soap; most of them like it. "At Port Ivory, the workers are friendly and smell nice," Clines declares, "and plant safety includes eyewash fountains in case a stray squirt catches someone."

Other Clines columns take him to unusual places to make observations. For "Marriage Municipal-Style" (19 April 1977), he spent a day in the city of New York's municipal building in the marriage bureau, "a kind of motor vehicle department of the heart." He watches as Geraldine Sposato and Adolph Continanza wed in the windowless room that serves as the bureau's chapel. He interviews Sam Kessler, in charge of the chapel's waiting room, "a room which usually is mobbed on a Friday afternoon with scores of couples, babbling relatives and grains of rice crunching under foot." He watches as clerk "Myrtle Bradford puts love on the public record in three-quarter time" with a rotary rubber stamp. "Cha-gung, cha-gung, cha-gung she goes across the official document, numbering another license to marry, perchance to love." In "Birth by Remote Control" (15 April 1978) Clines visits the switchboard room of the city ambulance service and watches as city workers deal with crisis after crisis. Beryl Romano, a registered nurse and emergency-room veteran, is talking to a hysterical pregnant woman who is about to give birth alone in her Brooklyn apartment. "The lilting power of Nurse Romano comes across immediately" as she guides the woman through childbirth, Clines writes.

After three years of writing "About New York," Clines asked for another assignment. The three-times-a-week job of doing the column was wearing, and Clines wanted to do something different. "I just didn't want to become a minor institution," he recalled. "I always look on this business as something like vaudeville: You've got to rework your act every three or four years, or they'll bring the hook out." Clines asked in 1979 to transfer to the Washington, D.C., bureau of the *Times*. He covered the presidential campaign in 1979 and 1980 and remained in the Washington bureau until June 1986.

In 1986 Clines began his first job as a *Times* foreign correspondent, working in the newspaper's London bureau. He remained there until 1988, when he served a brief stint in the *Times* bureau in Jerusalem. In 1989 he became the Moscow correspondent for the *Times,* where he remained for three years, covering the rise of Mikhail Gorbachev, the fall of Communism, and an abortive coup. "It was great stuff," Clines said. "That was a lottery ticket, my asking for that." The Moscow assignment was the hardest assignment of his life but also the most exciting, he said. "I really had a great time," he said, partially because the job allowed a mix of hard news and feature writing. "I don't like to do just feature writing." Since 1992 Clines has been back in the Washington, D.C., bureau of the *Times*.

Clines's second wife is Alison Mitchell, also a reporter in the bureau, whom he married in 1995. Among the honors he has received are the Meyer Berger Award for feature writing, awarded to him in 1979 by Columbia University, and the Deadline Writing Award of the American Society of Newspaper Editors in 1988. Clines looks back on the "About New York" column as the turning point of his long career. "Well, I guess it kind of defined me," Clines said. "I think that's what got me noticed and gave me credit for being deserving of a place on the paper. People would remember my byline, I think, because of that column, because of the work I did there. It's never gone away, I'm kind of remembered for that, even though now, God knows, it's been quite a while. . . . I'm still identified for having done that." Or, as Clines reflects in the introduction to the collection of his "About New York" columns: "I have a new assignment now—new people in a different place—but New York will never be done with me. It will outlive all the people I love and all the stories I loved to tell, and it will survive as a memorial to us all, to all the ordinary people at its heart."

Richard Ben Cramer

(12 June 1950 –   )

Robert Schmuhl
University of Notre Dame

BOOKS: *Ted Williams: The Seasons of the Kid* (Englewood Cliffs, N.J.: Prentice Hall, 1991);
What It Takes: The Way to the White House (New York: Random House, 1992);
Bob Dole (New York: Vintage, 1995).

TELEVISION SCRIPTS: "The Choice '92," by Cramer, Thomas Lennon, and Michael Epstein, PBS *Frontline,* 21 October 1992;
"Tabloid Truth: The Michael Jackson Scandal," by Cramer and Lennon, PBS *Frontline,* 15 February 1994.

OTHER: "Prize Winner News/Deadline," *Best Newspaper Writing,* edited by Roy Peter Clark (Saint Petersburg, Fla.: Modern Media Institute, 1980), pp. 1–42;
"From Cairo (Egypt) in 1978," in *The Pulitzer Prize Archive,* volume 1, "International Reporting 1928–1985," edited by Heinz-Dietrich Fischer (München, London, New York, Oxford & Paris: K. G. Saur, 1987), pp. 291–298;
"What Do You Think of Ted Williams Now?," in *The Best American Essays 1987,* edited by Gay Talese (New York: Ticknor & Fields, 1987), pp. 16–51.

SELECTED PERIODICAL PUBLICATIONS–
UNCOLLECTED: "Report from the Mideast: A Human Drama," *Philadelphia Inquirer,* special supplement (1978);
"Portrait of a Family," *Philadelphia Inquirer Sunday Magazine* (21 October 1979);
"Inside the Afghan Rebellion," *Philadelphia Inquirer,* special supplement (1980);
"Feeding on the Hungry," *Philadelphia Inquirer,* special supplement (1981);
"The Strange and Mysterious Death of Mrs. Jerry Lee Lewis," *Rolling Stone* (1 March 1984): 22–25+;
"Can the Best Mayor Win?" *Esquire,* 102 (October 1984): 57–60+;

Richard Ben Cramer (Esquire Associates)

"Olympic Cheating," *Rolling Stone* (14 February 1985): 25–26+;
"The Ballad of Johnny France," *Esquire,* 104 (October 1985): 110–112+;
"The Valley of Death," *Rolling Stone* (24 October 1985): 29–30+;
"Beyond Mengele," *Rolling Stone* (21 November 1985): 67–68+;
"What Do You Think of Ted Williams Now?" *Esquire,* 105 (June 1986): 74–76+;
"Citizen Ueberroth," *Esquire,* 107 (February 1987): 69–72+;
"Fore Play: A Celebration of Golf the Glorious," *Esquire,* 107 (June 1987): 99–101;
"Men of Honor," *Esquire,* 119 (June 1993): 74–80+;

"Know Your Way Home," *Esquire,* 120 (October 1993): 81–82;

"Little England," *Esquire,* 120 (December 1993): 84–88+;

"A Native Son's Thoughts," *Sports Illustrated,* 83 (11 September 1995): 56–68.

Richard Ben Cramer's career as a literary journalist follows a traditional, indeed conventional, pattern: newspaper experience, magazine free-lancing, and, ultimately, the writing of books. In each phase, however, Cramer's work has challenged the traditions and conventions of the chosen genres as he finds new, imaginative ways to present his reporting and prose. That he has also become involved in the making of television documentaries shows the range of his skills.

Cramer was born in Rochester, New York, on 12 June 1950. At Brighton High School he was active on the school newspaper staff; later he received a liberal arts bachelor's degree in 1971 from Johns Hopkins University, where he edited the campus newspaper. He spent the next year at Columbia University, earning a master's degree in journalism in 1972. Following graduate school, Cramer became a reporter for the *Baltimore Sun,* covering metropolitan news and state politics. In a 6 July 1992 profile of Cramer in the *Washington Post,* a former *Baltimore Sun* colleague says: "He cut quite a figure and he was pure adrenaline. He came in every morning and stopped at the cafeteria to get five cups of coffee. He set them up on his desk and drank them, one after the other."

In October 1976 Cramer moved to the staff of the *Philadelphia Inquirer* as its transportation writer. Nine months later he went to the New York bureau of the *Philadelphia Inquirer,* writing about the Son of Sam murders, the free-for-all mayoral campaign (involving Ed Koch, Mario Cuomo, and Bella Abzug, among others), and a citywide blackout. In December 1977 Cramer was sent to Cairo to cover the peace negotiations between Egyptian president Anwar Sadat and Israeli prime minister Menachem Begin. What was supposed to be a two-week assignment turned into a several-year stint abroad as a foreign correspondent.

Cramer's work during 1978 from the Mideast established his reputation as a dogged, detail-driven reporter with the ability to compose compelling prose. In 1979 he received both the Pulitzer Prize in international reporting and the American Society of Newspaper Editors deadline newswriting competition for dispatches filed the previous year. Cramer approached his journalism differently from most other reporters filing stories about the Middle East.

People rather than policy dominated what he wrote, and he tended to focus on ordinary men, women, and children trying to cope during an unsettled and violent time.

In an interview for *Best Newspaper Writing* (1980), which reprints several award-winning articles, Cramer remarks, "I must confess I was never a great reader of foreign news. I figured out . . . that I never read it because I never got a sense of the people who were caught in it." By concentrating on the human perspective he was able to take readers closer to what they could identify with and to the consequences of governmental decisions and actions. Instead of gathering statements and statistics from "newsworthy" officials he collected quotations and anecdotes from people unaccustomed to receiving any news coverage.

One of Cramer's stories appeared in the volume of international reporting from 1928 to 1985 of *The Pulitzer Prize Archive* (1987). To describe democracy in the Republic of Egypt, he begins by singling out one voter. This dispatch, which the *Philadelphia Inquirer* published on 23 May 1978, opens:

> Slowly, with pain, Orani Mahmaud Daker climbed the stairs to the second floor schoolroom where he was supposed to vote. He propped himself with a stout wooden cane that was in his right hand. His grandson, Rashid, helped on the left. His breath came in short whooshes from brown cheeks, which were not so much wrinkled as folded where the absence of teeth let the skin go lax. Once Orani Daker was a tall, graceful man. But 32 years delivering water in Cairo, a liter at a time from a heavy leather gourd that pressed cold and damp against his back for 10 hours a day, had stiffened and bent him and used him up before his time.
>
> He looked as though he might not make it through the day.
>
> But it was an important morning, a referendum day. He closed his cigaret stand in Babalouk, near the alley of the watersellers, and made the long walk through Cairo's crowds to do his duty for President Anwar Sadat. He would vote, provided God willed it.

Sixteen vivid, short paragraphs about Daker set up what becomes a broader examination of the Egyptian electoral process, complete with the information that any registered male failing to vote is subject to a fine under the existing law. Women are treated differently and "not obliged to vote." Only one candidate appears on the ballot, with voters registering either a yes or a no. After this background Cramer returns to Daker and to some university students he interviews:

> These days, Cairo University is not the only place where fear and politics tend to go together.

There is a new police presence throughout the capital. The leftist newspaper has been banned and a wave of political arrests has chilled political discussion.

The message came from Sadat one week before the referendum, when he said of his political detractors: "I will crush them with democracy."

No one knows how far the crushing process will go.

The article ends by focusing on Daker as he shuffles off "toward the alley of the watersellers." Cramer lets his reporting and presentation leave the impression that democracy in Egypt is a far cry from what takes place in a more open society, such as in the United States. Facts speak for themselves, making commentary unnecessary. The organization of this story is illustrative of Cramer's technique in much of his other work for the *Philadelphia Inquirer* and later for magazines. Precise rendering of a specific person introduces a subject, with historical background for context coming afterward. Emphasis on the human element then becomes the principal concern to conclude and produces narrative unity.

In 1980 Cramer won the Ernie Pyle Award for foreign reporting and an Overseas Press Award for his coverage of the Afghanistan guerrilla fighters in their war with the Soviet Union. He traveled with the poorly armed but proudly nationalistic rebels to understand what they had to endure in battling a superpower for their homeland.

Assignments took him throughout the Middle East and Afghanistan as well as to Northern Ireland, Italy, and Africa. The distinctive quality of his reporting and writing prompted the *Philadelphia Inquirer* to publish three special supplements of his work: "Report from the Mideast: A Human Drama" (1978), "Inside the Afghan Rebellion" (1980), and "Feeding on the Hungry" (1981). "Feeding on the Hungry" exposes the corruption involved in a relief program established to combat starvation in Somalia. As with his other foreign reportage, Cramer keeps the plight of the victimized people central to his series of articles.

Cramer spent most of his nearly eight years with the *Philadelphia Inquirer* abroad. He came back to Philadelphia in 1979, however, to render what life was like for one American family trying "to stay one step ahead of hard times." The resulting article, "Portrait of a Family," encompassed almost the entire Sunday magazine for 21 October 1979. Engrossing in its faithful depiction of individuals bedeviled by the "routine of poverty," the story of the Monroe family is one of a day-to-day existence with slim prospects for economic improvement. Despite their circumstances, the Monroes keep looking ahead and do what they can to make life better. Cramer's atten-

tion to detail and his desire to treat a specific subject at considerable length foreshadows what he does years later as a magazine writer and author.

Cramer left the *Philadelphia Inquirer* in April 1984. In "Backstage at *Esquire:* Our Man in Baltimore" in *Esquire* (October 1984), an article by Lee Eisenberg about Cramer, he said he departed from daily journalism after twelve years to "write things you can't write in newspapers." Working as a freelancer, he published several lengthy stories in *Esquire* and *Rolling Stone* during the 1980s. Although he continued to rely on extensive reporting as his foundation, Cramer shifted his attention to dealing with prominent rather than ordinary people. He also provided more of his own perspective or attitude on a subject. The newspaper apprenticeship proved valuable, but at the age of thirty-three he sought greater development as a writer.

The 1 March 1984 issue of *Rolling Stone* included "The Strange and Mysterious Death of Mrs. Jerry Lee Lewis," Cramer's nearly twenty-thousand-word account of the premature demise of Shawn Michelle Lewis, age twenty-five. Jerry Lee Lewis, a wealthy and influential performer whose previous wife also died mysteriously, has the nickname of "The Killer," and frequent usage of the nickname by Cramer conveys a definite suggestion that the official finding of "no foul play" should not be the final word in the case.

Cramer's first contribution to *Esquire* in October 1984 was a profile of William Donald Schaefer, the colorful mayor of Baltimore at that time. "Can the Best Mayor Win?" was nominated for a National Magazine Award. The beginning shows an engaging combination of specific facts and the writer's viewpoint:

How will they ever make a statue of him? They'll have to, you know. He saved the town.

But how could they bronze that stubby little body, the melon head, the double chin? Put him on horseback? Ha! One foot up on a pediment, with those clunky shoes he buys on sale? Gazing over a book? He doesn't read, I guarantee you.

No. If they really want him, they've got to get him mad. And paint the whole head rosy, and put glitter in his eyes. And a couple of guys in suits cowering. That'd do it, and they could carve on the base:

Mayor Annoyed

The Best Mayor in America, For A While

Cramer's admiration for the mayor is evident, yet a reader learns that Schaefer's "obsessive attention" to his city's concerns comes at a price: no friends and little to life besides work. The thorough reporting of the piece receives attention in the introductory article about Cramer, "Our Man in Baltimore." Recalling his early days as a *Baltimore Sun* staffer, he notes: "A reporter got points for *details*. Details made a story worth writing. Accuracy was important, but in detail there's *truth*." As Schaefer is "obsessive," so too is Cramer. Strategically presenting telling details has been a hallmark of Cramer's work since he began in journalism.

Although he published four articles in *Rolling Stone* during 1984 and 1985, Cramer started to appear with increasing regularity in *Esquire* in subsequent years. "What Do You Think of Ted Williams Now?" came out in the June 1986 *Esquire* and took on a life of its own. Reprinted in *The Best American Essays 1987,* the profile of the baseball Hall of Famer was subsequently expanded to provide the text for a lavishly illustrated book, *Ted Williams: The Seasons of the Kid* (1991). That the article was selected for inclusion in a collection of essays suggests Cramer's use of the first person and the presence of his perspective throughout.

Combining factual background about Williams's accomplishments as an athlete with reporting about what the man is like in retirement, Cramer portrays the complexity of a person who "wanted fame . . . but could not stand celebrity." Quotations of Williams as he reacts to questions and his surroundings in his home in the Florida Keys reveal the former star as a moody bundle of contradictions. A well-developed ego in need of constant attention competes with a strong urge to be left alone.

The conclusion of the *Esquire* article conveys a sense of sadness and rage. Williams contemplates the purchase of a car for his son. As he thinks about doing this, his mind shifts to consider problems he had with his daughter. The volume and profanity of his anger is reflected in Cramer's rendering of the words, complete with capital letters and ellipses. The writer, too, is a recipient of the fury.

Something has turned in his gut, and his face is working, growing harder. There's a mean glitter in his eye, and he's thinking of his elder daughter, walking away from him. . . .

"SLAM OUT . . . LIKE MY DAUGHTER USED TO . . ."

His teeth are clenched and the words are spat. It's like he's turned inward to face something we cannot see. It is a fearsome sight, this big man, forward, stiff in his chair, hurling ugly words at his vision of pain . . . I feel I should leave the room but too late.

". . . THAT BURNED ME . . ."

The switch is on. Lou [the woman with whom Williams lives] calls it the Devil in him.

". . . A PAIN IN MY HAIRY RECTUM!"

"Nice," says Lou. She is fighting for him. She has not flinched.

"Well, DID," he says through clenched teeth, "AND MAKES YOU HATE BROADS! . . ."

"Ted. Stop." But Ted is gone.

". . . HATE GOD! . . . "

"TED!"

". . . HATE LIFE!"

"TED! . . . JUST . . . STOP!"

"DON'T YOU TELL ME TO STOP. DON'T YOU EVER TELL ME TO STOP."

Lou's mouth twists up slightly, and she snorts: "HAH!"

And that does it. They've beaten it, or Lou has, or it's just gone away. Ted sinks back in his chair. His jaw is unclenched. He grins shyly, "You know, I love this girl like I never . . ."

Lou sits back, too, and laughs.

"SHE'S IN TRAINING," TED SAYS, "I'M TEACHIN' HER . . ."

"He sure is," Lou says, like it's banter, but her voice is limp. She heads back to the kitchen, and Ted follows her with his eyes.

Then he finds me on the couch, and he tries to sneer through his grin: "WHEN ARE YOU LEAVING? HUH?

". . . JESUS, YOU'RE LIKE THE GODDAMN RUSSIAN SECRET POLICE!

". . . OKAY, BYE! YEAH, SURE, GOODBYE!"

Ted walks me out to the driveway. As I start the car, Lou's face is a smile in the window, and Ted is bent at his belly, grabbing their new dalmatian puppy, tickling it with his big hands while the dog rolls and paws the air. And as I ease the car into gear, I hear Ted's voice behind, cooing, very quiet now: "Do I love this little

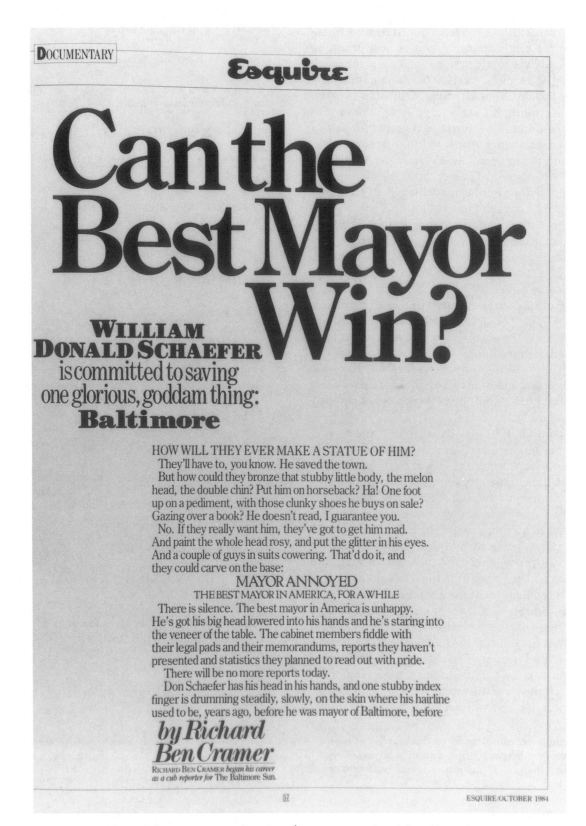

First page of Cramer's first contribution to Esquire. *The piece was nominated for a National Magazine Award.*

dog, huh? . . . Yes, this little shittin' dog. Yes, yes I love you . . . Yes, I do."

Besides being significant to his career, the article was discussed in almost every journalistic story about Cramer for the lengths to which he went to have his entire manuscript—all fifteen thousand words of it—appear in the magazine. When two thousand words were cut for space reasons, he returned at night after his editors left work and told the art, production, and copy departments they had last-minute permission to reduce the size of the type to restore every word. As a consequence of his intervention, *Esquire* no longer allows writers in the art department. Although the book version of his Williams profile came out in 1991, Cramer's writing did not appear in newspapers or magazines during the late 1980s and early 1990s.

For nearly six years, from 1986 until 1992, he was preoccupied with the research and writing of a book about several people who decided to run for president of the United States in 1988. An enormous reporting project—he focused on two Republican and four Democratic candidates—the 1,047-page work, *What It Takes: The Way to the White House* was published on 4 July 1992. In its allegiance to in-depth reporting and complete explanations, the book is the opposite of the brief sound bite or thirty-second spot so often debated during the 1988 campaign. *What It Takes: The Way to the White House* provides running biographies of George Bush, Bob Dole, Michael Dukakis, Gary Hart, Joe Biden, and Richard Gephardt, in intermingled accounts that yield larger lessons about the modern presidency and American political life. Cramer describes an electoral system out of control. Seeking the White House is an almost dehumanizing experience. To win is to lose one's life as one knows it.

Cramer renders his representative men with specificity and sensitivity. He captures their strengths, limitations, habits, and idiosyncrasies, and even seems to empathize with them for what they are forced to endure. The politicians, in fact, have a stature just short of heroic. With Hart, in particular, the treatment is so positive that the former senator's foibles never come into clear focus. Hart, according to Cramer, is unlike the other candidates; he has definite ideas and a coherent plan for governing. He is also different in not wanting to give up his life to secure the nomination.

Cramer devotes seven chapters to Hart's alleged extramarital affair and its aftermath. The account exposes more monkey business by journalists than sexual shenanigans by the former Colorado senator. Scent of scandal is stronger than verifiable proof, but the intense coverage is enough to make Hart withdraw. Hart's experience allows Cramer to focus on the importance of character and the involvement of the media in presidential politics. Calling character "the coin of the realm," Cramer repeatedly notes that the meaning of character has the stability of mercury. Journalists, who are referred to as "the Priests of the Process" and "Karacter Kops," form a hounding pack, making a serious campaign impossible.

Cramer's extensive reporting and reconstruction of what happened to Hart leads to the conclusion that the media blackmailed him and ultimately forced his departure. Biden, too, suffers a similar fate. He is the victim of press coverage that thrives on probing questions—but does not wait or work hard enough to provide fair, complete answers. Biden dropped out in the wake of media charges that he plagiarized statements of other political figures in his speeches. Cramer gives names of reporters he thinks engaged in questionable acts. Former colleagues in daily journalism share with political consultants the role of villains in this massive and unconventional work.

Cramer imposes a loose chronological order on his narrative, beginning in 1986 when the six started to plan their races and ending in late spring of 1988 with Bush and Dukakis about to be nominated as the Republican and Democratic standard-bearers. Flashback chapters recounting the candidates' lives before 1986 appear strategically for context, and a thirty-page epilogue provides a brief report of the fall campaign as well as postelection vignettes about the one winner and five losers. Despite the challenge of doing justice to portraits of all six figures, Cramer weaves his material so that few seams show. In all there are 130 chapters—the longest running thirty pages, the shortest but a single page—however, the development is deliberate, with repetition of specific metaphors or phrases unifying the work as a whole. The word *bubble* describes the enclosed environment of a presidential campaign. Influential journalists appear as "big-feet." Political consultants are "gurus."

The prime virtue of the book's length is the opportunity to reconstruct detail by detail what happened to these six public figures as they sought the nation's highest office. Each had a shot at winning. The reader, of course, knows the outcome, but Cramer creates drama by exploring previously unreported aspects of well-known occurrences. Indeed, there is so much new material that a reader begins to reconsider several "what-might-have-beens" for the 1988 election. For example, in the treatment of Hart and Biden, Cramer raises legitimate questions whether they were run out of the race without true cause. Dole and Gephardt clearly would have had greater chances of victory if they had more capable campaign organizations. In a certain way the book becomes a journalist's revisionist account of how journalists portrayed the 1988 campaign.

What It Takes is essentially a multiperson biography, a book of lives. In the "Author's Note" Cramer explains that he interviewed "more than a thousand people" and that he went back to some family members and aides "literally, fifty or sixty times." Getting that close to the figures results in full-length portraits. In each case the public persona and private self come together so that one sees, and, more important, understands, what drives someone to want to be president.

The portrait that emerges of the winner, George Bush, is of a man for whom friendship is everything. Chatting with people, writing countless thank-you notes, and sending out thirty thousand Christmas cards are personal and political efforts that helped Bush succeed. Cramer shows that when Bush first ran for office (as a senate candidate from Texas in 1964), he "didn't have a program," he just adopted the views of Republican presidential nominee Barry Goldwater. Lacking a program—what Bush as president tried to dismiss as "the vision thing"—is a defining absence of the man. He spent his career being and selling himself, widening the circle of "friends." As Cramer notes, "He didn't want to be President to *do* this or that. He'd do . . . what was *sound*." With neither a program nor direction, leadership becomes hollow, a void "friends" cannot fill. Cramer captures the complexity of Bush's compulsion for friends by writing:

The funny thing was, everybody heard Bush use that word, "friend," a hundred times a day, but they never could see what it meant to him.

By what extravagance of need and will did a man try to make thirty thousand friends?

By what steely discipline did he strive to keep them—with notes, cards, letters, gifts, invitations, visits, calls, and silent kindnesses, hundreds every week, every one demanding some measure of his energy and attention?

And by what catholicity (or absence) of taste could he think well of every one of them?

He could not.

But they would never know that.

The funny thing was, the friendship depended not on what Bush thought of them, but what they thought of him, or what he wanted them to think. If they thought well of him, then, they were friends.

For much of the book Cramer juxtaposes Bush and Dole. Two men seeking the same office could not be more different. Dole gives the word *driven* new meaning. It is work, work, work, attention to detail, and sleep be damned. There is no time for friends, and Christmas cards get sent to a hundred or so people. Cramer poignantly recounts Dole's recuperation from a crippling and almost fatal injury during World War II. That experience and "his private vision of hell"—returning to Russell, Kansas, to sell pencils from a wheelchair—trigger a commitment to success on his own demanding terms. Like Bush, Dole has no vision for the country, but he knows hard work can solve most problems. The Bush team prevails, but the reader wonders whether the best man won.

The least engaging figure portrayed in *What It Takes* is Michael Dukakis. The unemotional, robotic person who won the Democratic nomination in 1988 seeks control to such an extent it is the man's dominant trait. He is the furthest thing imaginable from the candidate as "a happy warrior." Interestingly, though, intrigue and mystery surround him. Campaign aides do questionable things on his behalf—and then hope their boss will not find out. The nominee's wife, Kitty, continues a diet-pill addiction and takes up binge drinking when her husband is not around. In a revealing anecdote the then-governor of Massachusetts decides to go grocery shopping instead of taking part in a high-powered discussion of arms control because "Dukakis does not like to be the dumbest guy in the room. Michael is always the smartest guy in the room."

Despite the book's length Cramer holds a reader's attention by sculpting mountains of notes into literary journalism with compelling characterization, vivid scene-setting, and dramatic tension. Cramer's eye for detail and his ability to extract telling information from people create the foundation of his writing. One learns that Dukakis went to his high school's senior prom alone and worked checking coats. One sees just how incompetent Dole's campaign is when his staff prepares several color-coded briefing books, and he has to tell them he's color-blind. The narrative reveals that the late and powerful congressman, Wilbur Mills, had a pet name for the first-term representative from Texas who filed a bill regarding birth control. Mills always called George Bush "Rubbers"—a manly endearment among "friends."

In most places the prose pulls a reader forward through the portraits and particulars. Cramer is deft in using concrete language. For instance, he compares Bush and Hart: "If, say, George Bush's intelligence was a silken windsock, so supple, so brightly sensitive to the currents of air around him, Hart's was something harder, unyielding—industrial-grade, a diamond-pointed tool on the landscape." Of Biden's penchant for exaggeration during his law school days at Syracuse University, Cramer notes: "if Biden could have sucked as hard as he blew, Syracuse would have been a seaport." The Dukakis campaign plane is "an aged commercial airliner that smelled inside like the stuff men spray in their gym shoes."

Throughout the book Cramer meticulously reconstructs intimate conversations of years ago and presents the thoughts and feelings of many people at critical times in 1988 or earlier. One paragraph in the chapter about Hart's attraction to Oletha Ludwig, who later became his wife, illustrates the method:

And he knew . . . it was that ease of hers that drew him, the wonderful way she had of plunging in—on the hockey field, in a group of friends—she didn't think twice . . . it was beautiful to him. God knows, there was no one more acutely aware of Gary's social unease . . . than Gary Hartpence. If the Good Lord had suddenly appeared to him, and asked him what was the *one thing* . . . well, of course, the way Gary was, he'd take it *seriously,* and ask for Salvation for All Mankind, or something . . . but if the Good Lord had *snuck up* and asked, well, the one thing Gary would have wanted, what he coveted, was to be able to fit in, or even better, to lead, *without even thinking,* just as a matter of natural grace. That was his lack, his one mortal envy, that ease of belonging, and Oletha had it, in her every move at Bethany, that sense of acceptance, that sense of right without thinking . . . and she liked *him.* It was intoxicating.

Cramer vows that for "every case, thoughts attributed to the characters in this book have been checked with them, or with the people to whom they confided those thoughts." He makes a similar statement about the quotations he uses. The techniques of fiction, including an emphasis on paced storytelling, three-dimensional individuals, and relevant details or statements, are critical to Cramer's approach and execution. The final result is different from any campaign book written since Theodore H. White created the genre with *The Making of the President 1960* (1961). Cramer's book received generally favorable reviews when it appeared. Walter Shapiro (in *Time,* 13 July 1992) called it an "artful reworking of the too-dispiriting-for-words 1988 presidential campaign." Joe Klein of *Newsweek* (6 July 1992)

termed it "a bizarre, belated, often brilliant, defiantly egregious" book that is "far more insightful about pols and political tradecraft than the common run of campaign effluvia." In the 5 July 1992 *New York Times Book Review* Laurence I. Barrett wrote, "Provocative insights and compelling vignettes . . . flicker like gas lamps in this dark maze of a book." To conclude, though, Barrett noted: "It is a shame that Mr. Cramer strains so hard for originality that he lapses too often into verbose eccentricity. That mars an otherwise serious, information-filled work. Perhaps the author needed better handlers to help him shape his message."

Maureen Dowd found less merit in *What It Takes* than other commentators. In the July/August 1992 *Washington Monthly* she observes: "With a prose style more irritating than entertaining, the author takes [Tom] Wolfe's faded New Journalism technique and sends it into fifth gear–VRO-O-O-OM! VRO-O-O-OM!–dousing each page with italics, ellipses, exclamation points, sound effects, dashes, hyphens, capital letters, and cute spellings. It's never 'character cops' when it can be 'Karacter Kops.' Bob Dole rarely starts a sentence without an 'Aghh' or 'Gggaahh.'" Dowd's criticism extends beyond presentation to the substance. The tartly opinionated writer for *The New York Times* says: "While I've occasionally used the gimmick of getting inside George Bush's head for a humor piece, the notion of using it for an entire book is disquieting. It's not possible to really know what's in anyone's head, no matter how close you are to him, how much he tells you, or how much research you do. Attempting to recreate the streams of consciousness of Bush and Dole when they thought they might die in World War II is a bit of a stretch."

Such criticism aside, throughout the 1992 presidential campaign and subsequently Cramer has been sought by reporters for his opinions on candidates and the process of running for the nation's highest office. Ironically, perhaps, given what he says about the media in *What It Takes,* the longtime journalist has himself become a frequently cited source as a result of a book that finds political reporting sorely wanting—and a serious problem to contemporary self-governance.

After finishing the book Cramer moved to Europe for a year to work on articles for *Esquire,* which had published three excerpts from *What It Takes* in 1991 and 1992. "Men of Honor"–about a Sicilian Mafia boss and the judge who worked to expose him and his associates–appeared in June 1993. As he did with other subjects in his earlier work, Cramer gets inside both the Cosa Nostra and the Italian justice system. The frightening portrait of

Mafia evil is juxtaposed against the consuming effort to make the law work. The gravity of the substance is reflected in serious, straightforward prose. In "Little England" (*Esquire,* December 1993) Cramer surveys the decline of the British Empire by making frequent use of tabloid newspaper coverage of the questionable doings of the royal family. Humor pervades what is really a not-so-jolly report of contemporary malaise and diminished prospects for the future.

Returning from abroad, Cramer took up residence in an old farmhouse in Maryland. As he describes it in "Know Your Way Home," a short essay for *Esquire* (October 1993), his time had come to settle down. "Newspapering was about impermanence," he recalls, and the years of freelancing as well as the extensive travel to do the reporting for *What It Takes* had taken their toll. In 1994 he shifted from writing for publication to working on the script (and serving as narrator) of a television documentary, "Tabloid Truth: The Michael Jackson Scandal." Broadcast on PBS on 15 February 1994 as an edition of the *Frontline* series, the report is a case study of the blurring lines between genuine news and hyped sensationalism. Money is at the heart of the phenomenon, with a person's reputation of little concern. In the *Washington Post* (15 February 1994) Tom Shales commented, "Both the writing of the narration and Cramer's delivery are boldly punchy and hard-edged. At times Cramer's voice sounds somewhat reminiscent of the young Orson Welles. . . . Is there a slight tabloid tinge even to 'Tabloid Truth'? Maybe just a little." This documentary followed an earlier one for *Frontline.* Cramer helped compose the script and narrated "The Choice '92," a two-hour examination of the lives of George Bush and Bill Clinton, which aired 21 October 1992. Cramer shared with two others an award from the Writers Guild of America in the category "documentary, current events" for "The Choice '92."

In "A Native Son's Thoughts" (*Sports Illustrated,* 11 September 1995) Cramer returned to his longtime interest in baseball with a profile of Cal Ripken Jr., the Baltimore Oriole who broke the Major League record of 2,130 consecutive starts in 1995. Interestingly, Ripken never grants an interview to Cramer, so the article revolves around the writer's research about his subject and impressions of him. Cramer—rather than Ripken—is the "native son" of the title, but Baltimore and baseball are two subjects Cramer knows well. A reader is led to believe that Ripken's self-absorption keeps him at a distance from the media. Maybe he has gotten too big for his uniform. However, Cramer concludes with a telling description of the star staying after a game for almost two hours to sign autographs and pose for pictures with fans. These are his people, and the scene (complete with Ripken at the end giving his hat to a boy) rounds out as well as tempers the portrait.

Dealing with one baseball star reluctant to talk could serve as a prelude to a biography Cramer is working on about the former New York Yankee center fielder, Joe DiMaggio, well known for media shyness and protecting his privacy. "I think DiMaggio occupies a wonderful place in the American century," Cramer told the *Washington Post Book World* (26 March 1995). "He is a hero of a kind we don't have anymore."

With Bob Dole the front-runner for the 1996 Republican presidential nomination, Cramer excerpted the minibiography of the Kansas senator from *What It Takes* and published it as a book, *Bob Dole,* in the fall of 1995. The fifteen-page introduction provides new information gathered during a speaking trip and interview with the senator. The opening paragraph is as much about the author and his memory as about the appearance of someone he has closely studied.

> I see him again—first time in three years—steaming through the double doors of a big Florida hotel ballroom, straight up the aisle, past five hundred prosperous pink men, making for the head table and his speech. From across the room, he looks the same: still, there's not a wrinkle in his dark Brooks Brothers suit; his silk tie is knotted tight against the smooth collar of his white shirt; his hair is dark, softly in place (four strokes with the barber comb, still in his back pants pocket); his face is still handsome, tight with perpetual tan. (It's like even his skin is practiced: Dole can get a tan on the way from his car to the hotel door.)

Later, Cramer describes how Dole reacted to being defeated by George Bush in the critical New Hampshire primary of 1988. Unable to sleep, Dole leaves his hotel room to brood:

> He lay there all night, tried to lie still . . . until he couldn't try anymore, and it was five o'clock and there was no reason to lie in bed. That's when Dole came down to the lobby of his hotel, and sat—no one around, he just sat. Pen in his hand. Careful suit. Perfect shirt, tie. And no one around. What would he have said, anyway? He was sorry? Sorry was the only thing in him.

> He knew loss—God knows, he could handle . . . why couldn't he handle *this?* . . . why couldn't he stop his head? Things that could've been different—all the things he'd done . . . probably wrong—half the things . . .

> But the worst part wasn't things he'd done. It was the pictures of Bush—that was what he couldn't stop—*pictures*

of Bush! In his head! Bush throwing snowballs, driving trucks, forklifts . . . unwrapping his Big Mac. Dole never wanted to see that in his head. And he never wanted to say, even in his head . . .

It would not leave him alone . . . five in the morning! Had to come down to the lobby . . . but he couldn't get away from it. For the first time in his career–first time in thirty years–Bob Dole said to himself:

"Maybe I could have done that . . . if I was whole."

Dole's war wound, so important to every aspect of the senator's life, is once again an important factor in what happens to him–or at least he thinks so. This revelation helps to set up Cramer's sympathetic re-creation in the biography itself of how Dole struggled against long odds and persistent pain to be as "whole" as he could be. Winning the White House continued to be the ultimate challenge. As Cramer notes after offering a general description of the campaign process, "That's What It Takes. It Takes Your Life." Cramer's opinion of Dole is generally favorable and different from his expectation. As he told the *Washington Post Book World* (26 March 1995), "I was possessed of the conventional Washington wisdom that he was sharp and sometimes mean-spirited. I found him to be kind and, in his personal history, inspiring. The conventional Washington wisdom is always wrong about everyone."

What It Takes and its progeny–the documentary "The Choice '92" and *Bob Dole*–enhanced Cramer's reputation as a detail-oriented reporter who writes with imagination and originality. The people he selects to write about are at the heart of his work, and they frequently come to life as characters in a well-wrought piece of fiction do. His willingness to test established journalistic forms yields creative approaches that a reader sees from his earliest newspaper days to his magazine articles and books. Journalism often simplifies complexity. With Cramer's in-depth probing of subjects, clear and precise explanation illumines what is complex, and the presentation is engagingly distinctive.

Interviews:

Lee Eisenberg, "Backstage with *Esquire:* Our Man in Baltimore," *Esquire,* 102 (October 1984): 7;

Martha Sherrill, "The Man Inside the Hopefuls' Heads," *Washington Post,* 6 July 1992, pp. D1, 4;

Cheryl Lavin, "Following the Bumpy Road to the White House," *Chicago Tribune,* 14 July 1992, sec. 2, pp. 1–2;

Mike Capuzzo, "What It Took," *Philadelphia Inquirer,* 2 September 1992, pp. E1, 5.

References:

Donald K. Fry, "The Presence of Richard Ben Cramer," *Style,* 16 (Fall 1982): 437–443;

Robert Schmuhl, "Richard Ben Cramer," in *A Sourcebook of American Literary Journalism: Representative Writers in an Emerging Genre,* edited by Thomas B. Connery (Westport, Conn.: Greenwood Press, 1992), pp. 331–341;

Schmuhl, "Richard Ben Cramer and 'People Journalism,'" *Style,* 16 (Fall 1982): 444–447.

Harry Crews

(7 June 1935 –)

David R. Davies
University of Southern Mississippi

See also the Crews entries in *DLB 6: American Novelists Since World World War II, Second Series* and *DLB 143: American Novelists Since World War II, Third Series.*

BOOKS: *The Gospel Singer* (New York: Morrow, 1968);

Naked in Garden Hills (New York: Morrow, 1969);

This Thing Don't Lead to Heaven (New York: Morrow, 1970);

Karate Is a Thing of the Spirit (New York: Morrow, 1971; London: Secker & Warburg, 1972);

Car (New York: Morrow, 1972; London: Secker & Warburg, 1973);

The Hawk Is Dying (New York: Knopf, 1973; London: Secker & Warburg, 1974);

The Gypsy's Curse (New York: Knopf, 1974; London: Secker & Warburg, 1975);

A Feast of Snakes (New York: Atheneum, 1976; London: Secker & Warburg, 1977);

A Childhood: The Biography of a Place (New York & London: Harper & Row, 1978; London: Secker & Warburg, 1979);

Blood and Grits (New York & London: Harper & Row, 1979);

Florida Frenzy (Gainesville: University Press of Florida, 1982);

Two (Northridge, Cal.: Lord John, 1984);

All We Need of Hell (New York & London: Harper & Row, 1986);

The Knockout Artist (New York & London: Harper & Row, 1988);

Body (New York & London: Poseidon, 1990);

Madonna at Ringside (Northridge, Cal.: Lord John, 1991);

Scar Lover (New York & London: Poseidon, 1992);

Classic Crews: A Harry Crews Reader (New York: Poseidon, 1993; London: Gorse, 1995);

The Mulching of America: A Novel (New York: Simon & Schuster, 1995).

SELECTED PERIODICAL PUBLICATIONS—
UNCOLLECTED: "Getting It Together," *Writer,* 84 (June 1971): 9;

Harry Crews (photograph by Maggie Powell)

"Buttondown Terror of David Duke," *Playboy,* 27 (February 1980): 102;

"The Violence that Finds Us," *Playboy,* 31 (April 1984): 98;

"Fathers, Sons, Blood," *Playboy,* 32 (January 1985): 111;

"The Mythic Mule," *Southern Magazine,* 1 (October 1986): 21;

"What Mama Knows," *Southern Magazine,* 1 (May 1987): 49;

"Wisdom of the Groin," *Playboy,* 36 (February 1989): 88;

"Sean Penn Lives to Tell," *Fame,* 3 (November 1990): 93.

Though best known for his often-bizarre Southern fiction populated by an array of deformed, grotesque characters, Harry Crews has, between novels, turned to journalism, producing essays filled with an equally unusual cast of true-to-life eccentrics: alligator poachers, cockfight promoters, skirt-chasing college professors, obnoxious drunks, carnival hustlers, and down-and-out race-car drivers. Like his novels Crews's nonfiction reflects both his varied interests—ranging from blood sports to hawk training—and his own strongly held opinions, both forged from years of hard drinking and hard living.

"People that read me," Crews said in an unpublished interview on 18 July 1996, "either like me or really hate me or think I'm a sham." In forcing readers to confront violence and the bizarre, Crews's journalism parallels his work as a novelist, which, as he told interviewer Susan Ketchin, "means you spend most of your time thinking about, meditating upon, trying to dissect and understand just those aspects of the human animal that other human beings try their damndest never to think about."

Crews's nonfiction has appeared mostly in *Esquire,* for which he wrote a Southern-oriented column called "Grits" in 1976–1977 and contributed many articles in the 1970s and 1980s, and in *Playboy,* though scattered works have appeared in *Fame, Sport,* and other periodicals. Much of his nonfiction has been collected in two books, *Blood and Grits* (1979) and *Florida Frenzy* (1982); a third collection, *Glimpses into a Keyhole,* is planned. His one book-length nonfiction work is *A Childhood: The Biography of a Place* (1978), a memoir of his gritty childhood in the hardscrabble back country of Bacon County in rural south Georgia.

Crews's childhood was difficult, even tragic, as he documents memorably in *A Childhood.* Born on 7 June 1935 to Ray and Myrtice Crews, tenant farmers in Alma, Georgia, on the edge of the Okefenokee swamp, Crews grew up so poor that he sometimes ate clay for its mineral content. When Crews was just twenty months old, his father died, and his mother's subsequent remarriage to another tenant farmer was marred by violence. Crews and his younger brother often fell asleep at night to the sounds of fistfights and crashing furniture. At age five Crews fell victim to infantile paralysis, and his legs curled far under his body until his feet touched his thighs. Young Crews had just begun to walk again when he fell into a pot of boiling water while playing pop the whip with playmates. His deep burns required months to heal. "Never once did I ever think that my life was not just like everyone else's, that my fears and uncertainties

were not universal," Crews wrote in *A Childhood.* "For which I can only thank God."

Crews's childhood did, at least, instill in him a strong sense of place and southern identity, as well as a love of storytelling. Crews has traced his interest in writing to his earliest memories of hearing adults swap stories on the front porches of Bacon County. Crews first practiced his storyteller's art using the only book in the Crews household, the Sears Roebuck catalogue, which he and childhood friend Willalee Bookatee used as a springboard for weaving detailed stories. To young Harry and Willalee, the unbelievably perfect faces of the Sears models were a sharp contrast to the imperfect inhabitants of Bacon County. "[A]ll of the people that Willalee Bookatee and I knew were maimed, mutilated, crippled in some fashion. We were in the rickets, the hookworm belt, of the South," Crews told interviewer A. B. Crowder in *Writing in the Southern Tradition: Interviews with Five Contemporary Authors* (1990). "All of us were poorly fed, poorly clothed, without benefit of doctors much at all. So we made stories about perfect people out of the Sears Roebuck catalog. And that's how I came to write stories."

After Crews graduated from high school in Bacon County he entered the United States Air Force, mustering out of the service as a sergeant in 1956, and then enrolled at the University of Florida under the GI Bill. He took eighteen months off during his undergraduate days to wander the country on a motorcycle, but he returned to Florida to take two degrees, a bachelor of arts in 1960 and an M.S. in education in 1962. During his college years he married a fellow student, Sally Ellis, and had two sons, Patrick and Byron. Crews and his wife divorced, then remarried, then divorced again after Patrick died in a swimming pool accident at age three.

While at the University of Florida, Crews studied under Andrew Lytle, a leader of the southern Agrarian movement, but Crews's background and writing style were far different from that of his teacher, who had been reared as a southern aristocrat. "Mr. Lytle was sort of like a father to me at one time, and he sort of disowned me," Crews told Crowder. "Our views of the world were so different. It doesn't mean we can't communicate; it just means that I can't talk their language because I don't know it."

In Crews's first attempt at writing he read and reread a Graham Greene novel, *The End of the Affair* (1951), taking it apart piece by piece and then constructing a novel that exactly matched Greene's style and form. The result was practically worthless, but Crews persisted, writing regularly but selling little. At the same time, he began a long career teaching

Dust jacket for Crews's first collection of essays

writing, first at Broward Community College in Fort Lauderdale (1962–1968) and then at the University of Florida (1968–1990). Crews's persistence at writing eventually paid off with the publication of *The Gospel Singer* (1968), which established him as a talented, quirky young novelist. Afterward, Crews wrote a steady stream of novels in a distinctive writing style in which tortured, emotionally and physically deformed people search for meaning in their lives. In *Car* (1972) a man gains worldwide attention with his effort to eat a Ford Maverick piece by piece; in *The Gypsy's Curse* (1974) legless deaf-mute Marvin Molar's obsession with a gorgeous woman eventually leads him to murder; and in *A Feast of Snakes* (1976) miserable former high-school football star Joe Lon Mackey shoots down a crowd gathered for a rattlesnake roundup and is hurled into a rattlesnake pit by the survivors. In all, Crews has published fourteen novels since 1968, all of them displaying his unique perspective.

For years Crews's own lifestyle reflected the tumult of hard drinking and hard living endured by the characters in his fiction. "The world pissed me off so bad that if I didn't have a drink to tilt, I couldn't take it," Crews told the *Palm Beach Post* (15 May 1994). Crews's love of bars and of alcohol resulted in several arrests—in Saint Augustine, Florida, in Texas, and elsewhere—and frequent adventures, many of

them described in his nonfiction. While touring Valdez, Alaska, for a writing assignment, Crews once awakened to find the image of a hinge tattooed on the inside of his right elbow. At home at the University of Florida, Crews was never a typical mild-mannered academic, either in appearance or behavior: for a time he sported a tapered mohawk haircut and mirrored sunglasses. On his right arm he wears a tattoo of a skull and crossbones with the inscription "How Do You Like Your Blue-Eyed Boy, Mr. Death?," a quotation from e. e. cummings. Crews's favorite campus-area hangouts were two bars, Lillian's Music Store and the Winnjammer. But Crews gave up alcohol in 1987 after spending time in a rehabilitation unit. "The truth of the matter is," he admitted to the *Post*, "it's made things much more difficult. Taking the world entirely straight, with no buzz at all, man, that's hard duty."

Crews's only book-length nonfiction work is, in fact, the autobiography of his childhood: *A Childhood: The Biography of a Place*. Critics generally responded favorably to the book. "Why Mr. Crews should wish to remember Bacon County is a puzzle," wrote reviewer P. L. Adams in the *Atlantic* (November 1978). "That he should successfully arouse in the reader both interest in the place and sympathy for its benighted inhabitants is a near miracle." In *The New York Times Book Review* (24 December 1978) Robert

Sherrill found Crews's reminiscences "different, fresh, and very touching." Crews is a "unique Southern raconteur," Sherrill concluded, one whose memoir succeeds because "he does not romanticize the kind of cruelty, crudeness, and poverty that were endemic to that region before World War II."

Crews's journalistic essays are also part autobiography. While many are based on solid reporting, all are filled with his own reactions and emotions and dotted with experiences often germane—and sometimes not so germane—to the topic at hand. Virtually all of his essays are part journalism, part autobiography, with the proportion of each changing from article to article. "As a matter of fact, I write about myself about as much as I do the person I'm dealing with, because it's my reaction to him or her and my reaction to where we find ourselves, and what I see and what we do, that I feel that I've been sent to get," Crews said in an unpublished interview in 1996. "If they hadn't wanted mine, they'd of gotten somebody else."

For Crews nonfiction is a secondary interest that he fits in only between novels. "Writing nonfiction for me is considerably easier than writing fiction," Crews said. With fiction, authors often do not know exactly what they are writing about until they are well into a writing project, according to Crews. By contrast, nonfiction is far less daunting. "You have a subject already, know what you want to cover, and if you didn't have some attitude toward that subject you wouldn't be doing it anyway. And the only problem that you've got is to put it in the best language that you can summon, the most concrete and specific language, and to organize it so that it has coherence and integrity."

In *Blood and Grits,* his first collected book of essays, Crews demonstrates the range of subjects and approaches he takes in his nonfiction. In several pieces, most of which appeared in either *Playboy* or *Esquire,* Crews plays the part of a bemused, wry observer in an odd, skewered world. In "L. L. Bean Has Your Number, America!" a bewildered Crews stands outside the Freeport, Maine, headquarters of the old, prosperous mail-order firm and wonders at the appeal of rugged outdoor wear to a nation of pampered urbanites and drugstore cowboys. In a short tour of Freeport, Crews observes the "country store tacky" in L. L. Bean's retail store, tours the company's computer-automated factory, and interviews visitors from across the United States who have traveled to Maine to see the mail-order headquarters firsthand, including a Chicagoan in a lavish motor home ending his annual L. L. Bean pilgrimage. Crews's exasperation at this state of affairs is interwoven with detailed reportage: on L. L. Bean's founding, its rapid rise to worldwide success, its varied and high-quality products. The essay's mixture of detailed journalism and hilarious comment is vintage Crews.

Others of Crews's short essays are not journalism but simply a forum for the author's observations on his day-to-day world. In "Tuesday Night with Cody, Jimbo, and a Fish of Some Proportion" Crews recounts the disagreement of two barroom patrons over the weight of a fish, the quick escalation of the argument into a truck-pulling contest, and the evening's significance for the deep friendship of the two men. In "The Wonderful World of Winnebagos" Crews and a companion tramp through Shenandoah National Park in Virginia, dodging motor homes and growing increasingly chagrined at the vehicles' occupants, who kidnap raccoons, chase deer and bear, hit golf balls, and frequently annoy everyone around them. In "Running Fox" Crews tries to cheer up a drinking companion by taking him on a night of drinking and "running the dogs."

Even in his lengthy journalistic pieces Crews injects much of himself into the story line. In "Television's Junkyard Dog," a profile of actor Robert Blake during the heyday of his television show *Baretta,* Crews writes empathetically of the actor's long effort to come to terms with his career, his childhood, and his family. But this is not a typical movie-star profile: it is also about the tremendous kinship that Crews strikes with Blake, the multifaceted demands that creative pursuits have placed upon both of their lives, and the similarities in how each man has coped with them. Crews's essay is about two tortured lives—his own and Blake's—and the revelatory moments that have saved each of them. Blake describes his years in therapy and the emotional day he recognized his own unanswered longing for his mother's touch. Crews, in the most provocative and moving section of the essay, recounts an epiphany from his earliest days as a novelist: the moment he recognized that the humiliation of his childhood, horrible as it was, had molded his personality and should be revered, not loathed. "Once I realized that the way I saw the world and man's condition in it would always be exactly and inevitably shaped by everything which up to that moment had only shamed me, once I realized that, I was home free," Crews writes.

In "Carny," also collected in *Blood and Grits,* Crews and his actions are woven into the story he has to tell. The author's best and lengthiest essay is about his travels with a carnival, his exploits with carnival insider Charlie Luck, and the hidden machinations of the small-time hustlers who move with the carnival from town to town. Crews spends his time popping pills and downing beers, sharing in the carnies' pleasure at bilking the "marks" who cruise the midway, advising Charlie Luck in his love affair with a dancing girl of unusual talents, and offering his van for use in the carnies' many sexual liaisons. The essay, much like Crews's earthy re-creations of barroom scenes, is laced with profanity—it is the language of the carnival, after all—and with graphic description of the girlie shows and the carnival's other seamy attractions. The description and the profanity are not gratuitous, however; they serve to bring the grimy atmosphere to life. With the carnies as with the other subjects of his essays, Crews is sympathetic and understanding, always looking beyond the hustlers' and barkers' dreary surroundings to find inner qualities that merit respect and dignity.

Crews's humor, and he is nearly always funny, can be biting, though seldom cruel and rarely taken at the expense of individuals. His ire, if it can be called that, is directed more at the absurdity of modern values than at the individuals who express them through their lives. He sees that absurdity reflected as much in himself as in those he writes about. In "The Knuckles of Saint Bronson," a profile of actor Charles Bronson, Crews ridicules the film industry and America's fascination with it even while expressing admiration for Bronson, one of its icons. On the set with Bronson, the actor's gritty individualism and his refusal to play movie-star games impress Crews at the same time the crass commercialism of other industry insiders depresses him. "Hollywood is a huge, extremely complex, multimillion-dollar machine whose sole purpose is to put the skin on baloney," Crews observes. But he then admits to succumbing to movie-star magic himself. "It *is* fantasy. It *is* magic," he writes. "And none of our dreams are safe from it. We are all—all of us—part of the wild tribe of baloney eaters." Crews therefore carefully avoids mockery in describing barroom patrons reduced to trembling upon seeing Charles Bronson's autograph.

Crews re-creates lengthy conversations from barrooms and other venues in his stories. His ear for dialogue, which he calls one of his greatest strengths as a novelist, is put to use in his nonfiction to establish atmosphere and provide humor. On assignments Crews collects dialogue with a tape recorder, and he often re-creates it at hilarious length, whether it's particularly relevant to the story or not. In his piece on Bronson, for example, Crews reproduces verbatim one woman's offer to accompany him to his motel room for a purpose she explains in brief but unmistakable detail. Crews declines her offer, however, saying he is working. "You always drink this much when you're working?" she asks. In much of the Blake essay the actor tells his own story in paragraph after paragraph of direct quotation.

As in the essays about Blake and Bronson, Crews's pieces are most personal when he is writing about subjects and people with whom he feels empathy. In "The Trucker Militant" he writes sympathetically of Mike Parkhurst, magazine publisher and advocate for independent truckers. When Parkhurst speaks of independent truckers as sharecroppers to the national trucking companies, Crews is understanding; these are terms the author can understand. "Sharecropping," Crews writes, "can make a good man dangerous."

Critics were generally kind to Crews in weighing the quality of the nonfiction in *Blood and Grits,* though some balked at the degree to which he consistently injected himself into his essays. Ted Morgan, reviewing Crews's collection in *The New York Times Book Review* (25 March 1979), praised Crews for avoiding formulaic magazine writing and applauded his ability "to turn every assignment into a picaresque adventure." But Morgan wrote that his enthusiasm for reading Crews's magazine pieces had faded once the writer's essays were collected in book form, where Crews's idiosyncrasies in dialogue and topic selection were more apparent. "Mannerisms and methods that one was willing to overlook in a monthly column become glaring," Morgan wrote. But Nelson Canton, writing in *Time* (5 March 1979), applauded Crews's idiosyncrasies and praised his stories as giving the reader "a sense of triumph." Readers are uplifted, Canton wrote, by watching Crews and his "gallery of odd personae" grapple with and overcome their fears.

Published in 1982, *Florida Frenzy* features a selection of Crews's work set in his adoptive state; mostly essays printed in magazines, the book also includes a few excerpts from two novels, *Naked in Garden Hills* (1969) and *The Hawk Is Dying* (1973). The essays include two particularly personal essays, "Teaching and Writing in the University" and "Why I Live Where I Live." In the former Crews discusses his teaching philosophy and in so doing displays the gentle side of his personality that—despite all his tough-guy bravado—is so often evident in his work. Crews writes that unlike many other writers, he believes that teaching helps his writing, primarily by maintaining in him a sense of accomplishment even when his writing is not going well. "When I walk out of the room or lecture hall," Crews writes, "a little voice in the back of my head says, 'Son, you may cain't write, but you sure as hell can teach.'" Crews's approach to students is gentle; he doesn't mark up their papers with red ink but talks to them instead, in an effort to push students to excel without crushing their spirits. A good teacher, he says, is like a good editor, one who is always trying "to discover what

Crews in 1979 (photograph by Charné)

the writer had in mind in the first place and then by indirection force the writer to see for himself where he went wrong." In "Why I Live Where I Live" Crews lists the multiple attractions that Gainesville, Florida, offer him: proximity to beaches, good bars, good libraries, and a competent hypnotist, all at a manageable but comfortable distance from his south Georgia roots.

Similarly, other stories in *Florida Frenzy* reflect disparate elements of Crews's day-to-day life in and around Gainesville. In "The Hawk Is Flying" Crews nurtures a badly injured hawk back to health. In "The Unfeminine Mystique" the author visits his favorite bar and finds himself in a hostile tête-à-tête with a female patron over his offhand complimentary remark about the barmaid's backside. "The Goat Day Olympics" is not about the Olympics at all but about the events before, during, and after an all-day barbecue put together by Crews and his friends. The festivities begin at Lillian's Music Store, the Gainesville bar, where a goat and a pig are packed into Crews's van while he and his friends soak up whiskey inside. The Olympics continue with a thirty-mile ride to a lake outside Gainesville, where the goat and

the pig are slaughtered and cooked in preparation for the carloads of men and women who will soon arrive for an all-day picnic. It is the kind of gathering that Crews finds most satisfying. "We had once again made ourselves purified and holy," Crews writes of the day's end, "under a bright sky on a killing ground older than any of us would ever live to be."

Several journalistic essays in *Florida Frenzy* are showcases for Crews's love of blood sports. In "A Day at the Dogfights" Crews accompanies Skete, a breeder of pit bull dogs, to south Florida as he and his dog, Mr. Pryde, prepare for a dogfight near Boca Raton. Crews, a lifelong dogfighting fan, complains that the truth is seldom written about the sport, which, while violent, he nonetheless defends as an activity typical of a violent American culture. Crews attends the dogfight but misses its final moments when, while jockeying for position outside the pit, he insults and is punched in the throat by a fellow member of the audience. "I woke up in the back of the Dodge van with Mr. Pryde lying beside me, snoring away," writes Crews, now covered with blood and barely conscious from a slight concussion. "All in all, it had been a grand evening."

On another, less pleasurable night that is the subject of "Poaching Gators for Fun and Profit," Crews accompanies an alligator poacher on a hunt. But Crews is clearly not as enthusiastic about this particular blood sport; he passes up several offers from the poacher to take a shot at passing gators. Characteristic of Crews, however, much of the essay is told in the poacher's own words, in lengthy direct quotations. "A tourist, a game warden, and a gator's all got about the same size brain," opines the poacher as the hunt winds down. "Just a little bigger than a good-size peanut."

Crews's uncollected essays run the gamut from journalism to personal essays to ruminations upon body parts. Much of his uncollected work was written in the 1980s, after the publication of *Florida Frenzy,* and Crews said in an interview that some will be reprinted in his forthcoming collection, *Glimpses into a Keyhole.* Like his work from the 1970s, many of his works in the 1980s appeared in *Playboy.* "It's never bothered me much where my stuff appears," Crews said in a 1996 interview. "Who published it or where it appeared cannot possibly affect what I wrote."

Crews's journalism from the 1980s is among his best. In "The Buttondown Terror of David Duke," Crews describes his days spent following Ku Klux Klan leader Duke and the race hatred that Duke is able to conjure in Klan audiences and in casual conversations with passersby. Crews records in detail the foundations of Duke's racist beliefs, the high-level security that always surrounds him, and the skill with which Duke clothes his race hatred in smooth respectability. A consistent theme throughout the piece is Crews's worry that Duke's racism was attracting adherents and gaining credibility—that Duke's affability and media savvy were obscuring a dangerous race hatred. "I liked Duke and many of the other members of his organization," Crews writes. "When they broke out of their racial monologues and rampant paranoia, they were great guys to travel with or talk with or eat with. But I always had the feeling that if you took a Phillips-head screwdriver and loosened the four little screws that held the plates on the backs of their heads and looked inside, you would see that at least two fuses were burned out."

As in earlier decades, Crews's work in the 1980s was far-ranging. In 1989 some editors at *Playboy* who were putting together a special issue on love asked Crews to write an entry on the groin. "The Wisdom of the Groin" appeared in the February 1989 issue. Ostensibly, the story is about a married college professor caught naked on his apartment house roof as he is surreptitiously making his way to a graduate student's apartment for a late-night tryst. But the piece is really about the place of desire in human life. After all, Crews relates, "It has been the knowledge and the language of the groin that have kept the race alive." But that language has no value without perspective, he writes. "God save us all from those who believe we exist only from the navel up, and save us, too, every mother's son and daughter, from those who would have us believe we exist only from the navel down." The essay, as Crews said in an interview, is about "what the head knows, what the heart knows, and what the groin knows, and the language each of them speaks." Crews said he liked the essay so much he gave a copy to his son.

A particularly personal piece written by Crews in the 1980s concerns the death of his young son, Patrick. *Playboy* editors had approached Crews to write an essay about fatherhood because many readers were considering becoming parents. In "Fathers, Sons, Blood" Crews re-creates the sense of loss he felt upon the death of his son Patrick; the writer's subsequent rededication of himself to his second son, Byron; and his ultimate conclusion that fatherhood, despite its heartaches and pitfalls, is indeed worth the trouble.

In 1996 Crews said:

When I start to write nonfiction I have a tendency to do the same thing I do when I'm writing fiction, that is to find a strong narrative line. I would say that all of the so-called craft that is used in fiction I use in my nonfiction. There is dialogue inevitably in my nonfiction, and there is a story line, and there are people doing things to other people in a place and time out of whatever motive they have. And so the two are very closely related to me.

Crews said he takes writing assignments from magazines only if they don't interfere with his fiction writing. "If I've ever been in the midst of a novel and magazines have called me to ask me to take an assignment, I've always turned it down," Crews said. "I don't like to leave a novel once I've started it. I like to stay in touch with it." Crews said he also turns down assignments that don't suit his fancy. An editor once badgered him into doing a profile of the writer Walker Percy, and Crews called it off after concluding that his friend Percy had better things to do than "fooling around with me for some damn magazine." Crews also refuses any pieces that seem to take advantage of a subject's troubles. "I can't stand to go bury people or butcher people or beat up cripples or that kind of thing," Crews said. "That's why I work best if a guy will just let me hang around for two or three days and we just talk about this and that."

Crews said that despite his commitment to fiction he continues to write nonfiction because it introduces him to new sights and sounds. "It gives me a chance to experience things I never would otherwise have experienced, meet people I never would have met otherwise, and I think that can't do anything but be good for a writer, or be good for this writer, anyway." Of his nonfiction he said, "There's some of it I'm really proud of. There's some of it that pleased me as much as anything I've written in fiction."

References:

Nelson Canton, "Triumphant Victim," *Time* (5 March 1979): 88;

A. B. Crowder, *Writing in the Southern Tradition: Interviews with Five Contemporary Authors* (Amsterdam: Rodopi, 1990), pp. 79–115;

Scott Hiaasen, "The Fierce and Funny World of Harry Crews," *Palm Beach Post*, 15 May 1994, p. J1;

Susan Ketchin, "Harry Crews: The Writer as Shaman," in *The Christ-Haunted Landscape: Faith and Doubt in Southern Fiction*, edited by Ketchin (Jackson: University Press of Mississippi, 1994), pp. 326–351;

Ted Morgan, "Occasional Pieces," *New York Times Book Review* (25 March 1979): 30.

Sara Davidson
(5 February 1943 –)

Ginger Rudeseal Carter
Georgia College & State University

BOOKS: *Loose Change: Three Women of the Sixties* (Garden City, N.Y.: Doubleday, 1977);
Real Property (Garden City, N.Y.: Doubleday, 1980);
Friends of the Opposite Sex (Garden City, N.Y.: Doubleday, 1984);
Rock Hudson: His Story, by Davidson and Rock Hudson (New York: Morrow, 1986).

SELECTED PERIODICAL PUBLICATIONS–UNCOLLECTED: "Kids in the Fast Lane," *New York Times Magazine,* 16 October 1988, p. 73;
"Love with a Proper Cowboy," *New Woman,* 25 (April 1995): 94.

Since she first wrote for the newspaper at the University of California, Berkeley, in the 1960s, Sara Davidson has been taking the pulse of her generation. Davidson's work spans not only four decades but also diverse media. She has moved from newspapers to magazines, from nonfiction to fiction, and from print to television. Her creative work seems to fit whatever medium is most popular at the time, and her subjects seem to be reminiscent of the mood of the decade in which they appear.

At least once every ten years she publishes an article that serves as her benchmark for that decade. From *Loose Change: Three Women of the Sixties* (1977), her book that evokes the chaotic period of the 1960s, to her article "Love with a Proper Cowboy" (1995), her work as a literary journalist has provided a vivid illumination of the times she describes. In the more than thirty years since she was first published Davidson has covered subjects that include the Vietnam War and its protesters, the assassinations of President John F. Kennedy and Sen. Robert Kennedy, the women's movement, family lifestyles in the 1980s, and cowboy poetry contests. Davidson has written for such magazines as *Esquire, Life, Harper's, Ms.,* and *Rolling Stone.* She grants few interviews, preferring to include her observations in her own writing.

Sara Davidson was born in Los Angeles on 5 February 1943 to Marvin H. Davidson and Alice

Sara Davidson (photograph by Glen Strauss)

Wass Davidson. In her first book, *Loose Change: Three Women of the Sixties,* Davidson writes about her life in post–World War II Hollywood, calling it "a city where the surf report was read with the morning news." She remembers that "I did not know, until I was seventeen, that the rest of the country was different. I was unaware that people in other regions of the country do not eat their salad first or paint Christmas trees orange." Davidson's grandfather, a Hungarian immigrant, moved to Los Angeles from New York in 1915, and her mother was born the next year. This "makes me something of a rarity: a second generation native," Davidson writes. "While my mother was growing up, the city came to a stop at what is now Beverly Hills."

Davidson grew up in the 1940s around her parents' store, MarvAl, where her father installed radios in automobiles. Davidson recalls in *Loose Change* that she was the first on her block to have a television set. In the 1950s, she writes, "my mother started selling real estate, and was soon earning more than my father. She pressed him to sell the radio business. She didn't want him crawling under cars any longer." Davidson's father eventually became a memorial counselor, selling burial plots for a Jewish cemetery.

Davidson entered the University of California in 1960, serving as an editor to the campus paper, the *Daily Cal.* She graduated in 1964 with a bachelor of arts degree, then pursued her master of science degree at Columbia University, graduating in 1965. She joined the *Boston Globe* that same year as a reporter, then became the paper's New York correspondent in 1967. While at the *Boston Globe* Davidson covered the political conventions of 1968 and the assassination of United States senator Robert Kennedy. Davidson also covered subjects related to youth, the counterculture, and rock music. In the introduction to *Loose Change: Three Women of the Sixties* she writes that the decade of the 1960s disenfranchised her as a writer: "In the Sixties, I often felt that I was caught between two worlds, the Establishment and the counterculture. In the first, I was viewed as a youth spokesman and in the second, I was seen as a representative of the bourgeois capitalist press. I could move in both worlds, but I did not fit in either."

On 26 January 1968 Davidson, then just days shy of her twenty-fifth birthday, married Jonathan Schwartz, a disc jockey in New York. She left the *Boston Globe* to be a freelance writer, and her work began appearing in *Esquire, Harper's, Atlantic, Life,* and *Rolling Stone.* The transition from news reporting to literary journalism was a self-conscious one. "Anyone who has come up from a newspaper has a great deal of self-consciousness about even writing the word 'I,'" she told Norman Sims, as he reports in his book *The Literary Journalists* (1992). "I don't remember when I first used it, but it was just in one little paragraph, a trial balloon. The more I did it the easier it got and also I found I could do more with it. It enabled me to impose the storyteller on the material."

In 1972 Davidson was in an elevator when she ran into a former roommate from Berkeley. As she writes, "It was this meeting which led me to seek out others from my past, to see if by tracing our stories, I might piece together a social history of the Sixties and gain an understanding of what happened to us—and our country—in this time." The result was *Loose Change: Three Women of the Sixties.* For this book she interviewed two former roommates and a cast of other friends. Davidson spent six months interviewing the two whom she called Natasha and Susie. "We would meet once a week and spend all day,"

she writes in the introduction. "Often I would ask them to go very deep." What the two did not remember Davidson filled in herself from her own memories of the 1960s. "I had to invent it, invent all that texture, from what I knew of Susie at that time, and what I knew of Berkeley," she writes. "Which gets to the question of: is it still nonfiction? I decided it was, if you were using the facts and details that were real and if you were taking the plot from history. But I was certainly filling it out, filling in the skeleton, with my memory."

Davidson also filled out one-third of the book's characters with her own account, titled "Sara" in the book. In chapter 29 she deals with her painful divorce from Schwartz, whom she calls Michael in the book. She recalls their meeting to settle terms in 1973: "The symmetry of it all was unnerving. On January 23, 1973, I had walked in the kitchen to fix supper for myself and flicked on the radio. 'Ladies and gentlemen, the President of the United States.' I had not known the President would be on the air, only that it was 6 p.m. and safe to turn on the radio and not hear Michael." Davidson adds that she noted the day in her journal with the words "I have seen a historical era begin and end." This comment mirrors her marriage to—and divorce from—Schwartz.

Loose Change was filled with intimate descriptions, heart-wrenching break-ups, sex, drugs, abortion, enlightenment, and rock and roll. In spite of its candor, the book met with mixed reviews. Victoria Rudin, in the *London Observer,* wrote that Davidson's "new-journalistic reliance on faked dialogue, her cliff-hanger chapter endings, and her use of pulpy leitmotifs (Tasha always laughs her 'tinkling laugh'; Rob twinkles his blue eyes) threaten to ground the story in coyness." Rudin added, though, that the book "stands as a painful document of what it was like to be young, female, middle class and American during the sixties."

Erica Jong, a writer whose style Davidson was charged with emulating, gave the book a weak review in 1977 in *The New York Times Book Review.* Jong, known for exploring a similar theme of women coming of age, wrote of the book's "formlessness, its easy topicality, its false sense of conveying history when it is really only dropping names of historical events, as one might drop the names of famous people." Another reviewer called the book "like a loaf that has been taken out of the oven too soon—crisp and brown on the outside, rather runny and shapeless within" and criticized Davidson for her "failure after four years of researching and writing the book to analyze the meaning of the event."

Davidson noted in the epilogue of her book, "I am afraid I will be criticized for copping out." She adds that she did not find all the answers and she had forgotten the questions. "The point is," she writes, "we all used to believe in certain interpretations that explained everything. When one interpretation wouldn't work, we'd change and get another. I've grown weary of explanations. No explanation ever closes all accounts."

Loose Change became a best-seller and was distributed by the Literary Guild. In 1978 it was adapted as a popular NBC miniseries. All this attention, Davidson told Sims for *The Literary Journalists,* had its costs. The subjects of the book, whose names had been changed, were easily recognizable to those who knew them. "They turned on me," Davidson told Sims. "Quite understandingly. They couldn't escape it. It didn't blow over. It's hard to describe their pain. It haunted them for two years. What bothered me was I caused pain to other people, to my husband, to the women, who went through hell."

Davidson vowed never to write so intimately about her life again. But in 1980 she wrote her second book, *Real Property,* which gives her account of her life after her divorce, when she lived in Venice, California, where she moved in 1974. The tone of *Real Property* is distinctly different from that of *Loose Change,* much as the music of the 1960s is different from that of the 1970s, more hip and knowledgeable, less bare and vulnerable. The change is also materialistic, as the quote from Ron Koslow at the beginning of the article suggests: "What marijuana was to the sixties, real estate is to the seventies." The subject matter for the book came from Davidson's journals and the articles she wrote for *Esquire* and *Rolling Stone.* Each section featured a different glimpse into 1970s lifestyles. The stories feature people she knew, but Davidson herself was usually the focus of each chapter. She describes her life at this time early in the book: "I live in a house by the ocean with an outdoor Jacuzzi. I owned, until an embarrassing little accident, a pair of roller skates. I still own a volleyball, Frisbee, tennis racket, backpack, hiking boots, running shoes, a Mercedes 240 Diesel and a home burglar alarm system. But I cannot say I am satisfied."

Davidson also writes about other characteristics of the times, such as the growing women's movement. In a section called "Birth Pains" she describes the early divisiveness in the movement. Davidson covered the early years of the movement for magazines such as *Life* and *Esquire* and

faced reactions from feminists that left her "wounded and enraged." Although *Life* had a large circulation, feminists considered it a "mom and apple pie" magazine unfriendly to the cause of feminism. The audience of *Esquire,* feminists argued, was largely male.

"Today," Davison writes, "when terms like 'sexism' and 'male chauvinism' have been so diluted that they have lost their charge, it is difficult to remember that in the beginning, anyone who declared herself an advocate of women's lib met with abuse and ridicule. Members of women's groups were afraid their ideas would be distorted by the press, and they would be labeled dykes, man-haters and lunatics." Davidson also marked her own rite of passage in *Real Property* when she wrote of her return to Los Angeles in 1973. She bought a house in Venice, and her words echo the remorse of someone who has made a major commitment of money to walls and plaster:

> During the interim years, I grew to have contempt for people who spent money on houses and furniture, expensive cars and first-class airline tickets. I thought it was more interesting and adventuresome to travel second class, if not to hitchhike. I visited and wrote about communes where "free land" was the ideology. It sounded right; no one should be able to own the land, any more than people could own the sky or the sea.

By the time *Real Property* was published in 1980, Davidson had remarried. She gave birth to two children, Andrew and Rachel, in 1981 and 1983. These changes brought with them another journey—this one literary. While Davidson continued to write nonfiction articles for magazines such as the *Los Angeles Times Magazine,* she moved away from books that could be called literary journalism and moved toward other forms of writing. Her first novel, *Friends of the Opposite Sex* (1984), is a story of friendship, romance, and travel abroad to countries that include war-torn Israel. The themes are reminiscent of both *Real Property* and *Loose Change* jumbled together.

But *Friends of the Opposite Sex* did not receive as much attention as Davidson's first—or next—work. In 1986, barely a year after his death, Rock Hudson and Davidson shared a byline on his authorized biography, *Rock Hudson: His Story.* Davidson spent twenty-nine days before Hudson's death with him at his Beverly Hills home, The Castle. He talked as freely with Davidson as his illness permitted, and more important, he encouraged his friends to do the

Cambridge, Massachusetts, 1965—one of the first mass marches calling for an end to the war in Vietnam, covered by Davidson for the Boston Globe *(photograph by Peter Simon)*

same. In the introduction to the book Hudson writes: "I've always been a private person. I've never wanted to write a book. I've never let my house be photographed and I've never let the public know what I really think. Now that's changed—there's a lot I want to say and not too much time left. I want the truth to be told, because it sure as hell hasn't been told before. So I've asked those who know me best—my real friends—to work with Sara Davidson in telling my story." This statement, signed by Hudson, was Davidson's letter of introduction to his friends. Davidson wrote that this was a difficult task for them to grant, since Hudson, as she observes, "had trained his friends to observe 'total silence' especially with writers."

In Davidson's introduction she records that she "had no idea, at the onset, how complex and fascinating" her job of writing about Hudson would be. She found an actor who had been loved by many friends. She also found around the man a circle of close friends who had helped him shield his homosexuality for more than forty years. "On screen, he projected the image of a simple soul, not ambivalent or tortured. He was warm and good and pure. He seemed completely

what he was at the moment: completely in love, completely brave, completely repentant," she wrote. "Yet in life, Rock was anything but simple. He was a master of illusion, devious and secretive, capable of being extremely kind and utterly heartless. Like the Trickster, he appeared to different people in different guises." The book is not graphic about Hudson's homosexuality, but it is frank. Davidson does not avoid talking about the men who filtered through the actor's life, but she keeps details discrete and minimal. Hudson is pictured as a Hollywood playboy, hard drinking, and sexually voracious, all of whose love interests are men.

Of her first meeting with Hudson, his friends, and his household staff, Davidson writes: "I drove out of the front gates feeling panicky, disoriented." She then notes: "It was one of the most bizarre scenes I'd ever witnessed: the old lover and the new lover brushing elbows in the hall, the old lover reclaiming his place while the new one refused to give ground. Friends gathering in the living room, laughing and telling stories while the movie star lay dying of a terrifying disease—the plague of our time. The eighty-year-old gardener eating ice cream in the kitchen. The butler in his towel. What was I getting into?"

Reviews for the book were mixed. Since the biography was published within weeks of another, unauthorized biography, the two were compared by Julia Cameron for the *Chicago Tribune* (22 June 1986). "Davidson had the advantages—and disadvantages—of access to Hudson," Cameron noted. "Even as he was succumbing to his disease, she was succumbing to his charm. There is a resultant warmth to her book even when the revelations it makes about Hudson's life are chilling." For although America knew Hudson was gay and had AIDS, it was still difficult to read about. "In the final telling," Cameron wrote, "it appears it was circumstances, not character, which forced Rock Hudson's belated heroism upon him."

By 1988 Davidson had made yet another media move, this time to dramatic television. While in the hospital giving birth to her children, Davidson came up with the idea of a television series about a women's medical clinic. The series was called *HeartBeat,* and it was produced for Aaron Spelling Productions by Esther Shapiro and George Eckstein. Shapiro told the *New York Daily News* that "These women in the clinic respect other women. They handle every kind of case from head to toe involving women, including cancer and pregnancies. Sara Davidson, when she came to us with the idea, said she got it while bedridden with her pregnancies." The series was short-lived, but Davidson did not leave television. She became co-executive producer of *Dr. Quinn, Medicine Woman,* a CBS series that premiered in 1994.

Perhaps not to leave the decade of the 1980s without providing a commentary on her own life, Davidson wrote "Kids in the Fast Lane," an account of her life with children in Los Angeles that appeared in October 1988 in *The New York Times Magazine.* The article is about children of yuppies, with Davidson and her children the perfect yuppie group. Andrew, age four, is taking karate and carrying kiwi for lunch to preschool. Rachel loves froufrou dresses and faux pearls. Mom writes for television and movies, and Dad drives twenty miles on his lunch hour to get Andrew a Nintendo for a birthday gift. Davidson quotes teachers and psychologists, as well as other parents, on the difficulty of parenting in the 1980s. After lamenting that her son's four-hour-a-week karate lessons will eat into her time, Davidson decides to take private lessons while Andrew is in class. This, she writes, will allow her some needed exercise and a bonding experience. "This plan is a little eccentric," she admits, "but I have come to see my foray into martial arts in California as a metaphor for the lifestyle of a certain group of parents—baby-boomers with substantial incomes—who are raising children."

Davidson, born in 1943, is not technically classified as a baby boomer by age, but she fits herself in the group experientially. "We are fascinated with the children, and, because we delayed having them, have had our chance to travel, stay out all night, flirt with wild ideas and people and are now content to settle in with our families," she writes. "No longer young, we're raising the young. Forget the joy of sex, we've replaced it with the joy of parental love, and we have made our child-raising the No. 1 event going on in our world."

The most humorous account in the article concerns the lunch pail of the 1980s. "It's lunchtime at pre-school, and the food that comes out of bags and boxes is something to behold," Davidson writes. "Sure, a few kids have peanut butter sandwiches, but others have spaghetti with pesto, tiny bunches of champagne grapes, sliced nova on a bagel. One girl eats from take-out containers: pasta salad, Chinese chicken salad, shrimp."

As her television writing and production career flourished in the 1990s, Davidson's second marriage failed. She and her children stayed in Los Angeles, and she continued to write for national magazines. In 1995 she published two articles that profile her life as a woman in her fifties living in the 1990s. The first, "Git Along, Little Doggerel," appeared in *The New York Times Magazine* on 15 January 1995. It is an account of the Cowboy Poetry Gathering in Elko, Nevada. The article describes the many cowboys and their words. "I don't believe . . . that I would have traveled five hours to attend a festival of stockbroker poetry," Davidson writes. "But 'cowboy poetry'—the very words are seductive, suggesting the unlikely and irresistible marriage of macho with the artistic."

But the underlying story of the gathering defines another change in Davidson's life. While at the contest she met a cowboy. In "Love with a Proper Cowboy," an article in *New Woman* (April 1995), she describes how she met and began a relationship with Zach. Davidson admits in the magazine's introduction that she had always wanted to meet a cowboy. "When we started dating, I felt as if we were from different galaxies," she writes. "But now, one-and-a-half years later, it doesn't feel absurd any more. It feels natural."

The article, which breaks her promise after *Loose Change* never to write about deeply personal subjects, hearkens back to her more than thirty years of work and is almost an anniversary celebration. The fears of her twenties, the freedom of her thirties, the conformity of her forties, and now, the assuredness of her fifties are reflected in her words as she describes falling in love with a man eleven years her junior from a polar-opposite background:

I felt twinges of fear. Why this person? I thought. He's a being from another planet, he doesn't wear a watch or read a newspaper. He's never heard of King Lear. If a phrase comes to me from the play and I want to share it with him, I'll have to explain who Shakespeare was and what King Lear was about and then tell him the phrase and what it means. I don't have the patience; I'll go crazy. I told Zach, "it's hard for me to let people close." He looked in my eyes for quite a while. "Well," he said, "I'm here."

"Love with a Proper Cowboy" is part of a new, book-length work of literary journalism in progress. Davidson, like her writing and her subjects, has grown and matured over her years as a journalist. After several decades of work she continues to write with the same depth of research and immersion-style reporting that first marked her work as literary journalism in the late 1960s.

Reference:
Norman Sims, *The Literary Journalists* (New York: Ballantine, 1992).

Joan Didion

(5 December 1934 –   )

Paul Ashdown
University of Tennessee

BOOKS: *Run River* (New York: Obolensky, 1963; London: Cape, 1964);

Slouching Towards Bethlehem (New York: Farrar, Straus & Giroux, 1968; London: Deutsch, 1969);

Play It As It Lays (New York: Farrar, Straus & Giroux, 1970; London: Weidenfeld & Nicolson, 1971);

A Book of Common Prayer (New York: Simon & Schuster, 1977);

Telling Stories (Berkeley, Cal.: Bancroft Library, 1978);

The White Album (New York: Simon & Schuster, 1979; London: Weidenfeld & Nicolson, 1979);

Salvador (New York: Simon & Schuster, 1982);

Democracy (New York: Simon & Schuster, 1984; London: Chatto & Windus, 1984);

Miami (New York: Simon & Schuster, 1987; London: Weidenfeld & Nicolson, 1987);

After Henry (New York: Simon & Schuster, 1992);

The Last Thing He Wanted (New York: Knopf, 1996).

MOTION PICTURES: *The Panic in Needle Park,* screenplay by Didion and John Gregory Dunne, 20th Century Fox, 1971;

Play It As It Lays, screenplay by Didion and Dunne, Universal, 1972;

A Star Is Born (remake), screenplay by Didion and Dunne, Warner Brothers, 1976;

True Confessions, screenplay by Didion and Dunne, United Artists, 1981;

Up Close and Personal, screenplay by Didion and Dunne, Buena Vista, 1996.

SELECTED PERIODICAL PUBLICATIONS– UNCOLLECTED: "Alicia and the Underground Press," *Saturday Evening Post,* 13 January 1986, p. 14;

"Unforgettable Women: The Startling Vision of Robert Mapplethorpe," *Esquire,* 112 (September 1989): 214–223;

"Uninvited Friend," *American Health* (June 1992): 37;

Joan Didion (photograph by Mary Lloyd Estrin)

"Eye on the Prize," *New York Review of Books,* 24 September 1992, pp. 57–66;

"Trouble in Lakewood," *New Yorker,* 26 July 1993, pp. 46-50+;

"The Golden Land," *New York Review of Books,* 21 October 1993, pp. 85–88.

Joan Didion told an interviewer in 1992 that she "started out thinking things were pretty coherent. Then I was surprised when they weren't. I decided I better tell people." Didion tells stories of disorder in minimalist novels, lyrical reportage, and personal essays. "We tell ourselves stories in order to live," she writes in *The White Album* (1979). In realizing this existential imperative, she probes the narrative borderlands. Didion confides in *Slouching Towards Bethlehem* (1968) that when keeping a journal she "always had trouble distinguishing between what happened and what merely might have happened, but I remain unconvinced that the distinction, for my purposes, matters." As a novelist she can go so far as to appear as Joan Didion in her own story. As a literary journalist, however, Didion practices what Michael J. Kirkhorn calls a "scrupulous professional self-consciousness." Didion's lapidary phrasing and acute sensitivity to any kind of cant, counterfeit reality, or political rhetoric informs her best work. When her reportorial persona becomes excessively solipsistic or didactic, her work loses some of its power.

The daughter of Frank Reese and Eduene Jerrett Didion, Joan Didion was born in Sacramento on 5 December 1934. She comes from a family that has been rooted in northern California since 1848. Some of her best writing is about the pioneer legacies left to her native state, where the past becomes coeval with the present. Her great-great-great-grandmother came to California with the ill-fated Donner-Reed party but left the group before it became stranded and resorted to cannibalism. Didion insists on "wagon train morality," a code that values survival and responsibility over utopian ideals. For Didion, the Donner Pass always lies just ahead.

Raised in Sacramento, Didion, in the essay "On Going Home" in *Slouching Towards Bethlehem,* describes her family as "difficult, oblique, deliberately inarticulate," while sharing a love of nature, independence, and community. Through childhood "some nameless anxiety colored the emotional charges" between Didion and the place she came from. She believes her generation may be the last to "find in family life the source of all tension and drama."

Didion is most self-conscious in her personal journalism. Hers is an imaginative, moralistic, and often desperate vision charged with a strong sense of loss and the pain of self-inflicted separation and banishment. It is important to Didion to confront self-awareness continually, "to keep on nodding terms with the people we used to be," as she writes in "On Keeping a Notebook" in *Slouching Towards Bethlehem.*

Didion received her undergraduate degree in English from the University of California at Berkeley in 1956, then moved to New York after winning both a literary prize, the Prix de Paris, and a job at *Vogue* magazine. In 1963 she left *Vogue* and married *Time* magazine editor John Gregory Dunne, with whom she moved to Los Angeles in 1964. Didion and Dunne collaborate on screenplays, columns, and other projects. In 1966 they adopted a daughter, Quintana Roo.

Didion's first novel, *Run River* (1963), is the story of two proud families, the McClellans and the Knights, who live in the Sacramento Valley of Didion's childhood. The novel explores the changes brought about by World War II and its aftermath and how those changes affected people who live out the mythologies and illusions of their pioneer ancestors in a lost Eden they are unable to escape.

Didion narrows the epic vastness of this changing California landscape in *Slouching Towards Bethlehem* (1968), an admired collection of twenty reports and essays, many of them previously published in the *Saturday Evening Post.* The book contains a preface followed by three sections. "Life Styles in the Golden Land" contains eight stories dealing with western figures; five "Personals" are more intimate reflections; and "Seven Places of the Mind" unifies the external and interior landscapes of the two previous sections.

The preface is both a commentary and evidentiary brief in support of Didion's epigram and title, taken from William Butler Yeats's poem "The Second Coming." The poem was written almost half a century earlier in the aftermath of World War I. Didion does not suggest that disorder is new but that for her it has become a personal imperative to locate and confront its source. When she cannot find proper words to render experience, she imagines she has suffered "a small stroke, leaving me apparently undamaged but actually aphasic." Didion's stories suggest that America, too, seems to have suffered a neurological interruption, with a resulting loss of language and a diminished capacity for complex thought. Katherine Usher Henderson observes that Didion identifies so strongly with the national condition "that when her nation suffers violence and aimlessness, she becomes ill herself, driven to the edge of madness by the vast chasm between her expectation of order and the chaotic reality."

After spending time in San Francisco's Haight-Ashbury, Didion found that for the first time she had "dealt directly and flatly with the evidence of atomization, the proof that things fall apart." Michelle Carbone Loris has argued that by providing personal testimony to what she witnesses, Didion's essays become prophetic. When her evidence and proof were misconstrued by some to be merely a social history of a localized topical phenomenon and not a prophetic warning of a deeper and more universal disintegration, Didion feared that writing might be an irrelevant act.

"Some Dreamers of the Golden Dream," the first essay, deepens the prophetic intentions of the overall work with its first sentence: "This is a story about love and death in the golden land, and begins with the country." Didion surveys a wasted landscape, alien, haunted, devastated, where "Every

Dust jacket for the collection of essays Didion wrote for Esquire *from 1968 to 1978*

voice seems a scream" in the "season of suicide and divorce and prickly dread." Lucille Miller, like earlier Californians, is in search of a dream, but her dream is largely the creation of television and the movies. What had once been a search for a land to sustain life was now only a search for lifestyle. Lucille ostensibly conspires to kill her husband in a staged car accident to collect on an insurance policy and continue an adulterous affair, and she is subsequently convicted of the crime. Lucille's ambitions overreach her morality. At some point "the dream was teaching the dreamers how to live," and Lucille and her lover begin to sound like characters out of a movie. The story more closely resembles a fictional narrative than straight reportage. Tom Wolfe included "Some Dreamers of the Golden Dream" in his anthology *The New Journalism* (1973). Following this inclusion Didion came to be regarded as a preeminent literary journalist as well as a novelist.

Further lifestyles are explored as Didion interviews very different westerners: the legendary actor John Wayne, recovering from a cancer operation while continuing to make films; folk singer Joan Baez, "a personality before she was entirely a person"; and Michael Laski, the twenty-six-year-old

general secretary of a Marxist-Leninist Party. Didion writes that she feels comfortable interviewing those such as Laski "who live outside rather than in, those in whom the sense of dread is so acute that they turn to extreme and doomed commitments; I know something about dread myself, and appreciate the elaborate systems with which some people manage to fill the void." Laski, "a minor but perilous triumph of being over nothingness," is certain she is a spy.

"7000 Romaine, Los Angeles 38" is about reclusive billionaire Howard Hughes. Didion's thesis is that Americans make folk heroes out of antiheroes like Hughes because they are independent and self-reliant, the same qualities that brought people across the country to seek something better. She finds a difference between those whom Americans say they admire and those whom they really admire. In another piece the Center for the Study of Democratic Institutions under Robert Hutchins is described as a fatuous think tank operating as an academic vanity press, its bloviating pundits subsisting on contributions from putative celebrity policy makers underwriting the "California Dreaming" of the essay's title. "Marry Absurd" examines Nevada's tawdry wedding chapels, symbols of American vulgarity.

The title essay, "Slouching Towards Bethlehem," chronicles emblematic serial ills besetting the culture, signs that the center is not holding and that the American Dream is fading into a darker reality. To capture this disintegration, Didion invents a prose style that mirrors the hallucinogenic images of the counterculture. As Didion travels this desolate landscape, an urban counterpart to the wasteland announced in "Some Dreamers of the Golden Dream," she hears the nihilistic voices of the drifting children of the 1960s. Didion discovers a primitive religious consciousness coexisting with youthful consumerism. The despair and moral emptiness that pervade San Francisco suggest a romantic movement empty of content and slouching toward further disorder and eventual authoritarianism. The press sees the movement as a series of unremarkable buffooneries "immaculate of political possibilities." For Didion, what ails American society is a growing loss of community caused by materialism, media, militarism, self-indulgence, the loss of heroes, and the absence of belief. As the culture disintegrates, subcultures arise in an attempt to restore community. A troubling sign of the social discord is the corruption of language, creating "an army of children waiting to be given the words."

The "Personals" are organized as meditations in the midst of disintegration. Many are meant ironically, as she considers self-respect, morality, going home, keeping a notebook. "Seven Places of the Mind" begins with "Notes from a Native Daughter" in which Didion explores her relationship to her native state and helps illuminate *Run River*. Hawaii is yet another failed paradise, its mood ominously martial. By contrast, she finds an abandoned Alcatraz congenial, "clean of human illusions, an empty place reclaimed by the weather." In Newport, Rhode Island, she finds a curiously western ambiance. "Goodbye to All That" is a memento mori, a romantic lament for her youth as a New York writer.

Critics generally liked *Slouching Towards Bethlehem,* but the book had its detractors as well. In *The Christian Science Monitor* (16 May 1968) Melvin Maddocks, while praising Didion's originality, saw her insistence on converting themes into myths, dreams, and symbols as a journalistic conceit. In the *National Review* (4 June 1968) C. H. Simonds attributed to Didion "a perfect eye for detail and an unfoolable ear," while T. J. O'Hara complained in *Best Sellers* (1 June 1968) that most of the essays "suffer from a lack of relevance or depth when they are not smothering under the heavy hand of irony." Dan

Wakefield, in the *New York Times Book Review* (21 July 1968), found the book "a rich display of some of the best prose written in this country."

Didion's most successful novel, *Play It As It Lays* (1970), became a best-seller and was nominated for a National Book Award. Maria Wyeth, an actress separated from her husband, a self-absorbed film director, seeks a traditional family but is unable to find meaning or security in the moral vacuum of the cinema capital, Hollywood. Maria is raised to think opportunistically and dualistically, knowing the existence of good and evil but not truly understanding either. In the end she winds up "holding all the aces" but wondering "what was the game?"

A Book of Common Prayer (1977) is the story of Charlotte Douglas, a mysterious socialite who becomes involved in the political life of an imaginary Central American country while seeking her eighteen-year-old daughter. Boca Grande is a frontier outpost for the American Dream. Grace Strassner Mendana, a Colorado anthropologist who has married into the Boca Grande aristocracy, attempts to tell both the history of Boca Grande and of Charlotte Douglas but is frustrated in understanding either. All the characters in the novel are in some way touched by political violence, which seems the end product of the chaos of the 1960s. The title, taken from the Episcopal prayer book, suggests a litany for Charlotte Douglas, who acts out a liturgy based on a progressive set of values in a world that has no use for those values. Grace attempts to be Charlotte's witness but in the end finds she is not the witness she wanted to be. In a world devoid of apparent meaning, it is only by choosing to love one another that life becomes redemptive. *A Book of Common Prayer* is the most existentially powerful of Didion's novels.

Telling Stories (1978) contains an essay and also three short stories Didion wrote in 1964. Didion dismisses these stories as minor works because she feels she lacks the facility for writing brief epiphanies. Also in 1978 Didion and Dunne moved to Brentwood Park in Los Angeles, where she completed *The White Album* (1979), Didion's threnody to the late 1960s and early 1970s. The book is organized in five sections containing a total of twenty magazine stories, most of which appeared in *Esquire* between 1968 and 1978. The title essay is followed by "California Republic," "Women," "Sojourns," and "On the Morning After the Sixties."

The White Album begins improvisationally with Didion in confusion and despair. In 1968 she had been described in a psychiatric report, which she includes in the preface, as alienated, pessimistic, and depressed. Didion's state of mind seems appropriate to the events she writes about. News events impose a surreal narrative over ordinary experience. Connections become suffused with irony, and attempts to draw narrative meaning become increasingly difficult. Didion meets Linda Kasabian, a participant in the Charles Manson trial, and other cultural icons such as The Doors, Janis Joplin, and Eldridge Cleaver. Through these encounters and interviews she further beholds the disorder she began to document in *Slouching Towards Bethlehem.* Issues no longer matter. She finds only disorder for the sake of disorder. For Didion the 1960s came to an end in 1971 when she moved to Trancas, a coastal town near Los Angeles. Her new house, like Didion, seemed haunted with memories of the previous decade.

The California section offers Didion a sanctuary where she can reconnect with childhood memories. Her essay on Episcopal bishop James Pike shows the keen sense of absurdity that marked the profiles in *Slouching Towards Bethlehem,* as Pike strides "through every charlatanic thicket in American life." She sees Pike as quintessentially American in having the hubris to think he can reinvent himself without memory or apparent consequences. In "Many Mansions" Didion contemplates a new residence for the governor of California, "a case study in the architecture of limited possibilities." She finds the flaccid design malevolent in its populist affectations, without any of the distinctive character of the old governor's mansion that she visited as a child.

Didion's critical essay on the women's movement, which generated controversy when it first appeared in the *New York Times Book Review* in 1972, attempts to separate the movement's political, social, historical, and moral dimensions and is followed by profiles of Doris Lessing and Georgia O'Keeffe. "Sojourns" moves across a landscape from Hollywood to Hawaii to Bogota. The final section attempts to connect the impressionistic essays. Didion reasserts the failure of narrative to come to terms with change. In "On the Morning After the Sixties" she moves, in a series of vignettes, beyond self to shared community and returns to the moral center of her work.

In *Time* (20 August 1979) Lance Morrow found *The White Album* "mellower than *Slouching Towards Bethlehem*" while still "full of the bizarre details, the eye for blinding weirdness" that made the earlier volume a 1960s icon. Ann Hulbert contended in the *New Republic* (23 June 1979) that instead of the "often insightful, ironic, deft stories of her first collection, her new essays tend to lose their shape and sharpness in her angst." Martin Amis in *The Moronic Inferno and Other Visits to America* (1986) called *The White Album* "a volatile, occasionally brilliant, distinctly female contribution to the new New Journalism, diffident and imperious by turns, intimate yet categorical, self-effacingly listless and at the same time often subtly self-serving." He adds that only "someone fairly assured about certain of her bearings would presume to address her readers in this (in fact) markedly high handed style. The style bespeaks celebrity, a concerned and captive following."

Salvador (1983), Didion's most successful reportorial work, was originally published as two articles in the *New York Review of Books* in October 1982 and was nominated for a Pulitzer Prize. Ostensibly a report on the war in El Salvador, based on a two-week visit with Dunne to the embattled republic in June 1982, *Salvador* reprises Joseph Conrad's *Heart of Darkness* (1902). *Salvador* contemplates the meaning of existence when one confronts absolute evil.

Taken only as a short, impressionistic report on the war, *Salvador* would be a slight work. Something much more is intended, however, than telling the facts about El Salvador. Like Conrad's tale, *Salvador* is a journey into the interior of the human soul. Conrad's novel begins with an optimistic official report in praise of colonialism but ends ominously with the deranged Kurtz annotating the report with the sinister marginalia: *"Exterminate all the brutes."* Didion's journalistic report begins with at least a measure of confidence that the situation can be comprehended but ends with the reporter in flight from the country in a state of terror and despair. *Salvador* is ironic because in this landscape there can be no salvation. The powerful imagery is exemplified by Didion's visit to an unfinished cathedral in which "the unlit altar seemed to offer a single ineluctable message: at this time and in this place, the light of the world could be construed as out, off, extinguished."

Salvador's distress is in part attributable to the American presence, although Didion is less interested in politics than in probing more deeply into the region's heart of darkness. Salvador is a country always acted upon, a country with little self-awareness or identity. In creating her narrative Didion uses a wide range of sources to emphasize the evidence of the senses. Anything can be used to help explain the situation. Her sources include physical evidence of atrocities, the statements of ordinary citizens, commercial texts, and public art.

But it is primarily language that interests her as she decodes the political and diplomatic argot of the war and looks for metaphors. She abandons the natural journalistic tendency to frame dispa-

Dust jacket for Didion's 1992 esssay collection, the title piece of which is a tribute to editor Henry Robbins

rate events into a story. She finds no issues, but plots and personalities, with disappearances the essential feature of *la situacion*. She challenges the relentless quantification she finds in military documentation, concluding that much of what occurs is ineffable. Numbers frustrate those who try to understand them literally rather than as conjectural propositions. Didion abandons induction as she comes to realize that facts will not lead to any kind of explanation. Salvador is a country that cracks Americans.

Carolyn Forche, who has written on the war in El Salvador, praised the book in the *Chicago Tribune Book World*: "Alternately detached and compassionate, this slim essay is many things at once, a sidelong reflection on the limits of the now-old new journalism; a tourist guide manque; a surrealist docudrama; a withering indictment of American foreign policy; and a poetic exploration in fear." Gene Lyons found little to distinguish *Salvador* from Didion's previous work, observing in *Newsweek* (28 March 1983) that "ghastliness and pointlessness are Didion's invariable themes where she goes." Other critics complained of inaccuracies in the text and characterized Didion's reporting as less about Salvador than about its author's obsessions.

Democracy (1984) is the story of Inez Christian Victor, the wife of a United States senator with presidential ambitions. The novel deals with the CIA, politics, and murder in 1975. Didion enters the story as a reporter-narrator who is writing an unfinished novel. Her journalistic persona seems to authenticate the text while confounding the classification of the book as a work of fiction. Phoebe-Lou Adams argued in the *Atlantic* (May 1984) that while the mixing of reportorial and novelistic styles is "an unusual way to construct a novel . . . the method works because the milieu that the author describes is itself a disjointed, far flung muddle of hypocrisy, stupidity, obfuscation, and underhanded maneuver."

Miami (1987), less absorbing than *Salvador,* attempts to unravel the complex political structure of the Florida city, which received much media attention during the 1980s. Didion seeks to understand the city in terms of its most politicized Cuban population. In Miami *el exilio* (the exile) serves as the explanatory metaphor as *la situacion* served in Salvador. But what works for *Salvador* does not work equally well for *Miami.* In *Salvador, Heart of Darkness* serves to frame the subject allegorically. In *Miami,* where "Havana vanities come to dust," Didion can only prowl Woodlawn Park Cemetery, pondering the graves of Cuban presidents.

Didion penetrates Miami more deeply as a reporter, but with a loss of the intuitive perceptions and ironic detachment that enrich *Salvador.* There are fewer emblematic resonances and more raw data. The bibliographic citations she appends to her report are unnecessary in *Salvador.* She largely misses Miami's self-referencing capacity for conspiratorial parody. Miami had become the Casablanca of the Americas, and the popular television series *Miami Vice* had turned the city into an art form. Accordingly, Didion's Miami is too preciously atmospheric, "not a city at all but a tale, a romance of the tropics, a kind of waking dream." One source of the dream is the *Miami Herald,* and Didion discovers that "It was even possible to enter the waking dream without leaving the house" just by reading the *Herald.* In her narrative Miami, since the coming of Fidel Castro to Havana in 1959, is linked referentially "to Caracas and Mexico, to Havana and to Bogota and to Paris and Madrid," connected domestically only to Washington. This is the Miami of the political thriller. Didion is less interested in Miami than she is in establishing the cloak-and-dagger relationship between the militant exiles and the duplicitous Washington intelligence establishment. While *Miami* begins where *Salvador* leaves off, Didion is less successful as an ironic prophet with a cold eye for the absurd.

George Russell observed in *Commentary* (January 1988) that what Didion "seems most interested in doing, screenwriter-fashion, is confecting a portrait of ethnic menace. Miami is of less concern to her than her own mood, in which the ordinary becomes sinister, in which the hand of a nefarious right-wing conspiracy is subtly evident. Sometimes, her attempt to conjure a sinister relationship into existence topples over into outright ludicrousness." Paul Stuewe, in *Quill & Quire* (December 1987), thought that while "on balance, its virtues outweigh its vices, it is still likely to disappoint anyone expecting the precisely calibrated revelation of *The White Album* and *Salvador.*" *USA Today* ranked *Miami* as one of the worst nonfiction books of 1987.

Didion's book *After Henry* (1992) is a collection of essays, most of which first appeared in *The New Yorker* and the *New York Review of Books. After Henry* is divided into four sections, the first containing the title essay and the subsequent sections titled "Washington," "California," and "New York." In the title essay Didion pays homage to her late editor, Henry Robbins, a literary craftsman who nurtured Didion and left her with the knowledge that she could carry on without him. The three essays in the Washington section explore the presidency and the presidential campaign in terms of theater and narrative imagery. In "In the Realm of the Fisher King" Didion assesses Ronald Reagan's triumphalism. Reagan is portrayed as a kind of counterfeit mystical populist, a westerner with no real sense of place who, through abstractions and images, becomes the political grail-keeper of Arthurian romance.

"Insider Baseball" reviews the 1988 presidential campaign, which Didion sees as a process remote from any real connection with democracy or the actual life of the country. The campaign becomes a spectacle manipulated by a professional culture of political and media insiders, a narrative that has little relationship to the issues the campaign claims to address. "Shooters Inc." briefly examines foreign policy as diversion. Officials use "other nations as changeable scrims in the theater of domestic politics."

Reviewing Patricia Hearst's *Every Secret Thing,* Didion, in the *New York Review of Books,* hears in Hearst's narrative of her abduction and survival the nuances of the Donner Party and the overland crossing. Hearst, like Lucille Miller, is another dreamer, another "Girl of the Golden

West." Like Didion, Hearst is "tainted with survival." Hearst is not an idealist but a "California girl, and she was raised on a history that placed not much emphasis on *why*."

"Pacific Distances" is a lyrical collage of images about places from New York to Hong Kong. Didion finds she is no more able to come to terms with disorder than she was as a bemused college student in 1954. Several Los Angeles essays define a city "in many ways predicated on the ability to deal with the future at a rather existential remove." Again the essential "otherness" of California, with its "protective detachment" from the rest of the country, its climate and its entertainment industry, its talismanic criminal cases, and its transient dream-driven population, symbolizes for Didion an inscrutable landscape open only to those who can frame its ambiguities in the context of native kinship. Didion explains the history of the Chandler family and its *Los Angeles Times* empire, and the transition of the paper to a more market-driven style of journalism. Didion admires the old *Times* style, which she defines as giving readers details that everyone knows but seldom reads in a newspaper. These details provide tone and subtext, also evident in Didion's own approach to journalism.

After Henry ends with Didion's return to New York, where she took up residence in 1988. The final essay, an astute blend of journalism, literary and cultural criticism, and rhetorical analysis, examines an assault on a jogger in Central Park. The incident becomes a sentimental narrative of New York public life, a "conflation of victim and city." The press, by creating narrative, creates sentimentality. News becomes for Didion a popular literature of the absurd. The jogger story gained attention because it played to middle-class fears of crime. Stories promising retribution and resolution blur the edges of insoluble problems and act as a source of natural morphine. New York's deeper problems lie in class differences, an underlying criminal ethic, and a rigged economy. Crime is intrinsic, not just an aberration, and not comprehensible rhetorically.

After Henry suffers from a lack of unity. While the theme of disorder remains, Didion's somewhat turgid Washington reports are not especially original or incisive, rooted less in place than in political circumstance. In the *National Review* (22 June 1992) David Klinghoffer complained that Didion had practically ceased being "one of the most devastating reporters in America" and had become instead a media critic. He predicted that "readers of her earlier, and more exhilarat-

ing, work will . . . miss the greater comedy and sadness of real lives observed at first hand. Won't someone pull the chair out from under this woman?" R. Z. Sheppard was among many critics who praised *After Henry*, noting in *Time* (29 June 1992) that readers "should welcome the chance to savor the vintage sotto voce style that more than 20 years ago distinguished this careful writer from New Journalism's noisier competition."

Sheppard correctly places Didion's literary journalism in a singular category, but Klinghoffer undervalues the relationship between her itinerant reporting and her media criticism. Her unorthodox reporting style is a counterpoint to the way the news media frame narrative reality. Unlike most reporters, Didion freely talks with journalists, quotes newspaper accounts, listens carefully to table talk, and moves against the nimbus of reportorial consensus. What the news fails to report is the area of greatest meaning to Didion. Her work speaks directly to the major concerns of her time. She tries to discover what Americans value, the moral codes they live by, and the way they come to terms with a fragmented and unstable world. Her collections of essays and reports define and interpret three critical decades in American life.

Critic Mark Royden Winchell, who deeply respects Didion's work, fears, as he writes in *Joan Didion* (1989), that Didion's reputation peaked in 1980 and that her more recent work "has done nothing to enhance her critical stature." He ranks *Salvador* and *Miami* as "embarrassingly modest failures." He sees Didion's defining work as the interpretation of the 1960s and the transformation of the Sacramento Valley. He speculates that she may find the grist for her future work in the time and setting of her youth rather than in giving an appellation to another decade. But this seems unlikely, for Didion's recent reportage contains some of the best literary journalism being written in America. Didion will likely continue to probe contemporary American life through fiction and personal journalism. As for her previous work, *Slouching Towards Bethlehem* and *Salvador* will each stand as classic works of literary journalism.

Didion's lyrical reporting is a long fugue for America. The woman who talked about rivers with her family in "Notes of a Native Daughter" and who learned early "the absolute mutability of hills and waterfalls and even islands" sees all that is solid washing away. Yet her moral courage and tenacious search for truth deeply honor American values. No literary journalist currently writing is better able to shape the shards of American disorder into a living history of this time.

Interviews:

Alfred Kazin, "Joan Didion: Portrait of a Professional," *Harper's,* 243 (December 1971): 112–122;

Sara Davidson, "A Visit with Joan Didion," *New York Times Book Review* (3 April 1977): 1, 35–38;

Martin Torgoff, "Joan Didion," *Interview* (June 1983): 36;

James Atlas, "Slouching in Miami," *Vanity Fair* (October 1987);

James Reginato, "Joan Didion's Backward Glance," *Women's Wear Daily* (27 April 1992): 12.

References:

Martin Amis, *The Moronic Inferno and Other Visits to America* (London: Cape, 1986; New York: Viking, 1987), pp. 160–169;

Sandra Braman, "Joan Didion," in *A Sourcebook of American Literary Journalism: Representative Writers in an Emerging Genre,* edited by Thomas B. Connery (New York: Greenwood Press, 1992), pp. 353–358;

Katherine Usher Henderson, *Joan Didion* (New York: Ungar, 1981);

Michael J. Kirkhorn, "Journalism's Guilty Secret," *Nieman Reports* (Summer 1992): 36–41;

Michelle Carbone Loris, *Innocence, Loss and Recovery in the Art of Joan Didion* (New York: Peter Lang, 1989);

Mark Royden Winchell, *Joan Didion,* revised edition (Boston: G. K. Hall, 1989).

Joe Eszterhas
(23 November 1944 –)

Jack Lule
Lehigh University

BOOKS: *13 Seconds: Confrontation at Kent State,* by Eszterhas and Michael D. Roberts (New York: Cornwall Press, 1970);
Charlie Simpson's Apocalypse (New York: Random House, 1974);
Nark! A Tale of Terror (San Francisco: Straight Arrow Books, 1974).

MOTION PICTURES: *F.I.S.T,* screenplay by Eszterhas, United Artists, 1978;
Flashdance, screenplay by Eszterhas, Paramount, 1983;
Jagged Edge, screenplay by Eszterhas, Columbia Pictures, 1985;
Hearts of Fire, screenplay by Eszterhas, Lorimar, 1986;
Big Shots, screenplay by Eszterhas, 20th Century-Fox, 1987;
Betrayed, screenplay by Eszterhas, United Artists, 1988;
Music Box, screenplay by Eszterhas, Tri-Star, 1989;
Checking Out, screenplay by Eszterhas, Handmade Films, 1989;
Basic Instinct, screenplay by Eszterhas, Tri-Star, 1992;
Sliver, screenplay by Eszterhas, Paramount, 1993;
Nowhere to Run, screenplay by Eszterhas, Leslie Bohem, and Randy Feldman, Columbia Pictures, 1993;
Showgirls, screenplay by Eszterhas, M-G-M, 1995;
Jade, screenplay by Eszterhas, Paramount, 1995.

SELECTED PERIODICAL PUBLICATIONS-UNCOLLECTED: "The Massacre at My Lai," *Life,* 67 (5 December 1969): 36–44;
"Charlie Simpson's Apocalypse," *Rolling Stone* (6 July 1972): 34–56;
"The Strange Case of the Hippie Mafia," *Rolling Stone* (7 December 1972): 28–34; (21 December 1972): 48–56;
"Death in the Wilderness: The Justice Department's Killer Nark Strike Force," *Rolling Stone* (24 May 1973): 28–34, 44–54;

Joe Eszterhas (photograph by Blake Little)

"The Curse of San Clemente," *Rolling Stone* (30 August 1973): 34–47;
"Claw Men from Outer Space," *Rolling Stone* (17 January 1974): 26, 38–47;
"The Prisons of War," *Rolling Stone* (28 March 1974): 30–40; (11 April 1974): 46–58;
"The Getty Kidnapping," *Rolling Stone* (9 May 1974): 32–45;
"A Footnote to the Book of the Dead," *Rolling Stone* (1 August 1974): 42–47;
"King of the Goons: Deliver Us from Evel," *Rolling Stone* (7 November 1974): 40–58, 68–73;
"The Nature of Chief Perkin's Fury," *Rolling Stone* (8 May 1975): 5;
"Dulcinea," *Rolling Stone* (25 December 1980): 16–22.

By the 1990s Joe Eszterhas had evolved from a radical journalist to a successful screenwriter. His scripts for taut, sexual dramas such as *Basic Instinct* and *Sliver* earned him $3 million per picture. His writing was in such demand that Eszterhas became the first Hollywood writer to sign a long-term contract guaranteeing a percentage of "first dollar gross," a deal only granted to the biggest directors and stars.

Eszterhas also overturned the traditional anonymous status of the Hollywood writer. With his long hair, bushy beard, and heavy boots, he has projected a kind of mountain-man image, achieving a celebrity status and social profile on a par with the actors and actresses of his films. Maureen Dowd wrote in *The New York Times* that Eszterhas "has almost single-handedly changed the image of screenwriter from martyr to macho, banishing old images of Dorothy Parker in Hollywood moaning into her martini, 'I used to be a poet.'" His divorce and subsequent marriage to Naomi Baka, the former wife of a Hollywood producer—who had left her for the actress Sharon Stone—was yearlong fodder for tabloids and newsweeklies.

Eszterhas's glamorous, million-dollar screenwriting in the 1990s stands in stark contrast to his previous work in the 1970s: radical, alternative journalism. Less than two decades before he titillated audiences with scenes of Sharon Stone wielding an ice pick, Eszterhas was engaging readers with political, controversial literary journalism. With his first articles he rose to the top ranks of literary journalism in the early 1970s. His talent for language and narrative may not have been surpassed by any of his colleagues. And the connection between the alternative journalist and the millionaire screenwriter may not prove to be so surprising: Eszterhas's career consistently has been marked by his talent for creating powerful and compelling drama.

Eszterhas was born on 23 November 1944 in Czakanydoroszlo, Hungary. He was one year old when he and his parents fled the war-torn state. The family spent the next five years in East European refugee camps before immigrating to America and the poor Hungarian community in Cleveland, Ohio. Eszterhas's father sold insurance and wrote novels about his homeland. Eszterhas recalled at first rejecting literature for baseball and a life on the streets. But a serious street fight eventually drove him to books. A youth made fun of his accent, and Eszterhas responded with a baseball bat to the head. The boy was hospitalized; Eszterhas retreated from the streets and found his outlet in books.

Driven by the desire to write, Eszterhas took journalism courses in local colleges before finding work in 1967 as a reporter for the *Cleveland Plain Dealer*. Before long his penchant for creating dramatic scenes earned him notoriety and an eventual Supreme Court rebuke. In 1968 Eszterhas covered the collapse of an Ohio River bridge in West Virginia that killed forty-four people. Sensing the dramatic possibilities, Eszterhas followed up his coverage with a feature story on a victim's family for the Sunday magazine. He and a photographer visited the Cantrell family, and although the widow, Margaret Cantrell, was not home, Eszterhas interviewed the children.

The resulting article, however, gave the impression that Eszterhas had indeed interviewed the widow. He described her as "wearing the same mask of non-expression she wore at the funeral." The article, which also stressed the abject poverty of the family, offended Margaret Cantrell, who sued for false-light invasion of privacy. Years later the suit eventually reached the Supreme Court. In *Cantrell* v. *Forest City Publishing* (1974) the Court upheld a $60,000 judgment, affirming the article contained "calculated falsehoods," and the family was placed in a "false light through knowing or reckless untruth." Eszterhas, however, had left the paper by the time of the decision.

His writing skills at the *Plain Dealer* were obvious and impressive. Within a year he had landed a compelling, national freelance assignment: a ten-page account for *Life* magazine of the My Lai massacre, in which U.S. servicemen deliberately slaughtered old men, women, and children. Eszterhas's riveting writing accompanied by exclusive photographs by Ronald L. Haeberle brought the massacre home to the American people.

The article was gripping and skilled but traditional in structure and form. Through extensive interviews with eyewitnesses, Eszterhas uncovered incredible details: a large pile of dead bodies; a "really tiny little boy" holding the hand of one of the dead; a GI dropping to his knees and killing the boy with a single shot; and a black GI, who could not stomach the slaughter any longer, shooting himself in the foot so he could be flown wounded out of My Lai. Two weeks later *Life* filled two pages with a special section of letters and interviews devoted to the My Lai article.

Not long after the My Lai story Eszterhas was on the scene to follow up another cataclysmic event: the 4 May 1970 killing of four students by National Guardsmen at Kent State University. In the ensuing weeks Eszterhas and fellow reporter

Dust jacket for Eszterhas's first book, a collection of accounts of the 4 May 1970 shootings at Kent State originally published in the Cleveland Plain Dealer

Michael Roberts interviewed hundreds of students, family members, and National Guardsmen and put together detailed accounts for the *Plain Dealer* that eventually were collected in *13 Seconds: Confrontation at Kent State* (1970). The subject was explosive, but the style was traditional, though descriptive. At times, though, the writing was colored by deep political conviction. "It was one thing to assemble all the known facts of what took place at the moment the National Guard lifted and fired their rifles," the final chapter states. "It was another to attempt to trace the twisting circumstances that stretch deep into the very viscera of the society."

Though neither the My Lai nor Kent State account contains the experiments and experience of literary journalism, the language of Eszterhas's early, traditional journalism does hint at his future style. His writing includes detailed reporting, long quotations to reveal character and issues, unflinching acceptance of the complexity of human acts, honest attempts to discover and report motives and consequences for all parties, and beneath the surface a real feeling of outrage, revulsion, and pain.

In 1971 Eszterhas left the *Plain Dealer*. His departure was less than amicable. The Cantrell lawsuit still had not been decided. Some colleagues at the paper told reporter Jerry Carroll that Eszterhas was "better with fiction than facts." At times Eszterhas has even said he was fired for columns critical of the news media. But his time at the paper provided him with his first real grounding and experience in journalism. He also met and married his wife, Geri, a police reporter, who left with him for the West Coast.

Within months of his departure from Cleveland, Eszterhas appeared in the offices of *Rolling Stone,* then published in San Francisco. Publisher Jann Wenner recalled that when the clean-cut midwestern man "came to the loft offices to purchase back issues, the mailroom guys were certain he was a narc." But Wenner looked at his writing and assigned him work. By the end of 1972 Eszterhas's work was appearing regularly in *Rolling Stone*. He rapidly moved through the ranks, becoming a full-time correspondent, an associate editor, and eventually a senior editor, sharing space for a time at the infamous National Affairs Desk with Hunter S. Thompson and Timothy Crouse.

The years were full of tumultuous change for Eszterhas. A former colleague told *Time* that Eszterhas first showed up wearing "a 9-to-5 haircut and polyester suits" but soon switched to buckskins and long hair and "would stab a hunting knife into the conference table to emphasize his story ideas."

The biggest change occurred in his writing. Unquestionably, the move to *Rolling Stone* developed Eszterhas's literary journalism. The magazine allowed, even encouraged, Eszterhas to pursue his two passions: language and politics. At *Rolling Stone* Eszterhas used the language of literary journalism to confront the politics and policies of the early 1970s. Politically and socially charged topics dominated his work. He captured the battle in a midwestern town between longhaired youths and fearful town elders; he immersed himself in the use of informers in narcotics enforcement; he considered the bizarre cultural implications of Evel Knievel; and he embraced the anguish and agony of a prisoner of war returned home.

Eszterhas's literary journalism for *Rolling Stone* experimented with writing and structure and challenged the traditional language of journalism. More than a question of style or technique, a change in language is a political act—an attempt to alter how the world is perceived and understood. Through the change of a single word such as "colored" to "black," literary journalism challenged the forms of experience, the ways in which traditional journalism observed, portrayed, and understood the world.

In his work for *Rolling Stone* Eszterhas broke free from the conventions and restrictions of a report and portrayed his subjects in a manner akin to that of a fairly modern novelist. He experimented with approaches and techniques usually found in fiction. He employed stream of consciousness, realistic dialogue, myriad points of view, scene-by-scene construction, and first-person narration. He suddenly showed up in his own stories, ornery and obnoxious, causing events to occur.

Eszterhas took pains to point out differences between himself and other reporters. He explicitly questioned journalistic claims to authority and objectivity, ignored or violated conventional practice, challenged the idea of a *report,* and offered a very different kind of mediation and meditation upon social life. He used language to confront language.

The emphasis on language and politics can be seen in Eszterhas's first major effort for *Rolling Stone*—"Charlie Simpson's Apocalypse," a searing story of rebellion in the heartland in which tensions between local youths and village elders of Harrison-

ville, Missouri, culminate in Charlie Simpson's running amok through the village square, bearing an M-1 semi-automatic carbine with which he kills two policemen and a bystander before he puts the gun barrel in his mouth and blows his own head away.

The article is an extraordinary exemplar of literary journalism. The words violate rules of reporting; they ignore usual assumptions; and they abuse the canon. One immediately recognizable mark of Eszterhas's literary journalism is the detailed, dramatic creation of scenes. In "Charlie Simpson's Apocalypse" Eszterhas reconstructed events from interviews and presented those events not as attributed quotations but as dramatic scenes, as if he himself had observed them. Eszterhas re-creates the centerpiece of the story—the rampage by Simpson—with precision:

> Charlie Simpson saw Orville Allen across the street, a man in faded khaki pants he had had never seen before, and aimed his carbine. The burst caught Allen in the chest. He dropped to the pavement, twisted on the ground, turned his bleeding chest to the sky, and clasped his hands in prayer. "God," he moaned. A trail of blood trickled across the street toward the sheriff's office.

The last scene illustrates another startling difference between traditional journalism and the Simpson story. Eszterhas himself becomes a character in the story: "I got into Harrisonville about two weeks after the shooting." Then he relates how he got the story. He tells how he deceived the older townspeople—how he slicked back his long hair with "a bottle of gooey hair-oil," donned a tie and blue blazer, walked around "with a fat Special Corona 77 cigar sticking out" of his mouth, and bought the people beer and malt liquor to get them to talk. Eszterhas, also in a nontraditional act, confesses in the first person his own mixed feelings about events:

> The fire was roaring and Rise Risner's red Volkswagen, which had been pulled as close as possible, played Dylan, Hendrix, and, what the hell, Jose Feliciano. The people here were Charles Simpson's best friends. We were talking about a man who had killed three innocent people in cold blood. They were calling him a brother and telling me how much he loved people and how he believed in The Cause. . . .

> It had been a long few days and I had scrutinized too many vivid details of four vicious killings and something in my mind flailed out now—Jesus Simpson, murderer, cold-blooded killer, compassionate, sensitive, sentimental. It could have been the fatigue or the Missouri weed or the beer mixed with wine, but I saw too many grotesqueries leaping about in that blazing bonfire.

In philosophical terms the story becomes reflexive as Eszterhas exposes the creation of meaning and its influence on him. Tom Wolfe contrasts Eszterhas's technique in the Simpson story to that of Truman Capote, "who was determined above all to write nonfiction according to the conventions of the twentieth-century novel." By suddenly introducing himself, Wolfe writes, Eszterhas "decides to tell you how he put the story together. Far from being like an epilogue or anticlimax, however, the device leads to a denouement of considerable power."

The editors at *Rolling Stone* quickly recognized Eszterhas as a valuable talent. They encouraged him to rework the Simpson article into a book. (*Charlie Simpson's Apocalypse* was published in 1974 and was nominated for a National Book Award.) They also gave him the time and resources to follow the Simpson story with another explosive political topic: the zealous investigation, indictment, arrest, and prosecution by Orange County authorities of members of Timothy Leary's Brotherhood of Eternal Love. "The Strange Case of the Hippie Mafia" was a two-part story appearing in December 1972. The series is notable for its use of long quotations—ten and twelve paragraphs—in which sheriffs, informers, and drug users present their views on the arrests. Once again Eszterhas himself appears at the end of the story.

Eszterhas followed the Brotherhood article in February 1973 with a more traditional *Rolling Stone* effort—a profile of the rock group the James Gang. However, Eszterhas found a personal and malicious angle to the profile: he depicted the James Gang as fighting to overcome the stigma of hailing from Cleveland. He was merciless on the town he had left just two years before: "Cleveland is a faded outpost of the barren flatland, a place where the river burns, murderers romp, and elections become theaters of slapstick absurdity. Cleveland is shrouded in some sort of gothic haze."

Eszterhas's efforts continued to be recognized by the magazine. He was added to the masthead as associate editor and again was given the time and money for large efforts. In May 1973 Eszterhas returned to the subject of drug busts with "Death in the Wilderness: The Justice Department's Killer Nark Strike Force." A litany of young people killed during narcotics raids, the article runs for a full sixteen pages.

It opens with a dramatically re-created scene: a young woman is awakened by her lover who has had a nightmare about death by an execution squad. Adding to the power and immediacy of the scene, however, is Eszterhas's choice of third-person point of view—presenting the scene through the eyes of individual characters. This technique, an important method in literature, is used little in journalism, which often limits itself to the unseen reporter or sometimes the first person. Eszterhas pushed point of view to the limit.

He first presents the young woman's thoughts as she is awakened by her lover's nightmare. Then he switches immediately to the nightmare itself, leaping inside the head of the doomed man, and finally returns again to the perspective of the woman. Dramatic and foreboding, the scene is also heavy with foreshadowing. Soon after the nightmare the young man is shot and killed during a raid by narcotics agents.

Eszterhas's finely rendered scenes, accomplished through extensive interviewing and observation and then rendered through his experimental use with perspective, provide impact and immediacy. Yet Eszterhas was working to do more. He also began to experiment with structure. Like a novelist he tells "Death in the Wildnerness" by stringing scene after scene together, choosing an achronological, Faulkner-like order, which forces the reader to piece the story together and allows a more personal and powerful *experience* of the story.

In a few months Eszterhas was again promoted and given the title senior editor. He was having two books published from his magazine articles: *Charlie Simpson's Apocalypse* and *Nark! A Tale of Terror* (1974). His work was attracting national attention to *Rolling Stone* and its efforts at promoting this new journalism.

Eszterhas's next assignment for *Rolling Stone* was a first-person travelogue. He traveled down the coast to Orange County and San Clemente, the Western White House of Richard Nixon. "The Curse of San Clemente," published on 30 August 1973, had an obvious affinity to the black comedy and armed defiance of colleague Hunter S. Thompson.

> You can't be too paranoid in horizonless Orange: There's always the chance bloodthirsty Minutemen will come rampaging from the hills; or that some manic-depressive Birchite, agonizing over John Schmitz's presidential wipeout, will gun his vinyl-roofed Camaro right at you, chalking one up, zipping one bodybag, against Appeasement, Alienism and God knows what else. So I've come prepared: There's a .22 Beretta automatic packaged alongside the tape-recorder in my black CREEP-standard-issue briefcase.

In January 1974 Eszterhas returned to small-town America for "Claw Men from Outer Space." The article recounted the consternation in a Mississippi town when two of its citizens claimed to have been visited by aliens. The first paragraph is a lusty embrace of culture and dialect:

> You crazy, countryboy? Comin in heuh like a whinnyin nigguh glugged up on moonshine cocktails . . . jabberin this rot about what you seen down by the rivuh in the devil's own pitchblack with them bloodfat blowflies stingin at yo eyes . . . these *Whatchamacallems* you says you seen.

Eszterhas was becoming known for his ability to turn out stories quickly. He threw himself deeply into research and writing and pounded out stories, one finger at time, on an old typewriter. His speed and reliability were not small commodities at a magazine that had to drag stories out of its other star, Eszterhas's colleague and friend Thompson.

In less than two months Eszterhas was back with a major political effort: "The Prisons of War," another epic, two-part series. It tells the story of Rick Springman, a GI in Vietnam who walked away from his unit without a gun because he did not want to fight, was captured by the Viet Cong, and eventually escaped from them to return to America as a disgraced deserter and a heroic prisoner of war.

Besides its stirring subject matter, the series is notable for Eszterhas's continued experimentation with third-person point of view. After a brief introduction, each of the two articles was written primarily from the viewpoint of its characters: the members of the Springman family. The characters "speak" in the first person, but without quotations. At first the words seem to be long, direct transcriptions from interviews. But soon the skilled language and dramatic descriptions lead the reader to see that Eszterhas has abandoned journalistic convention and embraced the fictional technique of taking wholly the perspective of the characters. For example, Eszterhas presents Springman's decision not to carry a gun in Vietnam:

> I thought about my own role and about those kids getting gunned down by the Guard [at Kent State] and about the things I'd seen over there. I realized I had to stop and look at my own morality and say—Now, really, where's it at, man? And what's the best thing you can do in this situation? And I figured out what I'd do.

> I wouldn't carry a gun. I'd never carry a gun again. I would eliminate myself from the conflict.

Through the use of perspective, Eszterhas allows the reader to feel the terror and triumph of Springman, the fear and misery of his mother, the consternation and pride of his father, and the confusion of his brother.

Eszterhas was also capable of producing traditional journalistic scoops for *Rolling Stone*. He secured a long interview with kidnap victim Eugene Paul Getty, the grandson of Jean Paul Getty, then the richest person in the world. "The Getty Kidnapping," published on 9 May 1974, tells the story of the youth's terrible ordeal in which the kidnappers cut off his right ear to send to the grandfather and the boy's eventual release when a $2.9 million ransom was paid.

Eszterhas was now confirmed as one of the top talents in literary journalism. He and Geri had settled into a home just outside of San Francisco and were making plans to start a family. An August 1974 article found Eszterhas looking back from where he had come. Inspired by Alexander Solzhenitsyn's *Gulag Archipelago, 1918–1956* (1974–1978), "A Footnote to the Book of the Dead" mixes first-person autobiographical material with Eszterhas's interviews with Hungarian refugees in Cleveland.

> My childhood was filled with the victims of Soviet prisons, the haggard, hollow men who chain-smoked cigarettes with rheumatic fingers and told us haltingly of what they'd seen. Theirs were the stories I grew up with, so this summer I took *Gulag* back to as many of these timeworn men as I could find and asked them to tell me again the stories of my childhood. I want to share some of their accounts with you because in a very personal way they are a footnote to *Gulag*.

Eszterhas found inspiration in wildly different places. He followed his inner ruminations on Solzhenitsyn with one of his most acclaimed pieces, "King of the Goons: Deliver Us from Evel," an acerbic, biting profile of Evel Knievel, self-proclaimed daredevil acrobat and motorcyclist. Eszterhas portrays Knievel as a bullying fraud who beat up a press cameraman and took money in golf bets from the ailing boxer Joe Louis.

Stylistically, the article is notable for Eszterhas's use of the first person once again to confound the canons of journalism. Midway through the article, after having reported Knievel's assault on the NBC cameraman, Eszterhas brings himself into the story. He recounts a press conference attended by dozens of reporters—none of whom mention the assault. Eszterhas finally brings the conference to a halt by asking promoter Bob Arum if Knievel plans to apologize. His appearance in the story serves to make explicit the opposition between him and the traditional reporters. Better than any academic treatise on differences and distinctions, the episode dramatizes the rebellion of literary journalism against the tradition and canon of journalism.

In May 1975 Eszterhas returned to his favored turf: small-town America. In "The Nature of Chief Perkin's Fury," an account of a crazed rampage by a police chief in McCall, Idaho, Eszterhas gives full vent to his creative forces. Rather than taking on the perspective of his characters, he invents a character to carry the primary narrative: "I forget his name, but he is a man who's lived in McCall for many years."

This was to be Eszterhas's last effort at literary journalism. By the time the story was published Eszterhas was already deep in negotiations with others interested in his writing talents. A United Artists executive wanted to make a movie about the American labor movement. She had seen the Evel Knievel piece, was intrigued by the writing, and contacted Eszterhas at the San Francisco offices of *Rolling Stone* in early 1975.

He was asked first to do a novel that would be developed into a screenplay. But in the midst of his research the studio told him to work full time on a screenplay. The money was good: $30,000 for a first draft, $30,000 for a second, $28,000 when filming was under way, and 2.5 points in the film. The money came at a good time. A baby, Steven, had been born. (Another baby, Susie, was to be born in two years.) Eszterhas knew he was at a crossroads. He informed Wenner that he was going to pursue the script.

It was not an easy decision. Myriad changes in directors left Eszterhas wondering if he had made the right move. By January 1976 Eszterhas was writing the script while still unsure if the movie was going to be made. "At this point I was really getting nervous," he told *Esquire*. "I had left *Rolling Stone*. I had a lot riding on it. If it didn't work out, I knew I would have to crawl back to Jann Wenner." The movie, *F.I.S.T.* (1978), eventually was made, but not before Sylvester Stallone, who played the lead character, had edited the script and fought long distance with Eszterhas over screenwriting credits.

Though *F.I.S.T.* was not a commercial or critical success, Eszterhas had seen enough to convince him to become a full-time screenwriter. After less than three years in which he helped revolutionize journalistic writing, Eszterhas's career in literary journalism was over. As a screenwriter he produced some spectacular successes in the 1970s and 1980s. Some early efforts include the highly successful *Flashdance* (1983), with its blue-collar concern for its young dancer; *Jagged Edge* (1985), about a murderous, hugely rich publisher; *Hearts of Fire* (1986), about an aging rock star; *Big Shots* (1987), about two boys, black and white, who overcome prejudice and fear; *Betrayed* (1988),

about the rise of white supremacist groups in the heartland; *Music Box* (1989), about a woman who confronts the past of her father, a former war criminal; and *Checking Out* (1989), about a man afraid of dying. In the 1990s the scripts for the spectacularly successful sexual dramas *Basic Instinct* (1992) and *Sliver* (1993) placed Eszterhas among the Hollywood elite. Many other scripts by Eszterhas continue to be placed in production.

For most of his Hollywood career Eszterhas was able to avoid the fast-lane politics of that town. He and Geri lived and raised their two children in northern California. Eszterhas flew down to Hollywood only when needed. But success brought Eszterhas into the spotlight. First, he made Hollywood headlines following his successful but highly publicized split in 1989 from the Creative Artists Agency and its powerful head, Michael Ovitz. Then, following his successful scripts, his hardball negotiations, which resulted in his million-dollar deals, gave him increased status. His messy and public divorce provided him with even more Hollywood notoriety.

In December 1980 his short story "Dulcinea," a traditionally told tale in which two high-school friends look for love after graduation, appeared in *Rolling Stone,* but Eszterhas did not return to literary journalism. How to reconcile the millionaire screenwriter and the rebellious, experimental journalist? Rather than a radical departure from his early work, his film career drives home the point that literary journalism, for Eszterhas, was an expressive vehicle, a channel for his narrative and dramatic talents.

Like other literary journalists, Eszterhas found the structures and strictures of traditional journalism too confining for telling his stories. His attempts to create scenes, to experiment with perspective and voice, to stretch the limits of language were reactions against those restrictions. His work simply could not be confined to the conventional news story. The traditional journalistic report is derived from language determinedly dispassionate and apolitical. No doubt the language of conventional journalism has been a potent force. Its conventions and traditions provide order for reporter, editor, reader, and viewer; influence what events are reported and in what ways; and, in doing so, shape an important part of social experience. Literary journalism, though, challenged the monopoly of that language. It challenged that way of observing, portraying, and understanding the world.

Language orders experience, Eszterhas knew, and he resisted having his experience ordered in traditional ways. His work can be understood as a challenge to the benefit and possibility of objective, unbiased, apolitical reporting. Instead, he celebrated passion, commitment, and engagement. The writing of Joe Eszterhas makes the confrontation between traditional and literary journalism difficult to ignore. His precise rendering of scenes, his experimentation with point of view, and his dramatization of differences with other reporters—all these challenged conventions of journalism and showed once again the power of a story well told by its teller.

References:

Jerry Carroll, "A Night in Hollywood," *San Francisco Chronicle,* 5 June 1994, pp. 6, 21;

Maureen Dowd, "Bucks and Blondes: Joe Eszterhas Lives the Big Dream," *New York Times,* 30 May 1993, II: 9;

Jeffrey Ressner, "Gonzo Screenwriter," *Time* (31 May 1993): 64–65;

Jean Vallely, "Stallone's Latest Fight," *Esquire* (9 May 1978): 78–82;

Jann Wenner, "Introduction," in *The Best of Rolling Stone: 25 Years of Journalism on the Edge,* edited by Robert Love (Garden City, N.Y.: Doubleday, 1993), pp. xi–xiii;

Tom Wolfe and E. W. Johnson, eds., *The New Journalism* (New York: Harper & Row, 1973).

Richard Goldstein
(19 June 1944 –)

A. J. Kaul
University of Southern Mississippi

BOOKS: *One in Seven: Drugs on Campus* (New York: Walker, 1966);

The Poetry of Rock (New York: Bantam, 1969);

Goldstein's Greatest Hits: A Book Mostly about Rock 'n' Roll (Englewood Cliffs, N.J.: Prentice-Hall, 1970);

Reporting the Counterculture (Boston: Unwin Hyman, 1989).

Richard Goldstein's precocious career in literary journalism in the 1960s filled the underground niche of counterculture reportage and rock and roll criticism. His "Pop Eye" column in *The Village Voice* was credited with helping launch serious and incisive popular criticism of rock music and the counterculture of the 1960s. The "counter-reportage" he invented probed the images of what he called "pseudo events," creating "a field of his own in which to exercise his critical faculties." His controversial assessment of the Beatles' *Sergeant Pepper's Lonely Hearts Club Band* in *The New York Times* in 1967 cost him some credibility as a rock critic; nevertheless, Ellen Sander maintained in the *Saturday Review* (31 July 1971) that by the end of the 1960s Goldstein had become generally recognized "not only as the most astute rock critic of his times and one of the decade's most promising young writers but as one of the most creative, colorful, and scholarly journalists alive."

Richard Goldstein was born on 19 June 1944 in New York City, the son of Jack Goldstein, a postal worker, and Molley Maurer Goldstein. He earned a bachelor's degree from Hunter College of the City University of New York in 1965 and a master's degree from the Columbia University School of Journalism in 1966. During these years the literary journalism of Norman Mailer, Gay Talese, and Tom Wolfe had, in Goldstein's words, "rocked my assumptions about the boundary between fact and fiction," yet his abiding obsession was rock and roll. "To my mind," said Goldstein in his introduction to *Reporting the Counterculture* (1989), "'jungle music' and 'parajournalism' made a perfect fit: both were red-light districts of renegade sensibility–junk

evolving into art." Rock music harnessed to literary journalism offered new possibilities to incorporate, Goldstein believed, "the mythmaking power of fiction and the credibility of reportage," but his journalism professors were hostile to his efforts to blend the two forms. "My attempts to enrich the obit with Faulknerian melancholy did not sit well with the professors, nor did my lengthening hair, or the pieces about rock I infused with the breathless tropes of Tom Wolfe, who was then the Great Satan of journalism schools." A journalism professor wrote across one of Goldstein's assignments: "I don't know what this is–but you owe me a story."

Goldstein's first book, *One in Seven: Drugs on Campus* (1966), met the tame standards demanded by the professors of conventional "straight" journalism even though, as Goldstein writes in the introduction, the "names and identities of all students quoted in this book have been changed." Goldstein's investigations of the campus drug scene at schools in the Ivy League ("What Is a Harvard Pot Party Like?"), at schools in the Midwest ("How You Gonna Keep Them Down on the Farm After They've Tried LSD?"), the West Coast ("The Psychedelic Scene in California Explored"), and New York City's "asphalt campus" ("What Is 'Cool' on a City College Campus?") all deployed the traditional "Five 'W's" of who, what, when, where, and why. Goldstein glibly concludes in *One in Seven* that drugs on the nation's campuses represent "Alienation a' Go-Go" in the American youth culture.

Goldstein joined *The Village Voice* in 1966, telling editor Dan Wolf, "I want to be a rock 'n' roll critic." "What's that?" replied Wolf, who agreed to pay the twenty-two-year-old journalist twenty dollars an article to write about whatever he wanted. *The Village Voice,* founded in October 1955 with financial assistance from Mailer, was, in Wolf's words, "conceived as a living, breathing attempt to demolish the notion that one needs to be a professional to accomplish something in a field as purportedly technical as journalism. . . . We wanted to jam the gears of creeping automatism." In the editorial indifference of *The Village Voice* to what Wolf in his foreword to The Village Voice *Reader* (1963) called the "dull pieties of official liberalism with its dreary, if unspoken, drive to put every family in a housing development and give each child his own social worker," Goldstein discovered a congenial and chaotic milieu of what he describes as "existentialism and roses." His job, he is delighted to note, involves "no editing to speak of, no stylebook . . . no story conferences or headline meetings"—and allows him to "invent a form and a persona, and in the process, re-create myself."

The persona of Goldstein's self-created rock critic found expression in hyperbolic paeans to popular music and a daring embrace of the pedestrian that declared rock "an artform-without-portfolio." "We like our culture classy," Goldstein writes in his second book, *The Poetry of Rock* (1969), an anthology of rock lyrics to which he adds his commentary. "But it is my opinion . . . that mass culture can be as vital as high art." Popular culture, he admits, often walks "a delicate line between camp and revelation," but America, after all, is "clown guru to the world." Rock music had transformed the American landscape, insinuating itself deeply into the culture. "Rock is de rigueur," he writes. "San Francisco is a teenybopper's holy land; London, a plastic Lourdes. Even Plato's Cave has become a discotheque."

In *The Poetry of Rock* Goldstein rattles off a critical colloquy of counterculture pieties: "Slang is to rock what classical allusions are to written poetry." Chuck Berry produced "an authentic rock libretto of America in the fifties," Goldstein writes, and "Elvis Presley was the Rasputin of rock." The Beatles' "A Day in the Life" was a "poetic statement of contemporary despair" in which "deadened crowds, the clutch and kitsch of pop culture, and the vision of a non-hero overwhelmed by non-demands" are all "images [that] owe their lineage to T. S. Eliot and his peers." Goldstein asks:

> Do these images really amount to art? Does Wordsworth speak to Donovan from the great beyond? Is John Lennon's wordplay truly Joycean? Is Bob Dylan the Walt Whitman of the jukebox? In a sense, assertions like these are the worst enemy of liberated rock. They enslave it with an artificial heritage. . . . Rock is, and always has been, the sacred squeal of now.

Thirty-seven critical essays written between 1966 and 1968 were collected in Goldstein's third book, *Goldstein's Greatest Hits: A Book Mostly about Rock 'n' Roll* (1970). The anthology traces his viewpoint and tone from, as Goldstein writes in the introduction, "wonder in my early columns to the re-

serve which came later, when being a 'critic' had already become a profession and a task." The essays reflect his virginal innocence and his captivation with popular culture. "I don't think I'll ever feel blasé about the polar-bear genius who destroyed his music because he thought it might start fires," Goldstein comments in one essay, to which he adds:

> Or the spade goddess who farted in the middle of an interview. Or the record company executive who offered hashish from a bronze butterfly. I've seen a lot of people with their heads gloriously shattered. I learned to take notes while stoned. I learned to read press releases without opening the envelopes. I learned to put myself in corners and fade into the entourage. Most important, I learned that I could never function as a superstar-by-proxy.

Goldstein's Greatest Hits opens with "Gear," a poignant vignette describing the plight of being a self-conscious, fourteen-year-old, middle-class male adolescent "with braces and bony fingers and a bump the size of a goddam coconut on your head." "Gear" evokes the juvenile posturing of a prototypical American teenager awkwardly coming to terms with his sexual identity. Goldstein relives a moment in which his younger self stands before a mirror in his bedroom:

> He checks hair, nose, braces, nails and pants. He likes the pants. They make him look hung. He reaches into his top drawer and pulls out a white handkerchief. He opens his fly and inserts the rolled cloth, patting it in place, and closing the zipper over it. He looks boss. Unfuckinbelievable.

Fashionable clothes offer a stylish antidote to the insecurities of adolescent identity. Goldstein's tour de force explains the phenomenon via internal monologue from the youth's own perspective: "Because clothing IS important. . . . And especially if you're fourteen. Because . . . ask anyone. Fourteen is shit." Tom Wolfe singled out "Gear" for inclusion in *The New Journalism* (1973) to represent the journalistic sketch, a form traceable to such nineteenth-century masters as Charles Dickens, William Makepeace Thackeray, and Stephen Crane and attractive to many journalists in the 1960s. The sketch's light presentation of "a realistic picture of a current character-type" offers "a single, central insight into the type," Wolfe observes, and qualifies as journalism "only because it aspires to nothing more than to give an accurate picture of a type of person rather than a specific individual."

With compression, insight, and style Goldstein's essays in *Goldstein's Greatest Hits* interpretively focus on many of rock music's icons: Janis

DRUGS *ARE* ON CAMPUS

- **THE USER:**
  your child or theirs? your friend or you?

- **THE STUDENT POT PARTY:**
  what it's really like.

- **THE SCHOOL:**
  big or small, East or West—which ones?

- **COLLEGE ADMINISTRATORS:**
  what they don't know and won't know.

- **THE PROBLEM:** a nationwide tragedy or bungling myopic law-making? Today thousands of students get away with it but there are some unlucky ones who will spend a few semesters in jail. Your roommate, perhaps, or, if you are a parent, your child. Everyone is a victim, the haunted student, the fearful parent, the perplexed administrator, the overworked police — victims of an unwillingness to face facts. This book sets out these facts with daring frankness.

"In the heart of every parent lies the hidden fear that this terrible tragedy could come to one of his own children—as indeed it could."
Governor Nelson A. Rockefeller

"Dean David B. Truman (of Columbia) said . . . that he 'would not be totally astonished' if the number of students who had experimented with some drug or another was as high as one third of the school."
The New York Journal-American

"The chief psychiatrist at the Berkeley campus of the University of California says that up to 20 percent of the students there may be smoking marijuana."
The New York Times

"A lot of us have been sweeping the problem under the rug, and the rug is getting pretty lumpy."
A university President quoted in The New York Times

WALKER AND COMPANY / 720 Fifth Avenue / New York, N.Y. 10019

1 in 7
drugs
on campus

goldstein

WALKER

1 in 7
drugs
on campus
by richard goldstein

Dust jacket for Goldstein's first book, a series of investigations of drug use in American colleges

Joplin, Mick Jagger, Jim Morrison, and Bob Dylan, among others. Blues-cum-rock singer Janis Joplin and her San Francisco–based band, Big Brother and the Holding Company, were, according to Goldstein, "nurtured in the roots of the Hip renaissance" and were also a "glorious throwback to a time when the primary aim in rock was 'to get people moving.'" Joplin's guttural howling is "no Patti Page regatta, no Connie Francis sob-along, but mangy backwoods blues, heavy with devotion to Bessie Smith. She still smears Bessie Smith across everything she sings, making it possible for a whole generation of us to hear beyond the scratches in those old records." The Rolling Stones' lead singer Jagger arrives in New York City as "Shango Mick," the African god of thunder, in a Goldstein column based on a press reception aboard a yacht circling Manhattan island. Later, two hundred young women pursue the band members when they make their way from the yacht to an underground garage that explodes, Goldstein writes, in "shrieks of brakes and ecstasy." "Real tears are shed," he notes. "Hands are quivering. . . . Outside, an African sun shines over the Sea Panther. Muffled sound of drumbeats

from the river. Burst of thunder from the motors. And a girl with merging freckles asks: 'Dijuh touch him? Dijuh touch Mick Jagger?' Morrison and the Doors offer "an inner theatre of cruelty" whose "musical dramas have made fear and loathing part of the rock lexicon," Goldstein observes in "The Shaman as Superstar," adding about Morrison that:

> Violence is his major motif. . . . His central symbol, the Great Snake . . . is a phallic liberator, extolling an act of creative desecration. . . . Most Doors songs plead with us to reject all repressive authority and embrace the Great Snake, with its slippery equation of freedom and violence. It is an equation we are eager to make, rendering holy what is simply unrestrained.

Dylan "writes shields around himself," Goldstein says in a review of the *John Wesley Harding* album. Goldstein then urges his reader:

> Stop to think about his songs and they grab you by the neck—strangling, slashing, putting you on. The put-on has become such a virile form of self-defense that we prefer it to pursuing meaning. We love to watch a great

poser like Dylan making magic charades. It's so easy to experience a joke when the victim is a square Other.

The hip intellectualism of the celebrity gurus of the 1960s fascinated Goldstein, providing his *Goldstein's Greatest Hits* with material that went beyond rock iconography. When Marshall McLuhan was hyping *The Medium Is the Massage* (1967), a "teleological coloring book" then topping the bestseller lists, Goldstein called the Canadian literary scholar "the James Joyce of Madison Avenue." McLuhan is, says Goldstein, "the Wizard of Oz, and we are all Dorothys from flat, clean Kansas, uprooted by the electric cyclone and thrust into emerald cities with button-down priests, instant ritual, and napalm liturgy. . . . His theories spread in whirlpools. There is no logical progression, no Hegelian synthesis, but an instant, almost pentecostal revelation." When psychedelic drug guru Timothy Leary's quixotic mantra ("turn on, tune in, drop out") was chanted during weekly "psychedelic celebrations," commercialized pseudoreligious rituals staged amid swirling light shows in New York's second-largest theater, Goldstein warned of "The Psychedelic Psell." The commercialization and merchandising of acid culture and the psychedelic gospel of "Psychedelic shoes. Acid TV commercials. LSD greeting cards. Marijuana brownies. Mandala shopping bags" prompted Goldstein to wonder about the prophet's profits. The "blood and body are being drained from Timothy Leary's eucharist and—in mercantile transubstantiation—are being mass-produced as love beads," writes Goldstein, who adds: "There is no Judas in Leary's garden of Gethsemane; treason is within the prophet himself. . . . The time has come for the guru to draw a line between revelation and merchandising. . . . Timothy Leary has until the first psychedelic Ban Roll-On commercial to do something about all this."

Finally, Goldstein challenges "the Dale Carnegie approach" to "the politics of salvation" that the Maharishi Mahesh Yogi offers as the way to world peace through transcendental meditation. "Are we to teach the National Guard bliss consciousness so they can perform their duties with inner peace," he asks. "Are we to meditate between strafings? Can we ever transcend America?. . . Can an honest man still be a fraud? If he allows himself a fraudulent role—yes."

The commercialization of rock music and underground culture set the critical tone for Goldstein's disenchantment with the loss of vitality in popular culture. In a piece titled "Giraffe Hunters" Goldstein describes a film he had seen in college in which African tribal hunters tracked down and killed a giraffe, ate the testicles for power, drank its blood, and put the head on the chief's hut as a trophy. "Rock 'n' roll is the giraffe," he writes. "Public relations men, disc jockeys, emcees, executives, socko-boffo copy boys, fabulous blondes, prophets, frauds, fakes, takes, connect-the-dot copies, and under-assistant West Coast promo men hunt with their snares and bolos, cut, castrate, slice up the meat, and hang shaggy heads in trophy." In Goldstein's judgment, the Beatles' elaborately produced special-effects studio album, *Sergeant Pepper's Lonely Hearts Club Band,* considered by many rock aficionados to be the group's great achievement, fell into the giraffe's trap. "When the slicks and tricks of production on this new album no longer seem unusual, and the compositions are stripped to their musical and lyrical essentials, *Sergeant Pepper* will be Beatles baroque—an elaboration without improvement," he writes. Again: "For the first time, the Beatles have given us a package of special effects, dazzling but ultimately fraudulent. . . . I sense an obsession with the surrogate magic of production, and a new sarcasm masquerading as cool."

By the end of the Summer of Love in 1967, subterranean hippie culture had disintegrated into violence, death, and media hype. In the murders of two flower children in the East Village, Goldstein saw the apotheosis of the Age of Aquarius. "We are all victims of symbols," he writes in "Love: A Groovy Idea While He Lasted." "Events breed their own ritual. Maybe that is why the murders of James Leroy Hutchinson and Linda Fitzpatrick read like Act Three of an off-off-Broadway play. The truest theatre of the '60's lies spiked across the city desk, slugged 'slay.'" The New York press eulogized Hutchinson, nicknamed "Groovy," and his woman, turning their tragic tale into an allegory of estranged flower power, but Goldstein maintains that:

> Flower power began and ended as a cruel joke. The last laugh belongs to the media men who chose to report a charade as a movement. In doing so, they created one.

> By the thousands the real victims of flower power poured into slums on both coasts. *Life-Look* filled its pages with technicolor testimonials to the young dropouts living the love ethic their leaders were wary of. There was a bizarre camaraderie between the fourth estate and the fifth dimension.

The media hype showered on middle-class hippies brought vicious reprisals from those trapped in the urban slums. Goldstein drives home this point, quoting from remarks made to *The New York Times* by a young black East Sider: "The hippies really bug us . . . because we know they can come down here

Dust jacket for a collection of Goldstein's essays on rock music

and play their games for awhile and then escape. And we can't, man." With the spectacle of violence in the underground culture came fear and the prospect of leaving. "And only as the Summer of Love chills into a violent harvest," Goldstein writes, "is there talk of getting out." Hippies began heading for the country—and the suburbs. Left behind in the urban ghettos is Groovy's legacy, a "new slum hippie" toughened by violence and toting guns. "Love: A Groovy Idea While He Lasted" is a compact mirror image of Joan Didion's tour de camp of San Francisco's hippie haven in "Slouching Toward Bethlehem." Didion had found in the Haight-Ashbury district anomie and atomization that resulted from the "the desperate attempt of a handful of pathetically unequipped children to create a community in a so-

cial vacuum." Like Didion's West Coast counter-culture that had eluded the media, Goldstein's East Village hippie murders represent victims of those distorted media symbols.

In his piece titled "Why the Blues?" Goldstein calls the blues revival in popular music "the first cultural appointment of the Nixon administration" and argues that the revival signals the loss of rock music's creative energy and vitality. "Singing the praises of pop seems to resemble a kind of futile nationalism to me now," he laments. "All my bags are packed, and I'm casing out frontiers, trying to choose the best point to make a border crossing." At the age of twenty-eight Goldstein no longer experienced the magic of popular culture that had enchanted him; he decided to leave writing about rock and the counterculture to others and to fade from the scene. "The blues revival we are witnessing now is a requiem for rock," he declares. "The simple fact is that the entire pop renaissance of the mid-'60s has failed to sustain itself beyond that first, shattering tonal wave."

Reporting the Counterculture (1989), Goldstein's fourth book, reprints many of the essays collected two decades earlier in *Goldstein's Greatest Hits*. The book begins with an insightful retrospective introduction, "First Person, Past Tense," that deftly situates Goldstein's writing in historical and literary perspective. A generation after writing those dispatches from the counterculture, Goldstein recognizes their underlying theme: "the struggle for subjectivity." "Subjectivity meant imposing a narrator on the news," he writes, "a voice that could openly address the meaning of events." According to Goldstein, New Journalism's "central premise," which he defines as "the individual is the true register of events," was a premise by which writers consciously sought to subvert conventional journalism's bland standardization of experience. "It's embrace of subjectivity was an attempt to resist . . . processed consensus," he writes.

From Goldstein's vantage point the 1960s counterculture spawned a hybrid form of journalism, a "counter-reportage" infused with hip jargon and hyperbole, a mix of essay, narrative, criticism, and memoir that became "the voice of mobility on the margins." His own writing about the counterculture evolved into an extended case study of hip culture's commercial co-optation in an expansionist economy. "The pseudo event became my beat," he writes, "but the closer one got to the hot center, the more this revolution resembled spectacle for the sake of Publicity. . . . Time and time again, I watched the struggle to assert community collapse in the face of fortunes to be made." Goldstein's counter-reportage was, like his brief career in literary journalism, a magic moment in the experimental journalistic style of the 1960s. "When the moment passed," he observes, "so did the style."

References:

Kevin Michael McAuliffe, *The Great American Newspaper: The Rise and Fall of the Village Voice* (New York: Scribners, 1978);

Daniel Wolf and Edwin Fancher, eds., *The Village Voice Reader* (New York: Grove, 1963).

Robert Bernard (Bob) Greene Jr.

(10 March 1947 –)

Ginger Rudeseal Carter
Georgia College & State University

BOOKS: *We Didn't Have None of Them Fat Funky Angels on the Wall of Heartbreak Hotel, and Other Reports from America* (Chicago: Regnery, 1971);

Running: A Nixon-McGovern Campaign Journal (Chicago: Regnery, 1973);

Billion Dollar Baby (New York: Atheneum, 1974);

Johnny Deadline, Reporter: The Best of Bob Greene (Chicago: Nelson-Hall, 1976);

Bagtime, by Greene and Paul Galloway (New York: Popular Library, 1977);

American Beat (New York: Atheneum, 1983);

Good Morning, Merry Sunshine: A Father's Journal of His Child's First Year (New York: Atheneum, 1984);

Cheeseburgers: The Best of Bob Greene (New York: Atheneum, 1985);

Be True to Your School: A Diary of 1964 (New York: Atheneum, 1987);

Homecoming: When the Soldiers Returned from Vietnam (New York: Putnam, 1989);

Hang Time: Days and Dreams with Michael Jordan (New York: Doubleday, 1992);

He Was a Midwestern Boy on His Own (New York: Atheneum, 1992);

To Our Children's Children: Preserving Family Histories for Generations to Come, by Greene and D. G. Fulford (New York: Doubleday, 1993);

All Summer Long (New York: Doubleday, 1993);

Rebound: The Odyssey of Michael Jordan (New York: Viking, 1996);

Chevrolet Summers: Dairy Queen Nights (New York: Viking, 1997);

The 50-Year Dash (New York: Doubleday, 1997).

SELECTED PERIODICAL PUBLICATIONS–
UNCOLLECTED: "A Streetwalker at 13: Fear Was Her Escort," *Chicago Tribune* (12 April 1978), "Tempo" section, p. 1;

"Bob Greene Tells How He Fell for Hoax," *Chicago Tribune* (14 April 1978), p. A2;

"The High Price of Being Michael," *Newsweek,* 122 (18 October 1993): 71;

Bob Greene (photograph by Karen P. Pulfer)

"The Question That Will Some Day Come," *Chicago Tribune* on America Online (25 June 1995).

Bob Greene is a columnist for the *Chicago Tribune* who has been offering his quick observations and pithy descriptions of the world since he wrote his first column in high school in 1964. Currently syndicated in more than two hundred newspapers in the United States, Greene regularly produces work that reflects the thoughts and emotions of everyday Americans. Since he became a columnist—first for the *Chicago Sun-Times* in 1971, then for the *Chicago Tribune* in 1978—he estimates that he has written between four thousand and five thousand columns about the famous and the infamous, beginnings and endings, birth and death, and happiness and sadness.

Robert Bernard Greene Jr. was born on 10 March 1947 in Columbus, Ohio, the eldest son of Robert Bernard and Phyllis Ann Harmon Greene.

His father was a business executive with the Bron-Shoe Company; his mother was a homemaker for a family that included Greene's sister, Debby, and a brother, Timmy. The family lived in Bexley, a Columbus suburb that Greene describes in *Be True to Your School: A Diary of 1964* (1987) as a "town of approximately fifteen thousand people, virtually all of them white." It was, he notes, "the kind of suburb where teen-agers generally didn't have to worry about where their allowance money was coming from. By and large, Bexley, like so many of the suburbs of the Sixties, was composed of stable families where the fathers brought home 'comfortable' paychecks every week."

Greene said in an interview in *Contemporary Authors* (1988) that he knew he wanted to be a journalist when he was twelve years old. "In seventh grade, we had this little punch-out test, the Kuder Performance Test, that tells you what career you're supposed to go into. Mine said I was supposed to be either a forest ranger or journalist," he recalled. Greene worked on both his junior- and senior-high school papers, and when he was a rising senior at Bexley High School he was offered his first paid newspaper position as a $65-a-week, noon-to-nine, summer copy clerk at the Columbus *Citizen-Journal*. According to Greene, there was no particular person who influenced his career at this period—he was just curious from the start. "Where I grew up, there were no really big famous writers working in the area," he said. "You could read the local bylines in the local newspapers. I guess I was a kid who would hang around and see stuff and wish I had a way to tell a lot of people about it. Sometimes you see a small moment and you want the world to know about it."

One of these small moments occurred while Greene was doing a weekend "fire run" for the paper: a man had been rushed to the hospital after sawing open a liquid nitrogen golf ball to see how it worked, and the liquid hit the man in the eye. The headline for Greene's piece was "Golf Ball Strikes Back," and in *Be True To Your School: A Diary of 1964* Greene writes that the piece ran on the bottom of the obituary page. "I felt so proud," he remembers. "I even showed it to Mom and Dad when they woke up."

On Saturday, 21 November 1964, a year after the assassination of President John F. Kennedy, a column that Greene wrote for a Columbus teen magazine was reprinted in the *Citizen-Journal* under the headline "A Teen Remembers JFK." In *Be True To Your School* Greene writes about the reaction to his column that Saturday morning:

I kept thinking as the phone continued to ring. . . : Isn't this something? A couple of weeks ago an idea popped into my head about President Kennedy. If I would have just kept it in my head, no one would have known that I was thinking about it. But because I wrote it down, everyone's going crazy. It's like the things I think about don't matter until I write them down.

Greene was coeditor of his high-school newspaper his senior year and a contributing writer to *Junior Prom*, a teen magazine. In the fall of 1965 he entered the journalism program at Northwestern University. The summers between his sophomore and junior years in college brought Greene back to the *Citizen-Journal*, first as a sports department intern, then as a city-side reporter. Ironically, as he said in an unpublished interview in July 1996, he did not work for the college paper, *The Daily Northwestern*, until his senior year. "I applied my senior year without ever having been on the staff, and I was named associate editor and columnist there. But I didn't work there before then. I felt there was this group who just worked there and didn't live. I could see more living than I could when I was just reporting it." Still, Greene said, he did not regret his decision.

In the summer of 1969, having recently graduated from Northwestern with a bachelor of science degree in journalism, Greene took a job as a reporter with the *Chicago Sun-Times*. "I had an offer from the *Tribune* for a full-time job that paid more money, but the *Sun-Times* seemed to be doing better," he recalled in an interview in 1995. Greene had already enrolled in the master's program at Northwestern, but after a summer with the *Chicago Sun-Times*, he said, "I stayed on. The Chicago 7 conspiracy trial was going on. Why go back to college when you can cover a story like that?" He immediately began to make an impact as a general assignment reporter. Only twenty-two, Greene brought fresh insight to the stories he wrote. "It was unusual," he said. "People would react to my ideas, react to my by-line. They had people asking about this 22-year-old kid." In 1971 Greene began a column at the *Chicago Sun-Times*, first twice a week, then four days a week. While there he produced four books. The first, *We Didn't Have None of Them Fat Funky Angels on the Wall of Heartbreak Hotel and Other Reports from America* (1971), a collection of magazine-length articles, was described as "an unusually perceptive look at cafe society and its discontents." His second book, *Running: A Nixon-McGovern Campaign Journal* (1973), viewed the political "road-show" of the 1972 campaign. Reviewers found Greene's writing filled with the wonderment of the political campaign and

Dust jacket for the 1983 collection of essays that includes Greene's interviews with Richard Nixon and Richard Speck

rich with sharp observation but offering only casual political insight.

In 1973 Greene joined Alice Cooper's band for its Holiday Tour, thereby combining two of his great interests—rock and roll and writing. *Billion Dollar Baby* (1974), his third book, showed facets of the flamboyant Cooper's tour. Greene joined the show, playing a Santa Claus who was beaten and stomped by the band at the end of the show each night, and reported the different sides of Cooper and his band. In one excerpt Greene describes Cooper's purchase of new clothes while in Montreal: "He came down the stairs wearing his purchase of the day. It was a gray flannel suit, cut very conservatively and severely. 'It was the only thing I could stand,' he said."

After five years as a columnist Greene published his first collection of columns, *Johnny Deadline, Reporter: The Best of Bob Greene* (1976). Critics said Greene had a knack for making the people and the issues of the city come alive. His formula for the column—then and now—remains the same: bring out the people who will not make page one. "So many columns in this country really exist for the person who wrote them," Greene said in 1995, adding:

Politics revolves around reading the bylines of The New York Times or Washington Post. Most columnists in this country write about the same things every day. And it all comes off the front page of a couple of major newspapers and they comment on it. That's probably when I won't write about them.

Instead, Greene said he looks for the personal angle: "It really has to interest me as a person more so than a journalist," he says, adding:

It's the kind of thing that I would come home at the end of the day and pick up the phone and call my best friend and say, 'You won't believe what I saw today,' or 'You won't believe what I heard today.' To me, the columns come from genuine curiosity. If there is something I think I'm interested in as a person, I will try to put it in the newspaper column.

On 9 April 1978 the *Chicago Tribune* ran a one-paragraph teaser: "He's the author of five books, the winner of the 1977 National Headliner Award as the best columnist in the United States, and the subject of a pop song. He's Bob Greene, and beginning Monday his new home is in Tempo." Greene said the switch came then because "it seemed like a good time to switch." The *Chicago Tribune,* he added, had always been the dominant paper in Chicago. His first column was about Larry Flynt, publisher of

Hustler magazine. Later that week he interviewed Ringo Starr about the Beatles.

That same week Greene had something happen to him that had never happened in his career: he became the victim of an elaborate hoax. "Professionally, it was one of the worst things that ever happened to me," he notes. While he was still at the *Chicago Sun-Times,* a thirteen-year-old girl Greene gave the pseudonym "Lindy" phoned and said she was a prostitute, trapped in a harsh life by a brutal pimp. Greene invited the girl to come to the newspaper office and he would help her. She refused but said she would be in touch. A few weeks later, after he had joined the *Chicago Tribune* staff, Greene received another call, this time from someone who identified herself as "Lindy's" mother and told Greene the girl had been killed in California. The caller then read a letter filled with gut-wrenching detail of the young prostitute's life. In the letter, which Greene excerpted in the column, "Lindy" told her mom to call Greene and thank him for his help. She ended the letter begging to come home. "Lindy's body now lies beneath a gravestone bearing a false name. She was 13 years old and she wanted to come home. She got her wish," Greene wrote on 12 April 1978 in his piece, "A Streetwalker at 13: Fear Was Her Escort."

While gathering information for a follow-up column, Greene discovered that a troubled thirteen-year-old girl had made up both characters and had portrayed both "Lindy" and her mother in separate phone calls. The next day Greene wrote a news story explaining how he fell for the hoax. "I felt horrible!" he writes in "Bob Greene Tells How He Fell for Hoax" (14 April 1978). "What a mistake! But one of the guys in the city room said, 'you know, this could happen to us every time we pick up the phone and take an obit.' It never occurred to me it wasn't real." The article explained the hoax, and Greene ended simply, "I am sorry."

The 1980s marked the release of five more books for Greene plus the beginning of a monthly column for *Esquire* magazine and regular appearances on ABC television's *Nightline.* In 1983 he released *American Beat,* another compilation of his best columns. The book drew its name from the column he had written for *Esquire* since 1981 and contained columns written at the *Chicago Sun-Times,* the *Chicago Tribune,* and *Esquire.* Greene writes in his introduction that the name *American Beat* "was no coincidence," explaining that he writes about the whole country.

Some of Greene's most renowned columns are reprinted in *American Beat.* These include "Speck," his interview with convicted killer Richard Speck; "Fifteen," the story about two teenage boys roaming the mall in Schaumburg, Illinois; "Michael Testifies," about the sixteen-year-old boy who was shot while going for ice cream and who testifies against the two teenage gunmen; "Reflections in a Wary Eye," Greene's interview with former president Richard Nixon; and "Kathy's Abortion," which details a trip inside an abortion clinic. Of his columns Greene writes in *American Beat,* "I am neither a pundit nor a political philosopher. I try to be a storyteller; I try to go out and explore something that interests me, and then—after hanging around and watching and listening and asking questions—I try to give the reader some sense of what it was like to have been there." Years later, Greene said, people were still trying to figure out "Kathy's Abortion," the column in which he describes holding the hand of a young woman undergoing an abortion. "Kathy lay on the operating table," Greene writes in the column:

> There were three other people in the room: the doctor, the nurse, and the newspaperman. All three were dressed in surgical scrub suits and masks. Kathy was on her back; surprisingly, the radio was playing, even in the operating room. As she waited for the operation to begin, the Bee Gees sang "Stayin' Alive" from the movie *Saturday Night Fever.*

"It was neither pro nor con," Greene said later of the abortion stance of the column. "But readers were up in arms about it, since it was controversial. But they read into it. But the facts were just there." Of the interviews with Nixon and Speck, Greene said that time had not dimmed the appeal of the stories. At the time each interview was a journalistic coup. "Those were people I wanted to talk to. I was pleased with the way the stories came out, but mostly those were people at the time who were supposed to be impossible to get to," he noted.

Good Morning, Merry Sunshine: A Father's Journal of His Child's First Year (1984) marked a departure from Greene's usual work. Published after the birth of his daughter, Amanda Sue, the book became a best-seller and was excerpted in magazines such as *Redbook, Reader's Digest,* and *Esquire.* It was hailed by critics, but some noted that it was somewhat ironic that Greene should write such a book since, as one writer observed in *Contemporary Authors,* "Greene has never revealed much about his family or private life in his columns." Eleven years after its publication Greene refused to talk about the book or his family, adding, "I prefer to keep my personal life to myself. I just decided a long time ago that you have to draw a line somewhere. I just decided a while back that there should be some place where you put your personal life in one place and public life in another."

Cheeseburgers: The Best of Bob Greene (1985), another compilation of columns, followed *Merry Sunshine*. Like the other compilations, material for *Cheeseburgers* was drawn from the *Chicago Tribune* and *Esquire* columns.

By 1987 Greene had taken the cryptic scrawling in his 1964 diary and produced the best-selling *Be True to Your School: A Diary of 1964.* Of all his work so far, Greene is exceptionally proud of *Be True to Your School.* In the introduction he writes:

> Working on this book has been as much fun as any writing project with which I have ever been involved. No matter what problems were going on in my 1980s daily life as I wrote the book, there was a time each day when I would pull the original diary out, go over the events of 1964, and then try to get them down on paper. It has been like stepping into a daily time machine; I have been able to walk sway from the world I live in now, and walk into 1964.

For the reader the book offers a trip down memory lane, and, no matter when that seventeenth year occurred, one is easily transported back to that earlier, carefree era. As Greene told *Contemporary Authors,* "Everyone was 17 once, and the emotions you feel at that age are universal."

Greene's writing in *Be True to Your School* is crisp and fresh. In "1964," a column in *American Beat,* Greene recalls his failing status on the tennis team, recording his original diary entry: "Coach Weis said that I'm down to fifth doubles—I pray so much that I can go back to my old position—I need that letter—without it I'm just nothing again." In *Be True to Your School,* he merely fleshes out the ideas from his diary, keeping the key words.

Homecoming: When the Soldiers Returned from Vietnam (1989), Greene's eleventh book, was critically acclaimed. For this book he asked veterans a series of questions such as, "Were you spat upon when you returned from Vietnam?" The book includes the responses received. "Vietnam veterans as represented in this excellent selection of letters are a national resource," *The New York Times Book Review* critic and Vietnam veteran Doug Anderson wrote of Greene's book (22 January 1989). "Our country's loss of innocence was experienced most acutely by them."

If the 1980s was the decade for Greene's diaries, the 1990s became his decade for different subjects and emotions. Greene's fourth compilation of columns, *He Was a Midwestern Boy on His Own* (1991), was published to mixed reviews. The title deeply reflected his life. "That really describes me now," he said of the Bob Seger verse. (He interviewed Seger in the 1980s, and the column appears in *American Beat.*) Greene talks freely about his allegiance to Ohio and the Midwest, saying, according to *Contemporary Authors* in 1988, "Chicago's fine, but I consider myself much more midwestern than from Chicago. After all these years of having my home in Chicago, when people say 'where are you from,' I say, 'Columbus' or 'Ohio.'"

Hang Time: Days and Dreams with Michael Jordan (1992) marked the beginning of a departure from Greene's book formula. For this work he went on the road with basketball star Michael Jordan for two championship seasons. Although the book has biographical moments, it is not an authorized biography of the famed Chicago Bulls guard. Of this book Greene said in 1995:

> People misunderstand *Hang Time.* Michael had no editorial say in that book and no financial gain. It was really the best of both worlds. It was all the freedom and independence you would have with an unauthorized biography, and all the access you would have with something authorized. It was sort of unbelievable. Jordan put me in his life with total access, but the book is mine. He didn't read it before it came out, and he had no financial part in it.

The book received mixed reviews but sold well. Greene said he heard Jordan liked it, but he also said he himself would never ask. *Hang Time* made Greene an unofficial spokesman for Jordan, and Greene observes that, "every time there's big news in his life, they sort of turn to me."

The paperback version of *Hang Time* appeared on the stands in November of 1993, only a month after Jordan announced his retirement from basketball and three months after his father, James, was murdered in North Carolina. In "The High Price of Being Michael," in *Newsweek* (18 October 1993), Greene writes about the fact that Jordan was trying to reclaim his life and observes that "For so long he has made millions of other people happy; now it is time for him to try to find some of it himself." In August 1995 Greene, on vacation from the *Chicago Tribune,* was completing *The Rebound: The Odyssey of Michael Jordan* (1995). According to Greene, the book is about what has since happened to Jordan, starting with the day of his father's murder. Greene added, "I didn't think I would be doing another book, but this thing has gotten pretty interesting."

Greene published two hardback books in 1993 that were as polar opposite as two books could be. The first, *To Our Children's Children: Preserving Family Histories for Generations to Come,* was a collaboration with his sister, D. G. Fulford, a columnist for the *Los Angeles Times.* Early reviews failed to note the family connection. In fact, Greene said most do not know

Dust jacket for Greene's book about Vietnam veterans' experiences upon their return to the United States

his sister is also a journalist. "She came to it very late," he said. "But she's very good at it." *To Our Children's Children* was "unlike any book I have written before," Greene said, adding, "I think that book will be around forever." The 192-page book contains lists of questions to use when conducting a family history. Greene and his sister got the idea for the book from their parents. According to Greene, "Our mother had written her family history for us, and our father didn't like to write, so he talked into a tape recorder. And it was such a precious gift," he said. "I talked to my sister about it and thought most families would do this if they had the opportunity." Questions in the book include holiday rituals, sibling and family memories, and even hygiene notations like "What kind of toothpaste do you use?"

The second book in 1993 (published in paperback in 1995) was *All Summer Long,* Greene's first work of fiction. Those who read *All Summer Long* and *Be True to Your School* will find certain similarities between the novel and the events in Greene's own life. The plot of *All Summer Long* takes three best friends from high school on a summer-long trip across the country. The three live markedly different lives— Ben Kroeger is a journalist; Michael Wolff is a high-school English teacher; and Ronnie Hepps is a corporate CEO—but they have remained friends for more than twenty-five years. Each drops his summer plans, and the story begins.

One feature in this work of fiction is Greene's journalistic attention to the details of locations. Greene was uncomfortable putting his characters in places he was unfamiliar with, so he researched each stop on the vacation. According to Greene:

> I realized that since I had never written fiction, I wasn't comfortable making the settings up. So I went to Wrigley Field and, for the first time, I went into the clubhouse with the ball players but didn't write a story about it. Then when I sent the three fictional guys in *All Summer Long* into Wrigley Field I actually had them in the clubhouse with the major leaguers. I had been there so I had the details right.

He said he also stayed in the Elvis Suite at the Las Vegas Hilton: "So when these three guys went to Las Vegas and I put them in Elvis' suite, I had the freedom to make the fictional guys do whatever fictional things they were going to do, but it had that solid base. I knew this was what Elvis' suite felt like 'cause I slept there for a while." Greene is as proud of *All Summer Long* as he is of any of his nonfiction works. "I loved writing that book," he said. "It was about as much fun as I'll have with a writing project."

Throughout the publication of his books, however, the four-times-a-week columns for the *Chicago Tribune* have continued. Since 1993 Greene has taken a special interest in the Illinois case of "the child known as Richard," a story that received national media attention at its culmination in the spring of 1995. In more than one media account Greene appeared as an expert on the story. The case of Richard revolved around the child's being put up for adoption under false pretenses by his birth mother. When the birth father, Otakar Kirchner, found out the child was alive, he sued for custody. Kirchner was reunited with the woman, whom he later married. The couple then sued for the return of their son. The child involved, who came to be known as Richard in the court case, was returned to the Kirchners by the Illinois Supreme Court after the United States Supreme Court refused to hear the case.

Greene said he saw the columns on Richard as being similar to others he has written in that the subject was not, in the beginning, front-page news. He learned of the story in 1993 from a judge and wrote his first columns on it at that time. By the end in 1995 Greene was center stage in the battle, fighting on behalf of the adoptive parents, and his columns had a strong impact on the Chicago community as well as the case itself. One judge accused him of "journalistic terrorism." Above all, it seemed to many readers that these columns were the work of a different Bob Greene—the columnist had, in effect, stepped out from the shadows to take an active part in the story. "Every person who has the chance to help this child and be merciful to him and did not, must live with the knowledge for the rest of their days," he wrote in his column on 25 June 1995, eight weeks after Richard was returned to the Kirchners and after thirty-one consecutive columns on the subject. "Thank you for your encouragement, support and extraordinarily kind words during all of this, but in some cases trying hard is not enough, and I live with the full knowledge that in the end I have failed him, too."

In 1995 Greene observed, "It is gratifying that people feel that I put myself into them. I certainly feel very strongly about the horror of what has been done to [the child.] But if you look at [the columns,] the strength of the columns is not that I put myself into them, it's the strength of the reporting. That is what is paradox about them." Greene reflects that:

> What I am the proudest of about this particular story is that I have been writing about it for two years, and every day it is moving forward. But you can't do that by telling people how emotional you are, you have to do it the other way: you have to lay out the stack, day by day, build it day by day. Tell them what you have found out, what you have seen, what you have reported.

Greene said he was pleased by the judge's angry reaction to his columns "because that judge did this reprehensible thing to a child." He added, "All the judge cares about is what is said about him. All he could do was quote what was said about him. The outrage is missing. Where is his outrage for the child?"

In the body of Greene's work several common themes emerge. First, Greene is a traditionalist. Throughout his works he is the champion of the "little guy." From "the child known as Richard" to the woman who was fired from John Deere for photocopying her buttocks on the new copy machine ("Backing into the Unemployment Roles"), he zeros in on the little things, which to him are the things that matter. He has a strong sense of justice, fueled above all by his self-confessed midwesternness. "I'm a traditionalist at heart," he has said. "No way around that."

This traditionalism is fueled by Greene's remarkable memory. A column in *American Beat* about two couples who met at the White House Restaurant in Valparaiso, Indiana, resurfaced in 1995 when the restaurant went out of business. The column, originally written in 1976, was not a story that made big news, but Greene remembered it. On another occasion the death of tennis great Pancho Gonzales triggered Greene's memory of having served as Gonzales's ball boy during a tennis match in Columbus, when Greene was a teenager. His memory also helped him to create an accurate reconstruction of the year 1964 in *Be True to Your School.*

Second, Greene is generally reticent, throughout his work, about private matters. In *All Summer Long,* for instance, when he refers to sexual activity between the men and women in the book, he foregoes details. Since the publication of *Good Morning, Merry Sunshine,* he has also worked hard to keep his own private life private. This privacy keeps the eyes of the reader focused on what really matters—the column. Greene's work is not overshadowed by a flashy lifestyle—few really know anything about his lifestyle, and he prefers it that way.

Greene is preeminently a journalist with an eye and ear for a good story who transforms the seemingly ordinary into the extraordinary. Although he has written thousands of pieces in his first twenty-five years as a columnist, he is always looking toward the next one. He still wants to write columns more than anything else, preferring the format to any other. Nevertheless, Greene says:

> About once a year, I think I'm not going to do this anymore, I'm going to retire. Or I think, "let's just write books or take a couple of years off." But then I think there is something about the column that it is there. The thing is, we all have things we would like to say to the world once in a while.

Greene worries, in fact, what he would do without his column, reflecting that:

> When I had a thought I wanted millions of people to see every day I'd have no place to put it. The number of people you reach with the newspaper column is just amazing. If the only time I can talk to people, tell them my stories, is once every 18 months or two years when I had a book coming out, well, that's a long time. So I have to do it every day.

Having his work considered literary journalism, Greene has said, is flattering, and he believes that the two terms need not be mutually exclusive.

> I would hope that the best journalism equals the impact of the best literature. And clearly, it works the other way around too. Literature has the power to move people and stir them in the way that the most effective reporting does. So it's a pretty powerful combination—journalism with the tools and impact of literature and with the devices of literature. I just think that if you do solid reporting and then do the writing with the same care and craftsmanship that those who do toil in the field of literature, whatever that is, it stands out a little bit.

References:

Doug Anderson, "How Many People Did You Kill Over There?," *New York Times Book Review,* 94 (22 January 1989): 18;

Mark Fitzgerald, "Journalistic Terrorism?," *Editor & Publisher,* 127 (23 July 1994): 12.

Michael Herr
(1940 –   )

Donald J. Ringnalda
University of St. Thomas

BOOKS: *Dispatches* (New York: Knopf, 1977);
The Big Room, by Herr and Guy Peellaert (New York: Summit Books, 1986);
Walter Winchell (New York: Knopf, 1990).

PLAY PRODUCTION: *Dispatches, a Rock-War Musical,* adapted and with music composed by Elizabeth Swados, New York, Public Theater, 18 April 1979.

MOTION PICTURES: *Apocalypse Now,* narration by Herr, Zoetrope Studios, 1979;
Full Metal Jacket, by Herr, Stanley Kubrick, and Gustav Hasford, Warner Brothers, 1987.

From the first review to the most recent assessment, critics have lavished praise on *Dispatches* (1977), Michael Herr's book about the Vietnam War. Major literary scholars of that war are unanimous in their judgments that this "rock 'n' roll" work of literary journalism is perhaps the single most powerful book to come out of that war, and the book is almost universally considered a landmark. Dust jacket blurbs rarely reflect a scholarly consensus, but they do in the case of *Dispatches.* Gloria Emerson claimed that Herr surpassed Stephen Crane in writing about war. Tom Wolfe still maintains that *Dispatches* rivals Erich Maria Remarque's 1929 masterpiece, *All Quiet on the Western Front.* Hunter S. Thompson says that Herr's book "puts all the rest of us in the shade." Robert Stone says, "I believe it may be the best personal journal about war, any war, that any writer has ever accomplished." Finally, John Le Carre calls it "the best book I have ever read on men and war in our time." All this near hyperbole is for a writer whose previous experiences were limited to working on the literary magazine at Syracuse University (where he dropped out), a nonpaying film-criticism job at the *New Leader,* from which he was fired after a year for liking all the wrong movies, and a job writing travel pieces for *Holiday,* which he quit after a short time. Then almost overnight Herr became a celebrity after *Esquire*

Michael Herr (photograph by Don McCullin)

published his lone dispatch from Vietnam, "Hell Sucks," in August 1968.

The book has had detractors. Feminists generally have attacked the book because it allegedly promotes the technology of modern warfare as a proving ground for male validation. In an interview with Herr in the *Los Angeles Times* (15 April 1990) Paul Ciotti observes that "The doctrinaire right was offended by the way [Herr] ridiculed the platitudes of what he called the Saigon 'Dial-soapers,' the starched and self-deluded brass. . . . And leftists piled on, too, calling him a war freak enraptured by the ecstasy of battle." Herr's response to the detractors typifies the independent, noncompany spirit that informs *Dispatches:* "I was deeply thrilled. . . . I knew I had succeeded. I offended everybody."

Herr has always been far less thrilled by the fallout from critical approval. The extreme success of *Dispatches* put him in the public eye, where he never wanted to be. Affable, but an intensely private person, he loathes being photographed, rarely grants interviews, and when he does, it is with almost palpable discomfort. In the 1990 interview with Ciotti he admits that "The aftermath of the publication of *Dispatches* was really heaven and hell. . . . The reception couldn't have been better, frankly—it couldn't have been more wonderful. It totally changed my life. But it also blew my cover." Ciotti adds, "To Herr it seemed as if everyone wanted a piece of him," including television, but "the idea of going on television," Herr tells Ciotti, "just fills me with dread and horror." So after writing the voice-over for the film *Apocalypse Now* (1979), Herr fled the United States and became an expatriate in London for more than a decade, living quietly with Valerie, his English wife, and their two daughters. In the early 1990s they returned to his hometown of Syracuse, where he was born in 1940; they settled in the country in upstate New York, where Herr remains something of an enigmatic recluse.

In her 31 May 1990 article-interview in the *Washington Times* Cathryn Donohoe relates a story that captures Herr's diffidence. While living in Greenwich Village in New York City, desperately trying to finish *Dispatches,* he went every day to the Buffalo Roadhouse, a restaurant near Sheridan Square. Donohoe writes, "Arriving at the restaurant just before noon each day, he had his own chair and his own corner table where he sat with his Jack Daniels looking out on Seventh Avenue. . . . It was two years before he said a word to anyone."

Why, then, in late 1967, at the age of twenty-seven, did this virtual agoraphobe go to the carnival and carnage of Vietnam? Why did a young man who described himself in the Ciotti interview as a "nice, middle-class, educated Jewish boy who as a kid had every nervous tic and allergy possible," decide to attend to the terrors of war? Herr admits in *Dispatches* that the search for adventure was certainly one of his motives. But adventure can take many forms besides the intensity and danger of being in a combat zone. Arguably, Herr's trail to Vietnam began when he was barely a teenager. Working in the record department of his father's Syracuse department store, he watched with moth-to-flame frightened zeal as rock and rollers such as Elvis Presley and Little Richard revolutionized popular music and youthful thinking in America. In his 12 June 1990 interview with Henry Allen of *The Washington Post,* he describes himself as:

> A kid in Syracuse . . . working in a record store and watching between 1954 and 1957 the walls break down, you know, and seeing these kids come in who were new kids. This isn't Archie and Veronica and Henry Aldrich coming in, man, this is like the new bit—it was terrifying to a lot of people. And to me. But attractive. . . . It wasn't long before I was on the other side of the counter.

Like many middle-class kids in the 1950s, Herr was infatuated by all those who rebelled against this decade of repression. (In fact, he has argued that the Vietnam War was caused by this repression.) His heroes included the new cult of rock stars and the early Norman Mailer, James Dean, and the Beats. Already in the late 1950s Herr saw a massive paradigm shift taking shape in the United States. But while the shift eventually thoroughly penetrated the ranks of the common soldiers in Vietnam, it never managed to wrinkle the uniforms of those whom Herr called the "Dial-soapers"—the people in charge, the people telling Americans what Vietnam was supposedly all about. This is the real reason Herr went to "the other side of the counter," to Vietnam: at best, the media were translating the terrifying attractiveness of the war as if it were being experienced by the cartoon characters Archie and Veronica on a bad day; at worst, as the media repeatedly talked about "progress" and "light at the end of the tunnel," it represented the "new bit" as Archie and Veronica on a normal day. Herr sensed the lid was being kept on. In *Dispatches* he writes, "something wasn't answered, it wasn't even being asked. . . . Hiding low under the fact-figure crossfire there was a secret history, and not a lot of people felt like running in there to bring it out." His probing for the dark secret history of Vietnam is reminiscent of a recurring scene in Joseph Heller's *Catch-22* (1961). Throughout the novel Yossarian, the main character, flashes back to a scene during a bombing run where he carefully tends to a serious but not at all life-threatening hip wound suffered by Snowden, the bombardier. Yossarian is convinced he has thoroughly treated the wound, yet Snowden becomes more and more deathly pale. Yossarian finally removes Snowden's flak jacket, and his viscera come sliding out.

During and after the Vietnam War conventional journalism (and writing about the war in general) busily attended to Snowden's hip wound. By contrast Herr's *Dispatches* removed the flak jacket, which makes it one of the most frightening, upsetting, and truthful books of the war. Even after multiple readings it maintains the capacity to unsettle the reader, perhaps much as Jimi Hendrix—whom Herr repeatedly refers to—unsettled his listeners at the Woodstock Music Festival when he deconstructed the "Star-Spangled Banner." Like Hendrix, Herr is a guerrilla sapper infiltrating the well-guarded perimeters of middle-brow decorum and rational consciousness. Herr reminds those who try to look away and persuade themselves that the news gets the news and the war is safely in the past that "in back of every column of print you read about Vietnam there was a dripping, laughing death-face; it hid there in the newspapers and magazines and held to your television screens for hours after the set was turned off for the night, an after-image that simply wanted to tell you at last what somehow had not been told." Hendrix's antiestablishment *Are You Experienced* album is a barometer of what was not being told. A bible-for-grunts album, it was never, Herr claims, played over the "company" airwaves, the Armed Forces Radio Network.

In the twenty years since the fall of Saigon on 30 April 1975 Herr has never retreated from his conviction that Americans have not been told the real story of Vietnam. At least part of that story, which he eventually reveals in *Dispatches,* is that there was nothing new about American behavior in Vietnam: "There'd been nothing happening there [in Vietnam] that hadn't existed here, coiled up and waiting." Herr traces the beginning of the Vietnam War back through the Cherokee Indians' Trail of Tears in the nineteenth century all the way to the Puritans "who found the New England woods too raw and empty for their peace and filled them up with their own devils." In the 1992 interview with Eric James Schroeder, Herr says:

> America has never come to terms with Vietnam. Vietnam is big in the culture now. It's right up there on the surface. I suppose that *Dispatches* broke it as a story in the culture. But that's still not quite dealing with it. There are these twelve-part PBS series and treatments of it. And I suppose that's useful—it's better than pretending that it never happened. But there is some profound way in which it is not going to be dealt with. We are not a great introspective or retrospective people. It's not in our nature. We're very ignorant of our history. We're great perverters of our tradition.

A moment later in the interview he adds, "we're not great at telling the truth about certain kinds of national behavior. The war sure twisted us. We haven't felt the same about ourselves since Vietnam. We're haunted by it, but we won't name the shape of the ghost; we won't say what it is."

The massive death toll Herr witnessed in Hue during the Tet offensive made it impossible for him not to "name the shape of the ghost." The war be-

came even more personal for him eighteen months after his return to the United States. In quick succession three close photographer friends were either killed or reported as missing in action in Vietnam: Larry Burrows from *Life;* Dana Stone from Associated Press; and Sean Flynn, son of actor Errol Flynn—and the freelancer's freelancer. This gave the "death-face" familiar features that Herr could not ignore. The sheer rapidity of the losses wiped him out. In the interview with Ciotti he confesses, "I experienced a massive physical and psychological collapse. I crashed."

Right after *Dispatches* was published, Herr, still close to the crash, admitted to Joyce Wadler of the *Washington Post* (4 November 1977) that he often holed up in his tiny Village apartment for a week or more at a time, getting stoned. "Grass, yeah, grass was the nail in the coffin that kept me paralyzed. I couldn't wait to get stoned every day, not high, Stoned, unconscious. The terror I felt, it was worse than Vietnam." Anyone who thinks that Herr was merely a member of the self-absorbed drug culture of the time should recall the words of Peter Braestrup, who covered the war for the *Washington Post* and told Cathryn Donohoe: "Most people develop calluses. Herr did not have many calluses, and he didn't develop them in Vietnam. And I imagine he didn't do it afterwards." What he did instead, John Le Carre maintains in the *Critic* (July 1978), was go "to the limit in order to make himself a part of the monstrosity he visited." The losses of Burrows, Stone, and Flynn seem to have been the catalysts that committed Herr to tell the untold story of Vietnam. Of his interview with Herr, Ciotti said, "20 years later, this is hard for Herr to talk about. His speech slows down, and his voice turns grave." Herr tells Ciotti that once these losses happened, "other things started to happen, too; other dark things that I had been either working too hard or playing too hard to avoid just became unavoidable."

To appreciate fully Herr's singular achievement in *Dispatches,* one needs to place the book in the context of journalism's monumental, monolithic success in *avoiding* that "dripping, laughing death-face" that Herr describes. One needs to return to that something that was missing, that was not answered or even asked by conventional journalists. In one of his book's many celebrated one-liners, Herr writes, "Conventional journalism could no more reveal this war than conventional firepower could win it." The comparison is not gratuitous. Herr saw an organic relationship between the way Americans fought the war and wrote about it.

Conventional wisdom—for both doves and hawks—failed to recognize this relationship between revealing and fighting the war. According to an

Dust jacket for Herr's first book, an examination of the Vietnam war

amazingly stubborn myth, the United States lost the war in Vietnam in part because the media did such a good job (or anti-American job, depending on one's perspective) in revealing the dark sides of the war. The myth would have the public believe that television and print journalists were against the war from the beginning and that they rather quickly galvanized public outrage, student protests, and marches to Washington, thereby crippling the military's ability to wage war effectively. The myth further claims that the military might have won the war if censorship had been practiced. Daniel C. Hallin counters this claim in the title of his book *The "Uncensored War"* (1986). The ironic quotation marks indicate that the media were censored–but largely by themselves. In John Hollowell's *Fact & Fiction* (1977) literary critic Robert Scholes says, "Perhaps the credulous believe that a reporter reports facts and that newspapers print all of them that are fit to print. But actually newspapers print all of the 'facts' that fit, period–that fit the journalistic conventions of what 'a story' is (those tired formulas) and that fit the editorial policy of the paper." Perhaps this is why Herr says that "as a group, newspapermen were not necessarily any more observant or imaginative than accountants." In fact, from 1962 until the Tet offen-

sive of 1968 American journalists essentially functioned as cheerleaders for the war effort, even propagandists. In *Between Fact and Fiction: The Problem of Journalism* (1975), Edward Jay Epstein writes that as late as 1967 a *Newsweek*-commissioned Harris poll discovered that "64 percent of the nationwide sample said that television's coverage made them *more* supportive of the American effort. . . . *Newsweek*'s conclusion was that 'TV had encouraged a decisive majority of viewers to support the war.'" Epstein adds that the nightly newscasts of the first half of the war reinforced "the main impression . . . of American progress" and "the dominant impression is one of continuous American successes and mounting enemy losses."

After the stunning Tet offensive, reporters and their editors began criticizing the war in large numbers. Some, like Braestrup, became severely critical of the way the war was being run, but this kind of criticism was not substantive and fundamental. As Phillip Knightley observes in *The First Casualty* (1975), even late in the war most journalists never got beyond the "subversive" news that the United States was losing the war: "the correspondents were not questioning the American intervention itself, but only its effectiveness." Similarly, Hallin points out that to the end the journalists' quarrel was only about *how* the United States was waging the war, not that it *was*. Even during the huge buildup between 1965 and 1967 the so-called uncensored war was delivered to American living rooms with a structure that was unimaginative and, Hallin writes, "simple and traditional: the forces of good were locked in battle . . . with the forces of evil. What began to change . . . was the conviction that the forces of good would inevitably prevail." The "dripping, laughing death-face" was nowhere to be seen.

Herr does not so much attack conventional journalism as he recognizes its extreme inherent limitations in dealing with death and horror. The reporters often did not even see a "death-face" to report. No doubt this is partly due, as Herr says, to the fact that "they worked in the news media, for organizations that were ultimately reverential toward the institutions involved: the Office of the President, the Military, America at war and, most of all, the empty technology that characterized Vietnam." This results in a tautological trap: reporters file stories that dovetail with the values and assumptions of the institutions toward which they are reverential, thereby legitimizing them to the point that they eventually forget what they have done. Herr calls this "a cross-fertilization of ignorance," which he attributes to a fictive reality deeply embedded in the American psyche because of overexposure to mediated truth: "We'd all seen too many movies, stayed too long in Television City, years of media glut had made certain connections difficult."

Much of Herr's book is about how language and reality stayed hooked into the circuit of "Television City." Repeatedly Herr talks about how language and reality were sanitized and made to make sense. At one point he quotes a British correspondent who compares the official rhetoric of the war to the captain of the *Titanic* saying, "There's no cause for alarm, we're only stopping briefly to take on a little ice." Herr himself adds:

> Spokesmen spoke in words that had no currency left as words, sentences with no hope of meaning in the sane world, and if much of it was sharply queried by the press, all of it got quoted. The press got all the facts (more or less), it got too many of them. But it never found a way to report meaningfully about death, which of course was really what it was all about. The most repulsive, transparent gropes for sanctity in the midst of the killing received serious treatment in the papers and on the air. The jargon of Progress got blown into your head like bullets.

Herr was less a victim of what Matthew C. Stewart calls in a 1990 essay an optimistic, "almost indelibly stamped . . . " "framework of consciousness" because he was not a certified member of the press. (Herr is fond of telling the story about how the Vietnam press corps was introduced during a reception for Ted Kennedy as "The gentlemen of the press, and Michael Herr.") Originally Herr planned to send only a monthly dispatch to *Esquire*, but after just a few days "in country" he realized that this was not the kind of war that could be neatly divided into discrete monthly columns. In fact, during his year in Vietnam he sent only the one dispatch. However, despite the latitude he enjoyed as an outsider with no ties to New York, Herr knew that he too was circumscribed by media and mythic versions of reality. He recalls looking at pictures of war casualties in *Life* and being unable to get himself to believe that the people in the photographs were really dead. Soon after his arrival in Vietnam he saw a fellow helicopter passenger fatally shot by ground fire. Again, he could not get himself beyond viewing the event as a movie scene. So the most difficult task before him—one that took him almost nine years of virtual insanity to complete—was to deconstruct his own mediated mind. Perhaps the most important sentence in *Dispatches* is, "A lot of things had to be unlearned before you could learn anything at all." Sometime between his arrival in Vietnam in late 1967 and the book's publication in 1977 Herr figured out that the highest level of learning often is predicated on the subtraction of mental habits, not the addition of yet more information. Lying at the center of Herr's achievement as a literary journalist is what he learned *not* to think. Put another way, Herr, in Stewart's words, "had to develop ways of freeing himself from the system's 'war stories' and finding his own."

The effort to free himself from the standard interpretations of the war, not the war itself, is the real subject of *Dispatches*. Thus, the matter of what Herr learns to avoid is inseparable from what he achieves. At the beginning of *Dispatches* Herr offers a microcosm of the primary "framework of consciousness" that most Americans carried with them to Vietnam: a rage for order and control over the inscrutable Vietnamese and their tortuous landscape. Herr points to two primary means of creating the illusion of order in Vietnam, namely, the military's reverence toward maps and its related enthusiastic use of chemical defoliants, especially Agent Orange. On the first page Herr uses the word *map* or *maps* six times. The problem, Herr soon discovered, was that Americans made the classic mistake of substituting the map for the territory, the menu for the meal—as surely as the Armed Forces Radio Network substituted Johnny Cash and The Beach Boys for Jimi

Hendrix and The Mothers of Invention. As an outsider Herr could see what many could not: "even the most detailed maps didn't reveal much anymore; reading them was like trying to read the faces of the Vietnamese, and that was like trying to read the wind." Other times, in less patient moods, Herr lashes out at commanders who routinely substituted orderly "mapped" realities for the actual chaos and destruction. After listening for days to army and marine "cheer-crazed language" describing U.S. disasters as "excellent," "real fine," "outstanding," and "first rate," Herr says, "it was all you could do to keep from seizing one graying crew-cut head or another and jamming it deep into the nearest tactical map."

Earlier, Herr notes that "The terrain above II Corps, where it ran along the Laotian border and into the DMZ, was seldom referred to as the Highlands by Americans. It had been a matter of military expediency to impose a new set of references over Vietnam's older, truer being. . . . And if it effectively obliterated even some of the most obvious geographical distinctions, it made for clear communication." Herr's tone here clearly is ironic, for he was fully aware that this "clear communication" actually was an intricate, self-sustaining maze of self-deception perpetuated until the map became the only thing real in the minds of Americans. Physically, Herr has been described by Joyce Wadler as a "myopic teddy bear," but intellectually he never lost sight of the severe disjunction between the war itself and the ways it was represented to Americans.

The military—and often the news media—never really gave up the effort to map the inferno and its indigenous residents. Onto the mythic, cyclical, seamless Tao of Vietnam was superimposed a geometrician's game plan. Arriving from what Herr described as a "carpentered" America of "engineer-straight" lines and right angles, the U.S. military leaders became "cartomaniacs" in Vietnam. As a result, Herr believes, "All in-country briefings, at whatever level, came to sound like a Naming of the Parts, and the language was used as a cosmetic." He later specifies one of the frames of consciousness he needed to unlearn if he were to tell his own story: "Since most of the journalism from the war was framed in that language or proceeded from the view of war which those terms implied, it would be as impossible to know what Vietnam looked like from reading most newspaper stories as it would be to know how it smelled."

The reverence for maps was related to the enthusiastic use of Agent Orange. Each seeks to simplify the landscape, figuratively and literally. Vietnam's terrain did seem to invite simplifying. Herr frequently describes the landscape of the Highlands, as if sensing that in its erratic contours it was itself that secret history that no one wanted to go in and get:

> The Highlands of Vietnam are spooky, unbearably spooky, spooky beyond belief. They are a run of erratic mountain ranges, gnarled valleys, jungled ravines and abrupt plains. . . . In the highlands . . . sudden contrary mists offered sinister bafflement. . . . The Puritan belief that Satan dwelt in Nature could have been born here, where even on the coldest freshest mountaintops you could smell jungle and that tension between rot and genesis . . . Oh, that terrain! The bloody, maddening uncanniness of it!

Early in the book Herr observes, "You could also fly out of places that were so grim they turned to black and white in your head five minutes after you'd gone."

At the end of his first week in Vietnam, Herr met someone who was emblematic of the American paradigmatic will to defeat the maddening uncanniness of Vietnam, its people, and the craziness of the war itself. Herr writes:

> I met an information officer in the headquarters of the 25th Division at Cu Chi who showed me on his map and then from his chopper what they'd done to the Ho Bo Woods, the vanished Ho Bo Woods, taken off by giant Rome plows and chemicals and long, slow fire, wasting hundreds of acres of cultivated plantation and wild forest alike, "denying the enemy valuable resources and cover." . . . It had been part of his job for nearly a year now to tell people about that operation; correspondents, touring congressmen, movie stars, corporation presidents, staff officers from half the armies in the world, and he still couldn't get over it. It seemed to be keeping him young, his enthusiasm made you feel that even the letters he wrote home to his wife were full of it, it really showed what you could do if you had the know-how and the hardware.

The U.S. defoliation of the landscape is more than tangentially analogous to the simplified understanding and reportage of the war. The violence to language is as much an instrument of willfully imposed order as are Agent Orange and Rome plows. It is no coincidence that the Twenty-fifth Division's tour guide for Dupont's Agent Orange is also a purveyor of "information." Language is his M-16. In *Writing After War* (1994) John Limon argues that "writing *is* war" because of its "aesthetic violence done to reality." Herr observes that "Nothing so horrible happened upcountry that it was beyond language fix and press relations. . . . You'd . . . meet an optimism that no violence could unconvince." Pervasive in Vietnam was a "linguistic technology"

A scene from Full Metal Jacket *(1987). Herr drew on his experiences in Vietnam to co-write the screenplay of the Stanley Kubrick film (Warner Bros., Inc.).*

every bit as destructive to real complexity as Agent Orange was to the flora and fauna. Herr had more contempt for the language-scrubbing "Dial-soapers in Saigon" than he did for the forest-scrubbing defoliation "Ranch Hands" who bragged "only we can prevent forests."

U.S. military officials prevented forests in Vietnam on a massive scale and not just as a tactic to deny cover to the enemy. They also tried to replace the forests with what amounted to gigantic industrial parks. Trying to re-create Vietnam in America's image, they transformed tens of thousands of acres of Herr's spooky terrain into billions of dollars worth of "engineer-straight" roads, airstrips, buildings, and bases. In a telling observation Herr says, "Nobody builds bases like Americans." They planted cities on the forests. Instead of utilizing the landscape according to the tactics of guerrillas, they tried to pave it over. These technological "improvements" were both enthusiastically reported by the media and mirrored by their own proclivity for imposing squares and rectangles on the Vietnam War morass.

In *The Perfect War* (1986) James William Gibson writes that Americans in Vietnam "became mesmerized by the spectacle of American construction." Gen. William Westmoreland himself was mesmerized by the spectacle of the Rome plows turning huge tracts of jungle into wastelands ready to receive American squares and rectangles—and not just in a figurative sense, according to Gibson: "War managers . . . tried to create a physical terrain

equivalent to the abstract mathematical space of 1,000 by 1,000 meter grid squares necessary for jets and artillery to find orientation." Without this kind of Western geometry, orientation was perceived to be impossible. Georgia governor Lester Maddox was not all that far from the consensus of American culture in calling for Vietnam to be turned into a parking lot. Agent Orange was more than a chemical compound whose principle ingredient was dioxin; it was an indelibly stamped cultural paradigm whose enemy was disorder.

What helped fuel the linguistic, epistemological Agent Orange of the war's novelistic, journalistic, and tactical thinking was, again, a framework of consciousness, namely, the Cold War fixation. The Domino Theory was a beautifully designed, if sinister, linear narrative that Americans of all political persuasions subscribed to with religious fervor. Like poet Wallace Stevens's jar in Tennessee, (which Herr refers to), it took dominion everywhere. Americans were entranced by the Euclidean black-and-white clarity of the forces of good standing up to the aggressive advances of the forces of evil. Hallin reminds his reader that "the journalists [in Vietnam] themselves were as deeply steeped in the ideology of the Cold War as those they wrote about. Its images pervade their language; its assumptions guided their news judgements. Its power can be seen both in the 'framing' of the events that were covered and, equally important, in the things that were *not* covered, that fell through the conceptual gaps of the world view the journalists accepted as common sense." As a character says in Tim O'Brien's Vietnam novel *Going After Cacciato* (1978), "What you remember is determined by what you see, and what you see depends on what you remember. A cycle. . . . A cycle that needs to be broken." The cycle rarely was broken during the Vietnam War, so the "conceptual gaps" and maps remained in place for the duration. Thus, Vietnam veteran and writer John Clark Pratt's observation is not surprising: "[The war] was being conducted and reported and understood the way people used to write traditional novels." So, too, Vietnam War narratives were and are being written the way the war was waged–conventionally.

Herr notes that most people, inside and outside the military, were trapped in this closed, self-perpetuating Cold War narrative. Anything that complicated, compromised, or contradicted this narrative was unconsciously edited out, which resulted in some preposterous abuses of good sense, such as one major's claim that "We had to destroy Ben Tre in order to save it," or General Westmoreland's claim that the tactical and strategic disaster of Khe Sanh was "a Dien Bien Phu in reverse." According to the logic of the American can-do narrative mindset, Westmoreland was able magically to transform into a U.S. victory what Herr calls "a non-operation devised to non-relieve the non-seige of Khe Sanh." When America's simplistic frontier myth collided with the obdurate, complex reality of the war and the Vietnamese people, the myth always won. Everything about the war, the land, and the people was so *other,* so alien to the American epistemological repertoire that one of Herr's characters claims he cannot possibly get wounded in Vietnam because "it don't exist." As Hallin says, "An ideology defines not only what people see, but also what they do not see. What Americans saw in Vietnam was aggression; what they did not see and could not see, given the political concepts available to them, was revolution." Even more important, they could not see that they could not see. One can infer from *Dispatches* that this lack of metaconsciousness, because of the seductive power of the Cold War narrative, lies at the foundation of conventional journalism's failure to reveal the war truthfully. Herr himself sarcastically refers to what might be called "narrativitis" as "overripe bullshit": "tumbling dominoes, maintaining the equilibrium of the Dingdong by containing the ever encroaching Doodah."

Conventional journalism during the war shared with Military Assistance Command Vietnam (MACV) an insistence upon control. Agent Orange, maps, linear narratives, and "objective" reports of MACV briefings all provided illusory control but not much effective running of the war or truth telling about it. At one point Herr says:

> That fall, all that the Mission talked about was control: arms control, information control, resources control, psycho-political control, population control, control of the almost supernatural inflation, control of terrain through the Strategy of the Periphery. But when the talk had passed, the only thing left standing up that looked true was your sense of how out of control things really were. Year after year, season after season, wet and dry, using up options faster than rounds on a machine-gun belt, we called it right and righteous, viable and even almost won, and it still only went on the way it went on.

The key element in the greatness of *Dispatches* is Herr's willingness and ability to step outside a mediating system of signification that dictated its own optimistic results. This meant accepting disorder and loss of control not only as his starting point but also as an epistemological constant. He claims that "if you were one of those people who always thought they had to know what was coming next, the war could cream you." Herr was himself one of those people, and this may have been the most difficult thing he had to unlearn before he "could learn anything at all."

Robert Graves, a veteran of World War I, ends his poem "In Broken Images" with the lines: "He in a new confusion of his understanding, / I in a new understanding of my confusion." The poem's "He" characterizes the mind-set of all those who rely on Agent Orange, literally or figuratively. Conversely, the poem's "I" characterizes a small handful of novelists, poets, journalists, and military strategists who recognized that the only way to understand this war was by articulating and riding out their confusion. In *Dispatches* the certitude of epistemological firepower gives way to a perilous, surrealistic journey of unlearning. Instead of explicating chaos with linguistic Agent Orange, Herr explores it.

In his commentary on *Dispatches* in the *New York Review of Books* (8 December 1977) Roger Sale astutely notes that "at his best . . . Herr shows and reminds us there are some things we had best not pretend to understand with such ease." A few weeks before Sale wrote these words, Herr told Joyce Wadler in an interview for the *Washington Post* (4 November 1977), "I want people to be confused so they won't be so smug. I want them to abandon definitions. I wrote that book more with my chest, with my heart, than with my mind, because I don't feel facts tell the truth. I saw facts changed into lies."

More recently, following the 1990 publication of his novel *Walter Winchell*, Herr told Ciotti, "I feel ambivalent about just about everything. If my feelings aren't mixed, I don't really trust them."

Those mixed feelings are the key to Herr's way of representing himself and the Vietnam War, for in order to do an end run around the "cross-fertilization of ignorance" he needed to create, in Peter Stoicheff's words, a "metafictional narrative of chaos" in which "the process of self-interrogation is built into the narrative, freeing it from . . . tautological determinism." Eschewing this process, most representations of the Vietnam War end up being acts—as Lynne Hanley says in *Writing War*—"not of remembering but of forgetting war."

In this self-interrogative reliance upon ambivalence and epistemological doubt Herr developed what Philip D. Beidler calls in *American Literature and the Experience of Vietnam* (1982) a "distinctively new and original architecture of consciousness." In so doing, he distinguished himself not only from conventional journalists but also from most literary journalists. In his illuminating article "The New Journalism and the Image-World: Two Modes of Organizing Experience," David Eason designates these two modes of New Journalism as "ethnographic realism" and "cultural phenomenology." Herr clearly operates in the second mode. Whereas the first mode assumes that the reporter can make sense of the world by putting new wine in old bottles, the second assumes a radical epistemological crisis. Ethnographic realism is fine tuning; cultural phenomenology is a total overhaul of cognition and consciousness. According to Eason:

> Whereas ethnographic realism, like other forms of journalism, reveals the act of observing to be a means to get the story, cultural phenomenology reveals observing to be a vital part of the story. Observing is not merely a means to understand the world but an object of analysis. . . . Ethnographic realism represents style as a communicational technique whose function is to reveal a story that exists 'out there' in real life. Cultural phenomenology represents style as an epistemological strategy that constructs as well as reveals.

Herr's immersion in the Vietnam War forced him into the overhaul mode. It did not take him long to experience, in Eason's language, "what it feels like to live in a world in which there is no consensus about a frame of reference to explain 'what it all means.'" Because of this crisis of meaning, *Dispatches* necessarily is as much invention as it is reportage. This upsets the credulous who cling to the illusion that real journalism is unmediated and prints all the news fit to print—as opposed to the news that fits.

Those who cling to the illusion are annoyed when they find out that parts of *Dispatches* are made up. In the Ciotti interview Herr says:

> Oh, yeah. A lot of *Dispatches* is fictional. I've said this a lot of times. I have told people over the years that there are fictional aspects to *Dispatches*, and they look betrayed. They look heartbroken, as if it isn't true anymore. I never thought of *Dispatches* as journalism. . . . A lot of the journalistic stuff I got wrong. . . . You know, this unit at this place. But it didn't bother me. There is no shortage of regimental histories.

Shortly after his arrival in Vietnam, Herr heard the inscrutable and now-celebrated Lurp story: "Patrol went up the mountain. One man came back. He died before he could tell us what happened." Herr seems to have decided then and there that no kind of journalism he was familiar with could meaningfully reveal the insanity of the war. Hungry for conventional meaning, he says, "I waited for the rest, but it seemed not to be that kind of story; when I asked him what had happened he just looked like he felt sorry for me, fucked if he'd waste time telling stories to anyone dumb as I was." Herr comes to the conclusion that his epistemological training had ill prepared him for the wacky reality of Vietnam. He arrived in Vietnam believing that if something was inscrutable it simply needed to be restated more clearly. He was used to a language of "defoliation" that had imperialistic control over the formless and the inconclusive. So rather than pledging allegiance to an illusory world of nonfiction, Herr plunged into a more promising world of self-conscious artifice. He has even said on several occasions that what *Dispatches* really is about is the writing of a book. Within that artifice Herr is less an author in charge than he is a character trying to articulate the contours of his nightmare journey to the American heart of darkness.

It is possible that Herr saw himself as a contemporary version of Joseph Conrad's voyager, Marlow. In a celebrated passage in *Heart of Darkness* (1902) the external narrator, just as he is about "To hear about one of Marlow's inconclusive experiences," explains the difference between the way Marlow and other men of the sea tell stories: "The yarns of seamen have a direct simplicity, the whole meaning of which lies within the shell of a cracked nut. But Marlow was not typical (if his propensity to spin yarns be excepted), and to him the meaning of an episode was not inside like a kernel but outside, enveloping the tale which brought it out only as a glow brings out a haze, in the likeness of one of these misty halos that sometimes are made visible by the spectral illumination of moonshine."

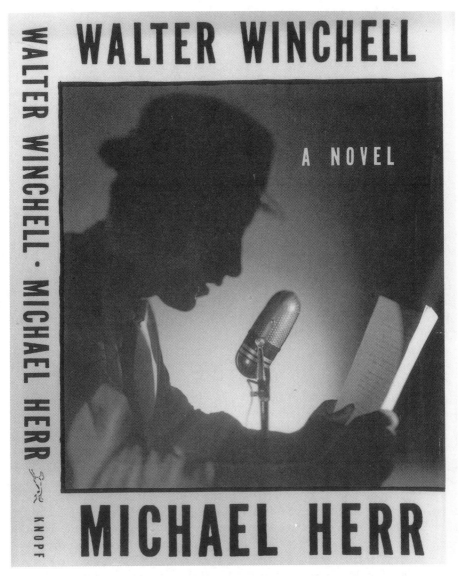

Dust jacket for Herr's novel, a fictional account of the life of the gossip columnist and radio journalist

This description sheds a great deal of "moonlight" on the story Marlow is about to tell and the one Herr tells much later. Herr's reportage is as different from conventional journalism as Marlow's is different from conventional sea tales. Because their experiences—both in the jungle and in storytelling—run so parallel, it is not surprising that Herr was the natural choice to write the voice-over for Francis Ford Coppola's version of Marlow (Captain Willard) in the 1979 film, *Apocalypse Now*.

Both Herr and Marlow realized that what they had witnessed in the heart of darkness was simply beyond the dimensions of conventional storytelling and perhaps beyond even unconventional storytelling. Their experiences had been altogether too dark or, because of what they reveal about Western behavior in Third-World coun-

tries, altogether too light. All "straight history" and straight reporting became seriously compromised. Morality became profoundly problematical. In one of Herr's great lines for Willard the audience hears, "Charging a man with murder here is like handing out speeding tickets at the Indy 500." Therefore, the only illumination Herr did experience was the well-lighted disintegration of his confidently straight Western consciousness; *Dispatches* is like tracer rounds illuminating objects targeted for destruction, and they include Herr's own rage for order.

Once this was destroyed Herr realized he could not possibly structure the episodes of *Dispatches* on a linear continuum, so instead he moves pulsatingly from one damp critical mass to another. One hundred and sixty-seven pages into *Dispatches* Herr suddenly finds himself newly arrived in Vietnam. On page 243 he is "Back in the World now, and a lot of us aren't making it." On page 256 he is whiplashed back to his first days "in country." Time and meaning for both Marlow and Herr came to resemble the muddy serpentine Congo River or the ominous, unmappable Central Highlands of Vietnam. Instead of kernels, both of their stories are swirling strobes eerily illuminating spooky shadows.

Thinking back on his experiences, some of which were "a translucent blur," Herr recalls that everything stood in "a strange light; the light told the story, and it didn't end like any war story I'd ever imagined." He says the experience of horror leaves one "changed, enlarged and . . . incomplete" because "I'd performed half an act." As Conrad's participle *enveloping* suggests, the glowing haze is a process in which experience past and experience present are interwoven. Neither storyteller relates a story that already exists. It comes into being as it is being told. To a great extent the process is the content. Their past experiences are less things in themselves than they are catalysts for a future act. As Paul Fussell says in *The Great War and Modern Memory* (1975), "it is only the ex post facto view of an action that generates coherence (an understanding of one's confusion) or makes irony possible."

Heart of Darkness and *Dispatches* are ex post facto collages that provide Marlow and Herr their only way of knowing their horrifying experiences. As Herr expresses it, "Plant you now, dig you later; information printed on the eye, stored in the brain." Or, "The problem was that you didn't always know what you were seeing until later, maybe years later, that a lot of it never made it in at all, it just stayed stored there in your eyes. Time and information, rock and roll, life itself, the information isn't frozen, you are."

Herr needed to immerse himself in time, memory, and the creative act in order to thaw himself out. "Immersion" is one of the primary hallmarks of literary journalism. Both Marlow and Herr were immersed beyond their wildest imaginations. (Herr was so immersed that, as he ends his book, he says, "one last chopper revved it up, lifted off and flew out of my chest"). But the crucial kind of immersion is the secondary one, after the fact, when the writer does not recollect, nor even re-create, so much as he or she correlates, creates, and images the fragmentary raw material of the first immersion. So Herr is not really speaking hyperbolically when he says he had only performed half an act. (The second half of the act—writing the book in Greenwich Village—proved to be far tougher and took much longer than the first half.) This brings up two paradoxes of Herr's and Marlow's literary journalism. First, the storyteller achieves immersion with distance—in both space and time. Herr wrote the greater share of *Dispatches* twelve thousand miles from Hue and Khe Sahn—years after the fact. Marlow created his story aboard the *Nellie* more than four thousand miles from the Congo, also many years after the fact. Conrad himself needed nine years after his sojourn in the Congo to write *Heart of Darkness*—almost to the month, the amount of time Herr took to write *Dispatches*.

The second paradox is that both Marlow and Herr scooped their stories by delaying the telling. By abjuring deadlines and wire services (literally, in the case of Herr), they assured an exclusive for themselves. To emphasize just how slow Herr was in getting the "news" out, he calls his only in-country dispatch to *Esquire* "a lost dispatch from the Crimea." Thus, it is paradoxically appropriate for Ward Just, Vietnam novelist and former reporter for the *Washington Post,* to call Herr the premier war correspondent from Vietnam even though Herr rarely corresponded with anyone back in the states.

Perhaps the best way of getting at Herr's alternative to "just-the-facts" conventional fighting and writing is to view him metaphorically as a Viet Cong (VC) writer. He is like a guerrilla sapper infiltrating the perimeters of our rational consciousness. Herr's unconventional writing emulates the unconventional fighting of the VC. First, *Dispatches* is off the main roads. Herr often "crashed" in Saigon and Danang, but his remembered and consciously mediated material mainly comes from the grunt operations in the jungles and in the devastated Imperial City, during Tet, and at the Khe Sanh outpost. He eschewed the light of civilization in the official press clubs of the major cities; he stepped outside into the tangled geography of Vietnam and his imagination. He refused to use what James William Gibson in *The Perfect War* (1986) both figuratively and literally means by "the old trails," which led only to the destruction of serious intellectual and artistic inquiry, just as literal trails ominously ensured the likelihood of ambushes, Bouncing Betty leg removers, and other assorted booby traps.

Actually, the U.S. military did utilize select troops who, like the VC, avoided the old trails. They were called Long Range Reconnaissance Patrols (known acronymically as Lurps). Emulating the VC, they spent many days at a time observing the enemy in the darkness of the far reaches of nowhere. Similarly, Herr's Lurp book pushes itself and the reader off the old trails and away from the artificially cleared landing zones of convention. *Dispatches* avoids the blunder of giving cover to the guerrillas; instead, it explores the cover. The book is a deep-reconaissance probe into murky questions about who one is and how one knows. Herr replaces the language-fixing, laundered narrative of old-trail realism and conventional journalism with a "dropped camera" in the bush, where it catches the weird, secret subtext of the war and its "smaller darker pockets."

In Vietnam a grunt learned to live in the bush; Lurps and the VC, on the other hand, learned to *be* bushes. Herr's book is a bush. Coppola has said that his *Apocalypse Now*, on which he and Herr collaborated, is not *about* Vietnam–it *is* Vietnam. Some people would no doubt debate both claims. But to a great extent Herr's dark imagination–in the book and the movie–does mirror the Vietnam landscape rather than impose a controlling narrative on top of it. His jerky camera images of the war underscore the slippery, treacherous ground his writing traverses. He saves a special Vietnam memory for near the end of his book that serves as an analogue for his endeavor. He goes up in a Loach (a wasplike, speedy, agile helicopter) with the First Cav's star flier, noting:

> We flew fast and close to the ground, contour flying, a couple of feet between the treads and the ground, treetops, hootch roofs. Then we came to the river where it ran through a twisting ravine, the sides very steep, almost a canyon, and he flew the river, taking us through blind turns like a master. When we cleared the ravine he sped straight toward the jungle, dipping where I'd been sure he would rise, and I felt the sharp freezing moment of certain death. Right in there under the canopy, a wild ship-shaking U turn in the jungle, I couldn't even smile when we broke clear, I couldn't move, everything looked like images caught in a flash with all the hard shadows left in.

The second way that *Dispatches* parallels unconventional fighting is axiomatic to VC tactics. An often-repeated maxim already found in that most prophetic of novels, Graham Greene's *The Quiet American* (1955), about which Herr says in Eric James Schroeder's *Vietnam, We've All Been There* (1992), "If you want to travel light, you don't need any other books about Vietnam," is that the day belonged to the Americans (to the French in Greene's novel), the night to the VC. "Debriefed by dreams," Herr presents a night vision. Described by Le Carre as the "black recording angel of the Vietnam war," Herr takes the reader on nightmarish, postmodern journeys into regions where one can only hope for what Bruce Weigl in *Song of Napalm* (1988) calls "black understanding." The light one does experience is, according to Vietnamese poet Yusef Ko-

munyakaa in *Dien Cai Dau* (1988), from a spooky moon that ". . . cuts through / night trees like a circular saw." Flares reveal, rather than explicate, chaos. Readers, so to speak, can either quit reading or become guerrillas themselves in the profusion of the landscape.

Third, as Herr says, the underground belonged to the VC, the ground above, to Americans. But Herr's brand of journalism clearly is underground. A "tunnel rat," he low crawls into the dark, subterranean texts of the American love affair with violence and the imperialistic mapping of reality. As Le Carre says in his 1978 review of *Dispatches*, "[Herr] takes you inside his own besieged and leaping brain, into his shivering bed; he makes you share his restless, bottomless fear. Just as Edgar Allan Poe, in the words of D. H. Lawrence, 'was an adventurer into vaults and cellars and horrible underground passages of the human soul,' so Herr as a good journalist . . . went to the limit."

Fourth, like the VC who were "equipped" with black pajamas, a rice ball, fish sauce, and a rifle, Herr "travels light," without the cumbersome "field pack" that U.S. soldiers and journalists strapped to their backs. Incongruous in the impenetrable jungle and often weighing more than sixty pounds, the field pack can be seen as a ubiquitous symbol of the will to impose a civilizing control on the wilderness. The weight of the packs' many technological items, ranging from insect spray to claymore mines to C-4 heat tabs, was directly related to the preponderant mental framework that dictated American thinking during the war. Within that framework it was impossible to think of the jungle as anything other than a damnable obstacle, which the field pack–in reality and in the imagination–would minimize. More often than not, the kinds of operations that the field pack represented resulted in what Herr calls a "crazed expenditure" both of ammunition and of "cheer-crazed" rhetoric. So when Herr notes that "Charles [the VC] really wrote the book on fire control, putting one round into the heart of things where fifty of ours might go and still not hit anything," he may have unwittingly signified the literary fire control of his own book. On a literal level Herr traveled with the clothes on his back and a notepad–never with a camera or a tape recorder. More important, his frugality mirrors his unique "architecture of consciousness" that enabled him to see America's metaphorical field pack for what it was: an emblem of illusory control and wishful thinking amidst the surreality of the war.

The fifth parallel concerns the problem of identification. Who was the VC guerrilla? A barber, PX worker, rice farmer, launderer, prostitute, hootch maid, drug dealer, Kit Carson scout, sapper, sniper, or booby-trap expert? More often than not, he or she was more than one of these, which outraged U.S. soldiers. Similarly, Herr transcends narrow specialization. Literarily, he refuses to be pinned down to what the army calls one's Military Occupational Specialty (MOS). He especially refuses to be penned in by the conventional boundaries of genre. What is *Dispatches*? It has been called New Journalism, memoir, a verbal collage, even a novel. In fact, in France it has always been considered a novel. Within the book itself Herr frequently calls it his "movie." His "novel," *Walter Winchell*, shatters the boundaries of genre with even greater resolve. In the introduction Herr writes:

> The book that you are about to read began its life as a screenplay.... It was written in prose instead of in standard screenplay form. In other words, its first intentions were cinematic, but its impulses and energies must have come from someplace else.... You could call it a screenplay that's typed like a novel, that reads like a novel but plays like a movie. Maybe it's a completely new form, or a wrinkle on an old form, or a mongrel. Maybe it's just a novel with a camera in it.

Just as the VC wore no military uniforms, so Herr's writing up to this point has necessarily avoided the uniformity of any single genre.

The sixth and final parallel concerns the ingenuity of the VC, particularly in their adeptness at scrounging American junk and waste and putting it back together in new combinations for new purposes to make crude but effective weapons and other essentials for survival: rubber tires became sandals; Coke cans became grenades; scrap metal became shrapnel; exhaust pipes became primitive mortar tubes; and so on. Even today water-filled bomb craters are profit-making fish ponds, and the notorious Cu Chi tunnels have become a low-tech amusement park. Something similar happens in *Dispatches*. It is poetic junk, composed of rock-and-roll riffs, the leftovers, excesses, fragments, and debris of technology and the frontier myth. It is black pop art, and Pablo Picasso's "sums of destructions." In the *Washington Post* (12 June 1990) Henry Allen says that Herr's prose has a "cool moist, ironic heft to it, like a good combination of rock music and some kind of prime meat marinated in marijuana." In a word, *Dispatches* is a collage. Like the VC, Herr literally makes do with this underground piecing-together of fragments. Rather than squander the waste, Herr scrounges from it. Most important, within Herr's genre-straddling book is an actual collage that serves as an analogue for his whole book. It belongs to Davies, a flipped-out outsider door gun-

ner scrounger that Herr met in Vietnam. Scrapping the Newtonian linear order that Americans brought to Vietnam, Davies's collage is a hip spatial emblem of cultural phenomenology, a nonlinear equation that lumps together grotesque "coefficients."

This collage is a microcosm of Herr's book in that it makes disturbing connections not seen by the conventional military and press. Among its startling juxtapositions are a created-in-Hollywood Ronald Reagan and the narcotic, cannabis; the procreative genitalia of machismo and the destruction of bombs; Cardinal Spellman and a Huey gunship; patriotism and money; the myth of the warrior-hero and hog butchering; and the beautiful ugliness of "one large, long figure that began at the bottom with shiny leather boots and rouged knees and ascended in a microskirt, bare breasts, graceful shoulders and a long neck, topped by the burned, blackened face of a dead Vietnamese woman."

Obviously, these seemingly disparate correlations are testimony that there was more than containing the Dingdong of the Doodah going on in Vietnam. Herr engages in no self-righteous posturing; indeed, he admits more than one wishes to the alluring correlation of eroticism and violence, like being in a firefight and "undressing a girl for the first time," or intensely hating and loving the war, almost simultaneously. One feels uncomfortable with Herr's oxymoronic connections. But that is the whole point: the mythic die that stamped America's Vietnam into existence is so deeply rooted in what men love to loathe that it is very hard to part with.

If the content of Davies's collage reveals much about the counterepistemology of Herr's cultural phenomenology, so too does its placement within *Dispatches*. First of all, it appears in a book that itself is a collage of colliding memories and free associations as the writer crisscrosses Vietnam in the omnipresent, oxymoronic "saver-destroyer, provider-waster, right hand-left hand" collective metachopper. Second, it appears in the middle of a frenzied collagelike section called "Illumination Rounds." In it, in the space of twenty-one pages, "dipping where [one is] sure he would rise," Herr rapidly fires off sixteen vignettes that seemingly do not correspond with each other. The reader feels caught in an *L*-shaped ambush. This section likely makes writers of straight history squirm because it offers them no kernel, no hook, no linear progression, and no angle—actually, far too many angles. But as Thomas Myers has said in *Walking Point: American Narratives of Vietnam* (1988), these vignettes "bring momentarily darkened history into view. As the fading suggestion of each image hangs in the textual air, he launches a new one to bring the reader closer to the historian's problem of focusing on and correlating within individual imagination the plenitude of suggestions, of dealing aesthetically with the nonstop accumulation of quick glimpses and possible correspondences."

Like the hit-and-run operations of the VC, Herr's discontinuous and unpredictable vignettes are designed to harass the master narrative that America tried to inscribe on Vietnam. This is why Davies's collage is the heart of *Dispatches*. As a collage within a collage within a collage, it aggressively undermines the wish-fulfilling linear power of narrative. Herr discovered in Vietnam that he "was leaking time," so that it was possible to experience "a fabulous warp where you took the journey first and then you made your departure." Because these "distortions" were real for Herr, the historian's problem is not a problem at all for him—no more so than the inability to fight a conventional war is a problem for guerrillas. In fact, the problem is an asset, a solution. The narrativistic, sense-making, map-making power that Herr gives up is the greatest strength of *Dispatches*.

One final correlation in Davies's collage goes a long way toward summing up what Herr discovered in his struggles as a cultural phenomenologist. In one part of the collage Davies has superimposed a reversed map of Vietnam over a map of California, the shape of which resembles a mirrored Vietnam. Rather than continuing the mistake of seeing Vietnam in America's image, this cartographical countergesture would have America see its image in its own Vietnam, an "East-West interface, a California corridor cut and bought and burned deep into Asia." It would have American readers demystify the most recent progenitor of their frontier mythology—Hollywood, forever "facing west," as Richard Drinnon puts it in *Facing West: The Metaphysics of Indian-Hating and Empire-Building* (1980), the Hollywood that is forever making movies, defoliating and sanitizing whatever gets in the way. If the information officer who proudly shows off what is left of the Ho Bo Woods is a synecdoche for the whole philosophy of the U.S. war effort, then Davies's collage is a synecdoche for *Dispatches*—Herr's replacement postmodern map.

To paraphrase Eason, Davies's gesture would have Americans admit the disorienting truth that in their trillion-dollar movie they all were actors, not audience. Thus, the final words of *Dispatches*: "Vietnam Vietnam Vietnam, we've all been there."

Walter Winchell, Herr's second book (in *The Big Room* (1986) he merely wrote extended captions for Guy Peellaert's paintings of Las Vegas celebrities), is "a novel with a camera in it." Its hybrid construction thoroughly divided the critics; some loved it, while others viewed it as a silly, self-indulgent game. A *Dispatches* it is not, at least in terms of sales and critical reception. But beyond its failure in the marketplace, many have wondered why Herr wrote it at all. In real life (and in the "novel") Walter Winchell was a pompous, vicious, gossiping powermonger, always addicted to publicity. He was exactly everything Herr is not. Henry Allen in the *Washington Times* describes Winchell as a "failed song-and-dance man, Broadway blabbermouth, creator of the gossip column, 197-words-a-minute radio tattle tale, crusher of enemies, husband and father in absentia . . . [who] practically invented the hype that makes Michael Herr cringe."

One way to explain why Herr wrote *Walter Winchell* takes the reader back to his distrust of unambivalent feelings. Herr had a terrifying attraction to the insurrection of rock and roll in the late 1950s. In the same vein, throughout his life Herr has admired—even emulated—Ernest Hemingway (who has a bit part in *Walter Winchell*). Yet he readily admits that these feelings make him uneasy. Herr felt both mind-numbing fear and erotic pleasure when in a firefight. Finally, Herr presents Walter Winchell as a man with few (if any) virtues, yet as a magnificent pariah whom people loved to hate.

Something else may have attracted Herr to *Walter Winchell*. The novel is a kind of phenomenology of celebrity-construction in America, and it may have provided Herr with a means to name the shape of a different ghost—his own heaven-and-hell celebrity status that has haunted him since the publication of *Dispatches*. In his conversation with Allen, Herr names the ghost: "[H]e [Winchell] was the architect and the inventor of the end of private life, the end of any kind of private internal life . . . and it weighs on all of us, it oppresses—the media, you know, the incessant, you know, promiscuous, endless river of facts and distractions and gossip, and, so, the people, it's like you're never alone, you're never alone, you're never left alone." Herr elaborates on this in his preface: "If people go around today treating themselves like celebrities because not to be a celebrity is just too awful, we may have Walter Winchell to thank." Reading between the lines of *Walter Winchell*, one senses that it may well say as much about the fears of Herr as it does about the excesses of its title character.

In part because of his sustained privacy and in part because he disappears from the literary radar screen for long periods of time (during the 1980s one often heard the phrase "missing in action" applied to him), it is hard to predict where Herr will go from here. He said in his 1990 interview with Ciotti that he had "kissed [Vietnam] goodby" and was at work on an "unambiguous novel . . . about a friendship that spans 25 years," which does not sound altogether promising. By now it is clear that he will never—in terms of output—be a Mailer, a Wolfe, or a Joan Didion. He is sensitive to this and rather defensive. As the interview with Ciotti closes, Herr says, "It means much more [to me] to have children than to have something that is read after my death. . . . [Publishing] doesn't seem to be the overriding motivating force of my life. I sometimes have thought that it would never really matter if I never published another book." Even if his career does wane, that should not in the least minimize the singular and astounding achievement of *Dispatches*. Stephen Crane also wrote only one great book, about a different divisive war, and one hundred years later his fame remains secure. Many believe that *Dispatches* will have similar staying power.

Interviews:

Joyce Wadler, "Michael Herr's Stark Naked Account of Terror," *Washington Post*, 4 November 1977, p. D1;

Paul Ciotti, "Michael Herr: A Man of Few Words," *Los Angeles Times Magazine* (15 April 1990): p. 22;

Cathryn Donohoe, "The Many Hells of Michael Herr," *Washington Times*, 31 May 1990: p. E1;

Henry Allen, "The Hipster and Walter Winchell," *Washington Post*, 12 June 1990, p. E1;

Eric James Schroeder, "We've All Been There," in *Vietnam, We've All Been There*, edited by Schroeder (Westport: Praeger, 1992), pp. 33–49.

References:

Philip D. Beidler, *American Literature and the Experience of Vietnam* (Athens: University of Georgia Press, 1982), pp. 64, 141–148;

Maria S. Bonn, "The Lust of the Eye: Michael Herr and Gloria Emerson and the Art of Observation," *Papers on Language and Literature*, 29, no. 1 (1993): 28–48;

Evelyn Cobley, "Narrating the Facts of War: New Journalism in Herr's *Dispatches* and Documentary Realism in First World War Novels," *Journal of Narrative Technique*, 16, no. 2 (1986): 97–116;

David Eason, "The New Journalism and the Image World: Two Modes of Organizing Experi-

ence," *Critical Studies in Mass Communication*, 1 (1984): 51–65;

John Hellmann, "The Hero Seeks a Way Out," in *American Myth and the Legacy of Vietnam* (New York: Columbia University Press, 1986), pp. 150–160;

Hellmann, "The New Journalism and Vietnam: Memory as Structure in Michael Herr's *Dispatches*," *South Atlantic Quarterly*, 79 (1980): 141–151;

Dale W. Jones, "The Vietnams of Michael Herr and Tim O'Brien: Tales of Disintegration and Integration," *Canadian Review of American Studies*, 13, no. 3 (1982): 309–320;

John Le Carre, *Critic*, 37 (July 1978): 4–5;

John Limon, *Writing After War* (Oxford: Oxford University Press, 1994);

Thomas Myers, "The Writer as Alchemist," in his *Walking Point: American Narratives of Vietnam* (Oxford: Oxford University Press, 1988), pp. 146–171;

John Clark Pratt, panelist, audiotape, *Back in the World: Writing After Vietnam* (New York: American Arts Project, 1984);

Donald J. Ringnalda, "Michael Herr," in *A Sourcebook of American Literary Journalism: Representative Writers in an Emerging Genre*, edited by Thomas B. Connery (Westport: Greenwood Press, 1992), pp. 281–295;

Ringnalda, "Michael Herr's Spectral Journalism," in his *Fighting and Writing the Vietnam War* (Jackson: University Press of Mississippi, 1994), pp. 71–89;

Roger Sale, "Hurled into Vietnam," *New York Review of Books* (8 December 1977): 34–35;

Matthew C. Stewart, "Style in *Dispatches*: Heteroglossia and Michael Herr's Break with Conventional Journalism," in *America Rediscovered: Critical Essays on Literature and Film of the Vietnam War*, edited by Owen W. Gilman Jr. and Lorrie Smith (New York: Garland, 1990), pp. 189–204;

Peter Stoicheff, "The Chaos of Metafiction," in *Chaos and Order*, edited by N. Katherine Hayles (Chicago: University of Chicago Press, 1991);

Marshall Van Deusen, "The Unspeakable Language of Life and Death in Michael Herr's *Dispatches*," *Critique: Studies in Contemporary Fiction*, 24, no. 2 (1983): 82–87.

John Hersey

(17 June 1914 – 24 March 1993)

Dan R. Jones
University of Houston

See also the Hersey entry in *DLB 6: American Novelists Since World War II, Second Series.*

BOOKS: *Men on Bataan* (New York: Knopf, 1942);
Into the Valley (New York: Knopf, 1943);
A Bell for Adano (New York: Knopf, 1944);
Hiroshima (New York: Knopf, 1946; Harmondsworth, U.K.: Penguin, 1946);
The Wall (New York: Knopf, 1950);
The Marmot Drive (New York: Knopf, 1953; London: Hamish Hamilton, 1953);
A Single Pebble (New York: Knopf, 1956);
The War Lover (New York: Knopf, 1959);
The Child Buyer (New York: Knopf, 1960);
Here to Stay (London: Hamish Hamilton, 1962; New York: Knopf, 1963);
White Lotus (New York: Knopf, 1965; London: Hamish Hamilton, 1965);
Too Far to Walk (New York: Knopf, 1966);
Under the Eye of the Storm (New York: Knopf, 1967);
The Algiers Motel Incident (New York: Knopf, 1968; London: Hamish Hamilton, 1968);
A Letter to the Alumni (New York: Knopf, 1970);
The Conspiracy (New York: Knopf, 1972);
My Petition for More Space (New York: Knopf, 1974; London: Hamish Hamilton, 1975);
The President (New York: Knopf, 1975);
The Walnut Door (New York: Knopf, 1977);
Aspects of the Presidency (New Haven, Conn.: Ticknor & Fields, 1980);
The Call (New York: Knopf, 1985);
Hiroshima: A New Edition with a Final Chapter Written Forty Years after the Explosion (New York: Knopf, 1985);
Blues (New York: Knopf, 1987);
Life Sketches (New York: Knopf, 1989);
Fling and Other Stories (New York: Knopf, 1990);
Antonietta (New York: Knopf, 1991);
Key West Tales (New York: Knopf, 1994).

OTHER: *Ralph Ellison: A Collection of Critical Essays,* edited by Hersey, Twentieth Century Views

John Hersey (photograph by Richard de Combray)

Series (Englewood Cliffs, N.J.: Prentice-Hall, 1974);
The Writer's Craft, edited by Hersey (New York: Knopf, 1974).

SELECTED PERIODICAL PUBLICATIONS–UNCOLLECTED: "The Battle of the River," *Life* (23 November 1942): 99–116;
"AMGOT at Work," *Life* (23 August 1943): 29–31;
"Engineers of the Soul," *Time* (9 October 1944): 99–102;
"Dialogue on Gorki Street," *Fortune* (January 1945): 149–151;

"Kamikaze," *Life* (30 July 1945): 68–75;

"A Reporter at Large. Long Haul with Variables," *New Yorker* (8 September 1945): 44–57;

"Letter from Shanghai," *New Yorker* (9 February 1946): 82–90;

"Letter from Chungking," *New Yorker* (16 March 1946): 80–87;

"The Death of Buchan Walsh," *Atlantic Monthly* (April 1946): 80–86;

"Letter from Peiping," *New Yorker* (4 May 1946): 86–96;

"A Reporter in China. Two Weeks' Water Away," *New Yorker* (18 May 1946): 59–69; (25 May 1946): 54–69;

"The Pen," *Atlantic Monthly* (June 1946): 84–87;

"A Reporter at Large. The Communization of Crow Village," *New Yorker* (27 July 1946): 38–47;

"Red Pepper Village," *Life* (26 August 1946): 92–105;

"A Fable South of Cancer," *'47–The Magazine of the Year* (April 1947): 113–141;

"Alternatives to Apathy," *United Nations World,* 1 (May 1947): 20–21, 70–76;

"A Short Wait," *New Yorker* (14 June 1947): 27–29;

"The Novel of Contemporary History," *Atlantic Monthly* (November 1949): 80–84;

"The Mechanics of a Novel," *Yale University Library Gazette,* 27 (July 1952): 1–11;

"Test of Heart and Mind," *Life* (4 September 1964): 62–64;

"The Legend on the License," *Yale Review,* 20, no. 1 (Autumn 1980): 1–25;

"A Reporter at Large. Homecoming," *New Yorker* (10 May 1982): 49–79; (17 May 1982): 46–70; (24 May 1982): 44–66; (31 May 1982): 47–67;

"A Reporter at Large. Assymetry," *New Yorker* (7 September 1987): 36–53.

John Hersey, the author of more than a dozen novels as well as many sketches, commentaries, articles, and essays, has a well-earned reputation as one of America's most important novelists of the post–World War II period, but it is his work as a journalist that comprises his most significant legacy to American literature of the second half of the twentieth century. In particular, his nonfiction account of the atomic bombing of Hiroshima in 1945, which awakened America to the human consequences of nuclear warfare, is significant both as a literary accomplishment and as a cultural event. *Hiroshima,* first published in August 1946 and reissued in 1985 with an update on the fates of its characters, is often cited as a seminal example of the nonfiction novel in America, a predecessor of the genre later developed and refined by Truman Capote, Tom Wolfe, and other so-called New Journalists. Hersey's account of the lives of six survivors of the world's first atomic bombing of a major city helped America take its first halting steps toward coming to terms with the significance of what it had done to end World War II.

John Richard Hersey was born 17 June 1914 in Tientsin, China, the youngest son of Roscoe and Grace Baird Hersey, who had come to China in 1905 as YMCA missionaries during the great "Social Gospel" wave of the late nineteenth and early twentieth centuries. Hersey attended British and American schools in China until 1925 when his father became ill with encephalitis during a trip on a mule cart through a famine-stricken region of China, forcing the family to return to the United States to seek medical treatment. Hersey's father eventually died from the illness, and Hersey later struggled to come to terms with the significance of the family's sacrifice to a cause that he had come to view in morally ambiguous terms.

Hersey entered Yale in 1932 and worked as a writer on the *Yale Daily News.* He played football under the direction of a recent Yale graduate and rookie coach, Gerald Ford, whom Hersey met again nearly forty years later in the Oval Office while gathering material for a book on the presidency. Following his graduation in 1936 Hersey studied English literature at Cambridge University for a year, returning to work as Sinclair Lewis's secretary during the summer of 1937. Claiming never to know of Lewis's serious problems with alcohol, Hersey found the older writer charming, entertaining, and eccentric, although the manuscripts that Lewis gave Hersey to edit revealed that Lewis's talent was waning.

Hersey joined the staff of *Time* in the fall of 1937, the magazine he later described as "the liveliest enterprise of its type," according to David Sanders in *John Hersey* (1967). Hersey and Henry R. Luce, publisher of *Time,* formed an instant bond based in part on the fact that though nearly a generation apart in age, both were children of American missionaries to China. Luce appreciated Hersey's understanding of Chinese culture and in 1939 sent him to the magazine's Chungking bureau, providing Hersey a platform from which to watch the war in the Pacific unfold.

Luce enforced both literary and political uniformity on his writers, strictures that ultimately led to Hersey's split with his employer. Much of what Hersey contributed to *Time* and *Life* during these early years, from 1939 to 1942, consisted of unsigned dispatches gathered from his own observations and contributions from contract stringers, including Theodore White, then a recent Harvard

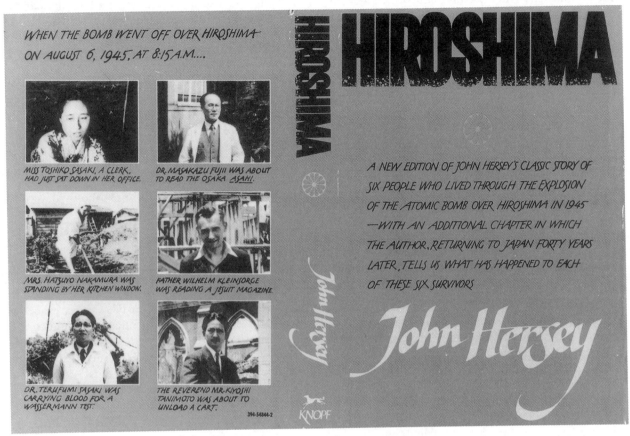

WHEN THE BOMB WENT OFF OVER HIROSHIMA ON AUGUST 6, 1945, AT 8:15 A.M...

MISS TOSHIKO SASAKI, A CLERK, HAD JUST SAT DOWN IN HER OFFICE.

DR. MASAKAZU FUJII WAS ABOUT TO READ THE OSAKA *ASAHI*.

MRS. HATSUYO NAKAMURA WAS STANDING BY HER KITCHEN WINDOW.

FATHER WILHELM KLEINSORGE WAS READING A JESUIT MAGAZINE.

DR. TERUFUMI SASAKI WAS CARRYING BLOOD FOR A WASSERMANN TEST.

THE REVEREND MR. KIYOSHI TANIMOTO WAS ABOUT TO UNLOAD A CART.

HIROSHIMA

A NEW EDITION OF JOHN HERSEY'S CLASSIC STORY OF SIX PEOPLE WHO LIVED THROUGH THE EXPLOSION OF THE ATOMIC BOMB OVER HIROSHIMA IN 1945 —WITH AN ADDITIONAL CHAPTER IN WHICH THE AUTHOR, RETURNING TO JAPAN FORTY YEARS LATER, TELLS US WHAT HAS HAPPENED TO EACH OF THESE SIX SURVIVORS

John Hersey

KNOPF

Dust jacket for the updated edition of Hersey's best-known work

graduate in Chinese studies whom Hersey had recruited. Hersey's dispatches presented straightforward and candid accounts of Japanese military advances during the early months of the war, although his work was often blended, according to Sanders in *John Hersey Revisited* (1990), with the work of other writers into general reports and "grave summaries" by the editorial staff at *Time*.

Returning to New York in 1942, Hersey combed the files at *Time* and *Life,* searching for information to expand his understanding of the rapidly developing military situation in the Philippines. He interviewed other correspondents as well as returned servicemen and their families and compiled this material in his first nonfiction book, *Men on Bataan,* published in July 1942. Compared with his later work, Hersey's first piece of extended nonfiction is amateurish and unrefined. An unapologetic celebration of the toughness, dedication, and resilience of American troops in general and Gen. Douglas MacArthur in particular, *Men on Bataan* was a critical success despite its flaws and secured Hersey's reputation as a promising young writer. Reviewing the book in *The New Yorker,* Clifton Fadiman described Hersey's writing as heroic poetry

and praised Hersey for presenting soldiers as vital living creatures rather than as anonymous battlefield statistics. Fletcher Pratt's review in the *Saturday Review* is particularly interesting for its observations regarding Hersey's synthesis of personal experience and objective journalism, signaling that even at this early stage in his career Hersey was exploring the literary potential of combining the techniques of fiction with the substance of fact.

As Hersey's political liberalism sharpened in later years he regretted having written *Men on Bataan* and asked his publisher to delete it from the list of his published works, claiming, as Sanders noted in *John Hersey Revisited,* that it was "too adulatory of MacArthur." Nonetheless, the book is a prelude to the journalistic style and reportorial stance Hersey refined in later works. Hersey begins the book with a clear statement of purpose: "This book proposes, in the interests of perspective, to understate the General. It will lay some of his myths to rest, and wherever the authenticity of accepted stories is questionable, they will be labeled as legends." Hersey's penchant for understatement became a defining element of his literary journalism; he never placed more weight on his facts than he thought they could bear. Hersey chose subjects that were deeply moral and often complex, yet his purpose in dealing with them was less to render judgment than to explore their human dimensions.

Men on Bataan furnishes early signs of how Hersey translated this journalistic principle into practice. His portrait of MacArthur as an American military hero is carefully balanced by somewhat less-than-flattering details about the general's West Point days, where he was viewed as an overachiever and something of a prig by his classmates, and by other mildly embarrassing facts about his personal and professional life. Hersey's characterization of MacArthur is intended, therefore, not to provide the hero of a war story but to humanize an important public figure known hitherto only as a series of images attached to events.

Hersey also provides brief sketches of various military personnel he had encountered in the field, the men of *Men on Bataan*. The sketches serve no real narrative or ideological purpose; they are included because they provide a sense of the human substance that lies behind popular images of the war. Always suspicious that his presence in the narrative might constitute a violation of journalistic integrity, Hersey nonetheless allows himself the privilege of a first-person introduction of his subjects, as in these opening lines of a sketch of an army chaplain: "I think you ought to meet Chaplain Brown. He was from Seattle." This introduction is followed by biographical details that are interesting not as pieces of a wartime narrative but simply for their own sake: "His grandfather crossed the plains to the great Northwest by oxcart in 1852 and later became a saddle-back preacher, traveling from place to place carrying the mail and preaching the gospel."

In addition to people, Hersey's sources for *Men on Bataan* are documents: speeches, letters, memoranda, reports, and other official and unofficial records of the war. He quotes from these texts at length, complete with misusages and grammatical flaws. His practice gives the book a documentary texture and anchors his observations and descriptions in objective source material. This documentary "feel" underscores Hersey's unswerving allegiance to factual authenticity in his literary journalism. By including actual documents Hersey enriches the historical record and makes his work a text of the war.

Following the publication of *Men on Bataan* Hersey returned to the Pacific theater, spending time aboard the carrier *Hornet,* where his interviews with pilots yielded material for several dispatches for *Time* and, later, a novel. From there he went to Guadalcanal, where he was assigned to cover the campaign to capture the Solomon Islands, part of the American counteroffensive to turn back the Japanese invasion of the Pacific.

On 8 October 1942 Hersey accompanied a company of U.S. Marines as they engaged in a "small skirmish" on Guadalcanal, part of a larger effort to secure a line of defense around Henderson Field, a jungle airbase that had been built by the Japanese and captured by the Americans. *Into the Valley,* published in February 1943, is his account of that experience. As in *Men on Bataan, Into the Valley* strives for understatement. Far from being a celebration of a just cause, Hersey's brief account describes a mission that, in his words, "was to be doomed before it got very far under way." In fact, Hersey declares, "if I had had any understanding of what Company H might meet, I never would have gone along." As the marines slowly move toward their objective, sniper shots ring out, and the tension in the air becomes palpable. Hersey's subject is not the details of a military action but the thoughts and emotions that accompany battle. In such an environment life is reduced to its barest terms: "Here in the jungle a marine killed because he must, or be killed. He stalked the enemy, and the enemy stalked him, as if each were a hunter tracking a bear cat."

As the day progresses the group encounters more Japanese mortar and sniper fire; almost simultaneously, communication with the company with which they were to coordinate their movements breaks down. After many strained moments the order to withdraw is passed back through the line, and the objective of the mission changes from victory to survival. Hersey assists in the task of retrieving the dead, near-dead, and wounded and closes the book with an account of a farewell conversation he has with the members of the company, each of whom gives him instructions on the favors he is to do for them when he returns to the United States.

Into the Valley received uniform praise, including a favorable comparison to Stephen Crane's *The Red Badge of Courage* (1895) and a declaration that Hersey was "a new Hemingway" by *The New York Times. Publishers Weekly* reported that the book had been designated "Imperative Reading" by the Council on Books in Wartime and that it was being vigorously promoted by its publisher to libraries and bookstores. Hersey received a commendation from the secretary of the navy for assisting those wounded in the battle. Although it appeared within months of *Men on Bataan, Into the Valley* is nonetheless a considerably more sophisticated example of literary journalism. Still supportive of the American war effort, it is driven less by patriotic impulse than by the immediacy of human experience. It confirms that Hersey's journalistic gift was his ability to make humans, not events, the basis for journalistic texts.

Hersey continued to write dispatches and short feature articles for *Time* and *Life,* having earned sufficient recognition to merit frequent by-lines. For one of these projects Hersey spent time with Maj. Frank E. Toscani, the military governor of Licata, Sicily, following the island's liberation by the Allies. The citizens of Licata told Toscani that the symbol of their community, a church bell, had been taken by the Nazis and melted down to provide metal for armaments. Toscani helped locate and secure a replacement bell from a navy destroyer and earned a place in the folklore of the village.

Hersey's sketch of Toscani and the village appeared in the 23 August 1943 issue of *Life,* titled "AMGOT at Work"; AMGOT is the acronym for Allied Military Government Occupied Territory. Hersey expanded and fictionalized the tale and published it as *A Bell for Adano* in 1944. Licata became the fictional village of Adano, and Toscani became Maj. Victor Joppolo, described in the novel as "a good man, though weak in certain attractive, human ways." Presumably it was one of these attractive human weaknesses—Joppolo's affair with a young Italian woman—that led Toscani to sue Hersey for libel. The suit was dropped after Hersey and Toscani met for dinner at a New York restaurant named for the novel.

A Bell for Adano received wide critical praise and won the Pulitzer Prize for fiction in 1945. Malcolm Cowley, reviewing the novel for *New Republic,* compared Hersey favorably with Ernest Hemingway and John Steinbeck; several reviewers praised the book for its rich depiction of the elements of human community. Other critics, however, were less comfortable with Hersey's fictionalization of actual people and events. Diana Trilling, writing in *The Nation,* charged that Hersey engaged in "conscious falsifying and purposeful simplification" of his subjects, casting doubt on the integrity of the book's ideas. Some felt that the novel drew too heavily on sentiment and emotion, causing Hersey to overlook fundamental moral questions surrounding the war. None of these concerns detracted from the popular appeal of the book, which was made into a play and a successful motion picture in 1945.

Sanders, author of the first book-length work on Hersey, has characterized Hersey's wartime writing as the work of a "man who had had to write too much too soon." Much the same could be said of many correspondents assigned to cover World War II for whom the demands of wartime reporting, both political and journalistic, dictated the production of supportive, morally unambiguous chronicles of the

Dust jacket for Hersey's collection of essays about survivors of disasters

war effort. Hersey's journalism of this period was intended to reinforce, rather than interpret, the images and understandings of the war his readers had gathered from a variety of popular sources. Had he not encountered a subject worthy of challenging and expanding his abilities both as a journalist and literary stylist, he likely would be remembered primarily as one of a host of correspondents who translated their experiences and perceptions into popular yet transitory accounts of the war.

By 1945, although still a correspondent for *Time* and *Life,* Hersey began to sense that his interests and ambitions were leading him to pursue projects that lay beyond Luce's control. He traveled to China and Japan in September 1945 on assignment for both *Life* and *The New Yorker.* It was an unusual arrangement that provided him an outlet for material that may not have fit Luce's editorial expectations; that freedom, plus the lifting of wartime military censorship, provided the conditions for a highly productive phase in Hersey's writing career. One of the more interesting products of this period was the result of a visit to his hometown of Tientsin, where he struggled to make sense of the changes that had come to China. "Red Pepper Village," a description of life in a Chinese communal village, appeared in the 26 August 1946 issue of *Life.* As in much of his literary journalism Hersey's article seems prompted by a quest for explanations but ultimately becomes a detailed sketch focusing on human beings and the communities that give their lives significance.

The idea for Hersey's most celebrated work of literary journalism, *Hiroshima,* published in 1946, emerged from a discussion with *The New Yorker* editor William Shawn. Hersey and Shawn agreed that a thoughtful and compelling article could be built around a first-person account of the condition of the devastated city and its people based on Hersey's own observations and punctuated by interviews with survivors of the blast. Hersey read all that he could find that might give him insight into the event and its consequences. One of these documents, the *Jesuit Report to the Holy See,* was a report by the Jesuit order in Hiroshima detailing the damage the mission had suffered and describing its plans for rebuilding. Hersey traveled to Tokyo to interview the author of the report, Father Wilhelm Kleinsorge, who was in a hospital recovering from radiation sickness.

Father Kleinsorge introduced Hersey to several other bomb blast survivors: the Reverend Mr. Kiyoshi Tanimoto, minister of the Hiroshima Methodist Church; Miss Toshiko Sasaki, a young clerk in the East Asia Tin Works; and Dr. Terufumi Sasaki, a young surgical resident at Hiroshima's Red Cross Hospital. In all, Hersey interviewed thirty atomic blast survivors for the project, choosing these four and two others—Dr. Masakazu Fujii, a physician in private practice; and Mrs. Hatsuyo Nakamura, a tailor's war widow—as subjects for his book. Although Kleinsorge and Tanimoto spoke English, interviews with the other sources required the assistance of an interpreter. Hersey realized that differences of language and culture would present obstacles to a full understanding of the event, both for himself and for his readers. He responded in a manner which by now had become characteristic of his literary journalism: focusing on the immediate actualities of human experience as reported to him by the firsthand participants of the event he was chronicling. The result is an unadorned narrative which draws its considerable power from understatement.

The basic narrative structure of the book is chronological: the account opens a few hours before the bombing and closes almost exactly one year later. The chronological scheme provides a simple, easily conceived frame for guiding the reader's perceptions. Hersey achieves a sense of authenticity by adopting an almost clinical tone in his prose. Missing from *Hiroshima* are the moral reflections of *Into the Valley* and *A Bell for Adano;* in their place are spare and meticulously documented details gleaned from close observation and careful research. The exact location of the center of the blast, for example, is identified as "a spot a hundred and fifty yards south of the torii and a few yards southeast of the pile of ruins that had once been the Shima Hospital." Although this fact is of little interpretive value, it helps establish a quantifiable context within which the reader may view this otherwise incomprehensible event; precise description becomes an instrument of comprehensibility.

The six survivors Hersey chose as his subjects are decidedly unrepresentative of the general population of Hiroshima. For example, Hiroshima, with its population of 250,000, had only 150 doctors; two of these appear in *Hiroshima.* Likewise, even though Christians numbered fewer than 1 percent of predominantly Buddhist and Shintoist wartime Japan, two of Hersey's subjects are Christian clergymen. Yet the very qualities that make Hersey's survivors atypical of Japanese culture also make them recognizable and even sympathetic to American readers. Hersey's choice of subjects is thus consistent with the book's basic agenda: to provide a frame for comprehending the incomprehensible reality of the atomic bomb blast. Because Hersey's nonfiction novel is populated with figures who, though Japanese, nonetheless conform to American social types, the characters become guides to understanding the event.

The survivors' attempts to comprehend the function and effects of the bomb and their uncertain progress toward that end trace an important narrative movement in the book in which readers participate. Rumors abound, such as the theory that the destruction was the result of gasoline or magnesium dust sprinkled over the city and then ignited; an exact understanding is never achieved. Although technical explanations were available to Hersey, he does not include them. Rather, he allows the bomb to remain ultimately inexplicable since that is how it appeared to the characters in his book.

In addition to locating figures who adequately symbolized the reality of the atomic bomb blast, Hersey was faced with the task of translating Japanese culture into a vocabulary familiar to Western sensibilities. He does this by choosing as settings for the book institutions common to both Japanese and American cultures: churches, banks, a police station, a lower-middle-class home, hospitals, and doctors' offices. When he can, Hersey describes Japanese life by using terms familiar to Americans; Hiroshima's outlying residential districts, for example, are referred to as "suburbs." When no adequate terms exist for describing a uniquely Japanese custom or institution, it is labeled an oddity and explained, often in detail. Dr. Fujii's single-doctor hospital is described as "a peculiarly Japanese institution;" an explanation of Japanese customs for ministering to the sick follows. The city of Hiroshima thereby assumes a quality of everyday life that readers may associate with their own lives. Hersey's journalistic agenda is thus not only to report the facts of the event but also to accommodate the habits and needs of his American readers by providing a perceptual frame within which the event assumes significance.

In 1985 Hersey published a fifth chapter to *Hiroshima* in which he documents the fates of the six survivors. Two–Dr. Fujii and Father Kleinsorge–have died, while the others have encountered various fortunes and misfortunes. Dr. Sasaki, the idealistic young surgeon who worked tirelessly in the days following the initial blast to care for the wounded and dying, has become wealthy, while Mr. Tanimoto, the equally selfless Methodist minister, has met with mixed success and much disappointment in his efforts to teach the world about the horrors of the atomic bomb. The updated accounts bring the reader no closer to a comprehensive moral understanding of the bomb, and Hersey skillfully avoids using the new stories to bring narrative closure to the original text. To do so would violate his original journalistic agenda: to translate the reality of the bomb into terms salient to Western habits of mind while declining either to justify or condemn its use. The true achievement of *Hiroshima,* then, and that which sets it apart from Hersey's earlier writing, is that its journalistic credibility is not diminished by the injection of moralistic sentiment.

Hiroshima was widely read and generously praised. Albert Einstein reportedly ordered a thousand copies that he distributed personally; newspapers throughout America sought rights to serialize the book. Hersey agreed but accepted no payment in return, requiring instead that the newspapers contribute to the American Red Cross. The book prompted an editorial in *The New York Times* calling attention to its publication, and Lewis Gannett, writing for the *New York Herald Tribune,* characterized *Hiroshima* as "the best reporting" of the war. Some critics felt that Hersey should have used the book to make a stronger statement against nuclear weapons. Hersey's own views toward the bomb notwithstanding, the publication of *Hiroshima* marked the beginning of a decades-long discussion concerning the moral significance of the bomb. Murray Sayle, writing in *The New Yorker* fifty years after the blast, noted that *Hiroshima* "broke more than a year's silence" by the American press on the subject of the bomb.

Hiroshima also marked the end of Hersey's association with Luce. Claiming to be angry that Hersey had chosen to publish *Hiroshima* in *The New Yorker* rather than *Time* or *Life,* Luce was actually far more disturbed by what he perceived to be the book's pacifist message and made it clear that Hersey would no longer be contributing to Luce publications.

Following the publication of *Hiroshima,* Hersey turned his attention to fiction, producing a series of novels during the 1950s, including the highly acclaimed *The Wall* (1950), which describes conditions in the Warsaw ghetto during the German occupation. *Here to Stay,* first published in London in 1962, was Hersey's next venture into literary journalism. The book is a collection of nine tales of survival–from war, natural disasters, concentration camps, and other extreme situations. The complete text of *Hiroshima* is included as the last piece. The stories are collected from a variety of sources. Some are products of Hersey's World War II experiences, such as "Joe Is Home Now" and "A Short Talk with Erlanger," both of which address the problems of returning war veterans. Other stories in the collection were included because they typified for Hersey the theme of survival. An example is the first story in the collection, "Over the Mad River," which chronicles the experiences of an elderly survivor of the floodwaters spawned by Hurricane Diane in Connecticut in 1955.

Hersey opens his preface to the 1988 edition of *Here to Stay* with the following statement: "The great themes are love and death; their synthesis is the will to live." The statement not only provides a unifying theme for the stories in the collection, but also may offer some insight into Hersey's motivations as a writer of nonfiction. Also in the preface he writes:

> I could wish that a great secret could have been embedded in these tales, so that a reader could unriddle it between the lines–a clear answer of some kind to the most mysterious of all questions, the existential question: What is it that, by a narrow margin, keeps humankind going, in the face of its crimes, its follies, its greed, its passions, its sorrows, its panics, its hatreds, its hideous drives to pollute and waste and dominate and kill?

The stories provide no final answers. While claiming to remain faithful to the factual demands of journalism, Hersey imbues his tales with a parable-like

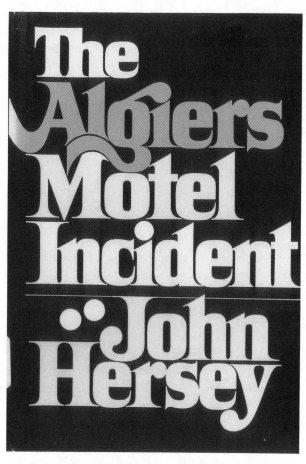

Dust jacket for Hersey's account of the murders of three young black men during the Detroit riots in 1967

quality consistent with the thematic character of fiction.

The Algiers Motel Incident (1968), an account of the murders of three young black men during the Detroit riots of 1967, was Hersey's next attempt at extended literary journalism. The book consists of carefully transcribed interviews with witnesses to the shooting, family members of the dead, the police and legal authorities involved in the shooting, and a host of secondary figures. There are also court transcripts, media accounts, and other official records, all linked by Hersey's narrative. While presenting a tremendous amount of data about the shootings, the book suffers from some flaws, not the least of which is Hersey's appearance in the narrative. Unlike *Hiroshima,* in which the narrator does not appear, and *Here to Stay,* in which he appears only in the preface and introductions to individual stories, Hersey enters directly into the telling of *The Algiers Motel Incident.* Early in the text he explains that while he has always "stayed out of my journalism" as a matter of principle, "this account is too urgent, too complex, too dangerous to too many people to be told in a

way that might leave doubts strewn along its path." Presumably, Hersey is freeing himself to make judgments on the facts he presents, but this rationale does not justify Hersey's failure to recognize the moral complexity of the tale. His blame for the police involved in the shooting is unequivocal; their victims were guilty, he says, of no more than "being, after all and all, black young men and part of the black rage of the time"—despite the fact, as *Atlantic* reviewer Edward Weeks observed, that most had police records, and all "had a cynical contempt for the legal process."

Such behavior hardly warrants murder, of course, and Hersey's moral judgments may have been correct, if only in a legal sense. Yet the book was published long before the legal issues in the case had been settled, and in any event, credible literary journalism must do more than assign blame. Hersey was unable to accomplish in *The Algiers Motel Incident* what he could do in both *Hiroshima* and *Here to Stay:* the conversion of a set of factual incidents into true-to-life parables of survival and endurance. *The Algiers Motel Incident* is presented as a parable of race relations and the malignant effects of prejudice, but the victims are not sufficiently ennobling, nor are the perpetrators sufficiently malicious, to reduce the tale to these terms. Ironically, it may be Hersey's integrity as a journalist that prevents *The Algiers Motel Incident* from being a more compelling story. Hersey was driven to uncover every scrap of available data in his quest for the truth behind the murders at the Algiers Motel, yet the circumstances and issues of the case he revealed turned out to be too complex to fit the parable-like narrative he seems to have envisioned for the book.

Hersey wrote *The Algiers Motel Incident* while serving as master of Pierson College at Yale, a post he held from 1965 to 1970. He continued to teach techniques of fiction and nonfiction at Yale for many years. Throughout his career he was active in various educational and writers' organizations and actively supported various liberal causes. In 1965 he was a sponsor of a march in Washington in protest of the Vietnam War.

In 1975 Hersey was invited to spend a week with President Gerald Ford, his former football coach at Yale. The invitation was intended to demonstrate the unelected president's commitment to openness and candor, although it is doubtful that Ford and his first press secretary, Jerald terHorst, would have conceived this somewhat unusual arrangement had they not been prompted by Jack Rosenthal, Sunday editor of *The New York Times,* soon after the president had been sworn in. The idea lay dormant for several months until Rosenthal suggested it again to Ron Nessen, terHorst's successor, in early December 1974. Rosenthal and Nessen worked out a set of understandings for the assignment: the president would make the final decision over who was chosen and would also be responsible for setting ground rules. Hersey was nominated for the assignment and met with Ford in early February.

The dates of the visit were 10–15 March 1975, a week Hersey describes as "typical" for the president. It was a week that witnessed no history-making events or decisions, although events in Southeast Asia and the need for tracking important bills in Congress made it a busy one for Ford. Hersey's perennial journalistic concern, that his presence at or participation in events upon which he was reporting might affect their outcomes, turned out to be baseless. As he writes in *The President* (1975):

I was fearful that my mere presence might distort the discussions in the Oval Office, just as a known electronic bug might; but after the first day or so I felt I had been absorbed into the furniture. Sometimes the President would explain my presence to strangers; more often I think I was taken for a staffer whose job it apparently was to keep scribbling madly in an effort to record all Oval Office transactions, now that the infamous tapes were no longer being made.

Hersey employs familiar techniques in the book. As in *Hiroshima*, he records events chronologically; as in *The Algiers Motel Incident*, he provides actual clock times to mark the occurrence of incidents, both large and small: meetings with visiting heads of state, a reception for the Cotton Queen, the entrance of staff members into the Oval Office, departures for luncheons and official events, even early morning exercise routines and dental appointments. As in all of his literary journalism, Hersey's concern is with the immediacy of human experience; thus, we learn not only when the president eats lunch each day but also what he has: a scoop of cottage cheese topped with A-1 Steak Sauce, followed by a small dish of butter pecan ice cream. While such details help to humanize the president, Hersey also reports on more significant events, including high-level discussions involving the military situation in Cambodia, agricultural price supports, and civil rights legislation; discussions with presidential advisors, including Henry Kissinger, Donald Rumsfeld, and Brent Scowcroft, are transcribed, largely without comment or interpretation.

While far from Hersey's best work, *The President* is interesting for the narrative stance he assumes. Hersey avoids the temptation to position himself as a political sage who has been granted a rare privilege. Rather, he becomes the reader's stand-in, a journalistic Everyman whose questions and perceptions are likely to be those of his readers, as in the following description of the emotions he experiences while standing alone in the Oval Office:

Re-entering the Oval Office alone, I feel its great force. This room is an egg of light. I have seen that each person who comes into it is lit up in two senses: bathed in brightness and a bit high. . . . there are dazzling parabolas of power here; authority seems to be diffused as an aspect of the artificial light in the room, and each person who comes into this heady glow seems to be rendered ever so slightly tipsy in it and by it—people familiar with the room far less so, of course, than first-time visitors, some of whom visibly goggle and stagger and hold on tight as they make their appeals[.]

Reviews of *The President* were lukewarm. While the book was praised for its narrative craftsmanship, some critics wondered whether Hersey should not have used his rare opportunity to spend a week with the president to probe more incisively into the inner workings of the White House or to challenge Ford's political positions. Ultimately, *The President* demonstrates that Hersey's strength as a journalist lay not in his investigatory skills but in his powers of observation.

In 1982 Hersey published a series of four articles in *The New Yorker* about his return to Tientsin, his first return trip to China since 1946. The articles, appearing under the heading "A Reporter at Large. Homecoming," constitute a personal travelogue mixing history, culture, and reportage with reminiscence. As Hersey wanders about the city of his youth he searches for reminders of his childhood and occasionally finds them. Familiar environments have changed, partly from the passage of time, more often as a result of political and cultural upheaval. Hersey seeks out his childhood home and is excited to find it still standing. His nostalgic discovery quickly turns to disappointment, however, when he finds that it is now occupied by twenty-four people. "I felt as if I had seen a cosmos compressed into my old home," he writes; the room in which he was born was now occupied by an entire family.

"I suppose we all lose our childhoods," Hersey observes, "But now I suddenly felt . . . as if my whole childhood had been unfairly and violently snatched away from me." Hersey's sense of psychological dislocation provides a frame for his reportage. As he tours the city, tracking down old family acquaintances or, more often, their descendants, he engages in a gentle reexamination of the political and cultural circumstances that led to his parents' decision to become missionaries and the effect of

ALFRED KNOPF AND JOHN HERSEY, 1973

ISBN 0-394-57784-1

Dust jacket for Hersey's last nonfiction collection

that decision on his own sensibilities. At first repulsed by the changes that have come to his hometown, Hersey comes to realize how sheltered his childhood had been and how protected he and his European playmates had been from the harsh realities of Chinese life. His experience becomes an emblem of the problems Americans face in trying to grasp cultural and political realities that lie beyond the boundaries of their own experience. Through an engaging mixture of observation and introspection Hersey suggests that if the reader hopes to understand the subtle and complex changes that have come to Tientsin, to China, and to the world, he or she would do well to begin by surrendering deeply held yet obsolete perceptions and understandings.

Though primarily a practitioner, Hersey occasionally theorized on the nature of literary journalism. At Yale he taught courses in creative writing, dealing in alternate semesters with fiction and journalism. In an article titled "The Novel of Contemporary History," which appeared in the November 1949 issue of the *Atlantic Monthly,* he defends the use of literature as a "clarifying agent" for the chronicling of world events and says that fiction may be a more effective instrument for understanding history

than is history writing itself. Further, Hersey identifies the qualities that the writer of historical novels should possess, including a need for understanding, a desire for communication, "anger," and a "will for world citizenship." The essay reveals more about Hersey's attitude toward the handling of fact than he perhaps intends; it is his self-conscious attempt to demonstrate anger, for example, that makes *The Algiers Motel Incident* an ultimately unsatisfactory account of a historically significant event.

Hersey's headnotes to the individual stories in *Here to Stay* offer additional insights into his practices and beliefs as a nonfiction writer. He includes in almost every headnote a statement of how the information for the particular piece was gathered as proof of its authenticity. For example, at the beginning of "Flight," a story about a family of Hungarian refugees following the 1956 suppression of Hungary, he includes the following statement: "I became acquainted with the Fekete family in Austria, at a teeming refugee camp, a few days after the family's eruption from its homeland, and it was there that the gaunt paterfamilias told me most of this story; I lived parts of its last chapters with him." Similar statements of Hersey's fact-gathering technique appear in the headnotes to most of the stories, assuring the reader that the fictional quality of the tales included in the collection should not be considered inconsistent with the journalistic integrity of the facts they present.

In the headnote to the section "Strength from Without" Hersey offers a further defense of his literary handling of factual material, in this case, his creation of composite characters and situations in the stories "Joe Is Home Now" and "A Short Talk with Erlanger." "Something needs to be said about the reportorial technique used in this story and the one that follows," Hersey writes, adding that his technique in these two stories is different from that used in the "orthodox journalistic tales that constitute the rest of the book." His explanation is as follows:

> These two accounts . . . are dovetailings, in each case, of the actual experiences of a number of men. . . . The story of [Joe's] struggles is not "fictionalized," because nothing was invented; it is a report. Joe does say and do things that were actually said and done by various men with whom I talked; I simply arranged the materials.

Again, Hersey demonstrates that the literary quality of his writing does not detract from its journalistic authenticity, yet the technique he is defending–the blending of composite characters and situations into a single narrative line–is not a conservative one. In general, Hersey's approach to the construction of journalistic narrative is much more traditional than the technique he employs in these two stories.

In a 1980 essay titled "The Legend on the License" Hersey declares that "Journalism is on a sickbed and is in a very bad way." The article attacks Truman Capote's *In Cold Blood* (1965) and offers stinging rebukes of Tom Wolfe for bending the rules of journalistic objectivity in *The Right Stuff* (1979) and of Norman Mailer for tampering with documentary evidence in *The Executioner's Song* (1979). Hersey concludes with what he considers a simple dictum: "The writer of fiction must invent. The journalist must not invent." Such an edict has the ring of common sense about it but does not go far toward clarifying the relationship between factual content and fictional technique that he himself employs in his best literary journalism.

Hersey's last nonfiction collection, *Life Sketches,* was published in 1989. It consists almost entirely of previously published material, much of it from early in his career. Hersey's selection is highly eclectic: profiles of John F. Kennedy and Harry S. Truman alongside those of George Van Santvoord, the headmaster of Hotchkiss School, which Hersey attended as a boy; and Pvt. John Daniel Ramey, an illiterate World War II Army recruit who learned to read and write at a special army training facility. The collection is a reminder that Hersey's journalistic talent lay in his ability to find extraordinary expressions of humanity in everyday experience, whether that experience belonged to a president or to an uneducated army private.

Although most of the stories in *Life Sketches* are products of earlier phases of Hersey's development as a literary journalist, the introduction was written especially for the volume and indicates a maturation in Hersey's views toward the relationship between journalistic factuality and fictionlike storytelling. Gone are the pronouncements of "The Legend on the License" in which he suggested that the lines between fact and fiction are absolute and not to be transgressed. In their place is a gentle observation on the mutability of human memory and perception; given these limitations, any attempt to use language to render the immediacy of human experience must inevitably be less than exact. As Hersey writes: "I feel, often, as if I am making my life sketches not with a fine pen or a sharp pencil but with a thickish piece of charcoal. The best I can hope for is that the smudged and blurred lines will lie on the page in such ways as to hint at, even if they cannot really represent, the amazingly clear pictures that I believe I have seen in my mind. " *Life Sketches* constitutes Hersey's wistful recognition that good reporting owes much of its force to good storytelling; as such, it is a tacit acknowledgment that his best work consists of the artful union of the two.

While Hersey devoted his final years primarily to fiction, the work of this period displays a masterful blending of historical fact, personal experience, and fictional form. *The Call,* published in 1985, remains for many critics his most accomplished novel. The story of an American missionary in China in the first half of the century, *The Call* is based on exhaustive historical research fueled by vivid and imaginative transformations of Hersey's own memories and experiences in what he referred to as his "natal land." The protagonist of the novel, David Treadup, is, like Hersey's own father, a YMCA "Social Gospel" missionary. Unlike the quiet and bookish Roscoe Hersey, however, Treadup is a driven man, blinded to political and cultural realities by fierce devotion to his evangelical mission. Following the outbreak of World War II, Treadup is imprisoned in a Japanese concentration camp. Deprived of the means with which to carry out his spiritual pursuit, he submits himself to a searing self-examination that reveals the complex patterns of tyranny embedded deep within the missionary impulse. As a novel *The Call* represents Hersey's most accomplished interweaving of factual content and fictional form.

Blues, published in 1987, is a curious blend of objective fact, folklore, and observations gleaned from Hersey's twenty years of fishing for bluefish along the coast of Massachusetts. Set as a series of dialogues between a seasoned fisherman and a novice identified only as "stranger," the book is a personal exploration of the author's fascination with the sea revealed in a series of dramatic revelations opened to the stranger as he learns to fish. While *Blues* can hardly be considered literary journalism, it is nonetheless an engaging concatenation of scientific data, folklore, and wisdom set in a literary frame.

Hersey's final work, *Key West Tales* (1994), was delivered to his publisher six weeks before his death in 1993. These short stories consist of imaginative recreations of life in Key West, where Hersey and his wife were part-time residents in his final years. Like some of Hersey's best literary journalism, the stories in *Key West Tales* have a fablelike quality, focusing on the compelling significance of everyday experience. In their seamless interweaving of fact and fiction one finds examples of some of Hersey's most mature writing. As a collection they display Hersey's finely honed eye for detail, his keen sense of narrative, and his shrewd understanding of the ingredients of human character.

Hersey died in Key West on 24 March 1993. He was survived by his wife, the former Barbara Kaufman, whom he married in 1958, two daughters, three sons from a previous marriage, six grandchildren, and his brother, Arthur Hersey.

Hersey's most substantial accomplishment as a literary journalist is still one of his earliest. *Hiroshima* represents Hersey's most successful blending of literary technique with journalistic content. While some reviewers criticized the book for what they took to be Hersey's lack of moral concern, *Hiroshima* is nonetheless a deeply moral text. In a *New Yorker* article commemorating the fiftieth anniversary of the dropping of the bomb Murray Sayle described Hersey's book as displaying a "realism all the more heartrending for being quietly understated." Hersey scrupulously avoids the simple moral judgments which he might have called upon to characterize the event. Consequently, the novel provides an honest and compelling account of a morally ambiguous event in a journalistically credible fashion as well as in aesthetically and dramatically effective terms. Hersey was not bothered by those who charged that his later work did not equal his earlier achievement. In 1985 Hersey remarked that some works "have had a life of their own, and some haven't and that's the way things go." Perhaps unwittingly, Hersey provided in *Hiroshima* one of the seminal examples of contemporary literary journalism.

Bibliography:

Nancy Lyman Huse, *John Hersey and James Agee: A Reference Guide* (Boston: G.K. Hall, 1978).

References:

Kelsey Guilfoil, "John Hersey: Fact and Fiction," *English Journal,* 39 (September 1950): 355–360;

Nancy Lyman Huse, *The Survival Tales of John Hersey* (Troy, N.Y.: Whitston, 1983);

David Sanders, *John Hersey* (New Haven, Conn: Yale University Press, 1967);

Sanders, *John Hersey Revisited* (Boston: Twayne, 1990);

Sanders, "John Hersey: War Correspondent into Novelist," in *New Voices in American Studies,* edited by Ray Browne (Lafayette, Ind.: Purdue University Press, 1966), pp. 49–58;

Tom Spain, "PW Interviews: John Hersey," *Publishers Weekly* (10 May 1985): 232–233;

Michael J. Yavendetti, "John Hersey and the American Conscience: The Reception of *Hiroshima,*" *Pacific Historical Review,* 43 (February 1974): 49.

Tracy Kidder
(12 November 1945 –)

David Bennett
University of Southern Mississippi

BOOKS: *The Road to Yuba City: A Journey into the Juan Corona Murders* (Garden City, N.Y.: Doubleday, 1974);
The Soul of a New Machine (Boston: Little, Brown, 1981);
House (Boston: Houghton Mifflin, 1985);
Among Schoolchildren (Boston: Houghton Mifflin, 1989);
Old Friends (Boston: Houghton Mifflin, 1993).

Four celebrated nonfiction books in a little more than a decade—*The Soul of a New Machine* (1981), *House* (1985), *Among Schoolchildren* (1989), and *Old Friends* (1993)—have propelled Tracy Kidder to rarefied heights, revealing a writer of rare intelligence and virtuosity. Not only have critics applauded each of these books, but Kidder was also awarded the Pulitzer Prize for *The Soul of a New Machine* and has been heralded as one of the most gifted voices of his generation. Since 1974, when "The Death of Major Great," Kidder's masterful short story about the horror of Vietnam, appeared in the *Atlantic Monthly,* he has often dazzled the literati, crafting exquisite narratives that ennoble and celebrate the daily activities of ordinary people and artfully weaving stories drawn from the rich milieu of common human experience.

The polished grace of Kidder's prose reminds one of Joseph Addison's prose in its unassuming elegance. Like Addison and John McPhee, his closest literary kin, Kidder writes with great warmth about the people who inhabit his books, endowing them with strength and nobility. He unearths nuggets of profound truth in seemingly mundane human endeavors; he clothes the common with dignity, exalting old and familiar ways, as he demonstrated with *House* when he observed carpenters and an architect at work for eight months, and with *Among Schoolchildren,* which required him to sit in a classroom with twenty fifth-graders for another nine months, during which he missed only two days of class. Out of those experiences Kidder produced

Tracy Kidder (photograph by Bob Riddle)

nonfiction masterpieces, works that rank with the best of this era. In *The Literary Journalists* (1984) Norman Sims characterizes the literary journalist as one who "confirms that the crucial moments of everyday life contain great drama and substance." This is precisely what Kidder does.

Born 12 November 1945 in New York City, the son of Reine Kidder, a high-school teacher, and Henry Maynard Kidder, a lawyer, John Tracy Kidder has fond memories of his childhood. He remembers his mother reciting Charles Dickens and Herman Melville to him, nurturing his early love of reading, which, he says, is "an experience that leaves you in some small way transformed." He began writing short stories at Harvard, where he majored in English, modeling them after the styles of those writers who have most influenced his career: McPhee, A. J. Liebling, and George Orwell. In his work one can find McPhee's meticulous attention to detail, Liebling's stylistic grace, and Orwell's intellectual skepticism.

Kidder admits that he draws freely from the work of each. "I certainly don't mean in any way to compare myself to them," he said in an interview with David Bennett on 3 October 1995. "They're just wonderful. So, too, is another writer I greatly admire, Joseph Mitchell. And I'm also a fan of Richard Rhodes; he's a fine talent. I also read a lot of fiction . . . I like [John] Updike and [John] Cheever, Peter Matthiesen, and a fellow named Stuart Dybek. . . . And I've always been a fan of [Norman] Mailer, [Truman] Capote, [Herman] Melville, and many others."

Kidder served in the army from 1967 to 1969, becoming a first lieutenant in Vietnam, where he worked in intelligence. Unlike Michael Herr, John Sack, David Halberstam, and Philip Caputo, all of whom were scarred and transformed by the war, Kidder emerged relatively unscathed, both physically and emotionally. He wrote artful stories about Vietnam for the *Atlantic Monthly* in the 1970s, receiving high acclaim, but he admits the war did not affect him the way it did many other writers:

> Of course, whenever you're in an experience like Vietnam, it is bound to influence your work; it's inevitable, but I really don't think it greatly shaped me as a writer. I was young and didn't pay much attention to what was going on around me. Certainly the war didn't influence me the way it did others, others who, incidentally, produced superb work about that experience. I guess Vietnam touched me in some way, but it had no lasting influence on my writing. For one thing, I was never in serious danger there—I wasn't in combat. Basically, I was just a kid growing up.

Kidder's stories about Vietnam belie his words; he has produced extraordinary portrayals of his intrigues there and the men he met along the way. "The Death of Major Great" (1974), "Soldiers of Misfortune" (1978)," and "In Quarantine" (1980), all published in the *Atlantic Monthly,* are superb essays that resonate with insight and compassion, each ranking among the finest reporting to come out of Vietnam.

After returning from the war Kidder married Frances Toland in 1971; they have two children. Unemployed and having little success as a writer at this time, Kidder enrolled in the University of Iowa Writers Workshop, hoping to learn that special magic that makes words come alive on the page. He aspired to be a writer—essentially the only thing he ever wanted to be—but his prose needed polish, and Kidder needed seasoning. The workshop helped: he wrote his first book, *The Road to Yuba City: A Journey*

into the *Juan Corona Murders* (1974), while still a student. He earned a master's degree after three years, finishing in 1974, and gained a deep respect for the magic of language.

"The best thing about that place is that it's a nice refuge," Kidder said in a 1983 interview in *Contemporary Authors*. Kidder, who now lives in Williamsburg, Massachusetts, in the heart of his beloved New England, added about his experience at Iowa that "being there made me realize that there were an awful lot of other people in the world who were trying to do what I was attempting to do. It was good in that way. Humiliating, so to speak. Iowa gave me some feeling of legitimacy. At least I was earning a little money and I could call myself a writer."

Connections he made at Iowa also helped advance his career. He met Dan Wakefield, a contributing editor for the *Atlantic Monthly* who recommended Kidder to the magazine, which commissioned his work on *The Road to Yuba City,* an investigation of Juan Corona, a labor organizer accused of murdering twenty-five migrant farmworkers in California. Kidder immersed himself in the assignment, hopping trains to California, living among the poor and downtrodden in decrepit shanties and boardinghouses, hanging out and eating in seedy missions, mingling with migrant workers. He took a job as a tree thinner, hoping to gain deeper insight into what he calls "the subculture of migrant farm workers, a world of rootlessness, exploitation, and despair."

Kidder came to know the key players in the case well: he interviewed Corona at length, talked daily with Corona's flamboyant lawyer, Richard Hawk, who bungled Corona's defense at critical times, especially during closing arguments when Hawk, who had promised to contradict the prosecution's most damaging evidence, simply rested the case, sealing his client's conviction. Kidder also conversed often with the sheriff's deputies and detectives involved in the investigation and established a rapport with the farmworkers, though he was never able to penetrate their private lives.

Despite Kidder's unabashed enthusiasm, *The Road to Yuba City* suffered because of his inexperience. He failed to develop his characters fully and to paint vivid pictures of the bizarre world into which he had ventured. The writing, stilted and pedestrian, bore little resemblance to the prose in *The Soul of a New Machine* or in any of Kidder's other major works. Critics panned *The Road to Yuba City,* calling it the work of a novice. "In the end, Kidder's book is a sad one, both thematically and stylistically," John M. Coward wrote in his essay on Kidder in *A Source-*

Dust jacket for Kidder's account of Data General Corporation's struggle to create a thirty-two-bit superminicomputer in eighteen months

book of *American Literary Journalists: Representative Writers in an Emerging Genre* (1992). Coward concluded that "In spite of Corona's successful prosecution, the murders were so bizarre, the evidence so disputed, and the major figures so disappointing that the book was bound to leave readers unsatisfied."

Kidder never attempted to defend the work—for the most part, he agreed with the critics. He used the first person awkwardly, as if he were intruding rather than reporting, and wrote a book that was shallow, timid, and transparent. He now uses the first person sparingly; straightforward omniscient narration better showcases his talent, as his major works have shown. *The Road to Yuba City* was "the first piece of journalism I had ever done, and I really

didn't know what I was doing," Kidder said in 1995. "I can't say anything intelligent about that book, except that I learned never to write about a murder case. The whole experience was disgusting, so disgusting, in fact, that in 1981 I went to Doubleday and bought back the rights to the book. I don't want *The Road to Yuba City* to see the light of day again."

He quickly rebounded, writing "The Death of Major Great" even before *The Road to Yuba City* hit the bookstands. Kidder recounted the murder of a hated American commanding officer by his own troops, weaving the killing into an account of his travels through parts of Vietnam with a sidekick, Pancho, an enlisted man who hated "lifers" and officers, during which the two encountered a myriad of horrors that included savagery, thoughts of suicide, deaths, and senseless atrocities. In the story Kidder crafted a chilling tale: in three pages, he captured the madness of the war, evoking memories of Ernest Hemingway with terse representation of fact, rigid detachment, and understatement of emotion. After the slaughter of civilians in a village, Kidder and Pancho looked in the doorway of the shack and inside on a straw mat a naked man and woman in intimate embrace lay bleeding." Kidder refused to elaborate; he let the sentence stand on its own, preferring spare description, a literary ploy he used to great effect throughout the story.

Consider his flirtation with suicide: "As we traveled on, my tongue found out a sore inside my lip. When it vanished, nothing. Then my hair began to fall. Despondent, I tried to murder myself, but Pancho caught me and took away my weapons." No affectation, no belaboring the point: Kidder weeded out the unnecessary, the minutiae that would detract from a powerful, riveting story. The reader knows that Kidder is in great despair, though he never says this explicitly; the reader knows, too, that Kidder is deeply disillusioned, though he never says it. He explains in his 1995 interview: "A writer I admire once told me that when you write about time, you never use the word 'time.'" He fashioned a compelling narrative, a gripping account of the insanity in which he found himself, fusing elegant understatement with spare yet precise prose. Critics noticed. Kidder won the Atlantic First Award for best short story, a redemption of sorts after *The Road to Yuba City* failure.

He spent the remainder of the 1970s refining his skills, writing a series of impressive essays for the *Atlantic Monthly*. He explored such diverse subjects as railroads, nuclear power, solar energy, water pollution, and life in the Caribbean while also revisiting his Vietnam experience for two acclaimed pieces, "Soldiers of Misfortune" in 1978 and "In Quarantine" in 1980. He polished his journalistic skills, becoming a consummate reporter, a talent that served him well when he began work on *The Soul of a New Machine*, his first book after the failed experiment with *The Road to Yuba City*. Somberness, melancholy, and a tortured sense of desperation fill Kidder's accounts of his Vietnam service. He writes often about Pancho, a sleazy misfit, an enlisted man who hates the military and everything about it. Drawn together by the war, they are a strange couple, complete opposites: Kidder is elegant, refined, Harvard educated, and dignified; Pancho is short, chubby, foulmouthed, uneducated, and lacking even the most rudimentary social grace. He calls fellow grunts "flatdicks," curses first sergeants, and loathes officers. Their relationship is a metaphor for

the war, a strange conjoining of disparate elements. Kidder chronicles their experiences in "In Quarantine" as they traverse the jungles and paddies of Vietnam, planning an escape from the war by catching a boat and riding to California. They fail miserably, simply riding around in circles for a few days before they land on the China Sea coast. They wander for several days before encountering a group of soldiers who have been quarantined because of an outbreak of contagious herpes—soldiers who are now *profiles*, a military term for the sick and infirm who are no longer able to fight.

Pancho concocts an outrageous plan to rescue the profiles and spread herpes on a global scale. Kidder explains Pancho's scheme: "He paced, drinking beer with one hand and waving the green gun with the other, telling me that he would liberate the 'flatdicks' from the 'big lifer's' tyranny, then lead his profiles back to 'the world,' where the ones who still could would start epidemics, beginning at the homes of the first sergeants and officers whose addresses he had memorized." This raw, primal, insane scheme is, to Kidder, Vietnam in microcosm. Nothing there made much sense; it was a strange, surreal world, a world of madness—and Kidder admits he did not see the worse of it, isolated as he was, away from heavy combat.

Kidder reached back into his Vietnam experiences for another memorable story, "Soldiers of Misfortune." Published in the *Atlantic Monthly* in March 1978, it details the shameful treatment veterans received after the war. Kidder visited Max Cleland, head of the Veterans Administration, a vet who had been horribly ravaged in Vietnam, suffering massive injuries that almost killed him. In a corner of Cleland's office Kidder observed that an "odd bronzed object sits in one corner. It looks as if it might have been some medieval instrument of torture, and I felt embarrassed to stare at it. At its base is a squarish foot. A short, hollow, conical leg, about the size and shape of an inverted wastebasket, rises from it. A few inches above the top there is a medal hoop, wired to the device like a halo. This is one of the prosthetic training legs—he called them 'little stubbies'—in which Max Cleland clumped around for too many months after he got back from Vietnam."

On a hilltop at Khe Sahn, near the end of his tour of duty, during which he had distinguished himself as a signal officer with the First Air Cavalry Division, Cleland reached down to pick up what he thought was a spent grenade. In a microsecond the explosion shattered his world. "Cleland came from Georgia," Kidder writes, adding:

He was a pretty good basketball player at Stetson College. When he reached down for the grenade, he was six foot three, a fair-haired, husky youth with the sort of glorious designs on the future that JFK inspired in many well-bred boys. A moment later, even before he had even touched the fragmentation grenade, an awful metamorphosis took place. He was knocked backward. His ears still ringing from the explosion, he looked at himself and saw that his right hand and wrist were no longer there. His right leg was gone, and he could see his left foot sitting a little distance away in his jungle boot. Eventually the whole leg would also have to come off. He didn't look again.

Kidder lamented the sad plight of veterans. He visited them in VA hospitals, crafting moving accounts of the problems they faced, the demons they could not exorcise, and the nightmares they could not escape. He won the Sidney Hillman Foundation Prize for "Soldiers of Misfortune," one of the most passionate and sympathetic pieces ever written about the survivors of Vietnam.

He also tackled highly technical subjects for the *Atlantic Monthly,* writing splendid essays about nuclear energy and solar power. In "Tinkering With Sunshine" (1977) he explored the feasibility of using solar power on a massive scale, concluding that the possibilities appeared limitless. He argued the merits of using natural sources such as the sun and wind for energy, positing that fears of energy shortages would abate because solar energy is "invulnerable to nation-crippling accidents and sabotage." Kidder next turned his attention to the debate on nuclear power, crafting a fine essay, "The Nonviolent War against Nuclear Power" (September 1978). He centered the article on a group of antinuclear activists, the Clamshell Alliance, focusing on Sam Lovejoy, "the Trotsky of the no-nuke movement."

His articles in the *Atlantic Monthly* about the environment ("Sludge," 1975), life in the Caribbean ("Winter in St. Lucia," 1976), railroads ("Trains in Trouble," 1976, and "Railroads: Aboard the Ghost Trains," 1978) padded his résumé and expanded his range, preparing him to write clearly about esoteric subjects, a skill he put to great use in the late 1970s when he sat down to compose *The Soul of a New Machine.* Kidder feels the experience he gained writing for the *Atlantic Monthly* was invaluable when he tackled the strange subculture of the computer world, where the jargon is largely incomprehensible to laymen, where engineers deal in geometric schematics, Boolean algebra, binary arithmetic, integrated circuitry, Booth's Algorithm, and microsequencing. Unfamiliarity with the subject matter did not faze

Kidder. "I was used to that," he said in his 1983 interview:

> I had done some articles for the *Atlantic Monthly* on technical subjects that I previously knew nothing about. If you're a journalist who doesn't cover a single beat, it's a familiar feeling to know nothing about what's going on. So, it wasn't all that unusual. It is a rather painful feeling not to know what the people around you are talking about. But that's also an impetus to figure it out. This topic was a little more forbidding than some things, that's true.

Kidder worked for two and a half years on the book, chronicling the struggle of engineers at Data General Corporation to create a thirty-two-bit supermini computer in eighteen months. He spent eight months at the corporation, watching the "Hardy Boys," the hardware specialists, wire and reconfigure the computer so that it would be compatible with the microcodes developed by the "Microkids," programmers who developed the code that fused hardware and software. Chief project engineer Tom West and his top lieutenant, Carl Alsing, directed the activities of the young college graduates working under them, relentlessly driving the kids to produce the "Eagle," a supermini computer West thought would capture the market, overtaking Digital Equipment Corporation's "VAX." West's ultimate goal was lofty: he aspired to build a computer that would not only topple the competition but also vault Data General into the Fortune 500.

Intense, driven, and obsessed, West, head of the Eclipse Group, demanded total allegiance to the project, hiring only recent college graduates who would devote themselves body and soul to the assignment. Over and over he stressed what he considered a vital point: the engineers building the Eagle were not just constructing a new computer; they were designing a product that would transform the computer industry, building a powerful new state-of-the-art machine that would make others obsolete. They were involved, West said, in a historic project, one that would revolutionize human communication.

The Hardy Boys and Microkids responded to West's exhortations; they sacrificed hobbies, free time, friends, even family in their zeal to build the machine, working fourteen- to sixteen-hour days, basking in the creative freedom they enjoyed. Kidder described them in 1995 as "eccentric knights errant, clad in blue jeans and open collars, seeking with awesome intensity the grail of technological achievement." Most thrived on the pressure; a few cracked, such as the young engineer who left a note on his computer: "I'm going to a commune and will deal with no unit of time shorter than a season."

West and Alsing at times felt guilty, but never for long. "I felt like one of those old supervisors from the 1800s who used to hire children and work them eighteen hours a day," Alsing said in *The Soul of a New Machine*. The quote contained great truth; even though the young engineers were intelligent, highly skilled, and among the best young graduates in the country, they had acquired an assembly-line mentality, trapped by the orthodoxies and rigidities of a highly structured machine, the corporation. Corporate structure often inhibits creativity, and several of the kids succumbed to the demands imposed on them, simply walking away from the job.

The project consumed West, who, Kidder writes, "was forty but looked younger. He was thin and had a long narrow face and a mane of brown hair that spilled over the back of his collar. These days he went to work in freshly laundered blue jeans or pressed khakis, in leather moccasins, and in solid-colored long-sleeved shirts, with the sleeves rolled up in precise folds, like the pages of a letter, well above his bone elbows." From the project West led, Kidder spun a masterful tale, a story of high intrigue and compelling drama. *The Soul of a New Machine* reads like a fictional thriller with one notable exception: all of it is true. "I don't invent dialogue and I don't use composite characters," Kidder said in his 1995 interview.

Critics raved. In *The New York Times Book Review* (29 November 1981) S. C. Florman wrote that Kidder had endowed the story "with such pace, texture and poetic implication that he has elevated it to a high level of narrative art." Kidder's ability to render highly technical subject matter comprehensible to laymen drew universal praise. Yet, during his undergraduate days at Harvard, Kidder refused to take courses in science or technology—he felt they were beyond his comprehension and avoided them at all costs. He shed his fears, however, when the time came to research *The Soul of a New Machine*. "Technology seems so forbidding, I suspect, because of all of its trade jargon," Kidder said. "It's a handy shorthand—but it's also a formidable veil. It's possible for almost anyone to understand it once he gets through that veil."

Richard Todd, Kidder's editor at the *Atlantic Monthly*, first suggested the book. Ambivalent about tackling such a complex subject, Kidder drew strength from his journalistic models, McPhee, Orwell, and Liebling, reasoning that any of the three would have succeeded masterfully in telling such a tale. He came to understand that a large and complex subject could best be understood by focusing on what he called "its smaller aspects." Critics later compared *The Soul of a New Machine* to Aleksandr Solzhenitsyn's *The First Circle* (1970), Robert Pirsig's *Zen and the Art of Motorcycle Maintenance* (1974), and Tom Wolfe's *The Right Stuff* (1979). Other critics wrote that Kidder's sensitive handling of a complex subject evoked memories of McPhee and Mailer, both of whom wrote with great expertise about esoteric subjects.

In 1995 Kidder noted that he had not read *The Soul of a New Machine* in "seven or eight years, probably more." Furthermore, he had read it only once. Over the years he has developed an aversion to dredging up the past; he tends "to kill things off and move on." He prefers not to read past works. "I've always regretted it when I go back and reread," he said. "So I stopped doing it. I see things I could have done a lot better, or things I did well then that I'm having trouble doing now. It's depressing." Despite all the hoopla over *The Soul of a New Machine*—and the subsequent rise in computer sales—Kidder refused to use a computer until the late 1980s when he was working on *Among Schoolchildren*. "I don't need one," he told an interviewer in 1983. He continued:

> I have an electric typewriter. I have my own way of doing things, and I'm a little superstitious, perhaps, a little bit set in my ways. I see no reason to change . . . if I were a daily reporter, I'd feel very differently about it; if speed were of the essence, you know. Sometimes my deadlines seem excruciating, but when I'm doing articles I usually have a month or more, so I really don't need one of those things.

Kidder now admits that even though he uses one, he is still "not so keen on computers. I think they distract from the writing process. . . . I usually start writing my books in longhand. It's just something I feel comfortable with."

He admits that the timing of *The Soul of a New Machine* was fortunate, coming when computers were just beginning to appear everywhere. "The personal computer market was opening up," he recalled, "and people were making a whole lot of money off them. In fact, the book still has a following; I continue to hear from people who still talk about it." *The Soul of a New Machine* won the Pulitzer Prize and the National Book Award. It remains one of the most acclaimed nonfiction works of this generation, a book that gained worldwide praise, vaulting Kidder into literature's stratosphere. Since its success, he has been on a white-hot binge, becoming one of the preeminent voices in contemporary nonfiction.

Kidder is not given to overstatement and refuses to engage in hyperbole. Told that his book helped ignite the "computer revolution," he merely shrugged, then disagreed, saying, "*Revolution* is a funny word: every time anything changes, every time there's anything new, there's somebody around who's willing to call it a revolution." He added: "Revolution implies a great social and political upheaval, and I think that in those terms the computer is a conservative instrument. . . . Like most new things, it's used by the people who are in power to increase their power. I'm not denouncing it on those grounds necessarily, but that's a fact."

The aesthetic of building a house—the initial excitement of prospective owners, the creativity of the architect, the daily grind by carpenters and construction workers to meet deadlines, the give-and-take between members of different social classes working to achieve a common goal—was the next subject that captured Kidder's attention. Few writers would attempt to describe the building of a house; it seems too mundane, too simple—and yet Kidder viewed it as a challenge. Thus inspired, he wrote *House,* which, like *The Soul of a New Machine,* dazzled critics, revealing a writer who could transform the most ordinary human experience into a rich, provocative narrative.

Symbolic realities pervade *House*—the book is as much about social class and class distinctions as it is about building, as Kidder admits. Larger truths and higher meanings emerge as the owners of the home, Jonathan and Judith Souweine, supervise construction of their dwelling on the Holyoke Range, on the outskirts of Amherst, Massachusetts. Kidder avoids talk about symbolic realities, reasoning that they sound like "a coat of paint on a piece of writing, added later to achieve academic respectability"—a belief not shared by Rhodes, also a Pulitzer Prize winner and a friend of Kidder's, who admitted in an unpublished interview with Bennett on 10 May 1995 that symbolic realities are "terribly important" to his work, that "the universe does indeed show forth in a writer's work, whether he's aware of it or not." Kidder thinks more in terms of "resonance." He says the "best works of literature have a close attachment to the particular. You pluck a guitar string and another one vibrates." "Resonances" and "symbolic realities" are essentially the same thing, paths to the same destination separated only by semantic differences.

"*House* is about social class," Kidder said in 1995, adding:

It's about how people from different economic and social backgrounds are able to come together for a common purpose. And it's my favorite book. I enjoyed the research, hanging out with the carpenters, getting out-

side, watching the construction process from start to finish. . . . You start with this empty piece of ground and wind up with something beautiful. I know it seems mundane, but I found it very enjoyable.

Kidder traces the activities of seven people—the Souweines (whose house is being built); architect Bill Rawn; and four counterculturist builders, the Apple Corps—from the first blueprints to finished product. Rawn, a Yale graduate, won a Boston Architects Society Award for the house, the first he ever designed and the first the Souweines ever owned. They had shared a duplex for eight years with another couple; now they seized an opportunity to buy land from Judith Souweine's parents, purchasing a site with what Kidder describes as:

a deep-looking woods on one edge. On another, there's a pasture, which turns into the precipitous, forested, publicly owned hills known as the Holyoke Range. And to the north and east there's a panorama. Look north and you see a hillside orchard topped with two giant maples locally known as Castor and Pollux. Look a little to the east and your view extends out over a broad valley.

It is a picturesque view, one the Souweines will enjoy. Jonathan is an Ivy Leaguer who received his undergraduate degree at Columbia University before attending Harvard Law School. Judith, with a doctorate in educational psychology, has written books, lectured, and delivered papers at conferences and seminars. The Apple Corps, four equal partners in a small building company that includes Jim Locke, Alex Ghiselin, Ned Krutsky, and Richard Gougeon, are free spirits, talented but not particularly driven, and efficient. They pride themselves on the work they have done around New England—they helped build roughly two hundred houses in a decade. They do not advertise, do not even list their company's name in the phone book. Word of mouth keeps their business alive; they are good, and other builders know it, recommending the Apple Corps to prospective clients. Money does not drive them—each partner averages about $20,000 a year.

House centers on the building of relationships between the architect, the builders, and the Souweines. Kidder crafts masterful portraits of the individuals involved; he paints wonderful pictures, showing clear class distinctions among the participants. The builders understand that they inhabit a different world from that of the Souweines, that their lives are different in profound ways. Yet class differences do not impede the building process, though the builders argue and haggle with the Souweines over costs and chastise Rawn for underdeveloped de-

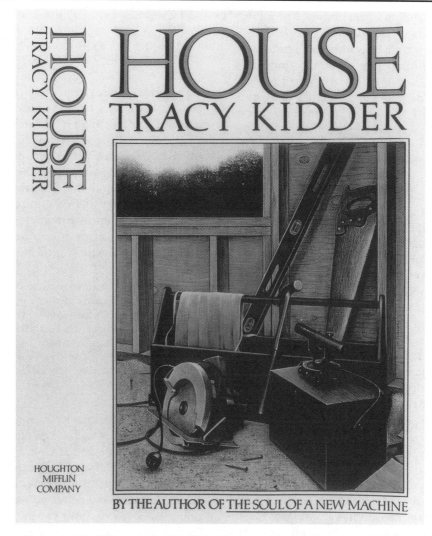

Dust jacket for Kidder's exploration of the relationships formed during the building of a new house

signs on a staircase. Construction costs eventually hit $146,000; the Apple Corps and the Souweines dicker over the final payment of $660, the Souweines claiming they do not owe it, the builders protesting that they indeed do. In the end the Apple Corps clears just $3,000.

According to Paul Goldberger in *The New York Times Book Review* (6 October 1985) Kidder tells his tale "with such clarity, intelligence and grace it makes you wonder why no one has written a book like it before. In the way that a well-told story of a marriage, or of a love affair or of a child's coming of age fills you with a sense that you are reading about a fundamental human experience for the first time, so it is with *House.*"

The most endearing characters are the four builders, whom Goldberger describes as "men in their mid-30's who, more or less by themselves,

built the Souweines' house . . . [and] are somewhere between businessmen and what were once called hippie carpenters." Kidder, who became particularly fond of the four men, hanging out with them for eight months and getting to know them well, said, "It was great being outside, watching these guys, talking to them. I really got to like them." With reviewers praising Kidder's virtuosity, *House* became an instant hit, and critics again applauded, heralding Kidder as one of the most eloquent of the literary journalists.

His next project, *Among Schoolchildren,* published in 1989, earned Kidder even greater acclaim. He spent nine months in the classroom of Chris Zajac with twenty fifth-graders at Kelly School, in the "Flats" of Holyoke, Massachusetts, a depressed area beset by unemployment and poverty. Kidder attended school from the first day to the last, missing one day because he was sick, another because he simply played hooky. Like the students, he arrived each morning at eight o'clock and remained throughout the day. He sat in a desk in front of the classroom, next to Zajac's, and observed. He took a staggering ten thousand pages of notes and grew particularly fond of Zajac. "She was thirty-four," Kidder writes in the book, bringing her into focus by adding:

> She wore a white skirt and yellow sweater and a thin gold necklace, which she held in her fingers, as if holding her own reins, while waiting for children to answer. Her hair was black with a hint of Irish red. . . . She strode across the room, her arms swinging high and her hands in small fists. Taking her stand in front of the green chalkboard, discussing the rules with her new class, she repeated sentences. . . . Her hands kept very busy. They sliced the air and made karate chops to mark off sentences. They extended straight out like a traffic cop's, halting illegal maneuvers yet to be perpetrated.

Kidder wrote the book from Zajac's point of view, sharing with her the triumphs of teaching, the heartbreaks, the joys, and the futility. Passionate, devoted, indomitable, she taught with exuberance, praising when she should, chastising when she had to. So dedicated to her profession that she spent large parts of her free summers preparing for the coming year, Zajac despaired when her students, about half of whom were Puerto Rican, fell short of their potential and worried when they became lax in their preparation. She chided and encouraged, using the means available to her to push students to their best. At times her best efforts, all her preparation and worry, did not work; students simply were too ill prepared to grasp what she taught, as they are in most schools across the United States. Kidder celebrates Zajac's teaching while also indicting the American education system for its many shortcomings.

"I became quite fond of her," Kidder said of Zajac in his 1995 interview. "She was a dedicated teacher who wasn't getting much help, something that happens in schools all over America. The sad thing was that some of these kids never had a chance to begin with; their futures had already been predetermined. And it's sad to see, because these kids can't help it that they were born into poverty or into situations in which learning simply didn't matter, wasn't even talked about." Kidder also confessed that *Among Schoolchildren* became one of his toughest assignments–it exhausted him, frazzled him. He explained: "The research was grueling. I was there each morning at 8, and I'm not used to institutional

controls. I'm not good in situations like that; I could never work a 9-to-5 job. It would drive me crazy. And I had a hard time writing the book. All those notes to go through, so much to remember. It was a hard job." After the experience he insists that there must be educational reform: administrators too often ignore the plight of the teacher in the classroom. "Most efforts at reform usually are conducted independently of the experience, knowledge, wishes of teachers," he said. "And that's a terrible mistake . . . since, for better or worse, education is what happens in these little rooms."

Zajac emerges as a noble figure, a heroine, a symbol of all that is good and rich and honorable in education. Kidder lavishes her with praise. He also shares with the students "their joys, their catastrophes, and their small but essential triumphs." They often test Zajac's will and patience. Pedro, who can barely read, causes her deep concern; Clarence, hyperactive and disruptive, frequently interrupts the daily rhythms of the classroom, forcing Zajac to discipline him again and again. She nevertheless plows ahead, dispensing wit and wisdom, though she knows that she has no control over the parents who never come to conferences, the indifference to education she sees in Holyoke, or the poverty in which some of her students live. She understands that it is terribly difficult for fifth-graders to study in rat-infested apartments, especially if they are hungry, most especially if they have been told that no amount of studying will help them overcome their poverty. Across the nation dismal test scores, crime in the classroom, and escalating dropout rates plague the American educational system, and Kidder urges change, presenting as a good starting point for reform, Chris Zajac, one good teacher in a system plagued by ineptness. Kidder reserves for her devotion to teaching a deep reverence. Critics again lauded Kidder, calling *Among Schoolchildren* his most important work.

Kidder's books read like novels; he infuses them with all the tools of fiction. He bridles, however, when someone suggests that he is a novelist, as an editorialist once did, writing, "Tracy Kidder . . . has won a Pulitzer Prize for his novel, *The Soul of a New Machine*." Norman Sims, chair of the department of journalism at the University of Massachusetts and a friend of Kidder, explained in *The Literary Journalists* (1984): "Kidder read it and shook his head in disbelief. A *novel*, an invented narrative. It was a little irritating to him after he had practically lived in the basement of Data General Corporation for eight months, and spent two and a half years on the book. Kidder took great pains to get the quotations right, to catch all the details accurately."

Of all contemporary literary journalists Kidder's work comes closest to Tom Wolfe's notion of what literary journalism should be: journalism that, as he says in his introduction to *The New Journalism* (1973), "reads like a novel," journalism that shows the reader "the subjective or emotional life of the characters." By combining such literary techniques as narrative voice, point of view, scene-by-scene construction, and extended dialogue with in-depth, exhaustive reporting, Kidder creates journalism that is virtually indistinguishable from fiction. He acknowledges that he depends heavily on the tools of the novelist, though he argues those tools are not the exclusive property of fiction and never have been. "There are all sorts of tools available," Kidder said in 1995, admitting that:

> Point of view, voice and other devices are all important to my work. I never believed those tools belonged exclusively to fiction; they belong to story telling, and that's what writing is. There is a lot more to nonfiction writing than just taking notes and being honest. I do write a little fiction now and then, and I know that the tools available to the fiction writer are the same tools available to the nonfiction writer. What it really comes down to is that there is writing that is alive on the page and writing that is dead.

Though Kidder may not be aware of it, a strong proletarian sensibility pervades his work—strangely, it seems, given his background of privilege as a Harvard graduate and the son of a successful lawyer. He seems to distrust large corporations and systems inherently. Perhaps his Vietnam experience touched him far more deeply than is generally known. Perhaps the 1960s shaped him in profound and significant ways. Whatever the reasons, Kidder often aligns himself with working-class people rather than executives and CEOs. Consider, for example, that in his 1983 interview he calls the computer a "conservative instrument . . . used by the people in power to increase their power."

His liberal leanings manifest themselves in *Old Friends,* published in 1993, his fourth major hit in a little more than a decade. In this work Kidder writes with grace and sympathy about two strangers, Lou Freed and Joe Torchio, thrust together as roommates in the Linda Manor Nursing Home in Northhampton, Massachusetts, and reminds his reader "of the great continuities, of the possibilities for renewal in the face of mortality, of the survival to the very end of all that is truly essential about life." In this immensely important book about old age in America, Kidder confronts many of the problems faced by the elderly: a sense of uselessness, of abandonment, of being cast aside by a society that devalues age; he again spins a wonderful tale, a paean to the strength and abiding hope in the human heart. Among other things Kidder chronicles the difficulty of finding a suitable nursing home. Too often, he writes, people dump the elderly in:

> places where the stench of urine got in one's clothes like tobacco smoke, where four, sometimes five, elderly people lay jammed in tiny rooms, where residents sat tied to wheelchairs or strapped to beds, where residents weren't allowed to bring with them any furniture of their own or to have private phones or to use the public pay phone without nurses listening in. One woman, on a recent tour of a nearby place, had been shown a room with a dead resident in it.

Joe and Lou, Kidder's central characters, forge a strong friendship. Joe, seventy-two, at first has reservations about rooming with a ninety-year-old, but Lou quiets his fears. Lou, in fact, is healthier than Joe; he has glaucoma, cataracts, and occasional angina, and he has trouble negotiating Linda Manor. But his problems are not as severe as Joe's, who suffers from diabetes, has had a stroke, is partially paralyzed, and has undergone a series of operations for various problems. The two meet after Lou's wife, to whom he was married seventy years, dies in the nursing home, leaving Lou alone in deep grief. He and Joe become roommates out of necessity and immediately establish a rapport that grows into love as the months go by. Both had been proud, productive men in their earlier lives. Joe had been a man of influence, the chief probation officer for the district court in Pittsfield, Massachusetts. Now, Kidder writes, "he lived in the care of strangers, exiled by illness from his family and friends."

Lou worries about Joe's swearing. Joe worries about the Boston Red Sox, who have not won anything worth mentioning in decades. Kidder details their day-to-day activities, weaving a powerful narrative that comments eloquently on the plight of the aged in American society. The book is profoundly redemptive, a poignant testament to the resilience of the human soul. Kidder nevertheless found the book difficult to write. "It was an almost impossible project," he said in 1995. "The research was very hard because basically nothing goes on in a nursing home most of the time. But I'm happy with the book; I achieved most of what I set out to do."

Critics again applauded. Kidder had now written four consecutive highly acclaimed books, enhancing his stature as one of the premier talents in contemporary American literature. The books came at four-year intervals: in 1981, 1985, 1989, and 1993. Kidder, an inveterate researcher, researches each book tirelessly, taking great pains to "get it right." And though he is not as prolific as many other nonfiction writers, what he writes dazzles, as critics have long agreed. Kidder is happiest while composing prose, unlike many other writers who find the actual writing process an excruciatingly painful ordeal. Kidder realized how much he liked the aesthetic of daily writing when he accepted a position as visiting professor-writer in residence at Northwestern University in Evanston, Illinois, in 1995. Although he enjoyed teaching, the fact that it did not leave him enough time to write helped confirm how vital the writing process had become.

Except for his one critical failure, *The Road to Yuba City,* all of Kidder's books have been set in Massachusetts, near his beloved Williamsburg. Like William Faulkner in Yoknapatawpha County and John Steinbeck along the California coast, Kidder does not venture far for material. His portraits of everyday life have vaulted him to the front rank of American literary journalism. Writing of hope and sorrow, love and despair, he has, along the way, elevated reporting to a high art, clothing the common with dignity and the familiar with nobility.

References:

John M. Coward, "Tracy Kidder," in *A Sourcebook of American Literary Journalism,* edited by Thomas B. Connery (New York: Greenwood Press, 1993), pp. 375–386;

Norman Sims, ed., *The Literary Journalists* (New York: Ballantine, 1984), p. 15.

Jane Kramer

(7 August 1938 –   )

John J. Pauly
Saint Louis University

BOOKS: *Off Washington Square: A Reporter Looks at Greenwich Village, N.Y.* (New York: Duell, Sloan & Pearce, 1963);

Allen Ginsberg in America (New York: Random House, 1969); republished as *Paterfamilias* (London: Gollancz, 1970);

Honor to the Bride Like the Pigeon That Guards Its Grain under the Clove Tree (New York: Farrar, Straus & Giroux, 1970);

The Last Cowboy (New York: Harper & Row, 1977);

Unsettling Europe (New York: Random House, 1980);

Europeans (New York: Farrar, Straus & Giroux, 1988);

Whose Art Is It? (Durham, N.C.: Duke University Press, 1994);

The Politics of Memory: Looking for Germany in the New Germany (New York: Random House, 1996).

SELECTED PERIODICAL PUBLICATIONS–UNCOLLECTED: "Founding Cadre," *New Yorker,* 46 (28 November 1970): 52–56+;

"Letter from the Elysian Fields," *New Yorker,* 63 (2 March 1987): 40–42+;

"Neo-Nazis: A Chaos in the Head," *New Yorker,* 69 (14 June 1993): 52–56+;

"The Politics of Memory," *New Yorker,* 71 (14 August 1995): 48–54+;

"The Invisible Woman," *New Yorker,* 72 (26 February/4 March 1996): 136–147.

Jane Kramer (photograph by Thomas Victor)

In her thirty years at *The New Yorker* Jane Kramer has written shrewd profiles of Italian peasants, Moroccan teenagers, Texas cowboys, German skinheads, New York City artists, and European heads of state. Reviews of her books in popular magazines and newspapers have praised the grace and clarity of her writing. Yet this cosmopolitan body of work, with an intellectual depth unmatched in contemporary journalism, has received almost no scholarly attention. Such recognition is long overdue, for Kramer has written eloquently about the politics of cultural identity—about the human migrations, genera-

tional disruptions, counterculture strivings, fading nationalist mythologies, gender wars, battles over artistic representation, and lapses of public memory that have characterized the late twentieth century.

Kramer was born on 7 August 1938 in Providence, Rhode Island, to Louis and Jessica Shore Kramer. Her father was a physician, and her writings hint at an upbringing that was quiet and conventional. She attended a Quaker girls' school in Providence, then in 1959 graduated Phi Beta Kappa with a bachelor's degree in English from Vassar College. After graduation she opted for the adventure of New York City where she entered the graduate program in English at Columbia University after working for six weeks at a publishing house. She received her master's degree in 1961 and in the fall began writing for the *Morningsider,* a recently founded Upper West Side neighborhood newspaper. Norman Mailer noticed her work and showed it to Dan Wolf, editor of *The Village Voice,* who offered Kramer a job at *The Village Voice* for thirty dollars a week. She accepted and began writing for that paper in June 1962.

Out of that work at *The Village Voice* came Kramer's first book, *Off Washington Square: A Reporter Looks at Greenwich Village, N.Y.* (1963). Written in a bright but conventional feature style, it explores the Village as a cultural habitat. *Off Washington Square* includes profiles of well-known public figures such as the urbanologist Jane Jacobs and the mime Marcel Marceau; lesser-known figures such as the crusading newspaper publisher J. David Stern and Father Flye, longtime confidant of the writer James Agee; and pure eccentrics such as Raymond Auger, a scientist and engineer who has invented a machine that paints abstract pictures automatically. The book's first story, "Practical Man's Guide to Washington Square," includes a hand-drawn diagram of the park showing how various groups claimed the square as their own. Other stories describe the Village's arts scene—a publisher's party, the naming of a dance studio in honor of Martha Graham, responses to an exhibit of the *Mona Lisa,* and the biannual Washington Park art show. Still others discuss Village politics—the bid of Ed Koch (later mayor of New York City) for a state assembly seat, the activities of the Fair Play for Cuba committee, and the work of an anti-Robert Moses group on behalf of parks and playgrounds.

Kramer experiments with her stance as narrator in these early stories. She variously maintains an unobtrusive distance, or notes her presence in the story in passing, or includes snippets of her own conversation. Occasionally, she inserts a tart observation, as when she notes of Jane Jacobs that "critical generalities, other than her own, amuse her." Kramer's ever-present wit, sharpened to a critical edge in her later work, appears in *Off Washington Square* as a youthful cleverness. When a group of visiting Brazilian students gathers in Kramer's apartment to discuss American life, she describes one young man's attempt to pick her up: "'You are my first American leftist,' whispered the law student from Bahia. 'I would like to talk with you about socialism—alone—later.' "

By early 1964 Kramer's work at *The Village Voice* had caught the attention of William Shawn, editor of *The New Yorker.* He offered her a job at the magazine; she agreed; and her first two bylined articles appeared in 1966: "The Skin Game," on the United Nations Security Council debate over Rhodesia, and "Man Who Is Happening Now," on New York art patron and taxicab tycoon Robert Cooper Scull. In 1968 *The New Yorker* printed Kramer's two-part profile of the poet, religious prophet, and peace activist Allen Ginsberg, and in 1969 that profile was published as Kramer's second book, *Allen Ginsberg in America.*

Allen Ginsberg was more widely reviewed than *Off Washington Square* had been, though not always with much sense of Kramer's aims. The poet Kenneth Rexroth, a friend and sometime competitor of Ginsberg's, writing in *The New York Times Book Review* (11 May 1969), patronizingly noted that Kramer's book was "obviously written with affectionate sympathy and a large half measure of understanding." According to Rexroth, she had not taken Ginsberg seriously as a religious prophet and artist. Instead, she had reduced him to the sort of *"hallucination publicitaire"* produced by the newsweeklies and picture magazines. Ironically, the *Time* review of Kramer's book, written two months later, illustrated Rexroth's complaint. The anonymous reviewer praises Kramer for not taking Ginsberg too seriously since "personality rather than poetry is certainly Ginsberg's bag."

Other reviewers periodically found Kramer guilty of associating with *The New Yorker.* They charged that the magazine's editorial *persona* shackled writers. The magazine's genteel audience expected polished, smooth, and soothing work—work that the critics found politically and theoretically frail, like a fine but delicate antique table that could not bear the weight of a meal. As Rexroth put it, the magazine spreads a "Winnie-the-Pooh whimsey" over its topics and "turns it all into something synthetic made of polyesters and cloying soybeans." Kramer had tried to tame Ginsberg, Rexroth charged, but "it is quite impossible to domesticate a person like this, even in the most sophisticated stately homes of Scarsdale where *New Yorker* Profiles go when they die."

Rexroth's stereotype of *The New Yorker* style misrepresents Kramer's work and politics. He, like others, struggled to place Kramer's writing in a suitable framework. Whose writer is she? Her books make ample use of scholarship in literature, history, politics, anthropology, and sociology, yet are not written in an academic mode. She discusses social conflict, but in a seamless, elegant, elliptical style. She sometimes spends weeks or months with the most ordinary people—French peasants, migrant workers, cowboys, impoverished Arabs—in order to write articles for the educated readers of upscale magazines like *The New Yorker, Vogue,* and *House and Garden.* Her politics seem leftist, though her personal opinions tend to seep through her texts rather than to flood them with polemics.

Critics did not know what to make of *Allen Ginsberg in America.* It was neither a biography, nor a

Dust jacket for the profiles of four European families that
Kramer wrote for The New Yorker between 1971
and 1979

duction, "Ginsberg had put years—and a great deal of anguish—into his own freedom. . . . He had worked for his mysticism, and it was bound to be different in its stubbornness and its substance from the quick-vision ecstasy of a runaway fourteen year old." Kramer considers Ginsberg the moral center of a *household,* not just an individual artist or prophet (a perspective more strongly implied in the title of the book's 1970 British edition, *Paterfamilias*). He sees himself as a "wise Jewish patriarch type with a family." In scene after scene Ginsberg playfully accepts his role as peacemaker, mediator, and interpreter. He refuses to play the part of tormented artist, rebellious son, or counterculture celebrity. His personal example, Kramer implies, offers a moral still point amid the unrest roiling America in the 1960s.

On 30 April 1967, about a year after her first bylined article appeared in *The New Yorker,* Kramer married the anthropologist Vincent Crapanzano, who was teaching at the Graduate School of the City University of New York. In 1970 their only child, Aleksandra, was born. The intellectual careers of Kramer and Crapanzano have often crossed in intriguing ways. They have written articles together for popular magazines, written their own books on the same group of Moroccan mystics and peasants, and written entirely separate books and articles on the same intellectual themes—in particular, the problems of interpreting culture.

Kramer and Crapanzano's first collaboration emerged from a field trip to Meknes, Morocco, in 1968. Under a grant from the National Institute of Mental Health, Crapanzano was studying the *Hamadsha,* a Moroccan religious brotherhood given to pilgrimages, ecstatic dancing, trances, and mystical cures. In 1969 Crapanzano and Kramer jointly published an article titled "A World of Saints and She-Demons" in *The New York Times Magazine* on the rituals of the *Hamadsha.* Crapanzano was interested in the ideological and psychological roles played by traditional, mystic brotherhoods in Morocco's modernization, and he later published his findings in *The Hamadsha: A Study in Moroccan Ethnopsychiatry* (1973). Kramer found her story in the everyday lives of a particular family of poor Moroccans and published it first as a three-part *New Yorker* series in 1970 and then as a book, *Honor to the Bride Like the Pigeon That Guards Its Grain under the Clove Tree* (1970).

One critic called *Honor to the Bride* a nonfiction novel, and the book does resemble similar work by other writers of that era, such as Mailer and Truman Capote. Kramer writes a factual story in a fictional style, using extended dialogue, building characters, and working within a limited third-person

critical analysis of his work, nor the usual account of Ginsberg as a cultural celebrity. The book unfolds episodically with each chapter set in a different place—at a Human Be-In in San Francisco, with friends in San Francisco's Haight-Ashbury, at home in his New York City apartment, on the college lecture circuit, in the living room of his father and stepmother's house in New Jersey, and at a radical chic party in a penthouse at the New York Hilton. Kramer mixes extended dialogue with background details about Ginsberg's education, entrance onto the Beat scene, and public reception.

Scenes pass before the reader with little direct comment, and Kramer's discretion often creates comic effects that Rexroth may well have interpreted as disrespect for Ginsberg's artistic accomplishments. Kramer's Ginsberg emerges as a man of good sense, generosity, and moral wisdom. Whether talking to radical students or a visiting Hindu swami or a dismayed party host, he remains the one adult in any room. As she notes in the book's intro-

point of view, though she resists the more flamboyant strategies used in other nonfiction novels of the period. She refuses to build the story around her own participation as Mailer does in *Armies of the Night* (1968), nor does she purport to speak from the interior spaces of her subjects as Capote does in *In Cold Blood* (1966). She records what she sees and hears and relies heavily on her subjects' interpretations. Kramer and Crapanzano appear in the story under pseudonyms as the young American couple Monsieur and Madame Hugh (Kramer disguised all the actual names in *Honor to the Bride,* as she later did in *The Last Cowboy* [1977]). Mostly, she and Crapanzano serve as comic foils—mystified outsiders who offer inappropriate advice and never fully understand what the Arabs are up to.

In the introduction Kramer calls hers a story about "shame, face, favors, and the pocketbook." As the book opens, Khadija, the thirteen-year-old daughter of Omar ben Allel and his wife, Dawia, has disappeared while the family is on a pilgrimage. Her parents later discover that their daughter was apparently violated and held hostage in a brothel for several weeks. After much finagling and bribery they recover their daughter. Unhappy that the dowry value of his daughter has been damaged, Omar schemes to pass Khadija off as a virgin in order to save himself the expense of keeping her in his household.

Many outsiders would find these events horrifying and tragic, as do some of Kramer's informants. But *Honor to the Bride* reads like a dark comedy of Arab manners. It explores the religious, legal, and cultural fictions of a world in which even virginity might be recovered with the right kind of performance. Kramer's Moroccans rehearse what to tell the neighbors to explain their daughter's dilemma and how to approach the police to guarantee the kind of justice they want. They explain away misfortune by invoking the she-demon, Aisha Quandisha. They tell and interpret their dreams. In order not to shame themselves or others they ask obliquely for what they want. Though no one ever fully establishes the actual facts of the incident—was Khadija seized or seduced?—in order to avoid shame and to be able to ask for a dowry from Khadija's future suitors Omar and Dawia maintain that their daughter was abducted.

All ends well, after a fashion. Omar finds a husband for his daughter and receives a modest dowry for her. Dawia faces her neighbors with pride. Khadija seemingly wins her freedom, though she discovers that her new husband plans to put her to work caring for his mother and his three sons from a previous marriage. The morning after the wedding night, to the amazement of the partygoers, bloody underwear is produced as evidence of Khadija's virginity, and Omar's friend, Musa, sings a Berber song celebrating the event: "Honor to the bride like the pigeon that guards its grain under the clove tree." Omar tells an amazed Crapanzano that "There is a saying. . . . It is that he who speaks last speaks truth."

Honor to the Bride was reviewed warmly if sparsely. Critics enjoyed its novelistic feel and praised Kramer for gaining access to the closed world of poor Arabs. By the early 1970s Kramer had won some measure of public recognition. Her success at *The New Yorker* inspired *Mademoiselle* in January 1969 to name her one of twenty-four young women who in 1968 had "carved niches for themselves often behind the headlines, beyond traditional areas." Among the other women, ages seventeen to thirty, cited that year were Laura Nyro, Joyce Carol Oates, Sandra Locke, and Jane Alexander.

Kramer began splitting her time between New York and Europe in the 1970s, reporting regularly from overseas on behalf of *The New Yorker* and often bringing her young daughter along on her travels through Europe. Four of her 1970s reports were eventually published in a collection titled *Unsettling Europe* (1980). But her next book was actually written during an interlude in the United States. *The Last Cowboy,* originally published as two profiles in *The New Yorker* in 1977, was set in the Texas Panhandle. "For years, I had been writing from other countries," she writes in her introduction. "I wanted—and needed—to look at America again, and it had seemed to me then that a cowboy's camp might be the proper place to start." Kramer's interest in culture and myth now drew her to Texas, as it had to Greenwich Village, Haight-Ashbury, Morocco, and Europe. She wanted to understand how cowboys made "thin but workable arrangements with the life they led." One cowboy in particular moved her. Henry Blanton, as she named him, "had settled into his life but could not seem to settle for it."

As a text *The Last Cowboy* juxtaposes the idealized West of public memory with the bureaucratic West of cattle processing and marketing. The first world lives by its speech, as enacted in handshake deals, the camaraderie of the trail, the remembrances of Blanton's grandfather Abel, and "expressin' right," the distinctive gift of Hollywood cowboys such as Glenn Ford. The second world obeys the written word, as inscribed in contracts, cattle futures, and property relations. *The Last Cowboy* constantly shifts between those worlds, describing first the economic system within which men like

Dust jacket for the 1988 collection of Kramer's essays on European politics and cultural identity

Blanton work, then the small turns of phrase, habits of dress, and acts by which Blanton daily urges his cowboy ideal into existence. Kramer positions Blanton's life within several contexts—the history of the cowboy as an economic, social, and mythical figure, the history of the Texas Panhandle region where Blanton lives, and the changing economics of cattle ranching. But her ultimate interest is in how Blanton and his wife Betsy make their lives in a world indifferent to their ideals.

At stake in Blanton's life, as in the lives of the Moroccan peasants, is a conception of honor. The Texas and Morocco families both feel bound to a code of morality that they can never fully meet; Henry Blanton feels trapped by his. For the Moroccans, at least, *hshuma* (shame) creates shared public expectations. Moroccans realize that in private they and others may scheme to evade their obligations,

but in public they must respect certain codes of behavior. Blanton's situation is more tragic, for no common moral principle governs his public and private worlds. Honor—the myth of the simple, hard-working, modest cowboy enacted in movies and pulp novels—counts for nothing in the economic calculations that govern cattle ranching. Hshuma does not deter Henry's absentee boss from reneging on his promises.

Henry's pleasures, such as they are, come hard. He sits alone in his pickup truck drinking from a whiskey bottle he has hidden under the front seat; or he loses himself in the dirty chore of dehorning cattle; or, coming upon two urban cowboys in a store, he and his brother Tom pick a fight to force the strangers to remove their cowboy hats out of respect for real ranch hands. Betsy, his wife, wants to nurture Henry's dream but feels the pressure of the marketplace. Henry encourages her to play the role of loyal ranch wife and prepare big breakfasts and lunches for his crew. She would like to earn some cash and feel more independent by working at a job off the ranch. Betsy respects Henry's desire to live off the land but takes pride in the small consumer items she can buy for her kitchen and bath. In her quiet moments she reads Kahlil Gibran's *The Prophet* (1923).

The Last Cowboy won a 1981 American Book Award for best paperback nonfiction book. Critics praised its careful descriptions of setting and character but sometimes mistook Kramer's larger intellectual goals. Diane Johnson, writing for *The New York Review of Books,* improbably treated *The Last Cowboy* as a work of travel literature. Larry L. King, author of the play *The Best Little Whorehouse in Texas* (1978), writing in *The New York Times Book Review* on 22 January 1978 suggested that "the worst [Kramer] can be accused of is freshly presenting an old idea." King noted that he and Larry McMurtry (and several other male writers) had already discovered and told the story of the "last cowboy" many times. At least one critic, John Leonard of *The New York Times* (24 January 1978), better understood Kramer's method. He noted similarities between *The Last Cowboy* and *Allen Ginsberg* and praised her sympathy toward her subjects: "She is incapable of contempt, although the sadness has spurs."

By the time Kramer sat down to write the introduction to *The Last Cowboy,* she was back in Italy doing research on a rural peasant family. That piece was the last of four profiles written for *The New Yorker* between 1971 and 1979 and republished in *Unsettling Europe.* These stories announce the subject matter that engaged Kramer for much of the 1970s and 1980s–Europeans' attempts to conjure away the shadows of World War II and construct new forms of social and political identity that would transcend the old nationalist ideologies. What interested Kramer, however, was not the self-confident rhetoric of the European Miracle or Common Market but the hard, sad lives of recently displaced new Europeans, such as the exiles from former colonies in Africa or migrant workers from Yugoslavia and Turkey.

Unsettling Europe challenges a familiar convention of feature writing by taking the household or family, rather than the individual, as the writer's unit of analysis. In each story Kramer subtly shifts the point of view from one character to another while maintaining a single narrative voice. Her story of the San Vincenzo cell, for example, starts with the life of the father, Mario, but devotes long sections to his wife, Anna, and his son, Alfredo. Kra-

mer ends with a scene in which all three sit around with other members of the cell, playing cards and dreaming about Italy's future. This way of blending characters owes its pedigree to the novel, of course, and Kramer has particularly acknowledged the influence of the British novelist George Eliot on her work. As a style of reporting, this way of blending characters' lives and voices owes much to sociology and anthropology; it is the elegant journalistic equivalent of a careful researcher's field notes.

Unsettling Europe won much praise from critics, and the story, "The Invandrare," won the 1977 Front Page award for best feature in *The New Yorker.* Yet some critics continued to note Kramer's theoretical deficiencies. *The New York Times Book Review* again set this tone. Rexroth had once declared Kramer too straight to understand Ginsberg, and King had declared her too eastern and female to understand cowboys. Now Irving Howe, in what was largely a favorable and perceptive review on 18 May 1980, complained that she was not sufficiently polemical. He appreciated that Kramer's book "defies conventional modes of historical explanation" but found her "oddly hesitant" about interpreting European politics. Like Rexroth and King, Howe attributed her hesitancy to the demands of *The New Yorker* style, which encourages, he said, "an excessive concern for smoothness of verbal surface, an unwillingness to let passion break through or argument flare up, a desire to be modestly, professionally serious without becoming 'too' serious in the way of unruly or combative intellectuals."

Critics writing for smaller publications saw Kramer's work from a different vantage point. Thomas Flanagan, in the *Nation* (31 May 1980), wrote that "Kramer's intention is to break down the exhausted, conventional categories in which sociology and journalism solicit us to consider contemporary Europe, by creating for us the bitter, absurd, fractured lives of 'people who fell into the cracks of history.'" Kramer, he said, establishes the meaning and significance of her subjects' lives by "juxtapositions of telling detail" rather than by reference to a purportedly higher level of theoretical abstraction. Similarly, Robert Walch, reviewing *Unsettling Europe* for the Jesuit magazine *America* (1 November 1980), praised Kramer for her "family studies." "Families like these are a social, political, and economic reality, a fact of modern European existence many people refuse to acknowledge or concretely deal with."

Critics so regularly interpreted Kramer's early works as a retreat from theory and abstraction that Kramer herself grew wary of claiming too much. In a 1980 interview with *Contemporary Authors* Kramer said her strong points as a writer were her ability to

Kramer in 1988 (photograph by Aleksandra Crapanzano)

sketch a character and extract dramatic meaning from a large body of material. But she called herself "terrible at abstraction. . . . You'll notice that even my analytic pieces on Europe are grounded in observation and detail." Despite her modesty Kramer does have a theory—not the overarching political ideology Irving Howe was looking for but a theory of storytelling. As Flanagan and Walch recognized, the key choice was not between detail or theory, character or analysis, and surface or substance, but between two kinds of journalism, one indifferent to and the other cognizant of its own literary conventions.

Most feature writers take for granted the choices they make; they assume the importance, significance, or celebrity of an individual as well as the social typology purportedly represented by that person. (Scholarly writing operates with its own canons of taste, which it uses to distinguish serious writing about society and politics from mere journalism.) In *Unsettling Europe* Kramer invents a more fully social style of feature writing that can accommodate scholarship as well as in-depth interviewing and observation. Her stories respect an individual character's acts but give greater weight to social, political, and historical forces than journalists commonly do.

Kramer understands the theoretical implications of her narrative art, as the introduction to *Unsettling Europe* clearly suggests. That introduction is the most elaborate she has ever written, for it must explain what four stories about Italian Communists, Yugoslav migrant workers, Ugandan Muslims, and former French Algerians might have in common. These stories, Kramer writes, are about "Europeans whom Europe never expected to accommodate." Her characters have been betrayed by public policy—by political parties, imperialist dreams, capitalist convenience, or nationalist mythology. In place of the "easy abstractions" of "newsmagazine cliche and conference jargon" Kramer offers densely personal accounts. She confesses her admiration for the courage of her subjects: "It is the triumph of these private people over their public sociology that interested me." Finally, she acknowledges that all her subjects have been stigmatized, ignored, or shunted to the margins. "The pathos of their longing is that it is so often merely for belonging, for some corroboration by the world around them."

The first essay in *Unsettling Europe,* "The San Vincenzo Cell," chronicles the effect of post–World War II political changes on Italian peasants. Mario Cecchi's family belongs to one of the last Communist cells in Italy and to the rural dairy cooperative it founded. Now, however, the central party is more interested in protecting its network of political favors than in promoting its ideology and so discourages activists such as the Cecchis. The party has made its peace with the Christian Democrats in the hope of strengthening its own claims as padrone. The peasants, however, miss their old ways and wonder whether their solidarity has faded with the modernization of the village. In the second essay, "Invandrare," Predrag Ilic, a migrant worker, labors as an auto worker in Sweden, saving money to return to Yugoslavia each August to work on a house he is building in the country. In Sweden he and the other *invandrare* are paid well but treated as invisible. After almost eight years in Sweden, Ilic still does not feel he belongs, but the longer his family stays there they also feel less at home in Yugoslavia. In "The Uganda Asians" and *"Les Pieds Noirs"* former colonists flee the violence as old European empires collapse. The Asians (mostly Muslims, Hindus, Sikhs, and Ismailis originally from India and Pakistan, recruited once to work on British colonial projects in East Africa) flee to England after Idi Amin takes control in 1971. The pieds noirs, poor French citizens and political outcasts who immigrated to Algeria in the nineteenth century, return to France when Algeria wins independence in 1962, after a long and brutal war in which they found themselves terrorized by both the French OAS and the Algerian FLN.

Common themes run through all these stories. None is about a single individual. Each nominally begins with one person—Mario Cecchi, Predrag Ilic, Akbar Hassan, and Mme. Martin—and then traces that person's life through an ever-widening network of spouses, children, and neighbors as well as ethnic, religious, and nationalist identities. Stylistically, the profiles in *Unsettling Europe* set the model for much of Kramer's subsequent work. In *Washington Square, Allen Ginsberg,* and *Honor to the Bride* Kramer uses an event, a person, or a setting to frame her narrative. In *Unsettling Europe* she begins to control the narrative line more firmly, deciding for herself the order in which she will recount events and switching frequently between times, places, and characters. This technique allows interpretation but avoids obvious editorializing. A strong authorial presence controls the story, but the text opens itself to multiple voices.

Europeans (1988), Kramer's next book, paints this same portrait of Europe in deepening and more-varied shades. Whereas *Unsettling Europe* focuses on four families of quite divergent backgrounds who share a common plight, *Europeans* mixes a wider variety of pieces that Kramer wrote for *The New Yorker* between 1978 and 1988. It includes seven portraits of ordinary Europeans (generally similar to the people encountered in *Unsettling Europe*); sketches of five major European cities; a series of short comic pieces written over two years about Mme. Goncalves, Kramer's concierge in Paris; eight long stories about controversial current events such as the Kurt Waldheim scandal, a British coal strike, and anti-NATO protests in Germany; a series of short obituaries and sketches of renowned Europeans such as Pierre Mendès France, Nathalie Suraute, and Christo; and eight shorter reflections about events and people in the news, such as Klaus Barbie's extradition to France to stand trial for his war crimes.

Europeans is also Kramer's first book to contain a foreword by another writer—in this case, William Shawn, editor of *The New Yorker* for thirty-five years and the man who hired Kramer. Asking Shawn to write the foreword and dedicating the book to *The New Yorker* staff may have been Kramer's discreet way of honoring Shawn at the end of his career and protesting recent changes at the magazine. On 12 January 1987, after years of organizational turmoil, Shawn was replaced as editor, much to the consternation of many longtime *New Yorker* staff writers. Though she was not one of the writers most publicly opposing the change, Kramer greatly admired

Shawn. "There is no one in the world like Bill Shawn, with his gentle and amazing instinct for the very peculiar way a writer works," Kramer had written in her introduction to *The Last Cowboy*.

Shawn's foreword explains Kramer's place in *The New Yorker* tradition of journalism as he understood it. He calls her method "odd"—a compliment that praises Kramer for approaching her subject "obliquely and idiosyncratically" and for choosing topics for no other reason than "profound personal interest." Humor and irony, for Shawn, are crucial components of Kramer's style: "At the center of her writing is wit, and at the center of the wit are a powerful intelligence and an elegance of diction." The "beauty and clarity" of her writing, Shawn argues, marks it as literature. He attributes to Kramer the cosmopolitan qualities to which *The New Yorker* has long aspired: wit, elegance, and an idiosyncratic, even dilettantish, curiosity (the same qualities to which Kramer's critics have occasionally objected).

Predictably, perhaps, Shawn thinks of Kramer as a writer rather than a journalist. "Ostensibly," Shawn says, "she writes factual reports on timely matters. Again and again, however, she crosses over into the literary realm; the timely becomes timeless, and her work can be read with rapt interest years after it was written." This assessment highlights Kramer's accomplishments as a writer but obscures her skills as a reporter. Kramer herself is much more conscious about the research and interpretation that goes into her work. She told *Contemporary Authors* that she typically spends weeks with her subjects, alternately following them around and gathering background information in nearby locales. By any reasonable public standard Kramer may be the most learned and well-read literary journalist working today. Her essays in *Europeans* regularly cite the work of historians, artists, philosophers, and critics such as Pierre Bourdieu, Claude Lévi-Strauss, Phillipe Aries, Roland Barthes, René Wellek, and Gregory Bateson.

Reviewers agreed that *Europeans* was a superb piece of writing; they called it "masterful," "exquisite," "polished," "distinguished," and "brilliant." Some, however, criticized the book for being neither timely nor timeless enough. Certain journalists, such as those reviewing Kramer's book for the *Economist* and the *Christian Science Monitor,* found some of the articles dated or complained that Kramer had not reconsidered some of her earlier judgments in the light of recent political changes. A former University of California, Berkeley, comparative-literature professor who reviewed *Europeans* for the *Los Angeles Times Book Review* on 11 December 1988 (and was himself the author of a book subtitled "Understanding Europeans") complained that Kramer's work "fails to rise to the level of timeless literature." Such criticisms underscore reviewers' inability to fit Kramer's work into familiar categories of journalism or literature. Her writing is timely only in the loosest sense; she thinks in terms of years rather than days or hours, and she avoids the geopolitical prognostication so beloved by foreign correspondents. Nor does she imagine herself producing timeless work; Shawn's distinction between timely and timeless is one she herself has never invoked, and reviewers' use of it probably owes more to their reading of Shawn's introduction than of Kramer's stories.

Europeans interprets the politics of cultural identity as it is played out in national policy, cultural mythology, news coverage, local prejudice, and family history. Kramer understands European politics as a symbolic drama and treats political events as cultural texts. Particularly new and notable are the book's ambitious profiles of five major cities—Hamburg, Paris, Zurich, London, and West Berlin. These city essays are among the most accomplished and opinionated pieces Kramer has ever written. Here she reconstructs nothing less than the cultural climate of time, place, and nationality. In less capable hands these city pieces would fall into stereotyping and journalistic cliché: for example, the French, Swiss, and Germans are like this, this, and that. But Kramer listens carefully to how Europeans describe one another—especially to how the French and Germans act upon their imagined cultural differences—and she supports her observations with a great deal of evidence.

Besides writing political analysis for *The New Yorker,* Kramer turned her experience living overseas into a series of handsome, short feature articles for upscale consumer magazines. During the 1980s *House and Garden* commissioned stories from Kramer and other well-known writers as part of the publisher Condé Nast's campaign to attract a more upscale audience for the magazine. Between 1983 and 1989 *House and Garden* published six of Kramer's articles describing French cooking, entertaining, Christmas rituals, and gardening; camping on a safari in Botswana; and New York City's hierarchy of taste. These features unselfconsciously appeal to the tastes and interests of a well-to-do audience. They probe less deeply than Kramer's other work, but their style sparkles and each contains a healthy dose of Kramer's wit and insight.

Kramer turned back to the United States again for her next book. *Whose Art Is It?* (1994), which originally appeared as a single long article in *The New Yorker* in 1992, recounts a battle over publicly

funded sculpture in the Bronx. In its scope and development it resembles "The San Vincenzo Cell." It is essentially a nonfiction novella, a small book told in one take, built around a single controversial incident, featuring a cast of interesting characters. A stylistic tour de force and winner of the 1993 National Magazine Award for feature writing, *Whose Art Is It?* displays the dense, graceful, complex narrative that Kramer has spent years perfecting. Unlike her previous books, which had been published by trade houses such as Harper and Row, Random House, and Farrar, Straus and Giroux, *Whose Art Is It?* was published in 1994 by Duke University Press as part of its new "Public Planet Books" series, which Kramer, Dilip Gaonkar, and Michael Warner edit. According to the prospectus, the series intends to publish "narratives of public culture" and to "open the scholarly discourse on contemporary public culture" with sophisticated books that combine "reportage and critical reflection."

Whose Art Is It? analyzes public art as a contested cultural practice. John Ahearn, an internationally known sculptor, wins a commission from New York City's Percent for Art Program to install three statues on pedestals outside a new police precinct house in the Bronx. The statues depict a man in his thirties in a hooded sweatshirt kneeling next to his beloved pit bull, a husky man in his twenties standing shirtless with a basketball under one arm and one foot on a boom box, and a gangly teenage girl on roller skates. Even before the statues are erected, however, protesters complain that the figures stereotype and demean the neighborhood and its residents. The conflict ends when Ahearn voluntarily takes down the statues only five days after they are erected.

Contradictions abound in this tale. Ahearn sells his sculpture to upscale clients through swank midtown galleries but lives in the South Bronx. Ahearn's critics argue that his statues misrepresent the community even though the statues are life-size molds of actual residents. Some critics even argue that Ahearn cannot speak for the community because he is not African American even though many of the neighborhood's residents are Latino and the critics themselves, unlike Ahearn, are professionals who live in Manhattan. Neighborhood activists want to display positive role models rather than troublemakers and lawbreakers; they think that statues of college students or white-collar professionals would be more appropriate even though such people are rare in the neighborhood.

Ultimately, *Whose Art Is It?* examines the social conflicts often referenced by shorthand terms such as *multiculturalism* and *political correctness.* Catherine

Stimpson's introduction to the book addresses these issues in a more explicit way than Kramer herself does. *Whose Art Is It?* offers many questions but few answers. Who has the right to decide what will count for "public" art? Does an artist owe allegiance to actual, local neighbors or to "higher" principles of artistic freedom? What does it mean to belong to a community? Who has the cultural authority to speak on behalf of that community? Kramer adds layers of nuance to each of these questions until the reader experiences the conflict as intellectually and emotionally vexing in the same way that the participants themselves did.

Kramer has continued to write for *The New Yorker* on political issues in France, Italy, Germany, and, occasionally, Latin America in the tradition of her "Letter from Europe." Her 1987 article "Letter from the Elysian Fields" discusses Brazilian priests who practice liberation theology and their continuing conflicts with the Vatican. She has explored Germans' quest for meaning in the wake of reunification in her 1993 article, "Neo-Nazis: A Chaos in the Head," and her 1995 article, "The Politics of Memory." However, she has remained unusually silent on one issue—feminism. By contrast, many other contemporary women writers have used the personal essay to discuss issues of gender, politics, and identity. Kramer, for her part, has lived a feminist's life, working in Europe, traveling widely, and writing self-confidently and incisively about political issues that men have traditionally assumed were theirs. Similarly, her style of writing suggests a feminist sensibility with its focus on the household rather than on the individual and its habit of shading one character's voice into another's to re-create the density of social life. And yet for the most part, despite the occasional personal reflections found here and there throughout her work, Kramer has addressed feminist concerns indirectly.

She admitted as much in a telling autobiographical essay titled "The Invisible Woman," published in the much-debated 1996 *New Yorker* special issue on women. Kramer begins that essay by recalling one of her earliest stories for *The New Yorker,* "Founding Cadre." Published in 1970, that story profiles a group of talented and contentious New York City feminists who founded one of the nation's first consciousness-raising groups. As always, Kramer's story draws together many themes—her own introduction to feminism; the women's reaction to her presence and her reactions to them; women's struggles with one another; her own experiences in Morocco while writing *Honor to the Bride*; her upbringing in the comfortably middle-class world of Providence and her education at a Quaker girls' school and an all-female Vassar College; generational differences in the types of feminism practiced by her and her grandmother, mother, and daughter; and the current conservative attack on feminism.

Kramer says that she thinks of herself as a good feminist, "even a militant feminist," but resists self-revelation. "Confessionals make me uncomfortable—blue collar or bourgeois, other people's or my own." Instead, she defines feminism as a critical principle, "a way of thinking . . . that is juicy, subversive, and severe." She defends the accomplishments of educated, well-to-do women and objects to the "Roseanne fallacy," the assumption that "getting battered in a trailer park gives a woman more insight into women's lives than a tenure battle at Harvard Law School." Looking back on the months she spent with the women in 1970, Kramer says she "saw the light, and went off to live my life while other women made the revolution for me." She recognizes her debt to such women: "Today, I owe them."

The title of Kramer's article, "The Invisible Woman," speaks to her career as a journalist as well as her relation to feminism. Over three decades she has developed one of the most elegant and distinctive voices in American literary journalism. She has written with depth and sophistication about an extraordinary range of topics. She has earned the admiration of careful readers and other professional writers. She has refused to traffic in celebrity, speculation, or shallow controversy. She writes eloquently of her subjects' virtues and vices, regardless of their social standing. Yet for all the praise of her beautiful writing style, Kramer remains underappreciated as a reporter and analyst. If she were a man, if she wrote in a more ponderously theoretical style, if she wrote more about Americans and less about foreign people, if she more forcefully declared her personal politics, if her books regularly reached *The New York Times* best-seller list, if she promoted herself as shamelessly as others do, she would find herself being heralded by the newsweeklies as a "public intellectual."

Kramer writes in "The Invisible Woman" that in 1970 she and other women of her generation often felt marginal, even within the antiwar movement and counterculture. So she made her marginality into a career because "the margins were not such a bad place for a reporter to be." "The margins," she says, "gave you a kind of critical space, a shrewd, unimplicated distance from which to look at power and the people who used and abused power." This experience of marginality and invisibility have not been Kramer's alone, of course. The profession of journalism is mythically devoted, in equal measure, to objectivity and publicity, to detachment and fame, and journalists, like women, struggle to make themselves visible. The worst journalists settle for notoriety, serving as television pundits, currying favor with the powerful, surfing the tides of public opinion. The best, like Kramer, cherish their independence but want something more. They seek to make their presence felt, to serve as witnesses rather than remain just observers. Writing from a farmhouse in Italy, Kramer watches a "fat male pheasant" strut outside her window. The pheasant, she says, "has been casing my house for the past two weeks and has just installed his hen and their chicks in a field by the pond. Other people might admire his markings, but I am watching to see how he treats his hen and how she treats him and who looks after the babies. I want to know if the hen is free."

References:

Steve Jones, "Jane Kramer," in *A Sourcebook of American Literary Journalism: Representative Writers in an Emerging Genre,* edited by Thomas B. Connery (New York: Greenwood Press, 1992), pp. 323–329;

Kevin M. McAuliffe, *The Great American Newspaper: the Rise and Fall of the* Village Voice (New York: Scribners, 1978), pp. 71–73.

Mark Kramer
(14 April 1944 –)

Jim Collins
Dartmouth College

BOOKS: *Mother Walter and the Pig Tragedy* (New York: Knopf, 1972);
Three Farms: Making Milk, Meat, and Money from the American Soil (Boston: Atlantic-Little, Brown, 1980; revised edition, Cambridge & London: Harvard University Press, 1987);
Invasive Procedures: A Year in the World of Two Surgeons (New York: Harper & Row, 1983);
Travels with a Hungry Bear: A Journey to the Russian Heartland (Boston: Houghton Mifflin, 1996).

OTHER: *The Growth of Industrial Art,* compiled by Benjamin Butterworth, introduction by Kramer (New York: Knopf, 1972);
Literary Journalism: A New Collection of the Best American Nonfiction, edited, with introductions, by Kramer and Norman Sims (New York: Ballantine, 1995).

Mark Kramer (photograph by Barry Nigrosh)

Books like Mark Kramer's *Three Farms: Making Milk, Meat, and Money from the American Soil* (1980), wrote Noel Perrin in *The New York Times Book Review* (1980), are "the true 'new journalism.' What's new is not the use of novelistic technique, but the use of truly exhaustive research, the shift from quick and easy reporting to the complete tracing of an ecosystem." Indeed, in setting out to answer the question of why so many American farms are being lost each year, Mark Kramer spent close to a year in libraries gaining background on American agricultural history, trends, and policy. He spent much of the next three years living on farms in Massachusetts, Iowa, and California before writing *Three Farms*. In the process of his research he became expert enough on the history and politics of agriculture to be offered a position teaching the subject at the University of Massachusetts, even without a doctorate. Since the publication of *Three Farms,* Kramer has published two more exhaustively researched books and dozens of magazine articles. *Immersion journalism* is a term he sometimes uses to describe his craft.

Mark William Kramer was born in Brooklyn, New York, on 14 April 1944. Books were an integral part of the family's life. Kramer's father, Sidney B. Kramer, was an executive in paperback publishing. His mother, Esther B. Schlansky Kramer, was a bookstore owner in Westport, Connecticut, where the family moved when he was six. Mark remembers that his father was the last one each day off the commuter train from New York. In explaining his success in the publishing business, the elder Kramer was fond of saying, "All of the other men just watch the bottom line. I watch them." His family paid attention to psychology and motivation, and that interest later came to distinguish Mark Kramer's nonfiction.

Sidney Kramer also wrote a local newspaper column, but it was Esther who may have had more

149

influence on Mark's eventual career. Esther was a brilliant storyteller who loved telling long, involved jokes filled with irony and surprise. She shied away from writing, but in her stories she set vivid scenes, using just the right language and carefully drawing her characters. "If I was half the story-teller she was," says Kramer, "I'd be twice the writer I am." As part of a Jewish family in suburban Connecticut, Mark learned what it was like to grow up "on the edge of things." That margin, he feels, forced him to learn the skills of an interested but detached observer.

Kramer graduated from Brandeis University in 1966 with a B.A. in English. He concentrated primarily on poetry, notably in courses taught by Ruth Stone, a well-known poet, and Alan Grossman, who later was named a McArthur Fellow. "It was from them I learned to think about the music of sentences," Kramer says. He was managing editor of the student paper. He also took courses in sociology, the subject in which he received a master's degree in 1968 from Columbia University.

He returned to poetry for graduate work at Indiana University the following academic year. "I considered myself a writer of verse until I was about 25," he says. At Indiana, though, two events led him to shift that assessment. His first real experience in front of a classroom, teaching writing to freshmen, convinced him he wanted to teach. Then he "caught politics." The war in Vietnam was raging. He helped edit an underground newspaper on campus, then gave up his graduate study to move to New York and write for the Liberation News Service. An unexpected event shifted his direction yet again: a lump mysteriously appeared on his left hip. The lump, removed by surgery, proved to be benign, but the effect it had on Kramer was profound. To recover from the surgery he left his job with the Liberation News Service and moved to a tiny hill farm in western Massachusetts. In a short time he began writing a regular "letter from the country" column for the *Cambridge Phoenix*. He received strong support from Harper Barnes, new editor of the *Phoenix,* later a novelist and an editorial writer for the *St. Louis Post-Dispatch*. "He was the person who gave me my start," says Kramer.

Kramer's first book, *Mother Walter and the Pig Tragedy* (1972), grew out of those newspaper columns. By the time of his tenth column he had already received inquiries from four book publishers. He settled on Knopf and edited thirty of his columns to work together as a book. Many of the essays touched on the rural life he saw disappearing around him and the juxtaposition of the new wave of young, urban back-to-the-landers and the local, old-line Yankee farmers. In 1972 a reviewer for *Publisher's Weekly* wrote, "Actually his book is an evocative half-acre of revealing digres-

sions about the hardships, horrors and austerities of the farming life, warmed and leavened by Kramer's profiles of vinegary village characters, helpful farm folk, and revolting snowmobilers come wintertime. . . ."

While the personal-essay form of the book is not considered literary journalism, that trait of "revealing digressions"–breaking away at an important moment in a scene for a discussion of, say, economics or the evolution of milking stanchions or the locals' attitude toward communes–became a hallmark of Kramer's later, more journalistic work. The technique is central to what he calls "extended digressive narrative nonfiction" rather than the now-accepted term *literary journalism.*

In *Mother Walter and the Pig Tragedy* the frank, intimate voice that distinguishes Kramer's reportage gives the reader the sense of being in the hands of a trustworthy, tell-it-like-it-is host. Kramer writes,

> There's no question that Hubert fit into the respected citizen category. For as many years as he wished the job, he was the judge at the local fall fair for all manner of horse-drawing contests. He still carries a reputation as a first-rate plowman, won in the days when horses were used for farm work. His barn was always freshly whitewashed, his empty grain sacks folded and stored in numbered bundles, his mangers never showed the matted signs of yesterday's feed. He kept his barn like he was a fussy old widower–which, now that I mention it, is just what he was.

Another trait found in this book is the distance Kramer keeps from the subjects he writes about, his narrative stance. Even in these personal essays the reader gets a clear sense of a narrator who is enough apart from his subjects–the locals *and* the back-to-the-landers–to describe and comment on the ironies or inconsistencies to which true, unselfconscious insiders of either group might be blind: "There's no reason to suppose the good people of the town will cease their wondering just at the moment a dozen strangely accented and oddly dressed, long-haired, unkempt and unmarried kids move into the old Biddle place, or the Thomas brothers' lower farm, or wherever," he wrote. "Truism: everybody always gets talked about in a country village."

While living in western Massachusetts, Kramer became interested in the dairy farms disappearing around him; in many cases, excellent farmers were staggering along or being forced out by circumstances beyond their control. He realized that no deep understanding was possible without learning the history and context surrounding those farms–from what traditions they had grown, in what economic and marketing climates they now found themselves competing. That interest led to his first major work of literary journalism, *Three Farms*.

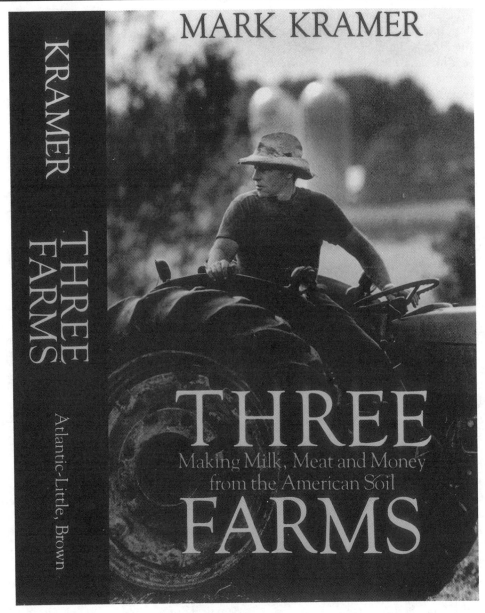

Dust jacket for Kramer's first major work

Kramer queried Richard Todd, then an editor at the *Atlantic Monthly,* who had favorably reviewed Kramer's first book. That contact had resulted in Kramer's first major magazine piece, a story about an Iowa county fair. (*Atlantic* would later publish two feature-length excerpts from *Three Farms.*) With encouragement from Todd, Kramer devoted the next five years to the research and writing of what became a book that looked at the state of American agriculture through the lenses of three distinct farms: a small, family-run dairy in Massachusetts; a large, subsidized hog farm in Iowa; and a giant, corporate vegetable farm in the San Joaquin Valley of California. A Humanities Fellowship grant

from the Rockefeller Foundation helped fund his research.

The book is divided into three sections, each corresponding to the individual farm profiled. The three farms, carefully chosen for their symbolic and real differences, gradually merge into a single portrait of America's changing farm industry, one increasingly dominated by technology, mechanization, and a small handful of powerful corporations.

According to Kramer's book, the meticulously run fourth-generation Totman dairy farm in northwestern Massachusetts, a state where fewer than two thousand family farms are left, has prospered through a combination of good land, careful transfer of ownership, intelligent farming, and the savvy use of emerging farm technologies. Ironically, Kramer notes, the Totmans' ability to coax more and more milk from their cows has forced many of their neighbors' farms out of existence, and along with them, a way of life.

The second farm is a typical hog and corn operation in Creston, Iowa, heavily mortgaged, capital intensive, where most of the five hundred acres are rented from absentee landowners. The motivation driving the farmwork is not so much improving production as meeting the payments on the land, supplies, and vast array of trucks, tractors, combines, spreaders, sprayers, cultivators, wagons, plows, and other specialized equipment. The farmer, Joe Weisshaar, encounters the dilemma faced by farmers across the Midwest: expand or perish. Yet expansion means increasing debt, purchasing still more machinery, and pushing the operation even farther away from family farming toward factory-style production.

The third section describes a modern corporate farm covering twenty-one thousand acres of irrigated land in central California. Here, the actual "farmer" is impossible to locate within the convoluted infrastructure of investors, subsidiaries, and holding companies. The farming is carried out according to spreadsheets, shipping schedules, and tax benefits, not according to weather and intimate knowledge of the crops being grown. The farm represents a radical shift away from the idea of farming as "craft" toward powerful, monopolistic agribusiness.

With the publication of *Three Farms,* Mark Kramer joined the select company of writers being referred to as "literary journalists." In *The New York Times Book Review* Noel Perrin wrote:

> Mr. Kramer does two remarkable things in this book. One is to capture the true feel of country life in a high-technology era. Most writing about the country is an exercise in one form or another of nostalgia, but this book is a vivid account of what really happens. Such a scene as Mr. Kramer's description of night harvesting in California—with the floodlights mounted on towers and machines straight out of science fiction, the row-crops supervisor talking on a mobile telephone and a repair crew rumbling across the field in the same kind of truck that services jets—shows a fine ear for American speech and a fine eye for detail. Mr. Kramer can be sad, funny and incisive in a single paragraph. The book reads as well as the best McPhee or Mitchell.

The summary in the *Kirkus Reviews* (1 April 1980) stated, "Profiles of three farms in the McPhee man-

ner, but with a cumulative, what-is-American-agriculture-coming-to effect."

The book received favorable notice in journals as diverse as *Harper's,* the *Village Voice,* the *Christian Science Monitor, Business Week,* and the *Nation,* among others. Writing in the July 1980 issue of *Harper's,* Jeffrey Burke concluded, "Besides knowing whereof he speaks, Kramer writes thereof with wit, economy, precision, and insight, and *Three Farms* reads better and rewards more than many novels." In another part of that review Burke refers to the "digressive" nature of Kramer's writing, "the self-contained short essay or narrative that either forms an integral part of the text or else stands apart as important background." These pieces, Burke says, "function structurally, they always delight and instruct, and the book abounds in them." In an interview for that review, Kramer said the painstaking research he did was "to assure himself that he was, in all he wrote about, as expert as the most expert reader, if only for the length of a paragraph's digression."

Three Farms, in addition to putting Mark Kramer on the literary map, provided other unexpected benefits. Dick Todd had passed on a copy of the manuscript to the poet Archibald MacLeish, who owned a home near the Totman farm. MacLeish liked the manuscript so well that he passed it on to Jill Kerr Conway, then the president of Smith College, who subsequently offered Kramer a writer-in-residence position at Smith. In the wake of *Three Farms* Kramer wrote and codirected an award-winning documentary about New England agriculture for public television. He also served for five years as a policy consultant for the Massachusetts Department of Agriculture.

During the time he was writing *Three Farms* Kramer met regularly to discuss his work and other aspects of writing with Dick Todd and Tracy Kidder, who lived in nearby towns. At the time Kidder was at work on *Soul of a New Machine* (1981), an outstanding work of literary journalism that would receive a Pulitzer Prize. The three men were valuable resources for each other, and that relationship still remains strong. The association with Todd has been especially important for Kramer. Todd served as an informal editor of Kramer's third book, *Invasive Procedures: A Year in the World of Two Surgeons* (1983), and edited Kramer's fourth book, *Travels with a Hungry Bear: A Journey to the Russian Heartland,* under his own imprint ("A Richard Todd Book," 1996).

In his prologue to *Invasive Procedures* Kramer refers to his own hip operation as a genesis for the idea of the book. Fifteen years after the operation, at the age of thirty-eight, Kramer's curiosity about surgery was stirred again. While at a party Kramer listened to a psychologist talking about an experiment he had performed on anesthetized patients. Kramer writes, "The conversation at the loud party reopened a closed topic and a few weeks later I was making plans to visit—to return, in a sense—to see, to touch and try to understand whatever had cut me open and moved me out of town."

The book is a detailed look at the world of two surgeons, describing their day-to-day lives, their obsession with their work, their power, their relationship with their colleagues and patients, and their perceived place in society. Along the way, as in *Three Farms,* Kramer investigates larger topics: the high cost of medical care, the psychological effects of the doctor-patient relationship, the nature of fear, and the politics, biases, and elitism of the healing profession.

Kramer's research for *Invasive Procedures* was exhaustive. He spent three years on the project, including eighteen months of fieldwork. In the process of his research he followed a vascular surgeon and a general surgeon through the course of more than one hundred operating room procedures, hundreds of office visits, and private time at home. He consulted with dozens of doctors, nurses, surgical technicians, hospital administrators, and other health personnel. The Ford Foundation provided funding in support of the project.

The book reinforced Kramer's position among the ranks of the best young literary journalists. Its characters, scenes, dialogue, digressions, and commentary are full of voice and tense, gripping narrative. In an early operating-room scene Kramer displays the literary journalist's skill at describing a scene and commenting on it at the same time:

> "Here's what Ponce de Leon was searching for," Andersson says, pointing to a wire of blood that squirts upward through a needle hole at the top of the graft. It takes half an hour to track down leaks and stitch them with filaments of thread. He closes the two leg incisions. He releases the intestines (the nurses, yielding up their retractor handles, look relieved), and runs them once again. He folds the wad of yellow fat comprising the potbelly back down into place, which seems a shame. He stitches closed the inner wall of the intestinal sac, and the supporting tissue. He stitches closed the subcutaneous fat. He stitches closed the incision, finally, with coarse black twine.
>
> When I had met Andersson before this day in surgery, he had seemed aloof from the world, affectedly genial, self-absorbed, and masking pride with a measured affability. In surgery, Andersson starts to make sense. In here, tensed, single-minded, and happy, he becomes graceful. It's like hearing a man with a Hungarian accent begin to speak Hungarian.

The *Atlantic Monthly* ran an eighteen-thousand-word excerpt from *Invasive Procedures* as a cover story, under the title "Benign Violence." The book drew a mixed review by Joe McGinniss in *The New York Times Book Review* on 18 September 1983. McGinniss described the book as "engrossing but uneven." He wrote of Kramer's "reportorial skill, combined with a prose style that (except for a certain cloying clumsiness in the use of the first person) is as clean and sharp as one of his subjects' scalpel blades." His conclusion touched on a definition of the literary journalist: "The irony is that it is as 'nobody special,' that Mr. Kramer functions best: as our guide into the very special world—mundane and at the same time almost occult—of the modern surgeon."

A section of the book was anthologized in *The Literary Journalists* (1984), a book whose introduction borrows heavily from Kramer's ideas and teachings about the craft. In his introduction to the excerpt Sims writes, "This excerpt gives a rare look inside the world of one of those surgeons by someone who is not a patient or physician. Kramer acts as our guide in this strange world. By revealing his own fears of cancer, he brings the subject into our world—if even our friendly guide can be afflicted, can we dare be complacent?"

A sequel to that anthology, *Literary Journalism: A New Collection of the Best American Nonfiction* (1995), coedited by Kramer and Norman Sims, includes separate introductions by both men. Kramer's introduction, "Breakable Rules for Literary Journalists," outlines rules for the craft derived from the common practices of the field's leading writers. He uses language and concepts he developed in his courses at Smith College, where he taught from 1980 to 1990, and at Boston University, where he has been a professor and a writer-in-residence since 1990.

Literary journalists immerse themselves in their subjects' world and in background research. "Literary journalists hang out with their sources for months and even years," Kramer writes. "The point of long immersions is to comprehend subjects at a level of 'felt life'—the frank, unidealized level that includes individual differences, frailty, tenderness, nastiness, vanity, generosity, pomposity, humility, all in proper proportion."

Literary journalists work out implicit covenants about accuracy and candor with readers and with sources. He writes, "Conventions literary journalists nowadays talk about following to keep things square include: no composite scenes, no misstated chronology, no falsification of the discernible drift or proportion of events, no invention of quotes, no attribution of thoughts to sources unless the sources

Dust jacket for Kramer's 1983 book, based on three years of research on the medical profession

have said they'd had those very thoughts, and no unacknowledged deals with subjects involving payment or editorial control."

Literary journalists write mostly about routine events, and literary journalists write in "intimate voice," informal, frank, human, and ironic. This nonacademic, noninstitutional voice "is the voice in which we disclose how people and institutions *really* are," Kramer writes. "It is a key characteristic of literary journalism, and is indeed something new to journalism."

Style counts, and tends to be plain and spare. Literary journalists write from a disengaged and mobile stance, from which they tell stories and also turn and address readers directly. In other words, literary journalists write from a perspective that al-

lows them to tell a story and comment on the story, and even comment on themselves as they tell it.

Structure counts, mixing primary narrative with tales and digressions to amplify and reframe events. Literary journalists develop meaning by building upon the readers' sequential reactions. "Successful literary journalists never forget to be entertaining," Kramer writes. "Readers should come to feel they are heading somewhere with purpose, that the job of reading has a worthy destination." Throughout the introduction reveals an extraordinary understanding of his craft. Many of his observations are backed with examples from the best literary journalists of the past fifty years.

Kramer's most recent book, *Travels with a Hungry Bear,* is an evocative look at the sad state of agriculture in the former Soviet Union. He attempts to answer the question "How can a country of eleven time zones of wheat fields not feed itself?" Again, Kramer serves the reader as host in a strange world–a world that dramatically shifted in the process of his writing about it. The result is a compelling tale that is part travelogue, part social and political commentary, part agricultural criticism, part historical document, and part psychological portraiture.

In addition to the hours spent on background and secondary research, Kramer made six trips to the Soviet Union while writing the book. He pushed the limits of a region famous for its closed access to journalists, benefiting slightly at times from the thawing of the Cold War. The timing, however, was not kind to the book. Kramer had just completed his first draft when the Soviet Union finally collapsed, making much of what he had written instantly out of date. "It was," he says, "as if I'd made a huge mosaic out of tiny pieces, and someone had come along and tipped the whole thing over, leaving the pieces in a jumble on the floor. I could use bits of the information I'd gathered, but now I had to start over and put them back together in a new order."

Kramer describes a typical event at the beginning of the book, one that symbolizes much of his experience being led from official state farm to official state farm. "Let us trudge down a well-worn garden path toward a lavish rosepatch planted in the middle of nowhere. Fat roses–red, white, yellow and pink, gaudy as cupcakes, wavered in file behind the burly shoulders of the delegation that marched forward to greet us in the dooryard of the Belgorad Slaughterhouse and Sausage Factory. The factory chairman, Andrei Michailovich Kozulin, held out a ham-sized hand, and looked welcoming and sincere and official." After guiding him along, the official shouts in his ear, "Please note that we have 1,500 rose plants, here in the yard in front of the cutting floor." He then whispers, "Regretfully, the production site is closed today. It is impossible to view it. But you will sample our excellent product."

Using his knowledge of agriculture, gained from his work on *Three Farms,* Kramer time and again is able to read between the lines of the official information he is fed (or to see through blatant lies by understanding exactly what he is looking at), to frame his observations of Soviet farming with U.S. practices and policy, and to put the information in context. The result is a condemnation of state-run agriculture on a large scale but a sympathetic portrait of everyday people who struggle to live within a system of entrenched bureaucracy, underground markets, and chronic shortages of everything from food staples to fertilizer and basic tractor parts. An example of that "felt life" reporting follows an incident in which Kramer realizes he has offended his hosts by offering a gift:

> I was amazed that this intersection was so intelligible to both of us, in spite of our having mimed most of it. How differently we'd filled our lives. Yet I could imagine being him; the basics were in place. There was his warm wife, who laughed at his jokes and raised children with him . . . I could imagine him sensing which boss respected him on the job, and which didn't. He worried about the advent of middle age, thought what more money would bring his family, what he could count as accomplishments. . . .

A major magazine article, drawn from the book's research, appeared in 1989 in *The New York Times Magazine* under the title "Can Gorbachev Feed Russia?" Other magazine pieces that qualify as literary journalism include "The Eternal Boyhood of an American Hero" in *The New York Times Magazine* (1983) and "Life on the Line" in *National Geographic* (1985). In profiling Tommy John–a religious, clean-cut major-league pitcher–Kramer chooses an opening whose setting is filled with telling detail and symbolic value. Kramer writes:

> In the bottom curl of the serpentine path, down past the piped-in stream that tumbles over the constructed waterfall, amid trimmed shrubs and freshly flowered succulents, next to the pool and Jacuzzi, and just below the triple-seater tree stump that has the ceramic owl perched on its back, it's family picnic time. The menu offered here in Anaheim, California, at the white lawn table under the beach umbrella, is the same as the one being grilled transcontinentally. . . . "We really out of hot dog rolls?" Tommy John asks. . . . "It's the Fourth of July."

In the course of his reporting Kramer attended several games, visited locker rooms, spent time with Tommy John away from the field, and even had John pitch to him so he could see the pitches as a batter would. Ostensibly a profile, the piece includes digressions into the nature of fame, hero worship, and the curious place professional athletes hold in our society.

In gathering information for "Life on the Line" Kramer spent three months along the two-thousand-mile border between the United States and Mexico. His vivid reporting portrays the bicultural world he found there, from the gritty, bustling markets of Tijuana to the nighttime raids on illegal alien crossings to the remote canyons of the Rio Grande. Discussions of immigration policy and the immigrant labor economy weave throughout the narrative.

Kramer has also written articles for *The Wall Street Journal, The Washington Post, The Chicago Tribune, The New York Times, Outside, Yankee, New England Monthly,* and other publications. He is currently at work writing a series of reports about Boston Harbor for *The Boston Globe Magazine.* He lives in Boston with his wife, Susan Eaton, and their son William.

In addition to his stature as a writer of literary journalism, Mark Kramer has distinguished himself by his teaching of the genre, both in the classroom and as a panelist and speaker. He has devoted years not only to the understanding of the craft but also to careful, systematic instruction of it. His devotion comes from more than the scholar's passion. At the end of his introduction in *Literary Journalism* Mark Kramer writes:

> I'll even claim that there is something intrinsically political—and strongly democratic—about literary journalism, something pluralistic, pro-individual, anti-cant, and anti-elite. That seems inherent in the common practices of the form. Informal style cuts through the obfuscating generalities of creeds, countries, companies, bureaucracies, and experts. And narratives of the felt lives of everyday people test idealization against actualities. Truth is in the details of real lives.

Reference:

Norman Sims, ed., *The Literary Journalists* (New York: Ballantine, 1984).

Norman Mailer

(31 January 1923 –)

Douglas Birkhead
University of Utah

See also the Mailer entries in *DLB 2: American Novelists Since World War II, DLB 16: The Beats: Literary Bohemians in Postwar America,* and *DLB 28: Twentieth-Century American-Jewish Fiction Writers.*

BOOKS: *The Naked and the Dead* (New York: Rinehart, 1948; London: Wingate, 1949);

Barbary Shore (New York: Rinehart, 1951; London: Cape, 1952);

The Deer Park (New York: Putnam, 1955; London: Wingate, 1957);

The White Negro: Superficial Reflections on the Hipster (San Francisco: City Lights Books, 1957);

Advertisements for Myself (New York: Putnam, 1959; London: Deutsch, 1961);

Deaths for the Ladies and Other Disasters (New York: Putnam, 1961; London: Deutsch, 1961);

The Presidential Papers (New York: Putnam, 1963; London: Deutsch, 1964);

An American Dream (New York: Dial, 1965; London: Deutsch, 1965);

Cannibals and Christians (New York: Dial, 1966; London: Deutsch, 1967);

The Bull Fight: A Photographic Narrative with Text by Normal Mailer (New York: Macmillan, 1967);

The Deer Park: A Play (New York: Dial, 1967; London: Weidenfeld & Nicolson, 1970);

Why Are We in Vietnam? (New York: Putnam, 1967; London: Weidenfeld & Nicolson, 1969);

The Short Fiction of Normal Mailer (New York: Dell, 1967);

The Idol and the Octopus: Political Writings on the Kennedy and Johnson Administrations (New York: Dell, 1968);

The Armies of the Night (New York: New American Library, 1968; London: Weidenfeld & Nicolson, 1968);

Miami and the Siege of Chicago (New York: New American Library, 1968; London: Weidenfeld & Nicolson, 1968);

Of a Fire on the Moon (Boston: Little, Brown, 1970; London: Weidenfeld & Nicolson, 1970);

Norman Mailer (photograph by Jerry Bauer)

Maidstone: A Mystery (New York: New American Library, 1971);

King of the Hill: On the Fight of the Century (New York: New American Library, 1971);

The Prisoner of Sex (Boston: Little, Brown, 1971; London: Weidenfeld & Nicolson, 1971);

The Long Patrol (New York: World, 1971);

Existential Errands (Boston: Little, Brown, 1972);

St. George and the Godfather (New York: New American Library, 1972);

Marilyn (New York: Grosset & Dunlap, 1973; London: Hodder & Stoughton, 1973);

The Faith of Graffiti (New York: Praeger, 1974); republished as *Watching My Name Go By* (London: Matthews, Miller, Dunbar, 1974);

The Fight (Boston: Little, Brown, 1975; London: Hart-Davis, 1976);

Genius and Lust: A Journey Through the Major Writings of Henry Miller (New York: Grove, 1976);

Some Honorable Men: Political Conventions, 1960–1972 (Boston: Little, Brown, 1976);

A Transit to Narcissus (New York: Howard Fertig, 1978);

The Executioner's Song (Boston: Little, Brown, 1979; London: Hutchinson, 1979);

Of Women and Their Elegance (New York: Simon & Schuster, 1980; Sevenoaks, U.K.: Hodder & Stoughton, 1980);

Pieces and Pontifications (Boston: Little, Brown, 1982; London: New English Library, 1983);

Ancient Evenings (Boston: Little, Brown, 1983; London: Macmillan, 1983);

Tough Guys Don't Dance (New York: Random House, 1984; London: M. Joseph, 1984);

Harlot's Ghost (New York: Random House, 1991; London: M. Joseph, 1991);

Oswald's Tale: An American Mystery (New York: Random House, 1995);

Portrait of Picasso as a Young Man (New York: Atlantic Monthly Press, 1995);

The Gospel According to the Son (New York: Random House, 1997).

After almost fifty years as a literary celebrity and a prolific writer of both fiction and nonfiction, Norman Mailer still defies critics and scholars to define his niche as a writer. Some interpreters periodically attempt to characterize him as "representative of his time," even as his timely work stretches from World War II through the Cold War and Vietnam to the breakup of the Soviet Union. Something in Mailer's work can be identified with each of these eras, with the latest connection involving Mailer's traveling to Russia to gather facts from the KGB for *Oswald's Tale* (1995), his investigation of the assassin Lee Harvey Oswald. Mailer's output totals more than three dozen books and collections, and his artistic involvement with his time promises to reach into the next century. Long recognized as a major figure in the American literary landscape, he continues, nevertheless, to write books that elicit contradictory critical assessments, and it has been said that he has evoked more invective than any other American author since Edgar Allan Poe. Mailer has elided his personal life with his literary reality, rehearsing

the voices, obsessions, conflicts, and existential explosions of his fictional characters. During the most legendary period of his writing he took center stage directly as a confessional, autobiographical storyteller. Even judiciously screened from the stormy publicity of his life, Mailer's art remains suspect to many literary traditionalists. His conventional fiction has had a mixed critical reception since the spectacular success of his first novel, *The Naked and the Dead,* in 1948. On the other hand, Mailer is widely acclaimed as a contributor to the movement in literary reporting that emerged in the 1960s as the "New Journalism," a recognition that came to Mailer at mid-career. The principal body of his work now lies irrevocably established in factual writing, although Mailer steadfastly has insisted he is essentially a novelist. Despite two Pulitzer Prizes and two National Book Awards, his achievement in journalism has sometimes been viewed as a consolation, even a dissipation of his literary talent. Almost at his own prompting, Mailer, in the eyes of his sharpest detractors, is a Faustian figure, an immortal legend but an unfulfilled artist.

In actuality Mailer abandoned nothing of his art to pursue journalism. When he assumed the role of a journalist, as Anna Banks notes in her essay on him in *A Sourcebook of American Literary Journalism* (1992), it was "more like that of a double-agent than a zealous convert." His literary journalism emerged as his most impressive work as he stretched his skills as a novelist to find meaning in actual lives and events, acting on his own vehement distaste for the performance of the mass press. As an alternative voice to traditional journalism, Mailer has produced examples of contemporary reporting that display the full range and energy of his creative powers as a writer.

As a young writer Mailer developed an admiration for Ernest Hemingway, legendary for beginning as a reporter and transforming his journalistic style into sparse, realistic fiction. Mailer's career and influence moved in the opposite direction. English novelist and critic Anthony Burgess suggested in 1985 that Mailer's writing, both in fiction and nonfiction, restored what Hemingway's style had swept away, a baroque prose salted "with new and dangerous condiments—existential violence, anal magic, Brooklyn street-boy expletives." Mailer's expletives are authentic enough, but the implication that his writing style was imprinted by a childhood on the mean streets of New York is somewhat misleading. By his own description Mailer was the "nice Jewish boy from Brooklyn," growing up since infancy in Flatbush and Crown Heights.

Dust jacket for the 1959 collection of Mailer's early journalism

Norman Kingsley Mailer was born on 31 January 1923 in Long Branch, New Jersey, the only son of Isaac Barnett Mailer and Fanny Schneider Mailer. His father was an accountant who had immigrated from South Africa. The family moved to Brooklyn in 1927, where Norman and his sister, Barbara, lived in a stable and conventional ethnic setting, treated as "important people" by their parents, Mailer recalls. With modesty "an old family relative," he exhibited no obvious early signs of the hipster he later concocted as an identity or of the existential "psychic outlaw" he defined in his writing and came close to imitating in life. He played rollerskate hockey, built model airplanes, and excelled in school. He demonstrated exceptional intelligence, an IQ of 165 as tested in grade school (later tested in the army at nearly 150).

Mailer entered Harvard at the age of sixteen to study aeronautical engineering. He received his engineering degree with honors in 1943, but he had been nurturing an ambition to be a writer since his freshman year. He was a disciplined and prolific writer from the outset, writing three thousand words a day as he learned the craft. He wrote for the literary magazine, the *Harvard Advocate,* and won a national collegiate fiction contest in 1941. Before he published his first novel he had written almost a million words. Just as important, Mailer was earnest in his pursuit of experiences to write about. He hitchhiked into the South one summer to gather material for a novel and worked briefly at a mental hospital during another break from school. Before the age of twenty he had developed a powerful alter ego on the written page, one he took through many guises and adventures. Like a method actor, Mailer was willing to commit his identity to the creative task. He loathed self-revelation during one phase of his career and celebrated it in another. He lived with a psyche at turns revealed, hidden, reconstructed, sacrificed, and resurrected in the process of writing. By any account of his life the practice took a heavy psychological toll.

Literary journalism provides a useful genre for understanding Mailer's adaptation of the conventional novel to tell fact-based stories. His name arises in any discussion of a "canon" of alternative journalism, especially the reportage associated with the New Journalists. He belongs to the most select group of New Journalism's contributing figures: Tom Wolfe, Truman Capote, Gay Talese, Hunter S. Thompson, and Joan Didion. He is the group's most prolific writer and its oldest. Since Mailer is also identified with the Beat writers of the 1950s, he can be considered a key transitional artist leading up to the developments of the 1960s. Although historians trace literary journalism back to the nineteenth century, its contemporary manifestation is both an aesthetic and political reaction against what George P. Landow, in *Elegant Jeremiahs: The Sage from Carlyle to Mailer* (1986), calls the culture's "wisdom literature," the established, institutional narratives of order in society. These narratives as day-to-day stories allow events to be sorted and interpreted according to an accepted pattern of meaning. The stories tend to be detached, even anonymous.

For the renegade journalist the traditional press is a powerful source of such conformist communication. Taking the objective stance of the press to be an illusion, literary journalism explores alternative practices to the standardized routines of institutional reporting. It accepts the subjective presence of the individual writer employing a set of literary techniques to capture the personalized reality of a story. The literary journalist also may give countercultural meaning to events and explore social deviance in ways that have little to do with helping the society at large cope with life. The literary journalist is just as likely to shock and disturb the mainstream consumer of information, jabbing needles and clashing threads into the fabric of a ready-to-wear culture.

For the "double-agent" novelist such as Mailer, literary journalism represents the entry of the literary practitioner into the arena of contemporary culture to compete in shaping the popular images of reality. The nonfiction novelist seeks to share the authority society currently grants to nonfiction over fiction, the journalist over the novelist. At the same time, writers such as Mailer also challenge that assignment of authority, devising strategies for engaging the participation of readers to decide the issue of reality for themselves. Literary journalism is both a pathway in journalism away from the institutionalized routines of the mass media and a crossroads in the development of the realistic novel. Even New Journalism now has its modernists and its traditionalists. Mailer frequently is set in contrast with writers such as Capote and Wolfe as an experimentalist who moves beyond realistic nonfiction to place reality at issue in the narrative itself. To Mailer, understanding the experiences of the writer is crucial for comprehending the events of a story.

Not all of Mailer's nonfiction is journalism. Not all of his journalism is as highly personal as *The Armies of the Night* (1968), his Vietnam-era account of a protest march on the Pentagon for which he was awarded the Pulitzer Prize. *The Executioner's Song* (1979), covering the final months of Utah killer Gary Gilmore, is akin to docudrama. For this book Mailer was awarded his second Pulitzer Prize, this time in the fiction category. Depending upon his involvement in gathering his own observations or relying upon those of others, Mailer has varied his presence as a narrator from effusive confessionalist to archivist or human tape recorder. In his more engaged journalism of the 1960s Mailer pursued "real" stories with the larger objective of making them "true" for the reader, at least in how they should strike the reader as reports of human experiences rather than mere observations.

Like all literary journalists Mailer adapted the narrative and structural techniques of fiction. But fiction became an elaborate metaphor for eliciting the appropriate emotions to make basic realities more acute as "hard facts." As he explains in *The Armies of the Night,* the most authentic story of an event might involve an interior drama that is "emotional, spiritual, psychical, moral, existential, or supernatural" in nature, requiring the intuition of the novelist. But no consistent journalistic style defines his approach to reporting. In *Advertisements for Myself* (1959) he describes himself as a "quick-change artist, as if I can believe I can trap the Prince of Truth in the act of switching a style."

His later journalism became more contingent in its point of view, achieving credibility by maintaining what might be described as a partisan open-endedness. Mailer's best journalism of the 1960s exploited the confessional, alternating between outrageous personal admission and profound insight, picaresque sins flickering with sage pronouncements like a revolving searchlight. In *The Executioner's Song* of the 1970s Mailer was a sort of psychic medium, allowing scores of voices to speak in the story. His own conception of his journalistic writing is that he attempts to bring fiction's entire world to journalism. Any discussion of Mailer as a journalist, even a literary one, is really talk of an exploratory relationship more than membership.

In 1948 Mailer's first novel, *The Naked and the Dead,* was published. In the early 1940s, when he was a student at Harvard, Mailer had known that World War II was the experience most likely to lead to the "great novel" that he aspired to write. But after graduating in 1943 he waited to be drafted, feeling an understandable, if ego-bruising, anxiety about becoming a soldier. In 1944 Mailer married his college girlfriend, Beatrice Silverman of Chelsea, Massachusetts, the first of his six wives. He was inducted into the army shortly after and sent to the Pacific. The aeronautical engineer with the honors degree from Harvard became a telephone lineman and clerk before volunteering as a rifleman with a

Dan Wolf and Mailer in the offices of The Village Voice *(photograph by Fred W. McDarrah)*

reconnaissance platoon. He saw combat in the Philippines and served in the occupation of Japan before his discharge in 1946. When *The Naked and the Dead* appeared in 1948, it was both a best-seller and a critical success, boosting Mailer, still in his twenties, into the first rank of young American writers.

The Naked and the Dead is notable for its realistic portrayal of combat and the sociological exactness with which Mailer developed his characters. The book is both plodding and terrifyingly electric in its detailed depiction of men fighting a horizonless jungle war. It has drawn comparisons with journalism as "a description in depth of an event in life," a novel achieving the effect of a newsreel. On another level the book is a political novel, presenting the war as a collective action that is totalitarian in its origins but also in the response of individuals drawn into it on either side. The individual is caught up in a "spiritual warfare" to maintain personal autonomy and dignity. Mailer describes his early politics as anarchist, a view suspicious of all political institutions. Mailer's role as a political writer is a role that links his fiction with his later nonfiction. To Mailer himself, the novel is more mystically symbolic than realistic, in the mold of Herman Melville's *Moby-Dick* (1851) in its exploration of an obsessive quest under conditions of great risk and uncertainty. Mailer sees his book as representative of the struggle between the beast and seer in man. Pursuing the promise of his early literary triumph was a journey that led to Mailer's own unleashing of the beast.

In 1948 Mailer attended the Sorbonne in Paris and began an influential friendship with Jean Malaquais, a Marxist philosopher and writer. At this time Mailer's politics gradually shifted to viewing collective action more favorably than he had earlier, a perspective that allowed for the activism of the artist rather than his withdrawal from society, and political engagement informed much of Mailer's writing for the rest of his career. When he returned to the United States he worked in the presidential campaign of the Progressive candidate, Henry Wallace, and took to the role of young radical with enthusiasm. It gave his celebrity status a purpose. He traveled in a tight circle of New York intellectuals of the Left who seemed destined to fashion a prominent corner of American politics and culture, if they ever resolved their endless infighting. Mailer's political attitudes were in a process of formation, and he inevitably offended some of his more seasoned and committed cohorts. Some interpreted his fluid political perspective as a betrayal, while others concluded that his ideas were incoherent and undeveloped.

The situation was not opportune for Mailer to attempt an overtly political novel to maintain the momentum of his glittering first strike as a novelist. But Mailer made exactly that move with *Barbary Shore* (1951), a book of tediously polemical characters sending Cold War rhetoric echoing down the halls of a Brooklyn boardinghouse. The novel received some of the worst reviews Mailer would see in his career. It became a candidate for everybody's exemplar of the bad second novel of a literary shooting star, or so the young author feared.

Mailer's marriage produced a daughter, Susan, but the marriage ended in mutual infidelity in 1952. Two years later Mailer married Adele Morales, a Spanish-Peruvian painter he met in Greenwich Village. During the years since the war he had lived in Massachusetts, Paris, Vermont, and Mexico, in addition to New York. He had worked briefly in Hollywood as a scriptwriter during 1949–1950 and attempted to draw upon that experience for his third novel, *The Deer Park* (1955).

The Deer Park rounds up the usual Hollywood suspects of sex, power, money, and dreams in a story of attempted artistic redemption. Several publishers turned down the work on grounds of obscenity. Like his previous book, the work drew its principal spiritual dilemma from the contemporary political scene, demonstrating Mailer's continued willingness to deal with ideas of broad social significance. His West Coast novel fared somewhat better with the public and critics than the disastrous *Barbary Shore*. But mixed reviews were not enough to allay Mailer's growing sense of failure. He drank heavily, brawled in streets and bars, and experimented with drugs. The reversal of favor was a traumatic blow for "the greatest writer to come out of his generation."

Mailer did not publish another novel for a decade. His response in writing, in effect, was to turn aside to the audience, like the actor responding to a scattering of hisses. His reaction burst forth in his nonfiction, a combative, chastising, confessional dialogue with critics, readers, and the nation itself, embarrassing, compelling, and brilliant writing on the edge, the exploration of what he called "new consciousness." Mailer had seen the success of his first novel as a lobotomy of his past, forcing him into "the war of the enormous present." His nonfiction was a turn to expression and commentary "in real time," where writing is an "event" relevant to the moment at which it is being created, like the stories evoked by psychoanalysis. Mailer's approach to nonfiction developed in a series of essays beginning in the mid 1950s, part of "a tangible influence in dragging America out of the Eisenhower years into the Aquarian age of the 60's and beyond," in the words of Carol Iannone.

Some of his earliest journalistic writing appeared in *The Village Voice,* the alternative newspaper Mailer helped to found and for which he provided the name. As a columnist in 1956 he waged his self-described "private war on American journalism" and other bastions of conformity and complacency. He offered highly personalized commentary

and practiced a kind of running shtick of insulting readers. A critic once observed that at his worst Mailer wrote like a small-town newspaper editor. But Mailer was moving toward a form of alternative journalism by first developing an appropriate persona and organizing a set of fundamental editorial attitudes. Writing for *The Village Voice* was an exercise in self-assertion that honed Mailer's taste for notoriety. The experience helped confirm his notion of reality as shaped by the willful individual rather than its existing as hard fact. Mailer also clarified his image of a new romantic spirit in America emanating from what he called a "mysticism of the flesh," energizing the rebellious hipster. He saw himself as a prominent exemplar. In fusing his own identity with a lustful, irreverent, and alienated radicalism, Mailer joined the Beat Generation in stride.

The best elaboration of Mailer's period slant on the meaning of the "Hip" versus the "Square" came in "The White Negro" (1957). The essay first appeared in the journal *Dissent,* where he was an editor. In the article Mailer's anarchism returns with a vengeance. The hipster embodies the American existentialist who renounces the allegiances of conventional politics and engages in personal resistance against rationalism, the bulwark of Western culture. In the philosophy of hip, the state's collective logic plots against the individual in schemes of increasing destructiveness. Life and death become absurdly meaningless. The normal logic of the individual compels submission and blindness to the situation for the sake of survival. For Mailer, accepting this condition is a failure of nerve and results in a loss of human dignity. The existentialist breaks the chain of reasoning by accepting the terms of death and living with its danger. Favoring intuition over intellect, the hip figure is a sensual dualist who is equally attracted to love and violence. His psyche develops a defense against the neuroses engendered by contemporary civilization by embracing the next stage of psychological progression, psychosis, and adapting it to serve the ends of the intuitive will. He learns to distinguish what is good for him and bad at precisely the moment a paralyzing habit of behavior is vulnerable to change. Thus he is able to act with decisiveness to alter his state of existence.

The hipster is a "psychic outlaw," but Mailer insists that he retains enough of the intellect to engage in narcissistic self-reflection. By philosophizing about the nuances of his motives, the hipster escapes the depravity of the conventional psychopath. Working with concepts at the fringes of human personality, Mailer refuses to make the distinction between the philosophical psychopath and his more mindless counterpart, the murderous psychopath,

Dust jacket for the third collection of Mailer's journalism

categorical. They share a common meaning to their lives that is beyond complete ethical contradiction. The pursuit of sex, drugs, and jazz, activities associated with the counterculture, characterizes the experimentation and freedom of the hip lifestyle.

In his essay Mailer associates the alienated existence of the hipster with the experience of the oppressed African American male. Symbolic of the quest, or perhaps its literal goal, is "love as the search for an orgasm more apocalyptic than the one which preceded it." Even more than the libertinism and the stereotyping of a "wise primitive" in the Negro, Mailer's apparent absolution of the psychopath who murders with "courage" to purge his impulses

and dare the unknown inflamed the sensibility of critics. Since the taking of a life represents the most extreme transgression of the state, Mailer might have set the limits of his existential psychosis at murder. But through a kind of calculus of social and political violence, Mailer suggests individual acts of savagery actually might subtract from the collective violence of the state, especially if the ultimate source of state violence is a repressed and inhibited culture. The hip hero exists as a feasible psychic outlet whose potential for individual violence is far more ethically acceptable than the collective murders of society. Through creative nihilism he is an agent of change and revolution. Such moral equivocation over violence was tolerable, if troubling, in fiction. Mailer was challenging the limits of responsible nonfiction.

What actually is going on in "The White Negro" has been a topic of much critical discussion. The article is considered one of the most influential essays in American postwar culture, a prelude to the radicalism of the 1960s. Mailer may have been engaging in a kind of intellectual slumming, pumping up an ideal of rebellious creativity with Harvard-accented street talk, more motorcycle rev than manifesto. He describes the hipster as fiction, yet real enough to be a profile of the revolutionary personality of the time. The essay's preoccupations with sex and violence are not unlike the exaggerated themes of contemporary commercial rap music. Stripped of their underclass mimicry and macho posturing, Mailer's arguments seem no more outrageous than what might emerge in a contemporary, freewheeling liberal debate on the redeemability of the human soul.

Mailer's position is a recognition of the absurdity and danger of holding that evil is a distinct category of existence that somehow cancels other traits of identity in a person. As Mailer recognized, such a simplistic notion of evil clouds any comprehension of its collective causes and effects. But the course of Mailer's own life belies simply framing the essay as intellectual antics, the writer's search for an expressive form or seeking a stimulation of creative energy. As the focus of Mailer's writing moved from fiction to exploratory nonfiction, his views seemed to be on some progressive path toward personal realization. His perspective hinted at potentialities in his own behavior. "The White Negro" changed Mailer's writing career. The essay also haunted Mailer as a flawed apologetic for himself.

Banks sees the source of Mailer's style of literary journalism in the play of hip language and in the deployment of an absurdist viewpoint for observing modern life. She suggests that Mailer's notion of *hip* as it is described and finds expression in "The White Negro" contributes to all of the narrative devices Tom Wolfe later described as defining New Journalism: scene-by-scene construction, full dialogue, a novelistic use of point of view, and the description of individuals in characterizing details of style. The piece achieved prominence as alternative journalism after it was reprinted as a segment in Mailer's compendium of his writing, *Advertisements for Myself* (1959).

This book as a whole is a plaintive response to Mailer's disappointments in trying to advance as an artist. Taking his own measure as a writer and as a man, Mailer compiled a collection of his work after nearly twenty years of writing, including stories, essays, poems, polemics, fragments, and letters. The pieces are joined by highly revealing personal comments, or "advertisements." The miscellany reveals an earnest, if uneven, journey through form and language. But a newly exposed talent runs through the commentary. Mailer is in turn baleful and defiant, angry and remorseful, demoralized and aroused, principally in feeling about Mailer. In self-therapy Mailer is compelling. With the book he refurbished his fame, if principally as a writer between novels. Among critics the work produced the major fault line of his career. On one side of the divide Mailer's detractors concluded he had descended into self-pity as a frustrated artist, indulging in self-promotion to maintain his ego. He had wandered pretentiously into journalism and other forms of nonfiction beneath his talent to sustain his celebrity and to make money. In the view of his sympathizers Mailer had come to terms with his own impulses and redefined the role of the artist. The writer has a responsibility to be a shock therapist of his own consciousness to achieve the "revolution in the consciousness" for society as a whole. The writer's struggle to create invokes the Emersonian paradigm of reality being shaped in terms of the living energy one is able to pump into it. To his admirers Mailer could lay legitimate claim to being the most energetic writer in America.

The large voice that Mailer found in his early journalism is that of both beast and seer, the apocalyptic prophet, possessed and with fist raised. Mailer himself accepted and developed the image. Landow suggests that, like many of the New Journalists, Mailer emerged in the culture as a modern Jeremiah with unwelcome truths. His vantage point on society is necessarily contentious. This kind of voice "resides at the periphery," "eccentric" and "off center." Like the oppositional sage, the alternative journalist has few resources of credibility to use with his audience except the force of his ideas wrapped in testimony about how they came into being from his experiences, emotions, and reflections. The journalistic prophet does not participate in a dialogue with the center as much as he or she records personal revelations. Seen in this light, Mailer's journalism, despite stylistic similarities, lies outside the press's own considerable range of subjective writing, from the storytelling of the human-interest writer to the musings and fulminating of the independent columnist. Mailer entered journalism as a nemesis, opposing the press as an institution wielding great power irresponsibly. "The shits are killing us, even as they kill themselves," he writes in *Advertisements for Myself,* implicating the media as the purveyors of Establishment lies. "Little lies, but they pipe us toward insanity as they starve us of our sense of the real." While Mailer himself no longer believed in a direct access to reality, the assumption of the realistic novelist, he condemned the media for conditioning society to live with images drained of feeling, complexity, and depth. Society had slipped into semiconsciousness, lulled into the illusion that pleasure could be separated from pain. Society was cutting corners "to cheat the heart of life." Mailer sought to restore the mystery of personality, if principally his own, to the mirror the writer holds up to society. Despite the egotistical bombast of his early journalistic style, he believed the authentic story of events lay in reporting the nuances of feeling, perception, and reflected meaning.

Mailer's confidence that he could ever be accepted as the prophet of his time was shaken in the wake of the most lurid incident of his life. On an early November morning in 1960, following a disruptive party at his apartment to celebrate his decision to run for mayor of New York, a drunken Mailer stabbed his wife, Adelle, with a penknife. She was taken to the hospital with one wound near the heart and another in her back. Mailer went on television the next day to announce his candidacy. He later turned himself in to police. After a medical evaluation that suggested he might be delusional, homicidal, and suicidal, he was committed to Bellevue mental hospital, where he remained for more than two weeks. He pleaded guilty to third-degree assault and was given probation when his wife refused to press charges.

If Mailer had brought his famous existential hipster to life and taken him to the edge of the ultimate abyss of violence, to his credit he never treated the experience as particularly liberating or ennobling. Perhaps he recognized the element of caricature in the affair, down to the two and a half inches of his knife blade and the unimaginative excuse that his wife had slipped on broken glass. To some observers, the episode illustrated an emotional makeup without subtlety or nuance, the very qualities he hoped to develop in his nonfiction writing. By most accounts Mailer took the affair as an acute embarrassment, finally, to a mind dulled to the meaning of extreme, an outrageous act. In his fiction, however, uxoricide, the murder of a wife by her husband, began the quest for spiritual rebirth of the existential protagonist of *An American Dream* (1965). The antihero of the novel not only chokes his wife to death when she taunts him and refuses his sexual advances but also sodomizes the German maid on the way out. Another literary response to the stabbing was a book of poems, *Deaths for the La-*

Mailer at a press conference in 1973, discussing his "novel biography" of Marilyn Monroe

dies and Other Disasters (1961). Mailer later wrote that the ineradicable impulses of human nature should not be suppressed "or anomaly, cancer, and plague will follow. Instead one must find an art into which it can grow."

The Mailers, who had two children, Danielle and Elizabeth Anne, were divorced in 1962. That same year Mailer married Lady Jeanne Campbell, herself an occasional journalist and the granddaughter of Lord Beaverbrook, the British newspaper magnate. The marriage ended the next year. The union resulted in a daughter, Kate. Mailer soon married his fourth wife, Beverly Bentley, an actress. Now forty, Mailer was supporting four, soon to be five, children from his various marriages. Journalism had become a financial necessity. The rise of New Journalism has been associated with the economic opportunities for nonfiction in magazines after the decline of the short story and the search for new market strategies to sustain a mass circulation. Mailer took advantage of the opportunities, taking assignments in commentary and reporting, and eventually becoming a columnist for *Esquire*.

A collection of Mailer's nonfiction work, *The Presidential Papers,* was published in 1963. The book employs a similar device to the one used in *Advertisements for Myself,* the connective introductions and commentary supplied by the impresario himself. With a flamboyant touch Mailer assumes the role of adviser or court jester to President John F. Kennedy, suggesting the book's selections were made to educate the president on how to be an existential leader. Some of his advice echoes his approach to journalism, such as the admonition to distrust the compact fact in favor of nuances. Mailer argues that Kennedy is too rational and objective in handling issues. Behind the fact are mysterious processes of open-ended change to be explored. The ploy of counseling the president lost much of its intended wryness with Kennedy's assassination shortly after the book's publication. The unfortunate coincidence probably subdued the book's critical reception.

Nevertheless, *The Presidential Papers* stands as one of Mailer's better collections of nonfiction. One noted journalistic piece is "Superman Comes to the Supermarket," Mailer's coverage of the Democratic National Convention in 1960. Originally written for *Esquire,* the article offers a profile of Kennedy in the convenient dramatic setting of his nomination. The essay frames Mailer's own longing for heroic leadership. The match in political outlook between the radical writer and his charismatic but mainstream captain is not precise, but Mailer views totalitarianism as the common enemy. Politics, like war, is an arena in which a man can rise to the challenge. Mailer was less than subtle in his purpose of promoting Kennedy's candidacy with the article. His effort at "bending reality like a field of space" was to affect a specific event, the upcoming election, just as certainly he was bending the candidate to fit his notion of the hip hero. Nonetheless, Mailer's journalism was developing rhetorical sophistication. His earlier writing for *The Village Voice* was journalistic taunt and brawl. His profile of Kennedy was an attempt at persuasion through the power of a compelling vision. Louis Menand attributes Mailer's political writing with helping to teach a "new generation of readers how to look at a politician." Robert Merrill suggests the piece as literary journalism advanced the use of such novelistic devices as the character sketch and analysis, the shifting of the order of occurrences, and the juxtaposition of contrasting story elements for ironic or dramatic effect.

In "Ten Thousand Words a Minute," another essay in the collection, Mailer indulged his fascination with prizefighting as a reporter at the scene of a heavyweight championship match in 1962. If Mailer had proven with Kennedy that he did not need a real superman to envision "a hero central to his time," he demonstrated with the Patterson-Liston title fight that he did not require an apocalyptic event to tell an epic story. Sonny Liston, a brooding ex-convict, won the fight easily in the first round over the smaller, if quicker, Floyd Patterson. Mailer identified with Patterson over the "outlaw" because of the underdog artistry of his style. His report of the fight is a highly symbolic tale of good versus evil, the earnest disciplinarian against the Faustian sellout, sex overwhelming love, liberalism losing its muscle tone, violence revealing true identity. The journalistic essay is considered one of Mailer's finest, although it does not offer a shared fantasy for all readers. Its extended sports metaphor drawn from a two-minute beating in the ring relies on an increasingly archaic code of meaning. The essay lies in the critical shadow of his later award-winning *Armies of the Night,* with which it shares many similarities, such as the dominance of Mailer's personality in the story and his direct participation in events.

While "Ten Thousand Words a Minute" can be seen as a transitional and developmental piece, it also colors how Mailer's later journalism can be interpreted. Both works depict episodes of spiritual passage for Mailer, but the earlier version is far less convincing and actually devalues the later epiphany as being rather formulaic. Mailer advances an existential story form in journalism at the expense of capturing the uniqueness of events. In the essay and the book Mailer displays what Alfred Kazin calls his persona of the "novelist-in-charge-of-practically-everything." In the more exclusive world of the prizefight Mailer is seen more clearly as an intruder whose cachet is celebrity and whose instinct is to crowd his way to the center. At the center is not simply the focus of attention, but disquieting violence. In the fight story Mailer seems caught up in the frenzy. He disrupts the press conference of the champion Liston in an act he finds redemptive.

"Ten Thousand Words a Minute" is a flashback of Mailer's more renowned story of defiance on the steps of the Pentagon. As much as the two examples of journalism are connected as points in a line of stylistic development, they also are episodes in a familiar course of behavior for Mailer when he is engaged in perceived tests of his manhood. A saving grace in the evolution of his style is his more persistent acknowledgment over time that he is indeed an eccentric figure, a mock hero, but one cleverly and fashionably demonstrating the absurdity, ambiguities, and implausibilities of the modern world. In a culture in which reality is dominated by the image there is potentially great significance in a writer's takeover of a press conference or in his arrest at a protest march. An even greater promise of effect lies in the impact of the writer's eventual stories about those occurrences. In traditional journalism the timeliness of news is derived from the relationship between events and when they are reported. As with much alternative journalism, the immediacy of Mailer's reporting is separate from the events themselves. Nothing significant happens until the writer creates a story. The "news" is in the reconstruction of events, their transformation as signifiers of meaning.

Working as a columnist for *Esquire* in 1963, Mailer decided to use the routine of magazine journalism to write a novel. He wrote on a monthly deadline, and the magazine published installments as the work progressed. A revised version of the serialization, *An American Dream,* including portions excised by the magazine as too pornographic, was published as a book in 1965. The work initially touches base with headline contemporaries such as Kennedy and Marilyn Monroe, Patterson and Liston, before launching into a surrealistic story of a man who seeks violent release from psychic bondage by killing his wife. The strategy recalls a reference in *Presidential Papers* to a "subterranean river of untapped, ferocious, lonely and romantic desires, the concentration of ecstasy and violence which is the dream life of the nation." To awaken a society enthralled by illusions of freedom and success, Mailer conjures up an alternative, latent fantasy of bestial license and fulfillment. Bravery, even if the risks of confirmation are reckless and exist only as avenues of self-discovery, emerges as more empowering than love. Mailer at middle age was hardly catching every wave of the new counterculture with its emphasis on flower power.

More Mailer journalism was collected a year later in his third miscellany, *Cannibals and Christians.* The book includes his reporting of another national convention, "In the Red Light: A History of the Republican Convention in 1964." The article offers an outsider's view of the American Right in its rallying around Barry Goldwater, whom Mailer manages to render as a seductive, if wholly unsuitable, national leader. The book is sarcastically dedicated to Mailer's more formidable political anathema, Lyndon Johnson. Mailer's opposition to the Vietnam War, public from the beginning in his journalism and speeches, flashes vehemently in yet another novel of identity crisis, *Why Are We in Vietnam?,* published in 1967.

The shock of this novel is linguistic, the perversion of a Huck Finn–like stream of colloquial speech in a scatological, present-day idiom. The narrator and protagonist is an eighteen-year-old Texan, D. J. ("Disc Jockey to the World," Dr. Jekyll), who speaks a kind of electronic patter. He is not only a child of the media wasteland but also a youth coming of age with a generation-gap awareness of his immersion in a society besieged by a corporate plague. The mass media are part of the technological abomination, wiring society together like a cage. On a hunting trip to Alaska, D. J. experiences but rejects the pursuit of game with the technological overkill used by his father, the equivalent of the hovering gunships and carpet bombing in Vietnam. He ventures unarmed into the wilderness, only to find a God who exhorts man to kill. Either violence is an ordained trait of nature that can be controlled but never eliminated, a familiar Mailer theme, or barbarism has reclaimed the myth of God in American culture. In either case D. J. has no spiritual basis for resisting the lure of going to Vietnam. "Vietnam hot damn" is the final refrain of the novel. The book was nominated for a National Book Award. In 1967 Mailer adapted his novel *The Deer Park* into a play and was elected to the National Institute of Arts and Letters.

Four days in October 1967 also provided the experiences for Mailer's most celebrated journalism of the 1960s. Mailer participated in a long weekend of protest activities against the Vietnam War, culminating in a mass march on the Pentagon during which he was arrested and briefly detained. He wrote an account of the event for *Harper's,* "The Steps of the Pentagon," an article he expanded into his book *The Armies of the Night* (1968). The book is highly praised for its innovative form. It is divided into two parts, "History as a Novel," basically the original magazine piece, and "The Novel as History," another account of the event, giving insight into the author's writing process. The book begins with a short journalistic account from *Time* magazine in which Mailer is personally ridiculed for his participation in the protest. "Now we may leave *Time* in order to find out what happened," Mailer writes, and the book is an exploration of that proposition, first through a personal history written with the structure and techniques of a novel and then in more detached fashion as a collective history.

Both versions of events are examples of novelistic nonfiction. Each claims allegiance to the facts. But the parts lean in different directions with regard to the writer's responsibility. In part 1 the writer represents himself. In part 2 he assumes a responsibility toward the participants who shared the experience as well as to the culture that must absorb it as history. "History as a Novel" is Mailer's own intimate story, a subjective report that purports to capture the feel of the event in terms of the sensibility of one individual. In "The Novel as History" Mailer

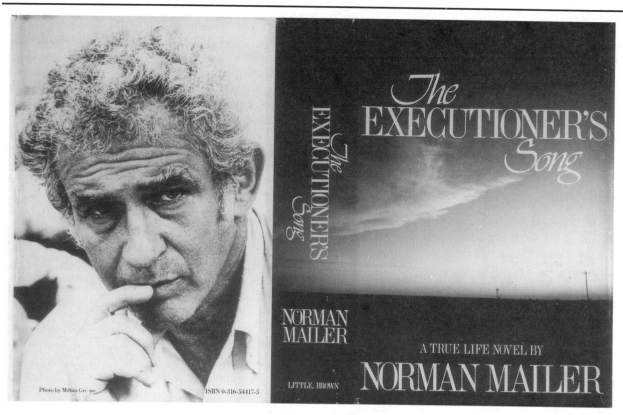

Dust jacket for Mailer's "true-life novel" about murderer Gary Gilmore

assumes the burden of the communal storyteller to provide a more general, representative account, "dutiful to all newspaper accounts, eyewitness reports, and historical inductions available." Mailer argues that the personal history informs and even gives authority to the collective report. Mailer offers a compelling case for the ability of the novelist to cross over the line of historical (and journalistic) inquiry and provide the "interior" view of reality. In part 2 Mailer graphically lowers the "cloak of an historic style" in order to "enter that world of strange lights and intuitive speculation which is the novel" at the moment of confrontation on the steps of the Pentagon. Here is a point in time and space, in existence and experience, the reader is to understand, at which conventional reportage fails.

Mailer's explanation of his writing strategy has been an influential defense of the subjectivity of literary journalism. *The Armies of the Night* is a legendary illustration of the approach. Other analysts draw even more significance from Mailer's juxtaposition of two versions of his reporting of the same event. The divided structure sets up a dialectic in narrative technique through which readers can play some role in deciding for themselves what happened. Mailer employs the same postmodern device in *The Executioner's Song,* where the effect of inviting

reader participation is even more striking because Mailer mutes his own rhetorical voice throughout the book.

Another feature of *The Armies of the Night* that obscures the border between journalism and fiction is Mailer's use of third-person narration. Avoiding the usual first person of the subjective eyewitness account, Mailer projects himself into the work like a character in a novel. He assumes an identity on the page as Norman Mailer and variously as the "Beast," the "Participant," the "General," and other appellations. The tactic blurs the presence of the author's renowned ego without, of course, actually diminishing it. Mailer plays on his public notoriety with humor and self-parody, making *The Armies of the Night* extraordinarily entertaining as satire. The writer's disreputable personality drives the story forward as if it were picaresque fiction. Mailer achieves believability by juxtaposing outrageous indiscretions with compelling insight that is grounded in the charisma of the romantic outlaw. Mailer's success with journalism in the third person is itself one of the great ironies in the development of alternative journalism. What is taken as a narrative breakthrough is a seamless transition from the prose of the *Time* article that opens *The Armies of the Night* in which Mailer is derisively portrayed as an "antistar" making a drunken fool of himself. Mailer turns the tables on establishment journalism by mimicking the style and winning a Pulitzer Prize.

The opening of the book reveals Mailer's sense of himself as a victim of journalism. His reputation as a journalist stings. In an often quoted exchange with the poet Robert Lowell, an episode recounted in *The Armies of the Night,* Mailer brushes aside the compliment that he is "the best journalist in America." He replies to his friend that "there are days when I think of myself as being the best writer in America." It is a resentful if also wistful response to all the critics who have considered his journalism a betrayal of the novelist's muse. Mailer's career-long attitude toward the mass media is that the press has gotten the world wrong, often at the behest of society's dark forces. Finding success at the very activity he finds morally suspect in others hardly sweetens the distaste.

The Pentagon march found the right Mailer at the right place at the right time. He is the jaded rebel who describes himself as a "Left Conservative." He is initially apathetic to the march. His opposition to the war is firm, but he is bordering on moral fatigue with some of the antics of his young allies, such as their burning draft cards. The aging hipster has not been transformed into a hippie. He frets about drugs when it comes to his own college-bound daughter. He skewers the liberal academics who hover around the protest movement like caterers. He is open to the movement's ambiguous and inane qualities while also appreciating and being sympathetic with its serious business of trying to affect the course of a disastrous war. Mailer's contradictions ensure a form of objectivity. He is at a point in his life to review the march as the chaotic street theater that it is while finding and illuminating its moments of transcending grace. In the process he is spiritually recharged. Reviewing the book for *The New York Times* (5 May 1968), Alfred Kazin compared *The Armies of the Night* with Walt Whitman's personal testimony on the Civil War in *Specimen Days* (1882). The times demanded a new form of political reportage. Mailer contributed to it.

Mailer wrote other celebrated pieces using a version of the same self-dramatizing protagonist. But *The Armies of the Night* itself could not lead to a journalistic encore. Despite its virtuosity, the book is very much a local piece. The same personified Mailer that is the source of comic vitality and insight in the book would have been highly offensive in the role of a war correspondent on a Vietnam patrol and perhaps even more so as a participant observer in a civil rights march on Washington or Selma. Traditional journalism claims that one size of reporting fits all events in the objective storytelling of concrete, observable facts. Mailer's greatest contribution to literary journalism is not the discovery of a more expressive universal form. Consistent with his fiction writing, Mailer in his nonfiction seeks the form and style that are most illuminating for the task at hand.

As he expresses his source of insight in *The Armies of the Night,* the key to discovery is "not in the substance of one's idea, but in what was learned from the style of one's attack." Mailer insists that he alters his style for every project of writing. The writer's relationship to reality constantly changes. What informs Mailer's whole body of journalism is the same experimental attitude that characterizes his seemingly erratic life. He is the ever-striving existentialist. As an existential writer, and by extension an existential journalist, he searches for meaning offered up in the experience of the moment. The grace of each moment is a mystery beyond most acts of ordinary attention. In *The Armies of the Night* he compares writing with impromptu public speaking, where truth "hovers on good occasions like a presence between speaker and audience." The writer's choices are to trick, seize, or submit to the grace of every moment, often a shift to the side of conscious intent. Mailer's impossible ideal as a writer has been to consider form as unique and varied as content. Nothing else sets his writing in such strong contrast with traditional journalism and its conventions of standardization.

Mailer did not repeat the success of *The Armies of the Night* for another decade. Yet the journalism between 1968 and the publication of *The Executioner's Song* in 1979 includes sporadic flashes of solid nonfiction writing. In *Miami and the Siege of Chicago* (1968) Mailer returns to what might almost be considered a regular beat, covering the national political conventions. The book won a National Book Award for nonfiction. He again entered the political ring himself in 1969, running for mayor of New York on a ticket that included a fellow journalist, Jimmy Breslin. Another noteworthy magazine assignment was the Apollo 11 moon shot that year, which provided the subject for Mailer's most searching examination of the role of technology in society, *Of a Fire on the Moon* (1970). Mailer the trained engineer proves amazingly adept at handling the technical complexities of the space program while at the same time probing what collective exploration means to the future of the individual spirit. Both works display the devices of the novel in descriptive sketches of scenes, characters, and action. But Mailer the reporter among the press pack is not a particularly effective dramatic focus. There is little feel of combat involved, and Mailer's ideas seem understimulated.

The fight is back in *The Prisoner of Sex* (1971), a troublesome book for Mailer in which he takes on the women's liberation movement. First appearing in *Harper's,* the extended essay refers to his own marital problems. Mailer uses his experiences of domestic rupture as a springboard for expressing his views on women while also defending himself against charges of male chauvinism. Mailer had been a prominent target in Kate Millett's *Sexual Politics* (1970). *The Prisoner of Sex* offers a view of Mailer grappling with a cultural phenomenon relevant to his life and writing. But his observations in the book often lack nuance and tact. Mailer coupled the essay with controversial public appearances, including a disastrous confrontation with the writer Gore Vidal on a national television talk show. His belligerent performance drew a derisive comeuppance from the quick-witted program host, one of the more memorable media happenings involving the literary scene of the early 1970s. Mailer's reputation among many feminists still awaits the imaginative revisionist. *St. George and the Godfather* (1972) was another run at political convention reportage. *Existential Errands* (1972) gathers his shorter journalism for the period. Each book contains some revealing character sketches, including an assessment of the boxer Muhammad Ali in the latter book.

Mailer attempted a full biography with *Marilyn* (1973). He was commissioned to write a preface to a book of photographs of Marilyn Monroe, who died in 1962, but the project developed into an in-depth analysis of her life and times. Most of Mailer's previous nonfiction had been from the perspective of a participant observer. He was credited with possessing exceptional awareness and recall, although his writing often was described as impressionistic. He was not considered a meticulous researcher. Mailer knew Monroe only as an exotic, cinematic icon. She had crossed into his literary world briefly as the wife of playwright Arthur Miller, but Mailer had never met her. This lack of firsthand acquaintance with a subject presages the circumstances of his later examination of the executed killer Gary Gilmore. In response to his absence as an eyewitness to Gilmore's crime spree and its aftermath, Mailer radically altered his journalistic approach by eliminating his highly personalized voice. In his treatment of Monroe, however, he considered her screen roles as a kind of presence, authorizing the same familiarity, if not the precise form, of his subjective journalism.

Mailer described his work on Monroe as a "novel biography." He conducted several important interviews for the book, but shortly before publication he was accused of plagiarizing from previous biographies. Controversy also arose from his speculations about the circumstances of Monroe's death. Yet another unfavorable national television appearance added to the notoriety of the project. In hindsight the affair seems distorted by publicity and misunderstanding. But Mailer himself had conditioned readers to take account of the author behind the text. Each of his books is a dual story, involving a subject and Mailer's coming to terms with the subject. Thus *Marilyn* is both a biography and another autobiographical episode in Mailer's life. It is a significant investigative work, although not of the fact-finding kind. Mailer sees himself and Monroe joined as kindred spirits. "Set a thief to catch a thief, and put an artist on an artist," he writes. He is again searching for the factual nuances that will reveal a pattern, using his own psyche as a template for understanding another human personality. For some reviewers Mailer is never able to portray her truly alone, with an intimacy that does not have the author breathing, sometimes heavily, close by. Others see the book as an unusual achievement for Mailer, a believable and sensitive reconstruction of a woman's life. At the other end of the scale as contemplations of gender identity are two other Mailer books of the mid 1970s. *The Fight* (1975) is an account of the Ali-Foreman heavyweight title match in Zaire. Mailer, past fifty, easily can be read into the aging Ali, the greatest love/hate symbol of sport. *Genius and Lust: A Journey Through the Major Writings of Henry Miller* (1976) is an anthology of the work of Henry Miller with Mailer providing extended comments. Critics point to the obvious parallels in the lives and identities of these two writers as well. Mailer had not made his existential journey without spiritual companions, at least on some level of interpretation. But in sketching their portraits he invariably represented them as variations of himself. In figures Mailer admired he saw a family resemblance, but the likeness was to a large degree his own reflection.

A little more than a decade after the triumph of *The Armies of the Night,* Mailer produced *The Executioner's Song,* his acclaimed chronicle of the final days of a defiant murderer. In both Pulitzer Prize–winning books Mailer attempts to convey an essential ambiguity or mystery, but with virtually opposite narrative strategies. *The Armies of the Night* has been described as a jeremiad wrapped in the carnivalesque. In *The Executioner's Song* Mailer writes in "a voice as flat as the horizon," in Joan Didion's apt phrase. He allows the story to unfold from a hundred different perspectives in many episodes and revelations gleaned from interviews, letters, and

Mailer and Truman Capote at a Random House party, circa 1980

other documents. The book runs more than a thousand pages. Mailer called his work a "true life novel," a factual account written for dramatic effect.

For all its complexities, the essential story unfolds in an amazingly compressed period of time. The book concerns the life of Gilmore from the time of his release from an Illinois prison in April 1976 to his execution in Utah nine months later. After the paroled Gilmore moved to Provo, Utah, to live with relatives, he entered a ruinous love affair. The relationship was a psychological factor in his killing two people in robberies on successive nights. Gilmore was soon captured, convicted, and placed on death row. The case drew national media attention when Gilmore refused to allow his death sentence to be appealed. No person had been executed in the country in ten years. Gilmore was a tall, laconic figure, someone who vaguely appealed to the culture's soft spot for stoic heroes. Utah's archaic method of execution, the firing squad, heightened the fascination.

"Let's do it," Gilmore told officials shortly before the bullets struck. The system took his life, but Gilmore seemed to exercise a final gesture of control.

Mailer's decision to write a book about the case came after he was approached by a freelance journalist who already was in pursuit of the story. Mailer was hired to complete the project. Adding to the journalist's material, Mailer conducted interviews on his own trips to Utah and other locations. The massive quantity of diverse information, much of it provided beforehand or existing in documents rather than gathered according to his own instincts as a reporter, presented Mailer with an unfamiliar creative challenge. He has admitted to being awed and initially paralyzed. He considered the story a "found object," like "gold." He felt a strange sense of stewardship, wondering if he really had the right to generalize the story. At the same time he worried about violating the fundamental integrity of the novelist's art by not providing a clear narrative voice. He questioned whether his persona had grown tiresome to readers and no longer provided the magnetic center for holding the elements of a story together. He considered the opportunity to attract a new audience by making his writing more direct. He came to realize that the transcripts and letters he possessed were as close as he would ever come to a reality about the people and events he wanted to write about. In the myriad of voices were the actual traces of the social drama he wanted to frame.

By allowing the participants to speak for themselves, Mailer relinquished much of the novelist's power to control characters, including his own role as a protagonist. Barbara Lounsberry observes that he also abandoned his favored novelistic device, the extended metaphor, to preserve the simpler imagery of his subjects. By moving his narration closer to the appearance of nonfiction, using the imagination of the novelist primarily to blend and juxtapose images and create a final dramatic effect, Mailer achieved another development in alternative journalism. *The Executioner's Song* is the greatest embodiment of his idea that the task of the literary journalist is to bring the whole world of fiction to the facts of journalism. With a style empty of his presence, critic John W. Aldridge writes, he managed to create the impression of people caught up in a violent tragedy "creating their own novel of what they were and did in real life."

Mailer's most penetrating insight into the story was to see the action progressing in two social stages: Gilmore before and after his national notoriety, before and after he became a media commodity and an ideological cause for lawyers with competing convictions to see him dead or alive. The first section of the book, "Western Voices," is the more intimate world of Gilmore and the people who came to abide briefly on that tragic orb spinning out of control. "Eastern Voices" is the din of the press and the impersonal vortex of the legal bureaucracy narrowing toward the final darkness. Gilmore is swept through and absorbed into the popular culture. Mailer's book as a portrait of Gilmore is evenhanded. He remains an enigmatic personality, although many critics note the similarities between Gilmore and the psychic outlaw, Mailer's familiar existential hero. Mailer belatedly was part of the media circus he criticized. The circumstances under which he came to write the book opened him to charges of "checkbook journalism." He later adapted the work into a television docudrama. As a social statement the book has been seen as a deflation of the western mythos, the region's epic history of prairie treks and mountain crossings ending in spiritual and emotional nihilism. *The Executioner's Song* also has been read as a story of resignation and endurance, fairness, commitment to principle, and compassion.

The beginning of the 1980s brought Mailer's domestic life a measure of stability. His estrangement from his fourth wife, Beverly, finally ended in divorce. The couple had two sons, Michael Burks and Stephen McLeod. Mailer had had an intimate relationship with Carol Stevens, a singer, but since the mid 1970s had been living with Norris Church, an artist from Arkansas. In 1980 he married Stevens to legitimize their nine-year-old daughter, Maggie. By arrangement they divorced a few days later, and Mailer married Church, by whom he had a two-year-old son, John Buffalo. The marriages were Mailer's fifth and sixth. The children were his seventh and eighth. Mailer remains married to his sixth wife.

Mailer returned to nonfiction with two biographies, *Oswald's Tale: An American Mystery* and *Portrait of Picasso as a Young Man,* both appearing in 1995. Mailer's experience in writing *The Executioner's Song* had a bizarre footnote. While working on the book he began a correspondence with a Utah prison convict, Jack Henry Abbott, who showed promise as a writer. Mailer helped Abbott publish his edited prison letters and wrote the introduction to the book, *In the Belly of the Beast* (1981). He supported Abbott's release from prison and brought him to New York as an assistant. Within weeks Abbott stabbed a restaurant waiter to death. Mailer testified at his trial and offered only equivocal comments to the press, renewing the debate over his attitude toward violence and the role art plays in redeeming the psychotic outcast.

In *Of Women and Their Elegance* (1980) Mailer revisited his fascination with Marilyn Monroe. The book is an "imaginary memoir" of the actress written in first-person narration. The work is a small tribute to the writer's versatility, although it was an odd release from the rigors of writing about Gary Gilmore. In 1983 Mailer published *Ancient Evenings,* his first major work of fiction since the 1960s. Between fictional engagements Mailer had experimented with every combination of fact and fiction imaginable. *Ancient Evenings,* which he spent a decade writing, was Mailer's return to his basic ambition as a literary artist, to write another significant novel. The book is a historical fantasy set in dynastic Egypt. The protagonist-narrator, Menenhetet, has discovered the secret of reincarnation and lives four lives. Mailer attempts to immerse the modern reader in a totally alien time and place with different boundaries between reality, myth, and mystical existence. The story contains its own set of values without reference to Judeo-Christian concepts. Many reviewers found the seven-hundred-page novel plodding and obscene. Defenders praised its daring and richly detailed execution. In the narrator's stories of himself the multiple identities blend in a kind of collective recall of the past. Biographer Richard Poirier notes that this narrative process parallels Mailer's own ongoing autobiographical project of perpetually reconstructing himself from earlier versions of his highly self-disclosing writing.

In 1984 Mailer was elected president of the American chapter of P.E.N., a worldwide organization of writers, and he presided over the International P.E.N. Congress in 1986. His next writing project was *Tough Guys Don't Dance* (1984), a murder mystery set in Provincetown, Massachusetts, the site of a Mailer residence on Cape Cod. In the book seven murders occupy a former bartender and writer. Jack Beatty, reviewing the book for *The New Republic* (27 August 1984), called it a "successful experiment in literary humiliation," although Mailer has described it as one of his favorite novels among his own fiction. He directed a movie version of the book, starring Ryan O'Neal, in 1987. The cinematic fling was not an entirely new adventure for Mailer. He had maintained an interest in filmmaking since his screenwriting days in Hollywood after the war. His first novel, *The Naked and the Dead,* was made into a movie in 1958. *An American Dream* was adapted in 1966. In 1967 Mailer produced his own underground movie, "Wild 90," shot in four days without a script and featuring Mailer and two friends as Mafia thugs. In another one of his productions, *Beyond the Law* (1967), he plays an Irish New York detective. In *Maidstone* (1968) he is a presidential candidate. Mailer played a minor part in the movie *Ragtime* in 1981.

Harlot's Ghost (1991) is another novel of epic length that elicited mainly weak reviews. The story offers an inside view of the CIA with fictional characters relating to actual historical events. After thirteen hundred pages the novel ends with the unexpected and not entirely welcome promise, "TO BE CONTINUED." *Oswald's Tale: An American Mystery* is the closest of his journalistic works to investigative reporting. He employs a familiar device of his nonfiction by dividing the book into two parts, each covering different material in a different style. The strategy is consistent with his writing philosophy that content and the writer's relation to it determine presentation. The first part chronicles Oswald's two and a half years in Minsk, Russia, and is written in a sparse narrative. June Oswald, quoted in a magazine article as having read portions of the book about her father, describes the experience as "a little like opening a family album you didn't know existed before." The latter half of the eight-hundred-page volume is an assemblage of testimony and other accounts, to which Mailer adds speculative asides. True to his perennial obsessions, Mailer again is engaged in exploring the violent soul and seeking meaning and understanding of a human tragedy. Again there is the obligatory arrant sex, a fanciful supposition that Oswald, while stationed in the Philippines, might have shot and killed a fellow Marine while performing fellatio. Mailer had impressed upon the reader in "The White Negro," the essay written more than thirty-five years earlier, that even the hoodlum who kills dares the unknown and is not altogether cowardly. As with Gilmore and Abbott, and now Oswald, Mailer continues to seek some slender thread of virtue in the violent outcast.

A consideration of Mailer in the company of literary journalists takes up his identity as a writer at the site of his most commonly acknowledged achievements. The full body of his work, although varying widely in quality, offers compelling evidence that he is the most versatile writer in contemporary American letters. Mailer brings to any subject or genre an adaptable prose style that, as he says, "takes mad chances and risks silliness to gain new tonalities and resonances." In his recent book, *The Gospel According to the Son* (1997), Mailer assumes the point of view of Jesus, certainly his most daring psychic possession to date. His labors in fiction, nonfiction, and sometimes something indistinguishably in between, are reconstructions of the writing craft and, in celebrated ways, of the writer himself.

Biographies:

Hilary Mills, *Mailer: A Biography* (New York: Empire Books, 1982);

Peter Manso, *Mailer: His Life and Times* (New York: Simon & Schuster, 1985);

Carl Rollyson, *The Lives of Norman Mailer: A Biography* (New York: Paragon House, 1991).

References:

Laura Adams, *Existential Battles: The Growth of Norman Mailer* (Athens: Ohio University Press, 1976);

Adams, ed., *Will the Real Norman Mailer Please Stand Up?* (Port Washington, N.Y.: Kennekat, 1974);

John W. Aldridge, "Documents as Narrative," *Atlantic Monthly,* 275 (May 1995): 120–125;

Chris Anderson, "Norman Mailer: The Record of a War," in his *Style as Argument: Contemporary American Nonfiction* (Carbondale: Southern Illinois University Press, 1987), pp. 82–132;

Jennifer Baily, *Norman Mailer: Quick Change Artist* (New York: Harper & Row, 1979);

Anna Banks, "Norman Mailer," in *A Sourcebook of American Literary Journalism,* edited by Thomas B. Connery (New York: Greenwood Press, 1992), pp. 297–306;

Robert J. Begiebing, *Acts of Regeneration: Allegory and Archetype in the Works of Norman Mailer* (Columbia: University of Missouri Press, 1980);

Harold Bloom, ed., *Norman Mailer* (New York: Chelsea House, 1986);

Leo Braudy, ed., *Norman Mailer: A Collection of Critical Essays* (Englewood Cliffs, N.J.: Prentice-Hall, 1972);

Philip Bufithis, *Norman Mailer* (New York: Ungar, 1978);

Anthony Burgess, "The Prisoner of Fame," *Atlantic Monthly,* 255 (June 1985): 100, 102–104;

Robert Ehrlich, *Norman Mailer: The Radical as Hipster* (Metuchen, N.J.: Scarecrow, 1978);

Joe Flaherty, *Managing Mailer* (New York: Coward-McCann, 1970);

Andrew Gordon, *An American Dreamer: A Psychoanalytic Study of the Fiction of Norman Mailer* (Cranbury, N.J.: Associated University Presses, 1980);

Stanley T. Gutman, *Mankind in Barbary: The Individual and Society in the Novels of Norman Mailer* (Hanover, N.H.: University Press of New England, 1976);

John Hellmann, "Journalism as Metafiction: Norman Mailer's Strategy for Mimesis and Interpretation in a Postmodern World," in his *Fables of Fact: The New Journalism as New Fiction* (Urbana: University of Illinois Press, 1981), pp. 35–65;

John Hollowell, "Mailer's Vision: 'History as a Novel, the Novel as History,' " in his *Fact & Fiction: The New Journalism and the Nonfiction Novel* (Chapel Hill: University of North Carolina Press, 1977), pp. 87–123;

Carol Iannone, "'Our Genius': Norman Mailer and the Intellectuals," *Commentary,* 80 (October 1985): 60–62, 65;

George P. Landow, *Elegant Jeremiahs: The Sage from Carlyle to Mailer* (Ithaca, N.Y.: Cornell University Press, 1986);

Nigel Leigh, *Radical Fictions and the Novels of Norman Mailer* (New York: St. Martin's Press, 1990);

J. Michael Lennon, *Critical Essays on Norman Mailer* (Boston: G. K. Hall, 1986);

Barbara Lounsberry, "Norman Mailer's Ages of Man" in her *The Art of Fact: Contemporary Artists of Nonfiction* (Westport, Conn.: Greenwood Press, 1990), pp. 139–189;

Robert F. Lucid, ed., *Norman Mailer: The Man and His Work* (Boston: Little, Brown, 1971);

Louis Menand, "Advertisements for His Self," *New Republic,* 192 (24 June 1985): 27–33;

Robert Merrill, *Normal Mailer* (Boston: Twayne, 1978);

Merrill, *Norman Mailer Revisited* (New York: Twayne, 1992);

Jonathan Middlebrook, *Mailer and the Times of His Time* (San Francisco: Bay Books, 1976);

Richard Poirier, *Norman Mailer* (New York: Viking, 1972);

Jean Radford, *Norman Mailer: A Critical Study* (New York: Harper & Row, 1975);

Robert Solotaroff, *Down Mailer's Way* (Urbana: University of Illinois Press, 1975);

Joseph Wenke, *Mailer's America* (Hanover, N.H.: University Press of New England, 1987).

Joe McGinniss
(9 December 1942 –)

Linda Steiner
Rutgers University

BOOKS: *The Selling of the President 1968* (New York: Trident, 1969);

The Dream Team (New York: Random House, 1972);

Heroes (New York: Viking, 1976);

Going to Extremes (New York: Knopf, 1980);

Fatal Vision (New York: Putnam, 1983);

Blind Faith (New York: Putnam, 1989);

Cruel Doubt (New York: Simon & Schuster, 1991);

The Last Brother: The Rise and Fall of Teddy Kennedy (New York: Simon & Schuster, 1993).

Because Joe McGinniss has experimented with different kinds of writing, criticism of his work has ranged across very different battlefields. From his first book, *The Selling of the President 1968* (1969), a critically praised and best-selling analysis of the 1968 presidential campaign, to his most recent work, *The Last Brother: The Rise and Fall of Teddy Kennedy* (1993), a "rumination" on the life and mythology of Sen. Edward Kennedy, McGinniss has been a lightning rod for concerns over nonfiction writers' more controversial methods. For example, *Fatal Vision* (1983) attracted attention when its subject, an army doctor convicted of murdering his wife and daughters, sued McGinniss for breach of contract. McGinniss had befriended Jeffrey MacDonald and had appeared to believe his protestations of innocence while McGinniss was researching the case. *Fatal Vision,* however, affirmed the court verdict of guilt and called MacDonald a "pathological narcissist." Some critics supported MacDonald's claim that McGinniss had betrayed him, and other McGinniss books have been the target of even harsher scrutiny.

By emerging definitions and standards in the scholarly criticism of literary journalism, McGinniss is not generally considered one of the more gifted practitioners of the form. Most of his books are lengthy and are based on comprehensive research, done lately with the help of diligent assistants. However, as Thomas Connery has pointed out, bulk is not a defining characteristic of literary journalism. Where McGinniss's skill does emerge is in his

Joe McGinniss (photograph by Nancy Doherty)

choice of subject. The readability of McGinniss's recent true-crime books relies on juicy, gripping stories rather than complex narrative architecture or elegant stylization. In contrast to literary journalists such as Truman Capote or Tom Wolfe, McGinniss has not engaged in attempts to carve out intellectual and aesthetic space for a new literary form. Yet most critics regard McGinniss as a literary journalist, and complaints about his methods have implicated the genre. A critical analysis of McGinniss can therefore contribute to the ongoing project of refining the understanding of literary journalism. Ironically, given that nearly all of McGinniss's books point to the disappointing or phony quality of authority figures, from mythological heroes to parents, McGinniss's reportorial stance raises questions about the nature of journalistic authority and authorship. His work lacks the sense of personal responsibility and moral commitment to the subjects of a story that have become characteristic of literary journalism. One of the important ethical problems inherent in McGinniss's work regards how or when a writer may legitimately use another person's life as the subject of a book. His work challenges readers to think about whose purposes and which purposes truth may be asked to serve.

McGinniss was born on 9 December 1942 in New York City to Mary Leonard McGinniss and Joseph McGinniss, a travel agent. He grew up in Rye, New York, where he attended parochial schools, and he graduated from Holy Cross College in 1964. Having been rejected by the graduate program in journalism at Columbia University, McGinniss worked briefly for small newspapers before going to the *Philadelphia Bulletin* as a sportswriter in 1966. He wrote for the *Philadelphia Inquirer* from 1967 to 1968. Since then McGinniss's name has appeared in newspapers far more often as topic than as byline.

McGinniss has attracted attention since the publication of his first book, *The Selling of the President 1968,* a vehemently critical and effective exposé of Richard Nixon's 1968 campaign and specifically of its use of modern marketing techniques and television to transform and sell the image of an otherwise unchanged politician. Its highly grounded, careful observations legitimately sounded the alarm about the implications for democracy of relatively new campaign strategies. McGinniss launched consideration of significant problems, especially the use of both technology and social science techniques to "package" candidates, that have since become even more unsettling.

Some media critics saw *The Selling of the President* as a malicious attack by a young know-it-all. Others denied that McGinniss had revealed anything extraordinary, although Nixon was certainly shocked at the exposure. Ironically, none of the contemporary criticism focused on McGinniss's journalistic methods per se. As McGinniss revealed later in the context of justifying his relationship with Jeffrey MacDonald, Nixon's campaign staff members never anticipated that the seemingly innocuous McGinniss might portray them as sinister. Therefore, he was freely allowed to attend meetings and planning sessions. (Hubert Humphrey had also hired a Madison Avenue advertising team, and the idea for McGinniss's project came from a serendipitous conversation with someone who worked on

Humphrey's behalf. But Humphrey rejected McGinniss's proposal to follow his campaign.) Even now, no one would challenge McGinniss's decision to exploit the naiveté of Nixon's staff or to withhold his judgments of Nixon over the course of the five months he spent on the trail. However, when asked for his advice, McGinniss as on-site researcher volunteered helpful suggestions to Nixon's people. Therefore, ethical questions arise concerning McGinniss's willingness to assist, albeit in an extremely minor way, in electing someone McGinniss later denounced in print; he participated in the same process of packaging and selling Nixon that he later condemned.

Arguably, these are false issues in the case of both *The Selling of the President* and *Fatal Vision.* Journalists may legitimately reason that if they have presented themselves as being on the job (that is, unlike undercover investigative reporters), then they are not further obliged to reveal their intentions or their working theories to their potential subjects, especially to those who are in the public eye or are relatively sophisticated about how journalists work. Second, although reporters, including literary journalists, do not typically interfere in the activities they cover, journalists who closely follow their subjects must interact with them.

The Selling of the President opens with a strong, vigorous narrative that invites readers to enter directly into the spirited debates among the television and advertising experts on how best to manipulate Nixon's image. In contrast, the book ends with a variety of source documents: extracts from Marshall McLuhan's *Understanding Media* (1964) that had been distributed to Nixon staffers, notes and memos from people working for and with Nixon on advertising strategy, and scripts for spot commercials. The appendix suggests that, following his more traditional journalistic instincts, McGinniss did not trust—or did not want readers to trust—his own observations. He resorted to more-conventional defenses and warrants for his logic.

The way McGinniss put it, the enormous success of *The Selling of the President* and the fact that he was, at age twenty-seven, one of the youngest nonfiction writers to reach the top of the best-seller list (a ranking the book enjoyed for four months) brought about considerable problems for him. It may also have brought on a measure of paranoia; he often claims that rivals resent the fact that he so quickly achieved fame and celebrity.

McGinniss's next project was a novel about an author on a book tour. The hero of *The Dream Team* (1972) was derailed by his fascination with women, drink, and horse racing. Years later, in an interview with Jean W. Ross published in 1989, McGinniss changed his mind and denied that success and personal dislocation were strongly connected in his case. In any case, the novel, a commercial failure, was soon followed with *Heroes* (1976), a nonfictional reworking of some of these issues. Here McGinniss describes treating his girlfriend rather badly, perhaps because of guilt feelings over his former wife and their three children. (Unlike the hero of *The Dream Team*, who eventually returns to his wife, McGinniss married girlfriend Nancy Doherty the year *Heroes* appeared.) *Heroes* combines maudlin confessions about his personal life with summaries of scholarly literature about hero worship and interviews with renowned men, including Eugene McCarthy and William Westmoreland. None of the putative heroes he interviewed was either forthcoming or enlightening on the nature of heroism. None appeared, under McGinniss's tortured scrutiny, heroic. Ultimately, ignoring the circular nature of pessimism and narcissism, he laments that heroic values have become obsolete.

James N. Stull, one scholar who is fairly appreciative of McGinniss's search for the antiheroic self, notes that *Heroes* appeared at a point when disenchantment with both political and parental authority had deepened and widened to a near-crisis degree. Forced to concede McGinniss's inability to achieve critical distance, however, Stull explains the author's self-absorption by reference to McGinniss's own descriptions of the frequent absences of his alcoholic father: "McGinniss's quest for the American hero appears in part to be a therapeutic search for more acceptable parental (authoritative) figures—particularly a surrogate father—with whom he can identify and by whom he can be accepted." The romanticized moodiness of McGinniss invites this psychological language. He brutally confesses his preoccupation with his unheroic self to the point of self-caricature. Describing how he silently rehearsed for his interview with Eugene McCarthy, McGinniss notes that what he really wanted to ask was what would happen to the two of them—McCarthy and McGinniss—as people who each had been displaced from the center of things. Later McGinniss told Ross: "I was trying to set myself up as a character [in *Heroes*] who was representative of rootless man in the post-heroic age without calling a lot of attention to the process."

McGinniss conceded that he was not as "out of control" as *Heroes* portrayed. Yet even in the chapters about public figures, McGinniss was painfully explicit regarding not only his domestic shortcomings but also his professional mistakes. For example, he got so drunk during an evening spent talking

with Daniel Berrigan that his notebooks were later found to contain only nonsensical scrawls instead of usable transcriptions of Berrigan's insights.

If most of the people who appear in McGinniss's books, including *Heroes*, were not dependent on journalistic attention, they were at least accustomed to being in the public eye. Others explicitly and even manipulatively invited McGinniss to tell their stories. However, McGinniss's next book represented a major exception to the pattern of dealing with people who were already subjects of attention. *Going to Extremes* (1980), therefore, cannot be defended with the same argument. This exploration of Alaska focuses on people who neither invited nor desired the author's attention. After writing *Heroes*, with its conclusion that no more heroic acts remained to be performed, McGinniss sought out heroic country in Alaska, where he toured for eighteen months.

Going to Extremes represents McGinniss's most literary, most lyrical writing. McGinniss, who had described himself in *Heroes* as having been "awkward, weak, and physically uncourageous," was energized and dazzled by the dramatic landscapes of Alaska. He gloried in the remote mountain range where he went climbing. Stull notes that McGinniss "transforms this culturally significant landscape into a metaphorical and personally meaningful setting in which the author can once again pursue his quest for the heroic self, or the model of the vanishing American frontiersman."

Yet *Going to Extremes* presents the entire population of Alaska—natives, newcomers, seasonal workers—as bored, cynical, or simply unable to cope with the challenges of the state, from harsh weather to modernity and urban life. The implicit analogies are striking: the gloomy McGinniss embarked on another romantic odyssey and met up with people who, for the most part, were themselves seeking refuge from personal problems and unhappiness. The difference between McGinniss and his subjects is that he could leave whenever he wanted—and did. McGinniss refused to engage with the people he met, and as with *Heroes*, his dismal sensibility says more about writer than subject. Not surprisingly in light of his earlier sourness, McGinniss left Alaska disappointed.

McGinniss was writing commentary for the *Los Angeles Herald Examiner* in 1979 when he struck a deal with MacDonald, who was then living and working in California, nine years after his pregnant wife and daughters were viciously stabbed to death in their Fort Bragg, North Carolina, apartment. MacDonald, who had been a doctor for a Green Beret unit, stated that knife-wielding intruders, chant-

Dust jacket for McGinniss's account of his eighteen-month tour of Alaska

ing "Acid is groovy," had slain his family while only slightly injuring him. Prosecutors believed otherwise. MacDonald had unsuccessfully contacted several writers about taking up his cause before he met McGinniss. Clearly assuming a book would exonerate him, MacDonald invited McGinniss to write his story. MacDonald promised McGinniss full and exclusive access to the deliberations and strategy planning of his defense team. MacDonald was to receive a healthy percentage of McGinniss's royalties and advance. More importantly—more fatefully—MacDonald promised in writing not to sue McGinniss for libel, "provided that the essential integrity of [his] life story is maintained." To protect the attorney-client privilege, McGinniss was named an official member of the defense team once he moved into the house they had rented in North Carolina.

McGinniss and MacDonald shared several interests and even personality traits and became friends. After MacDonald was convicted and imprisoned—by which time McGinniss had come to believe the doctor was guilty—McGinniss continued his research. He visited MacDonald, who was serving three consecutive life sentences, and listened to tape recordings MacDonald made from his cell. Until *Fatal Vision* actually appeared in 1983, they often corresponded. McGinniss's supportive, friendly, cheerful letters never hinted at his judgment.

Although MacDonald's suit against McGinniss ended in a hung jury, the publisher of *Fatal Vision* eventually settled out of court for $325,000. Janet Malcolm learned of the breach-of-contract case when McGinniss's lawyer contacted more than thirty journalists to warn them that MacDonald's claim threatened journalists' First Amendment freedoms. Intrigued, Malcolm interviewed McGinniss. But their discussions went badly and Malcolm, a writer even more controversial in her own right than McGinniss, went on to interview others involved in the case. Her 1990 book accused McGinniss of perfidy and bad faith in his relationship with MacDonald. In *Fatal Justice: Reinvestigating the MacDonald Murders* (1995) Jerry Allen Potter and Fred Bost went even further than Malcolm and supported MacDonald's claim that McGinniss's book and the television miniseries based on it injured MacDonald's chances for appeal.

Fatal Vision is massive: 665 pages, without the epilogue which was added later. It includes the text of the "Ballad of the Green Berets," the *Macbeth* passage from which the title was taken, biblical quotes, and a listing of medical textbooks. Structurally, *Fatal Vision* alternates between stories of the major characters and MacDonald's highly self-serving, first-person recollections. McGinniss refers to himself in the introduction, in order to explain how he met MacDonald, and then returns to first person only in the concluding section, where he offers an interesting and even plausible theory: he speculates that diet pills had triggered MacDonald's angry eruption. Otherwise determined to erase his own voice and submerge his authorship, McGinniss took Joan Didion's fascination with "physical fact" to an exhaustive, even oppressive, extreme. Gory details of the crime scene itself, for example, are recited in several contexts. Furthermore, pages and even entire chapters provide what amounts to transcripts of dialogue and testimony, with virtually no intervention by McGinniss. For example, nearly fifteen pages are given to the grand jury questioning of MacDonald's brother, a rather obstreperous, even bullish man who made clear his hostility to the proceedings. McGinniss offers a two-sentence description of the burly brother, whose name is not provided. From then on, McGinniss breaks into the transcript only twice to paraphrase.

Many readers may have willingly overlooked the lack of graceful or sensitive writing, since the story involved a handsome, sexy professional who murdered his pretty wife and blond children. The book shored up a case that was never in doubt, except in the mind of MacDonald. Even McGinniss himself told Ross that *Fatal Vision* "was really hardcore, rock-solid, old fashioned meticulous reporting, laying it down just as it was because of the kind of story it was." Unlike Capote's 1966 nonfiction novel, *In Cold Blood,* which echoed the naturalistic fiction of Theodore Dreiser, *Fatal Vision* recalls the sensationalism of the tabloid press. Whereas Capote grounded his story in chillingly amoral physical description, *Fatal Vision* was a bulky and often tedious report.

His next true-crime book, another best-seller, was far better written than *Fatal Vision,* although its central homicidal father was less charismatic and less glamorous. A classic page-turner, *Blind Faith* (1989) tells in seamless, straightforward prose of an outwardly successful insurance salesman in Toms River, New Jersey, who hired a thug to murder his wife so that he could pay off his considerable debts and settle down with his girlfriend on the proceeds of a $1.5 million insurance policy. Robert Marshall had arranged that the hired killer would hit him over the head convincingly. (MacDonald's wounds were superficial and, the jury decided, self-inflicted.) The youngest of Marshall's three sons accepted his father's lies. The boy's belief in his father's innocence, and a slight rewriting of a quotation from Herman Melville's *Moby-Dick* (1851) that McGinniss used for an epigraph, provided the title. Nonetheless, the police almost immediately suspected Marshall's involvement. Marshall was convicted and remains in prison.

Blind Faith, McGinniss's most novelistic work, offers fully developed, motivated characters. Each major player is introduced separately before moving on to act out a role in the plot that McGinniss deemed the "most plausible." McGinniss explains that he reconstructed dialogue and dramatically recreated scenes "in order to portray more effectively the personalities of those most intimately involved." A few people did object to McGinniss's portrayal. Yet, since McGinniss had changed the names of most of the minor players, as recognizable as they might be locally, they were effectively unable to dispute his version. One state senator who was "renamed" in *Blind Faith* told Wayne King of *The New York Times* that refuting McGinniss's implication that he had obstructed the murder investigation was like "fighting a ghost." Although *The Selling of the President* decried how television substituted a blandly attractive manufactured image for "reality," and although among the many demeaning things McGinniss said about the Marshalls' suburb was that life in Toms River "was lived at the mini-series level," *Blind Faith,* like *Fatal Vision,* became the basis for a television miniseries. Unlike MacDonald, the sons saw a prepublication draft, and they apparently had no complaints. One son helped the miniseries's producers.

Blind Faith is premised on a clear, if secondary, theme: the shallowness and moral impoverishment of Toms River. McGinniss, who lives with his wife and children in the Massachusetts community that is home to Williams College, saw the Marshall case as the "quintessential symbol of the consequences" of the consumerism and snobbery of towns like Toms River. The Marshalls' fascination with material goods gave McGinniss not only thematic fodder but also the opportunity for reporting on the "status details" that Tom Wolfe asserted were characteristic of New Journalism. Ironically, the two motifs—suburban social climbing turned extreme and innocent loyalty of sons betrayed—worked against each other both logically and emotionally. The warmhearted domesticity of Maria Marshall and her three sons existed in the same upper-middle-class community as the avarice and vileness of Marshall. The tragedy of the sons, whom Marshall had hoped would lie on his behalf at trial, was undermined by McGinniss's contempt for the New Jersey "country club set."

In 1990 McGinniss again faced murderous family secrets. Bonnie Von Stein and her husband had been brutally beaten and stabbed. Von Stein survived; her husband died on the floor of their bedroom. Given that a two-million-dollar inheritance was at stake, some people had initially suspected Von Stein of being behind the attack. On the other hand, some of Von Stein's relatives, including her brother, immediately suspected the involvement of her two children by a prior marriage. Angela Pritchard, age eighteen, had been sullen and unresponsive when informed of the attacks; she calmly told police that she had slept soundly through the night, although her bedroom was next door to her parents'. Chris Pritchard, a nineteen-year-old with a poor academic and social record, was then attending summer school some one hundred miles away. He eventually confessed that he had hired James Upchurch, a fellow Dungeons and Dragons player, to kill both his mother and stepfather. Pritchard avoided going to trial by pleading guilty to aiding and abetting murder in the second degree, and he was sentenced to life plus twenty years. Upchurch was tried by a jury and convicted of first-degree murder.

McGinniss had been contacted by Von Stein's lawyer, who himself had been local counsel for MacDonald and had apparently not liked *Fatal Vision*. Temporarily abandoning a biography of Edward Kennedy, a project not going well, McGinniss acceded to Von Stein's request that he play psychological detective. A quiet, undemonstrative woman who had closed herself off with a thick wall of self-protective mechanisms, Von Stein immediately hypothesized that since Pritchard might have been acquitted had he gone to trial, he had acted honorably by pleading guilty. In her view, he chose to tell the

truth out of a deep sense of remorse. Nonetheless, understandably astonished by her son's deeds, Von Stein asked McGinniss to "make comprehensible to her all that she had endured." Unlike MacDonald, she had no interest in financial compensation. Von Stein promised McGinniss total access to people and information. She insisted that others in the case speak freely to him and must have additionally encouraged people to speak openly with McGinniss's research assistant. The assistant, a former television journalist who was then a graduate student at Columbia University, interviewed more than thirty people.

The situation was thorny, but McGinniss managed to incorporate an analysis of several potentially confusing medical, legal, and ethical dilemmas into a highly readable narrative, *Cruel Doubt* (1991). Indeed, he showed considerable sensitivity. His writing and his moral attitude hinted at some degree of ambivalence and complexity. McGinniss's research led him to several speculations, including that Neal Henderson, who pleaded guilty to driving Upchurch to and from the Von Steins' home the night of the attack, was probably even more guilty, more involved than Henderson had admitted. McGinniss emphasized some glaring holes and contradictions in the prosecution of Upchurch. Von Stein herself told McGinniss that if she had been a juror she would have voted to acquit Upchurch.

However, McGinniss also underscored the logical, emotional, and physical evidence that Von Stein's daughter Angela was actively complicit. McGinniss's case against Angela was not implausible. But in proposing such a damning argument that Angela had helped the murderers, McGinniss put what he regarded as his commitment to "truth" above both moral justice and his relationship with a woman who had been horribly scarred. McGinniss's speculation that Angela had unlocked the door for the killer(s) could only hurt Von Stein, a woman who certainly had never doubted her daughter. McGinniss, who was respectful of Von Stein's psychiatrist and treated her psychoanalyses as authoritative, even quoted the psychiatrist warning him that to lose faith in Angela would be more than Von Stein could endure. Yet that loss was precisely what the book forced on Von Stein.

Especially given their conscious concern for developing relationships with their subjects, many literary journalists underscore a sense of mutuality, a concern for relational responsibility and connection. McGinniss's decision to privilege truth over individual human welfare subverted a fundamental, if still emerging and unstated, tradition in literary journalism to decenter abstract principle. Unlike the ethically motivated literary journalist, McGinniss obtained information from Von Stein in order to speak about her. It cannot be said that in *Cruel Doubt* McGinniss was interested in presenting evidence against someone so that justice could be served or so that evildoers would be punished. An article by Bob Greene reveals that McGinniss's publisher, having ordered a 375,000-copy first printing, told McGinniss its goal was to get *Cruel Doubt* quickly to number one on the best-seller list. The book, written and published at breakneck speed, was well reviewed in the popular press, although its clichéd moments were noticed.

After the book tour for *Cruel Doubt* McGinniss finally returned to the long-deferred Edward Kennedy project. In some sense he had long seen himself as tied up with the fate of the Kennedys and the Kennedy myth. He often measured his success by how close he could get to them. He left the *Inquirer* when its publisher, Walter Annenberg, editorially rebutted a column in which McGinniss linked the violence endemic in U.S. society to Robert Kennedy's death. He had also fruitlessly interviewed Edward Kennedy for *Heroes;* having ignored the advice of a congressional aide, McGinniss confessed, he posed precisely those questions that would cause Kennedy to freeze.

McGinniss faced the greatest critical derision and commercial scorn of his career with *The Last Brother: The Rise and Fall of Teddy Kennedy,* published in 1993. Ostensibly a biography of Edward Kennedy, the book depicts a great deal of maneuvering by and among other Kennedys, especially Joe, John, and Robert; much of this only tangentially had bearing on Edward. McGinniss widely blamed the savage criticism of *The Last Brother* on a conspiracy by the Kennedys. He speculated that since he had deflated the Camelot mythology on which the Kennedys financially and psychologically depended, they were pressuring reviewers to pan his book. Nat Henthoff was one of several critics to repudiate this accusation: not only were the majority of newspaper columnists pillorying *The Last Brother* more than the family could possibly control, but most of them were not even particularly enamored of the Kennedys. Also, many other books exposing Kennedy secrets had been, unlike *The Last Brother,* both well received and heartily purchased. Meanwhile, *The Last Brother* presented some logical contradictions. If, as McGinniss claimed repeatedly, "we" (sometimes referring to journalists, sometimes to Americans, sometimes unclear) were so willing to believe the Kennedy myth, then how had McGinniss suddenly and solely become immune to it?

The Last Brother appeared with a transparently defensive author's note to explain his methods. This note replaced a disclaimer that Simon and Schuster had felt the need to release a prepublication excerpt. McGinniss explained that he never intended *The Last Brother* as a formal biography. He asserted that "the writer should be permitted to employ any techniques he thinks best serve his purpose, so long as he informs the reader, unambiguously, of what he is doing." Quite sensibly, no Kennedy would talk to him. Therefore, with his two research assistants, McGinniss immersed himself in vast amounts of published material (listed in a bibliography) and notes from dozens of interviews in order to "distill an essence" and "make Teddy come alive for a reader as he never has in any of the previously published works." Quotations attributed to individuals, he said, "represent in substance what I believe to have been spoken."

In the note McGinniss further defends his decision to infer never-verbalized thoughts of people he never interviewed, from the post-stroke, bedridden, speechless Joe to the miserable, dumbstruck Joan Kennedy. Here he cites as precedent other biographies that included inference, such as Peter Gay's *Freud: A Life for Our Times* (1988). "I have tried to convey to a reader what it might have been like to be Teddy Kennedy," McGinniss said. "I have quite consciously written portions as if from inside his mind." How readers received such insights is difficult to determine, but reviewers lampooned assertions such as this one: "It had always been [Teddy's] belief that however junior and sometimes unsatisfactory a member, he was a part of the Kennedy family." McGinniss also claims to know the thoughts of Bobby Kennedy, who "had to have felt responsible" at some level for the assassinations of his older brother and of Martin Luther King Jr. The book is punctuated with phrases such as "it must have occurred to him" and "so it must have been."

The prose is filled with melodrama and sarcasm such as this: "Most of what Teddy knew about Vermont was that it was the place you went skiing when you didn't have time to get to Colorado or Switzerland." McGinniss also showed an especially strong preference for cliff-hanging rhetorical questions. For example, after John Kennedy's death, McGinniss figured, Robert Kennedy suffered not only grief but also "something like" fear: "Or could it have been, for some reason, guilt?"

More ominously, noted historians William Manchester and Doris Kearns Goodwin claimed McGinniss stole from their published work. McGinniss defended his lack of footnotes by saying "all the footnotes in the world cannot breathe truth and life into a misshapen portrait." Footnotes, however, would have allowed readers to distinguish what was lifted from authoritative sources such as Manchester's *Portrait of a President: John F. Kennedy in Profile* (1962) and *The Death of a President, November 20–November 25, 1963* (1967), and what McGinniss "learned" from what are otherwise regarded as far less credible sources. McGinniss's introduction is also substantially a reprint of his own chapter on Ted Kennedy from *Heroes,* although obviously the charge of plagiarism does not apply here.

McGinniss's note calls *The Last Brother* his "best effort at trying to engender in a reader not merely sympathy for Teddy Kennedy, but empathy with him." McGinniss concludes, "With considerable dignity and grace–despite many highly publicized lapses–Teddy Kennedy has endured thirty years of wrenching agony and relentless scrutiny." But only this late-entry apologia, out of 626 pages, says anything positive about any Kennedy. In every case *The Last Brother* accepts (or panders to) the worst-case speculations offered for the Kennedys' activities. Its single-minded recitation of scandals is one of several reasons the book has been branded an "odiography" or, more often, a "pathography," as Joyce Carol Oates calls that form of biography whose motifs are dysfunction and disaster. McGinniss portrays most of the Kennedys as evil, and the rest as stupid, or stupidly driven to evil.

The scholarship on literary journalism does not address what separates the inferior literary journalist from one who is altogether outside the category. As works by Norman Mailer and Truman Capote, among others, attest, the true-crime genre is not inherently antithetical to literary journalism. In contradistinction to Barbara Lounsberry's assertion that fine writing and polished language characterize literary journalism, sheer plot drives McGinniss's writing. Although it is saturated with detail, much of his writing is clichéd and ponderous. Nonetheless, when judged by aesthetic criteria and formal structure, McGinniss's books include many vignettes that might be seen as generally successful pieces of literary journalism.

People have criticized McGinniss's books for different and sometimes contradictory reasons. Then, too, McGinniss has written very different kinds of books. Unlike most works of literary journalism, some of his nonfiction books provide authentic sourcing; while they also offer McGinniss's own conclusions, *The Selling of the President* reprints documents, and *Fatal Vision* offers pages of verbatim testimony. The most severe attacks on his last book, on the other hand, focused on its rather unimaginative imaginings, its manufactured quali-

ties. With a half-man, half-myth subject such as Ted Kennedy, McGinniss has added, a writer "not only can but must" go beyond traditional and universally accepted approaches and techniques.

McGinniss is relatively consistent in his ethical commitments, which tend to be more like those of conventional journalists than literary journalists. Writers in the latter category do not present themselves as unlike or above everyone else; they tend to have a more fluid, more porous sense of authority and fidelity and a more egalitarian sense of community with both subjects and readers. In contrast, McGinniss assumes, as do many traditional-minded journalists, that his professional vision allows him to see what others cannot. For McGinniss, empathy for his subjects is not a virtue but merely a strategy. As he told a *Boston Globe* interviewer in 1989: "A writer has to be involved and detached. I totally immerse myself in my story. Empathy doesn't come hard to me. I can see the world through someone else's eyes. . . . But then you have to step away from the flesh-and-blood human being and step forward with your representation of that person." McGinniss's interest in detecting reality is also similar to the views of scientists and conventional-minded journalists who believe that the consequences of the search itself or of the achievement of "truth" are irrelevant.

After *Cruel Doubt* appeared in 1991, McGinniss told a *Publishers Weekly* writer that instances when family members cross the line "and do damaging things" intrigue him; nonetheless, he added, he hoped that his next project "doesn't involve people hurting people." Not surprisingly, given his obsession with the failures and failings of authority figures, in 1995 McGinniss attended the O. J. Simpson murder trial. McGinniss managed to obtain a much-coveted front-row seat by writing a personal letter to Judge Lance Ito. One irate journalist complained in the *Los Angeles Times* that "Ted Kennedy's unauthorized mindreader" enjoyed a reserved front-row seat while some reporters were forced to share seats at the back. In some sense McGinniss's most honest epigraph appeared in *The Last Brother,* which quotes an Adrienne Rich poem: "I came to explore the wreck. . . . I came to see the damage that was done."

Interviews:

Marian Christy, "The Writer as Loner," *Boston Globe,* 11 January 1989, pp. 65–66;

Anne Janette Johnson and Jean W. Ross, "Joe McGinniss," *Contemporary Authors,* new revision series 26, edited by Hal May and James G. Lesniak (Detroit: Gale, 1989), pp. 268–272;

Robert Dahlin, "Joe McGinniss," *Publishers Weekly,* (18 October 1991): 40–41.

References:

Gail Caldwell, "Virtual Biography," *Boston Globe,* 8 August 1993, pp. B1–B2;

Thomas B. Connery, "Discovering a Literary Form," in *A Sourcebook of American Literary Journalism,* edited by Connery (New York: Greenwood Press, 1993), pp. 3–37;

Bob Greene, "Joe McGinniss, at Bat Again," *Chicago Tribune,* 15 October 1991, V: 1;

Nat Hentoff, "Imagining Ted Kennedy," *Progressive* (November 1993): 16–17;

Michiko Kakutani, "Is It Fiction? Is It Nonfiction? And Why Doesn't Anyone Care?" *New York Times,* 27 July 1993, pp. C13, C16;

Wayne King, "It's Not Us, Toms River Says of Portrayal in Book," *New York Times,* 29 March 1989, pp. B1–B2;

Barbara Lounsberry, *The Art of Fact: Contemporary Artists of Nonfiction* (Westport, Conn.: Greenwood Press, 1990);

Janet Malcolm, *The Journalist and the Murderer* (New York: Knopf, 1990);

Bob Pool, "Back-Seat Treatment Rankles Many Journalists," *Los Angeles Times,* 25 January 1995, p. 13;

Jerry Allen Potter and Fred Bost, *Fatal Justice: Reinvestigating the MacDonald Murders* (New York: Norton, 1995);

Linda Steiner, "Joe McGinniss," in *A Sourcebook of American Literary Journalism,* edited by Connery (New York: Greenwood Press, 1993), pp. 367–374;

James N. Stull, *Literary Selves. Autobiography and Contemporary American Nonfiction* (Westport, Conn.: Greenwood Press, 1993).

John McPhee
(8 March 1931–)

Norman Sims
University of Massachusetts

BOOKS: *A Sense of Where You Are: A Profile of William Warren Bradley* (New York: Farrar, Straus & Giroux, 1965);

The Headmaster: Frank L. Boyden of Deerfield (New York: Farrar, Straus & Giroux, 1966);

Oranges (New York: Farrar, Straus & Giroux, 1967);

The Pine Barrens (New York: Farrar, Straus & Giroux, 1968);

A Roomful of Hovings and Other Profiles (New York: Farrar, Straus & Giroux, 1968);

Levels of the Game (New York: Farrar, Straus & Giroux, 1969);

The Crofter and the Laird (New York: Farrar, Straus & Giroux, 1970);

Encounters with the Archdruid (New York: Farrar, Straus & Giroux, 1971);

Wimbledon: A Celebration (New York: Viking, 1972);

The Deltoid Pumpkin Seed (New York: Farrar, Straus & Giroux, 1973);

The Curve of Binding Energy (New York: Farrar, Straus & Giroux, 1974);

Pieces of the Frame (New York: Farrar, Straus & Giroux, 1975);

The Survival of the Bark Canoe (New York: Farrar, Straus & Giroux, 1975);

The John McPhee Reader, edited by William L. Howarth (New York: Farrar, Straus & Giroux, 1976); revised as *The Second John McPhee Reader,* edited by David Remnick and Patricia Strachan (New York: Farrar, Straus & Giroux, 1996);

Coming into the Country (New York: Farrar, Straus & Giroux, 1977);

Giving Good Weight (New York: Farrar, Straus & Giroux, 1979);

Basin and Range (New York: Farrar, Straus & Giroux, 1981);

In Suspect Terrain (New York: Farrar, Straus & Giroux, 1983);

La Place de la Concorde Suisse (New York: Farrar, Straus & Giroux, 1984);

Heirs of General Practice (New York: Farrar, Straus & Giroux, 1984);

John McPhee (photograph by Joel Mednick)

Table of Contents (New York: Farrar, Straus & Giroux, 1985);

Rising from the Plains (New York: Farrar, Straus & Giroux, 1986);

The Control of Nature (New York: Farrar, Straus & Giroux, 1989);

Looking for a Ship (New York: Farrar, Straus & Giroux, 1990);

Assembling California (New York: Farrar, Straus & Giroux, 1993);

The Ransom of Russian Art (New York: Farrar, Straus & Giroux, 1994);

Irons in the Fire (New York: Farrar, Straus & Giroux, 1997).

SELECTED PERIODICAL PUBLICATIONS–
UNCOLLECTED: "It's Collegiate–But Is It Humor?" *New York Times Magazine* (25 May 1952): 17, 58;

"The Fair of San Gennaro," *Transatlantic Review* (Winter 1961): 117–128;

"Big Plane," *New Yorker* (19 February 1966): 28;

"Two Commissioners" by McPhee and Thomas Hoving, *New Yorker* (5 March 1966): 33;

"Coliseum Hour," *New Yorker* (12 March 1966): 44;

"Beauty and Horror," *New Yorker* (28 May 1966): 28;

"Girl in a Paper Dress," *New Yorker* (25 June 1966): 20;

"On the Way to Gladstone," *New Yorker* (2 July 1966): 17;

"Ms and FeMs at the Biltmore," *New Yorker* (2 July 1966);

"Eucalyptus Trees," *Reporter* (19 October 1967): 36–39;

"Ruth, the Sun Is Shining," *Playboy* (April 1968): 114–116, 126, 186;

"The License Plates of Burning Tree," *New Yorker* (30 January 1971): 20;

"Three Gatherings (Americans)," *New Yorker* (25 December 1971): 25;

"The Conching Rooms," *New Yorker* (13 May 1972): 32;

"The People of New Jersey's Pine Barrens," *National Geographic* (January 1974): 52–77;

"Sullen Gold" *New Yorker* (25 March 1974): 32;

"Flavors & Fragrances," *New Yorker* (8 April 1974): 35;

"Police Story," *New Yorker* (15 July 1974): 27;

"'Time' Covers, NR," *New Yorker* (28 October 1974): 40;

"The P-1800," *New Yorker* (10 February 1975): 30;

"The Upper 1," *Vogue* (April 1979): 248, 315;

"In Virgin Forest," *New Yorker* (6 July 1987): 21–23;

"Release," *New Yorker* (28 September 1987): 28–32;

"Outcroppings," *U.S. Air* (March 1989): 78–85;

"Altimeter Man," *New Yorker* (25 September 1989): 48–50;

"Travels of the Rock" *New Yorker* (26 February 1990): 108–117;

"Duty of Care," *New Yorker* (28 June 1993): 72–80;

"Other Snows," *New Yorker* (22 January 1996): 90;

"The Gravel Page," *New Yorker* (29 January 1996): 44–69.

John McPhee's career as a literary journalist has been tangled with the history of *The New Yorker* magazine since he became a staff writer in 1965. A list of classic literary journalism in the twentieth century would include several of McPhee's books, which range in subject matter from nuclear physics to oranges, from Russian art to the attempts of humans to alter the course of nature, and from Alaska to the history of the earth as seen in the geology of North America. His beautifully articulated structures, clear prose, and participatory voice have become a model for other literary journalists. McPhee's career coincided with development of *The New Yorker* under editor William Shawn as the premiere publication for literary journalism, although in recent years the magazine has seen the most pronounced changes in its history. Scientific topics such as nuclear physics and geology and regional portraits of New Jersey and Alaska seem to dominate his works. But just when a pattern starts to form, McPhee branches off to write a book about the merchant marine, or a collector of dissident Russian art, or a game warden in Maine.

McPhee's work thrives on narrative and characterization. In the January 1978 issue of the *Atlantic Monthly* critic Benjamin DeMott commented, after McPhee's thirteenth book, "There is not a bad book among them, seldom indeed a laxly composed page. In short, John McPhee . . . has become the name of a standard by which ambitious magazine journalism is now judged." The same could be said after his twenty-fourth book. Whatever his subject matter, McPhee finds a way to make it interesting and artistic. He once wrote a book about oranges that surprised a reviewer in *Harper's* in March 1967: "You may come to the end of it and say to yourself, 'But I can't have read a whole book about oranges!' . . . He writes like a charm, and without being cute, gimmicky, or in any way dull, he just tells you a lot about oranges." McPhee's four-book series on the geology of North America involves a natural subject full of rocks, yet he found a way to bring a human face to geology. In his literary journalism McPhee proves the value of what is often considered ordinary life, using writing techniques and a style that are far from ordinary. Organizing his material and structuring his narratives before he starts writing, McPhee uses this tightly controlled method to treat an unprecedented variety of subjects including basketball and tennis, art and airplanes, the New Jersey Pine Barrens and the wilderness of Alaska, atomic energy and birchbark canoes, oranges and farmers, the Swiss Army and United States Army Corps of Engineers, and the control of nature and the scientific revolution in plate tectonics that created modern geology.

"If you make a list of all the work I've ever done," McPhee said in an unpublished 1996 interview with Norman Sims, "and put a little mark beside things that relate to activities and interests I had before I was twenty, you'd have a little mark beside well over ninety percent of the pieces of writing." His early interests included sports, canoe camp in Vermont, airplanes, learning to write, and the subjects, such as geology, that he studied at Deerfield Academy and Princeton University. His relationship with Princeton has been an enduring one. He teaches there and prefers to write in his university office; he has followed the interests of other professors into his own books on nuclear bombs and geology.

John McPhee's father, Harry, was a doctor with a specialty in sports medicine who treated Princeton athletes and was a member of the faculty. His Scottish great-grandparents had married in 1858 shortly before they immigrated to the coal mining country of Ohio. Although they signed their marriage registry with an *X,* McPhee said, "they could certainly talk." He believes the family's Celtic verbality came with them from Scotland. "There's not so much difference between the Scots and the Irish," McPhee said, "except that the Scots are responsible." Harry was born in 1895. For twenty years he served as the United States physician at the Pan-American Games and the winter and summer Olympics. After an appointment at Iowa State University during which McPhee's brother, Roemer, and his sister, Laura Anne, were born, the family moved to Princeton. Harry McPhee died in 1984. McPhee's mother, Mary Ziegler, born in 1897, was a French teacher in Cleveland before and during the early years of the marriage. Mary Ziegler's father had been the editor of a book-publishing firm in Philadelphia. At the age of one hundred, she was still in good health.

John Angus McPhee was born on 8 March 1931. His parents' house stood on the edge of Princeton, New Jersey, with fields and woods beyond it, but they moved to the center of town when McPhee was still an infant. McPhee spent his childhood biking around campus and attending football and basketball practices with his father. The president of the university knew him by name. He attended elementary school at 185 Nassau Street in a building that the university later purchased and which now houses the creative-writing program in which McPhee teaches. When he was eight and nine years old he wore a Princeton football shirt and ran around at the games retrieving the ball after extra points and serving as the team mascot. When older, he practiced with the Princeton basketball team. "I grew up among the various sports," McPhee said in his interview with Sims. "That's all I cared about until I finished high school." In his early teens, during World War II, McPhee was an air spotter, watching for enemy aircraft from a little hut on

high ground and phoning in the sightings to New York. In high school he shot baskets in the backyard instead of doing homework, but he also encountered teachers who had a profound influence on his work.

One such teacher was Olive McKee, who taught him English for three years. She assigned three pieces of writing a week. "I feel a large and considerable debt to her," McPhee told Sims. "Every piece of writing you turned in had to have a piece of paper on top of it showing the structure. In her case it was Roman numerals and that kind of thing." As Ferris Professor at Princeton, teaching one writing course a year, he has adopted his former teacher's techniques, noting that "When I assign structural outlines with my students, it can be a drawing, but they have to show that they have an idea of the internal structure of the piece." In high school McPhee applied to only one college—Princeton University—and was accepted. Because he was barely seventeen and had grown up in Princeton, his parents sent him to Deerfield Academy in Massachusetts for an additional year of study before he entered college. There he was taught by Helen Boyden in chemistry and Frank Conklin in geology, and he was influenced by an English teacher named Robert McGlynn ("He got me excited about reading in a way I'd never been before").

He also discovered Frank Boyden, who became the subject of one of McPhee's earliest books, *The Headmaster: Frank L. Boyden of Deerfield* (1966). The book had a sentimental tone that was appropriate for a former Deerfield student writing about the headmaster, who was eighty-six. Boyden left his mark on the boys in the form of ethical standards, not academics. "His first-hand relationship with his boys has always been extraordinary," McPhee writes in *The Headmaster,* "and Deerfield students for sixty years have been characterized by the high degree of ethical sensitivity that he has been able to awaken in them." Boyden's ethics seem to have stuck to McPhee.

McPhee entered Princeton with the class of 1953, and spent his sophomore and junior years in the creative-writing program, then headed by Richard Blackmur. He studied not only with Blackmur but also with Randall Jarrell and Tom Riggs. He then proposed to write a novel for his senior thesis, but, he recalled, "I was an English major and they wouldn't hear of it. I argued all over the place and they finally let me do it."

Having decided at an early age to be a writer and wanting from the age of eighteen to write for *The New Yorker,* McPhee was interested in nonfiction writing in addition to the experience he was receiving in the fiction program at Princeton. "If you go back into the years when I was writing a novel for a senior thesis," he said in 1996, "I was also writing factual articles every week. Princeton had a feast of undergraduate publications, and any young writer ought to know that when you're in college you have an unparalleled opportunity to publish things, see yourself in print, see what it's like, grow in it. That's going to stop dead as a door-nail the day you graduate." At Princeton he worked for the *Nassau Sovereign,* the *Princeton Tiger,* and the *Nassau Literary Magazine.* In his senior year he wrote a one-page essay every week for the *Princeton Alumni Weekly* and was paid for it. He remembers it as "the single best piece of training I had as an undergraduate."

As editor of the *Princeton Tiger,* McPhee decided to create an imitation of *The New Yorker,* complete with a front section called "Spires and Gargoyles" that looked like "Talk of the Town" in *The New Yorker.* This issue caught the eye of a *New York Times Magazine* editor, who asked McPhee for an article about college humor publications. The article became his first professional piece of writing, full of adolescent barbs at the other humor magazines. It ran in *The New York Times Magazine* on 25 May 1952.

After graduating from Princeton, McPhee began a journey he compared in 1996 with a river trip:

> When a person is 21 or 22 years old and facing that great enigma about what to do, envying the law students or medical students who can get on a set of rails and run on it and know where they're going, the writer doesn't know. But a writer should also bear in mind there are numerous paths to this goal and they're all O.K. It's like a huge river with a lot of islands in it. You can go around an island to the left or right. You can go to this or that island. You might get into an eddy. But you're still in the river. You're going to get there. If the person expects the big answer at 21, that's ridiculous. Everyone's in the dark.

McPhee's path to his lifelong goal of becoming a writer took several turns. First, he went to Cambridge University for a year of postgraduate study in English, and while there he played basketball and worked as a stringer for *Time* magazine. Returning to New York, he tried freelancing and wrote short stories. One day he had an opportunity to watch rehearsals for a live television show in a warehouse on the Upper West Side. Without pay McPhee watched weeks of rehearsals for *Robert Montgomery Presents,* read old scripts, and began writing his own one-hour television plays, two of which were produced. For a while he wrote speeches for W. R. Grace and Company, a Wall Street firm, and did articles for the company magazine.

McPhee steadily submitted articles to *The New Yorker* and even interviewed for a position as a "Talk of the Town" reporter. Nothing happened. In the meantime he took a job writing for a mimeographed house organ called *FYI* at Time-Life. He moved up to the main magazine and stayed at *Time* seven years, writing articles for the show-business section and back-of-the-book pieces about people, art, show business, religion, education, and books. He wrote nine cover stories, including profiles of Joan Baez, Richard Burton, Jackie Gleason, Jean Kerr, Alan Jay Lerner and Frederick Loewe, Sophia Loren, Mort Sahl, and Barbra Streisand. He also wrote the cover story on the 1964 New York World's Fair. But he did not want to remain at *Time* indefinitely. He was writing short stories that were later published in *Playboy, Reporter,* and the *Transatlantic Review.* He wrote his short stories, as well as articles and poetry, in his free time. To young writers, McPhee suggests a similar path. "A writer ought to write in every genre," he said to Sims. "Try poetry. Find out how bad you can be at it, or good, but probably bad."

One day Harold Hayes, editor of *Esquire,* agreed that McPhee would write an article about playing basketball in England during his postgraduate year at Cambridge. "I wrote the piece and sent it to him. He said he didn't want it. He was sorry but it disappointed him. I thought, 'Hoooo!' I was so depressed," McPhee recalled in 1996. "Then . . . *The New Yorker* bought it." It was his first piece in that magazine. "Basketball and Beefeaters" appeared in 1963. But McPhee said that he "went on working at *Time.* It was the Bradley piece that changed my life."

As a freshman at Princeton, Bill Bradley, a six-foot-five basketball player from Crystal City, Missouri, had impressed McPhee's father, the doctor for the team. One winter day in 1962 McPhee's father called his son in New York and said, "There's a freshman basketball player down here who is the best basketball player who has ever been near here and may be one of the best ever." At the freshman game the next night against Pennsylvania the stands were filled and Dr. McPhee was holding a seat for his son. Three years later, in 1965, "A Sense of Where You Are" appeared in *The New Yorker* and proved to be a turning point in McPhee's career. That same year Bradley was named All-America, led his Ivy League team into the Final Four of the NCAA tournament, was named most valuable player in the tournament, and was the number one draft choice of the New York Knicks; Bradley turned down their lucrative offer in favor of a Rhodes Scholarship.

McPhee's profile used Bradley's skills, his dedication, and fan reactions to create the image of a superior basketball player. Bradley showed McPhee that the seemingly impossible–shooting without looking at the basket–was only a matter of practice, something Bradley had seen Oscar Robertson and Jerry West do many times. Bradley tossed the ball into the basket while looking McPhee in the eye, and then did it again. "The shot has the essential characteristics of a wild accident," McPhee writes, "which is what many people stubbornly think they have witnessed until they see him do it for the third time in a row." The participatory voice in the earlier sentence–Bradley looking McPhee in the eye–later came to characterize McPhee's writing. After playing the game a while, Bradley explained, "You develop a sense of where you are," and, likewise, McPhee always knows where the reader is.

McPhee published *A Sense of Where You Are: A Profile of William Warren Bradley* as a book in 1965. Bradley later helped the New York Knicks win two NBA championships, was elected to the Basketball Hall of Fame in 1982, became a United States senator from New Jersey, and was frequently mentioned as a possible presidential candidate. "The title of McPhee's book, *A Sense of Where You Are,* applies to both Bradley's play on the court and his life off the court," wrote critic James N. Stull. "In other words, Bradley has a sense of self, purpose, and direction in life, and this is true of almost all of McPhee's admirable subjects." McPhee followed up with a series of profiles for *The New Yorker.* First came "The Headmaster" (1966), a profile of Frank L. Boyden, headmaster of Deerfield Academy, followed by "A Roomful of Hovings" (1967), which focuses on Thomas Hoving, director-elect of the Metropolitan Museum of Art. McPhee published shorter profiles of Euell Gibbons, an expert on edible wild foods and the author of *Stalking the Wild Asparagus* (1962), and Robert Twynam, who grew the grass on Wimbledon's tennis courts. These profiles had complex inner structures, but they focus on a single person.

In 1982, sitting in his office at Princeton, McPhee drew on a blank piece of paper a structural pattern he was thinking about after he completed those profiles. "What developed in my mind for a long while was, 'What if you did the same thing with two people?' If you found two people and did all that for each of them, then things would start going back and forth in there." On the paper he drew the two individuals, each surrounded by dots representing the satellite figures in their lives–their friends, teachers, opponents, colleagues. He drew lines rebounding back and forth among the dots. He called this kind of planned structure "the single most important thing for me, other than the final writing itself." Each of McPhee's books has an archi-

tectonic plan; internally each book has a design that would impress his former English teacher McKee.

"One plus one just might add up to more than two," McPhee said, adding:

> I had this in my mind and I wondered just who these people might be. An architect and his client? An actor and a director? A pitcher and a manager? One day I was watching television, and there were Arthur Ashe and Clark Graebner in the semifinals of the first United States Open Tennis Championship at Forest Hills. Each twenty-five years old. Each an American. So they'd have to know each other very well because you could put all the good tennis players in the country in this room.

McPhee sat down separately with Ashe and Graebner and watched a film of the match over and over as each of them described his thoughts and feelings. The result was *Levels of the Game* (1969), a profile of the two men filled with portraits of their parents and coaches and multiple viewpoints on their development as players.

"When *Levels of the Game* worked out," McPhee said, "I got ambitious and thought, 'Well, if it works for two, how about more?'" He put a diagram on his wall that looked like this:

ABC
D

The plan was to let one person, D, relate to the other three. "This is not a promising way to develop a piece of writing," McPhee admitted.

> You don't do it backwards. This is an exception. I had no idea what the basic subject would be here, when this was already up on my bulletin board. But I'm interested in outdoor things and the conservation movement was starting up–this was in 1968. I went to Washington for two weeks, and went around talking to people in conservation organizations and to their 'natural enemies,' as I put it eventually. That's how *Encounters with the Archdruid* started out.

The pivotal figure, D, in McPhee's structural plan became David Brower, head of a conservation group called Friends of the Earth and former executive director of the Sierra Club. Brower's natural enemies were A, Charles Park, a geologist and mineral engineer who wanted to dig an open pit copper mine in the Glacier Peak Wilderness; B, Charles Fraser, a land developer with plans for a resort on Cumberland Island, Georgia; and C, Floyd Dominy, commissioner of reclamation, who wanted dams built in Grand Canyon National Park.

The dramatic tensions between these men were balanced by McPhee's even-tempered, objective portrayal of their opinions. Brower goes hiking with Park. He stays on Fraser's yacht off Cumberland Island and helps him review environmentally sensitive development plans. He rides a raft down the Colorado River in the Grand Canyon with Dominy. McPhee launched the participants on those encounters so he would have a narrative and something to describe. "Participation is a way of finding a narrative," he said, "a way to find something more interesting to report than a *Playboy* interview." In his essay on McPhee in *Literary Selves: Autobiography and Contemporary American Nonfiction* (1993), Stull notes that, in his writing, "McPhee may assume . . . the roles of limited participant, foil to more knowledgeable informants, and translator of arcane material to an intelligent but uninformed audience, but his most critical role is that of witness to his subjects' performances, which centers almost exclusively around their commitment to a job or calling."

Structure has been an important tool in McPhee's hands. Planned patterns are a creative force in McPhee's nonfiction. In *Levels of the Game* and *Encounters with the Archdruid* (1971) he created the external structures before he reported the real events. He imagined the structure, then went out and found Graebner and Ashe, and later, Brower and his "natural enemies." Of all the "absolutely legitimate" tools a nonfiction writer can use, including narrative, dialogue, character sketching, and metaphor, McPhee emphasizes structural innovation. He has a certain freedom of choice in his use of these tools. He is writing about "real people in real places," as he always reminds interviewers, and is limited by the demands of nonfiction form, but he selects the events he writes about and sometimes, as in sending Brower down the Colorado River with Dominy, he creates the events as well. The real people and real places are out there, but McPhee must turn nature into literature before an audience can read about them.

After "A Sense of Where You Are" appeared in *The New Yorker* in 1965, editor William Shawn named McPhee a staff writer. McPhee had achieved his goal. He held one of the most coveted positions in journalism, and his writing was well on the way to achieving the grace and fluidity that he described in Bradley's basketball game. Although he preferred to stand in the shadows as a narrator, McPhee still had a distinctive voice and total control of his narrative.

In 1990, in his living room in Princeton, McPhee thought back to the rush of energy that followed his arrival at *The New Yorker*, telling Sims:

"The next thing I did was to get up some ideas. I actually started work on three or four things lined up in a row. One was *The Headmaster*, one was *Oranges*, one was *The Pine Barrens*." Although a short book, *Oranges* (1967) demonstrates the literary power of solid research wedded to interesting characters and a limited involvement of the narrator. McPhee used a similar pattern in *The Pine Barrens* (1968), *Coming into the Country* (1977), and his four geology books.

Oranges was a whim, the result of a machine at Pennsylvania Station in New York where I went every day when I was commuting. I drank this orange juice and I noticed weird things. Fresh orange juice changes color across the winter. I saw an ad in a magazine that showed four or five identical-looking oranges with different names: Parson Brown, Hamlin, Valencia. I thought, "That's interesting. Maybe it would make a good short piece—go down there for four or five days, talk to growers and nurserymen and go home. Write a little piece." What made *Oranges* longer was when I stumbled into the Citrus Experiment Station at Lake Alfred, where they had forty-four thousand items in their library—books and papers about oranges—and they had men and women in white coats walking around who had Ph.D.'s in oranges. One had a heart-lung machine with oranges breathing in and out of it. I discovered the history of citrus, migrating westward along with the migrations of human-kind itself. I scarcely suspected I would learn anything like that. But when I did, it was interesting and I went into it, so it was a longish article.

McPhee proved he could write an interesting narrative about something as commonplace as oranges. *Oranges* combines the information he discovered at the experiment station in Florida with a narrative that made it fun. In an age when orange juice came in little frozen containers, a trip to Florida held the promise of fresh squeezed. Instead of delicious, fresh juice, McPhee found an industry in love with concentrate. The science of orange juice concentrate led him to the experiment station and its library. He went to a plant where fresh juice was reduced to concentrate. "When the evaporators are finished with the juice, it has a nice orange color and seems promising, but if it is reconstituted into 'orange juice' it tastes like a glass of water with two teaspoons of sugar and one aspirin dissolved in it," he writes in the book. McPhee finally got his glass of fresh orange juice from a conveyor belt moments before high-season Valencia juice entered an evaporator.

While dealing with information about oranges, McPhee started looking for literary tools that would support the weight. A device that carries information in a narrative McPhee calls a "set piece." In *Oranges* McPhee rides into a grove on the back of a tractor, and two pages later the reader is off on a set piece about the history of oranges, starting with the evolution of citrus in the Malay Archipelago about twenty million years ago and moving forward to orange trees in the Holy Land. It is a stylish prose trip, there on the back of the tractor, but it is set apart as a digression from the narrative. Eventually, each set piece in the book returns to the original narrative.

His miniature portrait of oranges grew into what McPhee calls a "broad canvas" containing a wealth of scientific research, historical sweep, character studies, and personal narrative. His perspective grew to regional proportions when McPhee took on the Pine Barrens, a wild, sandy area encompassing hundreds of square miles of New Jersey that is renowned for its abundant water supply and fabled residents. Writing about a regional culture proved daunting. According to McPhee, "I had wandered around talking to all kinds of people and I had no idea how to organize the material. I hadn't done it before." Pointing to the yard outside his living room windows, he added: "I spent two weeks on a picnic table right outside the window here lying on my back in agony and despair, staring up into the trees. I had no idea how I was going to tell the story of the Pine Barrens. I had miscellaneous stuff, sketches of people. Nowadays I would have an idea what to do with it."

The Pine Barrens opens with his first visit to Fred Brown, resident of Hog Wallow. Brown had no phone and no electricity. His yard was littered with eight cars, old vacuum cleaners, radios, cranberry boxes, "and maybe a thousand other things." He cooked McPhee a pork chop on a gas stove. McPhee writes: "He asked where I was going, and I said that I had no particular destination, explaining that I was in the pines because I found it hard to believe that so much unbroken forest could still exist so near the big Eastern cities, and I wanted to see it while it was still there. 'Is that so?' he said, three times. Like many people in the pines, he often says things three times. 'Is that so? Is *that* so?'"

McPhee asked Brown's permission to fill his jerry can at the pump in the front yard. "'Hell, yes,' he said. 'That isn't my water. That's God's water. That's God's water. That right, Bill?'" Bill Wasovwich, Brown's friend and neighbor, was also sitting in the kitchen at the time, although he was such a shy person one might not notice him.

"I *guess* so," Bill said, without looking up. "It's good water, I can tell you that."

"That's God's water," Fred said again. "Take all you want."

Fred became McPhee's central characters and guides to the history and geography of the Pine Barrens. They drove the sandy terrain on unpaved, unmarked roads with McPhee constantly scribbling in his notebook. One time, McPhee said, he was driving and Fred Brown said something interesting. McPhee slammed on the brakes and started writing in his notebook. "Fred," McPhee asked, "do you know what I'm doing?" "No," Fred said, "and I don't think you do either."

McPhee's hosts came to symbolize the native Pineys, a shy, self-sufficient, and maligned people. Never one to editorialize, McPhee nevertheless left his position clear in *The Pine Barrens:*

They are apparently a tolerant people, with an attractive spirit of live and let live. They seem to like hard work, if not steady work, and they like to brag about working hard. When they say they will do something, they do it. They seem shy, like the people who went before them, but when they get to know an outsider they are not shy and will generously share their tables, which often include new-potato stews and cranberry potpies.

By the mid 1970s three patterns formed in McPhee's books. In the first pattern he developed profiles of strong characters such as Bill Bradley, Thomas Hoving, and David Brower. Since then McPhee has used profiles of single characters in several books: *The Curve of Binding Energy* (1974) is about physicist Theodore Taylor; *The Survival of the Bark Canoe* (1975) features Henri Vaillancourt, an artist and craftsman who builds authentic birchbark canoes; and *The Ransom of Russian Art* (1994) focuses on Norton Dodge, who collected dissident Soviet art. "Above all else," wrote Stull, "McPhee's subjects are indeed expert craftspeople who demonstrate competence and an unparalleled skill that enables them to function successfully in their respective worlds, whether it be school-mastering, tennis, basketball, cooking, or geology." McPhee shares the commitment to craftsmanship found in his characters, according to Stull.

The other two patterns grew from *Oranges.* That book provides the first regional portrait, which he further develops in *The Pine Barrens* and later in his best-selling book about Alaska, *Coming into the Country.* "Each [has] a broad canvas, lots of people, lots of history and science," McPhee said of these books in 1996. *Oranges* also began a series of books dominated by scientific concerns, including his geology books. There has been considerable overlap among all three patterns, perhaps best represented in *Rising from the Plains* (1986), which contains a strong profile of geologist David Love, a re-

Dust jacket for the 1976 collection of McPhee's essays

gional portrait of Wyoming, and a discussion of the science of geology.

In the world of literary journalists McPhee belongs in the realist camp with writers such as Tom Wolfe and Tracy Kidder, who attempt to represent a real world for the reader as opposed to focusing on the process of storytelling as a way of creating reality. Realists have faith in the capability of traditional models of interpretation and expression to reveal the real. Although the reports acknowledge cultural relativism in their attention to the symbolic worlds of their subjects, this awareness is not extended to the process of reporting, which is treated as a natural process. If McPhee can understand a real world and the real people in it, he feels capable of bringing that world to the reader.

McPhee's literary journalism has a genealogy that includes Daniel Defoe, Joseph Addison, and Richard Steele and in this century such writers as Ernest Hemingway, George Orwell, A. J. Liebling, John Hersey, and Lillian Ross. McPhee has used increasingly complicated structures in his work while retaining a strict regard for realist assumptions about journalism. Ronald Weber, an American

Studies professor whose scholarly work has examined literary journalism from Hemingway to the New Journalists of the 1960s, wrote of McPhee's *Coming into the Country,* "The book's roots lie not so much in the effort to emulate the novel as in the attempt to extend the range of journalism while remaining within journalistic forms."

Until recently the literary qualities of nonfiction have been ignored by literary critics in favor of fiction and playwriting. McPhee, who has written plays and short fiction, was nevertheless drawn to nonfiction by its literary possibilities. "Remember the possibilities in nonfiction writing," he said in an interview, "the character sketching that stops well short of illegitimate invention." He added:

> There's plenty of room for invention, for "creativity," stopping well short of invading a number of things that only fiction can do. You can use fictional techniques: narrative, dialogue, character sketching, description, metaphor. Above all metaphor. Things that are cheap and tawdry in fiction work beautifully in nonfiction because they are true. That's why you should be careful not to abridge it, because it's the fundamental power you're dealing with. You arrange it and present it. There's lots of artistry. But you don't make it up. Nobody's making rules that cover everybody. The nonfiction writer is communicating with the reader about real people in real places. So if those people talk, you say what those people said. You don't say what the writer decides they said. I get prickly if someone suggests there's dialogue in my pieces that I didn't get from the source. You don't make up dialogue. You don't make a composite character. Where I came from, a composite character was fiction. So when somebody makes a non-fiction character out of three people who are real, that is a fictional character in my opinion. And you don't get inside their heads and think for them. You can't interview the dead. You could make a list of the things you don't do. Where writers abridge that, they hitchhike on the credibility of writers who don't.

McPhee's most financially successful work has been *Coming into the Country,* a regional portrait of epic proportions. Published in *The New Yorker* in eight parts, it actually tells three separate stories. The first story tells of a canoe and kayak trip in Arctic Alaska on the Salmon and Kobuk Rivers. In the second story McPhee accompanied a commission looking for a site for a new Alaskan capital. He went to Alaska for the first time in the summer and early fall of 1975, during which time he conducted the research for the first two stories. The third story took longer. He went back to Alaska in the spring of 1976 when the ice was breaking up in the rivers and stayed into the summer in the towns of Eagle, Circle, and Central in the Upper Yukon country north-east of Fairbanks. He returned to Alaska during the winter of 1977.

Coming into the Country sealed McPhee's reputation as one of the best nature and cultural writers in America. Writing in *The New York Times* on 25 November 1977, John Leonard said the book left him enchanted, dreaming of seal oil, caribou, the Yukon River, and grizzly bears:

> The time may come when nobody goes outside, when every American stays home in his "living center," his computerized cocoon, a bionic junkie with programmed dreams. And if it ever occurs to this sloth to wonder about the outside, about what the outside was like when there was an outside, why, all he will have to do is plug a cartridge into his communications console and read, if he can read, a book on his wraparound television screen. The book could be by John McPhee, or Edward Hoagland, or Edward Abbey, or Josephine Johnson—one of the people, anyway, who do our living for us. Remember, the book will say, when there were seasons?

Edward Hoagland in the *New York Times Book Review* (27 November 1977) called *Coming into the Country* a masterpiece. He said McPhee must have been looking for a "big, long, permanent book, written while he was still in the midst of life and could go after it, because in peripatetic journalism such as McPhee's there is an adventurous, fortuitous element: where the writer *gets himself* and what he *stumbles on.*"

In the third section of the book McPhee lived among the residents of the Upper Yukon country. These people came to Alaska, like many others, looking for gold, the challenge of survival, and land where they could build a cabin. The weather drives most of them away. Ed and Ginny Gelvin, who raised four children in the area, have taken their existence from Alaska into the modern age. Flying above the wilderness in their bush planes and studying old mining records, Ed and his son Stanley located a stream that might contain a placer deposit of gold. The Gelvins wanted to move thousands of tons of gravel, so they drove the largest bulldozer Caterpillar makes into the wilderness. They choked the stream and created a reservoir. They bulldozed forty thousand cubic yards of gold-bearing gravels into a metal sluice box and washed it through using a plume of water. This ecological disturbance was witnessed by McPhee the conservationist:

> Am I disgusted? Manifestly not. Not from here, from now, from this perspective. I am too warmly, too subjectively caught up in what the Gelvins are doing. In the ecomilitia, bust me to private. This mine is a cork on the sea. Meanwhile (and, possibly, more seriously), the rela-

tionship between this father and son is as attractive as anything I have seen in Alaska–both of them self-reliant beyond the usual reach of the term, the characteristic formed by this country. Whatever they are doing, whether it is mining or something else, they do for themselves what no one else is here to do for them. Their kind is more endangered every year. Balance that against the nick they are making in this land. Only an easygoing extremist would preserve every bit of the country. And extremists alone would exploit it all. Everyone else has to think the matter through–choose a point of tolerance, however much the point might tend to one side. For myself, I am closer to the preserving side–that is, the side that would preserve the Gelvins. To be sure, I would preserve plenty of land as well. My own margin of tolerance would not include some faceless corporation "responsible" to a hundred thousand stockholders, making a crater you could see from the moon.

McPhee located two modern-day pioneers, Dick Cook and Donna Kneeland, living ten miles up a stream on a subsistence diet of homegrown vegetables, moose, and fish. Their lives challenged some of McPhee's personal values and his ideals about wilderness. Cook was an expert in the survival skills needed for backwoods life. They left the door open when they were gone so grizzlies would make less of a mess getting into the place. "Bears are on my mind today," McPhee writes, because the next day he had to hike out alone to the Yukon River, where he would be picked up by a boat. He had been "strongly counseled" not to go into the woods without a gun. "Having never hunted, I have almost no knowledge of guns," he says, turning down the offer of a gun. On the hike into the cabin they passed bear scat. Every bear story McPhee had ever heard rushed through his mind. Once again, Alaska tested his conservationist values:

> Here I am about to walk through the woods the distance merely from Times Square to LaGuardia Airport and I am ionized with anticipation–catastrophic anticipation. I may never resolve my question of bears–the extent to which I exaggerate the danger, the extent of the foolishness of those who go unarmed. The effect of it all, for the moment, is a slight but detectable migration of my internal affections from the sneaker toward the bazooka, from the National Wildlife Federation toward the National Rifle Association–an annoying touch of panic in a bright and blazing day.

Dick Cook does not help McPhee's confidence when he tells him to remember that "the woods are composed of who's killing whom. Life is forever building from death. Life and death are not a duality." McPhee begins his two-hour hike to the Yukon River through closed-in willow thickets and soft muskeg. He thinks: "I can't accept anymore the rationale of the few who go unarmed, yet I am equally loath to use guns. If bears were no longer in the country, I would not have come. I am here, in a sense, because they survive. So I am sorry–truly rueful and perplexed–that without a means of killing them I cannot feel at ease."

Grizzly bears fishing in distant streams, placer mines gouged from the wilderness, gardens planted with "grass" and rhubarb, a dogsled sounding over dry snow like "the rumbling cars of a long freight," and the sun shining at 11:00 P.M.–these things are the real Alaska and emblematic at the same time. James N. Stull wrote: "While McPhee does write about some of the most pressing environmental concerns of his time, when we consider his fondness for wilderness and rural settings and timeless, out-of-the-way places, as well as the prototypical individuals who populate his world–individuals who are competent, trustworthy, and morally good–we enter a semi-idealized realm that reflects, more generally, McPhee the author's private vision of the world." Donald Hall, writing in *National Review* (31 March 1978), said, "It makes no difference what McPhee writes about; his subjects are irrelevant; we love him for his *form*. Oh, how he can shift his feet! Transitions are the *niftiest* things he does, moving from past into present, from present into past, shifting abruptly from one scene or set of characters to another." McPhee spends a lot of time *not* writing those graceful transitions; instead he allows his structures to juxtapose elements that need no bridges to link them together. "Two parts of a piece of writing, merely by lying side-by-side, can comment on each other without a word spoken," he observed to Sims.

McPhee's early study of the surface features of the earth at Deerfield Academy and his work on *Oranges, The Pine Barrens,* and *Coming into the Country* prepared him for the longest-running project of his career: four books on the geology of North America. In part, it began when Princeton geologist Ken Deffeyes answered a couple of questions McPhee had about how gold got into the mountains of Alaska. Later, McPhee called Deffeyes again. As a topic for a short "Talk of the Town" piece in *The New Yorker,* McPhee asked if Deffeyes could help him find a road cut outside New York City and describe what the world looked like when the rocks formed. Within two weeks McPhee and Deffeyes had planned a trip westward across the whole country looking at road cuts. "The next thing I know I'm in a pickup with Deffeyes in Nevada," McPhee said.

At one level his geology books deal with a twentieth century scientific revolution, the theory of plate tectonics and continental drift. "Ten years after plate tectonics came along," McPhee explained, "it was still very much controversial. I wanted to see how this science had settled down with its new theory." He envisioned a book about the geology of North America, a cross-section using the road cuts of Interstate 80 as windows into the rock. "When I embarked on the geology project in 1979 my idea was to do a single piece of writing," McPhee said in an interview. "After a year's travel, I came back to Princeton and made a structure for a single piece of writing, and then I realized it was too long for *The New Yorker* or for one book. Its structure naturally separated into four parts and each was published as a separate book. But they originated in a common structure." The full project with twenty thousand additional words will be published in 1998 as *Annals of the Former World.*

The first book, *Basin and Range* (1981), presents the theory of plate tectonics and is a primer in the modern geological sciences. The second book, *In Suspect Terrain* (1983), turns to Anita Harris, a geologist "who's clawing at the theory—not totally disbelieving but irritated with the gross extrapolations onto the continent of plate tectonic ideas to a point where they become, in her view, almost imaginative." In the third book, *Rising from the Plains,* McPhee concentrates on Wyoming and the dean of Rocky Mountain geology, David Love. The scientific focus is on the story of the building, burial, and exhumation of the Rocky Mountains. Love struggles with controversial topics in environmental geology and the economics of minerals, oil, gas, and uranium until, in McPhee's view, he becomes a one-man *Encounters with the Archdruid.* The human focus is on Love and his mother, a woman who had arrived from the East three-quarters of a century earlier. She had kept a journal in an articulate voice, and Love permitted McPhee to quote extensively from it in *Rising from the Plains.* The human characters here seem a match for the monumental geology. McPhee and his wife Yolanda sometimes do readings from the book with Yolanda reading the parts written by Love's mother. The fourth book in the series, *Assembling California* (1993), is about "the only place where this continent has a plate boundary on dry land."

The geology books have been widely adopted in college courses because they clarify a murky subject. Most readers, according to McPhee, are not students or trained scientists, and they do not necessarily have scientific interests. But they can absorb a scientific narrative and appreciate it. A topic such as geology, full of academic terms and complicated scientific theories, proved perfect for McPhee's approach to writing. He loves facts and the sound of names like *Paleozoic.* More important, he allows individuals such as Love and Deffeyes to represent and explain the theories. Love, for example, insisted on looking at rocks in the field rather than just using computer models of geology. Stull said, "Love's concern for first-hand experience with what he theorizes and writes about reflects McPhee's own belief in the primacy of experience. Witnessing the performances of his subjects enables McPhee the journalist to establish authority while simultaneously marveling at their ability both to perform a given task and navigate (see) their way through the world."

"One of the frustrations in it," McPhee told Sims, "is that a writer who seeks the multiple possibilities in a piece of nonfiction writing—character sketching and narrative and dialogue and description—is not well served by a subject like geology, which is extraordinarily demanding in one principal area: description. The pressure, the weight, and the opportunity in description are just out of proportion with everything else. This permits sentences to march along in ways that would seem inappropriate in other forms of writing, but are appropriate to the earth itself."

The reviewers fell into two camps: some felt geology was large and difficult enough to be worthy of McPhee's talents; others were simply bored. Evan Connell wrote a review of *Rising from the Plains* in which he appreciated McPhee's characters and natural description, but then concluded, "You need not have passed Geology 101 to enjoy 'Rising From the Plains,' but it might help." Herbert Mitgang, writing in *The New York Times* (10 November 1986), marveled at McPhee's handling of complex material:

> It would almost be unfair to make notes while reading one of John McPhee's fascinating books that explore some out-of-the-way corner of the American landscape and its inhabitants. They are comparable to Joseph Mitchell's model writing on the Mohawk Indians or the bottom of New York Harbor or any other subject that he has mined for nuggets of information. Among professional writers, there is an added pleasure in watching how authors in their class construct their factual narratives. By covering New York and America like some foreign country, they set a very high standard of originality for writers and readers.

McPhee's oldest daughter, Laura, said the geology project—spanning fifteen years of scientific inquiry, struggle with descriptions, and some negative criticism—had a powerful influence on McPhee. "The geology made him think about his own mortality and how brief human life is in relation to the earth," she said.

"It's the only piece of ground that we're ever going to inhabit," McPhee said simply. "I know that my own reflections on living and on being here changed considerably in the past few years. It's a perspective on our own position as a species with respect to space and time." McPhee looked up at the world geologic map on his wall for a moment. "Dammit, it's the only house we're ever going to have," he said emphatically. "It is some interesting thing, this earth and how it works. I could be somewhat evangelical about ideas in geology. I am permitted to talk about it at home ten minutes a day and no more. That's pretty rigid."

McPhee's geology books rank well on the list of his best-sellers. His top hardcover books have been: *Coming into the Country, Assembling California, Looking for a Ship* (1990), *The Control of Nature* (1989), *Basin and Range, Rising from the Plains, Table of Contents* (1985), and *La Place de la Concorde Suisse* (1984).

Paperback sales are a bit harder to track because some came through publishers other than Farrar Straus and Giroux, but the list looks something like this: *Coming into the Country, Encounters with the Archdruid, Basin and Range, The Pine Barrens, Rising from the Plains, Oranges, In Suspect Terrain,* and *The Control of Nature*. McPhee commented that the geology books rank high on those lists, and several people feel that *The Control of Nature* should be classified among his geology books. The four geology books are to be republished by Farrar Straus and Giroux as a single work titled "Annals of the Former World." McPhee will add another fifteen thousand words to the original books on the subject of the mid continent. "There's a significant gap between Chicago and Cheyenne," he said.

> This has always bothered me in the context of a North American cross-section. I want to write about the basement of the continent, the Canadian Shield, the Precambrian basement. The time that lies before the Cambrian is eight-ninths of the history of the Earth. The insights into those eons are considerable now because of gravity mapping, dating, and computing. They are getting a picture. It wasn't always there. There's a story to tell about when Colorado came in and landed.

The Precambrian eras began some 570 million years ago and extend back about 4 billion years before that.

McPhee stepped out of the pattern of the geology books when he wrote *The Control of Nature*. In it he deals with the vast forces of geomorphology that shape the earth's surface, the Mississippi River, volcanoes in Iceland and Hawaii, and the erosion of the San Gabriel Mountains near Los Angeles. These forces are also reshaping human communities, and humans are trying to control them.

About three hundred miles upriver from the mouth of the Mississippi a distributary called the Atchafalaya River draws off 30 percent of the water from the Mississippi River. The remainder continues down toward New Orleans through the "American Ruhr," an industrial district of great importance to the nation. The Atchafalaya, however, reaches the Gulf of Mexico in only 145 miles and has a steeper gradient than the main river. The Atchafalaya wants to change the course of the Mississippi, as has happened many times during the formation of the Louisiana Delta, but this time human industry hangs in the balance. In 1963 the Army Corps of Engineers built a control structure at the source of the Atchafalaya to maintain a constant 30 percent flow into the Atchafalaya and to guarantee that the main river would continue flowing toward New Orleans.

The tension in McPhee's story grows from the forceful patience of nature, which keeps trying to take the shortest route to the Gulf. In dramatic conflict McPhee casts the Corps of Engineers' control structure, already weakened by a major flood that nearly destroyed it. Downstream on the Atchafalaya sits Morgan City, Louisiana, surrounded by levees in a subsiding landscape. This human community sits beside the Atchafalaya like a tumbler in a sinkful of water. If the Atchafalaya wins the battle and captures the Mississippi, Morgan City may drown while industries fail beside a dry river bed near New Orleans. Controlling the Mississippi River would prove difficult. McPhee follows the river northward until his readers grasp the whole system of control on the Mississippi from the first levee the river encounters down to the delta and the Atchafalaya. Readers grasp that the river is stronger than humans are. The river is held at bay by the Army Corps of Engineers, flood after flood. But when the hundred-year flood hits three million cubic feet of water per second may have its way. Or maybe not. McPhee comes close to prediction but keeps one step away. Maybe the Corps of Engineers will win a few more battles in this war.

Two other fights between poorly armed humans and the elite forces of nature are described. In one case, Hawaiians and the residents of Iceland try to keep red hot lava flows out of their towns. In the other, Los Angeles suburbanites have moved up into the San Gabriel Mountains, one of the most shattered, most rapidly rising, and most rapidly eroding mountain ranges on earth. When winter rains bring five or ten inches of water in a deluge, rock from the mountains washes down in huge, muddy-debris flows. The flows rampage the newly built neighborhoods.

The Corps of Engineers trying to defeat the Atchafalaya's capture of the Mississippi River, Icelanders turning fire hoses on a lava flow, and the city of Los Angeles trying to hold back the San Gabriel Mountains possess the same symbolism. In a later work, *Looking for a Ship,* McPhee quotes Capt. Paul Washburn of the U.S. merchant marine, who said it best: "Anywhere in the world, if you fool with Mother Nature she's going to get you. This is not a political statement. It is just a fact." McPhee's geology books use the drift of crustal plates about the globe as a central theme. *The Control of Nature* deals with the generally uncontrollable forces that have shaped the surface of the earth. These struggles, although sometimes misguided or unnecessary, are monumental in their methods.

The geology books and his several works on subjects such as nuclear energy, Alaska, agriculture, canoeing, and the New Jersey Pine Barrens have given McPhee a reputation as an environmentalist. David Remnick, co-editor of *The Second John McPhee Reader* (1996), wrote, "Over time he has become the most effective literary advocate for environmentalism. . . . McPhee, however, does not preach, nor does he shout doomsday in a crowded room. He tells stories—stories that, in the margins, fairly bark the most important ecological questions."

In his 1994 work, *The Ransom of Russian Art,* McPhee again stepped away from his reputation as an environmentalist and nature writer. The book follows the work of an art collector and academic, Norton Dodge, who rescued thousands of paintings by dissident artists in the Soviet Union between 1956 and the glasnost period of the late 1980s under Mikhail Gorbachev. McPhee adopts what for him is an unusual stance as an investigative reporter. He grills Dodge on his connections with the CIA, asks how he smuggled nine thousand pieces of art out of the Soviet Union, and inquires where a college professor got $3 million to pay for this enterprise. When he does not get a satisfactory answer, McPhee goes to unnamed sources in the CIA for verification of facts. The answers to his questions are mostly innocent, involving embassy personnel who helped smuggle paintings as diplomatic items or involving lucky family stock investments. In a *New York Review of Books* essay on 2 March 1995 Remnick praised McPhee's reporting in *The Ransom of Russian Art* and noted that, apparently without having visited the Soviet Union himself, McPhee "has managed to deliver such a vivid picture of a distant and particular world. . . . [he] brings us into

rickety artists' lofts in Moscow, and I swear you can smell the turps and the bad cigarettes and the garbage down the hall."

A geologist looking at McPhee's life would find one large fault line and many layers of sedimentation. McPhee has always been active and appears capable of paddling a canoe all day or knocking samples out of a rock formation. He has lived in the same rambling, two-story house in Princeton township since 1963 when he was working at *Time* magazine. Four daughters from his first marriage, each two years apart in age, grew up in the house. Martha, the youngest, has published a novel, *Bright-Angel Time* (1996). Jenny occasionally writes book reviews for *The New York Times* and was an editor at Knopf. Martha and Jenny collaborated on a translation from the Italian of the best-selling book by Pope John Paul II, *Crossing the Threshold of Hope* (1994). Sarah is a professor of architectural history at Emory University. The oldest daughter, Laura, is a photographer and professor at the Massachusetts College of Art. McPhee and his first wife, Pryde Brown, separated in 1969 and later divorced. In 1972 McPhee married Yolanda Whitman, who had four children by her first marriage. Evidence of these eight children fills the house and competes for space with souvenirs of McPhee's writing projects—maps of the Saint John–Allagash Wilderness and Alaska, an Eastern coyote pelt from Maine, a chart of the structures associated with colliding crustal plates.

Since 1965 *The New Yorker* has given McPhee a remarkable degree of freedom. Its editors have encouraged literary journalism to a greater degree than any other American magazine, and Sharon Bass commented in *A Sourcebook of American Literary Journalism: Representative Writers in an Emerging Genre* (1992), "It may be that it is only because a publication like the *New Yorker* exists that a writer like John McPhee has been able to thrive." He has never been treated as a full-time employee with a W-2 tax form but is treated more like a freelance writer, writing whatever interests him and being paid only for what the magazine publishes. While this arrangement offers freedom, it provides what he calls "the financial security of a farmer." He has said that the new emphasis on current affairs at *The New Yorker* gives the offices there the feel of *Time* magazine when everyone is working on an airliner crash story. At one time it was estimated that *The New Yorker* brought the full text of fifteen books to subscribers each year, but now the magazine no longer publishes the eight-part series that brought *Coming into the Country* to its readers. Since the celebrated magazine was sold and Tina Brown became its editor, short, topical works have dominated. Brown steered away from pieces that required more than one issue to publish. McPhee's work continues to appear, although less frequently than before. *The Ransom of Russian Art* appeared in the magazine, and in 1994 McPhee wrote about the California earthquake, contributed a piece about a water crisis in Nevada, and in 1996 published an article about forensic geologists.

Despite changes at *The New Yorker* McPhee told Sims in 1996 that his own work "has not changed at all. It hasn't fit that well with the new approach to length and topic at *The New Yorker*. I continue to do what was on my agenda, without exception. It's been necessary for me to keep my vector going." He currently has a new collection of sub-book-length pieces called *Irons in the Fire* (1997). In 1996 *The Second John McPhee Reader* was published, and he has been putting together what he calls a "quilt" consisting of fragments that have never been republished. In all, the quilt will contain about seventy-five thousand words from the quarter of a million words in articles that have never been reprinted in any of his collections, including about 10 percent of the nine cover stories he wrote for *Time*.

McPhee's books and articles are regularly included as classics in anthologies of literary journalism. His structural innovation, spare and eloquent style of writing, understated voice, and ability to take on complex subjects and make sense of them for an uninitiated audience have ensured his position in the canon of the genre he has helped to establish. David Remnick suggested in *The New York Review of Books* that McPhee's choice of subjects—particularly Bill Bradley—have an autobiographical quality. "McPhee's virtues as a reporter and writer parallel Bradley's as a basketball player: thorough preparation in reading and reporting, an unmistakable sense of structure and form, an elegant and useful economy." McPhee has a large and devoted audience, and as Remnick noted, "He is a favorite of other writers and journalists." Another writer, Michael Pearson, said in 1993, "During the past three decades as a *New Yorker* writer, McPhee has defined the contours of the nonfiction story as much as E. B. White did the personal essay or John Cheever the lyrical work of short fiction."

"Writing is like a river meandering along," McPhee noted in 1990:

> It won't through time stay in the same banks. It cuts out new things and fills in other places. Sometimes it jumps across its own meanders. You wonder what you're going to be doing ten or fifteen years hence. . . . You might say my ambition is to write—as little as possible! My daughter Jenny tells me I overdo the negative aspects. I

grunt and groan about how horrible it is and how difficult the whole process is without talking about the good parts. In general, I do not wish to be writing anything different in genre than what I'm writing now. My ambition is to keep on writing.

Interviews:
Stephen Singular, "Talking with John McPhee," *New York Times Book Review*, 27 November 1977, pp. 1, 50–51;

Dennis Drabelle, "Conversations with John McPhee," *Sierra* (October–November–December 1978): 61–63;

Edgar Allen Beem, "John McPhee on Maine: Conversation with the Archjournalist," *Maine Times*, 1 November 1985, pp. 14–16;

Joan Hamilton, "An Encounter with John McPhee," *Sierra* (May–June 1990): 50–55, 92, 96;

Michael Pearson, "Twenty Questions: A Conversation with John McPhee," *Creative Nonfiction*, 1 (1993): 76–87.

Bibliography:
Joanne K. Clark, "The Writings of John Angus McPhee: A Selected Bibliography," *Bulletin of Bibliography*, 38 (January–March 1981): 45–51.

References:
Chris Anderson, *Style as Argument: Contemporary American Nonfiction* (Carbondale: Southern Illinois University Press, 1987);

John F. Baker, "John McPhee," *Publishers Weekly* (3 January 1977): 12–13.

Sharon Bass, "John McPhee," in *A Sourcebook of American Literary Journalism: Representative Writers in an Emerging Genre*, edited by Thomas B. Connery (Westport, Conn.: Greenwood Press, 1992);

David Eason, "The New Journalism and the Image-World," in *Literary Journalism in the Twentieth Century*, edited by Norman Sims (New York: Oxford University Press, 1990), pp. 191–205;

Edward Hoagland, "Where Life Begins Over," *New York Times Book Review*, 27 November 1977, pp. 1, 48–49;

William Howarth, Introduction to *The John McPhee Reader* (New York: Farrar, Straus & Giroux, 1976), pp. xii–xxiii;

Howarth, "Itinerant Passages; Recent American Essays." *Sewanee Review*, 96 (Fall 1988): 633–644;

Sally Lawrence, "Structure and Definition: Keys to John McPhee's Style," *Technical Communication*, 34 (November 1987): 296;

John Leonard, "Books of the Times," *New York Times*, 25 November 1977, I: 23;

Barbara Lounsberry, "John McPhee's Levels of the Earth," in *The Art of Fact: Contemporary Artists of Nonfiction* (Westport, Conn.: Greenwood Press, 1990), pp. 65–106;

Larry McMurtry, "Giving Good Weight," *New York Times Book Review,* 18 November 1979, pp. 3, 45;

David Remnick, "Notes from Underground," *New York Review of Books,* 2 March 1995, pp. 10–13;

Jack Roundy, "Crafting Fact: Formal Devices in the Prose of John McPhee," in *Literary Nonfiction: Theory, Criticism, Pedagogy,* edited by Chris Anderson (Carbondale: Southern Illinois University Press, 1989), p. 70;

Israel Shenker, "The Annals of McPhee," *New York Times,* 11 January 1976, XI: 20–21.

Norman Sims, "The Art of Nonfiction," Introduction to *Literary Journalism,* edited by Sims and Mark Kramer (New York: Ballantine, 1995), pp. 3–19;

Sims, "The Literary Journalists," introduction to *The Literary Journalists,* edited by Sims (New York: Ballantine, 1984), pp. 3–25;

Kathy Smith, "John McPhee Balances the Act," in *Literary Journalism in the Twentieth Century,* edited by Sims (New York: Oxford University Press, 1990), pp. 206–227;

Jeannette Smyth, "John McPhee of *The New Yorker,*" *Washington Post,* 19 March 1978, pp. Ll, L5–6.

James N. Stull, "Self and the Performance of Others: The Pastoral Vision of John McPhee," in *Literary Selves: Autobiography and Contemporary American Nonfiction* (Westport, Conn.: Greenwood Press, 1993);

William Warner, "The Call of the Running Tide," *Washington Post Book World,* 9 September 1990;

Ronald Weber, "Letting Subjects Grow: Literary Nonfiction from *The New Yorker,*" in *The Literature of Fact: Literary Nonfiction in American Writing,* edited by Weber (Athens: Ohio University Press, 1980);

Paul Zweig, "Rhapsodist of Deep Time," *New York Times Book Review,* 17 May 1981.

Joseph Mitchell
(27 July 1908 – 24 May 1996)

James Rogers
University of St. Thomas

Norman Sims
University of Massachusetts

BOOKS: *My Ears Are Bent* (New York: Sheridan
House, 1938);
McSorley's Wonderful Saloon (New York: Duell, Sloan
& Pearce, 1943);
Old Mr. Flood (New York: Duell, Sloan & Pearce,
1948);
The Bottom of the Harbor (Boston: Little, Brown,
1959; London: Chatto & Windus, 1961);
*Apologies to the Iroquois with a Study of the Mohawks in
High Steel,* by Mitchell and Edmund Wilson
(New York: Farrar, Straus & Cudahy, 1960);
Joe Gould's Secret (New York: Viking, 1965);
Up in the Old Hotel (New York: Pantheon, 1992).

Joseph Mitchell's work has proven crucial to
the development of literary journalism in the twentieth century. His use of characterization, dialogue,
and symbolism created a model for literary journalists, and he was widely respected as one of the best
reporters and interviewers of his age. Yet he published nothing between his last original work in
1964 and his final best-selling book in 1992. Even
during that absence he continued to influence the
work of succeeding generations of nonfiction writers.

In 1992 contemporary readers were introduced to the *New Yorker* prose of Joseph Mitchell
with the publication of *Up in the Old Hotel*. This collection of four earlier books, plus seven previously
uncollected stories and articles, appeared almost
twenty-eight years after Mitchell's last published
book; it made *The New York Times* best-seller list and
the "Books of the Year" list in *Time*. Reviewers were
effusive in their praise, declaring that Mitchell was
the best reporter ever to write for *The New Yorker,* or
even the best reporter of the century. Cultural critic
Harold Bloom included Mitchell's *Up in the Old Hotel,* James Agee's *Let Us Now Praise Famous Men*
(1941), Truman Capote's *In Cold Blood* (1965), and

Joseph Mitchell (photograph by Maryland Stuart)

Norman Mailer's *The Executioner's Song* (1979) as the
only nonfiction books on his "Twentieth Century
American Canon," listed in *Esquire* in September
1994 and consisting of "278 books you should have
read by now."

Mitchell's role in the development of literary journalism can be measured by his stature among noted writers. Lillian Ross, John Hersey, Mark Singer, and many others have cited Mitchell as a mentor or inspiration. The list of reviewers of *Up in the Old Hotel* reads like an honor roll of contemporary literary journalists, including Bill Barich, Roy Blount Jr., Joseph Epstein, Verlyn Klinkenborg, Noel Perrin, Luc Sante, Alec Wilkinson, and William Zinsser. In a *New Yorker* tribute to Mitchell by David Remnick, Calvin Trillin said, "I once dedicated a book to Joseph Mitchell as 'the *New Yorker* reporter who set the standard.' He was that to me and to a number of nonfiction writers I knew—inside and outside the magazine—during decades when most literate Americans might have had trouble placing his name." The two major anthologies of literary journalism that appeared in 1995, Norman Sims's and Mark Kramer's *Literary Journalism* and Gay Talese's and Barbara Lounsberry's *Writing Creative Nonfiction: The Literature of Reality,* each open with a selection from Mitchell.

Mitchell's course as a writer took him a long way from southeastern North Carolina, where he was born on 27 July 1908 to Averette and Elizabeth Parker Mitchell in the town of Fairmont. He had two brothers and three sisters. The Mitchell family had prospered as farmers since colonial days in this region of flat tobacco and cotton land, occasional timber stands, and swamps; it was assumed that Mitchell would also grow up to be a trader and a farmer.

By the time Mitchell was a student at the University of North Carolina he came to recognize some limitations. One was that he could never master the particular skills needed in his father's business, which was cotton trading. "In arithmetic, I think I'm a dyslectic," he admitted to Norman Sims.

> I knew when I was very small that I could never do it. I worked the cotton platform with my father, and he was always trying to teach me the cotton business—how to grade and sample cotton. . . . You have to be able to figure, as my father said, to deal with cotton futures, and to buy cotton. You're in competition with a group of men who will cut your throat at any moment, if they can see the value of a bale of cotton closer than you. I couldn't do it, so I had to leave.

Mitchell attended the university for four years, but the math stymied him again and he left before earning a degree.

While still a student Mitchell wrote and published dreamy short fiction in *The New American Caravan* and, later, *American Caravan IV.* He also began to write more-conventional features for newspapers in the region. He sold one article on the tobacco industry to the *New York Herald Tribune* in 1929, which led him into New York journalism. In *My Ears Are Bent* (1938), a collection of newspaper feature stories, Mitchell wrote that after leaving school, "I had an appendix operation and while getting over it I read James Bryce's *The American Commonwealth,* a book which made me want to become a political reporter. I came to New York City with that idea in mind." His apprenticeship as a journalist began in 1929 at the *World,* where he covered the Brooklyn police beat. Then he moved to the *Herald Tribune* for a brief time and finally to the *World-Telegram,* where he stayed for another seven years.

Mitchell's early work betrays no trace of his brief interest in political reporting. He occasionally makes fun of fatuous political speeches and depicts public officials in his first book, *My Ears Are Bent,* chiefly as meddlesome upholders of the status quo or as buffoons. The comic last chapter, "Our Leaders," introduces several venal officials, the most memorable of whom is stevedore-turned-politician Peter J. McGuinness, "the Fighting Alderman from Greenpoint, the Garden Spot of the World." He devotes his energies to "incessant warfare against women cigaret smokers, Chinese coolies, cabaret cover charges and the abolition of the Greenpoint ferry," and takes a Luddite's view of technology that displaces workers. Mitchell's editor, Stanley Walker, would send him to interview McGuinness on a slow news day, and Mitchell would bait the politician with questions about the latest advances to get him to start talking, until, "In the end, you don't know what the hell you said and what he came up with. That was one kind of hoax. There was a tradition of that sort of thing."

Mitchell had little stomach for the murders and shocking crimes that inevitably fell to a young reporter to cover, as he revealed in *My Ears Are Bent.* The first story he covered was "a Jack the Ripper murder in a Brooklyn apartment house" with the victim surrounded by lurid pictures. As a reporter he witnessed six electrocutions, had a stabbing victim die in his arms, and watched police torture a suspect while under interrogation. Along with swarms of other newsmen Mitchell covered the trial of Bruno Hauptmann, convicted kidnapper of the Lindbergh baby. The painful courtroom dramas of Anne Morrow Lindbergh identifying her child's sleeping suit or of Hauptmann receiving the death sentence were, to him, spectacles of "unnecessary inhumanity," even if the trial did provide "respite from the city room."

Pompous society women, self-made industrialists, cautious civil servants, and bowdlerizing copy

S.J. Perelman and Mitchell (photograph by Therese Mitchell)

editors bored Mitchell. His attitude toward conventional journalism can be seen in the photographs Mitchell included in his first book. Above the caption "Portrait of the Author," one picture shows Mitchell sitting on a couch, completely obscured except for his feet and legs by the newspaper he is reading. And on the last page Mitchell is shown sleeping face down on the same couch, newspapers strewn around him, above the caption "The Author's Opinion of the Sunday Newspaper."

Mitchell was nonetheless fascinated by the energies of city life and by what he called "common humanity." He soon began to specialize in features that portrayed the offbeat, and he introduced readers to what would be called "lowlife" characters: wrestling promoters, street evangelists, and strippers. Mitchell relished eccentricity and quirkiness. A chapter in *My Ears Are Bent,* "Cheese-Cake," collects six pieces about stripteasers and fan dancers.

These pieces demonstrate Mitchell's developing capacity to show respect for the people about whom he writes and to treat them with courtesy regardless of their distance from society's mainstream. He notes their professionalism: "Each chorus has a captain, a girl with a sense of responsibility, who can impose fines on her colleagues if, for example, she catches them chewing gum on the stage." And he records their humanness: "The girls work too hard for tabloid orgies. A girl who has jumped up and down a stage for twelve or fourteen hours a day does not want an orgy; all she wants is a quiet place to sleep." Mitchell's popular features were prominently advertised on the vans that delivered the newspapers.

In its attention to unfamiliar and gritty subjects, in passages of profound humor and in glimmers of eloquence, *My Ears Are Bent* foreshadows some of Mitchell's later writing. But it is not the work of a mature writer. Mitchell's glibness in this newspaper writing jars a reader familiar with his *New Yorker* style. In his later days Mitchell could never compose a sentence as heavy-handed as this one included in *My Ears Are Bent:* "There is one newspaper in New York City which prints acres of cheesecake, but you should see their holy, down-with-it articles about burlesque; in my opinion a pimp is a cherub compared with the two-faced editorial writer of this newspaper."

In the late 1930s several of the best feature writers in New York were hired by *The New Yorker,* many of them by Stanley Walker, who was managing editor for a brief time. They included Meyer Berger, A. J. Liebling, Richard O. Boyer, St. Clair McKelway, Alva Johnston, Joel Sayre, and, later, Lillian Ross. In 1938 editor Harold Ross and McKelway persuaded Mitchell to leave *The World-Telegram* and to join the staff of *The New Yorker.* In the more-expansive pages of the magazine Mitchell began to produce "Profiles" and "Reporter at Large" articles that would secure the reputation of the magazine for literate reportage. He thrived under the patient, even indulgent, editorial policy of *The New Yorker* that allowed him weeks and occasionally months to research and write a story.

Mitchell's relationship with the literary journalist and media critic Liebling deepened. A lifelong friendship had formed at the *World-Telegram* before they moved to the *New Yorker.* They both wrote about "lowlife" characters, and they had similar tastes in literature: Stephen Crane, Robert Louis Stevenson, George Borrow's books on the gypsies in Spain, François Villon, Ben Hecht's *Erik Dorn* (1921), François Rabelais, Ivan Turgenev, Fyodor Dostoyevsky, Sherwood Anderson, Robert Graves, and Mark Twain. Mitchell said his favorite writer was James Joyce, and critics later compared Mitchell's work on New York with Joyce's *Dubliners* (1914).

Mitchell and Liebling found themselves creating a new form of nonfiction. Instead of talking about the details of their work, they discussed Stendhal's *The Red and the Black* (1830) and other books and plays. "In talking about Stendhal's ideas, we talked about writing," Mitchell said in a personal interview. "We disagreed on a great many things, but I swear to God I can't remember what they were. It liberated me to talk to Joe about writing, and he gave me a great feeling. We walked a good deal coming up to the *World-Telegram.* He lived in the Village and so did I, and our wives were good friends. We talked a lot about books but not so much about our own writing. That was a private thing."

In a 1989 interview Mitchell elaborated on the development of his and Liebling's styles: "[Editor Harold] Ross insisted on certain things being up early in the article. But we'd say, 'You've taken all the surprise away.' He had the old newspaper lead concept: Put everything in the lead. But the newspaper story is not the magazine article. Narrative is all-important. It was a constant fight here with Mr. Ross, and his concept of the newspaper lead, which he thought was the greatest thing in the world. You've got to fight, and in doing so you learn what is, for you, a new technique."

In 1943 Mitchell gathered twenty of his *New Yorker* articles for his second collection, *McSorley's Wonderful Saloon.* He added seven articles and stories for its reissue in *Up in the Old Hotel.* The pieces in *McSorley's Wonderful Saloon* form a curious tour through the unconventional. Some explore exotic subcultures: calypso singers, gypsy families, and oyster fishermen among them. Probably the most vivid pieces are profiles of eccentrics, including some remarkable examples: Joe Gould, an unemployable Harvard graduate who claims to be writing a nine-million-word book (and also claims to converse with seagulls); A. S. Colborne, the "don't swear man," who founded the Anti-Profanity League and distributed six million cards scolding those who use vulgar language; Olga, the bearded lady, who appeared in the 1932 M-G-M horror classic, *Freaks;* and a strange Latvian named John S. Smith, whose cross-country hitchhiking is reconstructed only through a trail of worthless checks in amounts up to $600,000 given to strangers who have shown him minor courtesies.

Articles about lowlife characters caused endless difficulty for Harold Ross, who founded and edited *The New Yorker* for a sophisticated audience that might not appreciate freaks, fishermen, and hitchhikers giving out bad checks. Ross agonized for weeks after Meyer Berger published a "Profile" of a man who fished change out of sewer gratings near bus stops in New York. Then Mitchell and Liebling brought in literary portraits of a Bowery theater ticket taker and boxers that Ross could not turn down. In an interview Mitchell explained:

> At that time, Profiles were paid for here under a classification where a "highlife" Profile–somebody who was a celebrity–was paid more than a "lowlife" Profile–someone Meyer Berger might write about, or Liebling or me. Then, Ross said, "Look, this is a 'highlife lowlife.' You'll get a better rate on that." For example, in the Mazie Profile, he said, "I'll tell you what we'll do. You've got Fanny Hearst in there. She's a highlife. That makes it a highlife lowlife." And then he put another classification in, that if it was a "humorous highlife" it

got a certain amount, but if it was a "humorous highlife lowlife," that was as high as you could get.

What Mark Singer once described as a "Byzantine" structure for compensation at *The New Yorker* originated in these changes during the Ross era.

The story of a tough but tenderhearted theater operator on Skid Row that appeared in *My Ears Are Bent* under the wisecracking title "Except that She Smokes, Drinks Booze and Talks Rough, Miss Mazie Is a Nun" displays subtlety and depth in its 1940 *New Yorker* version, "Mazie." Mitchell's revised "Profile" precisely reports the details of her rough environment, the world of the Bowery to which she serves as a gatekeeper in her tiny ticket booth:

Mazie is small, but she is wiry and fearless, and she has a frightening voice. . . . Now and then, in the Venice, a stiff throws his head back and begins to snore so blatantly that he can be heard all over the place, especially during tense moments in the picture. When this happens, or when one of the drunks gets into a bellowing mood, the women and children in the reserved section stamp on the floor and chant, "Mazie! Mazie! We want Mazie!" The instant this chant goes up, the matron hastens out to the lobby and raps on the side window of Mazie's cage. Mazie locks the cash drawer, grabs a bludgeon she keeps around, made of a couple of copies of *True Romances* rolled up tightly and held together by rubber bands, and strides into the theatre.

If whacking the offender does not suffice, Mazie furiously chases him from the theater; however, "Mazie's animosity toward a stiff or a drunk usually lasts until she has driven him out to the sidewalk. Then, almost invariably, she becomes contrite and apologetic."

Structurally, "Mazie" moves the reader, first through her tiny cubicle, then into the larger but unfamiliar world of the Bowery, where legends and rumors circulate about Mazie's activities and her past. Finally, the story depicts her nightly routine of walking the streets looking after the destitute men sleeping and suffering on the streets. The world of the Bowery seems closed off from the rest of the world, and Mitchell keeps the readers' perspective at an ironic distance; the word *depression* never appears in the "Profile." Mitchell artfully balances Mazie's crassness and her kindness. His alertness to a detail such as the use of *True Romances* to clout an obstreperous drunk compresses the two worlds in which Mazie lives.

The elegiac quality of much of *McSorley's Wonderful Saloon* cannot escape notice. In virtually every piece at least one figure remarks on the vanished goodness of the past. Commodore Dutch, a salty old man who supports himself by arranging charity balls in his own behalf in "In a Sporting Man" thinks back on the barhopping of his drinking days: "I wasn't a teetotaler then by no means, and I would hit four or five gin mills and listen to the personalities, what they call celebrities nowadays, only a personality was somebody, but a celebrity, who the hell is he?" Johnny Nikanov, a Russian gypsy, regrets the coming of the automobile in "King of the Gypsies": "'Things have been getting worse and worse for gypsies ever since the automobile was put on the market,' he said. 'When I was a little knee-high boy the U.S. was gypsy heaven.'"

Mitchell expresses his love of the old-time saloon and the characters who hung out there in the opening piece, called "The Old House at Home," about McSorley's, the oldest bar in New York, just off Cooper Square. McSorley's clientele—restricted to men since the first owner—and proprietors have an abiding resistance to change. Mitchell describes the founder's son, second owner Bill McSorley, as someone absolutely dedicated to keeping the bar "exactly as it had been in his father's time," to the extent that he is reluctant to make even basic repairs: "After customers complained that they were afraid the flakes they found in their ale might strangle them to death, he grudgingly had the ceiling repainted."

Out of these profiles of eccentrics and freaks Mitchell discovered his attitude about the characters he encountered in the Fulton Fish Market, the Bowery, and Staten Island—an attitude that may define the difference between feature writing and literary journalism. "Some of the people I wrote about in the beginning were freaks in the sense the bearded lady was a freak," he said in an interview. "Then I began to see that wasn't what I wanted. I wanted not the unusual but the usual in the unusual. Or the extraordinary in the ordinary, you might say. I found that in the fish market and the old shad fishermen." He recalled talking with the photographer Diane Arbus, who specialized in photos of strange people. Mitchell felt that Arbus had accomplished exactly what he was trying to do: to recognize or acknowledge the freak inside the ordinary person. Mitchell never liked the term *lowlife*. He said, "You don't see that kind of Profile any longer because most of the reporters here have come to the same conclusion I did: The accepted is one thing and the freak is another. The freak living in the ordinary human being is what we're after. I could take some credit in that discovery."

Mitchell's next book, *Old Mr. Flood* (1948), collects three of what he called "stories of fish-eating, whiskey, death, and rebirth" that first appeared in

Dust jacket for the 1992 collection comprising four of Mitchell's books and seven previously uncollected stories and articles

The New Yorker. For this short book Mitchell created a crotchety, resolutely young ninety-four-year-old named Hugh G. Flood, who is convinced that he can live to the age of 115 by following a strict "seafoodetarian" diet. He lives in a waterfront hotel adjoining one of Mitchell's favorite haunts, the Fulton Fish Market. Through Mr. Flood, Mitchell opens a window on the exotic subculture of the fish sellers while at the same time giving voice to his feelings about aging and mortality: "Many aged people reconcile themselves to the certainty of death and become tranquil; Mr. Flood is unreconcilable."

In 1948 Mitchell said in the "Author's Note" of *Old Mr. Flood* that the main character is a composite—"combined in him are aspects of several old men who work or hang out in the Fulton Fish Market, or who did in the past"—and when the book was reprinted in *Up in the Old Hotel* in 1992 it was labeled as fictional. No such disclaimer accompanied the original pieces in *The New Yorker;* a wash drawing of the dapper nonagenarian accompanied the three pieces by Abe Birnbaum. Mr. Flood is fictional, but the book reflects diligent reporting. Mitchell based the book on years of research and loving immersion in the peculiar milieu of the fish market.

The three Mr. Flood articles had their origins in Mitchell's desire to create larger and deeper portraits of the city. "I had been trying to write this thing about the Fulton Fish Market in a kind of Melvillean way," he said. "I feel funny to say such a thing. I read *Moby Dick* in college and it had a great effect on me. I had often thought about a Melvillean background with the Fulton Fish Market." There were several old men in the market, particularly William A. Winant, whose family was among the original "Old Yankees" who once ruled the market—the people from Stonington, Connecticut, and New Bedford, Massachusetts, and Long Island, who came in to handle their own fish or sent a son to work in the market. Then the Irish, Jewish, and, finally, Italian interests entered the market. In one interview Mitchell recalled his initial difficulty in bringing together the story strands of the various people he talked to: "So I was talking to Mr. Ross about it one time. There had been a number of composite Profiles—a composite Profile of a policeman, for example, that McKelway had written. So he said, 'Why don't you write a composite?' I did. I developed *Old Mr. Flood.*"

When the first piece came out, visitors arrived at Mr. Flood's hotel asking for him. Mitchell asked the hotel clerks to say Mr. Flood was at his daughter's home in Norwalk, Connecticut. As Mitchell continued to explain in the interview, "I never intended to, what would you call it, foster a hoax, or anything. That was the *farthest* thing from my mind.

The idea was to get the spirit of the fish market. I couldn't do it by anybody in there. It had to be somebody on the outside looking in. . . . We began to feel strange about this. But Ross said, 'Oh, go ahead.' I don't think, except with his approval, that it would have been possible. We weren't trying to fool anybody really. The idea then of being between fiction and nonfiction—we weren't even thinking of such a thing."

Old Mr. Flood displays another Mitchell characteristic: his delight in the poetic languages of a subculture. "Mr. Flood's Party" includes a lengthy passage in which the old man recites a litany of the selections once available at Still's oyster house. Mr. Flood reels off dozens of names, concluding, "From New York—the finest of all—he had Blue Points and Mattitucks and Saddle Rocks and Robbins Islands and Diamond Points and Fire Places and Montauks and Hog Necks and Millponds and Fire Island Salts and Rockaways and Shinnecocks. I love those good old oyster names. When I feel my age weighing me down, I recite them to myself and I feel better."

Mitchell planned a fourth story in which Mr. Flood was going to disappear into Connecticut. Mitchell said he wished he had continued, but he got interested in other things, and "by that time I was appalled by the idea." He worried that it would cast doubt on his other articles. These stories were written at a time when composites were common, including John Hersey's "Joe Is Home Now," a collective portrait of returning war veterans. Mitchell said he thought Liebling later modeled his Colonel Stingo after Mr. Flood. The border between fact and fiction had been explored, and Mitchell learned how to use characters in a way that would enrich his later writing: "This old man that I more or less invented, and the other people, were able to tell the story. The people down in the market thought so. Sometimes facts don't tell the truth, you know."

Mitchell's next book, *The Bottom of the Harbor* (1959), contains six pieces written between 1944 and 1959. The earliest of these, "The Rats on the Waterfront," is atypical in its lack of human personality—it is more about rodents than people—but it bears the Mitchell hallmarks of exhaustive research in the portrayal of an aspect of the urban underbelly.

The Bottom of the Harbor may be the single book that best displays Mitchell's mature talents. For the most part, the dubious characters of his early works are missing from this collection. He directs his attention to men of innate dignity who preserve a vanishing way of life. The 1947 "Dragger Captain" portrays Captain Ellery Thompson of the trawler *Eleanor,* whose family has been working the waters out of Stonington, Connecticut, for three hundred years. Ellery, forty-seven, is single, opinionated, and unlettered, but he is brilliantly gifted as a fisherman, self-taught painter, amateur oceanographer, and designer of his own boat. He possesses an intimate knowledge of the sea and of marine life. Captain Ellery is splendidly out of sync with the pace of the modern world: "He abhors hurry; he thinks that humanity in general has got ahead of itself. He once threatened to fire a man in his crew because he worked too hard."

Any of the remaining four pieces in *The Bottom of the Harbor* might well be nominated as Mitchell's richest and most complex work. Each shows an increased awareness of mortality and decline. The 1951 piece that gives the collection its title is a meticulously researched survey of exactly what lies on the harbor floor, from the days of the Dutch down to the present. An immense amount of history lies under the water. In the final pages of the story Mitchell rides along on patrol with conservation officer Andrew Zimmer, whose duty it is to keep poachers out of the now-contaminated clam beds. They meet Roy Poole, a lifelong fisherman who is preoccupied with the harbor bottom, and, over bowls of oyster stew, the three men share harbor lore and wonder about its future. Poole has just had a troubling dream that an earthquake has drained the harbor like a bathtub and he is crawling around in the muck. Zimmer's timid optimism in new antipollution measures is no match for Poole's conviction that the water is "getting worse and worse. Everything is getting worse everywhere." Mitchell deftly ends the piece with the three men saying good-bye, and Mr. Poole's simple parting words can be read as a dark admonition: "Take care. Take care. Take care."

"Up in the Old Hotel" (1952) probes another unknown territory—this time, the abandoned floors of a six-story building near the fish market. Once the Fulton Ferry Hotel, the building is now home to Sloppy Louie's seafood restaurant on the ground floor. Mitchell dines there frequently, and in the course of chatting with the proprietor he learns that no one quite knows what is on the upper floors of the building. They can only be reached by a hand-operated elevator that has been unused for decades. Louie, the owner, turns out to have a powerful sense of the past and has in fact delved deeply into the history of the building. In the course of a long conversation—interrupted by the normal distractions of a busy restaurant—Mitchell, through Louie, provides an absorbing microhistory of this tiny corner of New York. The two men impulsively decide to explore the upper floors.

Mitchell and A.J. Liebling outside The New Yorker *offices on West 44th Street*

The experience is unsettling and disappointing. Louie, who comes from an ancient Italian fishing village, speculates romantically about linking the building to early New York. He hopes to find old hotel registers that will cement the connection, but the upper floors contain only bedsprings, rusty paper clips, hairpins, and other meaningless detritus. The previously unexplored past suddenly alarms Louie. After reading a religious placard in one abandoned room, "The Wages of Sin is Death," he abruptly cuts the tour short. The piece ends with Louie's disgust: "'The wages of sin!' he said. 'Sin, death, dust, old empty rooms, old empty whiskey bottles, old empty bureau drawers. Come on, pull the rope faster! Pull it faster! Let's get out of this.'"

"I was trying to write for years about the fish market as an institution in itself," Mitchell said in an interview. "And then, all of a sudden, going up there in the old hotel with Louie, I thought, 'My God, this will tell the story.' Out of all this knowing of the background of the fish market, it took all that to write this one little story."

The two other pieces in the book follow a similar pattern. Each opens with Mitchell pausing to take an interest in a familiar and thus easily overlooked community. "Mr. Hunter's Grave" (1956) explores an African American settlement on the South Shore of Staten Island; "The Rivermen" (1959) introduces the shad fishermen who set their nets in the Hudson River in Edgewater, New Jersey, opposite Manhattan. Mitchell's leisurely excursions into these communities gradually open up a long history which—though unknown to most New Yorkers—is still vivid to the men who live and work in these unexplored pockets of urban life.

Inexorably, Mitchell moves these stories toward a conclusion that involves a meditation on death. In the last pages of "The Rivermen" a group of fishermen gathered around an old photo point out those who have died, swap stories of a philandering fisherman who picked up women in cemeteries, and hear a friend's health complaints while nearby children recite the rhyme beginning "The worms crawl in / the worms crawl out" (which is also the epigraph of the book). The conclusion is inevitable: life is fragile, and like the shad, "the purpose of life is to stay alive and to keep on staying alive as long as you possibly can," as one of the rivermen put it. In the final scene of "Mr. Hunter's Grave" the old gentleman of the title tells how, because of a gravedigger's haste, he will actually be buried one plot over from his own headstone: "'Ah, well,' he said, 'it won't make any difference.'"

Mitchell's skills as a reporter and his use of dialogue, characterization, and symbolism are displayed best in the pieces collected in *The Bottom of the Harbor*. Mitchell explained his reporting techniques in an interview:

> My whole idea of reporting–particularly reporting on conversation–is to talk to someone long enough under different circumstances, like old Mr. Hunter down on Staten Island. I was always trying to reach his whole life. I couldn't really write about anybody until they spoke what I consider "the revealing remark" or the revealing anecdote or the thing that touched them. . . . I'm not easily bored. I can talk to the old man down on Staten Island all day long, and it doesn't bore me. The revelations that keep coming from his mind astonish me. I think, my God, here's Lear. Here's Lear on Bloomingdale Road in Staten Island.

Later in the same interview Mitchell added, "One thing you have to do, if you're going to write this sort of thing, is realize that people have buried their pain and have transformed experience enough to allow them to endure it and bear it. If you stay with them long enough, you let them reveal it to themselves, thereby revealing it to you." Mitchell said he recognized the revealing remark when he heard it in the same way "the archaeologist knows what he's seeing when he picks it up out of the dirt. I like to think of it as an archeological digging into the minds of these people."

In "The Rivermen" Mitchell meets an old woman in a cemetery tending roses on her family's gravesites–roses that originated with the Dutch settlers and survive now by sending their roots down into the graves. Later, the life cycle of the shad–bound together with the lives of the rivermen–becomes another symbol of the community and the attitude found among its residents. "In the beginning the idea of a literary journalism scared me because I thought the readers would expect too much," Mitchell said in an interview. "But then I began to realize the deeper you went into these people's lives, they were just as complex as people in novels. The creative aspect of it is the facts that you pick, and the conversations that you pick, and the fact you stayed with the man long enough to get a panoply of conversations from which you can take the one that you want." Mitchell felt readers dislike obvious symbolic or mythical elements in nonfiction. "But if it's

inherent and inescapable, then the reader will go along," he said.

Mitchell became legendary among his colleagues at *The New Yorker* for being a slow writer, to the point where, as his obituary in the magazine on 10 June 1996 noted, his "reputation for reluctance or perfectionism, or whatever it was, nearly eclipsed his reputation for what he had actually done." In his 1975 memoir, *Here at The New Yorker,* Brendan Gill wrote, "Mitchell, who is in his sixties, used to take months over a piece and now takes years. One consequence of that long period of composition is the interest it arouses among his editors and fellow-writers; everyone speculates about the nature of the piece upon which Mitchell is at work and about when it may be handed in. Nobody would dream of putting such questions to Mitchell directly." Gill added that Mitchell wanted friends to read his work only in its final published version, since even at the galley stage the meticulous author might change a word or two.

Mitchell's devotion to the craft of writing, as well as his fact checking and attention to detail, inspired something near reverence in his colleagues. Calvin Trillin said in an interview with Sims, "His writing has a 'magic slate' feel. You can't see him struggling with it. In narrative writing, getting yourself out of the way is a wonderful thing. He often has a lot about himself in it, but you can't see him being clever or striving or struggling. It reads as if it just happens. He's a simple presence, like Joe DiMaggio." Despite his skill at staying out of his own prose, Mitchell's later writing hints at a playful side. "When things get too much for me," he wrote in the lead sentence of "Mr. Hunter's Grave," "I put a wild-flower book and a couple of sandwiches in my pockets and go down to the South Shore of Staten Island and wander around awhile in one of the old cemeteries down there." And this side appears again in "The Rivermen": "One day in late February, the weather was surprisingly sunny and warm. It was one of those balmy days that sometimes turns up in the winter, like a strange bird blown off its course. Walking back to my office after lunch, I began to dawdle. Suddenly the idea occurred to me, why not take the afternoon off and go over to Edgewater and go for a walk along the river and breathe a little clean air for a change."

These asides suggest that Mitchell in his middle age was, at heart, still the young man who had fallen in love with the richness of life in and around New York. As he aged, his work came to be shaped by an awareness that the love affair must someday end. Increasingly, he was attracted to cemeteries. Mitchell said in an interview that Ross once told him, "'You know, you're a pretty gloomy guy.' I said, 'I know it. I think the only view I have of the world, the one I like best, is graveyard humor. I think the world's a terrible place.' By that time I was writing about old men and old women. When they started talking about how nothing turned out the way they thought it would, I said, 'I can respond to that.'" He never clearly defined what he meant by graveyard humor. One time he said it was not exactly laughing at death, "but it's an attitude I wish I could define to myself. It's whistling through the graveyard. But I developed that feeling as a reporter because I covered that kind of story during the depression."

After "The Rivermen" Mitchell's next signed "Profile" in *The New Yorker* was in 1964, when *Joe Gould's Secret* appeared in two installments. He had previously written about Joe Gould in *McSorley's Wonderful Saloon,* but this lengthy profile put Mitchell in a new role. Though he had expanded and reworked material before, in this case twenty-two years had passed. Before *Joe Gould's Secret,* Mitchell's reportage sometimes opened by speaking in the first person, but his presence often slipped away as the narrative developed. Here, Mitchell remains a part of the story from beginning to end.

Joe Gould's Secret tells the story of Mitchell's relationship with a celebrated eccentric. A New Englander of impeccable lineage, Joe Gould was a fixture in the bohemian life of Greenwich Village. The few of his early writings that found their way into print cast an impressive shadow: William Saroyan singled out a story of his for praise, and E. E. Cummings wrote a poem about Gould. In 1917 Gould professed to have had something like a vision of his life's work, the compilation of an Oral History of Our Time. The book was to be all-inclusive primary material for future historians, recording without commentary thousands of pages of overheard talk. Gould described his idea:

I would spend the rest of my life going about the city listening to people—eavesdropping, if necessary—and writing down whatever I heard them say that sounded revealing to me, no matter how boring or idiotic or vulgar or obscene it might sound to others. I could see the whole thing in my mind—long-winded conversations and short and snappy conversations, brilliant conversations and foolish conversations, curses, catch phrases, coarse remarks, snatches of quarrels, the mutterings of drunks and crazy people, the entreaties of beggars and bums, the propositions of prostitutes, the spiels of pitchmen and peddlers, the sermons of street preachers, shouts in the night, wild rumors, cries from the heart.

Gould was continually writing in notebooks, but he refused to show the Oral History to anyone. For decades, he lived on the streets, devoting his lifetime to the recording of ordinary conversation.

After the 1942 "Profile" of Gould, "Professor Sea Gull," Mitchell acquired more of Gould's friendship than he wanted. Gould dropped in at Mitchell's office to beg, talk for hours, and pick up the mail that he had delivered in care of *The New Yorker.* Too diffident to insist that he leave, Mitchell attempted to divert Gould by finding a publisher for the Oral History. Gould was strangely obstructive. The truth suddenly dawned on Mitchell: there was no Oral History. Gould's lifelong project was an utter fraud.

Joe Gould's Secret is alternately comic and pathetic. By itself, the story appears too slim to sustain a 150-page book. But Mitchell makes the story transcend mere anecdote by taking the risk of autobiography. Mitchell's involvement in the life of Joe Gould offers a cracked mirror in which to consider his own life's work. When Gould says, "In New York City, especially in Greenwich Village, down among the cranks and the misfits and the one-lungers and the has-beens and the might've-beens and the would-bes and the never-wills and the God-knows-whats, I have always felt at home," we can easily recognize the other Joe, the one who is writing. Gould was an exile from his family and his home, which was something Mitchell could understand. While Mitchell's family experience had been a loving one, his life's work was writing about New York City. He loved North Carolina, but he had to go elsewhere to earn a living.

When Mitchell discovers Gould's secret he is at first appalled. But he finds it impossible to stay angry. Instead, he begins to reflect on the plans he once had to write a great and ponderous novel that would do for New York what Joyce's *Ulysses* (1922) did for Dublin. "Almost every day, I would discard a few characters and invent a few new ones. But the truth is, I never actually wrote a word of it," Mitchell admits in *Joe Gould's Secret.* The few pages that Gould writes are surrounded by his obsessive secrecy; he revises the same slight essay on his father's death over and over for decades—all traits that have their parallels in Mitchell's own work habits. The difference, of course, is that Mitchell did write—not a colossal book, but a series of masterpieces that taken together approximate the Oral History that Gould talked about.

Even though he is the one person in the world who knows the secret, Mitchell cannot bring himself to expose his friend. Perhaps he sees too much of himself in Gould. Or perhaps Mitchell's fundamental courtesy keeps him from acting hurtfully toward anyone, no matter how great a sham or a misfit that person might be. In the closing paragraphs of *Joe Gould's Secret* Mitchell's friend Edward Gottlieb asks him to join a committee that will search for the missing Oral History manuscripts. Mitchell agrees, "continuing to play the role I had stepped into the afternoon that I discovered that the Oral History did not exist–a role that I am only now stepping out of." Thus, Mitchell's most self-reflective work ends with the suggestion that he was now beginning something different. The nature of that new role would never be determined, for Mitchell never again published an original work.

During the years between *Joe Gould's Secret* and *Up in the Old Hotel* speculation and mystery grew around Mitchell's writing. Roger Angell, a writer and editor at *The New Yorker,* told David Remnick:

> Knowing him as a colleague during this profound and elegant silence made you feel like an archaeologist forever on the brink of an extraordinary find. He hadn't stopped writing, that was always clear; he was busy on a piece that hadn't quite gone right so far. Each morning, he stepped out of the elevator with a preoccupied air, nodded wordlessly if you were just coming down the hall, and closed himself in his office. . . . Sometimes, in the evening elevator, I heard him emit a small sigh, but he never complained, never explained.

Janet Malcolm, a friend and colleague, said in Remnick's article, "In 1964, after writing his masterpiece, 'Joe Gould's Secret,' he undertook a work so labyrinthine and deep that at his death it was still not finished. Much has been made of the fact that Joe didn't publish anything for thirty years. To his friends this was not remarkable; it was simply another sign of Joe's seriousness about writing."

The mystery was compounded by the fact that Mitchell turned down all requests from interviewers, except two, between 1964 and the publication of *Up in the Old Hotel* in 1992. Yet his reputation among writers grew as his readers lost track of him. Mark Singer used to tell new "Talk of the Town" writers at *The New Yorker* to read Mitchell's *My Ears Are Bent*–not to imitate it but to be inspired by it. Calvin Trillin told a newspaper interviewer that he would "trade pretty much everything I'd written for a paragraph of 'Old Mr. Flood' or 'Joe Gould's Secret.'" Used-book stores could easily sell original copies of *McSorley's Wonderful Saloon* or *The Bottom of the Harbor* for more than $100 each.

In 1989, during an interview with Sims, Mitchell said he was working on a piece about Joe Cantalupo, who used to haul all the trash from the Fulton Fish Market. During another interview later that year he said he was writing an autobiography: "What I'm writing will explain it all. I'm going to try to explain this whole matter of personas and disappointments, interruptions, and the like." Except for *Up in the Old Hotel,* nothing new appeared.

Mitchell tried to explain the "mystery" of his life during the final thirty-one years. In one of his interviews with Sims, Mitchell said that after his father died in 1976 he helped his two brothers and three sisters manage the family farms. Of the many acres of land, about half was farmland and the other tracts were timberland, a great deal of it mature.

> I got very interested in reforestation, and still am. I would leave here and go down there. Nobody would know when I left. I would stay down there for pretty long periods. [William] Shawn was the editor then. He didn't mind what I did. It was a peculiar editor-writer relationship. He figured sooner or later I'd . . . well, I got sidetracked. There's no mystery about what I was doing in those years. Bill was amenable: 'Go and take as much time as you want.' Other people were mystified. I didn't want to talk about inherited land and that sort of stuff. So it's gotten to be a mystery.

Other interruptions included time researching the development of the South Street Seaport and six years as one of Mayor Ed Koch's appointees to the Landmarks Preservation Commission.

As for turning down all those requests for interviews, Mitchell said he had never given interviews. He told Sims he had resisted a friend's request to do one and thereafter felt obligated to avoid others; besides, he added, "I just feel the reporter shouldn't be in it [the public eye]. That's a very strong newspaper thing. The old expression is, 'You shouldn't get into that.'"

After Mitchell's death at age eighty-seven on 24 May 1996 his companion in the later years and his literary executor, Sheila McGrath, told Sims that Mitchell had never stopped writing: "He was forever taking notes and typing them up. He always had his folded note paper and pen inside his inner breast pocket. He never gave up. He had a sense there were things he would do." When it became clear that his cancer could no longer be treated or delayed Mitchell thought of works in progress, telling McGrath, "There was so much I still wanted to do."

As a child Mitchell had often traveled with his mother and aunts to small cemeteries in North Carolina where relatives were buried. Easter-egg hunts were held in cemeteries. Later, he would search for wildflowers in New York City cemeteries and incorporate visits to them in his work. His graveyard humor was connected somehow to these experiences. Later in his life he reestablished his connections to North Carolina, where many of his sensibilities formed. Mitchell is buried near Fairmont, North Carolina, next to his parents; his brother Jack; his wife Therese, with whom Mitchell had two daughters; and several aunts and cousins. McGrath told Sims that Mitchell's surviving brother, Harry, wrote in his notes for the graveside eulogy: "Joe loved New York City and he loved North Carolina."

References:

Christopher Carduff, "Fish-eating, Whiskey, Death & Rebirth," *New Criterion,* 11 (November 1992): 12–22;

Malcolm Cowley, "Joseph Mitchell: The Grammar of Facts," *New Republic,* 109 (26 July 1943): 113–114; reprinted in his *The Flower and the Leaf: A Contemporary Record of American Writing Since 1941,* edited by Donald W. Faulkner (New York: Viking, 1985), pp. 261–264;

Joseph Epstein, "Joe Gould's Masterpiece," *New Republic,* 153 (23 October 1965): 26–30;

Brendan Gill, *Here at The New Yorker* (New York: Random House, 1975);

Stanley Edgar Hyman, "The Art of Joseph Mitchell," in his *The Critic's Credentials: Essays and Reviews,* edited by Phoebe Pettingell (New York: Atheneum, 1978), pp. 79–85;

Joint Committee on North Carolina Literature and Bibliography of the North Carolina English Teachers Association and the North Carolina Library Association, *North Carolina Authors: A Selective Handbook* (Chapel Hill: University of North Carolina Library, 1952);

Malcolm Jones Jr., "The Paragon of Reporters: Joseph Mitchell Transformed Journalism into Art," *Newsweek* (10 August 1992): 53–54;

Pembroke Magazine, no. 26 (1994): 7–47; contains essays on Mitchell by Raymond J. Rundus, Sanford J. Smoller, and Norman Sims;

Noel Perrin, "A Kind of Writing for Which No Name Exists," in his *A Reader's Delight* (Hanover, N.H.: University Press of New England, 1988), pp. 20–24;

Perrin, "Paragon of Reporters: Joseph Mitchell," *Sewanee Review,* 91, no. 2 (Spring 1983): 167–184;

David Remnick, "Postscript: Joseph Mitchell: Three Generations of *New Yorker* Writers Remember the City's Incomparable Chronicler," *New Yorker* (10 June 1996): 78–83;

Norman Sims, "Joseph Mitchell," in *Literary Journalism: A Research Guide to a Developing Genre,* edited by Thomas B. Connery (Westport, Conn.: Greenwood Press, 1992), pp. 205–211;

Sims, "Joseph Mitchell and *The New Yorker* Nonfiction Writers," in *Literary Journalism in the Twentieth Century,* edited by Sims (New York: Oxford University Press, 1990), pp. 82–109;

William Zinsser, "Journeys with Joseph Mitchell," *American Scholar* (Winter 1993): 132–138.

P. J. O'Rourke

(14 November 1947 –)

Jack A. Nelson
Brigham Young University

BOOKS: *Modern Manners: An Etiquette Book for Rude People* (New York: Dell, 1983);
Republican Party Reptile: Essays and Outrages (New York: Atlantic Monthly, 1987);
The Bachelor Home Companion: A Practical Guide to Keeping House Like a Pig (New York: Pocket Books, 1987);
Holidays in Hell (New York: Atlantic Monthly, 1988);
Parliament of Whores: A Lone Humorist Attempts to Explain the Entire U.S. Government (New York: Atlantic Monthly, 1991);
Give War a Chance: Eyewitness Accounts of Mankind's Struggle against Tyranny, Injustice, and Alcohol-Free Beer (New York: Atlantic Monthly, 1992);
All the Trouble in the World: The Lighter Side of Overpopulation, Famine, Ecological Disaster, Ethnic Hatred, and Poverty (New York: Atlantic Monthly, 1994).

MOTION PICTURE: *Easy Money,* screenplay by O'Rourke, Rodney Dangerfield, Michael Endler, and David Blain, Orion Pictures, 1983.

OTHER: *The 1964 High School Yearbook Parody,* edited by O'Rourke and Douglas C. Kenney (Boston: National Lampoon, 1974);
Sunday Newspaper Parody, edited with contributions by O'Rourke (Boston: National Lampoon, 1978).

P. J. O'Rourke (photograph by Maxwell MacKenzie)

P. J. (Patrick Jake) O'Rourke is a satirist-humorist who sprang from the tradition of New Journalism espoused by Tom Wolfe, Norman Mailer, and Hunter S. Thompson. His literary journalism abandons any pretense of objectivity and instead offers a version colored by the reporter's immersion into the subject, with all the biases and emotions intact. *Time* magazine calls O'Rourke "an acerbic master of gonzo journalism and one of America's most hilarious and provocative writers," a conservative with libertarian leanings. His mixture of one-liners, wit, vitriol, cynicism, and outrage makes him capable of offending almost everyone. His melding of rock-and-roll wildness and conservative libertarianism evoke laughter even from his political opponents. Jeffrey Abbot of *The Times* (London) sees him as "the gunslinger of the eminently respectable school of American right-wing libertarian philosophers." His books, often collections of his magazine pieces, have appeared with some regularity on the best-seller lists.

Besides the other New Journalists, O'Rourke has been compared to H. L. Mencken, the journalistic curmudgeon who satirized American life of the 1920s and 1930s with his *American Mercury* magazine. O'Rourke's sharp and witty opposition to almost everything–particularly government–made him a best-selling author in such works as *Parliament of Whores: A Lone Humorist Attempts to Explain the Entire U.S. Government* (1991) and *Give War a Chance: Eyewitness Accounts of Mankind's Struggle against Tyranny, Injustice, and Alcohol-Free Beer* (1992). He has been a columnist for *Rolling Stone* and has contributed to *Harper's, Playboy, Vanity Fair, American Spectator, House and Garden, Wall Street Journal, Esquire, Car and Driver,* and *Automobile*. He is a member of the editorial board of *American Spectator*.

O'Rourke was born in 1947 in Toledo, Ohio, a son of Clifford Bronson O'Rourke, an automobile salesman, and Delphine Loy O'Rourke, a school administrator. He graduated with a B.A. from Miami University of Ohio in 1969 and earned an M.A. from Johns Hopkins University in 1970. His honors have included Woodrow Wilson Fellowship, 1969–1970; Merit Award from Art Directors Club, 1973; Gold Award, 1975; Merit Award from Society of Publication Designers, 1976; and other awards for visual excellence in *National Lampoon*.

With his Toledo upbringing and a father who was a car salesman, O'Rourke considers himself a typical American. "We lived in the 1950s version of suburbia–houses with lawns inside the city limits, like a working class *Leave It to Beaver*," he told *Publishers Weekly*. "It was an utterly ordinary, middle-America sort of upbringing, and one with no regionalism other than the tendency to put an intrusive *r* into 'Warshington, D.C.' And I also come at the very crest of the baby boom, so in terms of age, ethnic background, geographical background, my reference points are likely to be shared by a lot of Americans, probably even by a majority. All that gives me a sense of confidence that when I refer to something, a lot of people are going to understand that reference."

During the 1960s he dropped out with his colleagues to embrace the hippie counterculture while maintaining a conservative distance. He wrote two undistinguished novels in his early twenties, and his early efforts at experimental poetry attracted little attention. Scholarships helped him through college; he then migrated from the Midwest to a graduate creative-writing program at Johns Hopkins University. He loved Baltimore and found his niche–humor–writing for an antiwar underground newspaper, the *Baltimore Harry*.

O'Rourke's writing there consisted of what he calls "crazed, left-wing political nonsense. You know, lots of articles damning capitalism and praising dope." Although he avoided the draft during the Vietnam War, O'Rourke became aware of the flaws of ultraliberals when a Maoist group called Balto-Cong invaded the *Baltimore Harry* and held the staff hostage for a night while putting them through consciousness-raising sessions. "They had come to liberate us," O'Rourke explained to Chris Peachment in *The Times* (London). "This involved taking each of us upstairs and screaming at us that we were all running dog lackeys of capitalist pigs and so on. . . . After they had all gone, it fell to me and the staff photographer to guard the office each night, simply because we had a pistol each. He, it turned out, was an undercover cop who had been planted. The trouble was that when we discovered this fact, we realized that we all liked him a lot better than the Balto-Cong. And he liked us too. So he quit the cops and we all cut our hair and got jobs." Following that episode and a winter spent in England, O'Rourke says it became obvious "the whole Hippie thing was pretty stupid."

With the goal of becoming a writer, he moved to New York, working odd jobs to survive, then writing for a time for the *Village Other* and later the *New York Herald*. He also started freelancing for the *National Lampoon*. In 1973 the *Lampoon,* a training ground for smart-aleck parody writers, hired him as a junior editor, launching his career as a savage satirist. Each issue of the *Lampoon* focused on a theme, often dedicated to attacking the ethnic groups, women, and liberals beginning to assert themselves during the 1970s. With *Lampoon* founder Doug Kenney in 1974 he put out the highly successful *1964 High School Yearbook Parody* and in 1978 published *Sunday Newspaper Parody,* a similar spoof of Sunday papers.

His authorship of such articles for the *Lampoon* as "How to Drive Fast on Drugs While Getting Your Wing-Wang Squeezed and Not Spill Your Drink" won him the role of managing editor in 1978. His already-apparent conservatism did not play well with the *Lampoon* staff. In *Going Too Far* (1987), a book about the magazine by former staff member Tony Hendra, the author writes, "O'Rourke was a narc, a very good narc who hit all the right notes, but whose police-issue shoes showed beneath his bell-bottoms."

Part of O'Rourke's differences with the other *Lampoon* staff members came from a difference of class. They had gone to Ivy League schools while O'Rourke had gone to Miami University of Ohio. His car-dealer father had died when O'Rourke was only nine, and his mother had married a man that O'Rourke describes today as an "unaffable, drunk bum."

In 1981 O'Rourke left the *National Lampoon,* in part because he saw the magazine as being part of the 1970s, which had ended. After a brief stint in Hollywood collaborating with comedian Rodney Dangerfield, among others, on the film script *Easy Money* (1983), he took a *Harper's* magazine assignment to write an article on a group of left-wing *Nation* readers' trip to the Soviet Union. The result was one of his best travel pieces, a blend of his *Lampoon* style and a clear ideological approach—focusing mainly on the naiveté of peaceniks. His major impression of Russia was negative.

His account of that trip is ranked among his best writing. "The main point about his writing," notes London *Times* writer Peachment, "is that it tells the truth. His account of a trip to Russia is the most accurate I have ever read. . . ." O'Rourke's success with this *Harper's* piece led to a position at *Rolling Stone,* with book contracts to follow. His friends say that O'Rourke's charm and his approach allow him to get by with views that would attract brickbats to other authors. Part of O'Rourke's appeal lies in his eye for the bizarre. For instance, during student riots in Seoul, Korea, as roof tiles were raining around him, he took note of the spotless bathrooms.

A major reason for his success is an instinct for recognizing deeply felt public resentments and finding a market niche for them. A former colleague at the *Lampoon* writes, "A guy on the right wing with brains who's funny is so rare it's something he can do for years."

O'Rourke has been called a cultural analyst who plays to changing public prejudices. During the 1980s, with America cringing from the Iran hostage crisis and other worldwide humiliations, his ethnocentrism—often expressed in scatological terms—hit a familiar spark for a wide audience. Neither foreign nor domestic ethnic groups have escaped his rightwing wrath. His quips, a critic says, often are hysterically funny, but "they leave a tacky taste in the mouth." Foreign victims of his satire have been the easiest for him; favorite domestic targets are women, blacks, gays, and assorted racial minorities.

Modern Manners: An Etiquette Book for Rude People, written in 1983, was dedicated to the proposition that upper-class manners have unfortunately declined and that pseudomanners now have to suffice. A sample is "A hat should be taken off when you greet a lady and left off for the rest of your life. . . . Wearing a hat implies that you are bald if you are a man and that your hair is dirty if you are a woman."

As for humor, he says, "You always need a foil, you need a fool, you need someone who doesn't understand, somebody things have to be explained to. You need an idiot, and as long as I write in the first person, I've got one—and he can't sue."

His politics are a matter of conjecture. His publisher at *National Lampoon* writes, "The only person I know who claims P. J. O'Rourke is conservative is P. J. . . . I think P. J. is a humanitarian. He has classic liberal views about justice and humanity and economic and social justice and ethics." In his 1987 collection of magazine articles, *Republican Party Reptile,* O'Rourke writes:

> What I'd really like is a new label. . . . We are the Republican Party Reptiles. We look like Republicans, and think like conservatives, but we drive a lot faster and keep vibrators and baby oil and a video camera behind the stack of sweaters on the bedroom closet shelf. . . . We are in favor of guns, drugs, fast cars, free love (if our wives don't find out), a sound dollar, a cleaner environment (poor people should cut it out with the graffiti), a strong military with spiffy uniforms, Nastassia Kinski, Star Wars (and anything else that scares the Russkies), and a firm stand on the Middle East (raze buildings, burn crops, plow the earth with salt, and sell the population into bondage).

This uneven collection of essays also includes his now-infamous "How to Drive Fast on Drugs While getting Your Wing-Wang Squeezed and Not Spill Your Drink."

O'Rourke's 1988 *Holidays in Hell* is an outrageous account of his world travels to Europe and places like Lebanon and Nicaragua under the Sandinistas. His irreverent humor touches everywhere he mentions. About Nicaragua he writes, "I didn't think you could wreck a Central American country. I thought they came prewrecked from the time of the fall of classical Mayan civilization in 900 A.D. I didn't think you could make things any more depressing than they are in, say, El Salvador or the slums of Colon, Panama. But the Sandinistas had done it." He is equally scornful of Europe in the book. "The Europeans can't figure out which side of the road to drive on, and I can't figure out how to flush their toilets. . . . Plus there are ruins everywhere. The Italians have had two thousand years to fix up the forum and just look at the place."

After signing on with *Rolling Stone* in the early 1980s he traveled the globe chronicling civil unrest. This forum led to the Atlantic Monthly collection *Give War a Chance.* With some regularity he has written about the triumph of Western idealism. He admits he really did cry upon seeing an East German border guard reach through the Berlin Wall as it

Dust jacket for O'Rourke's essays on his travels to unpopular spots around the world

was being dismantled in 1989 to ask for a chip for a souvenir. "I was very affected," he says. "You know, any time you scratch a humorist, you find sentimental mush." He bears the title of foreign affairs desk chief for *Rolling Stone* that allows him the freedom to write in his "own style, to be able to express all those emotions, and never have to pretend to a journalistic omniscience–that great lie of objectivity."

In 1990 he married Amy Lumet, daughter of film director Sidney Lumet and granddaughter of singer and actress Lena Horne. For several years they split time between a sixty-acre farm home in Shannon, New Hampshire, and a spacious apartment in Washington, D.C. They divorced shortly after O'Rourke returned from the Gulf War.

Much of his writing is done on the New Hampshire farm in a home with five fireplaces, but he also keeps the apartment in Washington, D.C., where he records the foibles of American government. His 1990s books have focused on the U.S. government as a favorite target. *Parliament of Whores,* a scathing indictment of life on the Potomac, was on the best-seller lists for nearly a year and catapulted O'Rourke into the elite ranks of the Washington literati. In this volume he attacks the Supreme Court, the bureaucracy, and liberals. "A little government and a little luck are necessary in life but only a fool trusts either of them," he writes. "The whole idea of our government is: if enough people get together and act in concert, they can take something and not pay for it. . . . Every government is a parliament of whores. The only trouble is, in a democracy, the whores are us."

O'Rourke has long been considered one of the New Journalists, along with Thompson and Wolfe– who are also published regularly in *Rolling Stone*. He counts both writers as major influences on his own work, but he carefully distinguishes himself from Thompson. "Hunter and I are almost diametrically opposed in what we do," he told *Publishers Weekly*. "He takes a unique sensibility and uses it with very ordinary events–a police convention in Las Vegas, interviews with sports figures. I'm just the opposite: I take a very conventional, middle-aged, Midwestern sensibility to very peculiar places–busting crack dens, strange countries where people are shooting each other for semi-unintelligible reasons." A more important literary influence seems to be the writing of Mark Twain, especially in *Innocents Abroad* (1869).

The connection is one that O'Rourke himself intimates. The opening lines of his *Holidays in Hell* tell of Twain embarking in 1867 aboard the steamship *Quaker City* for a tour of Europe, Egypt, and the Holy Land with a group of tourists. The chapter is called "The Innocents Abroad, Updated." Twain was out to see the world with his own eyes and with good-natured scorn ripped away the romantic veil with which earlier travelers had adorned such exotic locations. As the forerunner and blood brother of the best literary journalists of all time, Twain was a worthy model for the jaundiced and cockeyed view of the world offered by O'Rourke.

During the Persian Gulf War, O'Rourke parachuted into Kuwait for ABC Radio News and *Rolling Stone* to get a firsthand view of the devastation left by the war and the jubilation of the liberation from Saddam Hussein's forces. His resulting chronicle, *Give War a Chance,* was one of the first books to have an eyewitness account of the Gulf War. He looked hard to find grounds for humor and eventually discovered a full complement of absurdities. Lack of alcohol, for example, O'Rourke says, caused him to lose ten pounds and meant a complete absence of bonding in the press corps.

All the Trouble in the World: The Lighter Side of Overpopulation, Famine, Ecological Disaster, Ethnic Hatred, and Poverty (1994) played the same notes as his earlier works. Many of the chapters are from his *Rolling Stone* articles. The book traces O'Rourke's travels around the world visiting the kind of places tourists avoid: Haiti, Somalia, Vietnam, Bangladesh, and the former Yugoslavia, where "the unspellables were shooting the unpronounceables." He observes that "overpopulation always has to do with people who look different from us–it never has to do with the Swedes or the French." He goes to great lengths to show that overpopulation in Bangladesh is less dense than in Fremont, California.

O'Rourke went to Haiti expecting to be revolted by the slums, but he found the citizens so courteous, charming, and law-abiding that he hoped that they could be swapped outright for South Florida's population of "crabby families in Winnebagos, drug smugglers, Disney executives, Palm Beach divorce lawyers, 2 Live Crew, Burt and Loni, time-share condo salesmen and the whole shebang."

He dwells on the point that the news media foist "fashionable worries" on the public. A good worry is one the media–who travel in packs, like lemmings–can make a good story out of, he writes. He is darkly skeptical of the ecological reporting that associates dwindling natural resources with impending disaster. "We run out of things all the time," he writes. "We're way out of whale oil."

Some reviewers of the book suggest that while O'Rourke is still funny he is not saying anything new. Mary Carrol of *Booklist* acknowledges that while some passages in the book are "as penetrating and funny as anything in O'Rourke's previous six books, the ax he has been grinding so long appears to be in danger of losing its edge." Others see his humor as merely bizarre. Carolyn See writes in *Book World* that O'Rourke is funny in an easygoing, mean-spirited sort of way. His mind is "in the barren steppes," she says, "so far to the right that if the political world were round, he might find himself in unmarked tundra belonging to the left."

Reminded that he keeps pointing out the world's problems without offering solutions, O'Rourke shrugs and says problem-solving is not part of his job description. "The beauty of being a journalist is that you get to point out problems, you don't have to solve them. You get to turn on the lights and watch the roaches scurry."

References:

Colin Covert, "The Court Jester of the Right," *Minneapolis Star-Tribune,* 5 April 1994;

Chris Goodrich, "PW Interviews: P. J. O'Rourke," *Publisher's Weekly,* 239 (16 March 1992): 60–61;

Bob Ickes, "Humor: P. J. O'Rourke–White Mischief," *New York,* 25 (21–28 December 1992): 126–127;

Florence King, "Damn Liberals," *New York Times,* 16 October 1994;

Peter Millar, "P. J. O'Rourke: Raving Reporter," *Times* (London), 27 November 1994;

Brian Wendell Morton, "Roving Stone: P. J. O'Rourke's Advocacy Is Fast, Funny and Offensive," *Washington Journalism Review,* 10 (September 1988): 22–25;

Sean Piccoli, "Taking on the Worrywarts," *Washington, D.C. Times,* 20 October 1994;

Michael Riley, "Of Cows, Scuds and Scotch," *Time,* 137 (15 April 1991): 58–59;

Carolyn See, "O'Rourke Sees World of Humor in Reality," *Chicago Sun-Times,* 2 November 1994;

Andrew Sullivan, "Is P. J. O'Rourke Squeezing Our Wing-Wang?" *Esquire,* 114 (August 1990): 126–130, 132;

Dick Teresi, "As Far from PC as Possible," *Wall Street Journal,* 18 October 1994.

George Plimpton

(18 March 1927 –   )

Sam G. Riley
Virginia Polytechnic Institute and State University

BOOKS: *The Rabbit's Umbrella* (New York: Viking, 1955);

Out of My League (New York: Harper, 1961);

Paper Lion (New York: Harper & Row, 1966);

The Bogey Man (New York: Harper & Row, 1968);

Mad Ducks and Bears (New York: Random House, 1973);

One for the Record: The Inside Story of Hank Aaron's Chase for the Home-Run Record (New York: Harper & Row, 1974);

One More July: A Football Dialogue with Bill Curry (New York: Harper & Row, 1977);

Shadow Box (New York: Putnam, 1977);

Sports!, text by Plimpton, photographs by Neil Leifer (New York: Abrams, 1978);

A Sports Bestiary, by Plimpton and Arnold Roth (New York: McGraw-Hill, 1982);

Fireworks: A History and Celebration (Garden City, N.Y.: Doubleday, 1984);

Open Net (New York & London: Norton, 1985);

The Curious Case of Sidd Finch (New York: Macmillan / London: Collier Macmillan, 1987);

The X Factor (Knoxville, Tenn.: Whittle Direct Books, 1990; revised, New York: Norton, 1995);

The Best of Plimpton (New York: Atlantic Monthly Press, 1990).

OTHER: *Writers at Work: The Paris Review Interviews,* 9 volumes, edited by Plimpton (New York: Viking, 1958–1992);

The American Literary Anthology, nos. 1–3, edited by Plimpton and Peter Ardery (New York: Random House, 1968, 1969, 1970);

Jean Stein, *American Journey: The Times of Robert F. Kennedy,* edited by Plimpton (New York: Harcourt Brace Jovanovich, 1970);

Pierre Etchebaster, *Pierre's Book: The Game of Court Tennis,* edited by Plimpton (Barre, Mass.: Barre, 1971);

George Plimpton *(International Portrait Gallery, Gale Research)*

Bernard Oldsey, ed., *Ernest Hemingway, The Papers of a Writer,* includes a chapter by Plimpton (New York: Garland, 1981);

Edie: An American Biography, edited by Plimpton and Jean Stein (New York: Knopf, 1982);

D. V., edited by Plimpton and Christopher Hemphill (New York: Random House, 1984);

Poets at Work: The Paris Review Interviews, edited by Plimpton (New York: Viking, 1989);

Women Writers at Work, edited by Plimpton (New York: Viking, 1989);

The Best of Bad Hemingway: Choice Entries from the Harry's Bar & American Grill Imitation Hemingway Competition, 2 volumes, edited by Plimpton (San Diego: Harcourt Brace Jovanovich, 1989–1991);

The Paris Review Anthology, edited by Plimpton (New York: Norton, 1990);

The Writer's Chapbook: A Compendium of Fact, Opinion, Wit, and Advice from the 20th-Century's Preeminent Writers, edited by Plimpton (New York: Viking, 1990);

The Norton Book of Sports, edited by Plimpton (New York: Norton, 1992).

SELECTED PERIODICAL PUBLICATIONS–UNCOLLECTED: "Dreams of Glory on the Mound," *Sports Illustrated,* 14 (10 April 1961): 112–114, 116, 118, 120, 122, 125–126, 128, 131–132, 134;

"Newport Notes: The Kennedys and Other Salts," *Harper's,* 226 (March 1963): 39–47;

"Miami Notebook: Cassius Clay and Malcolm X," *Harper's,* 228 (June 1964): 54–61;

"World Series with Marianne Moore," *Harper's,* 229 (October 1964): 50–58;

"World Champion Is Refused a Meal," *Sports Illustrated,* 22 (17 May 1965): 24–27;

"Celestial Hell of the Superfan," *Sports Illustrated,* 23 (13 September 1965): 104–106;

"But Why Me, Coach?," *Sports Illustrated,* 23 (13 December 1965): 18–21;

"Observations of a Rookie," *Saturday Review,* 49 (10 December 1966): 60–61;

"What the Deuce Is Going On?," *Sports Illustrated,* 27 (18 September 1967): 34–36;

"Strange Case of the Balls That Go Poof!," *Sports Illustrated,* 28 (22 January 1968): 28–31;

"Man, I'm Dropping Your Bag Right Here," *Sports Illustrated,* 29 (28 October 1968): 34–36;

"Stuff of Dreams," *Sports Illustrated,* 29 (4 November 1968): 36–38;

"Visions of Eight," *Sports Illustrated,* 39 (27 August 1973): 30–35;

"Pony Wars of Bloomfield Hills," *Harper's,* 247 (September 1973): 78–80, 82–84;

"Sportsman of the Year," *Sports Illustrated,* 41 (23 December 1974): 84–89, 93, 97, 98, 101;

"George Plimpton: Playboy Photographer," *Playboy,* 22 (January 1975): 189;

"But the Ivies Do Fight Fiercely," *Sports Illustrated,* 43 (8 September 1975): 29–39;

"World Series 1975, in Relief: Agony, Ecstasy, and Comedy," *Sports Illustrated,* 43 (3 November 1975): 28–30, 33–34, 36–37;

"Baseball Stories," *Harper's,* 252 (May 1976): 66–68, 70, 72;

"zzZZZZBOOMMM!! Aaaaaaahhhhhh!," *New York Times,* 30 June 1976, p. 37;

"Golden Fish Out of Water," *Sports Illustrated,* 45 (5 July 1976): 57–58;

"Final Season: Elegy for an Athlete Getting Old," *Harper's,* 254 (January 1977): 61–63, 66–67;

"Grand Old Hotels of the Orient, Part I," *Holiday,* 58 (March 1977): 42+;

"Grand Old Hotels of the Orient, Part II," *Holiday,* 58 (April 1977): 36+;

"These Sporting Poets," *Harper's,* 254 (May 1977): 76–79, 82;

"Plimpton's Peroration," *New York Times,* 30 June 1977, p. 19;

"Un gran pedazo de carne," *Audubon* (November 1977): 12–25;

"Bozo the Bruin," *Sports Illustrated,* 48 (30 January 1978): 54–60, 62, 64;

"First Family of Fireworks," *New York Times Magazine,* 29 June 1980, pp. 24–26;

"Costing Out Iran," *Harper's* (July 1980): 60–64;

"Paper Tourist: A Yank in Moscow," *Time* (4 August 1980): 32–33;

"A Frisbee over Moscow," *Time* (11 August 1980): 28–29;

"Islands of Paradise," *Reader's Digest* (November 1980): 207–214;

"Birds Thou Never Wert," *Sports Illustrated* (4 January 1982): 82–86, 88, 90, 93, 94, 96;

"Sly Stallone Scores Another K.O. with Rocky III–and Readies an Alter Ego for the Ring," *People* (21 June 1982): 92–93, 95, 97–99;

"Safecracking Leads to TV's Biggest Opening: The Safe of the Andrea Doria," *People* (20 August 1984): 121–122, 125;

"More Than Just a Token Effort," *Sports Illustrated* (23 September 1985): 30–32, 37;

"Literary Lair: Freddy and George Plimpton in Sagaponack," *Architectural Digest,* 44 (June 1987): 126–131;

"A Sportsman Born and Bred," *Sports Illustrated* (26 December 1988): 140–144, 146–148, 152, 154, 157–158, 160;

"The Wild Blue Yonder," *Sports Illustrated* (3 April 1989): 64–66, 71–72, 74;

"Across the River and into Harry's Bar," *New York Times,* 16 April 1989, VII: 1;

"The Creative Uses of Disability, the Restorative Functions of Art," by Plimpton and Jean Kennedy Smith, *New York Times,* 11 June 1989, p. 26;

"Poetry Man: Sonnets in Silicon," *Computerworld* (31 October 1989): 3–5;

"A Fired-Up 4th," *USA Today,* 3 July 1990, p. A1;

"Return to Spender," *Esquire,* 115 (1991): 50–53;

"How to Face a Firing Squad," *Esquire,* 115 (June 1991): 52–55;

"Don Juan of Gramercy Park," *The Independent* (17 November 1991): 32– ;

"Truman Capote's Black-and-White Ball: Was This the Greatest Party?," *Esquire,* 116 (November 1991): 134–140, 177;

"The Smaller the Ball, the Better the Book: A Game Theory of Literature," *New York Times,* 31 May 1992, VII: 16;

"Hanging Out: A Vote for Political Humor," *Esquire,* 118 (October 1992): 109;

"A Reluctant 'Mambo King,'" *USA Weekend,* 14 March 1993, p. 14;

"1970: The First Marathon," *New York,* 26 (19 April 1993): 122;

"Self-definition: Courage," *Self,* 15 (June 1993): 170;

"In the Night Kitchen," *People* (7 June 1993): 42–48;

"Always Stand on Ceremony," *Esquire* (October 1993): 84;

"Final Twist of the Drama," *Sports Illustrated,* 80 (11 April 1994): 86–88, 92, 94, 96, 98–99, 100, 102;

"On the 19th Hole," *New York Times,* 24 April 1994, VI: 30;

"Spotting the Literati in Their City Lairs," *New York Times,* 16 September 1994, C1;

"My Last Cobra: Stalking the Wild Prevarication," *Harper's,* 289 (September 1994): 73–77;

"Birds of Paradise," *Travel Holiday* (October 1994): 79–83, 104;

"The Goose Is Out of the Bottle," *Wall Street Journal,* 31 March 1995, A12;

"Smashing Game, But Not What It Used to Be," *Wall Street Journal,* 5 May 1995, A10;

"Golfing–In the Swing," *Gourmet,* 55 (May 1995): 70, 247–248;

"Playgrounds of Privilege," *Golf Digest,* 46 (June 1995): 108.

Among literary journalists George Plimpton is so unusual that he marches not just to a different drummer but more nearly to a different orchestra. His reputation rests on a unique assortment of accomplishments that began in his twenties when he became editor of a literary magazine, *The Paris Review,* and then extended at a gentlemanly pace into book and magazine writing. Most of his books con-

cern sports and their appeal, as do many of his articles. What makes his handling of this subject matter so unusual is his approach: that of a "professional amateur." By briefly participating in the sporting events he writes about, Plimpton is able to achieve a perspective different from that of the mere observer, an approach complemented by his droll, arch, patrician, essentially British writing style. Finally, he has achieved his widest fame via the true mass medium of the century–television–in specials aired on ABC in the 1970s and 1980s, most of which show Plimpton the participant, observer, and perpetual dilettante attempting to "play with the big boys" at various sports, in musical performances, and even on the flying trapeze. Throughout it all, everything he has touched has been marked with the indelible stamp of the individual.

George Ames Plimpton was born on 18 March 1927 in New York City, one of the four children of Wall Street corporate lawyer Francis T. P. Plimpton and Pauline Ames Plimpton. Unlike many other well-known authors, Plimpton has written little about his youth, possibly due to its ease and prosperity. He joined his parents for tennis at Cold Spring Harbor Beach Club, attended St. Bernard's School in New York City and Exeter Phillips Academy, where he wrote for the school paper, *The Exonian.* From 1945 to 1948 he served in the army, attaining the rank of second lieutenant. He then attended Harvard, where he wrote for and later edited the *Lampoon.* In a *Writer's Digest* interview Plimpton recalled having drawn a cartoon for that humor magazine so badly done that it was printed upside down. He was, he said, the only one to notice. He majored in English, taking one course from Archibald MacLeish. After graduating with an A.B. in 1950, Plimpton went on to King's College, Cambridge, where he earned two degrees: a B.A. in 1952 and an M.A. in 1954. While still at Cambridge, Plimpton, twenty-six, accepted an invitation to become editor in chief of a new literary magazine based in Paris. Its founders were Peter Matthiessen, who went on to write *The Snow Leopard* (1978) and *At Play in the Fields of the Lord* (1965), and Harold L. Humes, author of *The Underground City* (1958) and *Men Die* (1959). The first issue of *The Paris Review* appeared in spring 1953, and Plimpton has remained its editor since that time.

The Paris Review is said to have been conceived in a bar in Montparnasse, the Chaplain, a place about which William Styron remarked that one could write his name in the cigarette smoke with his finger. By the time Plimpton arrived in Paris to assume his new position, the watering place of choice was the Café de Tournon, located close to the make-

Whitey Ford, Plimpton, and a Yankee batboy after Plimpton's experience pitching to an all-star lineup of National League and American League players in 1961 (photograph by Garry Winogrand)

shift office of *The Paris Review* on rue Garancière. Among Plimpton's *Paris Review* colleagues were managing editor John Train, art director William Pene du Bois, operations manager Tom Guinzburg, and associate editor Eugene Walter. Matthiessen served as fiction editor, and the magazine's first publisher was Prince Sadruddin "Sadri" Aga Khan, half brother of the better-known Aly Khan and second son of the enormously wealthy Muslim ruler the Aga Khan. Though the prince took little part in the operation of *The Paris Review,* he convinced his father to endow an annual prize for fiction. Not only did the Aga Khan fund the competition, but he also promptly entered it with two short stories of his own. To his credit, he continued the prize even though his stories were not selected as winners.

Plimpton's first years as *The Paris Review* editor were spent in post–World War II Paris, which in that time of favorable exchange rates attracted a large and flourishing community of literary-minded expatriates who fell into three camps: the Beat Generation writers, whose guiding light was poet Gregory Corso; black writers such as James Baldwin and Chester Himes; and the writers who, like Plimpton, worked for the city's so-called little magazines. *The Paris Review* was but one of several such literary magazines published in the city at the time. Com-

petitors were the French *Les Temps Modernes* and two other American titles, Sindbad Vail's *Points* and *Merlin,* edited by Alex Trocchi and others. *The Paris Review* had the advantage of wealth behind it and was the only one of the English-language periodicals that was not short-lived. Plimpton and his cohorts were, in the main, well-supported, well-connected Ivy Leaguers, better able than their competitors to continue an enterprise that was foreordained by its very nature to remain innocent of monetary profit. Also, the concept of the magazine was to avoid taking strong ideological or political stands, to steer clear of the pedantry of university-style literary criticism (which has become even more ingrained thanks to the deconstructionists), and instead to print—and pay for—creative new material, both prose and poetry. The magazine's aims were explained in a preface to the initial issue by writer William Styron who wrote *The Confessions of Nat Turner* (1967), *Sophie's Choice* (1979), and who who also lived in Paris at that time.

Another unusual feature of *The Paris Review* was that in place of the usual literary criticism, Plimpton and his fellow editors decided from the first issue to embark upon a series of stories based on interviews with famous writers about writing. In the maiden issue appeared P. N. Furbank and

F. J. H. Haskell's interview with E. M. Forster, whom the American audience has learned to know better through movie adaptations of his novels *A Room with a View* (1908), *Howards End* (1910), and *A Passage to India* (1924). In the more than forty years that have followed that first issue *The Paris Review* interviews have included a rich array of literary lights, from William Faulkner, Robert Penn Warren, Françoise Sagan, Ezra Pound, Marianne Moore, T. S. Eliot, Aldous Huxley, Ernest Hemingway, and Mary McCarthy in the early years to the more recent additions of Rebecca West, Carlos Fuentes, Bernard Malamud, Philip Larkin, John Barth, and Philip Roth. These interviews in question-and-answer format have been collected as *Writers at Work: The Paris Review Interviews*. Only a few writers—J. D. Salinger, Aleksandr Solzhenitsyn, and Thomas Pynchon, for example—have refused the invitation to be interviewed.

The Paris Review has been an unusual literary magazine indeed: it has continued publication for more than forty years. Many such periodicals are stillborn, and most live a short and fitful life one step ahead of the bill collectors, their backers ever surprised that a large reading public does not share their interest in the delicate sensibilities of belles lettres. In his 1961 book *The Overreachers* Gay Talese briefly relates the role Plimpton played after he instead of Harold Humes who accepted the role of managing editor, was chosen as editor of *The Paris Review*. Certainly Plimpton was the better connected of the two—he had once escorted the future queen of England to a ball. Humes had returned to the United States by the time the first issue of the magazine appeared. Put out over Humes's refusal to perform his duties, the staff of the magazine removed his name from the masthead as managing editor and inserted it under advertising and circulation. According to Talese, Humes, apprised of this change, met the ship carrying the U.S. copies at the dock in New York and rubber stamped his name in its proper place on as many copies as he could.

After four years Plimpton and *The Paris Review* moved to New York City. Plimpton's bachelor apartment on East Seventy-second Street became known for its frequent parties attended by the literary set and beautiful people of other stripes.

Plimpton worked from 1956 to 1958 as an instructor at Barnard College. During this period he conceived the idea of a career based in part on writing as a participant-observer. In the introduction to his 1990 book *The Best of Plimpton* he remarks that he drew this idea from the much earlier book *Farewell to Sport* by sportswriter Paul Gallico, a man who had boxed with Jack Dempsey, golfed with Bobby Jones, and attempted an Olympic ski run—all in the interest of a better story. It occurred to Plimpton that he might carry this scheme further; he chose as his first venture a foray into the favorite sport of his youth—baseball. "Dreams of Glory on the Mound" in the 10 April 1961 *Sports Illustrated* described Plimpton's pregame pitching to both sides in a Yankee Stadium all-star game between players of the National League, led by Willie Mays, and the American League, captained by Mickey Mantle. *Sports Illustrated* offered a $1,000 prize to the team that scored the most runs. Soon thereafter Harper and Brothers published *Out of My League* (1961), a fuller account of this episode. Plimpton's version of being on the mound in such circumstances ("Mostly you hear your own voice—chattering away, keeping you company in your loneliness") and his simile-rich description of his fellow players, such as his catcher going after a pop-up, stomping around "with his face upturned like a Piute praying for rain," got good notices. Acting out Everyman's fantasy and describing the experience with self-effacing commentary and solid reporting laced with unusually detailed description and characterization gave his newfound career a strong start. They also made *Sports Illustrated* a regular outlet for his work, and in 1967 he was named a contributing editor.

Plimpton's earlier books had been limited and entirely different in subject matter from his later ones. His first effort was a children's book, *The Rabbit's Umbrella* (1955), which he wrote in Paris "to have something to do." He had also edited the first volume of *Writers at Work: The Paris Review Interviews,* which appeared in 1958. By 1961, however, the dual nature of his life as a writer-editor was set: his participatory adventures with their attendant books and articles on the one hand and his *Paris Review*–based literary editing on the other.

In "Newport Notes: The Kennedys and Other Salts," a March 1963 feature in *Harper's,* Plimpton took a mildly irreverent look at Newport, Rhode Island, "the place of the grand gesture"; the America's Cup yacht race; and President John Kennedy, who, with Plimpton and others, watched the races from aboard the destroyer *Joseph P. Kennedy Jr.* An especially nice touch in this account is Plimpton's juxtaposition of the patrician goings-on of the yachtsmen and the puerile rock music to be heard everywhere on transistor radios ("Sherry . . . won't you come out tonight?").

Jim Gibbons, Plimpton, and Nick Pietrosante on the Detroit Lions bench. His experiences as an understudy quarterback became the basis for his most successful book, Paper Lion *(1966) (photograph by Walter Iooss Jr.).*

Another noteworthy article for *Harper's* (June 1964) was "Miami Notebook: Cassius Clay and Malcolm X," a sort of color story built around the Sonny Liston fight. Plimpton contrasts the essentially good-natured theatrics of Clay with the bitter outlook of his spiritual adviser, Malcolm X. Plimpton continued his association with *Harper's* and in 1972 was named associate editor.

Plimpton demonstrates his range in a pair of *Sports Illustrated* stories that appeared in late 1965. The first was "Celestial Hell of the Superfan," a humorous look at individuals who go to any length to be around their idols—professional football players. Aside from the team owners, who must pay millions of dollars for this privilege, he introduces readers to the likes of Abraham Abraham, who held the job of retrieving footballs used for field goals and extra points for the Cleveland Browns, and Lovely Boatwright, a restaurant owner who attended San Francisco 49ers games wearing a Harpo Marx wig and carrying an air

horn. This humorous feature was followed three months later by the poignant "But Why Me, Coach?," an account of New York Giants backup defensive tackle Mike Bundra's "Blue Monday," the day he was cut from the squad.

Then in 1966 Harper and Row brought out Plimpton's most successful book, *Paper Lion*. Having practiced for three weeks with the Detroit Lions as an understudy quarterback and having learned several plays, Plimpton played in a preseason scrimmage. Wearing jersey number zero, a number symbolic of what he himself later termed his "eccentric flailings," he lost twenty-nine yards during the four plays he was allowed to run. The success of the article resulted from his training and playing in the game, which enabled him to "get inside the sport" in an unusual way and exercise his flair for vivid, almost sociological description.

Plimpton's second book as a participant-observer of football began as the idea of Detroit Lions offensive guard John Gordy, often referred to as "The Bear" due to his excessive body hair. Gordy wanted to do a how-to book for and about linesmen, players who often feel unappreciated compared to their teammates with more glamorous positions. Tackle Alex Karras, known as "The Mad Duck" because of his on-field gait, would write about defensive line play, Gordy about offense; Plimpton would serve as editor. Then in 1971 Plimpton began preparing for a televised special by training for a month with the Baltimore Colts, again as quarterback. Plimpton emerged as sole author, and the book became an account of his pigskin exploits, with Gordy and Karras providing colorful, often hilarious anecdotes. This time pitted against the Detroit Lions, Plimpton managed one six-yard gain out of several plays. The results were a Wolper Productions special, the book *Mad Ducks and Bears* (1973), and stories in *Sports Illustrated* and *Harper's*.

After his success with *Paper Lion* Plimpton turned his attention from football to golf, a game he had played since age twelve and at which he had an eighteen handicap. Through *Sports Illustrated* he arranged to play in three West Coast pro-am tournaments—the Bing Crosby, San Francisco's Lucky International, and the Bob Hope Desert Classic. Again, actually taking part, however ineffectually, allowed Plimpton to "get inside" the game, though the fun of his having done so was diminished somewhat for the reader because this time he was participating in a sport played by other people more nearly like himself rather than by the rougher, tougher, less tutored players of football or boxing. Still, with all new equipment and a diminutive caddy named Abe, he set out to match strokes with the pros–with predictable results. His golf book carried the playful title *The Bogey Man* (1968). Years later, in 1980, he played in the Crosby for a second time, having golfed so infrequently in the interim that he thought of his game, he wrote in "My Crosby" (*Sports Illustrated,* 2 February 1981), "as a distant family relative who may be all right but about whom rumors persist." His foursome included a fellow duffer, actor Jack Lemmon, who followed an especially inept shot with the quip "Life is an irreplaceable divot."

Plimpton's excellent social connections have resulted in, among other things, a variety of writings about the Kennedy family. The most extensive of these is a 1970 book, the first of two oral history projects Plimpton edited with interviewer Jean Stein. *American Journey: The Times of Robert F. Kennedy* presents the results of 347 interviews arranged to form an oral narrative of two journeys: Robert Kennedy's life as described by his friends and associates, and the funeral train from New York to Washington as related by those on board and by onlookers who watched the train pass. Much later, in the 7 June 1993 *People* magazine story "In the Night Kitchen," Plimpton, who had been a Harvard classmate of Kennedy's and who was walking just ahead of the senator when he was shot by Sirhan Sirhan, gave an inside view of the assassination and of Sirhan's capture.

In 1981 Plimpton spoke at a dinner commemorating the opening of the Hemingway Room designed by I. M. Pei at Kennedy Library outside Boston. The president's widow and about one hundred Hemingway scholars attended; Plimpton described to this audience a social evening at the White House during which the president surprised him with a story about Plimpton's maternal grandmother, whose father was Civil War Union general Adelbert Ames. Following the war Abraham Lincoln named Ames Reconstruction governor of Mississippi, and in his book *Profiles in Courage* Kennedy painted an unflattering picture of Ames. Plimpton's grandmother Blanche Ames took offense and sent Kennedy a steady stream of letters requesting a retraction. The president asked for Plimpton's help in getting her to stop. She did stop but wrote a book of her own, *Integrity* (1964), which she completed in her eighties. Plimpton also reported the story in "JFK and Hemingway," his chapter in *Ernest Hemingway, The Papers of a Writer* (1981), edited by Bernard Oldsey.

Finally, after the death of Jacqueline Kennedy Onassis, Plimpton wrote "Remembering Jackie," which ran in the "Talk of the Town" section of the 30 May 1994 *New Yorker.* Plimpton included his recollection of a party the first lady gave in 1965 for her two children and their friends at Newport. The festivities featured a buried treasure chest and a mock battle between parents on the shore and a longboat full of "pirates," one of whom was Plimpton.

On 28 March 1968 Plimpton married Freddy Medora Espy, who before their marriage worked in a New York photography studio. The couple have two children, a daughter and a son. Divorced in 1980, Plimpton married Sarah Dudley on 31 December 1992. Twin daughters were born on 14 October 1994.

Pierre's Book: The Game of Court Tennis, which Plimpton edited for Pierre Etchebaster, appeared in 1971. Court tennis, the ancestor of the modern game, was played by French royalty and called *jeu de paume.* Only a handful of courts still exist; two are in the Racquet Club on New York's Park Avenue. In 1974 Plimpton authored a less esoteric book–sans participation–on baseball great Hank Aaron's topping of Babe Ruth's thirty-nine-year-old record of 714 home runs. While *One for the Record* lacks the wit and sparkle of his participant-observer accounts, it nevertheless presents a vivid portrait of the unassuming, workmanlike Aaron as he moved in on the record.

With the publication of *Shadow Box* (1977) Plimpton's abilities at writing humor reached full flower. The book is an amalgam of boxing lore: boxing history from the great Jack Jackson to the English boxer Fainting Phil Scott, "the Horizontal Heavyweight," alias the "Swooning Swan of Soho," plus considerable material on Muhammad Ali. The heart of the book, however, is, in vintage Plimpton style, the account of his own exhibition bout with heavyweight champ Archie Moore. The author writes of his dislike of boxing, which dated from his school days when he and his classmates were required to box in gym class "with enormous gloves tied to our pipestem arms." He describes a malady from which he suffers–sympathetic response. In short, when he is hit, he weeps. Despite these drawbacks and a gentlemanly adulthood during which he had never been called upon to strike anyone, he had come to regard boxing as the ultimate contact sport, hence the ultimate challenge, and decided upon this sport for his next misadventure. Pictures of the bout in Stillman Gym (New York City) show the 6'4" author looking impossibly gangly next to the compact, muscular Moore, who entered into the spirit of the affair, only once hitting the writer hard enough to make his nose bleed.

Most of Plimpton's writing is marked by a reasonably generous amount of droll, self-deprecating humor, but his second humorous crescendo came some years later in *Open Net* (1985), the story of his experience on the ice as a goalie for the Boston Bruins. In this sport his problem was weak, wobbly ankles, an affliction that he described as rendering him the same height whether wearing skates or barefoot. The climactic moment of the book came when his teammates contrived to give the opposing team a penalty shot, which Plimpton would have to defend single-handedly. Windmilling out of the goal toward the shooter, Plimpton fell down, looking "like the collapse of an ancient sofa," and the puck hit one of his skates, missing the goal, perhaps the closest thing to success he had yet accomplished in professional athletics.

In an address he gave at a New York Philharmonic luncheon Plimpton told his audience that the most frightening experience he had had in participatory journalism was not being hit by three-hundred-pound linesmen or slugged by the light heavyweight champion, but facing the wrath of conductor Leonard Bernstein on those occasions in 1967 and 1968 when he was an honorary member of the percussion section of the orchestra. For this assignment the writer's background had been childhood music lessons and a modest ability at piano—he had once tied with an eleven-year-old girl for third place in an amateur competition at Harlem's Apollo Theater—in which the limit of his ability, he said, was "Deep Purple" and "Tea for Two." Touring with the orchestra in Canada in 1968, his rendering of the sleigh bells in Mahler's Fourth Symphony during a London, Ontario, performance so upset the maestro that he fired Plimpton on the spot. Bernstein later relented and allowed Plimpton to strike the gong in a Winnipeg performance of Tchaikovsky's Second Symphony. Bernstein directed Plimpton to look directly at the podium during the performance as he awaited his big moment, saying, "Don't look down at the music. We all know you can't read music. You don't fool anybody when you turn the pages." Luckily, Plimpton struck the gong a crashing blow at just the right moment, and thereafter, whenever Bernstein wanted fortissimo from the gong, he would demand "the Winnipeg Sound." On an earlier occasion Plimpton had told Garry Valk, publisher of *Sports Illustrated,* that his most intimidating experience had been playing a rubber

of bridge partnered with bridge maven Oswald Jacoby, who, like Bernstein, became upset. Plimpton added, "My sense of mental inadequacy was much more excruciating than pain."

A year prior to the publication of *Open Net,* Plimpton had authored a book on one of his favorite hobbies, fireworks. In *Fireworks: A History and Celebration* (1984) he presents various milestones, disasters, and disappointments, such as Princess Diana's dissatisfaction over her wedding fireworks display. In this well-illustrated book Plimpton also tells of his own pyrotechnic exploits, such as taking part in setting off the largest "bomb" ever built, Fat Man II, which weighed seven hundred pounds. *D. V.,* the story of Diana Vreeland, coedited with Christopher Hemphill, also appeared in 1984. In 1989 Plimpton published *Women Writers at Work,* a book of excerpts from *Paris Review* interviews.

As Plimpton's reputation grew he was increasingly in demand as a speaker. In late June 1977 he addressed Harvard graduates as Class Day speaker, telling them (according to "Plimpton's Peroration" in *The New York Times,* 30 June 1977) "Stop! Go on back to your rooms. Unpack! There's not much out here." As for himself, he continued to find new material. In November of that year *Audubon* magazine ran his story "Un gran pedazo de carne," a tale of high-profile birdwatching about his expedition to the remote mountains of western Mexico in search of the imperial ivory-billed woodpecker, the largest of that species in the world. The trip was led by serious professional birder Victor Emanuel, who had received reports of sightings of one of these rare and now probably extinct birds. Their search was unsuccessful. In a hard-to-reach mountain area they met a Mexican logger, and Emanuel asked in Spanish if the man had seen such a bird. The man replied he had shot it for supper, volunteering that it was "un gran pedazo de carne"—a great piece of meat. With typical anticlimax Plimpton added, "Victor said he couldn't bring himself to ask him how it had tasted."

From time to time Plimpton has returned to the topic of birding. "Birds Thou Never Wert" is a long *Sports Illustrated* article (4 January 1982) in which he describes the serious birders' custom of adopting a "nom de plume" (pun intended), usually that of a fairly rare bird. Plimpton himself is known as Hadada Ibis. The article constructs the "perfect bird"—a composite of the finest features of actual birds, then a similar composite of the world's worst bird. In the October 1994 *Travel Holiday* Plimpton regales the reader with another

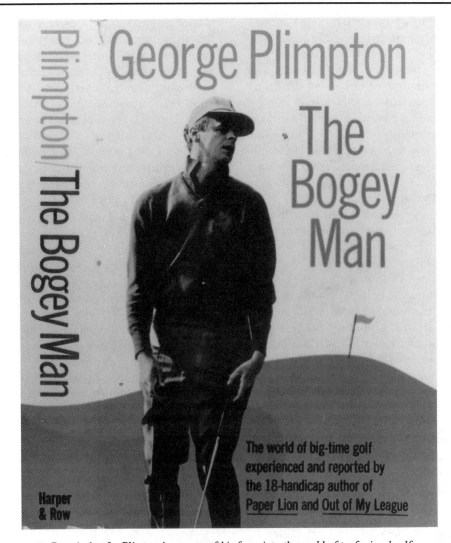

Dust jacket for Plimpton's account of his foray into the world of professional golf

Victor Emanuel–led tour, this time to Bhutan to view the rare black-necked crane. Such articles have made Plimpton a favorite choice of *The New York Times* book review desk for birding field guides, coffee-table bird books, and the like.

One of Plimpton's zaniest articles appeared in the November 1979 *Harper's*. His "The Snows of Studiofiftyfour," a discotheque in which the snow was not the usual kind, described writer Truman Capote supposedly just released from a fat farm, "his face lifted and perky as a jackal's under the bandages and his rear end tucked up and river-smooth." While there, Capote had begun his enemies list and, wrote Plimpton, had had to use the Dewey decimal system to arrange it. Bizarre footnotes identified John Kenneth Galbraith simply as "a tall crane-like economist" and Gore Vidal's latest book as a roman à clef "entitled *Roman a Clef,*" the story of "an Eskimo family's at-

tempt to settle in Old Westbury, Long Island. An absorbing treatment of a neglected theme."

Plimpton's love of the unusual again surfaced in the July 1980 *Harper's*. "Costing Out Iran" he represents as being about a friend who had once costed out the naval barrages fired by U.S. ships in Vietnam. The largest shells were called "Cadillacs" since the cost of one shell was nearly equal to that of a Cadillac. Plimpton raises the question of what would have happened had the navy dropped luxury cars into the jungles rather than shells. The remainder of the article asks what might have been done with the reported $13 billion spent to bring home the Americans held hostage in Iran. He suggests, tongue-in-cheek, a sort of pension fund and calculates that if the $13 billion had been used in this way, it could have netted each hostage around $2 million a year.

Desirous of finding a way to mingle the intellectual and the athletic in covering the 1980 Moscow Olympics—the games boycotted by the United States, *Time* magazine sent Plimpton as its representative. Time printed two color stories by Plimpton in August of that year. His first thought, he wrote, was to pack a few items to confound the Soviet customs authorities: a single boxing glove or a whoopie cushion, for example. He settled instead for a Frisbee, which he sailed from his hotel window under cover of darkness, commenting that "you think a lot about trajectories over there." As his means of communication he describes his reliance on "curious pidgin words, rather the way the Sioux talk in old western films."

The November 1980 *Reader's Digest* carried Plimpton's offbeat travel article "Islands of Paradise," condensed from its February 1979 appearance in *Sports Illustrated*. The story concerns the Seychelles, a group of islands off East Africa that had experienced an armed coup in 1977. Of this event Plimpton commented, "It is no big heroic deed to take over the Seychelles. Twenty-five people with *sticks* could seize control." Among other things he wrote about an island culinary "delicacy" called *chauve-souris,* made from a giant bat, and about his successful spotting of the rare black parrot that lives there.

In 1982 Plimpton helped edit *Edie: An American Biography,* the oral history story of willowy, beautiful, but troubled Edie Sedgwick, who died at age twenty-eight in 1971 after having spent the 1960s on the fast track as a *Vogue* model, would-be actress, and protégé of artist-filmmaker Andy Warhol. She came from a well-connected Massachusetts family whose prominence dates from the Revolution; a noteworthy relation of more recent vintage was Ellery Sedgwick, who edited the *Atlantic Monthly* around the turn of the twentieth century. Plimpton knew the Sedgwicks during his Long Island boyhood and helped Jean Stein edit the transcripts of the innumerable interviews she had taped in gathering information on Edie Sedgwick's pampered childhood, neurotic youth, and drug-laced twenties. The book captures something of the "swinging sixties," at least as lived by New York's artsy-drugsy crowd.

The X Factor (1990) is a slender volume in which Plimpton reflects on that hard-to-pin-down something that sets off the champion from his or her less successful competitors. Plimpton borrowed the term "X Factor" from tennis star Billy Talbert, who originated it in the 1950s. This elusive difference, Plimpton concludes, is a combination of singleness of purpose, ability to focus, positive thinking, intuition, toughness, and perseverance. Success in athletics is compared to success in business, a not unfamiliar theme, and this little book might be regarded as "Plimpton Lite." The book was published by Whittle Direct Books as part of its Larger Agenda series, featuring little books by big writers on topics of interest to business leaders. *The X Factor* is oddly interrupted by one-page advertisements for Federal Express. A more traditional revised edition was published by W. W. Norton in 1995.

Far more satisfying is Plimpton's other 1990 book, *The Best of Plimpton.* This collection is an excellent representation of his writing career and is organized into five sections: sports participations, people once interviewed (including poet Marianne Moore, literary agent Irving "Swifty" Lazar, actor Warren Beatty, and writers Hunter S. Thompson and Norman Mailer), places (Newport, Las Vegas, Elaine's Restaurant in New York City), indulgences (fireworks, birding, humor), and a coda (comments from the funeral of fireworks great Jimmy Grucci and from his own father's funeral). Readers unfamiliar with Plimpton's work might find this book a useful starting point.

In November 1981 *Sports Illustrated* ran a Plimpton color story written from the fan's point of view. Specifically, it tells of a "Christmas present" the writer gave his nine-year-old daughter Medora—tickets to her first Harvard-Yale football game. The game held scant interest for her, and Plimpton's account of his cheering for Harvard and her restless shivering includes the following bit of revealing dialogue:

> "Are they losing?"
> "I'm afraid so."
> "How much longer will it take them to lose?"

Father and daughter left early, of course.

People ran a Plimpton interview with action movie star Sylvester Stallone in June of the following year. The interview was conducted in the actor's Pacific Palisades home amid the "shine of the Nautilus machinery," the heavy punching bag, the wolf-skin rug, and the bronzes of fighting animals. The story was built around another Stallone "prop," however—an enormous Italian American heavyweight named Lee Canalito whom Stallone was grooming for a ring career. Canalito would be, Stallone told Plimpton, everything that the actor would like to be in reality but could be only on screen.

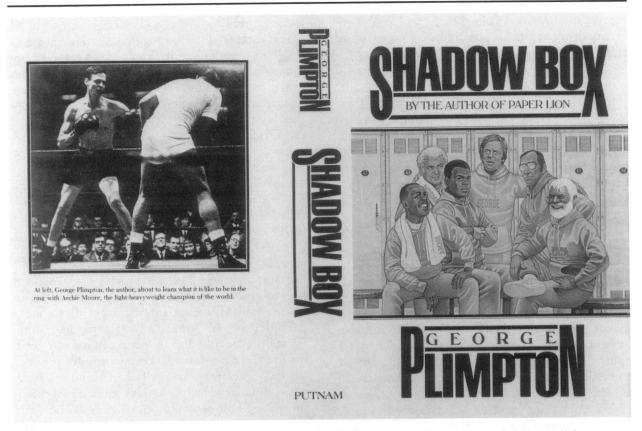

Dust jacket for Plimpton's book on boxing, which includes an account of his exhibition bout with light-heavyweight champion Archie Moore

Two months later Plimpton's work again appeared in *People,* this time an account of plans for the much-publicized televised opening of the safe from the ship *Andrea Doria,* which had collided with another vessel and gone down off Nantucket in 1956. Plimpton was to serve as master of ceremonies while master locksmith Sal Schillizzi of Queens, New York, cracked the safe, which had been salvaged and kept in a tank at the New York Aquarium at Coney Island. What, Plimpton mused, would he find to say if the safe contained nothing at all? His premonition proved true—only a few lira notes were found within.

These stories were pleasant enough but received little attention compared to the hornet's nest Plimpton stirred up with the fourteen-page April Fool's Day story he concocted in 1985 for *Sports Illustrated.* This elaborate hoax centered on one Hayden "Sidd" (for Siddhartha) Finch, an English orphan adopted by an eminent archaeologist who later died in a plane crash in Nepal. Finch, now twenty-eight, played French horn, had studied Zen at a monastery in Tibet, and, aided by mysterious mantras, had developed the ability to throw a baseball at 168 MPH, roughly 60 MPH faster than any pitch ever clocked. He had never

played baseball but had been hired, Plimpton wrote, as a rookie pitcher by the New York Mets. His stiff-armed pitching style was reminiscent of the way Goofy pitched in Disney cartoons. The Mets gleefully cooperated. Various players posed for photos that accompanied the story and gave the hoax added credibility, and Mets management helped string the media along before the spoof was unmasked. Although most of the blizzard of mail *Sports Illustrated* received about the put-on was positive, some fans and sportswriters were outraged that anyone would dare kid about the holy topic of baseball. Even though the first letters of the lead spelled out "Happy April Fool's Day" and no harm was done to anyone, much righteous blathering about alleged harm done to journalistic credibility issued forth from various journalists.

Two years later the *Washington Post Magazine* ran its own April Fool hoax. In this eleven-page account the Washington Senators, whose final game had taken place in 1971 before the team became the Texas Rangers, was returning to the nation's capital. Howls of protest resulted again. As for Plimpton, his character Sidd Finch went on to become the protagonist in the writer's first novel, *The Curious Case of Sidd Finch* (1987). Plimpton added a love interest, a blond surfer and Duke University dropout Debbie Sue, and a great deal more detail from the world of professional baseball.

Plimpton's magazine articles during the remaining years of the 1980s were a varied lot. "More Than Just a Token Effort" in *Sports Illustrated* (23 September 1985) found Plimpton trying out the New York subway system—not his customary mode of transportation—just in case the next World Series might pit the Mets against the Yankees. As in his sports participation adventures, the appeal of the story lay in the incongruity of the patrician riding with Joe Average Strap Hanger.

Architectural Digest ran "Literary Lair: Freddy and George Plimpton in Sagaponack" in June 1987. The story, written by Plimpton himself, showcases the couple's summer residence, which they had purchased from the poet Elizabeth Vreeland. Photos show views of the tastefully furnished house, though the article's main interest lies in Plimpton's discussion of the virtual writer's colony that had sprung up in that Long Island community. At night, he writes, "the word processors glow green in the windows."

A fifty-nine-hundred-word *Sports Illustrated* piece, "A Sportsman Born and Bred" (26 December 1988), is Plimpton's portrait of President-elect George Bush as the greatest sports enthusiast of all America's chief executives since Bush had taken part throughout his life in fishing, hunting, wrestling, soccer, tennis, golf, baseball, bicycling, and horseshoes. The writer summarized the favorite sports of other presidents from Lincoln to Reagan and devoted the rest of the story to portraying Bush's delight in sporting competition. Of special interest are the terms the Bushes employ to describe their games, such as calling out "Power outage!" after a weak tennis shot or characterizing an inept backhand that barely makes it over the net as "the falling leaf" shot. An eight-hundred-word sidebar in the same issue presents Plimpton's account of his defeat at horseshoes by Bush and his son George Bush Jr. Plimpton's book *The X Factor* tells the story of his equally unsuccessful rematch with President Bush at Camp David during a sporting weekend that also included golf, tennis, skeet shooting, and even tiddlywinks. This account was adapted for various newspapers, including *The New York Times* and the *San Francisco Chronicle,* in April 1994.

In April 1989 *Sports Illustrated* ran "The Wild Blue Yonder," a typically offbeat Plimpton story in which he takes his son Taylor to an ice hockey game at Madison Square Garden, where they sit within earshot of the lower-priced section known as "the blues" because of the color of the seats. Plimpton describes the deafening torrent of profanity that flowed from the blues and the outfits and other New York Rangers paraphernalia worn and carried by these vocal fans. The story is essentially a clash of eccentricities: gentleman eccentric observes blue-collar eccentrics.

In April 1989 Plimpton promoted the sale of his forthcoming book *The Best of Bad Hemingway: Choice Entries from the Harry's Bar & American Grill Imitation Hemingway Competition* (1989–1991) with a thirty-two-hundred-word piece in *The New York Times.* The story, headlined "Across the River and into Harry's Bar," attributes the 1978 origin of the contest to one Paul Keye, who was seeking a way to generate publicity for the Harry's Bar in Florence, Italy. Hemingway, one of the most parodied of all American writers, had mentioned the Harry's Bar in Venice in his own writing, so Keye conceived a competition to produce the best single page of really bad Hemingway. A panel of judges—including Jack Hemingway; Bernice Kert, author of *The Hemingway Women*; and California newspaper columnists Jack Smith and Herb Caen—culled twenty finalists from the twenty-five-hundred entries eventually submitted over the incredible eleven-year length of the contest. A sample of this work appeared in Plimpton's article under the subhead "The Pun Also Rises." The story includes lines such as "'Oh, pooh,' swore the girl. 'I can't bear it when you're like this'" and "Nick sat against the wall at Harry's drinking his dry martini with courage and with grace." But the far limits of the pun itself were surely tested in this snatch of contest dialogue:

"Do you remember George Tell?"

"Yes," said Frances. "He was a swell bowler, For whom does Tell bowl now?"

"Poetry Man: Sonnets in Silicon" appeared in *Computerworld* (31 October 1989), which describes its writer as "avowed nontechnologist, author and noted famous person George Plimpton." In this thirteen-hundred-word story Plimpton visits a computer-minded friend, Michael Newman, who had developed software called Poetry Processor that helps would-be poets follow the poetic form of choice: blank verse, Spenserian stanzas, or, in Plimpton's case, the Shakespearean sonnet. For his computer-generated sonnet Plimpton chose tennis as his topic. The sonnet was to be written from the point of view of the tennis ball. In just more than an hour Poetry Processor had generated such lines as:

> Green, fuzzy, hollow, are we, born to light
> But locked inside a gloomy tomb of tin.
> But then a hiss of air . . . the sun in flight
> We slap against the gut of cats, and spin.

The early 1990s brought three additional Plimpton-edited books. The first, *The Writer's Chapbook* (1990), rearranges material from *Paris Review* interviews into handy subject categories such as literary forms, writing techniques, and the like. Also in 1990 appeared *The Paris Review Anthology,* Plimpton's choices from among the four hundred fiction pieces and more than one thousand poems that had appeared in *The Paris Review.* Also included is a modest amount of nonfiction prose, among which is his own story "Vali," a 1950s portrait of a young Australian-born girl who lived *la vie Boheme* in Paris and did strange, Beardsley-like drawings.

Most recent is *The Norton Book of Sports* (1992), an anthology of quality sports literature selected by Plimpton. He used this book as a chance to rehash a brace of "theories" he had derived years earlier. The Small Ball Theory's thesis is that the smaller the ball, the better the literature. The Uh-Oh Theory asserts that the more dangerous the sport, the more memorable its literature. Having set up this structure, and having admitted its exceptions, Plimpton imposes the additional structure of seasons of the year when various sports are most often played. Then he makes his selections, which begin with Mark Twain's "The Celebrated Jumping Frog of Calaveras County," in which the "ball" used was tiny indeed: birdshot. Some of his choices were written by major literary figures such as Thomas Wolfe, Carl Sandburg, James Joyce, and Robert Penn Warren. Some were by writers known for their use of humor: James Thurber, Ring Lardner, P. G. Wodehouse, Don Marquis, and Woody Allen. Others were the work of journalists: Mike Royko, Paul Gallico, and Red Smith. He closes the book with his own adaptation of material from Lee Green's book *Sportswit* (1984), which presents well-known, sports-related quotations ("The bigger they are, the harder they fall," "Nice guys finish last," and "He can run, but he can't hide," for example) with the circumstances of their origin. Also included is the full script for comedians Bud Abbott and Lou Costello's classic comedy routine "Who's on First?"

"A Fired-Up 4th," in the 3 July 1990 issue of *USA Today,* found Plimpton, New York City's honorary fireworks commissioner, in a quandary as to where best to celebrate the Fourth of July. This article offers historical tidbits about the invention and development of fireworks and discusses several kinds of shells—Saturns, butterflies, willows, and strobes—plus their major manufacturers, most of which are family-owned firms of Italian origin. In the article's artful conclusion Plimpton remarks, "I can never remember the names of the Seven Lively Arts, but I know what the Eighth should be."

The November 1991 *Esquire* carried a lavishly illustrated feature story in which Plimpton recalls the formal ball that writer Truman Capote threw "for 540 of his closest friends" at New York's Plaza Hotel on the evening of 28 November 1966, ostensibly to cheer up *Washington Post* publisher Katharine Graham, who was guest of honor. Other revelers were Lee Radziwell, William Styron, Norman Mailer, John Kenneth Galbraith, Lauren Bacall, and William F. Buckley Jr. In addition to his feature stories Plimpton wrote an *Esquire* column, "Hanging Out," which ran from February 1991 to June 1992. Examples of topics are a visit to *Playboy* founder Hugh Hefner after the birth of his second child by wife Kimberly and a reflection on the on-court invective of tennis star John McEnroe.

Just prior to the appearance of Ben Sonnenberg's autobiography, *Lost Property: Memoirs & Confessions of a Bad Boy* (1991), Plimpton visited its author, who was bedridden with multiple sclerosis, and wrote "Don Juan of Gramercy Park" for the *Independent* (17 November 1991). Plimpton notes the irony that after a scapegrace youth as the dissolute son of a rich father, Sonnenberg went on to found the important literary magazine *Grand Street,* named for the Lower East Side street where his father lived after arriving, penniless, as a Russian immigrant. Sonnenberg and Plimpton shared the experience of having lived for a while in England. The most striking quotation coming out of this interview is Sonnenberg's remark about "the effortless rudeness of the English upper classes. It took my breath away." "A Reluctant 'Mambo King,'" an interview with 1990 Pulitzer Prize–winning writer Oscar Hijuelos, author of *The Mambo Kings,* appeared in *USA Weekend* (14 March 1993). Perhaps the strangest of Plimpton's recent interview stories, however, appeared in the Spring 1994 *Paris Review.* Its subject is Harvard-educated artist Walter Channing.

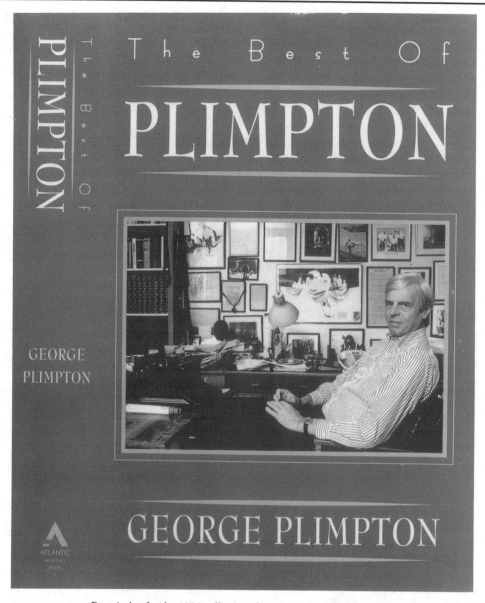

Dust jacket for the 1990 collection of representative Plimpton essays

Other recent magazine pieces include a one-pager in the October 1993 *Esquire*. "Always Stand on Ceremony" relates Plimpton's tips and reminiscences about the gentlemanly art of toast giving. One suggestion for anyone called upon to offer a toast is to use the Zulu equivalent of "Bottoms up," which, Plimpton reveals, is "Oogy wawa," certainly preferable to the garbled version of that familiar toast that Plimpton says was offered by a Russian diplomat at a state dinner: "Up your bottoms."

Cocktail party banter was responsible for another Plimpton article, "My Last Cobra: Stalking the Wild Prevarication," in the September 1994

Harper's. Plimpton had had his elbow lanced to relieve a bout of bursitis, and, tired of telling people the real reason his arm was in a sling, he told someone that he had been bitten by a small cobra while birding in Bhutan. The story relates his discomfort upon receiving various calls from people who heard this news, including his mother, his sister, and, worst of all, a Roosevelt Hospital poison expert who wanted all the details.

Finally, *The New York Times* (16 September 1994) printed Plimpton's "Spotting the Literati in Their City Lairs: a Guide." Mentioned are Elaine's, the modern Algonquin; the Knickerbocker; the Nuyorican Poets Café; Time Café;

Limbo; Anseo; the White Horse Tavern; and The Lion's Head—all favored by writers of one kind or another.

Plimpton's life and career have included many other unusual experiences. In a Harvard student prank he once leaped into the Boston Marathon two blocks shy of the finish line and still managed to lose. In 1954 he fought the bulls (actually calves) with Ernest Hemingway and on another occasion received an unwanted boxing lesson from that bellicose writer. He contrived to play a set of tennis against Pancho Gonzales, losing 6–0, and swam against Don Schollander. He went into a Boston Celtics game for two minutes, replacing John Havlichek. He performed as a stand-up comic in Las Vegas, in 1971 was "guest conductor" of the Cincinnati Symphony, and photographed the centerfold for the January 1974 *Playboy* magazine.

Plimpton has had several minor flirtations with Hollywood by doing bit parts. He played a Bedouin in *Lawrence of Arabia* in 1962, appeared in *The Detective* in 1968, was the mayor in *Beyond the Law* (1968), and was shot by John Wayne in *Rio Lobo* (1970), tried to seduce Diane Keaton in Warren Beatty's *Reds* (1981), played Tom Hanks's father in *Volunteers* (1985), and Richard Nixon's lawyer in Oliver Stone's *Nixon* (1995).

Plimpton became known to a wider cross-section of the American public via television specials on ABC. Most, but not all, have been extensions of his participatory journalism. Perhaps the most entertaining of the lot was *Plimpton! The Man on the Flying Trapeze* in 1970. Here, the 6'4" writer found his size and shape singularly unsuited to this line of work, yet the viewer simply had to admire his courage for trying. Each time the bar reached the bottom of its arc, Plimpton would sink like a stone into the safety net. Other television specials showcased his amateur film acting, stand-up comedy act, football, and the like. One in 1972 was about his safari into Kenya in an attempt to photograph an unusually large elephant. Also, in 1983 he began as host of a children's program, the Disney Channel's "Mouseterpiece Theater."

Plimpton has also lent his name and presence to several events, including an annual backgammon tournament in Los Vegas as well as the George Plimpton Celebrity Challenge Cup Harness Race. One of these, held in Pompano Beach, Florida, in spring 1987, was won by George Steinbrenner, owner of the New York Yankees. Other participants were two football stars, a champion pool player, and designer Oleg Cassini, who provided the contestants with special racing silks.

Time described Plimpton, who finished last, as "a tall, gangly man, who resembled a preppy, perpetually disoriented tropical bird."

Throughout his long, unusual career the Great Participator has remained popular and has, for the most part, managed to avoid crossing swords with anyone aside from his staged competitions. One exception was mentioned by Alexander Cockburn in his column "Beat the Devil" in the 10 June 1991 issue of *The Nation*. Plimpton had edited three volumes of *The American Literary Anthology*, wherein he published work taken from various "little magazines." The funding was provided by the National Endowment for the Arts. He was assailed by Iowa congressman William Scherley for spending tax money on reprinting a one-word poem by Aram Saroyan. The word was "lightht." Plimpton lost his grant but actively raised money for liberal Tom Harkin, who defeated Scherley in the next election.

Plimpton's career as a literary journalist largely has been founded upon the appeal of contrast. First, there is the internal element of contrast: on one hand, the serious editor of belles lettres, on the other, the purveyor of entertaining journalistic nonfiction and televised specials. Foremost is the contrast that he himself presents vis-à-vis the people he has competed against in his myriad adventures: the tweedy, genteel literary figure at play on the turf of rougher, more hardbitten types, the bon vivant amid serious athletes, and the amateur generalist head to head with professional specialists. He has delighted in this role—in his much-publicized participations and even in fantasy. For example, in *The Best of Plimpton* he details his "plan" to become a professional wrestling manager. He would hire a behemoth, call him "the Grecian Urn," and train him to quote poetry while hurling opponents to the mat. Plimpton has used the element of contrast in many of his stories, such as "Studiofiftyfour," in which he produces a parody of Truman Capote writing in the style of Hemingway—truly a contrast of personality types. Also appearing in *The Best of Plimpton* is his account of having introduced the frail, birdlike poet Marianne Moore to boxing great Cassius Clay, who promptly suggested that he and Moore write a poem together about his next fight. Taking turns, each writing a line at a time, they penned "A Poem on the Annihilation of Ernie Tyrell."

Plimpton has enjoyed a career unlike that of any other literary figure—journalist, author, editor, or otherwise. He still edits *The Paris Review*, a literary magazine that has printed early work by such writers as Philip Roth, Mary Lee Settle, and

Jay McInerney and that receives around fifteen thousand submissions a year. He has authored or co-authored fifteen books and has edited or coedited twenty-two more. He continues to entertain readers with articles in a variety of magazines and newspapers and in his on again–off again "other life" in television. His varied accomplishments render his career hard to sum up, but a quotation he himself used in *The Norton Book of Sports* from poet Donald Hall, who once, Plimpton-like, played with the Pittsburgh Pirates, says it fairly well: "Half my poet friends think I am insane to waste my time writing about sports and to loiter in the company of professional athletes. The other half would murder to be in my place."

References:

"All Yesterday's Parties," *New Yorker,* 70 (27 June–4 July 1994): 44;

Elliott Anderson and Mary Kinzie, eds., *The Little Magazine in America: A Modern Documentary History* (New York: Pushcart Press, 1978), pp. 525–534;

Alexander Cockburn, "Democrats, Trade, Workers," *Nation* (10 June 1991): 762–763;

Mark Fitzgerald, "An April Fools' Day Hoax," *Editor & Publisher* (20 April 1985): 7–8;

"Focus on George Plimpton," *Harper's Bazaar* (November 1973): 103, 134–135, 142;

David Jeffrey Gaines, "The Sun Also Sets: American Writers in Paris After the Second World War," dissertation, University of Texas at Austin, 1980;

Malcolm Jones Jr., "Major-League Man of Letters," *Newsweek* (14 January 1991): 22;

Pat Jordan, "In Florida: Sweet Charity," *Time,* 129 (13 April 1987): 9–11;

James Ledbetter, "Paper Literary Lions: The Paris Review Gets in Step," *Village Voice,* 36 (11 June 1991): 30;

D. Lloyd, "Interview with George Plimpton," *Writer's Digest* (June 1974): 17–18;

Alan Nadel, "'My Mind Is Weak but My Body Is Strong': George Plimpton and the Boswellian Tradition," *Midwest Quarterly,* 30 (Spring 1989): 372–386;

"Remembering Jackie," *New Yorker,* 70 (30 May 1994): 34–35;

Mordecai Richler, "The Paris Review Is a Movable Feast," *Gentlemen's Quarterly,* 59 (October 1989): 183, 186;

"A Swinging Walter Mitty," *Time* (7 April 1967): 40;

Gay Talese, *The Overreachers* (New York: Harper & Row, 1961), pp. 103–119;

Garry Valk, "Letter from the Publisher," *Sports Illustrated,* 23 (13 September 1965): 4;

Bruce Weber, "Spurious George," *Esquire,* 104 (November 1985): 243;

Clark Whelton, "Paper Plimpton," *Esquire,* 85 (January 1976): 115–117, 142, 144, 146.

Rex Reed
(2 October 1938 –)

A. J. Kaul
University of Southern Mississippi

BOOKS: *Do You Sleep in the Nude?* (New York: New American Library, 1968);
Conversations in the Raw (New York: World, 1970);
Big Screen, Little Screen (New York: Macmillan, 1971);
People Are Crazy Here (New York: Delacorte, 1974);
Valentines and Vitriol (New York: Delacorte, 1977);
Travolta to Keaton (New York: Morrow, 1979);
Personal Effects (New York: Arbor House, 1986).

Rex Reed's meteoric ascent into the media establishment in the 1960s was launched on a quick-fire reputation for being "the hazel-eyed hatchet man" whose "bitchy," "gossipy," "intimate," and "ferocious" first-person celebrity profiles rewrote the rules of interviewing. Celebrity profiles earned him star billing among an emerging coterie of New Journalists who redefined nonfiction writing and resurrected its literary status. In 1968, three years after his first celebrity interviews appeared in New York's elite press, *Time* magazine called the twenty-nine-year-old Reed "the most entertaining new journalist in America since Tom Wolfe and the most unprincipled knave to turn name dropping and voyeurism into a joyous, journalistic living." His novel and six collections of interviews and criticism have drawn harsh reviews from critics who chastised him for his "camp sensibility" and "smart ass" commentary on popular culture.

Born on 2 October 1938 in Fort Worth, Texas, Rex Reed is the son of an oil company field supervisor, Jimmy M. Reed, and Jewell Smith Reed. Because his father's job required extensive travel, Reed grew up in a succession of southern oil boom towns, attending thirteen different public schools before graduating from Natchitoches High School in Louisiana. Always being "the new kid" was "a terrible thing," he told a *Newsweek* magazine interviewer in 1968. "I withdrew from it all," Reed said, "and went to the movies every afternoon." In his introduction to *Do You Sleep in the Nude?* (1968) he recalls: "My memories of that period are all mixed up

Rex Reed (International Portrait Gallery, Gale Research)

with Betty Grable musicals and greasy pit barbecues and people dancing around bonfires doing the Bunny Hop." In 1956 he entered Louisiana State University in Baton Rouge, where he majored in journalism and wrote for the college newspaper. An anti-segregation editorial he wrote, "The Prince of Prejudice," prompted the local Ku Klux Klan to burn him in effigy.

Reed was more interested in drama and theater than journalism during his college years. "I was a peculiar student . . . getting involved in plays, painting scenery," he said in a *Writer's Digest* interview in 1973, adding:

> I only majored in journalism because it was the easiest thing I could do. . . . I made A's in everything except, ironically enough, Feature Writing. . . . I thought I was writing terrific stuff. . . . I'd start a piece by describing the color of the sky that day, and they'd say, "What is this? Nobody'll read this.". . . The only way to make any kind of name for yourself in journalism is to be totally original and fearless and throw your style in it—I mean just throw it at them. These are things journalism professors throw their hands up in shock over.

When he left Baton Rouge with a bachelor's degree in 1960, Reed headed straight to New York City to start an acting career, using his journalism skills to support his theatrical efforts. For five years he performed in what he called "that miserable streetwalking nadir that all actors find themselves in, looking for a job and trying to audition for people—walking out on stages and reading cold with two hundred other people—and that was a terrible time in my life because I was literally broke." He wrote public-relations publicity for entertainment-industry press agents, including a seven-month stint as a $56.50-a-week copy boy for 20th Century-Fox.

Freelance movie reviews for *Cosmopolitan* magazine's entertainment editor, Liz Smith, led to his first professional job in New York as the magazine's film critic. "I was riding on a crest of my own perfume," he observed about this period. The perfume faded fast. Two months later Helen Gurley Brown became *Cosmopolitan*'s editor, and she fired the opinionated film critic. "It was one of the more memorable encounters in my life," he recalled. "I remember going in and she was sitting on top of her desk in her Bonnie Doon panty stockings and her false wig and her false teeth and her false nose and her false breasts . . . and a little Pucci dress pulled up to her thighs, and she said:

> "Now dear, I don't want you to be personally insulted by the fact that I am firing you, because there are so many writers who will never be able to work for me because they have opinions, too. Gloria Steinem, Joan Didion. . . ." So I said, "And probably Gay Talese." She said, "No, I'll never be able to use her either."

Two celebrity interviews published in 1965 launched his writing career. He traveled to Venice, where he interviewed an old and fragile Buster Keaton—"The Last Interview Buster Keaton ever gave," Reed claimed. Reed typed the interview on the back of stationery stolen from the Venice Film Festival public-relations office and sent it with borrowed stamp money to *The New York Times,* which paid him

$125. Reed earned $150 for his interview with Jean-Paul Belmondo that the *New York Herald Tribune* published. "I had two checks in Venice—enough to pay my hotel bill and enough to get home on," he recalled. "And when I got back to New York I had all of these job offers, and I've never been out of work since."

Reed continued contributing to *The New York Times* and placed articles in *Esquire* and other magazines, a move calculated to increase his cachet in the New York media marketplace. In 1967 alone Reed earned $25,000 for the seventy-five articles he turned out, and *New American Library* paid a $5,000 advance for the collection of his interviews published under the title *Do You Sleep in the Nude?* "You know, it's really like the measles—once you get it everybody gets it, and when your name is published in New York there is this very circumspect little group of people in journalism who immediately take notice," Reed observed in an interview with *Writer's Digest* in September 1973. "I mean, all you have to do is to be published once in the *Sunday Times* or in *Esquire* and suddenly everybody is aware of a new writer on the scene." A stinging *Esquire* article published in August 1967, "Will the Real Warren Beatty Please Shut Up," boosted Reed's notoriety and so incensed the actor that he threatened to sue the magazine for libel. "Reed's trouble is that he leaves nobody cold," *Esquire* editor Arnold Gingrich commented. "There's usually a flap afterward and we have to go around cleaning up after him."

In 1968 *Newsweek* and *Time* magazines published gushing profiles of Reed in their respective "Press" sections. His articles are "a theater of cruelty" and "Swiftian examinations" of the famous that had "rewritten the rules of interviewing," *Newsweek* wrote. "He is part of the story. . . . Members of the fourth estate often complain that he had forfeited journalistic objectivity in his pursuit of involvement." *Time* (23 August 1968) called Reed "the Now Kid," "the jet set's latest instant celebrity," and "a fascinating gossip who has recast the interview format in his own bitchy image." Reed readily agreed with the assessment, telling *Newsweek* (8 January 1968):

> It was time for someone to step in and write the truth. . . . For years people didn't know celebrities went to the bathroom. They were always glossed over in cornball, press-agentry terms. The public won't settle for pap anymore. It wants its copy bitchy. I tell it like it is. Everybody knows that actors are the most neurotic people in the world so why write a piece that reads like "Snow White and the Seven Dwarfs?"

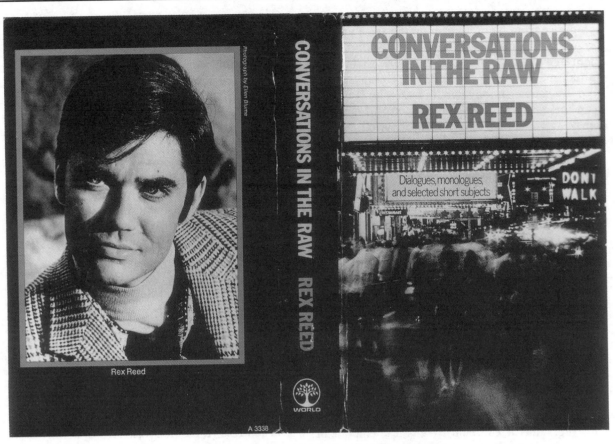

Dust jacket for Reed's second collection of celebrity interviews

The notoriety lavished on Reed opened more media doors to him: he became music critic for *Stereo Review* (1968–1975), film critic for *Holiday* and *Women's Wear Daily* (1968–1971), and film critic and syndicated columnist for the *New York Daily News* (1971–1975). Reed, who made appearances in the films *Myra Breckenridge* (1970) and *Superman* (1978), became in 1986 the critic for a public television series "At the Movies" and a columnist in the 1990s for the *New York Observer*.

Do You Sleep in the Nude? collected previously published celebrity profiles that established Reed's reputation as votary and executioner, revealing a personality that seemed to possess both a killer instinct and a genuine sense of compassion. Sympathetic portraits of show-business grande dames—Lucille Ball, Marlene Dietrich, and Angela Lansbury, among others—were matched with caustic profiles of Michelangelo Antonioni, Warren Beatty, and Barbra Streisand. In *Newsweek* Reed confessed to a fascination for stylish over-forty women: "The old broads are the ones who interest me the most. Nothing bores me more than these miniskirted girls with nothing on their minds." Critics chastised Reed for writing about some celebrities, notably Warren

Beatty and Barbra Streisand, with what they saw as personal animosity. "I have never set out to destroy anybody," he countered. "If I see somebody is basically an s.o.b. but underneath is real, then I say they're a nice s.o.b. I don't go to any interviews ever with a preconceived idea. I give people the benefit of the doubt and if they hang themselves that's their problem." To Reed, Beatty came across as boorish, childish, insecure, and self-possessed; he said Streisand looked like a spoiled, self-indulgent brat.

Reed's poignant profile of forty-four-year-old film star Ava Gardner, titled "Ava: Life in the Afternoon," drew the attention of Tom Wolfe, who included the article in his anthology, *The New Journalism* (1973), and declared that Reed "raised the celebrity interview to a new level through his frankness and his eye for social detail. He has also been a master at capturing a story line in the interview situation itself." Wolfe added that "Reed is excellent at recording and using dialogue." Reed's unique interview style came to be called the "Rex Reed treatment," referring to a mix of first-person commentary, observation, and extensive quotation candidly used to reveal the idiosyncrasies and foibles of the personalities he profiled.

Reed's collection *Do You Sleep in the Nude?* won high praise from Nora Ephron on the same page of *The New York Times Book Review* (21 July 1968) that celebrated Joan Didion's masterwork of literary journalism, *Slouching Towards Bethlehem* (1969). "Rex Reed is a saucy, snoopy, bitchy man who sees with sham eyes and writes with a mean pen and succeeds in making voyeurs of us all," Ephron writes. "If any of this sounds as if I don't like Rex Reed, let me correct that impression. I love Rex Reed." The piece that captured Ephron's attention was a "loving interview" with Carson McCullers, her last, during a visit to the Plaza Hotel in New York City. One quotation in the interview seemed a kind of epitaph and found its way into many obituaries after McCullers died on 29 September 1967. "Sometimes I think God got me mixed up with Job," McCullers said. "But Job never cursed God and neither have I. I carry on."

Reed's admiration for the author of *The Heart Is a Lonely Hunter* (1940) and *The Member of the Wedding* (1946) sprang from their friendship. "She read a lot of my fiction before she died," Reed told an interviewer in 1973. "She was very encouraging. She wanted me to write fiction." Reed's admiration for McCullers extended to an abiding respect for southern writers that he consciously sought to emulate in his literary journalism. "I've always admired that Southern school of writing which is heavily descriptive and uses imagery and uses metaphors and similes a lot," he said. "I've always liked that, and I've always thought that it could be applied to journalism to make it more interesting . . . and that's what I've tried to do." His journalistic influences include Gay Talese's profiles for *Esquire* magazine and Truman Capote's coverage of the "Porgy and Bess" tour of Russia, published as *The Muses Are Heard* (1956). "I also admired the economy and clean style of J. D. Salinger," Reed noted. "When I was growing up, he was my idol . . . and I used to write short stories about people committing suicide in Schrafft's and I would copy him, really try to write like J. D. Salinger."

Reed's second collection, *Conversations in the Raw* (1970), contained material previously published in *The New York Times, Holiday, Women's Wear Daily, Cosmopolitan,* and *This Week,* printed, according to Reed, "the way it was originally written instead of, in some cases, the way it was later published." *Conversations in the Raw* collected vintage Reed interviews. Of Bette Davis he says, "Froggy-eyed, lipstick-slashed or glowing like a Tiffany lamp, she is exciting enough . . . to make the nubile youth cultists about as interesting as a withered logarithm." About Jane Wyman he writes: "Joan Crawford sells Pepsi, Veronica Lake waits on tables . . . and when last heard from, Hedy Lamarr was still trying to get a new Diner's Club card. . . . Well, don't worry about Jane Wyman." Reed describes the admirers of James Earl Jones, then appearing in *The Great White Hope,* as people who are "worshipping at the shrine of that new 20th century hero, the black man who is 'making it.'" Following his interview with George Sanders, Reed portrayed the actor as a sad, if soulful, creature: "He sat back on the bed, spent, like a gruff child who has been lashing out at everyone because he stubbed his toe—sad, passionless, exasperating, but strangely touching. As I left, I wished him luck. 'Don't bother, I shan't need it. I have no friends, I have no interests, I have no plans. . . . I have nothing left to say. . . . I just want to be left alone.'" In the same book Reed describes a televised Miss U.S.A. beauty pageant as a "cattle auction." "The only difference is that the winning cow gets a movie contract," he quips. "You know what that means. Miss U.S.A. invariably ends up as a topless waitress serving cigars in the background of a Rock Hudson flick. Gives her something to tell her grandchildren." The fortieth anniversary of the Walt Disney Studio's Mickey Mouse cartoon character on network television turned into "a bloated billboard to advertise other Disney products," Reed observes. "Thanks to the greediness of commercial television advertising, he couldn't get a squeak in edgewise."

The celebrity profiles that garnered Reed his reputation as a literary journalist deflected attention from his descriptive evocation of geographic cultural icons. *Conversations in the Raw* closes with "Malibu," a vignette that deftly weaves historical backdrop and scenic description with a first-person social commentary and satire about the beachfront summer playground of Hollywood stars. "For nine months of the year, this ugly little collection of motels and empty Coke bottles looks like any other boring retirement center marked by a bright flag on a Medicare map." Reed continues:

> Then comes June, when it all starts happening. The movie stars and jet-set buddhas pack up their sneakers, their coconut oil, their martini mixers, their poodles and the kids from all their previous marriages, and head for the sea, descending on Malibu like sand crabs in their blue jeans and their Yves St. Laurent chain belts. Then, for as long as the summer sun lasts, they get stoned on pot, barbecue everything but the delivery boys from Western Union, and work like hell to make their summer rent money pay off.

Reed spent three months living and writing in Malibu, ending his sojourn with the conclusion that

ISBN: 0-440-09336-8

Dust jacket for the 1977 collection of Reed's interviews

"Malibu . . . is not so much a place to live as it is a way of life."

One critic, Henry Flowers, in *The New York Times Book Review* (9 November 1969) thought *Conversations in the Raw* was simply a remake of *Do You Sleep in the Nude?*, that it merely offered "big chunks of quotes running the gamut from bitchiness to nostalgia to that brand of superficial self-revelation show figures specialize in." The interviews and sketches in the book displayed Reed's talent, but, according to Flowers: "Reed's is a severely limited talent. He's not that sharp a reporter, and he is an erratic (at times hopelessly gushing) film critic." Reed, claiming to have "total recall," bristled at the criticism. "No one has ever been able to pin me down on anything inaccurate," he told *Writer's Digest* in 1973. "I've never misquoted anybody or anything." His "built-in encyclopedia of trivia" about his interview subjects, he claimed, was so extensive that he rarely needed to do any background research. "I usually just go cold and try to write a piece that's like a movie: I just try to photograph the whole meeting." His major credential as a film critic was having been a movie buff from childhood. "I think those are the only require-

ments for being a critic, anyway," Reed said. "All you need to know, really, is what movies are all about and you have to have a built-in history of the industry. You have to know everything everybody's ever done, seen most of the movies ever made, and I had that."

Reed's next book, *Big Screen, Little Screen* (1971), collected his film and television criticism from such publications as *Women's Wear Daily, Holiday,* and *The New York Times.* In a piece in *Women's Wear Daily* (1 March 1968) Reed challenges network television executives to clean up "the sado-masochistic bloodletting running rampant all over the dial" during Saturday-morning children's cartoon programming. He takes special notice of the cartoon "Road Runner," in which one of the characters "gets electrocuted, stampeded, knocked unconscious, and crucified week after week to gales of sweet childish laughter." A televised verbal joust between liberal novelist Gore Vidal and conservative publisher William F. Buckley–Buckley called Vidal "a producer of perverted Hollywood prose," and Vidal countered by calling Buckley "the Marie Antoinette of the right wing"–during the 1968 Republican convention prompted Reed to remark that they "ended up looking like *The Boys in the Band* impersonating two Ken dolls in heat."

Reed delights in pricking prime-time television entertainers with his acerbic wit, calling the star of a network television private-eye show "a prepackaged instant-defrost Italian caballero from the Polo Lounge of the Beverly Hills Hotel with the class of a chianti cork and the style of a store window dummy at Robert Hall." Former "Tonight Show" host Johnny Carson is "the most overrated amateur since Evelyn and Her Magic Violin," and singer Nancy Sinatra, star of a network special, is "a hash-slinger slumming it up in an Andy Warhol movie."

Reed unleashed some of his most strident invectives against pop artist Warhol and the camp sensibility of the underground cinema of the 1960s. In "The Home Movie as Porny Put-On" Reed explains the popularity of Warhol's profitable avantgarde films ("peep shows") as the world's "spoofing itself, sending itself up." He writes that "Commerce is a dirty word, sex without orgasm is as much an everyday experience as watering the geraniums, enthusiasm has been slowly and agonizingly replaced by ennui. . . . Warhol pictures were the next rung on the ladder toward the ultimate obscenity—the self send-up." In Reed's view, "Warhol was just a trend, a phase of our self-corruption." Characters in Warhol's films appear like "inmates trying to get out of the pages of Dante before they go to press . . . they make no statement, they make no point, they cannot be taken seriously." Warhol's first full-length film, *Chelsea Girls* (1966), is "a 3 1/2-hour cesspool of vulgarity and talentless confusion . . . about as interesting as the inside of a toilet." "Lonesome Cowboys," says Reed, is a "circus side-show of fag hags and homosexuals . . . improvising a piece of humorless trash on horseback. . . . The 'cowboys' look like Hollywood Boulevard drag queens who just looted Teepee Town. They get stoned on pot, talk about getting their hair done and ride around on worn-out nags on their last legs before the glue factory."

People Are Crazy Here, published in 1974, is a collection of forty previously published sketches and interviews with Hollywood film stars, rock performers, and writers. In the introduction to this book Reed declares that what he looks for in his interviews and profiles are "the eccentricities, ambiguities and irreparable ego damages that set famous people apart from the folks next door, make them controversial, and keep them dancing recklessly on the lip of the volcano." In "The Complete Guide to the Hollywood Society Game" Reed describes "the social caste system" in Hollywood as "the biggest thing since strip monopoly," something that Hollywood hostesses pursue with ledger books that clas-

sify the "in-crowd" based on the parties they have attended.

"Think of the Hollywood social scene," Reed advises, "as Vietnam—an expensive war game in which nobody wins." The social structure has three levels: "Group A" is comprised of "generals who map out the strategy . . . where all the action is (but not necessarily the fun)"; "The Fun Group" is commissioned officers who "couldn't care less about their social status as long as they are having a good time"; and "Group B" is "enlisted men who try too hard, name-drop, social-climb, and seldom relax or enjoy themselves."

Reed's interview with Tennessee Williams reveals a playwright who, according to Reed, is "convinced he has breast cancer only a doctor in Bangkok can cure." The best-selling author of *Valley of the Dolls* (1966) and *The Love Machine* (1969), Jacqueline Susann, whom Truman Capote once called a "truck driver in drag" on national television, took her revenge on Capote in a Reed interview, calling Capote "poor thing," and saying to Reed, "You realize, don't you, that he has never written a full-length novel in his life. . . . He hasn't written a book since 1965."

Critics called *People Are Crazy Here* (1974) "boutique penny candy" with a "fan magazine style" that nevertheless made many of the sketches "revealing and amusing." *Esquire* magazine film critic John Simon, in an article in the *National Review* on 5 July 1974, was unimpressed with the author's fourth collection. Simon said Reed's overblown reputation was based on a "clever bitchiness and supposedly revelatory interviews with aging prima donnas, an activity best described as mudpackraking." In Simon's view, Reed's interviews lack "much feeling for ambience," his portraits are deficient in concentrating unduly on his subjects' eyes, his "hearing is no sharper than his vision," and "his insensitivity to words remains his most disastrous feature." Simon accounted for Reed's popularity and success as "slaking the public's thirst for gossip" and mirroring "the public's vulgarity and sentimentality." Reed offers, according to Simon, "something for everyone, jetsetter or rube, oldtimer or child" and serves "the basic public dichotomy by crawling in both directions." Simon continued: "He has conned a lot of Americans into endowing their image of the critic with his mental and physical lineaments. Pascal defined man as a thinking reed; Rex, alas, is a Reed of another Sort."

Liz Smith, in her introduction to *Valentines and Vitriol* (1977), another collection of celebrity interviews, came to Reed's defense. "Rex Reed is a celebrity whose claim to fame is backed up by talent, guts, compassion, wit, just a soupçon of sardonic overkill, and the warmth of a real person behind the image," she writes, adding that "The single and best feature distinguishing Rex's work is his courage. . . . I've never known him to weasel . . . to be too flattered or overwhelmed by charm or position . . . [or] to back off from an important issue or an unpopular verdict. He plunges on without reservation, aware that his candor will get him barred, dropped, spat upon, ignored, attacked, and held up to ridicule."

If Smith's spirited defense of Reed was a candy valentine, John Lahr's review of Reed's fifth collection of celebrity profiles for *The New York Times Book Review* (22 May 1977) provided the vinegar and vitriol. "He scavenges the bones thrown to him by the rich and famous," Lahr wrote, adding:

> There is panic and fearful insecurity behind this frantic compulsion to mix with the famous and sniff the hem of power. But Rex sees neither the humor nor the mediocrity in a system that elevates his brand of witless ballyhoo to stardom. At the mention of the elegant and the famous, Rex's head swims and his prose sinks. . . . His gossip-column prose never flows when it can gush. . . . Rex's biggest valentine is to himself.

"Rex likes to pretend that he's part of an aristocracy of success," complained Lahr, whose unrelenting bashing of *Valentines and Vitriol* concludes with a stinging coup de grace:

> The Rex Reed Interview differs from the publicity handout only in its length. Rex doesn't probe, debate, or look farther than the glitter of the surface. The technique of his "valentines" is to kiss the hand that feeds him. . . . Rex calls himself a "critic," [which is] as much a misnomer as "sanitary engineer."

Two years later Reed's next book, *Travolta to Keaton* (1979), was greeted with a more tempered critical reaction. A *Booklist* critic noted that the thirty-four interviews avoided "the extreme swings from sacharinity to virulence" found in *Valentines and Vitriol*. Reed's sixth collection contained "much insightful commentary by a variety of actors about their profession, peers, and own abilities. The author's chatty, sometimes fawning remarks frame the revelations . . . in this popular survey of contemporary film people."

By the mid 1980s Reed had tired of interviewing celebrities and writing film criticism. The self-styled "Renaissance man in a rock-and-roll age" felt like a misplaced person who "came out of the wrong time tube." He confessed to being nostalgic for the

1940s, telling an interviewer in the *Philadelphia Inquirer* (9 March 1986):

> I like Big Band jazz, and I like ballroom dances under a revolving mirror ball, and I like to buy a girl a gardenia corsage. . . . I understand taffeta dresses, and I understand bow ties . . . and I understand short haircuts, and I understand saddle oxfords. And I understand the jitterbug. . . . And I understand the family unit, which has disappeared now. I understand the importance of working to get a good job and being a provider. I just think all these values have disappeared. People are just berserk now.

The superstar celebrity interviews had become boring to him. "To have to make them come alive and think up new adjectives, think up new ways to describe their hair and how they ate their salad . . . just drove me berserk," he said. A rash of "teenagers in heat" movies had soured him. "I think what's happening with movies is that they're all being made by children about what they understand—trying to get rid of acne and get laid and build a spaceship in their backyard," he lamented. "I'd much rather see June Alyson and Van Johnson tomorrow than anything I'm seeing today." During a monthlong publicity tour to promote his novel, *Personal Effects* (1986), Reed told an interviewer, "I'm sick and tired of journalism, and novels are the only way to make money."

The narrator of *Personal Effects* is a Reed surrogate, Hollywood gossip-columnist Billy Buck, who spins a tabloid-style mystery tale of a murdered movie star, one critic wrote, "in the grand tradition of trashy Hollywood fiction." The novel weaves through twenty-five years of intrigue in the lives of four fans that the murder victim, roughly modeled on a composite of Ava Gardner, Lana Turner, and Judy Garland, among others, had befriended. "It took me a long time to think up this plot," Reed said. "When you've seen as many movies as I have, you just think everything's been done. Every time I thought of a story I wanted to write, I suddenly remembered it was either 'Laura' or 'All About Eve' or 'The Bad and the Beautiful.'" Reed's turn to fiction allowed him to feel "the true power that comes from writing." "I controlled all those characters," he said. "I made them do whatever I wanted them to do. I wasn't reflecting on other people's work. I wasn't a conduit through whom other people's ideas flow. I really created this from my own imagination."

Karen Stabiner, in the *Los Angeles Times Book Review* (23 February 1986), found *Personal Effects* a "cream puff" compared to Nathanael West's grim Hollywood classic, *Day of the Locust* (1939). "If this book is destined to become a classic," Stabiner wrote, "it's strictly of the kitsch variety." Reed unraveled so many "interlocking cliches" that a diagram of the plot would look like, according to Stabiner, "the four-level intersection of the Harbor, Pasadena, San Bernardino and Hollywood freeways." Another critic branded Reed "the king of glitz" whose *Personal Effects* broke "absolutely no new ground in ultratrash" and was destined to become "a cheezwhip TV miniseries," with "every detail inauthentic (even the sex is forced), derived from pulp romances, and ten million light-years from observed life." Harsh reviews came as no surprise to Reed. "Any movie critic they assign is going to say horrible things," he said during his promotional tour. "He's going to write me right out of the human race."

Reed's meteoric reputation for being a "hatchet man" went hand in hand with his reputation for redefining the celebrity interview. His acerbic wit and whiplash writing pushed the celebrity profile and film and television criticism into candid new territory that went far beyond Hollywood press agentry. In a 1973 interview with *Writer's Digest* Reed was asked how he would like to be remembered. "With respect," he replied. "All I would like for them to do is respect my work. I would like my body of work to be looked back on as honest and flavorful, but with respect and dignity."

Few critics have bestowed upon his work the respect and dignity he hopes to earn. His notoriety and celebrity status may have prompted professional jealousies that found their way into the snide and caustic assessments of his writing. "There's so little room for fame in this profession," he commented in the *Minneapolis Star and Tribune* (11 March 1986), "and so many of them want to be famous, that they hate, loathe and despise anyone who does achieve any kind of fame. And nobody has quite the same name or reputation that I do." In the 1973 interview with John Brady, Reed threw his own distinctive style into his writing with a ferocious honesty. "I think I have a good following because of that—not because I'm as brilliant as somebody else . . . but simply because it's honest."

Interviews:

John Brady, "If you can't say something nice about somebody, let's hear it," *Writer's Digest,* 53 (September 1973): 10–21;

David Crumpler, "Bluntly speaking, that's Rex Reed," [Jacksonville] *Florida Times-Union,* 15 March 1985.

References:

"The Ax Man Cometh," *Newsweek* (8 January 1968): 47;

"The Film Critic of the New York Post Says Our Culture Is Disintegrating. (Just Look at Pie Crusts.)," *Philadelphia Inquirer,* 9 March 1986;

Bob Lundegaard, "Rex Reed," *Minneapolis Star & Tribune,* 11 March 1986;

"Rex Reed: The Hazel-Eyed Hatchet Man," *Time* (23 August 1968): 54–55.

Richard Rhodes
(4 July 1937 –   )

David Bennett
University of Southern Mississippi

BOOKS: *The Inland Ground: An Evocation of the American Middle West* (New York: Atheneum, 1970; revised and enlarged edition, Lawrence: University of Kansas Press, 1991);

The Ungodly: A Novel of the Donner Party (New York: Charterhouse, 1973);

The Ozarks, by Rhodes and the editors of Time-Life Books (New York: Time-Life Books, 1974);

Holy Secrets (Garden City, N.Y.: Doubleday, 1978);

Looking for America: A Writer's Odyssey (Garden City, N.Y.: Doubleday, 1979);

The Last Safari (Garden City, N.Y.: Doubleday, 1980);

Sons of Earth (New York: Coward, McCann & Geoghegan, 1981);

The Making of the Atomic Bomb (New York: Simon & Schuster, 1986);

Farm: A Year in the Life of an American Farmer (New York: Simon & Schuster, 1989);

A Hole in the World: An American Boyhood (New York: Simon & Schuster, 1990);

Writing in an Era of Conflict, by Rhodes and Thomas L. Friedman (Washington, D.C.: Library of Congress, 1990);

Making Love: An Erotic Odyssey (New York: Simon & Schuster, 1992);

Nuclear Renewal: Common Sense About Energy (New York: Whittle Books/Viking, 1993);

How to Write: Advice and Reflections (New York: Morrow, 1995);

Dark Sun: The Making of the Hydrogen Bomb (New York: Simon & Schuster, 1995);

Trying to Get Some Dignity: Stories of Triumph over Childhood Abuse, by Rhodes and Ginger Rhodes (New York: Morrow, 1996);

Deadly Feasts: Tracking the Secrets of a Terrifying New Plague (New York: Simon & Schuster, 1997).

TELEVISION: *The Loss of Innocence,* script by Rhodes, National Education Television, 1965;

The Osage River: Another Kind of Wilderness, script by Rhodes, KCPT-Television, Kansas City, Mo., 1973;

Richard Rhodes (photograph by Nancy Crampton)

A Wild Delight: Emerson on Nature, script by Rhodes, KCPT-Television, Kansas City, Mo., 1973.

OTHER: William C. Menninger, *Living in a Troubled World: Selections from the Writings of William C. Menninger,* edited by Rhodes and Bernard H. Hall (Kansas City, Mo.: Hallmark Editions, 1967);

Robert Serber, *The Los Alamos Primer: The First Lectures on How to Build an Atomic Bomb,* edited, with an introduction, by Rhodes (Berkeley: University of California Press, 1992).

Richard Rhodes emerged as one of the major nonfiction artists of this age with *The Making of the*

Atomic Bomb (1986), his sprawling, 886-page, Pulitzer Prize–winning saga that chronicles what he described in a 1994 interview as the "great epic tragedy of the twentieth century: mankind inventing the means of its own destruction." When he followed with two other highly acclaimed works, *Farm: A Year in the Life of an American Farmer* (1989) and *A Hole in the World: An American Boyhood* (1990), and then explored human sexuality in the controversial *Making Love: An Erotic Odyssey* (1992), he entrenched himself as one of the preeminent talents in contemporary American literature, a lyrical voice sounding unmistakable echoes of Herman Melville, Ralph Waldo Emerson, and Joseph Conrad.

In the 1991 revised version of *The Inland Ground: An Evocation of the American Middle West* (1970) Rhodes states that for him, writing "is done out of pain, and no amount of writing will take away the pain; the pain is to be alive." He is the quintessential tortured poet, driven by an almost obsessive need to explore human suffering. He shares with Conrad a fear of the darkness in men's hearts; each is deeply concerned with the duality in humanity of good and evil. Both tap universal themes and chords in seeking to understand the mysteriousness of the heart.

Five great themes—death and violence, darkness, destruction, betrayal, and survival—resonate through his body of work as Rhodes deplores the capacity of mankind for horrific cruelty and savagery. Over and over he confronts these dominant themes, exposing myriad abominations and egregious deceptions but always, as he said in an unpublished interview with David Bennett on 10 May 1994, finding a "small margin of hope" at the edge of disasters that happen to people. He reminds readers of the sorrow, despair, and fragility of life.

Born 4 July 1937 in Kansas City, Kansas, the third son of Arthur and Georgia Rhodes, Richard Lee Rhodes endured a hellish Dickensian childhood that profoundly shaped his literary career. His mother committed suicide when he was thirteen months old, using a 12-gauge shotgun in a bathroom next to Richard's bedroom. She was twenty-nine. After the suicide the family split up. Richard's oldest brother, Mack, went to live with relatives in the state of Washington while Richard and brother Stanley, two years older, stayed with their father, a railroad repairman. They lived for periods with relatives and friends, rented rooms in squalid boarding homes, and moved frequently as Arthur Rhodes struggled to provide food and shelter for the boys. The years were nevertheless happy ones, Rhodes recalls; their father nurtured and cared for the boys as well as he could.

The happiness turned to deep and unrelenting despair in 1947 when Arthur Rhodes married Anne Ralena Martin. Stanley was twelve and Richard ten. Their stepmother immediately introduced the boys to a new world of violence and fear, systematically starving, battering, and torturing them over a two-year period, inflicting deep psychological, physical, and emotional damage. Arthur Rhodes refused to intervene, intimidated by his wife. After taking as much as he could, Stanley notified the police, sneaking out of the house to avoid his stepmother. State authorities intervened and took the boys away, placing them in a boys' home called the Drumm Institute, located outside Independence, Missouri. At Drumm they farmed, performed daily chores, and submitted to stringent rules of behavior. In return they received schooling, room, and board. Rhodes immersed himself in books, reading everything he could find, from pulp fiction to the Bible. He stayed at Drumm until he was eighteen, and he earned an academic scholarship to Yale, which he attended from 1955 to 1959, graduating cum laude with a degree in intellectual history.

After brief stints as a writer trainee at *Newsweek* and as an English teacher at Westminster College in Fulton, Missouri, Rhodes became book-editing manager of Hallmark Cards in Kansas City, Missouri, from 1962 to 1970. He married Linda Hampton in 1960, and they had two children, Timothy and Katherine, before divorcing in 1974. Rhodes then married Mary Evans in 1976; they divorced in 1986. In October 1993 Rhodes married Ginger Untrif, his companion since 1987. They now reside in Madison, Connecticut.

While working for Hallmark, Rhodes occasionally reviewed books for *The New York Times, The New York Herald Tribune,* and *The Kansas City Star.* An editor at the *Tribune,* Dick Kluger, impressed by Rhodes's talent, remembered Rhodes when he became an editor at Atheneum. In 1967 Kluger asked Rhodes to write a literary study of the Midwest to be published in book form.

Rhodes froze in fear. Unable to exorcise the demons of his nightmarish childhood, he felt he had no right to speak; as he explained in the revised *The Inland Ground:* "Crucially, because of the violence of my childhood and the rage that violence engendered in me, I was afraid, grandiosely and delusionally, that if I revealed my feelings in writing I might somehow destroy the world." He was thirty years old, depressed, anorexic, unhappily married, drinking half a fifth of whiskey a night to ease the anxiety attacks that visited him daily, and considering suicide.

He attempted two chapters, both of which were flat, uninspired, and pedestrian. He worried that he could not find the words to make the book work or to release the fear and guilt he had harbored most of his life. A friend then invited him to go on a coyote hunt in central Kansas. During the hunt Rhodes watched packs of dogs rip coyotes to pieces as people smiled, callously indifferent; later, at a cockfight he watched birds tear each other's eyes and throats out with razor-sharp spurs, and again people smiled.

When Rhodes returned from the hunt, he got "thoroughly drunk," reread Ernest Hemingway's *Death in the Afternoon* (1932), then applied the techniques of literary journalism—dialogue, scene-by-scene construction, voice, and point of view—for the first time in his writing, expressing his horror of violence. What began as a simple description of a rather mundane coyote hunt became much more: a troubling commentary on the capacity of humanity for violence and savagery. The hunt revealed an essential evil in the American psyche; Rhodes's chapter, "Death All Day in Kansas," was eloquent, rich in allegory, and filled with larger truths. We are often the victims of our own strange greed and lust, Rhodes observed, a species bent on self-destruction.

"Death All Day," first published by *Esquire* in 1969, served as the centerpiece of Rhodes's first book, *The Inland Ground,* which helped launch him into the consciousness of the nation. Rhodes explored such diverse subjects as the suicide of a dear friend, a train ride in Kansas, the tenets of the Unity School of Practical Christianity, and the school of creative writing at the University of Iowa, weaving separate essays into an incisive commentary on the Midwest.

The book sold fewer than five thousand copies but was nonetheless a critical success; reviewers applauded Rhodes as a rich, idiosyncratic voice. Rhodes sold some of the individual chapters to *Esquire, Harper's,* and other magazines, getting paid twice for the same work as someone who wants to make a living from writing will try to do.

Vivid biblical imagery and Puritan thought saturate Rhodes's writings. His Protestant heritage (he studied to be a Methodist preacher during his six years at the Drumm Institute before severing most religious ties at Yale) manifests itself throughout his literary corpus. Jeremiads are prevalent in his work, appearing for the first time in *The Inland Ground* as Rhodes reproaches conventional morality and orthodoxy, abhorring the violence and darkness he witnessed in American society. Rhodes uses the jeremiad as a form of secular sermon; he possesses an evangelical impulse.

In an unpublished 2 February 1995 letter to David Bennett, Rhodes bridled at the word *jeremiad,* associating it "less with preaching than with preachiness, which I'd like to think I'm not guilty of even though I know well enough that I am." He added, "That is, those jeremiads aren't directed at the reader—it doesn't feel that way when I write them—they're directed at those whose m.o.'s fit the bill. I usually feel in solidarity with the reader in jeremiading and at the same time feel the reader and I are the miscreants together." In an interview with Bennett on 20 May 1995, however, he conceded that the jeremiad "is pervasive in my work. It's a very fine form."

Rhodes admits that his religious upbringing is clearly evident in his writings. "You have to remember that I was on the road to being a preacher when I was eighteen, until I got to college and realized there were some other cultural forms available," he said in a 1994 interview with Bennett. "That was what I knew up to then, what I had done a lot of reading (particularly the Bible) into."

The Inland Ground is a running commentary as Rhodes examines the people of the American Middle West, their customs and follies, their anxieties and delights, their morals and philosophies. He celebrates their decency, goodness, ingenuity, and inherent loyalty. Along the way, however, he discovers an egregious darkness in the heart. Mindless slaughter, callous indifference, conspicuous waste—this is, he reminds readers, the American character. In his travels through the Midwest he encounters malicious forces—hatred, greed, lust, violence, and savagery—and observes the "transparency of American life," the ceaseless striving for wealth and fame.

After publication of *The Inland Ground* Rhodes turned full time to writing, leaving his job at Hallmark. He spent the 1970s alternating between fiction and nonfiction, writing two novels, *The Ungodly: A Novel of the Donner Party* (1973) and *Holy Secrets* (1978); a travel guide, *The Ozarks* (1974); and more than seventy articles for *Harper's, Redbook, American Heritage, Esquire, Playboy, Rolling Stone, The New Yorker,* and *The New York Times Magazine*. He also published *Looking for America: A Writer's Odyssey* (1979), a collection of some of his best nonfiction from the 1970s.

In 1973 Rhodes, fascinated by the tragic journey of the Donner Party, turned to fiction, explaining that everything that could be written about the Donners in nonfiction form had already been written. And indeed the Donner Party has intrigued chroniclers for more than a century. But Rhodes found another way to approach the subject, a fictionalized approach that nevertheless remained true to the known facts. "I saw in the Donner Party all those themes that have been vital to my work—vio-

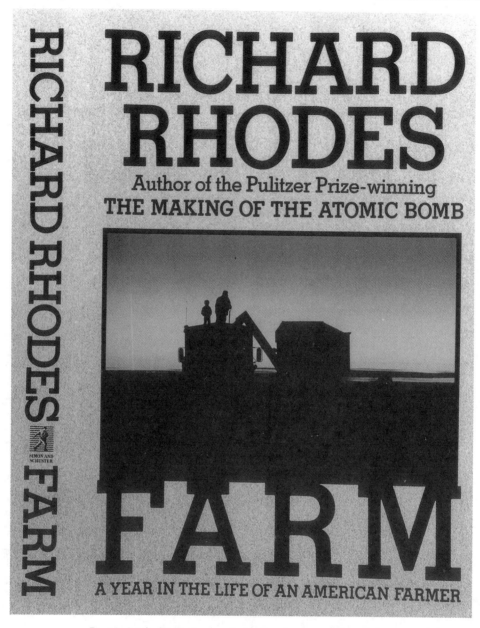

Dust jacket for Rhodes's account of a year spent on a Missouri farm

lence, destruction, death, survival, the miniaturization of the American Dream, man's need always and forever to move on," Rhodes said in his 1994 interview with Bennett.

As Rhodes depicts, members of the Donner Party shamelessly raped the wilderness. Seduced by the promise of comfort, all the free land they wanted, and wealth, the eighty-nine midwestern pioneers immigrated to California in 1846 but were trapped in the Sierra Nevada by one of the worst snowstorms in history. Along the way they callously littered the land, destroyed whatever got in their way, refused to listen to any advice except their own, and eventually turned on each other, quarreling, even killing, over minor misunderstandings. They were uniquely modern, Rhodes points out, people who believed it was their destiny, even divine right, to take their rich share of all the plentiful bounty God had provided for them in the wilderness. Instead they found terrible grief, and it drove them to cannibalism and madness. They resorted to eating their dead in order to survive the brutal winter.

Rhodes tells the story of the Donner Party in journal form, chronicling each day of the journey as a diary entry, from April 1846 when the emigration began in Illinois, to its tragic end in June 1847 when the rescue party of Gen. George Kearney arrived at the Donner camp in the Sierra Nevada to discover humans who now more resembled animals.

Of the eighty-nine people who began the trip, forty-one died. And yet, remarkably, none of them ever gave up, as Rhodes explains in *Looking for America:* "None committed suicide: [they] preferred slow death by starvation to suicide, preferred cannibalism to suicide. That fact alone must stagger us today with its implications of strength and trust in the ultimate benevolence of life. . . . We are, whatever the evolutionists say, some yet unexplained separate creation, most bloody and until recently most unbowed."

Rhodes ranks the book, his first published novel, among his best. "In fiction," he told Bennett in 1995, "my favorite work without question is *The Ungodly,* which was written in great haste, which was written under great pressure, but which I think is just about as good a novel as one can ask for. I'm very proud of it."

While Rhodes was working on *The Inland Ground* and *The Ungodly,* he was drinking heavily at night, after finishing his daily writing. As he explains in *A Hole in the World: An American Boyhood* (1990), he thought he did not have a right to speak; alcohol freed him from his inhibitions and insecurities, subduing the "lurching monster of overwhelming, intractable, involuntary rage that my mother's suicide, my father's neglect and my stepmother's violence instilled in me." The pattern, which started in the 1950s, led Rhodes to drink himself to intoxication almost every night for thirty years, when he would unleash his rage and pain onto what he perceived to be a hostile world. He quit drinking circa 1987 after he met and fell deeply in love with his current wife, Ginger Untrif. He thought his drinking would jeopardize his relationship with Untrif, and he was able to quit.

Sobriety produced a different writing style; gone, for the most part, are the extended diatribes, the scathing jeremiads, the harsh indictments that characterized Rhodes's early prose. "Much of that earlier writing came when I was drunk, and however difficult being drunk is in terms of writing, it has the one virtue that it frees up a kind of madness that you can then draw on for some of your associations and metaphors," Rhodes told Bennett in 1995. "As for the shift in recent years to a more rational style, that's implicit in writing history, I think, although sober writing is certainly different from drunk."

After *The Inland Ground* and *The Ungodly* the 1970s were fruitful though not prosperous years during which Rhodes produced an impressive body

of work that critics lauded. *The Ozarks,* a minor travel guide, reveals Rhodes's fascination with the wilderness. Written in the first person, it describes the changing of the seasons and the natural wonders that abound in the picturesque mountain chain that stretches from Missouri through Arkansas. Nature has much to teach humans and can show them that they are not far removed from the animals, Rhodes reasons. Larger truths and deeper meanings fill *The Ozarks.*

Rhodes draws heavily on symbolic realities, a characteristic that distinguishes him from most literary journalists. As Norman Sims told Bennett in an unpublished 27 April 1994 interview:

> The term "symbolism" has been used so often in analyzing fiction that nonfiction writers seem to be leery of it. Symbols have a certain abstraction. If you talk about symbolism referring to something outside of itself, nonfiction writers tend to distance themselves from it. Fiction carries with it the notion of made-up abstractions, and literary journalists tend to be very sensitive about that sort of thing. But Rhodes is an exception. He is probably the most symbolic of all the literary journalists. He tends to write about death and violence in symbolic ways.

Rhodes admits in Sims's *The Literary Journalists* (1984) that symbolic realities are "terribly important" to him, that "deep structures" within his stories invariably yield a larger truth, and that the universe does indeed show forth in a writer's work.

Symbolism is "always there," Rhodes elaborated in a 1994 interview. "I don't see how any writer who is writing seriously can't be—or try to be—attuned to all the reverberations that are in anything people do. One thing that is very central to the whole business of writing but also to the way the world works is the layeredness, the complexity, the interrelatedness."

Rhodes returned to fiction with *Holy Secrets,* detailing the struggles of a surgeon, Tom Haldane, caught up in a violent divorce. Rhodes's rage clearly surfaces: jeremiads and diatribes saturate the narrative. The novel chronicles Haldane's experimentation with cocaine and his loss of virginity in a New York City brothel—experiences drawn directly from Rhodes's life. Much of *Holy Secrets* is, in fact, autobiographical. Haldane's tragic vision mirrors Rhodes's: every human being, in Haldane's view, is "inherently insane" and "potentially a murderer."

Doubt and guilt torment Haldane, who shows further connections to Rhodes: his mother commits suicide, remorse tears at him, fears assail him. Haldane watches life cycle inexorably through destruction and death and becomes deeply disillusioned. He questions social myths, seeking to understand how they are sustained. He attacks notions of male superiority and female inferiority and laments the equation of femininity with weakness. Rhodes, an early profeminist, uses Haldane to denounce the absurdity of a male-dominated social hierarchy, to expose the "extraordinary scientific denial, against obvious evidence, of female sexuality itself."

Critics praised *Holy Secrets* as a work of rich intelligence and virtuosity. Nevertheless, Rhodes faced a dilemma: he had now written three acclaimed books—*The Inland Ground, The Ungodly,* and *Holy Secrets*—but he was still having to scramble for money, writing essays for magazines, living off grants. Nearly a decade would pass before he broke into the ranks of writers who earn a more-than-comfortable living with all of the attendant perks of celebrity.

He followed *Holy Secrets* with *Looking for America: A Writer's Odyssey,* one of the neglected nonfiction masterpieces in American literature. Richly diverse, it is a montage, a collection of Rhodes's best magazine writing in the 1970s. He demonstrates his breadth and depth, exploring subjects that range from the development of the atomic bomb to his first and last experiment with cocaine. Throughout *Looking for America* Rhodes examines his grand motifs: the restlessness and capacity for cruelty of the human heart, the duality in humanity of good and evil, the need for hope in the midst of terrifying adversity, and survival in the midst of horrific destruction.

Rhodes makes frequent reference to the wilderness in *Looking for America,* attempting to unravel the mysteries that confront man there. To Rhodes the wilderness is many things—spiritual, moral, physical, emotional, and psychological. It is often ominous and foreboding, a source of fear and anxiety; at the same time the wilderness is often a source of wonder and awe. Humans are, Rhodes says, "creatures who should not be allowed to touch a wilderness because, having touched it, we will destroy it if we possibly can." The rape of the Garden is a dominant metaphor in *Looking for America* as Rhodes laments the destruction of natural resources, the wanton disregard for nature. Man's unending quest for money, land, and prosperity has driven him for centuries to sacrifice those things most precious—pristine rivers, beautiful mountains—in order to build plants and factories. Technology has long enchanted; but, Rhodes argues, this same technology may one day destroy man as the pollution and decay he witnesses demonstrate.

Emerson's understanding of the interconnectedness of the universe and the wilderness it shelters has profoundly influenced Rhodes, who still rereads and quotes Emerson, considering him one of the most gifted voices in American literature. As Rhodes told Bennett in 1994: "Reading Emerson was very important because of his sense of the universe—it is something that is transcendent and in some sense transparent even in the midst of all the terrible opacity."

Rhodes's literary artistry finds its highest expression in certain chapters, particularly "The Death of the Everglades," "Loathe Thy Neighbor," "J. Robert Oppenheimer, Shatterer of Worlds," "Sex and Sin in Sheboygan," and "Coming Down Snow Mountain"—all minor classics, works destined to rank among the best American magazine writing ever produced.

In J. Robert Oppenheimer, the father of the atomic bomb, Rhodes found a kindred spirit, a man unable to conceal the painful humiliations and scars of a devastating childhood. His *American Heritage* article is sympathetic. Later, after Rhodes got to know Oppenheimer better, his opinion of the physicist changed; Rhodes discovered that Oppenheimer was repulsive, "afflicted with a pathological disgust with himself and a nearly pathological horror of the world."

Seconds after witnessing the first explosion of a nuclear device at the Trinity test in July 1945, the awed Oppenheimer remembered a quote from *The Bhagavad Gila:* Oppenheimer remembered "I am become death, the shatterer of worlds." When the first atomic bomb on Hiroshima fell, he realized that he had unleashed unfathomable horror on the world, that all those hideous corpses were largely his handiwork. Here was a tragic paradox—one of the authentic geniuses of the twentieth century had used his intelligence to build a horrible weapon of mass destruction.

"Oppenheimer certainly was not a hero of mine," Rhodes told Bennett in 1994. "Oppenheimer was a very cruel and nasty man. He had one moment of transcendence—when he got to be director (of the Manhattan Project)—and he was a good actor who played the role wonderfully. But he was not a very nice man."

Buoyed by critical reaction to *The Ungodly* and *Holy Secrets,* Rhodes returned again to fiction with *The Last Safari* (1980), a tale of intrigue set in East Africa, where three Americans are caught up in terrorist and guerrilla warfare that is taking place all around them. Rhodes paints superb pictures of the African landscape, describing in detail the majesty of the land and vividly portraying the frenzied struggle for life on the Serengeti Plains, where species feeds on species. The novel reveals touches of

Hemingway; Rhodes writes superbly about the splendors of East Africa while also delving deeply into two of Hemingway's great themes, death and savagery. Rhodes, in fact, makes frequent reference to Hemingway.

Rhodes also explores the incomprehensibility of human existence, much as Hemingway did. The vicious struggle for life he sees in the African wilds allows him to confront his main concerns, darkness and destruction. He attempts to postulate an explanation for man's fixed cycle of life before concluding that, as E. O. Wilson wrote, the "reflective person knows that his life is in some incomprehensible manner guided through a biological ontogeny. . . . He senses that with all the drive, wit, love, pride, anger, hope and anxiety that characterize the species he will in the end be sure only of helping to perpetuate the same cycle. Poets have defined this truth as tragedy."

Rhodes draws on his fascination with space travel in *Sons of Earth* (1981), his fourth novel. Red Wainwright, a famed astronaut, serves as the narrative voice. Wainwright describes the high price of fame and celebrity, wondering if adulation is worth the price it exacts. After he writes a book on the energy crisis that vaults to the top of the best-seller list, his son Chris is kidnapped and buried alive by a monstrous villain, Karl Loring Grabka, who demands a half-million-dollar ransom. The son, meanwhile, is slowly dying; the box he is buried in has only a limited life support system.

The "crouching animal" within man manifests itself in Grabka's actions. Rhodes launches into an extended jeremiad, arguing that man is driven by the same primal instincts that drive animals. He says that the animal in the human heart is capable of maiming and killing for pleasure, of committing wanton acts of murderous violence; and as cases such as Jeffrey Dahmer and Ted Bundy have shown, the human animal is a far more vicious killer than any animal in nature.

Rhodes went into virtual seclusion after *Sons of Earth,* taking refuge in the basement of his Kansas City home for five years while he researched and wrote *The Making of the Atomic Bomb* (1986). An epic tome that details the frenzied race by teams of scientists involved in the Manhattan Project to develop a perfect death machine, *The Making of the Atomic Bomb* became a great success, winning the literary equivalent of the Triple Crown: the Pulitzer Prize, the National Book Critics Circle Award, and the National Book Award.

Winning the Pulitzer Prize ratified a conviction Rhodes had harbored most of his life as a writer: that the creation of the first nuclear weapons represented the most tragic story of the twentieth century. Humanity now possessed the capacity to obliterate itself with the flip of a switch.

Rhodes risked his career on *The Making of the Atomic Bomb*. During the five years he worked in his basement, going through mountains of research documents and distilling them into a compelling narrative, money became so scarce that Rhodes canceled his newspaper and magazine subscriptions, mortgaged his home, and eliminated all but the essentials around his household. He almost went bankrupt until a grant from the Sloan Foundation bailed him out at the last minute. "Winning the Pulitzer certainly opened doors for me and changed things," Rhodes said in 1994. "But the financial struggle was terrible. I had two children in college at the time, and I had to make those tuition payments each semester. Simon & Schuster gave me a $75,000 advance on the book, and I received grants from the Ford Foundation and the Sloan Foundation which kept me afloat. But it was quite a struggle."

Although Rhodes had written substantial literary nonfiction in the 1960s and 1970s, *The Making of the Atomic Bomb* was his first book-length nonfiction work. It is a historical narrative, as he described it in *How to Write: Advice and Reflections* (1995), "a straightforward third-person omniscient narration." Despite his own feelings about the subject, Rhodes largely remains a dispassionate narrator, an objective historian, never taking sides on the nuclear debate, giving equal space to myriad points of view.

His interviews with survivors of Hiroshima are particularly absorbing. The bomb devastated the city, destroying or severely damaging seventy thousand of the seventy-six thousand buildings. It inflicted terrible damage, killing thousands instantly, leaving the rest to wander hopelessly, making death itself seem preferable to the lot of those who survived.

The Making of the Atomic Bomb draws much of its strength and vigor from Rhodes's reporting prowess. The narrative spans more than a century; Rhodes tracks the development of the atomic bomb from its earliest roots, back to the 1850s and 1860s when the notion of an electromagnetic field gained credence among scientists, to the 1920s and 1930s when a new field of research, nuclear physics, attracted brilliant minds into the discipline. He depicts the efforts of the giants of twentieth-century science—Leo Szilard, Edward Teller, John von Neumann, Oppenheimer, Niels Bohr, Otto Hahn, Ernest Lawrence, Lise Meitner, Ernest Rutherford, and Enrico Fermi—as they assemble all the intelligence and machinery necessary to build the most lethal weapon known to man.

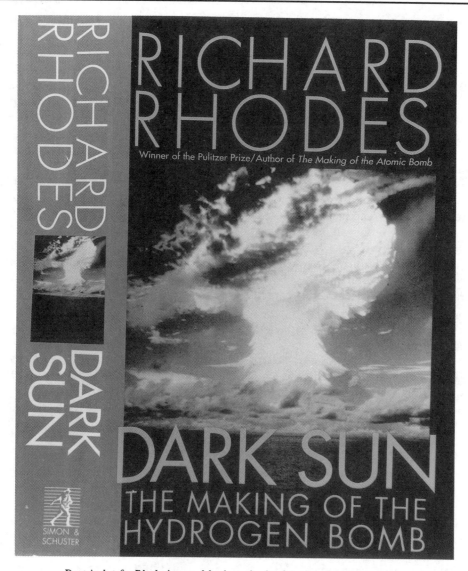

Dust jacket for Rhodes's second book on the development of nuclear weapons

Rhodes personalizes the main characters who developed the bomb, showing that they were not cold, uncaring automatons but rather men and women with common human failings, often tormented by doubt and filled with deep guilt and remorse. They argued that large moral responsibilities devolved upon the United States; many were stunned beyond speech by the horror of Hiroshima, while others, such as Szilard, Bohr, and Oppenheimer, wrestled with ethical dilemmas, even questioning the wisdom of producing so awful a weapon in the first place.

Apocalyptic imagery pervades *The Making of the Atomic Bomb*, which is, in essence, the story of the capacity of humanity to inflict suffering, explains Rhodes. He points out that there have been more than one hundred million man-made deaths in the twentieth century—far more than any sickness or disease has ever claimed. Technology will not save people; neither will intellect. Humans are flawed at the core—within the heart and soul—and trapped in a moral wilderness that even the most intelligent cannot escape, Rhodes reasons; original sin is a dominant metaphor throughout the book. His vision never strays far from the inescapable darkness that envelops humanity. Humans are all imperfect beings grasping to make some sense of the anarchy within their own hearts, Rhodes posits.

Soon after Rhodes finished *The Making of the Atomic Bomb* he spent a year on the Missouri farm of Tom and Sally Bauer (pseudonyms he used to protect their privacy), waking early each morning to milk cows, castrate bulls, plant seed, and harvest a thousand acres of wheat, corn, and soybeans. Rhodes filled forty-two spiral notebooks by the time his year ended, taking notes whenever a break from work allowed, jotting down additional details at night in the small apartment he rented. Out of those notebooks emerged the framework for one of the most critically acclaimed books of the decade: *Farm: A Year in the Life of an American Farmer,* Rhodes's purest example of literary journalism.

In *Farm* Rhodes becomes an unobtrusive, almost invisible character, standing in the background, watching, reporting what he observes, much in the manner of Gay Talese. Rhodes surfaces only once in the book, and then in the third person, as the "city man" who ventures along on a deer hunt.

Biblical terms abound in *Farm: redemption, resurrection, salvation, cleansing,* and *healing* resonate through the narrative. Getting back on the farm was like being "reborn." Writing the book took Rhodes back to his roots, to the days when he farmed at the Drumm Institute as an adolescent, after his stepmother's abuse drove him from home.

The Bauers were shrewd and frugal enough during the Reagan years to keep their land and make a profit from it—at a time when 25 percent of American farmers lost their farms—and Rhodes chronicles the daily struggles the family endures. Machinery breaks; weather threatens crops; bills mount as disposable income decreases; cattle die; and stringent government regulations cause farmers extreme anxiety. During the year Rhodes spent with the Bauers they grossed $152,000 by selling their crops and cattle but netted only $19,000 after expenses. Rhodes worked for free and paid the Bauers $50 a week for the food he ate and the time he took out of their schedules asking questions.

To the Bauers the land is a living, breathing thing—their shelter from an outside world that neither understands nor appreciates the immense complexity, and satisfaction, of farmwork. Tom Bauer becomes almost a mythic figure, a man of great strength and wisdom and pride, a latter-day Abraham. Rhodes reserves for Bauer a certain biblical reverence. In all of Rhodes's writings he accords few people such respect. The reason is simple: Rhodes sees in Bauer the older brother, Stanley, he so loved.

"His name is actually James Ruehter," Rhodes told Bennett in 1994. "He doesn't care if people know now; I think he kind of likes people to know he was the farmer in *Farm.* He was more like a big brother. Being with him was like being back with Stanley. He's a big, powerful man, yet he's also gentle. I really got to like him a great deal."

Rhodes's preoccupation with death and violence is clearly evident in *Farm;* he sees death wherever he looks. Animals are slaughtered daily as

farmers watch, coldly indifferent. Animals are also born—the flip side of death—for one reason: to be killed. Birth only begins the inexorable march toward death and destruction. Rhodes's childhood instilled in him a horror of violence, of which death is the ultimate manifestation.

When asked in a 1994 interview if he had a preoccupation with death, Rhodes said, "If you're dealing with violence you're necessarily dealing with death . . . there is that sense of absence in my childhood, of walking around in a universe where there seemed to be this great thing missing in the middle, my mother. If by preoccupation you mean morbid brooding, no. All my books are about how you survive, whether you survive. Death is the ultimate danger for the individual. Yes, it's a preoccupation but not an obsession."

Rhodes next told his "orphan story," the tale of his brutally abusive childhood in Missouri. *A Hole in the World: An American Boyhood* begins with searing intensity as in the first sentence of the book Rhodes recounts his mother's suicide. The memoir sizzles with rage and anger: Rhodes unleashes the hostility and hurt he suppressed for forty years. But *A Hole in the World* is also profoundly redemptive, a poignant testament to the strength and resilience of the human heart.

To understand Rhodes it is necessary to understand the shame and self-loathing he endured as a child; it informs everything he has written. Nevertheless, he apologizes for dwelling on his battered childhood and his mother's death: "I understand that the world is full of terrible suffering, compared to which the small inconveniences of my childhood are as a drop of rain in the sea."

Rhodes's Protestantism is more clearly evident in *A Hole in the World* than in any of his other writings. He has since denounced religion, rejecting its hypocrisy. But his memoir reveals deep religious convictions as if he were back at Drumm Institute studying for the ministry as he had done forty years before. Rich allegory built on Protestant belief fills his writing as he echoes familiar biblical refrains. He evokes memories of David, crying out in despair, wondering if he has been abandoned by God. Empowerment is one of Rhodes's great themes throughout the book; over and over he cries out for the strength to change his circumstances. When Rhodes finally arrives at Drumm, after years of torture and abuse, he embraces the healing simplicity of farmwork, comparing it to resurrection.

Rhodes's syntax in *A Hole in the World* is at times quite simple and straightforward, somewhat timid, even vulnerable, written largely through a child's eyes. This literary ploy is used for effect: the tender syntax operates as a metaphor for a child's vulnerability, capturing the distinctive resonances and nuances of a child's pain. Rhodes uses this syntactical strategy often; he changes prose styles for virtually every work.

Two metaphorical "saviors" emerged at Drumm to provide Rhodes with wisdom and moral instruction: Harry Nelson, the superintendent of the institute, and George Berkemeier, Nelson's assistant. They were stern and demanding but decent and strong, the first such men Rhodes had ever been around for any significant amount of time.

The Bible provided an escape for Rhodes; he read it incessantly, just as he read anything else that was available, ranging from science fiction to *National Geographic.* He quickly became the top student at Drumm, a gifted intellect capable of work that bordered on brilliant. The reading and academic preparation served him well, earning him the scholarship to Yale. Rhodes spent six years at Drumm, from ages twelve to eighteen, and credits the daily farmwork—raising cattle and hogs and chickens, planting seed, harvesting crops—for instilling in him a sense of discipline and purpose.

Rhodes admits that writing *A Hole in the World* was extremely difficult, an exercise that drained him psychologically and emotionally. He opened old wounds and dredged up old demons. But it was also cathartic and cleansing as Rhodes at last confronted fears and emotions that had tormented him for forty years. The journey has been painful—he leaves in his wake alcoholism, deep depression, crippling anxiety, and a death wish, while admitting in a 1990 *Washington Times* article that "there's an underlying sadness that doesn't really go away."

Three universally praised works in four years—*The Making of the Atomic Bomb, Farm, A Hole in the World*—made Rhodes white-hot, the newest darling of the American critical establishment, which marveled at his talent and range. When Rhodes explored human sexuality in *Making Love: An Erotic Odyssey* (1992), however, many critics turned on him, criticizing the shallow pretentiousness of the book.

Making Love, Rhodes's startlingly candid, shockingly explicit exploration of his own sex life, is the most intimate book ever produced by a literary journalist, perhaps the most provocative work ever produced by a "serious author." Rhodes sent shock waves from New York City to Los Angeles when he released the work; here, after all, was one of the major figures in American literature, a Pulitzer Prize winner, one of the most eloquent voices of this generation, discussing such things as his first orgasm, his favorite X-rated Marilyn Chambers film, and the size, color, and shape of his and his partner's

sexual organs. Evoking memories of Henry Miller, John Updike, Philip Roth, John Cheever, and Gay Talese, Rhodes describes in unflinching detail the most graphic moments and memorable milestones of his sexual odyssey.

Rhodes says he wrote the book for two reasons, one of which was personal—he used sex as a form of catharsis after his battered childhood—and the other literary. He points out that in the history of Western literature over the last thousand years, personal nonfiction narratives of sexual experience are exceedingly rare; Rhodes estimates there are fewer than five. He explained in *The Kansas City Star* in 1992: "Here is a field of human experience and human behavior that is enormously rich, something every human being on earth has some relationship to, but something that has been cordoned off for centuries from any sort of normal discourse."

The book ignited a maelstrom of protest and denunciation. While some critics cheered Rhodes's boldness, others lashed out at him for shameless self-indulgence. Critics complained about the "joylessness" in Rhodes's book, about his clinical approach to sexuality, about his degradation of women.

Rhodes gives new meaning to participatory research and immersion in a subject—and he refuses to apologize. He reproaches those who cling to archaic sexual beliefs, arguing that sex must be explored. He points to the high rate of sexual dysfunction in American marriages and claims that many marriages could be rehabilitated if sexual problems—premature ejaculation, impotence—were more openly addressed. "How much suffering is there simply because people don't talk about this subject?" Rhodes asked in the *Kansas City Star* article.

He admits in the same article that *Making Love* was written to other ends also, to provide a higher truth and a deeper reality, as all of his works invariably do. He contends that the sexual relationship between two people lying naked in a bed is "a microcosm for the whole political world that we enlarge from our relationships first of all with one person."

After the *Making Love* furor Rhodes returned to a familiar subject: nuclear energy. *Nuclear Renewal: Common Sense About Energy* (1993), which grew out of *The Making of the Atomic Bomb,* is a call for the continued use and efficacy of nuclear energy. Rhodes posits that nuclear power is the safest, cheapest, and most efficient way to produce mass energy. He argues that bungling mismanagement, not flawed technology, created the perception that nuclear energy is a dangerous liability. His voice resonates with anger and outrage; we have written off nuclear energy too soon, he laments. *Nuclear Renewal* is, in essence, a short manifesto in which Rhodes decries our lack of knowledge about nuclear energy. He shows how it has thrived in Japan and France; he closely examines accidents at Three Mile Island and Chernobyl, charting a series of mistakes that led to disaster; and he asks that we rethink our policies concerning nuclear energy.

In *How to Write: Advice and Reflections,* Rhodes dispenses cogent advice to aspiring writers, encouraging them to express themselves in print and warning them of the countless obstacles they may face. Rhodes understands the writer's struggle; he spent twenty years living from paycheck to paycheck until he finally broke through with a series of hits. For two decades, he points out, he averaged only $25,000 a year (in today's dollars). Now, he says, he makes about as much annually as "a general physician earns in private practice." Writers who become millionaires are extremely rare. "There probably aren't one hundred such writers in the world," Rhodes states.

Rhodes laments critical reaction to nonfiction prose (which he calls "verity"). He told Bennett in 1995, "It's very disappointing that verity is so lightly dismissed in the scheme of things." He explained, "There is a sort of hierarchy in people's minds about writing, with poetry at the top, fiction next, and verity, poor verity, dragging along behind."

Rhodes's primer touches on the basics—voice, point of view, precision, editing, rewriting, and research—and celebrates the joy of release writing can bring; for, Rhodes says, "silence is pain that writing relieves." He often quotes those literary figures who have most influenced his career: Melville, Emerson, John Donne, and Conrad.

Rhodes accepted an offer to write *How to Write* chiefly to finance the writing of *Dark Sun: The Making of the Hydrogen Bomb* (1995), which he had been working on for four years. "The advance (on *Dark Sun*) had run out," he said in a 1995 interview. "I needed to earn my daily bread, and here was a chance for three months of very pleasant work, to make enough money to finish *Dark Sun*." But he is quick to admit that "I would not have taken on the project if I didn't feel that perhaps I had accumulated over the years enough understanding of the process of writing and the business of writing and the culture of writing to have something useful to say."

In *Dark Sun* Rhodes weaves together three parallel books: the development of nuclear weapons in the Soviet Union under Joseph Stalin; postwar nuclear weapon development in the United States; and the development of the Strategic Air Command af-

ter World War II and the many intrigues it indulged in under the command of Gen. Curtis LeMay. As a subplot Rhodes examines the role espionage played in the nuclear arms race, focusing on Americans who spied. Rhodes hardly mentioned espionage in *The Making of the Atomic Bomb;* he presents a detailed exploration and narrative of it in *Dark Sun.*

Rhodes finds LeMay's role in the nuclear race particularly compelling. Given the task of defending against a first strike by the Soviets, LeMay tried unceasingly to provoke a response. During the Cuban Missile Crisis, LeMay urged John F. Kennedy to let him invade Cuba and then bomb the Soviets; he had seven thousand megatons of nuclear weapons in the air, ready to strike Russia. What LeMay did not know—what no one knew—was that there already were two dozen nuclear warheads in Cuba, aimed at the United States. "If LeMay had managed to drop those seven thousand megatons on the Soviet Union, he would certainly have provoked a nuclear winter over the northern hemisphere and killed us all," Rhodes said in a 1995 interview. "We were within hours of a nuclear war."

Rhodes produced ten pages a day, six days a week, to meet his August 1995 deadline, set to coincide with the fiftieth anniversary of the bombing of Hiroshima and Nagasaki and the end of World War II. He admitted to Bennett in 1995 that *Dark Sun* "was the hardest job I've ever done and is closer to what I wanted it to be than books usually are. I think it is actually a better book than *The Making of the Atomic Bomb,* better in terms of my depth of understanding, better in terms of containing a great deal more new information. The story of the atomic bomb had been told before. But the story of the development of the hydrogen bomb and to some degree the development of Soviet nuclear weapons has not been told. Nor really has the story of the Strategic Air Command been told."

In 1996, Rhodes and his wife produced *Trying to Get Some Dignity: Stories of Triumph over Childhood Abuse,* a collection of firsthand accounts that grew out of *A Hole in the World.* Rhodes has most recently published *Deadly Feasts: Tracking the Secrets of a Terrifying New Plague* (1997), which focuses on "prion" or protinaceous infectious diseases, particularly spongiform encephalopathy (in its bovine form, "mad cow disease"). He is also at work on *Lessons,* a fictional trilogy—*Judgment Day, The History of the World,* and *Long Afternoons in Heaven*—set "somewhere near the end of the world" and combining computer-generated images with prose narratives; another project is an examination of the causes of violent crime. "I feel very much at the height of my development as a writer," Rhodes said in 1995. "I'm very much in the middle of the most productive time of my life."

Few contemporary nonfiction writers explore the human heart—its cunning, its restlessness, its ceaseless striving, its capacity for cruelty and savagery—as relentlessly as Rhodes. He seeks to understand the darkness he witnesses in human experience, evoking memories of Conrad. "I wouldn't presume to compare myself with Conrad, of course," Rhodes told Bennett in 1995. "But if we're talking about themes, there certainly are a lot of similarities. He also was concerned with people on the edge, people confronting overwhelming forces that they had somehow to incorporate into their world." He added, "The darkness is one of the central mysteries I've spent many years trying to deal with. It's a very interesting mystery why human beings find ways to slaughter large numbers of their

kind. It's absolutely appalling what humans do to each other."

Interviews:

Molly McQuade, "PW Interviews: Richard Rhodes," *Publishers Weekly* (20 October 1989): 39-40;

C. Donohoe, "One Writer's Rage," *Washington Times,* 30 October 1990, p. G6;

S. Paul, "Richard Rhodes and the Making of a Sexual Being," *Kansas City Star,* 30 August 1992, p. D6.

References:

Norman Sims, ed., *The Literary Journalists* (New York: Ballantine, 1984);

Charles Trueheart, "Richard Rhodes: The Nonfiction Hat Trick," *Washington Post,* 1 April 1988, p. G4.

Ron Rosenbaum
(27 November 1946 –   )

Paul Ashdown
University of Tennessee

BOOKS: *Murder at Elaine's: A Novel* (New York: Stonehill, 1978);

Rebirth of the Salesman: Tales of the Song & Dance 70's (New York: Dell, 1979);

Manhattan Passions: True Tales of Power, Wealth, and Excess (New York: Beech Tree Books, 1987);

Travels with Dr. Death and Other Unusual Investigations (New York: Viking/Penguin, 1991).

SELECTED PERIODICAL PUBLICATIONS–UNCOLLECTED: "Ah, Watergate," *New Republic* (23 June 1982): 15–24;

"Too Young to Die?," *New York Times Magazine* (12 March 1989): 32–35, 58, 59, 61;

"Angel of Death: The Trial of the Suicide Doctor," *Vanity Fair,* 54 (May 1991): 146–151;

"Taking a Darker View," *Time* (13 January 1992): 54–56;

"The Most Hated Lawyer in America," *Vanity Fair* (March 1992): 68, 72, 77, 80, 84, 86, 88, 90, 92, 94;

"Hitler's Doomed Angel," *Vanity Fair* (April 1992): 178–186, 238, 240, 242, 244, 246, 248, 250–253;

"Return of the Wanderer," *Vanity Fair* (June 1992): 144–147, 162–167;

"Movies: Splendor in the Sorghum," *Mademoiselle* (September 1992): 78, 80, 86;

"Movies: About Face–Hollywood's New Look," *Mademoiselle* (October 1992): 52, 54, 56;

"Movies: Noir Lite," *Mademoiselle* (November 1992): 66, 74, 76;

"Riddle of the Scrolls," *Vanity Fair* (November 1992): 222–228, 286–294;

"Movies: Beyond Therapy–Analyzing Husbands and Wives," *Mademoiselle* (December 1992): 38, 42, 46;

"The F.B.I.'s Agent Provocateur," *Vanity Fair* (April 1993): 122–136;

"Seinfeld: Scary," *Harper's Bazaar* (August 1993): 78, 80;

Ron Rosenbaum (photograph by Janie Eisenberg)

"The Devil in Long Island," *New York Times Magazine* (22 August 1993): 21–27, 36–38, 42–43;

"The Know-It-All Nineties," *Harper's Bazaar* (September 1993): 172, 176;

Review of Carl Hiassen's *Strip Tease, Vanity Fair* (September 1993): 124, 126, 128, 132, 134, 136;

"Rescued by Rosanne Cash," *Harper's Bazaar* (October 1993): 136, 138;

"Non-Talk Talk," *Harper's Bazaar* (December 1993): 90, 92;

"The Rationalist and the Crystal Ball," *Harper's Bazaar* (February 1994): 76, 78;

"An Ode to Fat," *Harper's Bazaar* (March 1994): 190, 192;

"Kim Philby and the Age of Paranoia," *New York Times Magazine* (10 July 1994): 28–37, 50, 53–54;

"The Great Ivy League Nude Posture Photo Scandal," *New York Times Magazine* (15 January 1995): 26–31, 40, 46, 55–56;

"Explaining Hitler," *New Yorker* (1 May 1995): 50–70;

"Evil's Back," *New York Times Magazine* (4 June 1995): 36–44, 50, 58, 61, 72;

"The Revolt of the Basketball Liberals," *Esquire* (June 1995): 102–106;

"Among the Believers," *New York Times Magazine* (24 September 1995): 50–57, 62, 64;

"The Beautiful and the Damned," *Esquire* (March 1996): 102–111.

In his introduction to *Travels with Dr. Death and Other Unusual Investigations* (1991) Ron Rosenbaum tells how he amused himself in "the uneventful suburb of my childhood" by reading cartons of Hardy Boy detective mysteries. Having adventures and solving mysteries like the Hardy Boys, he writes after becoming one of the most prolific and well-respected magazine writers in America, "is what I thought a life in journalism would be about. Instead, while I found myself having more than my fill of adventures, the mysteries I was most attracted to rarely got solved." Rosenbaum turns his subjects into what Thomas Powers calls "a poetry of doubt." In explicating that doubt, Rosenbaum, Powers says, has become "one of the few distinctive voices of modern literary journalism."

Rosenbaum was born in Manhattan on 27 November 1946, the son of Henry Rosenbaum (1915–1990), a purchasing agent, and Evelyn Rosenbaum, a high-school teacher. He has one sister, Ruth. Rosenbaum grew up in the Long Island village of Bay Shore. In "The Devil in Long Island" (*New York Times Magazine,* August 1993) Rosenbaum reflects on the place: "I could talk about the peace of mind the lawns and trees brought to people like my father, who grew up in Brooklyn, lived through the Depression and the war and found the American dream on the same streets that became a nightmare of boredom to me." Long Island, for Rosenbaum, is a prototypical America of suburban sprawl, "a self-contained social organism. An organism whose socio-biological clock started ticking a little earlier than subsequent burbs." And so "when America

laughs at Long Island, it's laughing in the face of its own onrushing future."

Rosenbaum learned something about storytelling from a terrifying ninth-grade geometry teacher who, when confronted with a disingenuous pupil, demanded "an answer, sir. Don't give me a song and dance." And yet, Rosenbaum later reflected in *Rebirth of the Salesman: Tales of the Song & Dance 70's* (1979), we enjoy the song and dance for "the artistry of its prevarications which are–like literature–not so much lies as delightful evasions of the stern geometries that increasingly rule civilized life."

As a teenager Rosenbaum spent summers working in Bay Shore supermarkets, the low point "a hot-asphalt summer retrieving shopping carts on a vast King Kullen parking lot." Whatever the limitations of Bay Shore, Rosenbaum found ways to transcend them through reading and discussions with friends. One conversation he had as a seventeen-year-old in an all-night restaurant called the Peter Pan Diner, where he and a friend debated "such matters as the nature of Time before the creation of the universe and the mystery of the afterlife" before turning to speculation about the third Fatima prophecy, later became the opening for "The Subterranean World of the Bomb," an article published in *Harper's* and included in Norman Sims's anthology *The Literary Journalists* (1984) and in Rosenbaum's *Travels with Dr. Death and Other Unusual Investigations* (1991). Shortly after graduation from Bay Shore High School, Rosenbaum went to a theater near Gramercy Park in Manhattan and heard attorney Mark Lane lecture about the Kennedy assassination. Lane recently had testified before the Warren Commission and told the audience he had turned up evidence suggesting a conspiracy to frame Lee Harvey Oswald; the lecture fueled Rosenbaum's interest in mysteries.

Rosenbaum left Bay Shore in 1964 to attend Yale University as a Carnegie Fellow. In "The Last Secrets of Skull and Bones" in *Esquire* in 1979 he writes that he "always felt irrelevant to the real purpose of the institution, which was from its missionary beginnings devoted to converting the idle progeny of the ruling class into morally serious leaders of the establishment." At the beginning of his freshman year Rosenbaum received a summons to the gymnasium, where he was asked to strip for what he was told was a routine posture photo taken as a part of freshman orientation. Years later, while researching the article that became "The Great Ivy League Nude Posture Photo Scandal" (*New York Times Magazine,* January 1995), Rosenbaum learned that this procedure was common at most Ivy League schools as well as elite women's colleges and that

"Nobody writes better than Ron Rosenbaum, and this collection proves it." —ANDREW TOBIAS

"Ron Rosenbaum's penetrating and inventive portrait of the rich and powerful is also a portrait of our times. While *Lifestyles of the Rich and Famous* celebrates these people, Rosenbaum undresses them, one limb at a time." —KEN AULETTA

"Ron Rosenbaum is very smart, and he knows how to make people talk. Combine these two attributes, and you have the reason that *Manhattan Passions* is such a pleasure to spend time with." —BOB GREENE

"Rosenbaum is the right guy to be right here at the right time: a spy for the nineties. This is great stuff." —ROY BLOUNT, JR.

BTB
BEECH TREE BOOKS
WILLIAM MORROW
105 Madison Avenue · New York, N.Y. 10016

31F2   ISBN 0-688-06612-7

TRUE TALES OF POWER, WEALTH, AND EXCESS
Manhattan
Passions
RON ROSENBAUM

Dust jacket for the collection of articles Rosenbaum wrote on the rich and powerful of New York for Manhattan, inc.

many of the best-known American public figures had been similarly photographed. Rosenbaum discovered that the photographs had been made for anthropological research by Columbia University professor W. H. Sheldon and a Harvard colleague. He learned more from George Hersey, a Harvard art historian who had written a letter to *The New York Times* about the photographs: "What Hersey seemed to be saying was that entire generations of America's ruling class had been unwitting guinea pigs in a vast eugenic experiment run by scientists with a master-race hidden agenda." Rosenbaum discovered boxes of the photographs in the National Anthropological Archives at the Smithsonian Institution in Washington. Shortly after the article was published, the photographs reportedly were destroyed.

Later in his freshman year Rosenbaum took a philosophy course from Josiah Thompson, a Kierkegaard scholar who was writing *Six Seconds in Dallas: A Micro-Study of the Kennedy Assassination* (1967). While investigating the Kennedy assassination industry in 1983, Rosenbaum located Thompson, who had became a private detective in San Francisco. "And so with Thompson as my model," Rosenbaum writes in "Oswald's Ghost" in the *Texas Monthly* (November 1983), "I came to think of critics

of the Warren Report—the best of them anyway—as intellectual heroes, defying conventional wisdom and complacency to pursue the truth." Under the spell of Thompson, the philosopher-sleuth, Rosenbaum calls the world of assassination buffs "a carnival-sideshow underbelly of American life." Rosenbaum establishes a posture of skepticism toward the Kennedy assassination and calls himself "El Exigente of conspiracy theory culture," after "El Exigente, The Demanding One," a character in a famous television coffee commercial. The real legacy of the assassination investigation, he declared in "Taking a Darker View" (*Time,* January 1992), is a "much darker, more complex, less innocent vision of America, produced by the murk that has been churned up by the dissidents."

During his sophomore year Rosenbaum lived in the Jonathan Edwards residential college. Nearby was the strange tomb of the influential and secretive Skull and Bones Society. Early one morning Rosenbaum and a friend saw the thighbone of a large animal on the steps of the tomb. When his friend picked up the bone, the huge, triple-padlocked door to the tomb creaked open and a hand wrenched the bone from his grasp. In true Hardy Boys style the two fled to contemplate the mystery as the door clanged shut. "That dreamlike gothic moment

Dust jacket for Rosenbaum's 1991 collection, the title essay of which is an account of the trial experiences of a forensic pathologist

seems to me an emblem of the strangeness I felt at being at Yale, at being given a brief glimpse of the mysterious workings of the inner temples of privilege but feeling emphatically shut out of the secret ceremonies within," he reflects in "The Last Secrets of Skull and Bones." His humorous elegy about Skull and Bones was published in *Esquire* in 1977 and is included in *Travels with Dr. Death*. The story was used, however, by the *Manchester Union-Leader* during the New Hampshire primary in 1980 to embarrass George Bush, who had been a member of Skull and Bones. In 1988 the *Washington Post* wrote about Bush's connection with the secret society and found many members willing to talk, "a true measure," according to Rosenbaum, "of the decline of Skull and Bones—when the glamour of the White House overshadowed the mystique of the Tomb."

Rosenbaum eventually found his place in the English Department at Yale. He especially admired William Empson's *Seven Types of Ambiguity* (1930), which he later found useful in helping to explain counterintelligence mysteries. The historic association of Yale with the cloak-and-dagger trade prompted Rosenbaum to interview CIA spymaster James Jesus Angleton and to advance his own theories of double agentry.

After he graduated Phi Beta Kappa with an English degree in 1968, Rosenbaum was hired as a reporter by the *Suffolk Sun* and covered the Democratic National Convention. He then became assistant editor of the *Fire Island News*. His writing caught the attention of Rhoda Wolf, who mentioned Rosenbaum to her husband, Dan, a founding editor of *The Village Voice*.

Rosenbaum met Dan Wolf at a party during the summer of 1969. Ten days later Rosenbaum called Wolf and asked him for a job on the paper. Wolf turned Rosenbaum over to city editor Mary Nichols, who put him to work writing feature stories such as a profile of the SoHo neighborhood artists' colony and a tribute to the cheesecake at Junior's restaurant in Brooklyn. As he says in his introduction to *Rebirth of the Salesman,* he was "free to seek out peripheral epiphanies that reflected in some parabolic way the essence of the main event" and wandered "around city and country following my instincts to cover stories that appealed to me." He covered John Lindsay's campaign for mayor of New York and the Vietnam War moratorium rally, which drew six hundred thousand marchers to Washington in 1969. He also followed Arthur Goldberg's race against Nelson Rockefeller for governor of New York in 1970.

Kevin McAuliffe, whose history of *The Village Voice,* titled *The Great American Newspaper,* was published in 1978, called one of Rosenbaum's articles, "Troy Donahue Was Always Just Like He Is," published in *The Village Voice* in July 1971, "perhaps the most effective torpedo job ever done on anyone, or anything, in the *Voice.* The subject was Troy Donahue, that washed-up Warner Bros. TV star of the early sixties with the surfer-boy looks and the wooden acting technique, at the start of a media hype campaign for his 'comeback' starring role in a *roman à clef* movie about the Charles Manson Family."

Rosenbaum covered George McGovern's presidential campaign in 1972, "brilliantly crosscutting in his article between snatches of anecdotes from the last week of the botched campaign and what came over his car radio as he twiddled the dial driving through South Dakota on his way to McGovern's Election Night defeat party," according to McAuliffe. He served as the White House correspondent during the Watergate investigation, a subject he would return to with "Ah, Watergate" (*New Republic,* 23 June 1982), a tenth-anniversary assessment of the events. Writing in 1991, he said he found it remarkable that the original Watergate burglary remained unsolved.

Rosenbaum often brought a light, ironic touch to his Watergate coverage. For example, an essay about television advertising, "Three Tales of TV Commericals," recounts a visit to President Richard Nixon's first law office in Whittier, California. Rosenbaum was surprised to learn that the previous tenant had been a seller of false teeth who had gone bankrupt. From this piece of trivia Rosenbaum "began to notice the astonishing number of denture-aid ads on the nightly news and the Watergate-like structure common to most of them. We start with a cover-up." The denture wearer tries to hide his secret but is forced to decide the degree to which he can risk biting into something that will lead to embarrassment. "Fed perhaps by the insatiable post-Watergate appetite for exposure of the private lapses of public figures, certain denture-problem commercials have made a significant shift to the public humiliation of their porcelainized protagonists."

McAuliffe painted a generally unflattering portrait of Rosenbaum while acknowledging "an ease, a fecundity, a graceful glibness to his writing that no one else seemed to have." According to McAuliffe, Rosenbaum's contemporaries "were amazed at him, in more ways than one. He could write fast, and long, driving himself to stay awake for extended periods of time to finish something, and with such seemingly easy force, that they were dazzled by him. At other times he appeared to some of them to be a bit dazzled himself, and certainly acted that way." After Wolf was fired by new *Village Voice* owner Clay Felker in 1975, Rosenbaum resigned, claiming later in an interview with the *SoHo Weekly News* that *The Village Voice* had become "embarrassing, shrill and vulgar." Meanwhile Rosenbaum published in *New Times* a sensational interview with Abbie Hoffman, a fugitive from cocaine charges. Felker, Rosenbaum, and other journalists had differing accounts about the circumstances under which the story was written. Felker was critical of Rosenbaum at a meeting of the New York Deadline Club, and the controversy continued in the trade press.

After Rosenbaum left *The Village Voice,* he wrote *Murder at Elaine's: A Novel* (1978), that first appeared in serial form in six installments in *High Times* under the name "George R. Boz." According to McAuliffe, the character of Walter Foster, a magazine publisher who is the murder victim of the title, resembled Felker. A prologue, "The Apartment, a True Story," tells of the Golden Greek Affair, a plot that allegedly grew out of Richard Nixon's obsession with the possibility of Sen. Edward Kennedy's political challenge in the 1972 presidential elections. Supposedly, Nixon's people set up a trysting place in Manhattan equipped with cameras and recording equipment. The idea was to obtain compromising information that could be used for political purposes. The novel speculated that the "smoking gun tape" of the Watergate investigation reveals that Nixon approved retargeting the operation against journalists to obtain compromising in-

Rosenbaum in 1991 (photograph by Andrew Eccles)

formation that could be used to protect the presidency.

In Rosenbaum's clever story a reporter, Guy Davenport, supposedly notorious for taking LSD in President Gerald Ford's plane, tries to solve the puzzle of Charles Dickens's unfinished novel, *The Mystery of Edwin Drood* (1870). He thinks there may actually have been a plot to murder Dickens to keep him from publishing the last chapter of the book. *Murder at Elaine's,* a roman à clef, evolves into a send-up of New York journalism, investigative reporting, conspiracy theories, literary pretentiousness, and even the murder mystery genre. Rosenbaum pokes fun at himself, dropping names of editors and magazines and discoursing about New Journalism. "I'm just under a lot of pressure from the goddamn editors to act crazy," Davenport says. *Rolling Stone* is thinly disguised as *Argonaut* magazine. Rosenbaum mixes actual events, conspiracy theories, Watergate transcripts, and self-referential satire while explicating political, literary, and social mysteries. At one point Victor, a literary pimp, tells Davenport: "Under less infelicitous circumstances we could have had some provocative conversations about journalism and fiction and the deliberate confusion of the two realms you seem to delight in." Like Davenport, Rosenbaum too delights in confusing realms to produce what he calls "a hybrid kind of thing I do."

Tom Buckley, reviewing *Murder at Elaine's* for *The New York Times* (4 March 1979), found the novel "diffidently amusing" but added that "one has the feeling that the author and his editors were so

pleased with the initial inspiration that they neglected to subject the manuscript to the high-temperature refining and the painstaking shaping and hammering that alone can produce the impression of effortless wit and airy imagination." Nora Ephron and Roy Blount Jr. have attempted to develop the novel into an Off-Broadway production.

Rosenbaum also wrote for *Esquire* under Harold Hayes and was a contributing editor to the journalism review *MORE.* A collection of his articles, *Rebirth of the Salesman: Tales of the Song & Dance 70's,* was published in 1979. Seeking a unifying theme, Rosenbaum saw the 1970s as a decade of self-promotion–a decade best represented by the traveling salesman, an essential and enduring American type. Introductions to each of the dozen articles in the collection show the salesman's influence. The salesman is to be found among public relations and advertising agents, pitchmen, preachers, promoters, presidents, publishers, and even journalists.

Like Joan Didion, Janet Malcolm, and other literary journalists, Rosenbaum has reflected candidly on the art of interviewing and the inevitable deception in the reportorial enterprise. Rosenbaum describes himself as obsessive and says he tends to bring out the obsessions of other people, who talk to him freely. "The Ancient Mariners of the world have always singled me out to tell their troubled tales to," he notes in his introduction to *Manhattan Passions.* In other situations, however, as he observes in *Rebirth of the Salesman,* sources have to be encouraged to talk:

> To get people to talk to you, particularly people who are not public figures, who don't have anything to gain from talking to you, you have to win their confidence. They want to know who you are, why you're doing the story, what your angle is, why they should trust you with their privacy. After you speak to thirty people about the same story, this process of winning confidence inevitably becomes your pitch. . . . You learn to tell the story of your story; anecdotes are picked up from earlier interviewees and trotted out; personal reminiscences and past stories are offered up, all in the effort to sell the notion that you, the reporter, are no ordinary traveling salesman but a merchant of truth, understanding, and empathy–in exchange for which commodities the innocent interviewees are asked to pay with pieces of their privacy. If you're good at it, people fall for it. And they always tell more than they need to, more than what's good for them, leaving them open to feelings of betrayal.

In an unpublished interview with Paul Ashdown on 24 October 1995 Rosenbaum explained how he works. He tape-records all his interviews and has them transcribed. He then reviews the transcripts and looks for themes. "I guess I'm always looking for some pure storytelling element at the heart of things," he says. Rosenbaum prefers to write in the first person, finding "a kind of false objectivity of writing in the third person."

Many stories in *Rebirth of the Salesman* are entertaining and brilliantly rendered. "Secrets of the Little Blue Box," which first appeared in *Esquire* (October 1971), is an account of a network of "electronic con artists," many of them blind, who developed illegal devices to infiltrate and control long-distance telephone switching systems. Among the early users of these illegal devices were gamblers and securities swindlers, but also electronics geniuses and hoaxers, forerunners of the computer hackers. Rosenbaum confesses that he too acquired one of the devices and enjoyed using it.

Steve Jobs, cofounder of Apple Computer, told Rosenbaum that he and partner Steve Wozniak read this story as teenagers and began manufacturing the blue boxes in Jobs's garage. Thomas McMahon also may have been inspired to write the novel *Loving Little Egypt* (1987) after reading the article. Rosenbaum received so many phone calls from hackers seeking more information about the secret codes alluded to in the article that he had to get an unlisted number.

"The Corpse as Big as the Ritz" in *Esquire* (August 1973) probes the mysterious death of David Whiting, "a dreamer of Gatsbylike pretensions" and a press agent for actress Sarah Miles, during the filming of *The Man Who Loved Cat Dancing* in 1973. "Death & The Nite Owl" is a profile of Pat Doyle, the self-proclaimed "World's Greatest Police Reporter" of the *New York Daily News*. Rosenbaum expanded his theory about how good reporters "must be salesmen to their editors as well as to their sources. Promoting the misfortunes of the latter for the approval of the former is part of the game." Doyle, in Rosenbaum's story, is more storyteller than writer, phoning in most of his stories to the rewrite desk as he cultivates sources and prowls the city streets.

Rosenbaum overreaches his metaphors in some of these stories, but the collection ties together a series of seemingly unrelated personalities and events. One factor that makes his writing excellent literary journalism is that it makes the attempt to discover cultural tendencies and themes. As social history the book captures the essentially vacuous spirit of the 1970s, setting the stage for Rosenbaum's next book, *Manhattan Passions: True Tales of Power, Wealth, and Excess* (1987), a collection of articles published in *Manhattan, inc.* Rosenbaum explains in his introduction that he initially hesitated

when the magazine's editor, Jane Amsterdam, asked him in 1984 to write about the rich and powerful of New York, "the shadowy new Gatsbys of the roaring eighties." Rosenbaum protested that he generally preferred to write about outsiders with strange obsessions rather than power brokers. Amsterdam, whom he knew from his days as a Washington reporter, convinced him that stories about insiders with obsessions would be just as appealing. Most of the collected pieces involve discussions over meals, a motif Rosenbaum uses to link the stories together as if to emphasize the gluttony and greed that characterize the decade.

The first story in the collection, "The Shame of the Super Rich. Meet Felix and Elizabeth Rohatyn: Society Dissidents," caused controversy. Rosenbaum interviewed Felix and Elizabeth Rohatyn, two prominent New Yorkers active in charitable causes. The Rohatyns felt wealthy New Yorkers were not doing enough for the city's poor, were disingenuous in their charitable work and more interested in social climbing. Felix Rohatyn, a powerful investment banker, questioned whether democracy could survive in a society of extreme wealth and extreme poverty. After the article was published in May 1986 the Rohatyns were attacked by the social elite. *Newsweek* made note of Rosenbaum's interview, which appeared as a *Manhattan, inc.* cover story, and the ensuing controversy.

Donald Trump's interest in halting nuclear weapons proliferation was the subject of another story, "Trump: The Ultimate Deal." Trump told Rosenbaum he wanted to make a deal with the Soviet Union to limit further use of the technology. Rosenbaum suggested facetiously that it would not be unreasonable to put all nuclear negotiation in Trump's hands because he knows how to make deals. In other articles Rosenbaum discussed Teilhard de Chardin and Pelagius with New York governor Mario Cuomo; Robert Kennedy with attorney Roy Cohn; organized crime with James La Rossa, a trial attorney for alleged mob godfather Paul Castellano; and power, status, and the culinary arts with New York mayor Ed Koch. He was given a hasty exit from *Forbes* magazine publisher Malcolm Forbes's wine cellar after he asked a question about Ronald Reagan's policy toward the Sandinistas in Nicaragua.

A *Publishers Weekly* reviewer on 26 December 1986 called the collection "a brilliant group portrait of New York City's rich and famous of the 1980s," though the critic found some pieces "a bit lackluster" and thought Rosenbaum went too easy with his interview questions because he usually got to like his subjects. Bruce Nussbaum, reviewing for *Business*

Week (6 April 1987), said that "Rosenbaum's ear is so good and his interviewing skill so smooth that you simply can't believe what he gets people to say." However, he disliked Rosenbaum's intrusion into the stories: "His snide asides and 'look-at-me' cracks interfere with the cadences of his subjects."

A third collection of articles, *Travels with Dr. Death and Other Unusual Investigations,* followed in 1991. Two of the articles, "The Corpse as Big as the Ritz" and "Secrets of the Little Blue Box" had been published previously in *Rebirth of the Salesman.* "The Subterranean World of the Bomb" had been published in *The Literary Journalists* (1984), and Thomas Fensch included the title piece, "Travels with Dr. Death" (*Vanity Fair,* 1990), in an anthology, *Nonfiction for the 1990s* (1991). The inclusion of the articles in *Travels with Dr. Death* is appropriate and fortunate given the scope and structure of the book and its wider readership.

In the introduction Rosenbaum argues that the "investigation of the investigation" is the paradigmatic form the search for truth has taken in our time. Epistemologically, these investigations lead to "a despair of certainty" characteristic of the age. The Nuremberg trials, the Warren Commission report, and even the Woodward and Bernstein Watergate investigations all have left unanswered and perhaps unanswerable questions that remain before the public. The investigations themselves become the subject of yet more investigations. He points out that the Woodward and Bernstein Watergate stories began as a reinvestigation of a grand jury document. Although people have difficulty accepting the inevitability of doubt and the lingering paradox of uncertain knowledge, the investigations of investigations do contain much ancillary data that tell a great deal about the culture. The book, then, represents "an education in the varieties of contemporary uncertainty."

Rosenbaum establishes a philosophical structure by quoting John Keats's doctrine of negative capability: the capability of "being in uncertainties, mysteries, doubts without irritable reaching after fact or reason." But paradox is an uncomfortable position, so while keeping negative capability in mind he presses ahead with further investigations. Uncertainty, he argues, should not lead to the acceptance of conspiracy theories simply to have an answer, but should acknowledge the need for further inquiry. The stories "are efforts to map out the boundaries between what can be known and what can't, road maps that take us up to the borders of terra incognita, not infallible guides to the entities within it." What links most of the stories is that as individual entities they share "multiple identities." He cites

Thomas Carlyle's notion that man, a "fictile" creature, has an urge to create fictions and fictional selves. Rosenbaum, in turn, writes "factual stories about fictile people."

The book is organized into sections exploring public scandals, private investigations, clandestine subcultures, and a historical labyrinth. In "The Shadow of the Mole," first published in *Harper's* in 1983, Rosenbaum introduces his "notional mole" theory—a double-double-cross system to explain unanswered questions in the cloak-and-dagger contest between the CIA's "Yale-bred" former counterintelligence chief James Jesus Angleton and the British foreign service mole Kim Philby. Robin Winks gave Rosenbaum's theory attention in his book *Cloak & Gown* (1987). Rosenbaum expanded and updated his own theories in "Kim Philby and the Age of Paranoia," published in *The New York Times Magazine* on 10 July 1994.

In the title story, "Travels with Dr. Death," Rosenbaum accompanies Dr. James Grigson, a forensic pathologist known as Dr. Death because of his lethal testimony in more than one hundred death penalty cases, as he testifies in several trials in three Texas towns over two days. The doctor's area of expertise is the "poorly charted borderline realm between evil and madness." Another notable story, first published as "Dead Ringers" in *Esquire* in 1976, probes the mysterious deaths of two New York physicians, the Marcus twins. Rosenbaum claims that the title of a 1988 movie about the case was taken from the article. Other stories in the collection deal with Gen. Richard Secord and the Iran-Contra case; the murder of President Kennedy's mistress; a Brooklyn crack murder investigation; the "death awareness" movement associated with Elisabeth Kubler-Ross; the cancer cure underground; and Richard H. Roffman, a celebrity press agent.

Praise for the collection was widespread. Dave Shiflett, reviewing for the *Wall Street Journal* on 20 February 1991, said that, unlike most journalists, Rosenbaum "actually writes about things people care about: corpses and how they got that way." He described the book as "a creepy masterpiece." Thomas H. Cook praised the book in *The New York Times Book Review* (3 March 1991). Rosenbaum, he wrote, "may be in pursuit of the ineffable, but his methods are strictly down-to-earth—solid research and a laudable determination to be at the center of the landscape he explores." Robert Stone placed Rosenbaum "among the most thoughtful and insightful interpreters of our fractured fin-de-siecle society. He has a wonderful eye for paradox and always manages to find the significant detail and to suggest the most intriguing conclusion." Thomas Powers declared Rosenbaum "a master of the short form—the 5,000–10,000 word magazine article. They're all as easy to read as spy stories and beautifully written."

Rosenbaum, who lives in Manhattan, writes a column for the *New York Observer* called "The Edgy Enthusiast," which gives him a chance to praise topics within his wide range of cultural enthusiasms, from television to Latin poets. He also enjoys writing about advertising. Rosenbaum is collecting magazine articles he may publish in another anthology of his work. He has a book on Hitler in progress: a nonfiction work tentatively titled *Explaining Hitler,* forthcoming from Random House in 1998. A sample appeared on 1 May 1995 in *The New Yorker.* "To spend time, as I have for the past several years, with historians, psychologists, psychohistorians, philosophers, and theologians who have devoted themselves to the task of explaining Hitler," he writes, "is to realize how pervasive is the feeling of something still missing, something still inexplicable." Other factual material about Hitler has appeared in *Travels with Dr. Death* and in *Vanity Fair;* Rosenbaum has also discussed Hitler on network television.

In 1992 Rosenbaum visited Qumran in the Judaean desert with a group of American Christian scholars to study the Dead Sea Scrolls. In "Riddle of the Scrolls" in *Vanity Fair* (November 1992) he claims to be "the first non-scholar to read these fragments of the Qumran legacy in 1,900 years." Walking above the graves of the Qumran writers, he became fascinated by the historical pathos "that may be at the heart of their power to appeal to us: the urgent sense in their work of belatedness, of being—like us—in an apocalyptic holding pattern at the End of History, trapped in a pre-millennial moment,

helplessly enduring the cruel reign of the Children of Darkness, sensing that God is late, or worse, has fled."

His recent work increasingly explores the nature of evil. In "Evil's Back," published in *The New York Times Magazine* (4 June 1995), he tries to find a common thread in the Oklahoma City bombing, the Susan Smith murder case, the Jeffrey Dahmer murders, the Hitler atrocities, and other heinous acts. He interviewed theologians, philosophers, literary scholars, historians, and a talk show host, and he resumes his theological discussion with Mario Cuomo. Staring into the ruins of the federal building in Oklahoma City, Rosenbaum "found it difficult not to see the gaping holes in the building as a metaphor for the gaping holes in the fabric of our state of understanding of the Problem of Evil."

Rosenbaum's article "attracted an unusually swift and large response," according to an editor's note in the letters section of the 25 June 1995 issue of the magazine. "Rarely is reaction to articles so universally favorable. Hundreds of postal and e-mail letters offered praise for the article and extended reflections on the subject." The quest for answers to the ultimate questions lifts Rosenbaum's journalism from the tabloid pages to the highest temples of scholarly inquiry and faith.

References:

Thomas Fensch, ed., *Nonfiction for the 1990s* (Hillsdale, N.J.: Erlbaum Associates, 1991);

Kevin Michael McAuliffe, *The Great American Newspaper* (New York: Scribners, 1978);

Norman Sims, ed., *The Literary Journalists* (New York: Ballantine, 1984);

Robin W. Winks, *Cloak & Gown* (New York: Morrow, 1987).

Lillian Ross
(8 June 1927 –)

Thomas B. Connery
University of Saint Thomas

BOOKS: *Picture* (New York: Rinehart, 1952);
Portrait of Hemingway (New York: Simon & Schuster, 1961);
The Player: A Profile of an Art, by Ross and Helen Ross (New York: Simon & Schuster, 1962);
Vertical and Horizontal (New York: Simon & Schuster, 1963);
Reporting (New York: Simon & Schuster, 1964);
Talk Stories (New York: Simon & Schuster, 1966);
Adlai Stevenson (Philadelphia: Lippincott, 1966);
Moments with Chaplin (New York: Dodd, Mead, 1980);
Takes: Stories from the "Talk of the Town" (New York: Congdon & Weed, 1983).

Lillian Ross in 1942 (UPI/Corbis-Bettmann)

When the so-called New Journalism burst upon the scene in the 1960s, some critics were quick to note that the form was not really new; it had precursors, if not a tradition. Lillian Ross's *Picture* (1952), a dramatic account of the making of the film *The Red Badge of Courage* (Metro-Goldwyn-Mayer, 1951), was cited as a classic work of "new journalism" that preceded the 1960s version by about fifteen to twenty years, having first been published in *The New Yorker* in 1952. In one of the early studies of the genre, *The New Journalism in America: Other Voices* (1974), Everette E. Dennis and William L. Rivers placed Ross among a handful of writers who were "chiefly responsible for developing the new nonfiction." Since then it has been demonstrated that the New Journalism of the 1960s was part of a tradition of literary journalism predating Ross in the United States by almost one hundred years. Today her name is often linked with two of her *New Yorker* contemporaries, Joseph Mitchell and John Hersey, both of whom did much of their significant literary journalistic writing in the 1940s.

Ross was reportedly born 8 June 1927 in Syracuse, New York, to Louis and Edna Rosenson Ross. She began writing for *The New Yorker* shortly before the end of World War II, becoming a staff writer in 1948 or 1949, and she has worked for that magazine ever since. Although she established her career pri-

marily by writing about people, often producing biographical sketches full of facts and curiosities about her subjects, Ross has closely guarded the details of her own life. Interviews with her have been few, and information regarding her background is sparse, just as she prefers. She told *Time* in 1964 that she had made a mistake when she publicly revealed that she had been born in Syracuse; *Newsweek* in 1961 described her as "a short, quiet, friendly woman who does not care to be photographed"; and the *Boston Globe* in 1993 reported that she was "reluctant to discuss herself" and that she "refuses to divulge her age even to her son."

Ross's reluctance to reveal much about herself may be based, at least in part, on principles about writing and reporting that she holds dear. She discussed her reporting/writing approach briefly in the *Time* interview and in greater detail in introductions to two collections of her *New Yorker* pieces: *Reporting* (1964; the introduction appears in a 1981 Dodd, Mead edition) and *Takes: Stories from the "Talk of the Town"* (1983). In the *Reporting* introduction she insists that it is not possible to explain how she did the reporting in the book because "the 'how' of each writer's work resides somewhere deep in the fabric of that writer's being." Nevertheless, she then volunteers seventeen "principles" that she says have guided her work as a journalist.

Under her ninth principle she writes: "do not promote yourself; do not advertise yourself; do not sell yourself." A few lines earlier she says: "Actually, your attention at all times should be on your subject, not on you. Do not call attention to yourself." Of course, she is admonishing writers to keep themselves out of their articles; like some other authors before her, Ross views celebrity journalists as distractions to genuine reporting and counterproductive to depicting the truth of the persons, places, or events being covered. Thus, the less the reader knows about Ross, the more the reader is able to focus on her subjects.

Using television and the talk circuit to sell herself and her books in order to get people to read what she writes "would be the ultimate foolishness," she declares, and "a betrayal of the force within me that made me want to write in the first place." In the *Takes* introduction she emphasizes how much she enjoys writing the short, anonymous pieces that appear at the front of each *New Yorker* and that reveal a glimpse of people and life in New York City, calling the anonymity "very satisfying" because that work can "speak for itself in its own way."

Both introductions provided Ross the opportunity to attack indirectly some characteristics of the 1960s and 1970s New Journalism that she clearly found unsavory. Many of the best-known New Journalists, for instance, were self-promoters and often the main characters in their works. But in the *Reporting* introduction she also cautions against ambiguity, another characteristic of some New Journalism, saying it has a place in poetry and fiction but not in journalism. In *Takes,* referring to the "Talk" form, she says techniques more common to fiction may be used, but she emphasizes key limitations that make a "Talk" piece, and most journalism, difficult. For instance, she writes that, "contrary to what some writers believe today," it is impossible to report what is inside another person's head. Furthermore,

for Ross a "reconstructed" quote is not good enough; rather, the reporter had to be there to hear the speaker. That is part of being "bound to the *facts.*"

In *Reporting* she urges young writers to "get out from under the deluge of propaganda about doing what is 'new'" and instead "find what is a natural expression of yourself." In *Takes* she lists the great writers/reporters who are experts at "careful observation, significant details, characterization, insight into a character or situation," fictional devices that have been used in reporting, she says, "for centuries." It is these same characteristics, these tools of good writing, that mark Ross's own literary journalism.

These characteristics also appear in the journalism of two *New Yorker* colleagues she calls in *Takes* "two of the great reporters of the present," Joseph Mitchell and Berton Roueche. Although critics often speak of a predictable *New Yorker* style of writing, it would seem that Ross has been especially influenced by these two writers. Besides the rich, full detail and characterization, the writing styles of Mitchell, Roueche, and Ross have a similar tone that seems subtly placed somewhere between amusement and bemusement. The writing of all three is also marked by a sheer pleasure in the subject.

In the course of praising great reporters from the past, including John Aubrey, Ivan Turgenev, Henry Mayhew, and Daniel Defoe, Ross favorably quotes from Defoe's *A Journal of the Plague Year* (1722). Yet *A Journal* is entirely a reconstruction, since Defoe was about five years old when the Great Plague swept through London in 1665. This does not so much reflect a contradiction in Ross's thinking as her not knowing the true nature of Defoe's work. Nevertheless, it is revealing that Ross cites favorably a work she considers "a factual report in fictional form," which is another way to define literary journalism.

If there is a contradiction in Ross's views of reporting/writing, it would be in her contention that as long as she stands back from a scene and exhaustively records details for her readers, she remains a neutral observer and the facts tend to speak for themselves. Her primary reporting technique is to be as unobtrusive as possible, to listen and watch carefully, to use a fly-on-the-wall approach, as one critic has put it, and take lots of notes. She never uses a tape recorder. One of the actors on the set of *The Red Badge of Courage* remembered her tagging along "every time, practically in lock step, filling up her notebook." Her presence in an article is barely and rarely felt, except as the narrator who serves as the reader's eyes and ears. Her approach is perhaps best described by Gay Talese, who explained his own reportorial technique this way: "I try to follow my subjects unobtrusively while observing them in revealing situations, noting their reactions and the reactions of others to them. I attempt to absorb the whole scene, the dialogue and mood, the tension, drama, conflict."

This type of extended observation, what some might call immersion or saturation reporting, allows for the best works of literary journalism to be stories that inform thematically and emotionally at a level common to fiction. While such works accurately depict what the writer has seen or what the subjects have experienced, the selection of point of view, quotations, and various rhetorical and narrative elements, including tone, framing devices, and unifying themes, make the claim that the facts speak for themselves disingenuous.

This does not mean that Ross is wrong when she declares that she simply presents people objectively. "In my work I don't make judgments of people," *Time* reported her saying; "I think you should let them be the way they are." But her selection of details and behavior and the use of language to present those details and depict that behavior create one version of the subject—Ross's version. While Ross's reporting technique may be informed by a belief in neutrality and objectivity, her articles are naturally subjective—as is true of all literary journalism and perhaps all writing—because she has imposed a narrative structure on the material she may have gathered objectively. To a degree she recognized this in *Takes* when she praised writers who "tried to understand" but did not "overinterpret" in their writing.

Ross has felt compelled to make her claim of neutrality and objectivity at least in part because some readers and critics have considered her articles scathing attacks, embarrassing revelations, or both. For the most part the principal subjects of her pieces do not agree. The perception of Ross as a caustic writer primarily came about after publication of two of her works of literary journalism: *Portrait of Hemingway* (1961), first published in *The New Yorker* in 1950, and *Picture* (1952).

When *Reporting,* a volume that also includes both *Portrait of Hemingway* and *Picture,* was published in 1964, one reviewer noted several different contemporary views of Ross as "a disarmingly aggressive writer." Later, the same reviewer said Ross used a "scalpel for her palette knife" and talked of her subjects being "pinned to her butterfly board." *Time* quoted two people who had appeared in Ross

Jerry Epstein, Ross, and Charlie Chaplin

articles. One said, "She sits there like a little mouse, looking so cute, but there's nothing but vitriol in her typewriter." The other, Bill Mauldin, who had a part in *The Red Badge of Courage,* said, "Anybody who holds still for an interview by her is taking an awful chance, because he could very well lose a lot of skin." Writing in *The Saturday Review* in 1963, Granville Hicks referred to Ross's "malicious wit," and although he was reviewing a collection of Ross's fiction, *Vertical and Horizontal* (1963), he described her Hemingway piece as "painfully revealing if not deliberately malicious."

Yet a reader of much of Ross's writing over the past forty-five years would find such assessments puzzling and would conclude that they are misleading. The vast majority of Ross's work, particularly her "Talk of the Town" pieces, collected in two volumes, *Takes* and *Talk Stories* (1966), reveals her genuine curiosity about her subjects and, more often than not, her appreciation for them as artists, actors, or professionals of one sort or another. After all, two of her reporting/writing principles are: 1) Do not write about anyone who does not want to be written about; and 2) Do not write about anyone you do not like. That she likes nearly all her subjects, even when she finds their behavior amusing or quirky, seems perfectly clear.

In addition, even in her best work she ignores or avoids personal aspects of her subjects' lives, particularly if the matters in question would make the subject uncomfortable or would be controversial, too negative, or embarrassing. Anjelica Huston, daughter of John Huston, the focus of *Picture,* said in a foreword to a 1993 Anchor Books edition that her parents maintained a friendship with Ross long after *Picture* was first published. Huston even asked Ross to accept a Creative Arts Award for him in 1986 when he was recovering from eye surgery. Anjelica Huston said her parents loved, respected, and trusted Ross, adding that they said Ross was "different from other reporters." As she points out, her father had been described as a hedonist, a womanizer, and a gambler, but there is no hint of any of that in Ross's account because Ross "never sought to write gossip or to go beyond a particular line that she drew for herself in his personal life."

Many of Ross's "Talk of the Town" pieces are simply extended quotations from a single interview with the subject, generally reflecting favorably upon the subject. But the "Talk" sketches that qualify as literary journalism often have stronger narrative unity than such monologues, as well as an ironic or satiric element. For instance, the first piece in *Talk Stories,* which consists of "Talk of the Town" articles written between 1958 and 1964, is "Movement," a tiny literary journalistic gem. The "Movement" refers to the Beat Movement, and the focus of this "Talk" piece is a cocktail party sponsored by a publisher that has just produced an anthology of Beat writing edited by Seymour Krim, who serves as party host and who also tries to define and explain the movement to Ross, sounding a bit pretentious in the process. The party is conventional and low-key; everyone seems to be waiting for someone to appear or something striking or interesting to happen. The people Ross first encounters appear to be Beats, but she learns that they are just dressed like Beats and have been hired by the publisher "to inspire confidence." Ross allows readers to eavesdrop on bits and pieces of conversation that reveal the conventionality of those gathered to celebrate the revolutionary.

Many at the party are there to gaze at celebrities and are disappointed that Beat legends Jack Kerouac and Allen Ginsberg are absent. They seem pleased when Norman Mailer arrives, though Ross says he is "looking very conservative in a business suit and very much the elder statesman." A bartender's comments serve as ironic counterpoint to the comments of the guests, and near the end the bartender declares: "What kind of writers are they, they all talk the same? These kids, they are not Tol-stoy." But perhaps the most perceptive comment, and one that best reflects the satiric tone of the piece, comes from a Harvard student who declares: "This party looks like any old party at Harvard."

Another "Talk" article, "Switched," which allows the reader to be present as the recently selected Miss American Teen-Ager is given her trendy London wardrobe, has the same ironic tone and playful quality as "Movement." But while both sketches include a certain amount of deflating of the pompous and pretentious—or the loss of some skin, as Mauldin would have it—the depictions are neither cruel nor malicious.

Other "Talk" pieces that qualify as literary journalism are wonderful sketches in which Ross simply records two brilliant people sharing a scene. An example from *Talk Stories* is "Fugue," in which the pianist Glenn Gould and the violinist Yehudi Menuhin meet at Gould's request to view Gould's hour-long film, "The Anatomy of Fugue." In the opening paragraph readers meet an "unslept and unbarbered" Gould in his "baggy dark-blue suit" and "raggedy brown sweater," and a "pink-cheeked, chubby, trim and serene" Menuhin "neatly encased in well-tailored pin stripes and well-laundered supplementation." Ross allows readers to listen as the two men talk to one another, watch Gould's film, and continue their conversation. Ross makes evident the pure delight two musical geniuses take in one another's company and artistry.

"Bartok in the Morning," from *Takes,* presents a similar scene between Menuhin and Benny Goodman, joined by pianist Paul Coker, as they rehearse in Goodman's apartment for a concert appearance. In between playing they talk of back surgery and exercise and, of course, music. Ross's pleasure in witnessing the scenes in both "Fugue" and "Bartok in the Morning" radiates from her depictions. Readers see Ross's subjects as joyful and human and take pleasure with Ross in being allowed to drop in on these men. Ironies are not developed or acknowledged, nor is any possible discomfort, tension, or disagreement.

Just as Ross's pleasure in her musician subjects is clear in these short "Talk" pieces, becoming a part of the meaning and purpose of the articles, so supposedly should her delight in the Hemingway personality have been evident in that profile. Perhaps it is evident today. But when Ross's profile was published in *The New Yorker* in 1950, it caused a stir. In a preface to the book publication of the profile in 1961, the year Hemingway killed himself, Ross described the controversy over her piece as "strange and mysterious." Some readers admired the piece for the wrong reasons, she said. They did not like

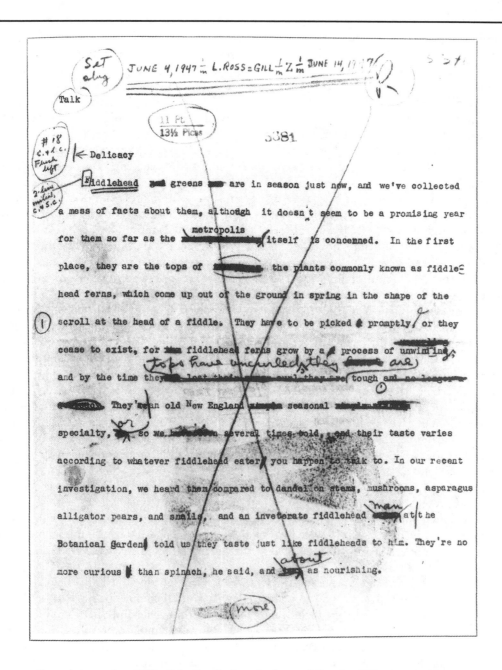

Typescript page for a "Talk of the Town" column by Ross and Brendan Gill, edited by Harold Ross
(from Brendan Gill, Here at The New Yorker, *1975).*

the Hemingway personality and thought she did not like it either; they believed Ross ridiculed Hemingway. Fans of Hemingway did not like the way Ross presented him, believing that a serious writer should not act and talk as Ross said Hemingway did. Ross said these readers "didn't like Hemingway to be Hemingway."

In a 1961 *New Republic* article on Hemingway's reputation, Irving Howe referred to the Ross profile and said, "nothing more cruel has happened to an American writer than the Lillian Ross interview . . . a smear of vanity and petulance that only a journal-

istic Delilah would have put into print." Ross responded to the Howe piece with a letter to *The New Republic* that took up nearly three full columns, almost a page, and called Howe's remarks "irresponsible, rather sordid, and absolutely wrong." She described her Hemingway profile as "an attempt to record as precisely as possible just how Hemingway, who had the nerve to be like nobody else on earth, behaved when he was in action, just how he talked, how he sounded and looked; it was a portrait of a great and lovable man." In the 1961 book preface she explains that she had intended to present Hem-

Ross with Ernest Hemingway, his family, and an unidentified friend in Ketchum, Idaho

ingway without judgment but that she now saw implicit in her "choice and arrangement of detail, and in total atmosphere created" her feeling of "affection and admiration" for Hemingway. Ross had even allowed Hemingway to read the profile before it was published, and both he and his wife, Mary, made corrections. Hemingway suggested a deletion and, according to Ross, said the profile was "funny and good." When the controversy arose after publication, Hemingway wrote to Ross and, referring to the profile's critics, said "the hell with them."

Ross had visited the Hemingways in Ketchum, Idaho, in 1947 on her way back to New York after interviewing a Brooklyn bullfighter in Mexico. The article on the bullfighter, Sidney Franklin, would be Ross's first *New Yorker* profile, published in 1949. She found the Hemingways warm and welcoming, and after her visit she corresponded with Hemingway, receiving encouragement and some praise for her *New Yorker* work. Ross said in her preface to *Portrait of Hemingway* (which ran in *The New Yorker* as "How Do You Like It Now, Gentlemen?") that the way Hemingway wrote in his letters and the way he talked made her feel good because "it was so fresh and wonderful."

So when Hemingway and his wife stopped in New York in late 1949 on their way to Europe, Hemingway had agreed to see Ross, suggesting that she meet them at the airport. Her profile covers two days with Hemingway, and the Hemingway character is revealed by showing him interacting with people in a series of scenes: at the airport gate and the airport bar; in the Hemingways' hotel room, first with just the Hemingways and Ross and later with Marlene Dietrich; the next morning in the hotel room again; at Abercrombie and Fitch as Hemingway buys a coat and runs into an old friend; at the hotel the next morning, where Hemingway's son, Patrick, has joined him; looking at paintings at the Metropolitan Museum of Art; and once more back in the hotel room, where Hemingway talked with Charles Scribner and signed a new book contract.

Although the profile includes bits of dialogue and conversation, much of it consists of Hemingway talking to Ross, who dutifully records it all. Yet a character emerges, a fascinating big man who does not care if he behaves as others would like or expect of one of the great writers of the world—and that is probably the main point of the profile. Sometimes Ross's Hemingway speaks in a type of broken English, repeatedly using boxing and baseball analogies; and he drinks alcohol almost constantly. He also seems knowledgeable about art and literature, although a bit too sure in the correctness of his opinions. He is gregarious, confident, and fun-loving, someone who clearly enjoys life, but he is also moody and avoids doing what he does not enjoy. Ross's careful and thorough selection of details, gestures, and quotations reveals the Hemingway personality and makes the man concrete and well defined.

When Ross meets Hemingway at the airport, the famous novelist has "one arm around a scuffed, dilapidated briefcase pasted up with travel stickers" and his other arm around "a wiry little man" who is perspiring "enormous beads." The man, whose name is Myers, turns out to have been Hemingway's seat companion on the flight, and Hemingway has had the man read the entire manuscript of *Across the River and Into the Trees* (1950) on the flight. Hemingway clutches the briefcase containing the manuscript to his chest, and, looking "bearish, cordial, and constricted," he holds onto Myers, who tries to "dislodge himself from the embrace." Then Hemingway speaks:

> "He read book all way up on plane," Hemingway said. He spoke with a perceptible Midwestern accent, despite the Indian talk. "He liked book, I think," he added, giving Myers a little shake and beaming down at him.
>
> "Whew!" said Myers.
>
> "Book too much for him," Hemingway said. "Book start slow, then increase in pace till it becomes impossible to stand. . . ."
>
> "Whew!" said Myers.

Overall, Ross's portrait of Hemingway is favorable; Ross loves her subject. Also evident in the exchange with Myers is Ross's genuine amusement in witnessing the scene and her ability to recapture its humor and the incongruity of Hemingway the writer and Myers, the befuddled businessman.

As the portrait unfolds, however, Ross also reveals a man conscious of his age, someone obviously trying to deal with getting old. Beneath the surface Hemingway is wrestling with whether he is able to write as well as he once did. Yet the recurring undertone is that he *can* still write and compete as one of the best living authors. The fact that different readers responded to the piece in quite different ways demonstrates just how well Ross succeeded in depicting the complexity of this human character. The response also indicates that this profile incorpo-

rates some of the ambiguity that Ross abhors in journalism but which is standard in good literature.

Ross's portrait of Hemingway has endured because of Hemingway's fame and continued interest in his writing. But *Picture* also endures, not because of the notoriety of the subject but because many consider it perhaps the best inside look at the making of a motion picture ever written. When it was republished in 1993, forty-one years after its original appearance, Charles Solomon, writing in the *Los Angeles Times,* said *Picture* "still ranks among the most revealing books ever written about Hollywood," while D. T. Max described it in *Variety* as "probably the best on-location reportage ever about Hollywood."

In the same *Variety* piece Ross was described as "John Huston's New York night-clubbing pal." Whether that is true or not, the point is that Ross knew her main character well as she conducted her reporting and writing, just as she already knew Hemingway when she reported and wrote that profile. One of Ross's earliest pieces for *The New Yorker* was "Come In, Lassie," which ran as an "Onward and Upward With the Arts" feature in February 1948. That piece primarily explores how Hollywood was coping with the House Un-American Activities Committee investigation. But included in the article is an account of a lunch with Huston and the cast of the movie *Key Largo,* including Humphrey Bogart, Edward G. Robinson, and Lauren Bacall. Thus, when Ross suggested to Huston that she report on the making of a movie, he readily agreed to give her complete access and supposedly said, "Honey, you just write what you want to write."

The result of that access fits any definition of literary journalism. *Picture* is a nonfiction novel for which Ross gathered the material in New York and Hollywood over the course of eighteen months. It has plot, character, drama, and theme. Ross told *Variety* that she thought of herself as a camera and that "the characters in the story were just like movie characters, and their setting out to make a movie was the plot."

The tension of the book derives from whether Huston and his producer, Gottfried Reinhardt, can make the movie they want and also make money for the studio, Metro-Goldwyn-Mayer, with it. The story has a strong, favorable central character in Huston and a host of secondary characters. Although the journalistic purpose of the book is to depict the making of a film, *The Red Badge of Courage,* the story is unified and driven by a central theme: the nature of, and the struggle between, art and entertainment in Hollywood and in a culture that relies on popular taste to determine success. In addition, Ross makes it clear that Huston is the good guy, the perceptive artist and honest creator, while several studio executives, the money counters whose only goal is to give the people what they want, come across as the bad guys. The book is also about power, time, and money, documenting a struggle for control between Louis B. Mayer, head of M-G-M, and Dore Schary, production head.

As in her other work, Ross again clearly and cleanly defines each character through a combination of precise description and selective use of the telling phrase or gesture. In addition, as she sketches in a character, the themes of her piece emerge and become clear. Here, for instance, is part of her description of the producer, Reinhardt:

> Reinhardt is a paunchy man with a thick mane of wavy brown hair; in his cocoa-brown silk shantung suit, he looked like a Teddy bear. There was a cigar in his mouth and an expression of profound cynicism on his face. A heavy gold key chain hung in a deep loop from under his coat to a trouser pocket. He speaks with a German accent but without harshness, and his words come out pleasantly, in an even, regretful-sounding way. "We promised Dore that we would make our picture for one million five or under, and that we would make it in about thirty days," he said, sitting down at his desk again. He put a hand on the estimate and sighed heavily. "The producer's job is to save time and money."

Louis B. Mayer's presence and importance also permeate the story, even when he does not directly appear. After describing Mayer's office, done in cream and peach colors and containing a marble M-G-M lion statue, a tintype of Mayer's mother, and a statuette of the Republican elephant, Ross presents Mayer himself: "His large head seems set upon the shoulders, without an intervening neck. His hair is thick and snow-white, his face is ruddy, and his eyes, behind glasses with amber-colored frames, stared with a sort of fierce blankness at Freed, who was showing him a report on the box-office receipts of his latest musical, then playing at Radio City Music Hall."

Mayer is ultimately portrayed as somewhat of a clown, almost a caricature of the one-dimensional, profit-driven studio head, someone who not only identifies with public taste but seems to be one with it. Ross later called him "an honest villain and I love an honest villain." Mayer was opposed to M-G-M making *The Red Badge of Courage,* but he allowed Schary to approve it; then he just waited for it to fail.

Huston's character emerges slowly, and during the first half of the book, especially, he is im-pressive and somewhat larger than life. One character observes early in the book that "Everyone in Hollywood wants to be something he is not," but that is clearly not the case with Huston. Ross spends more time introducing him than she does the other characters and then takes pleasure throughout the rest of the book in showing how he works as she fleshes out the lines and texture of his personality. Huston remains a cut above the other characters in the book. He is more original, more creative, and more legitimately confident and pure. When he first appears, he says "Hel-lo, kid" and shakes hands with Ross. After the greeting Ross specifically and vividly describes Huston, calling him a "lean, rangy man" who has "long arms and long hands, long legs and long feet." She depicts his clothing and mannerisms and posits that "the style of the Huston pictures, Huston being one of the few Hollywood directors who manage to leave their personal mark on the films they make, was the style of the man."

Despite her affection and admiration for Huston, as well as her obvious infatuation with his style, Ross does not depict him as a god or as infallible. For instance, although Reinhardt and M-G-M executives would prefer a movie with established stars, the decision to have Audie Murphy play the lead role in the film is entirely Huston's. Yet it is never clear that Huston made the right choice; when Murphy is introduced in Huston's office, the young actor is decidedly unimpressive. Furthermore, when the studio begins to gut *Red Badge,* Huston is on another continent, directing his next film, leaving Reinhardt to fight the powers that be.

Because Reinhardt the producer is the man in the middle—watching the budget for the studio bigwigs but also allowing Huston creative space, desperately wanting both an artistic and commercial success with *Red Badge*—he serves as an interesting barometer and commentator as the story unfolds. As it becomes clear in the first few pages of the book that some at M-G-M have doubts about whether *The Red Badge of Courage* should be made, Ross allows Reinhardt to explain what is at stake:

> " . . . you need the King's blessing if you want to make a picture. I have the King's blessing, but it has been given with large reservations." He looked at me over his cigar. "Our picture must be a commercial success," he said flatly. "And it must be a great picture."

The word *great* becomes a type of mantra for Reinhardt, a wish and a prayer more than an accurate

Dust jacket for a collection of Ross's contributions to The New Yorker *department*

description, and he uses it repeatedly throughout the book. Eventually Schary also uses it, calling the film "great, great," as Huston and Reinhardt complete it. And it does seem that Huston and Reinhardt succeed: they supposedly create a touching, powerful work of art that will probably draw moviegoers as well. After a showing of *Red Badge* at the studio, Huston, who has already pulled away from this project to work on *The African Queen* (United Artists, 1951), calls it the best picture he has ever made, and others agree.

Soon, however, the general manager of Loew's reminds Reinhardt that the greatness of a film "depends on how it is received by the public." But the audiences at two previews react negatively, and Mayer castigates Reinhardt. Eventually Schary begins cutting and rearranging *Red Badge,* and many of those who praised the film to Huston suddenly agree with Schary's newfound view that the film needs work. The final version is quite different from the one Huston finished, according to Reinhardt. The reader can surmise as much from the many scenes cut and altered—scenes that Huston had earlier declared central to his conception and that Schary and the others had once declared moving or profound.

Meanwhile, Huston was in Africa shooting *The African Queen,* having left Reinhardt to fight alone unsuccessfully for *Red Badge.* When Schary later writes to Huston that he hoped Huston had seen the edited picture and approved of the changes, Huston tells Ross that he had given his assent when he actually had not yet seen Schary's version. The book ends with movie executives declaring that they are showmen and that Schary was allowed to make *Red Badge* so he could learn from his mistakes. One of those executives, Dietz, explains to Ross that he is "not of the school that believes that popular entertainment need be art." Earlier in the book Ross had described Dietz as "a bland man with a bored air," the opposite of Huston the artistic hero. Readers are left with the clear indication that it is unlikely art will ever intrude into the American film industry unless it can make money.

Ross's writing about acting has not been confined to *Picture* and a few articles. Much of her writing has dealt with acting, actors, the stage, and film. She and her sister, Helen Ross, put together a collection of interviews with actors for a book called *The Player: A Profile of an Art* (1962). The Rosses interviewed more than "a hundred actors and actresses" and selected fifty-five "equally eminent and talented and devoted" performing artists whose background and views on acting are presented as autobiography. The sisters hoped to "make an aesthetic whole, and thus give a balanced and definitive picture of the art of acting." Most of the photos of the actors were taken by Lillian Ross. This book is not literary journalism.

Another book, however, *Moments with Chaplin* (1980), the text of which first appeared in *The New Yorker* in 1978, might be considered literary journalism. Although the book includes revealing scenes in which dialogue and gestures make real the personality of Charlie Chaplin, overall the book seems to be more a collection of scenes united by Ross's obvious admiration and affection for Chaplin and his family, and by Chaplin's celebrity and artistry, but not by much else.

If *Picture* is Ross's book-length masterpiece of literary journalism, her "The Yellow Bus" is a masterpiece of literary journalism as a nonfiction short story. This 1960 piece incorporates a natural narrative device that unifies the story and gives it movement. The article opens with a school bus containing the eighteen-member senior class of Indiana's Bean Blossom Township High School entering New York City for a two-day, three-night class trip and ends with the bus leaving the city.

Ross is there to follow the group as they try to see the sights of Manhattan, and she listens to squabbles over where to go, what to eat, the superiority of Bean Blossom over New York, and the fact that "everybody in New York was rude and all for himself." But while Ross documents the ups and downs of the visit, certain themes emerge, and the article becomes more than a journalistic telling. While Ross provides the facts of the visit, she also presents an amusing tale of cultures clashing: a story of what happens when the country visits the city and a familiar yet perceptive account of how people respond when they are plopped into a strange environment. What readers see are the uncertainties, insecurities, and fears of young people encountering something new, different, and big, and ultimately that is what the story is about: how people, particularly the young and unsophisticated, shy away from that which seems foreign. Readers see them trying to cope, primarily by clinging to one another and to their rural Indiana ways. They want New York to conform to their desires and habits; they have difficulty opening their senses and their minds to a different way of living.

Ross adds a layer of meaning and poignancy to her tale by noting that for most of the students the New York trip "was in the nature of a first and last fling." The students will return to Indiana for a life of jobs, marriage, housework, and child rearing. A couple of them will go to college. It seems unlikely many of them will ever again take this type of trip.

The bemused and occasionally ironic tone Ross maintains throughout the piece is evident when the Indiana travelers take a noisy, bumpy subway ride to Coney Island. They complain about the ride and New York, yet the narrative develops in a more interesting way when some of the students begin to assert their individuality. One young man's statement, "I sort of like Coney Island," is seen as "the first sign of defection from Indiana, and the others did not seem to know what to make of it."

Whether too many of Ross's quotations and scenes were selected to depict the Indiana high-school students as typical rubes to be laughed at is certainly open to debate. For instance, Nancy Prather, who did not like New York because the people were different, is one of several students depicted as intensely narrow-minded and ignorant. When a group of the students visit the Central Park Zoo and afterward go into the Metropolitan Museum of Art when they suddenly come upon it, Nancy describes the museum visit: "It was there, and it was free, so we did it. . . . There were these suits of armor and stuff. Nothin' I go for myself." Ross would defend such a portrayal by simply saying, as she has about her other work, that that is the way they were. One reader might call Ross's article funny and revealing of human nature, a keen depiction of middle-American high-school students in 1960; another reader would consider it a distinctly eastern viewpoint, condescending and mocking. That it can legitimately be read either way suggests its richness and ambiguity, and its kinship to a work of short fiction. But, like all literary journalism, it really happened.

Other pieces in the *Reporting* collection also would qualify as literary journalism: "Symbol of All We Possess," about the 1949 Miss America pageant, told with typical Ross irony and bemusement that lead to social satire; "The Big Stone," a 1954 story that depicts a man's complete obsession with inanimate objects, diamonds; and "Terrific," which offers an inside look at the planning for the New York City Junior League's Mardi Gras Ball in 1954.

Although *The New Yorker* under Tina Brown, who has been editor since 1992, has drawn criticism from some longtime *New Yorker* writers, Ross told the *Boston Globe* in 1993, "I like doing work for Tina Brown." Ross has continued to work for *The New Yorker* through the 1990s, contributing the "Talk" sketches that she loves. An April 1994 article took her full circle in her career, coming under the "Onward and Upward With the Arts" heading and plunging her again into Hollywood and actors as she profiled Tommy Lee Jones. The *Globe* called "Mr. and Mrs. Williams," another of her film articles, "one of the finest feature stories on the movie business." This September 1993 article is a look at film producer Marsha Garces Williams and her relationship with her husband, actor Robin Williams; the two had been working together on *Mrs. Doubtfire* (Blue Wolf/20th Century–Fox, 1993).

Although well done, Ross's recent writing has not replaced either *Picture* or "The Yellow Bus" as exemplars of literary journalism. It is because of those works that Ross undoubtedly will continue to be mentioned in any list of outstanding American literary journalists.

Interviews:

"'I Take a Lot of Notes,'" *Newsweek* (18 December 1961): 102;

"Reporting: The Invisible Observer," *Time* (1 May 1964): 67–68;

D. T. Max, "'Picture' Author Ross Remembers It Well," *Variety*, 35 (24 May 1993): 63.

References:

Everette E. Dennis and William L. Rivers, *The New Journalism in America: Other Voices* (San Francisco: Canfield Press, 1974);

Arthur W. Roberts, "Lillian Ross," in *A Sourcebook of American Literary Journalism: Representative Writers in an Emerging Genre*, edited by Thomas B. Connery (New York: Greenwood Press, 1992), pp. 231–237.

John Sack

(24 March 1930 –   )

James Stewart
Nicholls State University

BOOKS: *The Butcher: The Ascent of Yerupaja* (New York: Rinehart, 1952); republished as *The Ascent of Yerupaja* (London: Jenkins, 1954);

From Here to Shimbashi (New York: Harper, 1955);

Report from Practically Nowhere (New York: Harper, 1959);

M (New York: New American Library, 1967);

Lieutenant Calley: His Own Story (New York: Viking, 1971); republished as *Body Count: Lieutenant Calley's Story* (London: Hutchinson, 1971);

The Man-Eating Machine (New York: Farrar, Straus & Giroux, 1973);

Fingerprint (New York: Random House, 1982);

An Eye for an Eye (New York: Basic Books, 1993);

Company C: The Real War in Iraq (New York: Morrow, 1995).

SELECTED PERIODICAL PUBLICATIONS–
UNCOLLECTED: "When Demirgian Comes Marching Home Again (Hurrah? Hurrah?)," *Esquire,* 69 (January 1968): 56–59, 124–127;

"In a Pig's Eye," *Esquire,* 70 (November 1970): 91–94;

"The Dogs of Bosnia," *Esquire,* 127 (February 1997): 56–63, 108–110.

John Sack's devotion to accuracy and fairness places his writings among the best examples of the ability of literary journalism to capture truth. Working within a school of reporting often criticized for its use of literary license, Sack, one of New Journalism's pioneers, has built a career on accuracy. His stories are as vivid and compelling as those of others using that style, and yet, despite the assumptions of some critics, he has made it his practice not to fictionalize. In a half century of writing books and writing for magazines, newspapers, radio, and television, often on extremely controversial topics, none of the more than one thousand people whom Sack has written about have reported to him a serious error or distortion of fact.

John Sack (photograph by Cari Iri for Playboy*)*

John Sack was born 24 March 1930 in New York City to John Jacob and Tracy Rose (Levy) Sack. At fifteen he began reporting as a stringer for the *Mamaroneck* (N.Y.) *Daily Times* at Camp Siwanoy of the Boy Scouts of America; Sack eventually became an Eagle Scout. He graduated cum laude from Harvard University in 1951 with a B.A. in English.

As an undergraduate at Harvard, Sack was an editor of the *Harvard Crimson.* From 1949 to 1951 he was the Harvard stringer for both the United Press and the *Boston Globe*. In the summer of 1950, as a correspondent in Peru for UP, he covered a mountain-climbing expedition on Yerupaja, at the time the highest unclimbed mountain in the Americas. This project provided the material for his first book, *The Butcher: The Ascent of Yerupaja* (1952).

Sack's first full-time reporting job began after he volunteered for the United States Army in 1952. Requesting, and receiving, assignment to the Far East Command, Sack served as a frontline reporter covering the western front of the Korean War for *Stars and Stripes*. During that time he also published stories in *Harper's* and *The New Yorker*. In 1953 his status as a correspondent ended when he stowed away overnight aboard an American landing ship to interview Chinese prisoners of war; he was arrested by the American military police when the ship docked at Pusan, South Korea. As a result Sack, facing possible court-martial charges, was reassigned to a mailroom in Tokyo where his job was to hand out postage stamps to the Japanese. After a month there, with the army unable to find a specific violation with which to charge him, Sack was ordered back to Korea as an infantryman. Sack requested a meeting with the inspector general in Tokyo. Although he received no help from the IG's office, Sack used the one-day delay to find a job with the Voice of the United Nations Command writing radio news for translation into Chinese and Korean. When his Army enlistment expired in 1953, he immediately returned to Korea as a reporter for UP.

His experiences as a *Stars and Stripes* war correspondent provided material for his second book, *From Here to Shimbashi* (1955), which recounts his army life. And it was while serving in Korea that he began to lose faith in traditional reporting methods. In an unpublished interview with James Stewart, Sack recalled covering a press conference in Seoul at which a government official denied rumors of an ammunition shortage. "I was sitting there thinking, 'Bullshit. Of course there's an ammunition shortage. I know there's an ammunition shortage,'" Sack said. A week earlier he had been in a battle during which an American tank crew had run out of shells and was told at the ammunition dump, "Sorry, we're all out; we don't have any more." He had also attended a briefing where spotter pilots were told that, because of low munition supplies, there would be no artillery strikes on targets of fewer than fourteen enemy soldiers. Despite his firsthand knowledge, Sack was compelled to print the denial. "I was writing what I knew was a lie. But under the rules of journalism, that was all I could write," he said.

Sack continued reporting for UP in Korea, Japan, and Taiwan until 1954. From 1954 to 1955 he was a legislative correspondent for UP covering the New York State Senate. By 1953 he had started writing humor for *The New Yorker*, and over the next eight years he wrote more satire for the magazine than anyone except S. J. Perelman and James Thurber. In 1959 he published *Report from Practically Nowhere*, a lighthearted account of his tour through thirteen of the smallest independent nations of the world, including one, located in the same city as the Vatican, so tiny its borders were encompassed by a building about half the size of a football field. Over time, however, he became frustrated with working for *The New Yorker*, which would not let him address what he felt were socially significant issues. He left the magazine in 1961, but humor, though sometimes black, remained a thread in most of his later work.

After leaving *The New Yorker* Sack became a writer/producer for CBS News. In his first year at CBS he worked on *Eyewitness*, a weekly prime-time program, and in the second year he moved to *Calendar*, a daily show. After spending 1963–1964 in graduate school as a CBS Fellow at Columbia University, Sack returned to CBS as a writer/producer/special correspondent and spent the next two years working with the documentary unit of the network and on the *CBS Evening News* with Walter Cronkite. He also served as CBS bureau chief in Madrid.

Though his three earlier books included many of the elements that define New Journalism, Sack came of age as a New Journalist with *M* (1967). As Carol Polsgrove reports in her 1995 book on *Esquire* during the 1960s, a 1965 *Time* magazine article on the war in Vietnam that described soldiers leaping from helicopters as "lean, laconic, and looking for a fight" was the impetus for what is perhaps Sack's best-known work. After having seen war in Korea he could not accept that soldiers heading into battle were eager to fight. "Scared shitless was more like it," Sack told Eric Schroeder. "But all the reportage about the war in Vietnam was written in that same gung-ho World War II style, and I knew that's not the way the Army was. No one was writing about it the way it really was."

In 1966, as a correspondent for *Esquire* magazine, Sack followed an infantry company from training at Fort Dix, New Jersey, to its first battle in Vietnam. Headlined "M," the thirty-three-thousand-word October 1966 cover story was the longest article in the history of the magazine. Polsgrove wrote that with Sack's article the magazine began to cover the war more seriously: "In austere black and white, the 'M' cover was

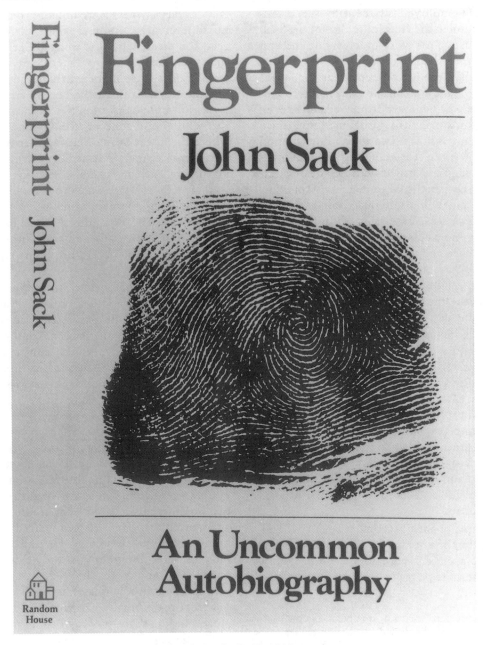

Dust jacket for Sack's 1982 memoir

like a formal announcement of a change of heart." The article was also among the first to appear in the mainstream media questioning the war. Sack returned to Vietnam to do a follow-up story on the main character of "M," Varoujan Demirgian, at the end of his one-year tour in Vietnam. By then Sack had expanded his *Esquire* material into a book, *M.*

The influence of Ernie Pyle's World War II reporting can be seen in "M," at the end of which Sack includes an alphabetical list of the names, ranks, and hometowns of the approximately two hundred soldiers who appear in the story. However, in "M," un-

like in Pyle's writing or in his own earlier books, Sack adopts a narrative approach found in many novels and short stories, telling the story through the eyes and thoughts of its participants. As Robert N. Sheridan wrote in *Library Journal* (1 February 1967): "Though he is merely reporting what others tell him about their thoughts and feelings, he gives the impression of having lived in each person's mind and body." Although some reviewers criticized Sack for overusing stream-of-consciousness writing in *M,* an examination of the book shows that Sack uses this technique considerably less than some literary journalists.

In *M* Sack employed the scene-by-scene construction common to the New Journalism style. Sack said that because of his work in television (he had originally planned the project as a television documentary for CBS), the use of scenes was so natural to him that he made no conscious decision to employ it. But while he benefited from the habits developed working in a primarily visual medium, those instincts also caused him to overlook a fundamental component of written storytelling. Upon reading a Michael Herr magazine article with rich description of sights and even smells, "I immediately thought, 'My God, I've left all that stuff out,'" said Sack, who was still in the process of writing *M*. In television there had been no need to describe the scene because the audience had a picture of it. After reading Herr's article, Sack added description to *M*. "It wasn't like putting in paragraphs of description. It was like maybe a line, every page or two, to try to capture the scene in just one sentence," Sack said.

While the inclusion of descriptive detail became second nature to Sack, he uses it subtly rather than overpowering the reader with information, choosing the one key phrase that captures the image. He compares those phrases to an icon on a computer screen where "you see a little square on one of the windows and you click on it and it expands to fill the whole screen. I'd like to think that I can give one little particular of description, and the reader will click on it, and that will expand like on a computer to fill the whole screen, and the reader will get a complete picture."

An example of Sack's techniques can be found in his description of a soldier in Vietnam who, as a firefight rages around him, cannot see the enemy and attacks a termite instead:

> When silver airplanes started to dive-bomb the trees, Demirgian could only lie behind his dike observing a colony of black termites eating a grey beetle. Taking his insect repellent from his pants pocket, Demirgian directed a fine needle spray at one of those conspicuous enemies of man, a termite who stopped in the midst of its verminous meal to look at Demirgian bug-eyed. Its shower bath continuing, the termite turned and fled to Demirgian's right, oblivious of the super saberjets that now dove in from there to drop their bombs with a spherical *boom* on the terrified evergreen trees.

M also illustrates Sack's passion for accuracy. His attention to detail cost him half a day in Saigon where he tried unsuccessfully to find the proper name of the "evergreen" trees. His notes (now part of the John Sack Collection at Boston University) include a pen-and-ink map of the termite's route.

Esquire lawyers were initially concerned about possible invasion-of-privacy suits when they first read the piece, which at times describes soldiers' thoughts. The magazine asked Sack to get release forms from the ten main figures in the story to demonstrate their faith in the reporter should a suit arise. To get releases from two of the men Sack had to fly to a war zone on the Cambodian border, where there was heavy fighting. Because the army would not assign air transport to fewer than five journalists, Sack persuaded CBS correspondent Dan Rather, Rather's two-man crew, and his own journalist girlfriend to travel with him. As the helicopter touched down at the soldiers' jungle location, a .50 caliber round from an enemy machine gun ripped through a rotor blade. Both soldiers signed the release.

One result of the narrative style Sack uses is that critics sometimes do not realize or acknowledge that he is writing nonfiction. He said that because "other people who write in scenes and write conversation, fictionalize, everyone assumes that I fictionalize." He does not use fictionalization, except for obvious hyperbole. Sack said that while there are times when "one really can get to a higher truth by fictionalizing, I'm trying as best I can to get to a higher truth by sitting there like a piece of furniture, by looking and listening for days, weeks, months, until I know exactly what's going on in people's minds." He added, "I'm absolutely not saying that writers who fictionalize are wrong. I'm only saying they're different from me. I am insanely compulsive about accuracy." He is also convinced that the truth always makes a better story. He finds that when he tells himself "'boy-o-boy, if only this or that had happened, wouldn't that be great,' it's never as good as when I put in a couple of hours of work and find out what really, really happened. It's always much more amazing than anything I could make up."

Although critics attack New Journalists for using literary devices and for lacking objectivity, Sack said, "I don't believe any other kind of journalism gets to the real truth." He does not believe in traditional notions of objectivity, explaining that efforts to achieve this mythical standard lead to shallow and distorted reporting. As a result, he said, reports of events which appear in the traditional press are "invariably half-wrong," something even journalists who have firsthand knowledge of the event recognize.

Using the literary journalism approach, Sack found the freedom to record the truth he had found lacking as a newspaper and broadcast reporter. "In those days I felt, here I am in possession of the truth and here I am writing stories that don't communicate the truth. Why do so many reporters become alcoholic and cynical in their old age? Because they've spent a lifetime knowing the truth and reporting something else." Sack finds it "bizarre," for example, that reporters do not want to get to know the people they are writing about. He said, "You might lose your so-called objectivity, but you get closer to the truth." Only by forming a personal relationship with someone, by getting past defense mechanisms, he said, can a reporter understand the motives behind the words and deeds. If that is accomplished, he believes, it results in a fairer, more accurate story, and subjects will not feel betrayed even when the story reports that they have done something that will bring societal disapproval. "Other reporters think that you get to the truth by asking people questions and by writing down what they say. I think that's madness," Sack stated.

An excellent example of Sack's way of forming personal relationships is seen in his story on Lt. William L. Calley Jr. Among Sack's first projects after becoming a contributing editor for *Esquire* in 1968 was a three-part article on the American army officer sentenced to life in prison in 1971 (though he was later released) for killing twenty-two unarmed Vietnamese civilians at the village of My Lai three years earlier.

Sack told *Esquire* editor Harold Hayes, who had already had three writers turn down the assignment, that before he could agree to write a story on Calley he had to meet him. Sack later explained to Schroeder that he needed to find out if Calley was "a homicidal maniac." Had that been the case, Sack said he would have had no interest in the story as it would have shown little other than sometimes "homicidal maniacs get into the Army." At that first meeting in the spring of 1970 Sack began a friendship with Calley which would develop over the intervening months through the trial and would continue long after all the stories had been published. Sack even risked a jail sentence for refusing to help prosecutors in their case against Calley. Despite warnings from the attorney at *Esquire* that he would not be protected by existing shield laws, Sack declined to answer questions by prosecutors when they called him to the stand, nor would he surrender his notes and sixty hours of taped interviews with Calley. Sack was subsequently arrested and indicted on federal felony charges for refusing to testify and refusing to deliver evidence. He did not go to trial because prosecutors, in their charges against Sack, swore that he had refused a direct order from the judge. Transcripts of the exchange between the judge and Sack, however, showed that the judge had never formally ordered the reporter to testify or surrender his notes or tapes. At risk of facing perjury charges themselves, prosecutors let the matter drop.

The articles, republished in book form in 1971 as *Lieutenant Calley: His Own Story,* are a sympathetic portrayal of Calley which Sack wrote in the soldier's own voice. In Sack's description Calley was not the cold-blooded monster depicted in the press, but was essentially a scapegoat for a system that ordered, or at least promoted, behavior such as Calley's.

However, the articles were sometimes misinterpreted as endorsement of Calley's deed, and Polsgrove reports that the coverage in *Esquire* provoked criticism even from within its own staff. The first installment, "The Confessions of Lieutenant Calley," was the cover story for the November 1970 issue. The cover photo was of a smiling Calley wearing his uniform and surrounded by four small Asian children. Some staff members were appalled by the cover and what they felt it suggested. Hayes's own secretary, Connie Wood, threatened to resign in protest.

According to Polsgrove, the magazine received criticism from outside sources throughout its coverage of the story. The first article cost the magazine $200,000 in lost revenues when some advertisers withdrew. Both Porsche and Volkswagen officials said they would never run ads in the magazine again, forcing Hayes, company vice president Jerry Jontry, and members of the business staff to meet with Volkswagen representatives in an attempt to change their minds. *Newsweek* published an article that not only attacked the appropriateness of the cover but also questioned the morality of paying Calley for the magazine rights to his story. Acknowledging that other news organizations had paid murderers for their stories, the author of the article argued that Calley's pay was excessive, incorrectly reporting that he had received $50,000 instead of $20,000. The magazine and Sack were later accused of perpetrating a publicity stunt by withholding discussion of the My Lai massacre itself until the third and final installment in the September 1971 issue.

Despite the attacks and accusations, the executives of the magazine stood by the story and its author. In response to the criticism and the volume of letters the magazine received following publication of the first installment, *Esquire* publisher Arnold Gingrich wrote a column defending the cover and story, arguing in the February 1971 issue (where the second installment appeared) that critics were allowing prejudices to cloud their judgment. Hayes denied claims that the magazine was waiting to publish the massacre story to coincide with the verdict in Calley's trial in an attempt to increase readership. Calley's lawyer had told him not to discuss the inci-

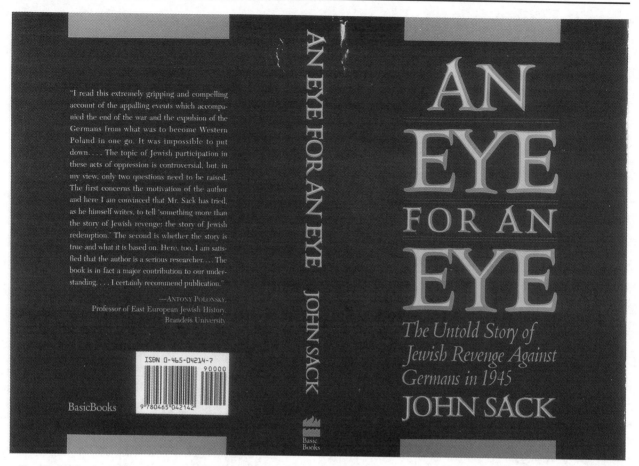

Dust jacket for Sack's controversial book alleging that more than sixty thousand German civilians died after World War II in Polish prisons and camps

dent until the conclusion of the trial out of fear that Sack would be called to testify.

The story on Calley not only illustrates Sack's policy of forming relationships with subjects, but also reflects a thread which runs through much of his work in New Journalism. Though the reporter said he does not consciously seek out projects to expound a particular message, many of his stories, at their heart, deal with people he sees as good who do things he sees as bad.

Sack has been trying to understand how ordinary people can bring themselves to commit horrible acts since the late 1950s when he took a trip to Poland. While in Warsaw he met a young woman who showed him a wall where, when she was four years old, she had been lined up with a group of other civilians by Germans. The Germans then began to machine-gun them in retribution for an earlier Partisan attack; but an Allied air raid interrupted the slaughter, allowing her to escape. Sack remembered asking, with tears in his eyes, how anyone could justify to himself shooting at a four-year-old girl with a doll in her arms. If the act is committed by an unbalanced or evil person, it means little, Sack said. If, on the other hand, the person truly believes that he or she is doing the right thing, then broader societal values must be questioned. The story then becomes a "criticism of a society as a whole rather than a criticism of one bad egg," Sack explained.

With *The Man-Eating Machine* (1973), a book based on four of his *Esquire* articles, Sack examined not only what he saw as the lunacy of the war in Asia but also its similarity to what was happening in America. In essence the book is a critique of the "System" or, as he defines it in his autobiographical book *Fingerprint* (1982), the insistence of American society on using the "one best way of doing anything."

Calley and Demirgian are two of the figures in *The Man-Eating Machine*. The remaining two were the subjects of stories on Vietnam veterans as they faced life at home after their tours of military duty. Vantee Thompson, the main character in "Making Contact in Baltimore" (*Esquire*, June 1969), is a black man who was a founder of the NAACP chapter in his hometown of Dunn, North Carolina, and had been arrested at seventy-two demonstrations there. He is sent to an army base in Georgia to receive riot-control training and finally finds himself in Baltimore as soldiers, armed with fixed bayonets, defend a shopping center from rioting blacks. Robert Melvin, the focus of "The Corporate N*gg*r" (*Esquire,* July 1970), is a twenty-seven-year-old black advertising executive who helps his company sell a mouthwash; he aspires to be put in charge of promoting a deodorant soap, and by the end of the article he is made responsible for selling a shampoo. He sacrifices his own identity to advance within the predominately white corporate hierarchy at his Madison Avenue firm; and on the very day of Melvin's promotion, blacks pleading for jobs take to the streets of Newark, New Jersey, in what Sack describes as the worst riot in two years. *The Man-Eating Machine* failed to gain wide acceptance among reviewers, and Sack himself said it is so awkwardly written that he asks friends not to read it.

Sack made a second, and much more successful, attack on the "one best way" with *Fingerprint.* Sack said, "I was trying to write a book so comprehensive that no one, especially me, would ever have to write another book again. And at the end of the book I thought I had done it." In *Fingerprint* Sack examines his birth, his childhood, his army service, and other important experiences. At each turning point Sack describes himself as struggling against a system that, in the name of a misplaced notion of efficiency, tries to impose the "one best way" on him. This mindless quest is sometimes carried to ludicrous extremes, as when Sack describes how his army boot-camp drill instructor yelled at him for having toothpaste in his footlocker rather than the required tooth powder.

In 1991, at sixty years old, Sack returned to *Esquire,* this time covering the Persian Gulf War and becoming the only person to cover every American war for the past fifty years. Following much the same procedure that he had used in *M,* Sack was attached to a company in the First Infantry Division (Mechanized) as the unit trained at Fort Riley, Kansas, during December 1990 in preparation for duty in Saudi Arabia. Soon after the unit arrived in Saudi on New Year's Day, Sack tried to rejoin it, once again running afoul of military edicts. Although Gen. Norman Schwartzkopf, supreme Allied commander, had previously given Sack permission to link up immediately with the company at its desert location upon his arrival in Saudi, he was still being held at headquarters in Dhahran, Saudi Arabia, when the air war began on 16 January 1991. So, in direct violation of military press restrictions, Sack

"bought a pair of green pants, a green shirt, and a green hat, and, rolling through all the checkpoints saying 'Good morning,' I drove eight hours in a Cherokee jeep out to the desert and Company C."

He spent the night hidden from authorities by soldiers of Company C before being discovered and ordered to Dhahran. He returned to the soldiers on 7 February, this time with military permission after members of the print media voted him into the combat pool on 3 February. After spending the intervening days living with the men and sleeping on the tops of sixty-three-ton Abrams tanks, Sack rode with the group at the spear tip of American invasion troops rolling across the Iraqi border on 24 February. He followed Company C as it fought in the Battle of Al Qarnain (with eighteen hundred Allied tanks involved, the largest armored battle American forces have participated in) and stayed until the fighting ended on 28 February. Of the fifteen hundred accredited journalists covering the conflict, Sack was the only one to stay with a frontline unit throughout the war. After leaving Saudi Arabia in March, Sack was at Fort Riley in May when Company C returned. During the time he spent with them he had amassed 135 hours of taped interviews, 575 pages of typed transcripts, and 950 pages of handwritten notes. Sack used the material he had gathered, as with *M,* for three *Esquire* articles: "The Salvation of Gunner Penn" (April 1991); "Captain John E. Busyhead and the Surrender in Indian Country" (May 1991); and "C Company" (December 1991). The material became a book, *Company C: The Real War in Iraq* (1995).

The 241-page book presents a view of the war unseen by most Americans, who formed their impressions of the conflict from television coverage. Far from the video-game image created by broadcast coverage, the combat, as Sack described it, was as brutal, confusing, and frightening as in any other war. Dick Lipsey, an Associated Press reporter who interviewed soldiers included in Sack's book, quoted Col. Greg Fontenot, Company C's battalion commander during the war, as saying, "I think the greatest tragedy of Desert Storm is that it has been made to appear easy. . . . If you want to understand what people feel like under extreme pressure and tension, this is a good book."

Two years before the book version of *Company C* was released Sack published what is arguably his most controversial book, *An Eye for an Eye* (1993). In fact, its subject was so politically and emotionally sensitive that seven years elapsed from the inception of the project to the point that a publisher, Basic Books, would print it. In *An Eye for an Eye* Sack reports that at the end of World War II between sixty

Dust jacket for the book publication of Sack's coverage of the Persian Gulf War for Esquire

thousand and eighty thousand German civilians, including women and children, died in Polish prisons and concentration camps that were run by Jews.

Sack first began working on the story following a 1986 meeting with Paramount Pictures producer Lynda Obst to discuss a movie deal for the writer's story on the Billionaire Boys Club. At the meeting Obst's secretary told Sack that her mother had been an inmate at Auschwitz during the war and, at its end, had been put in command of a Polish prison filled with former members of the German SS. Over the next two years Sack interviewed the mother, Lola Potok Blatt, and others with knowledge of the prison. *California* published the story, "Lola's Revenge," which had previously been rejected by ten magazines, including *Esquire, Rolling Stone,* and *The New Yorker,* as its lead in the May 1988 issue. Lola, as Sack refers to her in the story, helped promote it on National Public Radio, flying at her own expense to Washington, D.C. The article was included in *Best Magazine Articles: 1988* (1989, edited by Thomas Fensch).

However, problems began to mount when Sack started to expand the story for book publication. His agent at the time refused to represent it, as did five others before Sack signed with the Ellen Levine Agency in New York. Of the twelve publishers approached with the book proposal, only Henry Holt accepted it. But then Lola, who had earlier asked Sack to write the book, said she no longer supported it and threatened legal measures to halt it. Sack had to spend several thousand dollars on legal fees before he could continue. In February 1990 Holt canceled the book following the death of Don Hutter, Sack's editor. Sack, who had already spent two years on research, including interviews with more than two hundred people and trips to seven countries (several visited more than once), went $100,000 further in debt while doing the project on his own.

After the book was completed *GQ* in 1992 paid Sack $15,000 for "The Wrath of Solomon," the chapter on Shlomo Morel, the Jewish commandant of a postwar Polish camp for German civilians. Sack's ten-thousand-word article was fact-checked, libel-checked, and scheduled for the February 1993 issue, but two days before it was to be sent to the printer Sack received a call from *GQ* editor Art Cooper saying that it would be pulled. Cooper told Sack that the attorneys at the magazine were concerned about the libel laws in Great Britain, where the magazine would also be distributed.

The article was then rejected by *Harper's, Rolling Stone,* and *The New Yorker* before the *Village Voice* published it on 30 March 1993. More than twenty publishers rejected the book despite descriptions such as "extremely well-written," "extraordinary," and "important." In June 1993 Basic Books bought the manuscript and published it as *An Eye for an Eye* in November. The publication's travails were not restricted to the United States. Facing vocal criticism, Piper Verlag, a Munich publisher, canceled the German-language version in February 1995 and destroyed the six thousand copies that already had been printed. (Kabel Verlag would ultimately publish it.) The Polish edition was also accepted, then canceled, by one publisher before a second finally produced it.

At the outset of his book research in 1989, Sack had traveled to Germany for a reunion of one thousand people who had lived in the city of Gleiwitz (now Gliwice, Poland), the site of Lola's prison. There, he said, "I learned the first of many astonishing things: that Lola's prisoners weren't SS but German civilians; were German men, women and children, some of them thirteen years old, who had been beaten, whipped and tortured and often had died in Lola's prison. Later I learned that very few were ever accused of war crimes." During the next four years Sack amassed more than 300,000 words of typewritten notes from 140 interview tapes, about seven handwritten books of notes, and many file boxes filled with documents gathered from government archives. The book that resulted from this research describes in hauntingly graphic detail the mistreatment and death of German civilians at the hands of the Office of State Security. Its main characters are Lola, Morel, and Pinek Maka, the head of state security for Silesia.

Sack wrote in *An Eye for an Eye* that the director of the office in Warsaw and almost all of the department heads were Jews. Sack argued that Joseph Stalin had actually encouraged the selection of Jews for the office, which maintained 277 prisons and 1,255 concentration camps for 200,000 German prisoners.

After initial silence by the majority of the popular press, the book quickly came under attack. While not denying that Germans died in Polish camps and prisons at the end of the war, detractors challenged Sack's conclusions, his research methods, and his endnote system, as well as his writing style. The criticisms were at times virulent. Among these was a five-thousand-word attack on the book published by the *New Republic* in December 1993. Headlined "False Witness," the article was written by Daniel Goldhagen, a Harvard assistant professor of government and social studies. He described the book as tabloid journalism that "systematically and colossally exaggerates and distorts." Sack was accused of misleading readers and of inaccuracy, and at the conclusion of the review its author wrote, "I have no personal knowledge of John Sack. I know nothing of his motives. I am not saying he is an anti-Semite. For a student of anti-Semitism, however, the methods of John Sack's book ring a bell. Or more precisely, an alarm."

Some of the critical reviews contained assertions that were demonstrably inaccurate. In a special preface added to the 1995 Basic Books paperback edition Sack cited several reviews that made false claims about the contents of the book. In one attempt to illustrate what he described as inaccuracies Goldhagen claimed that Sack had asserted that 75 percent of the Office of State Security in Silesia were Jewish. Citing November 1945 figures from the office, Goldhagen stated that only 1.7 percent of the 25,600 members were Jewish. In fact, Sack had written that 75 percent of the officers—lieutenants, captains, and majors—in the city of Kattowitz in February 1945 were Jewish. Sack later pointed out in reply that he had also written that Jews began leaving the office by June 1945 and almost all were gone by

that December. He added, "If, as the Harvard professor wrote, there were 438 Jews in the Office as late as November 21, 1945, that's sixty times more than I'd ever mentioned in *An Eye for an Eye*." Sack, himself a Jew who had once been voted most religious in his Torah class, attempted to publish his response in a letter to the editor of the *New Republic,* which the magazine refused to run. He then asked to purchase an ad. The *New Republic* agreed to publish one for $425; however, after the ad had been set in type the magazine reversed its position. The *Harvard Crimson* also refused to run the ad.

Among the major complaints lodged against the book was the assertion that it drew comparisons between the events it examined and the government-sanctioned genocide that resulted in the deaths of six million Jews during the Holocaust. Critics argued that there was no evidence suggesting an organized program of vengeance by the Jewish community in Poland at the end of the war. In fact, however, the book made no such claim. "This [the persecution of Germans] was no Holocaust or the moral equivalent of the Holocaust," Sack wrote in the original preface. According to the book, Maka, the head of state security for Silesia and a Jew, issued standing orders specifically prohibiting mistreatment of prisoners. Sack's story is actually about individuals who fight an internal battle between the teachings of their faith and a natural human desire to seek retribution. The book includes many examples of Jews who refused to take part in any attempts to seek vengeance; who, despite the atrocities they had suffered, were in fact horrified by such acts as those committed by Lola and Morel. The Jews who did participate in acts of brutality were often racked by guilt; many were driven to alcoholism. The book arguably is about redemption, not revenge. At the end of the story Lola herself comes to the realization that what she did was wrong, and, at the risk of her own life, protects her prisoners from her Jewish and Catholic guards.

Another argument raised by critics was that the subject of the book demanded a more scholarly style of writing than the one Sack used. Jon Wiener wrote in the *Nation* that Sack "deserves credit for finding and doing the work on an important story, but his blood and guts style is singularly inappropriate, and his lack of skill as an historian is crippling. The publishers who turned his book down were exercising good judgment." Throughout eleven of the twelve main chapters Sack uses the third-person narrative approach developed during his more than twenty-five years as a literary journalist. In the final chapter and the twelve-page afterword he switches to the first person. Sack said the tone he used in the book "was the unavoidable tone of a Holocaust memoir," such as that found in Elie Wiesel's *Night* (published in the United States in 1960).

Although the book indeed lacks detailed discussion of the broad political and social conditions within which the events it depicts took place, it certainly includes personal context for its main characters. The first three of the twelve main chapters describe how these people, their family members, and their friends were brutalized and often killed by the SS. In the preface Sack wrote, "I decided that in *An Eye for an Eye*, I wouldn't report that a Jew had beaten a German, tortured a German, or killed a German until the reader could understand why the Jew had done it and even could think, *If I'd been that Jew, I'd have done it myself* [emphasis in original]."

Of all the criticisms he received, Sack told Stewart he was most surprised by those who denied the accuracy of his story. He noted that its main points have been repeatedly confirmed by others. Among those reports were stories by both *60 Minutes* and *The New York Times,* both of which found independent sources who corroborated his findings. According to the *60 Minutes* story, as early as 1946 both the British Foreign Office and the U.S. Congressional Record had reports on the mistreatment of German prisoners at Swietochlowice, the camp run by Morel. The television news magazine quoted a 1945 BFO report which stated that prisoners were routinely starved or beaten to death or were killed by being forced to stand in neck-deep frigid water. In *The New York Times* Craig Whitney quoted a survivor of the camp, who was fourteen years old when he was arrested and placed in Morel's concentration camp, as saying that Morel was "as I recall, driven by burning hatred. . . . When he picked out a prisoner for individual treatment, it usually amounted to a death warrant." In 1996 Poland issued an international arrest warrant for Morel, whom Sack said was "taking refuge in Tel Aviv as late as September 1997." By 1997, according to two unpublished letters Sack wrote to Stewart (on 10 April 1997 and 2 June 1997) some scholars, including Norman Davies and Istvan Deak, had begun to offer public support of Sack's findings.

Sack told Stewart that from the beginning he believed that, while painful, *An Eye for an Eye* was a story that must be told. He added that while he never set out to be a controversial writer, truthfully telling unpopular stories has made him the target of criticism at many times throughout his career. "What's the cause of all this controversy?" he asked. "It's really that we're living in times that are so politically correct that just to report the truth becomes controversial."

Interview:

Eric James Schroeder, "John Sack: Playing a Diabolical Trick on the Reader," in his *Vietnam, We've All Been There: Interviews with American Writers* (Westport, Conn.: Praeger, 1992), pp. 12–31;

References:

"The Commandant," *CBS News-60 Minutes,* transcript by Burrelle's Information Services, 26 (21 November 1993);

Daniel Jonah Goldhagen, "False Witness," *New Republic,* 209 (27 December 1993): 28–34;

Dick Lipsey, "Author Researches War Stories from the Front," *Fort Scott* (Kans.) *Tribune,* 20 May 1995, p. 1;

John Lombardi, "The Book They Dare Not Review: An Inconvenient Holocaust Story," *New York,* 27 (9 May 1994): 18–21;

Carolyn Toll Oppenheim, "Can We End the Cycles of Revenge?," *Progressive,* 58 (September 1994): 39–44;

Carol Polsgrove, *It Wasn't Pretty Folks, But Didn't We Have Fun? Esquire in the Sixties* (New York: Norton, 1995);

Craig R. Whitney, "Poles Review Postwar Treatment of Germans," *New York Times,* 1 November 1994, p. 3;

Jon Wiener, "Jews, Germans and 'Revenge,'" *Nation,* 258 (20 June 1994): 878–882.

Papers:

The John Sack Collection at Boston University includes drafts of manuscripts, research notes, audiotapes, videotapes, and correspondence from his career.

Mark Singer

(19 October 1950 –   )

Susan Weill
University of Southern Mississippi

BOOKS: *Funny Money* (New York: Knopf, 1985);

Mr. Personality: Profiles and Talk Pieces (New York: Knopf, 1989);

Citizen K: The Deeply Weird American Journey of Brett Kimberlin (New York: Knopf, 1996).

OTHER: Truman Capote, *In Cold Blood,* commemorative edition, introduction by Singer (New York: Random House, 1986);

A. J. Liebling, *The Honest Rainmaker,* reprint, foreword by Singer and Garrison Keillor (San Francisco: North Point Press, 1989);

Theodore M. Bernstein, *Miss Thistlebottom's Hobgoblins,* introduction by Singer (New York: Noonday Press, 1991);

Vincent McHugh, *I Am Thinking of My Darling,* introduction by Singer (New York: Yarrow Press, 1991).

Mark Singer

After more than two decades as a writer for *The New Yorker,* Mark Singer has earned the praise of critics for carrying on the tradition of literary journalism established by earlier *New Yorker* writers A. J. Liebling, Joseph Mitchell, and Lillian Ross. Singer has also won the respect and support of his contemporaries at *The New Yorker,* such as Susan Orlean, who admire his approach and his narrative voice. Singer has written more than 250 "Talk of the Town" pieces and many profiles since 1974; the subjects have been simply people who interested him. His first book, *Funny Money* (1985), which documents an Oklahoma bank failure, earned critical praise for his narrative style. *Mr. Personality* (1989), a selection of "Talk" pieces and profiles, was hailed by reviewers who enjoy his humor. His 1992 *New Yorker* article "The Prisoner and the Politician" (expanded and revised in 1996 as *Citizen K: The Deeply Weird American Journey of Brett Kimberlin*), an investigation into the possible reasons that allegations of marijuana purchases by a future American vice president were kept from the press, was a finalist for a National Magazine Award in reporting. As for a personal observation of his own writing career, Singer considers himself "a professional amateur."

Born 19 October 1950 in Tulsa, Oklahoma, Mark Singer is a son of Alex Singer, an independent oilman, and Marjorie Singer. His parents encouraged reading, emphasized the importance of education to their five children, and kept copies of *The New Yorker* around the house. Singer attended public schools and was interested in student politics and sports during his years at Thomas A. Edison High School in Tulsa. In an unpublished 2 April 1996 interview with Susan Weill, his older brother George, a Harvard-educated attorney and former chair of the Oklahoma Art Council, remembered Singer's sense of humor as one he has been fine-tuning over the years. Singer cultivated an interest in becoming a writer while attending Yale University, and he graduated cum laude in 1972 with a bachelor's degree in English. While at Yale he met Rhonda Klein, who continued her education at New York University School of Law and whom he married in 1973. Divorced in 1996, they have three sons: Jeb, born in 1981; and the twins, Reid and Timothy, born in 1986. In Singer's introduction to *Mr. Personality* he recalls how his interest in journalism was piqued when he worked as a reporter for the *Tulsa Tribune* in college: "My only other job offer was as a steamgunner in a car wash. I had never previously written for a newspaper or enrolled in a journalism course—to this day I haven't had the fundamentals explained to me by a certified professor of journalism. I took the job at the *Tribune* with the idea that this might be fun. The newspaper city room had air-conditioning."

In 1974, after a two-year stint with the *Yale Alumni Magazine,* Singer found himself in the office of William Shawn, then editor of *The New Yorker.* Singer had been sending some of his humorous writing to Robert Bingham, another *New Yorker* editor, and Bingham had set up a meeting between the young author and Shawn. Singer remembers in the introduction to *Mr. Personality,* "I knew that he was a shy, polite genius who had been the editor of *The New Yorker* for about as long as I had been alive and that the whole world called him 'Mr. Shawn.'" Singer was offered a position as a "Talk of the Town" writer. His first assignments were reporting a meeting of citizens opposed to the construction of a superhighway along the Lower West Side of Manhattan, and attending a convention of Beatles memorabilia collectors. After that he was on his own for story concepts, generating ideas from his daily activities in the city and learning to listen to people.

The New Yorker was founded in 1925 by Harold Ross to provide "humor, criticism, short fiction and reportage," wrote Norman Sims in *Literary Journalism in the Twentieth Century* (1990). Shawn joined the staff in 1933 to write "Talk of the Town" features, became managing editor by 1939, and stayed on at the magazine until 1987. According to Sims, "The magazine created by Ross and Shawn provided the institutional conditions that nourished literary journalism from the late 1930s: time, space, freedom and financial backing." John Hollowell wrote, "In the thirties and forties, St. Clair McKelway, Joseph Mitchell, Lillian Ross and A. J. Liebling virtually pioneered a new form of magazine journalism in the *New Yorker* 'Profiles.'" These writers, he added, "combined careful research, fictionalized scenes and

extensive dialogue to bring a new level of sophistication to the personality piece." Sims, who selected Singer for inclusion in both his anthologies of literary journalists, concurred that Singer "has followed in their footsteps."

Singer, with his own subtle, nonintrusive, first-person style, employs the primary techniques deemed necessary in describing a piece of journalism "literary," as defined by writer Tom Wolfe in his introduction to *The New Journalism* (1973): scene-by-scene construction portraying people in dramatic settings; complete dialogue; varying points of view; and status life details. David Eason further adds that such reporting is "characterized by the narrative techniques associated with the novel and the short story." Singer also remains true to the other characteristics that stamp a journalism composition "literary," as defined by Thomas B. Connery: individualistic structure; reportorial accuracy; personal narrative voice; a sense of responsibility to the subjects; and disclosure of the underlying symbolism of the narrative. Finally, Singer is known for immersing himself in each story he researches.

William Zinsser, a *New York Herald Tribune* writer from 1946 to 1959 and general editor of the Book-of-the-Month Club from 1979 to 1987, taught nonfiction writing at Yale in the 1970s; Singer studied under him. In 1992 Zinsser offered a nonfiction writing course at The New School in New York City, and he asked several of his former Yale students, including Singer, to teach the class with him. Zinsser wrote in *Speaking of Journalism* (1994): "The lively mixture of human and local detail in Mark Singer's work is a useful reminder that people and places are intertwined in good nonfiction writing—more closely than reporters sometime remember when they go out on a story and come back to write it." In an unpublished 1 April 1996 interview with Weill, Zinsser elaborated further on Singer's work. During his class session with Zinsser's students, Singer said that when he went to work at *The New Yorker,* he made special efforts to capture dialogue accurately, even taking a shorthand course for that purpose. Singer also told the students that he adheres to the literary journalism idea of scene-by-scene construction, building with exposition, narration, and dialogue instead of dumping everything on the reader at once. He advocated immersion reporting, becoming totally involved in one story at a time; but he warned that the dangers in such a method are taking too much time and losing interest in the subject.

While researching and interviewing Singer attempts to develop a narrative as he goes. "If I've witnessed a certain scene, I bring my shorthand notes

A REPORTER AT LARGE

THE PRISONER AND THE POLITICIAN

by Mark Singer

BRETT COLEMAN KIMBERLIN is a small thirty-eight-year-old man who has spent more than a third of his life confined to small spaces. He is five feet five inches tall and weighs a hundred and twenty-five pounds. He is clean-shaven and has short light-brown hair with blondish highlights, blue eyes, a pallid complexion, and a lean, muscled physique. He has been a ward of the federal Bureau of Prisons for the past thirteen and a half years, the last three and a half of them at a medium-security institution in Memphis. Before arriving in Memphis, he did time in, among other places, El Reno, Oklahoma; Chicago; Oxford, Wisconsin; Corpus Christi, Texas; Springfield, Missouri; Terre Haute, Indiana; and Indianapolis, his home town. Though he has generally accommodated himself to the standard routines and protocols of prison life, he has not enjoyed a minute of his life as an incarcerated person. Among his fellow-inmates, he has made a point of establishing few close friendships. He has never been drawn into a prison poker game or a pool game or allowed himself to be tattooed. Television doesn't interest him, but he does tune in at least once a day to news broadcasts on National Public Radio. Ever since he was charged with the crimes for which he is now being held—a series of bombings that occurred in Indianapolis in 1978—he has defiantly maintained his innocence.

The cell that Kimberlin occupies at present is shared with another inmate. It is six feet wide and nine feet long and has a sink, a toilet, a medicine cabinet, a mirror, a pair of three-and-a-half-foot-wide and seven-foot-tall storage lockers,

a desk and chair, an overhead light fixture, and a floor-to-ceiling window six inches wide. The ceiling is nine feet high, tall enough for a bunk bed. Kimberlin sleeps on top. To reach his bed, he steps first on the chair and then on the desk. He is fastidious about his health and his appearance. Most days, he dresses in sweatpants, a T-shirt, and tennis shoes, unless he is going to spend time in the visitors' area. On those occasions, regulations require him to wear a khaki uniform.

When certain visitors—attorneys,

Brett Coleman Kimberlin, at left, is serving time for a questionable conviction in Indiana's Speedway bombings. Would he be free today if he had kept quiet about Dan Quayle?

say, or journalists—make arrangements to see Kimberlin, he arrives at these appointments toting bulky stacks of legal papers and other evidence pertaining to the circumstances that landed him behind bars. He carries the voluminous documents without strain, because he is in extraordinary physical condition. Daily, he follows a rigorous exercise regimen. For twenty years, he has been a vegetarian and a practitioner of transcendental meditation. He says he has never drunk alcohol in his life. Though he is a convicted marijuana smuggler, he says he has not partaken of illegal drugs in more than twenty years. For his work detail, he has taught classes in nutrition, yoga, aerobics, weight maintenance,

smoking cessation, sensitivity and assertiveness training, and rational-behavior therapy—all part of a "wellness" curriculum that he helped develop and that has been adopted by other penal institutions within the federal system. His prison job pays sixteen dollars a month. He is matter-of-fact, neither modest nor immodest, about what he has achieved in prison: completion of a college degree (with a 3.9 grade average), a national ranking as a weight lifter, certification as a paralegal, and a reputation, buttressed by testimonials from distinguished attorneys throughout the country, as an exceptionally adroit jailhouse lawyer. He has a romantic relationship with a young Russian émigrée who now lives in Philadelphia. A few years ago, they began to exchange letters and phone calls. This was at a time when she was still living in the former Soviet Union, and shortly after she read an article about him written by an American correspondent for TASS. Kimberlin speaks more than passable Russian, which he studied while earning his college degree. Often, late at night, working at his desk, if he is not engaged in legal research or writing in his own behalf or for other inmates, he refines his Russian skills translating stories by Pushkin, Tolstoy, and Chekhov.

Kimberlin himself tells compelling stories—stories about his life, riveting yarns that are part Dostoyevski, part Erle Stanley Gardner, part Elmore Leonard. He tells them in a sober, uninflected, seemingly unembroidered manner that has the effect of impressing skeptical listeners—people with plenty of experience having their ear bent by convicts reciting dubious tales of perse-

First page of Singer's 5 October 1992 story for The New Yorker. *An expanded and revised version of the article became* Citizen K: The Deeply Weird American Journey of Brett Kimberlin (1996).

back to my word processor and try to reconstruct the scene that day," he told his students. "If I'm traveling I carry a laptop. It's a very clumsy kind of writing, not even a first draft. What I hope will begin to emerge is some kind of narrative logic. I find that inside each piece there is a chronological spine." Singer advised the students to immerse themselves in their story to get the story, but then to narrate from a storyteller perspective rather than as an active player. He feels the writer should not be

the central focus of a piece but should record the story and let readers form their own opinions.

In the summer of 1982, after Singer had been "gravitating toward more serious subjects," he returned to Tulsa to visit his family, a vacation that just happened to coincide with the collapse of the Penn Square Bank in Oklahoma City, a bank failure declared by the U.S. Department of the Treasury based on uncollectible loans to independent oil producers in the "good old boy" network. As Singer writes in *Funny Money,* "Too many of the bank's customers had borrowed more money than they could ever repay; liabilities considerably surpassed assets; the bank was bankrupt." He knew little about the oil, gas, or banking businesses, though his father and older brother George were both oilmen; but he recognized the potential of the story. Singer, his wife, and their one-year-old son, Jeb, left New York and lived in Oklahoma City for a year and a half while he worked on the book.

Funny Money was published in 1985 by Knopf and was on the *New York Times* best-seller list. Singer offered many possible scenarios for the bank's demise and provided in-depth historical background on the Oklahoma oil business, beginning with the first hole dug by a salt prospector on Indian Territory in 1859. He rendered stories from his youth depicting the "Okiesmo" attitude of the state's inhabitants, particularly the "wildcat" independent oilmen. Singer recounted the story of the people involved with the Penn Square Bank with a collage of conversations and descriptive scenes.

Reaction to *Funny Money* in Oklahoma was generally positive, according to George Singer. Though a few were offended by what they perceived as Singer's disdain for Oklahomans, most readers in that state recognized the milieu and the people described. National reviews of the book were varied. Susan Lee, a senior editor at *Forbes* magazine, wrote in *The New York Times Book Review* (23 June 1985): "Mr. Singer does a great job describing the yahooism, generally called Okiesmo, that captured Oklahoma City during the boom years. But although Mr. Singer has an eye for vulgar excess and an ear for self-serving bluster, he doesn't fit the gossip into a broader context." Other reviewers praised Singer's skillful reporting, rich description, and clear prose style. *Funny Money* has even been used as a textbook in business schools.

In 1986 Singer was commissioned by Zinsser to write a new introduction to a reprint of Truman Capote's *In Cold Blood,* a book first serialized in *The New Yorker.* In his introduction Singer explains that he began reading literary journalism "carefully":

> The proposition that there might be a legitimate "shifting, imaginative" hybrid of fact and fiction clashed with my belief that it was a reporter's duty to be an absolutist about facts—and that it was his further duty to *over* report, to accumulate great surpluses of raw factual material and direct observation. I also grasped that, in careless hands, even the facts were not sufficient to produce honest journalism.... Clearly *In Cold Blood* was a superior piece of reporting. Capote had accumulated all the facts and then a great surplus. What finally made it a classic was not artistry but legwork and stamina. *In Cold*

Blood was really two books: a work of imagination (all right, a novel), and a heroic feat of fact-gathering—and it was the latter book that dazzled me.

In 1989 *Mr. Personality,* a collection of Singer's "Talk" and profile pieces, was published. The book was dedicated to William Shawn, who had retired from *The New Yorker* two years earlier. The collection included "With Leo," about Leo Hoffman, a kitchen range repairman; "Mr. Personality," about Paul Schimmel, a printer who plays his clarinet during rush hour on the F train seven days a week; "Idea," about Robert Sparks and the portable upright-sleeping device he invented for long commutes by bus or train; "Avenue P," about one-wall handball players in Bensonhurst; "King of All Kings," about the proprietor of a sewer cleaning business; "Court Buff," about retiree Benjamin Shine, who spends his days observing primarily murder trials; and "Professional Doppelganger," about lawyer-turned-theatrical agent Sam Cohn, whose clients include actors Sigourney Weaver and Roy Scheider and who has the unusual eating habit of ingesting paper or cotton products such as the sports section of the *Daily News,* wads of tissue paper, and the collar of his shirt. The last line of the Cohn story leaves the reader reevaluating, as many of Singer's pieces do, the type of success that could possibly be worth the anxiety that is manifested in the nervous habit of publicly eating a book of matches: "And, for the moment, he looked unmistakably sad." Singer often uses his subjects' words in closing to confirm perceptions maintained throughout the profiles: the court buff "wants to see what's doing"; the range repairman proudly affirms, "I *fix.*"

Singer's first *New Yorker* profile, included as "Goodman Ace: Words Fool Me" in *Mr. Personality,* is about a radio and television comedy writer, who also happened to be Singer's maternal great-uncle. Singer told students in Zinsser's class that he used a tape recorder for this story in order to capture Ace's speech exactly; in most cases, however, Singer prefers simply to take notes. In "Words Fool Me" Singer uses anecdotes to describe the character of his uncle, including the tale of "some arcane duel" fought with his dinner date's cat.

New Yorker writer Susan Orlean told Weill in an unpublished 2 April 1996 interview that the Singer profile called "Supers," included in *Mr. Personality,* inspired her to become a writer. "It also motivated me to dream of writing for *The New Yorker.* I had never read anything like it. No story, just the lives of regular people, five brothers who were the building superintendents of luxury apartments on the East Side of Manhattan. I was hypnotized by the piece and I thought to myself, 'I want to write like that.'" Of the same story, Singer explained to Zinsser's students his method of reportorial immersion: "I was in their homes; I was in their offices; I attended family gatherings over a long period of time. We became social friends; when their mother had an eightieth birthday party I was there; when they had christenings I was there; on St. Patrick's Day, I was there."

Mr. Personality was well received. George Singer said the book is "a good cross section" of Singer's writing. Critics admired Singer's humor and his skill in depicting colorful characters. Richard Condon, author of nearly thirty novels, including *The Manchurian Candidate* and *Prizzi's Honor,* wrote a laudatory blurb for the dust jacket. John House, reviewing the book for *Seven Days,* wrote: "Singer deserves a wider audience. Apart from his own wry, oblique style, his most conspicuous talent is for capturing the special language people speak when talking about themselves. Among Singer's considerable skills are a greedy eye for detail and a deft hand with physical description."

Singer's profile of filmmaker Errol Morris, first published as "Predilections" in *The New Yorker* (February 1989), was chosen for inclusion in *Literary Journalism: A New Collection of the Best American Nonfiction,* edited by Norman Sims (1995). In the chapter preface Singer is quoted as saying, "You deal with people and their stories in an ironic way, or you can even deal with abstract ideas if you then try to fix a human narrative in an ironic way. I'm as proud of the Morris piece as anything I've done, for that reason. I was really caught up in the whole story." The lengthy first sentence of the piece offers a breathtaking synopsis of the story subject:

Among the nonfiction movies that Errol Morris has at one time or another been eager to make but has temporarily abandoned for lack of investor enthusiasm are *Ablaze!* (or *Fire From Heaven*), an examination of the phenomenon of spontaneous human combustion; *Whatever Happened to Einstein's Brain?* (portions of the cerebellum and the cerebral cortex are thought to be in the possession of a doctor in North Carolina, other parts are floating around here and there); *Road,* the story of one man's attempt to build across northern Minnesota an interstate highway that no one else wanted; *Insanity Inside Out,* based on the book of the same title, by Kenneth Donaldson, a man who, in his forties, was wrongly committed by his parents to a mental institution and got stuck there for fifteen years; *Weirdo,* about the breeding of a giant chicken; *The Wizard of Wendover,* about Robert K. Golka and his laser-induced fireball experiments in Utah; and a perusal of Yap, a South Pacific island where stone money is the traditional currency.

Morris developed a journalistic method for filmmaking that Singer seemed to admire, perhaps because of his own technique of letting his subjects tell him their own stories on their own terms.

In 1992 Singer wrote a reporter-at-large piece, "The Prisoner and the Politician." Published in *The New Yorker* on 5 October 1992, the article focused on Brett Kimberlin, a federally convicted drug smuggler who had made allegations during the 1988 presidential campaign that vice-presidential hopeful Dan Quayle had bought marijuana from him in the early 1970s. When Kimberlin attempted to hold a press conference at the federal penitentiary in Oklahoma where he was incarcerated, he was put in detention and the story was suppressed. Singer interviewed Kimberlin and decided to write his article because he believed Kimberlin's story was credible; he also questioned why Quayle should be held above suspicion and why Kimberlin's accusations against him were silenced. Singer told Zinsser's students that his piece "dealt with a violation of rights and an abuse of power at the federal level."

Within the first few sentences of "The Prisoner and the Politician," the reader has a vivid description of Kimberlin and encounters the mind of federal prisoner number 01035-079. Singer depicts an intelligent, self-disciplined individual who maintains that he is innocent in the 1978 bombings for which he has been imprisoned. Kimberlin also told Singer, and anybody else willing to listen, that his dealings with Quayle lasted from 1971 to 1973, when Quayle was in his mid twenties. But Singer's article centers mainly on Kimberlin and the reaction he received from prison officials when he attempted to take his story about Quayle to the news media. Singer probed deeply into the case, offering insights and possible motivations for journalists and prosecutors who insisted that Kimberlin was merely a lying felon. In the course of his research Singer talked with Erwin Griswold, former dean of the Harvard Law School and solicitor general under Lyndon Johnson and Richard Nixon, who was convinced of Kimberlin's honesty. Based on his own extensive study, Singer concludes in his article that Kimberlin "has become a political prisoner." "The Prisoner and the Politician" was published in the first issue of *The New Yorker* edited by Tina Brown and was a finalist for a National Magazine Award.

Singer then contracted with the Alfred A. Knopf publishing company to expand the article into a book, which was published in 1996 as *Citizen K: The Deeply Weird American Journey of Brett Kimberlin.* Singer's plan, when he began writing, was to tell the full story of Kimberlin's conviction, his accusations against Quayle, and the violations of his civil rights. However, as he engaged in further research, which included extensive conversations with Kimberlin and others to whom he referred, Singer began to doubt Kimberlin's truthfulness; soon he realized that he was being told complicated lies by the very person whose credibility he had defended. Singer, as he confesses in his book, learned to his chagrin that he had been "sucked whole and cast adrift inside Kimberlin's narcissitic universe, a black-and-white realm of dreams and schemes and factoids." Repudiating the conclusions he had drawn in his *New Yorker* article, Singer turns *Citizen K: The Deeply Weird American Journey of Brett Kimberlin,* in part, into a mea culpa in which he frankly admits to having been duped. By the end of the book he condemns Kimberlin as a fraud who was undoubtedly guilty of the crime for which he had been convicted and whose allegations against Quayle had been sheer fabrications.

Singer's book received mixed but generally favorable reviews in such publications as *The Nation* and *The San Francisco Review of Books.* Ben Yagoda, in *The New York Times Book Review* on 10 November 1996, found it remarkable that Singer, whom he praises as a first-rate reporter and a diligent reseacher, candidly placed himself in an unfavorable light as he spun his cautionary tale about the dangers inherent in the journalist's relationship to his source. Yagoda believed that the principal flaw in *Citizen K* lay in Singer's choice not to let the reader know until late in the narrative that Singer had realized fairly early in his research that Kimberlin was lying to him.

As he worked to complete *Citizen K,* Singer retained his humorous approach to articles for *The New Yorker.* In a "Shouts & Murmurs" piece, "Head Case" (13 November 1995), he symbolically compares reporters, such as himself, to head lice. Injecting personal experiences to make the point, he uses his immersion technique to best advantage and is willing to engage in self-deprecating satire, as when he observes: "When you're a journalist, you get used to being called a nitpicker—even a bloodsucking parasite."

As a literary journalist Singer ponders the dilemma of how a reporter "reconciles intimacy and distance." He admires Capote's ability to know everything about the story and yet keep himself out of it. As for what motivates Singer after more than twenty years at *The New Yorker,* he told his students at The New School, "What has always driven me as a writer is that I'm curious about people. I just want to know."

References:

Thomas B. Connery, *A Sourcebook of American Literary Journalism: Representative Writers in an Emerging Genre* (Westport, Conn.: Greenwood Press, 1992);

David Eason, "New Journalism, Metaphor and Culture," *Journal of Popular Culture,* 15 (Spring 1982): 142–149;

John Hollowell, *Fact and Fiction: The New Journalism and the Nonfiction Novel* (Chapel Hill: University of North Carolina Press, 1977);

Norman Sims, "Joseph Mitchell and *The New Yorker* Nonfiction Writers," in *Literary Journalism in the Twentieth Century,* edited by Sims (New York: Oxford University Press, 1990), pp. 82–109;

Sims, ed., *Literary Journalism: A New Collection of the Best American Nonfiction* (New York: Ballantine, 1995);

Sims, ed., *The Literary Journalists* (New York: Ballantine, 1984);

Tom Wolfe and E. W. Johnson, eds., *The New Journalism* (New York: Harper & Row, 1973);

William Zinsser, *Speaking of Journalism* (New York: HarperCollins, 1994).

Adam Smith
(George Jerome Waldo Goodman)
(10 August 1930 –)

John J. Pauly
Saint Louis University

BOOKS: *The Bubble Makers,* as George Goodman (New York: Viking, 1955);

A Time for Paris, as Goodman (New York: Doubleday, 1957);

Bascombe, the Fastest Hound Alive, as Goodman (New York: Morrow, 1958);

A Killing in the Market, by Goodman and Winthrop Knowlton (New York: Doubleday, 1958);

The Wheeler Dealers, as Goodman (New York: Doubleday, 1959);

The Money Game (New York: Random House, 1969; London: Joseph, 1969);

Supermoney (New York: Random House, 1972; London: Joseph, 1973);

Powers of Mind (New York: Random House, 1975: London: W. H. Allen, 1976);

Paper Money (New York: Summit Books, 1981; London: Macdonald, 1982);

The Roaring '80s (New York: Summit Books, 1988).

MOTION PICTURES: *The Wheeler Dealers,* screenplay by Goodman, M-G-M, 1963;

The Americanization of Emily, screenplay by Goodman, M-G-M, 1964.

OTHER: *The Money Managers,* edited by Gilbert Edmund Kaplan and Chris Welles, with an introduction by Smith (New York: Random House, 1969).

SELECTED PERIODICAL PUBLICATIONS—
UNCOLLECTED: "I Crashed Stalin's Party," *Collier's,* 128 (10 November 1951): 26–27+;

"The Goof-Offs," *New Yorker,* 31 (25 June 1955): 70–74;

"The Dominant Kite in Bangkok," *New Yorker,* 32 (3 November 1956): 188–193;

"The Unconventional Warriors," *Esquire,* 56 (November 1961): 128–132;

"Our Man in Saigon," *Esquire,* 61 (January 1964): 57–60, 144, 148.

Though George J. W. Goodman would achieve his greatest fame as a financial writer, best-selling author, and television host under the pseudonym "Adam Smith," in his forty-year career he has worked in nearly every venue available to feature writers. As the older mass magazines died, he found a niche in the expanding market for business journalism. During the 1960s he achieved fame as a practitioner of the "New Journalism" at the first and most influential of the new city magazines. With much less fanfare he directed a bold and irreverent trade magazine for investors and fund managers. During the 1980s his stylish columns helped redefine a struggling men's magazine. Through all this work has run an appealing and recognizable persona—that of a witty, urbane dinner guest, a droll observer of human affairs as comfortable discussing group psychology and cultural myths as he is business.

Goodman was born in Saint Louis, Missouri, son of Alexander Mark Goodman and Viona Cremer Goodman. His father was a lawyer in private practice, and his mother was a medical researcher. The family lived in Clayton, a suburb west of the city. Goodman has described an upbringing attentive to books, magazines, and fine music and indifferent to business. Known as Jerry to his friends, Goodman studied piano and attended a public high school where he participated in drama and varsity football. He won a scholarship to Harvard University where he majored in history and literature and served as an editor of the *Crimson.* After graduating magna cum laude in 1952, Goodman was awarded a Rhodes scholarship to study political economy at Oxford University.

Goodman's unusual final project at Oxford eventually became his first novel, *The Bubble Makers,* published in 1955. Thus began what Goodman imagined would be a traditional literary career. He published three other novels, all by age thirty—*A Time for Paris* (1957), *A Killing in the Mar-*

Opening spread of the 10 November 1951 article Smith (as Goodman) wrote for Collier's

ket (1958), with Winthrop Knowlton, and *The Wheeler Dealers* (1959)—as well as a popular children's book, *Bascombe, the Fastest Hound Alive* (1958). The novels demonstrate Goodman's familiarity with the upper middle class and his growing interest in life on Wall Street. Critics praised his fiction for its stylish, clever dialogue and comic turns—qualities future critics would note in his journalism as well.

One of Goodman's earliest ventures as a journalist created national news during the summer between his junior and senior years at Harvard. He and a fellow student had contracted with a magazine syndicate to provide stories and photographs of their journey to Europe in summer 1951, which was to take them to Paris, Italy, Austria, and West Germany. While in West Berlin that August, Goodman sneaked into a controversial Communist world peace festival being held in East Berlin. For a week he blended in with the American delegation, which included other students and members of the International Ladies' Garment Workers' Union. When festival officials discovered Goodman's ploy, they expelled him. But his exploits were reported in *The New York Times, Newsweek,* and on the front page of the *Saint Louis Post-Dispatch.* His own account of his charade appeared in the November 1951 issue of *Collier's.*

Upon returning from Oxford, Goodman was drafted into the army, receiving training in military intelligence and psychological warfare at the Special Forces camp at Fort Bragg, North Carolina. He later wrote about the army's difficulty in accommodating soldiers such as himself in a 1961 *Esquire* article, "The Unconventional Warriors." He wrote that the army hoped to train well-educated, cosmopolitan young men to combat Communist insurgency movements in Asia, Central America, and Africa. But the Special Forces mission was constantly being undermined by the traditional army bureaucracy. Local commanders refused to approve unconventional modes of training and routinely ordered soldiers out of language and counterinsurgency classes to police the grounds. As in his later business journalism, Goodman identified himself as an unconventional iconoclast at odds with a stodgy establishment.

After he left the army, Goodman began selling magazine stories to support his fiction writing. Two *New Yorker* articles in the mid 1950s opened the door to his magazine career. His 1955 autobiographical story "The Goof-Offs" described a summer job in Saint Louis he had held while still in college. As a "parking survey assistant" he had collected names and license-plate numbers of citizens who parked illegally along a Mississippi

River levee. Goodman said he eventually lost the job because he allowed delivery men to gather there for midmorning coffee breaks and conversation. The second article, "The Dominant Kite in Bangkok," described a kite-fighting contest in Thailand into which Goodman had wandered while on military leave. On the strength of "The Dominant Kite," the political journalist Theodore White would later claim, Goodman was hired in 1956 to work at *Collier's*. He was one of a group of young writers—including Peter Maas, Robert Massie, and Pierre Salinger—recruited during the last days of that failing giant. In 1957 Goodman moved to *Barron's* magazine and then from 1958 to 1960 to a job as associate editor with *Time* and *Fortune*. In 1961 he married Sallie Cullen Brophy, an actress who had appeared on television, in Hollywood films, and on the New York stage. They had two children, Alexander Mark and Susannah Blake.

Through the early 1960s Goodman pursued parallel careers as investor, scriptwriter, and magazine journalist. In 1960 he left *Time* and *Fortune* for a two-year stint as a portfolio manager for the Lincoln Fund in New York City. Goodman has said he never intended to go into business, but he had studied the markets for some time, seen friends who enjoyed the work, and thought managing investments could help support his career as a novelist. In 1962 he was invited to write the screenplay for *The Wheeler Dealers,* which was produced the following year as a comedy starring James Garner and Lee Remick. From 1962 to 1965 Goodman commuted between New York and Hollywood, working on other screenplays and television pilots, including a script for *The Americanization of Emily* (1964), for which Paddy Chayevsky eventually received the screen credit. During these years he continued to write for *Esquire,* including a 1964 profile of *New York Times* journalist David Halberstam titled "Our Man in Saigon."

"Adam Smith" was born after Goodman's return to New York in 1965. In the first chapter of *The Money Game* (1969) he explains the origins of his pseudonym. He had been asked by Clay Felker to write a column on Wall Street. Felker was the editor of *New York* magazine, the Sunday supplement first published in 1963 by the *Herald Tribune,* then (after the *Herald Tribune* merged with the *World-Telegram and Sun* and the *Journal American*) by the *World Journal Tribune* from September 1966 to May 1967. To protect his insider status Goodman decided to write the story under the pseudonym Procrustes. On the suggestion of Sheldon Zalaznick, the managing editor, and without asking Goodman, Felker changed the pseudonym

to "Adam Smith." The name stuck. Though Goodman had long been listed on the masthead as a contributing editor, it was not until several months after *The Money Game* hit the best-seller lists, that a *New York Times* reporter and friend publicly revealed the real identity of "Adam Smith."

In November 1967, six months after the *World Journal Tribune* had failed, a group of investors revived *New York* as an independent weekly magazine. Goodman, Tom Wolfe, Jimmy Breslin, and others from the original magazine became members of the new editorial board, with Felker as editor. The new owners told *The New York Times* that their magazine would focus on news, arts, and social issues and aimed to attract a "sophisticated, intelligent reader who is not afraid of colorful, impressionistic journalism." About half of *The Money Game,* Goodman's first nonfiction collection, originally appeared in *New York,* and for many readers that magazine came to personify the spirit of the New Journalism that Wolfe and others were proposing in the 1960s.

The Money Game proved an extraordinary commercial as well as critical success. It sold over thirty-two thousand copies in its first week. Excerpts appeared in the *Atlantic Monthly, Ladies' Home Journal, Washington Post,* and *Los Angeles Times* as well as *New York.*

Three weeks later *The Money Game* reached first place on the hardcover best-seller list of *Publishers Weekly* and stayed there for forty-two consecutive weeks, one of the longest unbroken spans in the number-one slot for any book in publishing history. In its first year more than three hundred thousand copies were sold; it was on *The New York Times* best-seller list for more than a year.

The "Adam Smith" stories represented a new form of business journalism. For centuries newspapers had published routine news of markets. By the early 1900s two styles of writing about business had emerged. On one hand, business periodicals such as *Dun's Review, Forbes, Barron's,* and *Nation's Business* praised the captains of industry and promoted free-enterprise ideals. On the other hand, muckraking magazines such as *McClure's* dramatized corporate corruption and villainy. In the 1930s *Fortune* broke new ground, employing talented liberal writers such as Archibald MacLeish, Dwight MacDonald, John Kenneth Galbraith, and Daniel Bell to write about the politics of big business and its battles with the New Deal.

Goodman was one of the first to cover modern business as a subculture, a curious world with its own ethos, cast of characters, and drama. Goodman's *New York* stories later set the style for writers at *Institutional Investor*. A decade later, as *The New York Times* was creating a new "Business Day" section, it encouraged reporters to do the kind of reporting Goodman had done at *New York*. A long series of nonfiction books on business published in the 1980s and 1990s, prompted by waves of corporate buyouts and growing middle-class investment, exploited the market Goodman discovered. The popularity of *The Money Game* and Goodman's other books convinced television producers that a small but significant well-to-do audience would watch an entertaining program about business.

The Money Game definitively established the subject matter, author's persona, and tone that have characterized Goodman's writing ever since. It described Wall Street as a stage upon which odd, compulsive characters played a game that many of them would eventually lose. "This is a book about image and reality and identity and anxiety and money," Goodman announced. "If that doesn't scare you off, nothing will." For "Adam Smith," Wall Street was a scene, a social world governed by its own fashions, fads, habits, and superstitions. It was not at all the mathematical universe of economists calculating the laws of supply and demand, nor was it the dreamworld of public relations conjuring images of confident, visionary businessmen leading the nation. The players were neither the rational actors hypothesized in the original Adam Smith's economic theory nor the solid citizens and community leaders portrayed in the old business magazines, but an odd array of cranks, obsessives, steel-blue gamblers, and true believers.

Like other New Journalists, Goodman also documented a generational shift. Older investment counselors had once dedicated themselves to preserving their customers' principal; the new go-go fund managers of the 1960s expected quick returns. They thought of themselves as players in their own right, not just as fiduciaries of the wealthy. In Goodman's comic narrative the faithful old family retainer who kept the candle burning year after year was displaced by hot, young mutual-fund managers such as Jerry Tsai, supernovas who burned brilliantly for a year or two and then collapsed into darkness. Managers and investors' rising expectations about what constituted a good return on investment had ratcheted up the anxiety level on Wall Street. Customers and brokers alike now competed to outguess the market. Chart technicians pitched their wares to middle-class customers who, for the first time, imagined that they, too, could make a killing in the market.

Confronted with the dullness of most business journalism and inspired by Tom Wolfe and his other colleagues at *New York*, Goodman tried to humanize and enliven these social changes. He often organized his stories around the experiences of pseudonymous characters: the Great Winfield, whose speculations in the cocoa market cost Goodman $5,000; Poor Grenville, the investment manager who found himself stuck with $25 million cash and no place to invest it; Scarsdale Fats, who invited bankers and fund investors to trade information over corned-beef sandwiches at his office; or the Gnome of Zurich, a cynical international gold speculator who prophesied the collapse of financial markets. Like other New Journalists of that era, such as Hunter S. Thompson and Norman Mailer, Goodman also cast himself as a character—surprisingly, in *The Money Game* as in his later work, as a hapless investor undone by his own naiveté.

The Money Game proved quite popular with reviewers as well as readers. *Time* praised the book's originality and called the stories "not only clear and authentic but also sharply satirical." A reviewer for *The New York Times* found *The Money Game* "lively, wise, horrifying, full of wonderful irreverent stories." In general critics admired Goodman's ability to explain dull, complicated business subjects in a simple and entertaining way for a lay audience. They were intrigued that so many of his stories stressed the irrationality of the market. For the most part reviewers enjoyed the persona Goodman had created. They found Adam Smith hip, flip, breezy, and freewheeling, though in reviews of his later books critics would wonder whether Goodman was more a wise guy than the wise man he hoped to be.

Goodman's Adam Smith pieces for *New York* caught the eye of Gilbert Kaplan, who offered him $10,000 a year and a share of the business to edit his new magazine, *Institutional Investor*. First published in March 1967, *Institutional Investor* was a trade magazine with attitude. It featured catchy and dramatic covers and snappy writing; it made heroes of the heretofore invisible men who managed large institutional portfolios. Goodman has said he wanted to bring adventure to the magazine: "We took four money managers and dressed them as Superman, Batman, Captain Marvel, and somebody else and put them on the cover. Nobody in the financial press had done anything like that." The irreverent style of *Institutional Investor* later provided a model for Goodman's television

Dust jacket for Smith's 1988 collection of essays on international finance and economics

show, "Adam Smith's Money World." He edited the magazine until 1972, when he sold his investment.

Goodman's next book, *Supermoney* (1972), explores the same themes as *The Money Game,* with a difference. Between 1968 and 1972 Wall Street had endured one setback after another. A bear market had erased many of the gains of the 1960s, creating a liquidity crisis. Brokerage houses discovered that $4 billion in stock certificates were missing, many of them stolen, others deliberately or accidentally misplaced. Confronted with customers' demand for cash and securities, many houses folded, including some respected older firms. Universities, which had been encouraged by the Ford Foundation to invest more in stocks, saw the equity portions of their portfolios drop precipitously. In 1970 the Penn Central Railroad, the sixth biggest company in the United States, filed for bankruptcy, sticking creditors with $200 million of bad debt and nearly precipitating a liquidity crisis. At an investment seminar that Goodman moderated that year, old-school investment counselor David Babson condemned the speculative mood that had turned the stock mar-

ket into a "national crap game." Babson proclaimed, "No greater period of skulduggery in American financial history exists than 1967 to 1969."

Supermoney was published in October 1972 after excerpts had appeared in the *Atlantic Monthly* and *New York.* It was promoted as an alternate selection of the Literary Guild and other book clubs. A week after publication *Supermoney* ranked seventh on the best-seller list of *Publishers Weekly,* 125,000 copies were in print and press, and it was selling five thousand copies a week. Two weeks after publication it moved to third on the list and became the leading nonfiction book at Scribners and Doubleday bookstores in New York City. By the end of November *Supermoney* had become the top-selling book on the *Publishers Weekly* list. It was also number one on the *New York Times* best-seller list. Nobel Prize–winner Paul Samuelson, who had called *The Money Game* "a modern classic," contributed a jacket blurb to *Supermoney,* saying that it was "as witty and profound as *The Money Game.*"

For all its comedy, *Supermoney* sounded a more somber note than *The Money Game.* Goodman portrayed a business system that had stared into the apocalypse and survived, in part by sheer luck. The title essay describes a form of wealth created when private businesses went public; the stock offerings often dramatically inflated the company's value out of all proportion to its actual earnings. In other chapters Goodman similarly ponders the increasingly phantom relation between market value and social worth. Some characters from *Money Game* reappeared in *Supermoney*—Poor Grenville and the Great Winfield—as well as new characters such as Odd-Lot Robert. As in *The Money Game,* Goodman admits his own investment mistakes—this time an improbable loss in a failed Swiss subsidiary of United California Bank. If Swiss banks were no longer a safe investment, Goodman asked, what was the market coming to?

Reviewers praised *Supermoney,* though less ebulliently than they had *The Money Game.* They still admired Goodman's sense of humor and found his writing intelligent yet entertaining. Peter Passell and Leonard Ross, in *The New York Times Book Review,* parodied Goodman's style in a friendly way, inventing an Adam Smith–style conversation with Harry the Hedge. Like other reviewers, Passell and Ross noted the worried tone that had crept into *Supermoney.* Goodman's own losses seemed to have drained the fun from the money game: "Between books Adam goes out and invests a bundle in a Swiss Bank run by Hans Kastorp and a bunch of hustlers. When the thing collapses under a tone of margin calls, suddenly the game isn't a game anymore." The reviews of *Supermoney* also began to position Goodman more permanently as a popularizer—someone with a gift for explaining complex economic issues to a general public, a man given to repartee and the bon mot—as well as a careful journalist.

The success of *Supermoney* allowed Goodman to pursue his personal interests in altered states of consciousness and self-awareness movements. No longer tied down to *Institutional Investor* or *New York,* he spent the next three years exploring the research on left brain–right brain processes, Eastern religion, biofeedback, meditation, sports zen, yoga, EST, and parapsychology. He would publish his findings in 1975 as *Powers of Mind.* Goodman framed his book as a personal journey through modes of alternative consciousness. "On the Road from the City of Skepticism," he writes, "I had to pass through the Valley of Ambiguity." The stress of the investment business had urged him on this quest. "On the first day of Christmas," he announces in the opening chapter of *Powers of Mind,* "my alleged true love gave to me a silver

pillbox." He imagines returning to the business world with new wisdom: "I would leave my nine-foot teak desk, my phone with all its buttons lit up, and my totally filled in Month at a Glance calendar, go find some answers, and be welcomed back to the business community, like the first Arapaho that came back to his horseless tribe with a Pawnee pinto."

Goodman spent three years writing *Powers of Mind.* The book does not seem to develop a cast of characters in depth, as Tom Wolfe's *The Electric Kool-Aid Acid Test* (1968) had, nor does it make Goodman himself a compelling character, as George Plimpton's nonfiction had. *Powers of Mind* collected a series of short, skillful descriptions of topics about the complex and controversial nature of the human brain. Goodman had wanted to publish the book under his own name, but the Random House editor reportedly insisted on marketing it as an Adam Smith book and asked him to insert more of his usual wryly witty persona.

Powers of Mind was praised by such writers as Lewis J. Thomas, author of *Lives of a Cell* (1974). The book was also favorably reviewed by R. Z. Sheppard in *Time,* and a 1975 review in *Publishers Weekly* said, "Smith reports on the scene [of mind research] with the same wit and intelligence he devoted to high finance. . . . The deadpan humor is stimulating—the book is a pleasure to read." Elsa First, a psychoanalyst who reviewed Goodman's book for the *New York Times Book Review,* observed that Goodman "writes with enough pizzazz, jump cutting, and Woody Allen one-liners to keep even the weariest commodities trader alert." She took issue, however, with what she considered its oversimplified accounts of certain topics, and the *National Review* critic found it "disjointed" and "bumpy." *Powers of Mind* was a main selection of the Book-of-the-Month Club and sold nearly two hundred thousand copies.

In the late 1970s Goodman continued his habit of working on several projects simultaneously. He helped launch *New Jersey Monthly* in 1976 and resumed his regular column, "American Journal," in *New York* until Rupert Murdoch purchased the magazine. He worked for a short time in 1977 as a contributor to *The New York Times* and was appointed a member of its editorial board. ("To write anonymous editorials and have them honed into a *Times* tone seemed to me to be a mismatch," Goodman later told an interviewer.)

By 1978 Goodman was deeply concerned about the growing political and economic influence of the Organization of Petroleum Exporting Countries and the inflation being fueled by high energy prices. After returning from a trip to the

Middle East with U.S. Secretary of the Treasury W. Michael Blumenthal, Goodman proposed an ambitious book on the social consequences of the world economy, inflation, and the energy crisis. The Atlantic Monthly Press offered him a $400,000 book advance on the project. In 1978 he published two cover stories for the *Atlantic Monthly,* one in February on his trip to the Middle East and one in December on hyperinflation. By January 1979, however, recognizing that his plan for the book was too sprawling and unfocused, he returned the advance.

The new Adam Smith book that emerged from this research, *Paper Money* (1981), represented a return to the content and style of *The Money Game* and *Supermoney*. In *Paper Money* the economic dangers appear more formidable—hyperinflation, the power of the OPEC cartel, the worldwide circulation of petrodollars, the unhinging of international currency from fixed exchange rates—but the answers seem less reliable. Goodman maintains his hip, irreverent tone, but the scale of the new global economy baffles him: "No big picture! The old faith has waned; the new has not yet arrived. No new star has risen in the east. The old conceptual scheme that bound the observations together has frayed with no successor." Americans fear that their currency is "losing its value, becoming meaningless."

In analyzing these issues Goodman called more frequently upon the expertise of professional economists. Paradoxically, however, he found even their knowledge inadequate. The forces wracking the economy—unpredictable acts by foreign leaders, natural disasters, cultural mythologies—were all variables that economists could not calculate. Though economists did not provide the answers Goodman was looking for, his interest in their accounts did noticeably alter the tone of his book. *Paper Money* offers fewer profiles of pseudonymous insiders and more conventional on-the-record interviews with named sources. Goodman's acknowledgments, for example, list dozens of professional and academic economists such as Blumenthal, George Ball, Alan Greenspan, Robert Lekachman, Lester Thurow, and Robert Solow.

Reviewers of *Paper Money* noticed this shift and did not particularly care for it. Some criticized him for underestimating economists' knowledge; others thought he had identified himself too closely with conventional wisdom. The reviewers continued to praise his ability to explain complex economic forces, but several confessed that they could find no intellectual center in the book.

Newsweek described a "Gloomy Adam Smith" who seemed to have fallen into a funk. *Business Week* noted that "Wall Street has moved away from [Goodman's] most notable skill. His forte is psychodrama. When it was people who moved the Street he was great. Now abstract forces move the money centers." In these new circumstances, *Business Week* said, Goodman's insights seemed merely conventional, at the same level as those of other observers. Though the reviews were lukewarm, *Paper Money* did restore Goodman's popularity with readers. The hardcover edition, released in February 1981, was named a Book-of-the-Month Club main selection. The paperback release in March 1982 featured a major advertising and promotion campaign as well as an author's tour.

Goodman's increasing use of experts to frame his stories, so evident in *Paper Money,* was actually a deliberate narrative strategy that he had developed while writing a column for *Esquire*. Goodman had served as an executive editor at *Esquire* from 1978 to 1981 and published a column called "Unconventional Wisdom" from 1980 to 1989. During the early years of his tenure that magazine was undergoing another in a seemingly endless series of makeovers, and Goodman was one of a talented group of columnists hired to help *Esquire* capture an upwardly mobile and affluent young audience. Goodman's column regularly appeared along with Bob Greene's "American Beat" feature profiles; columns by Harry Stein on "Ethics," James Wolcott on "Media" and "Books," and Geoffrey Norman on "Outdoors"; and an annotated Edward Sorel cartoon called "Movie Classics." Goodman compressed witty and intelligent analyses of the economy and American society into just two pages, month after month. Revised versions of his columns on housing prices, the oil crisis, and currency speculation ended up in *The Roaring '80s*. Over the years, however, he also wrote about popular social issues such as the rise of yuppies, the culture of MBAs, military disarmament, and the Bernhard Goetz subway murders.

Goodman's *Esquire* columns typically started with a comment by a friend or acquaintance of Goodman—a "very successful Boston lawyer," "an Arabist," "savants and directors," "a very smart economist at the First Boston Corporation," "a housing economist and a professor of management." This approach irked Goodman's critics, who considered it name-dropping and an example of his fondness for playing the oracle. Yet to some extent Goodman had always used this common journalistic technique; it was just that in his earlier Adam Smith stories his acquaintances inside Wall Street had seemed more bizarre and idiosyncratic. Now he moved in the company of more straight-laced and conventional members of the establishment. For better or worse, Goodman's success had propelled him into a different social orbit beyond even the well-to-do world in which he had been raised and educated. The people Goodman mentioned really were his friends and acquaintances. For the ambitious young audience *Esquire* hoped to attract, this intimation of inside knowledge and Goodman's invitation to join him behind the scenes was seductive indeed.

As personal and public debt levels exploded in the U.S. economy during the 1980s, Goodman found a topic for a new collection of stories. Published in 1988, *The Roaring '80s* continues the themes and style of his previous books. The worried tone of *Paper Money* became more insistent. Goodman asked what would happen to the meaning of productive labor if individuals, corporations, and the government were all leveraging the future so heavily. *The Roaring '80s* draws this theme through an even wider range of topics than *Paper Money* had. In short, loosely connected vignettes Goodman contemplates the prosperity of the Pacific Rim economies, Japanese styles of management, the nuclear arms race, baldness cures, the increasing gap between rich and poor, and leveraged buyouts. *The Roaring '80s* features the sort of interviews with well-known figures—investor T. Boone Pickens, management consultant Peter Drucker, writer William Whyte, fashion designer Liz Claiborne—that had become so common in his articles and books. But it also features short but candid interviews with several residents of Johnstown, Pennsylvania, a historic factory town where layoffs by the steel industry had thrown thousands out of work and deeply disrupted community life.

Susan Lee in *The New York Times Book Review* of *The Roaring '80s* praised Goodman for "his fine instincts—and amazing memory—for the telling fact." She added that one could not ask for "a more genial, knowledgeable companion for a tour of the national financial landscape." But she also echoed criticisms that others had previously directed at *Paper Money*. Goodman mostly describes rather than analyzes, she said; he capably explains complicated material for a general audience but perhaps without sufficient nuance; and he calls for a return to a time when markets reflected genuine value. Joseph Nocera, in the *Wall Street Journal*, complained that Goodman had become too much a celebrity himself and now spent too much time at lunch with VIPs. *A Newsweek* reviewer suggested that readers were now more sophisticated about business news and no longer wanted the sort of book that Goodman had become so adept at writing.

Goodman still reviews books on business and writes occasional features on the economy for *The New York Times*. But for the last decade he has turned his attention to broadcasting, with great success. His half-hour public television program on business, "Adam Smith's Money World," was first broadcast in 1984; by 1995 it was running on over 240 Public Broadcasting System stations in the United States. Goodman focuses on just one topic each week so that he can analyze an issue in more depth than other business news programs. In recent years the show has mixed coverage of issues such as biotechnology, sports marketing, derivatives, and flat-tax proposals with interviews of prominent authorities such as Treasury Secretary Robert Rubin, Henry Kissinger, and Sen. Daniel Patrick Moynihan. Goodman has adapted for television many of the techniques he developed as a journalist; the wry style, emphasis on storytelling, clever graphics (as in *Institutional Investor*), and intelligent interviewing are all familiar. The show has won particular praise for its programs on emerging markets in nations such as India, Mexico, Cuba, and China, and in 1997 it won the Overseas Press Award. In 1990 "Adam Smith's Money World" became the first American business program to be broadcast in the former Soviet Union. The show has won more awards than any other business program, including five individual Emmy awards for Goodman as best interviewer. It ran until May 1997, and a new program is being planned.

The career of George Goodman aptly demonstrates not only the literary possibilities of magazine work but also the compromises such work exacts. After a critically successful but unremunerative career as a novelist, Goodman put his writing skill, intelligence, and curiosity in the service of topical issues, tight deadlines, and target markets. As a result, future readers may find much of Goodman's writing dated (though *The Money Game* will likely remain a classic work of New Journalism). Yet in another sense Goodman's influence has greatly exceeded that of other literary journalists. He opened the eyes of publishers, writers, and readers to a feature approach now widely used by business journalists. He left a distinctive mark on every publication with which he was closely associated, from *New York* to *Institutional Investor* to *Esquire*. And, most improbably, he is the only noted literary journalist in U.S. history to have made an equally successful career in television. For historians, at least, there will be no telling the story of literary journalism in the late twentieth century without speaking about Jerry Goodman.

Interview:

"Interview with George J. W. Goodman," *Contemporary Authors,* 31 (Detroit: Gale, 1990), 160–163.

References:

John Quirt, "Tracing the Lineage," *The Press and the World of Money* (Byron: Anton/California Courier, 1993), 138–147;

Richard Scheinin, "The World According to Adam Smith," *Avenue,* 12 (October 1987): 110–125.

Papers:

Goodman's papers are found in the Special Collections, Mugar Library, Boston University.

Gay Talese

(7 February 1932 –   )

Barbara Lounsberry
University of Northern Iowa

BOOKS: *New York: A Serendipiter's Journey* (New York: Harper & Row, 1961);

The Bridge (New York: Harper & Row, 1964);

The Overreachers (New York: Harper & Row, 1965);

The Kingdom and the Power (New York: World, 1969; London: Calder & Boyars, 1971);

Fame and Obscurity: Portraits (New York: World, 1970);

Honor Thy Father (New York: World, 1971; London: Souvenir, 1972);

Thy Neighbor's Wife (New York: Doubleday, 1980);

Unto the Sons (Franklin Center, Pa.: Franklin Library / New York: Knopf, 1992).

OTHER: *The Best American Essays 1987,* edited, with an introduction, by Talese (New York: Ticknor & Fields, 1987);

Writing Creative Nonfiction: The Literature of Reality, edited by Talese and Barbara Lounsberry, with an introductory essay, "Origins of a Nonfiction Writer," by Talese (New York: Harper-Collins, 1996): 1–25;

The Penguin Book of Interviews: An Anthology From 1850 to the Present Day, edited by Christopher Silvester, preface by Talese (New York: Norton, 1996).

SELECTED PERIODICAL PUBLICATIONS–
UNCOLLECTED: "Caddie, a Non-Alger Story," *New York Times Magazine,* 12 June 1960, pp. 38, 56;

"Suspicious Man in the Champ's Corner," *New York Times Magazine,* 23 September 1962, pp. 40, 45, 47, 48, 50;

"White Man in Harlem," *Esquire,* 62 (September 1964): 123;

"Where's the Spirit of Selma Now?," *New York Times Magazine,* 30 May 1965, pp. 8–9, 41, 44–45;

"Charlie Manson's Home on the Range," *Esquire* (March 1970): 9–10, 193–195;

"An Autobiography of Style," *Esquire* (September 1982): 88–89, 91–92;

Gay Talese

"Men and Women Are Working Out, But Are They Working It Out?," *Esquire* (November 1984): 90–91;

"The Homeless Woman with Two Homes," *New York,* 22 (30 October 1989): 40–42;

"Walking My Cigar," *Cigar Aficionado* (Autumn 1992): 36–41;

"Where Are the Italian-American Novelists?," *New York Times Book Review,* 14 March 1993, pp. 1, 23, 25, 29;

"Gino's Long Run," *New Yorker* (17 April 1995): 35.

Gay Talese is known for his daring pursuit of "unreportable" stories, for his exhaustive research, and for his formally elegant style. These qualities, arguably, are the touchstones of the finest literary journalism. Talese is often cited as one of the founders of the 1960s New Journalism, but he has always politely demurred from this label, insisting that his "stories with real names" represent no reformist crusade but rather his own highly personal response to the world as an Italian American "outsider."

Talese was born 7 February 1932 on the small island of Ocean City, New Jersey, a resort town south of Atlantic City. The lives of his parents, Joseph Talese, a southern Italian tailor who immigrated to the United States in 1922, and Catherine DePaolo, a buyer for a Brooklyn department store, are chronicled in *Unto the Sons* (1992), Talese's memoir and history of Italian immigration to America. In "Origins of a Nonfiction Writer" (1996) Talese writes that he comes "from an island and a family that reinforced my identity as a marginal American, an outsider, an alien in my native nation." Talese was a minority within a minority, for he was an Italian American Catholic in an Irish Catholic parish on a Protestant-dominated island. Always a lover of history, he soon learned that his island home had been founded as a religious retreat in 1879 by Methodist ministers who wished "to secure the presence of God on the beach, to shade the summer from the corrupting exposure of the flesh, and to eliminate the temptations of alcohol and other evil spirits they saw swirling around them as freely as the mosquitoes from the nearby marshes." Talese's later exploration of "forbidden" subjects in such works as *Honor Thy Father* (1971) and *Thy Neighbor's Wife* (1980) is most likely rooted in his rebellion against the island's prohibitions.

Talese's profound identification with the unnoticed and his celebration of "losers" throughout his writing career stem from his own feelings of failure as a grade-school and high-school student as well as from his outsider, minority status. Journalism was to provide escape and the first success for the undervalued but always curious Talese. As often happens with life-changing events, his calling came in the most offhand, serendipitous fashion. One afternoon after his sophomore year in high school the assistant coach of his baseball team protested that he was too busy to call in the account of the games to the local newspaper, and the head coach asked Talese to assume this chore. "On the mistaken assumption that relieving the athletic department of its press duties would gain me the gratitude of the coach and get me more playing time, I took the job and even embellished it by using my typing skills to compose my own account of the games rather than merely relaying the information

to the newspapers by telephone," Talese wrote in "Origins."

Once he started, Talese was no ordinary high-school reporter, however. From his first article as a fifteen-year-old in June 1947 until his "Swan Song" column in September 1949 as he left the island to attend the University of Alabama, Talese wrote 311 articles and columns for the weekly *Ocean City Sentinel-Ledger*. After only seven articles his role as a *Sentinel-Ledger* sportswriter was expanded to that of high-school reporter and columnist as well. His "High School Highlights" column, which premiered 17 October 1947, enabled Talese to become the Balzac of his own miniature culture.

In "Origins" Talese pays tribute to his mother for modeling the listening and interviewing skills he came to practice as a literary journalist. Catherine DePaolo Talese ran the "Talese Townshop," the fashionable women's dress boutique over which the family lived. Talese recalls the shop as:

> a kind of talk-show that flowed around the engaging manner and well-timed questions of my mother; and as a boy not much taller than the counters behind which I used to pause and eavesdrop, I learned [from my mother] . . . to listen with patience and care, and never to interrupt even when people were having great difficulty in explaining themselves, for during such halting and imprecise moments . . . people are very revealing—what they hesitate to talk about can tell much about them. . . . However, I have also overheard many people discussing candidly with my mother what they had earlier avoided—a reaction that I think had less to do with her inquiring nature or sensitively posed questions than with their gradual acceptance of her as a trustworthy individual in whom they could confide.

Perhaps more than any other artist of nonfiction, Talese has made it his credo to return again and again to his subjects. This patient and unfailing solicitude has enabled him to gather and to verify extensive information, to observe change over time, and to know his subjects so well he can describe not only their actions but also their thoughts and feelings with confidence. Equally important, the trust he has cultivated has permitted him to be the first writer to enter the world of the Mafia and break its "code of silence" and to report on the private sexual lives of Americans—with their permission.

Talese wrote fifty-five "High School Highlights" columns and general stories during his junior and senior years and 258 sports stories or columns. During his senior year he became a double columnist for the *Sentinel-Ledger* when he inaugurated his "Sportopics" column. In his "Origins" essay he tells the heartening, Dickensian story of his acceptance by the University of Alabama following his rejection by dozens of colleges in New Jersey and surrounding states. He has described his college years as the happiest four years of his life. Away from the insular confines of home, Talese flourished for the first time as a student. "I chose journalism as my college major because that is what I knew," he recalls, "but I really became a student of history." Talese would reprise his high-school journalism scenario at the University of Alabama—but with an important difference. He wrote only twelve articles for Alabama's student newspaper, the *Crimson-White*, while establishing himself as a student during his freshman and sophomore years, but these were enough to win him the position of *Crimson-White* sports editor for his junior and senior years. In this role he immediately transformed his high-school "Sportopics" column into a more experimental and literary column titled "Sports Gay-zing," a conscious play on his own name and unconscious confession of his voyeur role. Tom Wolfe has written that he learned to write scenes from Talese's June 1962 *Esquire* article "Joe Louis: The King as a Middle-aged Man," but Talese's own signature subject matter and stylistic experimentations began much earlier—during his college days from 1950 to 1953. Talese was trying out his scenes even before Lillian Ross's *Picture* (1952) and Truman Capote's "The Muses Are Heard" (1956).

Talese read Irwin Shaw's 1951 novel *The Troubled Air* on the train carrying him to Alabama to start his sophomore year. The major difference between his high-school and college reporting is that in college Talese's journalism began to become literary. The short stories and novels of Shaw, Carson McCullers, John O'Hara, Ernest Hemingway, and F. Scott Fitzgerald provided the models for what Talese would seek to do in nonfiction. He noticed that while journalism forever focused on "winners"—the highest scorer, the big men and women on campus, the achievers—fiction writers were writing about ordinary people and their lives, subject matter highly congenial to Talese. His genius was to believe that he could do in nonfiction what Shaw and company were doing in fiction, that he could write "stories with real names." As he writes in his "Origins" essay, he wanted to write about "the overlooked non-newsworthy population that is everywhere, but rarely taken into account by journalists and other chroniclers of reality." This focus, of course, would often place him at odds with traditional news editors, and he began to see his career as an effort to slip his kind of writing into the newspaper.

Talese was a nineteen-year-old college sophomore when he attempted his breakthrough first scene in a feature story. Like much modernist fiction, it seemed to begin in medias res: "The smiling French professor, with a dapper tweed sports jacket, stylish

pair of basket-weave shoes, and windsor-knotted tie, asked the question again" (*Crimson-White*, 7 March 1951). Fully thirteen of Talese's seventy-one college columns and articles employ scenes or miniscenes. He often tried to evoke the atmosphere of athletes away from the glory of the playing field, as in this 7 November 1951 "Sports Gay-zing" item titled "Sunday Morning Bull Session":

> Rhythmic "Sixty Minute Man" emanated from the Supe Store juke box and Larry (The Maestro) Chiodetti beat against the table like mad in keeping time with the jumpy tempo. T-shirted Bobby Marlow was just leaving the Sunday morning bull session and dapper Bill Kilroy had just purchased the morning newspapers.

This could be fiction, only the actions and people were real. In his senior year Talese would combine scene with philosophical musing in an early exploration of one of his greatest subjects: fame and obscurity, which would become the title of his 1970 collection. As he would tell *Playboy* magazine decades later: "I'm not at all concerned with the mythology of fame and success but with the real *soul* of success and the bitterness of attaining [it] and the heartbreak of not attaining it." Resisting the hero-worshiping stance of sportswriters such as Grantland Rice, Talese began to turn his "Sports Gay-z" toward "losers" and the unnoticed. He wrote of seven-foot Eugene Jackson, an Alabama student who was not a basketball star (17 March 1953), and about old "Hooch" Collins, the African American locker-room attendant on Alabama's then all-white campus (12 May 1953).

Talese headed for New York City when he graduated from college in June 1953, but the only newspaper job he could find was as a nonwriting copyboy for *The New York Times*. However, his impeccable store manners and hand-stitched Italian suits impressed first the woman in personnel who hired him and then several editors who were inclined to use the stories the dapper "copyboy" began politely to feed them. Talese's later best-selling volumes are all foreshadowed in his earlier work; indeed his unsigned first article for *The New York Times* prefigures uncannily his first best-seller, *The Kingdom and the Power* (1969), a behind-the-scenes look at *The New York Times*. Talese is particularly drawn to the kind of story that is present yet ignored by everyone because they are following "the big story." In November 1953 his curiosity led him to climb the stairs of the Times Square building to interview and write about the man behind the famous five-foot headlines that revolve glittering around Times Square. Only Talese thought to look

Talese (second from left) as a reporter for The New York Times, *in a walking interview with Harry S Truman*

behind the facade ("Times Square Anniversary," 2 November 1953). In similar fashion, in 1954 he intrigued the newspaper's staid editors with a long feature article on the Boardwalk chairs of Atlantic City, which carried nearly ten million visitors a year (21 February 1954). Here again was something present yet unremarked upon until Talese turned his

gaze, his indefatigable research, and his respectful language upon it.

Talese's college days had unfolded during the Korean conflict; in preparation, all male University of Alabama students trained in the Reserve Officers' Training Corps (ROTC). Talese graduated from Alabama as a quartermaster and sought work in

New York knowing the army could commission him at any time. The call came in 1954, and he was sent to Fort Knox, Kentucky, to train in the Tank Corps. Mechanically maladroit but verbally savvy, he managed to get himself transferred to the Office of Public Information, where he quickly reinstituted a column titled "Fort Knox Confidential" in the local newspaper, *Inside the Turret*. Talese had quoted Red Smith in his college "Sports Gay-zing" columns and written parodies of William Shakespeare and Edgar Guest. He continued his literary exercises in his "Fort Knox Confidential" columns, beginning with a scene of a blonde in the PX among comic-book-reading GIs (20 May 1955), and progressing to an account of a parachutist's miracle survival written in the style of Jimmy Cannon ("You're Stanley Melczak and You Do Everything the Hard Way," 10 June 1955). The climax of these literary exercises was a tour de force telling one story in five different styles, including Hemingway's (24 June 1955).

Talese kept in touch with *The New York Times* during his military service, and when his tour of duty ended in mid 1956, the paper invited him to return, not as a copyboy, but as a reporter assigned to bring style to the sports pages. Those who know Talese only through his later best-selling volumes on *The New York Times,* Mafia families, sex and censorship in America, and Italian immigration are invariably surprised to learn that he spent nine of his first eleven years as a professional (1947–1958) writing primarily on sports. Talese himself insists he was never interested in sports per se, just as he was never interested in traditional journalism. Talese cared passionately about human character. Journalism and sports merely provided the vehicles for its exploration.

Of all the sports, boxing proved most suited to Talese's human and literary studies. Prize fighters tended to be minorities, outsiders often derided by society—as was boxing itself. Boxers, nevertheless, were striving for the prize. Talese could show their humanity in scenes that would strike most readers as the opening of a novel or short story rather than the lead of a sports article in *The New York Times*. Through boxing, Talese was able to introduce scenes and dialogue to a journalistic establishment wedded to fact plus substantiating quotation. Even dialogue designed to reveal mood rather than information might be accepted. Talese experimented with a diary structure within one *Times* boxing story (16 October 1958) and with Joycean stream of consciousness in an article on bare-knuckle fighter Billy Ray (23 November 1958). That Talese was systematically applying the techniques of fiction to nonfictional subject matter in these 1950s *Times* sports stories is an understatement.

Talese further expanded traditional journalistic practice in his efforts always to delay the "news peg," the factor which made the story "news," until as late in a story as he could manage. This tactic, of course, was the reverse of standard journalistic teaching, which called for the peg to be as near to the beginning as possible. Talese was happiest when he found a way to dispense with the news peg altogether. He did this, just as he eased names to the background in defiance of the venerable journalism maxim "names sell newspapers" because he sought to make his stories universal rather than specific. Talese had no wish to be timely; he was writing for eternity. His "Portrait of a Young Prize Fighter" (12 October 1958) represented a special triumph over newspaper convention, for he managed to withhold José Torres's name until the twenty-first and final paragraph of the story.

Journalists do not often write more than one feature story on a given celebrity. Even writing three or four stories over a span of years is an unusual occurrence. In 1957 Talese wrote the first of thirty-eight separate articles on heavyweight champion Floyd Patterson. Talese is often cited for his skillful use of interior monologue. He insists that his frequent return to his subjects makes this literary feat possible. By the time Talese wrote his celebrated *Esquire* article "The Loser" (March 1964), with its two extended monologues, he had lived with Patterson at his training camp and had jogged beside him during roadwork. "I had become almost an interior figure in his life," Talese recalls. "I was his second skin."

Talese did well as a *Times* sportswriter. He did so well, in fact, that in 1958 *The New York Times* gave him the plum baseball spring training road assignment and allowed him to write three substitute "About New York" columns for the vacationing Meyer Berger. By 1959 the editors thought he was doing so well that as a reward they dispatched him to Albany to cover Gov. Nelson Rockefeller and the New York General Assembly. They thus unwittingly moved him toward the "big story" and away from his signature subject matter. Talese countered by turning more and more to magazines and to books as offering the necessary freedom for his stories with real names.

In 1960 Harold Hayes of *Esquire* magazine stepped forward to offer Talese more writing freedom than he was ever to know at *The New York Times*. His first *Esquire* article, "New York/New York" (July 1960), was different from anything he had done before. It was a series of leads drawn from dozens of articles he had written on "the unnoticed," but now stitched artfully together:

> New York is a city of things unnoticed. It is a city with cats sleeping under parked cars, two stone armadillos crawling up St. Patrick's Cathedral, and thousands of ants creeping on top of the Empire State Building. The ants probably were carried there by winds or birds, but nobody is sure; nobody in New York knows any more about the ants than they do about the panhandler who takes taxis to the Bowery; or the dapper man who picks trash out of Sixth Avenue trash cans; or the medium in the West Seventies who claims, "I'm clairvoyant, clairaudient and clairsensuous."

This widely praised article, reprinted in *Reader's Digest* ("Offbeat Wonders of New York," October 1960), was the basis for Talese's first book, *New York: A Serendipiter's Journey* (1961). The title signals Talese's literary intentions. It links him to the eighteenth-century English essayist Horace Walpole, who coined the term *serendipiter* after reading the Persian fairy tale "The Three Princes of Serendip." According to Talese, the princes "in their travels were constantly finding valuable or agreeable things they did not seek." In *New York: A Serendipiter's Journey* Talese is a twentieth-century prince assembling the fortunate discoveries he has made tramping the streets and avenues of the city. Illustrated in its first edition with Marvin Lichtner photographs on almost every other page, the volume is divided into five sections: "New York Is a City of Things Unnoticed," "of the Anonymous," "of Characters," "of Odd Occupations," and "of the Forgotten."

The response to this volume was encouraging. Critics praised Talese's crisp, precise style and his gift for words. Reviewers only differed in their interpretations of the overall tone of the volume. Some saw Talese's work as a celebration of a strange but wonderful world. Others, however, saw the book as more sober and moody than celebratory. The perceptive *Newsweek* (29 May 1961) reviewer noted that "the colorful is most often melancholy." Indeed, the reviewer suggested that Talese's "preoccupation with the rootless and the lost has a funereal effect." Only this reviewer noted where Talese chose to end his *Journey:* in Potter's Field, where twice a week the bodies of 150 or so of the terminally unnoticed city dwellers were lowered into unmarked graves.

Death is also the backdrop for *The Bridge* (1964), Talese's second volume drawn from his work as a *Times* reporter. On 1 January 1959 he wrote the first of eleven stories on New York bridges which came to focus on the building of the Verrazano-Narrows Bridge linking Brooklyn to Staten Island ("Bay Ridge Seethes over Bridge"). "I knew books had been written about bridges, but never about the people who built them, the obscure people we see from a distance only in silhouette," Talese explained in a 1984 interview. From early 1960 to late 1962 Talese practiced what he calls "the fine art of hanging out." He recalls, "I was so regularly in attendance at the bridge in my off hours and vacations from *The Times* that I was practically considered one of the staff of U.S. Steel." Talese read all the books he could find on bridge building and on famous bridges and bridge builders. He interviewed O. H. Ammann, the designer of the new Verrazano-Narrows Bridge, then the largest suspension bridge in the world, and he walked across the narrow beams, wobbling in the wind, to feel the danger firsthand. Talese spent so much time with the bridge builders that he was invited to their homes, even those of the Native Americans who would race one hundred miles an hour on Friday evenings to reach the Caughnawaga reservation near Montreal.

The Bridge can be read as a bridge builder's manual. At the same time Talese records the recurring injuries and death inherent in the lifestyle of these American macho heroes. The ten chapters comprising this volume offer Talese's first extensive exploration of what will be an obsessive theme for him during his next twenty-eight years: the parental legacy. Throughout the range of subjects his work has covered, Talese tends to be drawn toward the parent-child relation. In these works he expands the specific question of how to honor one's father in a changing age to the larger issue of how to honor the national spirit, the American dream of our forefathers, in a similarly changing and diminished era. Thus the individual psychodramas of Talese's subjects become more universal.

In *The Bridge* Talese stresses the difficulty of sons trying to escape the dangerous family tradition of bridge building. Chapter 6 is titled "Death on the Bridge," and here Gerard McKee, a handsome, popular youth from a "boomer" family, falls to his death from the Verrazano span. Gerard has two brothers who are also boomers, and his father is well aware of the perils of the profession, having been badly crippled by a collapsing crane. At Gerard's funeral his father suffers most: "'After what I've been through,' he said, shaking his head with tears in his eyes, 'I should know enough to keep my kids off the bridge.'"

But McKee does not keep them off, and *The Bridge* ends with another son's death on the next bridge project. Both Talese and Hart Crane, from

Dust jacket for Talese's 1971 book about life in the Mafia

whom Talese borrowed the title, proffer the bridge as a symbol of hope for a permanent spanning to some national ideal, yet both show the modern negations which somehow prevent that goal. Death, failure, or, at best, a short-lived success are the fates of the sons of bridge builders. A further irony of Talese's title is that although a bridge is created to take one someplace, the boomer song used for the final line of this volume suggests the bridge builders are "*linking everything but their lives.*"

With only one exception reviewers were unanimous in their approval of *The Bridge*. Critics praised Talese's style, his evocation of humanity, and the black-and-white Bruce Davidson photographs and delicate Lili Rethi drawings that illustrated Talese's text. Only the *New Yorker* critic faulted Talese's focus: "The author tells something, but not nearly enough, of the problems and triumphs of modern bridge design, scanting the technical side of a great technological achievement in favor of anecdotes about the construction workers' risks and daring, which are, after all, fairly apparent."

The Bridge showed Talese could handle extended narrative—even sequential narration—as well as weave together serendipitous moments. He fol-

lowed *The Bridge* with *The Overreachers* (1965), a collection of twelve articles previously published in *Esquire, The Saturday Evening Post,* and *The New York Times Magazine,* capped by an evocation of New York through the changing seasons. For this third volume Talese took his title from Hemingway, who described "overreachers" as those who "take that extra step, climb too high, lean too far, go too fast, get too grabby with the gods." A prophetic article on George Plimpton and the *Paris Review* set, titled "Looking for Hemingway," was included in the volume, as were Talese's now-classic portraits of Floyd Patterson ("The Loser"), Joe Louis ("The King As a Middle-Aged Man"), and Joshua Logan ("The Soft Psyche of Joshua Logan").

Once again Talese found his work welcomed and praised. Frank Jones set the tone in his *Library Journal* (1 February 1965) review, observing that *The Overreachers* was "written with a real flair for language and with an urge to be utterly realistic. It displays feeling for the meanings of life, the social and racial tensions that underlie the newsworthy, and the forces 'simmering in the smithy' of the soul." *The New York Times* (8 April 1965) praised Talese's research methods. And in perhaps the first use of the term "the new journalism," Pete Hamill (*Book Week,* 12 June 1965) lauded the style and grace of Talese's writing.

The positive response to his magazine and book forays helped Talese finally break with *The New York Times* in mid 1965 and leave newspaper writing forever. He accepted a one-year $15,000 contract from *Esquire* to write six articles. Ironically, his first, in February 1966, was about *The Times,* a celebration of "Mr. Bad News," the obscure man who wrote the obituaries for *The Times.* Harold Hayes then suggested Talese write about Clifton Daniel, a more prominent *Times* executive. The enthusiastic response to this November 1966 article, "Kingdoms, the Powers, and the Glories of *The New York Times,*" equaled the response to Talese's now classic *Esquire* pieces "Frank Sinatra Has a Cold" (April 1966) and "Silent Season of a Hero" (July 1966) on Joe DiMaggio.

When Talese finished the Daniel article, he says, he saw for the first time the potential in his *New York Times* material. "I saw that Daniel was connected to other people," he recalled in a 1984 interview. He determined to do his next *Esquire* piece on Daniel's friend, Harrison Salisbury. The opening of this May 1967 article, "Public and Private Wars of Harrison E. Salisbury," compresses the whole history of *The New York Times* into six italicized paragraphs. These articles, of course, were eventually woven into Talese's fourth volume and first bestseller, *The Kingdom and the Power,* which is often called the first of the "media books."

This volume was Talese's most ambitious to date. "*The Bridge* was a footbridge compared to *The Kingdom and the Power* which was a major suspension structure," asserted Talese several decades later. "The organizational problems of that book were enormous. Hanging from that suspension structure are all kinds of self-contained units, yet they all are linked by the wiring and cabling of the structure." The *Times* building itself becomes a stage for Talese's twenty-chapter volume, for he retraces his steps as a copyboy from floor to floor and section of the newspaper to section, commemorating the lives and behind-the-scenes stories of the men and women who produce "all the news that's fit to print." Turner Catledge becomes the centerpiece of Talese's structure. "He was the man who bridged the old *New York Times* and the modern *Times,*" notes Talese. "I dealt with him in the present and then went back to his Mississippi forbears, one of whom fought in the Civil War. I was then able to describe how *The Times* covered the Civil War, and from there write a little about the man who founded *The Times* fourteen years before the Civil War. It is

through devices like this that writers can tell a story in a way that seems seamless."

For many readers *The Kingdom and the Power* is the most artistically satisfying of Talese's volumes. It also offers Talese's most complex vision of the struggle of America with its legacy as Talese gives national dimension to his "institutional history." He defines his central subject as the transmission of tradition of *The Times* from Adolph S. Ochs to each generation of his successors. Talese employs religious rhetoric to depict this *Times* tradition as a veritable patriarchal religion for its employees. Finally, Talese equates the tradition-religion of *The New York Times* with the secular vision of the U.S. Establishment. To the degree that Talese also continuously criticizes this establishment, particularly for its indifference to the lower classes, his book arraigns *The Times* as an example of the American dream gone wrong, of American idealism gone elitist.

In 1967 the World Publishing Company gave Talese an $11,500 advance to write *The Kingdom and the Power.* This was almost five times the $2,500 advance he had received for his first book, *New York: A Serendipiter's Journey.* Talese chose not to renew his contract with *Esquire* and wrote the story of *The Times* despite the fact that both World and Farrar, Straus and Giroux told him no one would want to read about newspaper people. Looking back, Talese recalls the publisher's discouragement when the first review of *The Kingdom and the Power* appeared. Christopher Lehmann-Haupt, *The New York Times* daily book critic, had received an advance copy of the volume. Disregarding the publication date six weeks away, he printed an attack on the book in *The Times* (21 May 1969). "I thought that would be the end of the book, for nobody would want to read it after reading that review, and there would be no voices countering this critic for six more weeks," recalls Talese.

What happened instead was that the *Times* review backfired. Its premature censure brought attention to the book, causing Murray Kempton of the *New York Post* to attack Lehmann-Haupt in a column two days later, giving a lively defense of the volume. "I suddenly became the center of a controversy and was interviewed by magazines and invited on radio shows," says Talese. "I was given a forum to defend myself against *The Times'* attack, and the book sold very, very quickly." Most reviews, in fact, were laudatory, and to the surprise of Talese and his publisher, *The Kingdom and the Power* became a bestseller, staying on the best-seller list for six months. The success of the volume spurred a torrent of imi-

Richard Castellano, Raf Vallone, Gay Talese, and Joseph Bologna on the set of the 1971 made-for-TV movie Honor Thy Father

tations. Journalism's inner workings were now understood to be of surpassing public interest.

Talese, however, was on to something new. In fact, throughout the writing of *The Kingdom and the Power* he had a parallel project in mind. Talese first saw the mafioso's son Salvatore "Bill" Bonanno in 1965 during his last days as a *Times* reporter. When Talese noticed Bonanno standing with his lawyer in a federal courthouse corridor, he might have been gazing at his double on the other side of the law. Talese was not yet aware of the many remarkable similarities in their backgrounds and experiences. But Talese saw enough to be curious, and after the reporters left he approached Bonanno's lawyer and indicated his interest in writing the Mafia son's story.

Such a subject was forbidden in both professional and personal ways for Talese—and therefore, perhaps, especially attractive. Journalistic consensus at that time was that the Mafia's "code of silence," their *omertà,* could not be penetrated. In addi-

tion, Talese's moralistic, law-abiding father was "horrified and embarrassed beyond explanation" by the presence of Italian Americans in the Mafia and, worse than that, by the publicity given them. This feeling was a primary reason for Talese's interest in exploring that world.

For four months following this first encounter, Talese wrote letters and made phone calls and office visits to Bonanno's lawyer, seeking, without success, an interview. Finally, his persistence prevailed. Bonanno met him for dinner at Johnny Johnson's Steak House on Second Avenue in New York. Then one night in 1966 a disheveled Bonanno appeared at Talese's door. He had been fired upon on the streets of Brooklyn and needed Talese to inform the media to assure greater police surveillance. "I called up *The Times* and leaked the story," Talese recalls, "and after that Bill disappeared to California. Every time I saw Bill, however, I would keep notes of my impressions. Finally, in 1969, I received a Christmas card from Bill inviting me out to his house in California.

I stayed in his home, rode unarmed with Bill and his bodyguards, and eventually wrote about family life in the Mafia."

Honor Thy Father (1971) begins with an "Author's Glossary" identifying Talese's nineteen-person cast of characters and defining "organized crime," "the Mafia," and "the Commission." The inside front pages present the Bonanno family tree while a set of ten sepia-framed photos of the early Bonannos gives readers the sense of holding an old family album while a later series of twelve unframed contemporary photographs hint at the contrasting modern life of Bill and his young family. The thirty-two chapters comprising *Honor Thy Father* are divided into four thematic parts: "The Disappearance," "The War," "The Family," and "The Judgment." Talese has called this the easiest of his books to write, for the material contained a ready-made suspenseful story line; however, he had to find interesting ways to depict the more mundane, ordinary aspects of everyday Mafia life.

The final scene of *Honor Thy Father* takes place in a federal marshal's office where there are two signs on the wall, one marked "civil," the other "criminal." These two signs remind us that, taken together, Talese's first two best-sellers represent the "civil" and "criminal" sides of American legacies. From 1965 to 1969, while Talese was giving primary attention to the success story of Punch Sulzberger and *The New York Times,* he was simultaneously keeping track of the dark side and dark son of the American Establishment, Bill Bonanno. *The Kingdom and the Power* and *Honor Thy Father* can be read as companion pieces showing the upper and undersides of the American Dream.

Honor Thy Father became an immediate best-seller upon its publication and was made into a teleplay starring Joseph Bologna as Bonanno. Talese dedicated *Honor Thy Father* to Bonanno's four young children "in the hope that they will understand their father more, and love him no less. . . . " He allocated the substantial income from foreign sales of the volume to trust funds for his own two daughters and for the four Bonanno children. However, Talese's efforts as generational go-between backfired when *Honor Thy Father* first appeared. After reading the book Don Joseph Bonanno stopped speaking to his son for a year, during which time the young man was in prison and, presumably, in even greater need of parental support. Time, however, has softened the paterfamilias. In 1983 Joseph Bonanno published his own autobiography, *A Man of Honor,* and in 1995 he invited Talese and his son to the elegant black-tie dinner celebrating his ninetieth birthday.

One of the truisms of literary nonfiction is that it often takes twenty years or more for a book to be read the way the author intends. This may be true as well for *Thy Neighbor's Wife* (1980), Talese's greatest financial success and sole critical failure. The project began one evening in 1971 when he investigated a neon sign advertising "Live Nude Models" on the third floor of a building near Bloomingdale's. Just as the Mafia represented a denied and forbidden subject to Talese as a boy, sexuality was, if possible, an even greater taboo. By associating for the next five years with "the obscene people of America," as Talese had wittily characterized his research, he was defying the sexual repression of his familial, religious, and social upbringing.

Talese believed the story of changing sexual mores in America was the biggest story of his time, and he has described *Thy Neighbor's Wife* as a "breakthrough" book for him which includes some of his best writing. The style he employs throughout the twenty-five chapters is exceptional, particularly alliterative passages and delicate descriptions of erotic acts. *Thy Neighbor's Wife* also encompasses a larger subject and historical period than either of his previous two best-sellers, as it treats the vast and complex topic of sex and censorship in America from the Puritans to 1980.

As in the fiction of Henry James, settings represent psychological states in *Thy Neighbor's Wife.* The book opens in Chicago, a city which for Talese embodies the religious, political, and sexual rigidity that is the formative experience of most of the inhabitants Talese depicts. The movement of many of these people away from Chicago and primarily to Los Angeles and the utopian Sandstone Community suggests a journey from repression to freedom. But Harold Rubin, whose story opens the volume, never escapes Chicago, and the Sandstone "utopia" does not survive; these two factors suggest the power of formative, restrictive forces. This point is underscored by the concluding setting—Ocean City, New Jersey, Talese's own "Chicago." Here, at the end of the volume, is a further artistic breakthrough: Talese's first effort to depict himself as a character in his work.

Perhaps the most important breakthrough, however, is the change in the filial stance of the younger generation. *Thy Neighbor's Wife* offers at least twenty portraits of "sons" and sixteen "daughters" seeking not to honor their fathers but to defy them. The important place *Thy Neighbor's Wife* holds in Talese's canon is as the first extended work in which sons move from submission to unrepentant rebellion. Talese, in fact, chooses to end this book with himself returning home to the insular island of

Dust jacket for Talese's memoir and history of Italian immigration to America

Ocean City, standing naked, defiantly eye to eye with the town fathers. "They were unabashed voyeurs looking at him," runs the final line, "and Talese looked back."

Thy Neighbor's Wife was an extraordinary financial success for Talese, marred only by the intensity of the hostile criticism directed at the book. Talese was faulted for failing to include all aspects of sexuality (such as homosexuality, incest, venereal disease, and contraception) and for giving women secondary status. Many reviewers were shocked and outraged by Talese's open attitude toward sexuality and by his widely publicized participatory research methods. What has not been said about the critical reaction to this book is that perhaps one reason the response was often so angry is because *Thy Neighbor's Wife* itself invites confrontation through its tone of unrelenting defiance.

The first words of *Thy Neighbor's Wife* are Talese's prefatory "Note to the Reader," stressing that "The names of the people in this book are real, and the scenes and events described on the following pages actually happened." Critics to date, however, have not yet adequately acknowledged the remark-

able reporting showcased in the volume. It presents scenes of marital infidelity using (with permission) the actual names of the participants. That Talese's method of returning again and again to his sources created the trust which made this detailed reporting possible is perhaps his greatest legacy to other writers. It implies there may be no subject beyond the bounds of human communication.

Talese was upset and angered by the reaction to *Thy Neighbor's Wife,* particularly by a censorious editorial in the *Ocean City Sentinel-Ledger* and by repercussions affecting his family. As a result of the Ocean City editorial and of insulting remarks addressed to his father on the local golf course, Talese contemplated selling his summer home in Ocean City and sparing his loved ones further embarrassment by never returning to the island. Professionally, his response to suggestions that he write a "respectable" book was a wish to write a sequel to *Thy Neighbor's Wife* instead.

Tensions between "respectability" and defiance continue within Talese to this day. In 1982 he turned away from an assured "respectable" fourth best-seller, the story of Lee Iacocca and the salvation of Chrysler Corporation, after four months of living and traveling with the Chrysler executive. "Iacocca was an Italo-American success story, but it was not my story," he told an interviewer in 1983. Instead, Talese's aging father drew the author's attention closer to home.

Thus, once again Talese turned from the "big story" to the unnoticed story, this time of Italian immigration to America, told through his own obscure family. Rather than the small book Talese's friends urged him to write after *Thy Neighbor's Wife, Unto the Sons* (1992) expands even further in historical and geographical scope. Talese's research included tracing his family name to the fourteenth century and his father's southern Italian village back to the ancient Greeks. He lived in the Calabrian village of Maida, interviewed his surviving relatives through an interpreter, and steeped himself in the history and lore of Italy from Saint Francis to Benito Mussolini.

The forty-eight chapters comprising *Unto the Sons* move freely back and forth, in Talese's signature seamless fashion, between his boyhood years in Ocean City in the 1930s and early 1940s and Maida and Italy across the water. Tension is created from the beginning, for World War II placed Italian immigrants such as Talese's father in a position of divided loyalty as their newly embraced nation waged war against Italy. As in *Honor Thy Father,* such continuing narrative suspense permits Talese to introduce into the volume the history of the current crisis: southern Italy overrun by one nation after another; Garibaldi and eventual Italian independence; and the subsequent poverty of the south that led to the flood of Italian immigration to America, including the stonecutter Gaetano Talese, the author's grandfather and namesake, followed eventually by Talese's father, the tailor Joseph. Talese's re-creation of World War I Italian battle campaigns recalls Hemingway's *A Farewell to Arms* (1929), and in the dramatic final chapters Allied planes during World War II prepare to bomb Maida, a national offensive that precipitates a final crisis between Joseph and his son.

Unto the Sons became Talese's fourth bestseller. The critical response was by and large both respectful and enthusiastic. *The Library Journal* (1 February 1992) reviewer sounded a common response in terming *Unto the Sons* "a grand epic along the lines of Alex Haley's *Roots*." Others wrote that the book was a masterpiece, and several agreed that Talese's volume would "resonate for parents and children of every nationality" (*Publishers Weekly,* 1 January 1992). As with Talese's first book, *New York: A Serendipiter's Journey,* however, critics emerged with differing senses of the tone of the volume. Is it bitter or affectionate? Several reviewers found Talese's attention to detail excessive, yet the very sections on asbestos manufacturing which were often condemned were the favorite of Book-of-the-Month Club Editorial Board member David Willis McCullough (*BookNews,* April 1992). Reviewers also differed in their responses to the mesh of history and memoir. While the majority found the interweaving "masterful," several preferred the personal to the panoramic.

The tension between personal and national history is just one of several Talese is exploring at this point in his career. Indeed, he appears to be at an artistic crossroads. The immigrant's son who made his career by writing of the ordinary, unnoticed, and forgotten people with whom he profoundly identifies has, by so doing, left their ranks and become a celebrity, a New York literary lion with a den at Elaine's. From this elevated position, can he continue to speak compellingly of the unnoticed and the forgotten? As a winner, can he truly speak today for losers?

Another burden is his current literary reputation (nurtured by *Honor Thy Father* and *Thy Neighbor's Wife*) as a best-selling writer on sensational, forbidden subjects. Talese's status among editors has risen greatly since the $2,500 advance for *New York: A Serendipiter's Journey*. In 1991 the prestigious publishing house of Knopf contracted to pay $2.5 million for *Unto the Sons* and Talese's next two books.

Talese's movement as a writer, however, seems to be toward continued exploration of the personal rather than the sensational. He wishes to carry forward his memoirs from World War II to the present, but wonders: can he find a national resonance in this personal odyssey—as he did in his other books? And can such personal subject matter attract the mass audience his publisher undoubtedly desires?

Fortunately, some things are inviolable. Fame and obscurity, and the national and the personal, have been the poles of Talese's odyssey from the 1950s onward. But a third beckoning flag has been the "forbidden." Complicating Talese's current crisis is the temptation he has felt since 1992 to put aside the continuation of *Unto the Sons* to pursue one more forbidden subject. This one would be the defiant sequel to *Thy Neighbor's Wife,* with all the potential for outraging reviewers once again. The unspoken subject for the 1990s is male impotence; indeed, as the baby boomers enter their fifties, the audience for this forbidden story grows larger and larger. Since 1992 Talese has made significant forays into the world of male impotence—the world of urology, implants, and John and Lorena Bobbitt. He covered both Bobbitt trials and was invited to John Bobbitt's Niagara Falls home.

But the pain of *Thy Neighbor's Wife* still lingers, causing Talese to hesitate at the door of this forbidden subject. Yet, a book entering the world of male impotence would further Talese's reputation as a best-selling writer on unspoken topics. Its subject matter alone might assure the large audience Talese has come to expect for his books and would justify Knopf's multimillion-dollar investment. This book could also press the frontiers of reporting that *Honor Thy Father* and *Thy Neighbor's Wife* began.

Matters of literary technique further complicate the issue. In *Unto the Sons* Talese pressed the boundaries between fact and fiction farther than he ever dared before. That he is a bit uncomfortable with the liberties he took is evident in his "Author's Note" which concludes the volume:

> my efforts to keep my . . . book within the boundaries of "nonfiction"–that is, to remain factually verifiable–do not meet the strict standards I have always followed in my previously published work. For the first time in my career as a nonfiction writer, in this latest book I have altered some of the personal names. These name changes do not apply to any of the major characters, including members of my own family, but I have deliberately falsified the names of some minor characters–either to avoid undue embarrassment and pain to their survivors or for legal reasons.

Critics to date have not been troubled by Talese's changes. Indeed, although noting that "historical"–and even journalistic–purists might complain that Talese could not possibly know [some of] the thoughts and conversations he reports" in *Unto the Sons,* McCullough writes in his *BookNews* review that "For me, the technique is acceptable simply because it works and works beautifully. Talese has created–or re-created or perhaps, at times, fabricated–a believable and breathing family whose progress, with its triumphs and its heartbreak, is a uniquely American story, at once wonderful and utterly ordinary."

Perhaps this response will fortify Talese to continue pressing the boundaries between fiction and nonfiction. Alternatively, he may follow Wolfe and write the sequel to *Unto the Sons* as fiction. Ultimately, however, decisions regarding form and subject matter will be his alone. Whatever direction he

pursues, his reputation for unlocking forbidden subjects, for exhaustive research, and for respectful celebration of the unnoticed is secure.

Interviews:

Leonard Wallace Robinson, "The New Journalism: A Panel Discussion with Harold Hayes, Gay Talese, Tom Wolfe, and Professor L. W. Robinson," *Writer's Digest* (January 1970);

"The View from Talese's Head," *Playboy* (September 1974): 152–153, 234–236, 239;

"Playboy Interview: Gay Talese," *Playboy* (May 1980): 75–116;

"The Conversation: Francis Coppola & Gay Talese," *Esquire Film Quarterly* (July 1981): 78–80, 82, 84, 86–87;

William Kelly, "Thy Neighbor's Life: From Books to Blue Laws Gay Talese Explains it All," *SandPaper* (21 August 1986): 22–23;

John Brady, "Gay Talese: An Inclusive Interview," *Writer's Digest* (January 1993): 28–31; (February 1993): 26–31, 56–58, 60.

References:

David L. Eason, "The New Journalism and the Image-World," in *Literary Journalism in the Twentieth Century,* edited by Norman Sims (New York: Oxford University Press, 1990), pp. 191–205;

Eason, "New Journalism: Metaphor and Culture," *Journal of Popular Culture,* 15 (Spring 1982): 142–149;

Barbara Lounsberry, "Gay Talese's Fathers and Sons," in her *The Art of Fact: Contemporary Artists of Nonfiction* (New York: Greenwood Press, 1990), pp. 1–35;

Carol Polsgrove, "Gay Talese," in *A Sourcebook of American Literary Journalism: Representative Writers in an Emerging Genre,* edited by Thomas B. Connery (New York: Greenwood Press, 1992), pp. 261–272;

Ronald Weber, "Subjective Reality and Saturation Reporting," in his *The Literature of Fact: Literary Nonfiction in American Writing* (Athens: Ohio University Press, 1980), pp. 89–110;

Tom Wolfe and E. W. Johnson, eds., *The New Journalism* (New York: Harper & Row, 1973).

Hunter S. Thompson

(18 July 1939 –)

A. J. Kaul
University of Southern Mississippi

BOOKS: *Hell's Angels: A Strange and Terrible Saga of the Outlaw Motorcycle Gangs* (New York: Random House, 1967);

Fear and Loathing in Las Vegas: A Savage Journey to the Heart of the American Dream (New York: Random House, 1971);

Fear and Loathing: On the Campaign Trail '72 (San Francisco: Straight Arrow Books, 1973);

The Great Shark Hunt: Strange Tales from a Strange Time (New York: Summit Books, 1979);

The Curse of Lono, by Thompson and Ralph Steadman (New York: Bantam Books, 1983);

Generation of Swine: Tales of Shame and Degradation in the '80s (New York: Summit Books, 1988);

Songs of the Doomed: More Notes from the Death of the American Dream, Gonzo Papers, Volume 3 (New York: Summit Books, 1990);

Better Than Sex: Confessions of a Political Junkie, Gonzo Papers, Volume 4 (New York: Random House, 1994);

Fear and Loathing in Las Vegas and Other American Stories, edited by Douglas Brinkley (New York: The Modern Library, 1996);

The Proud Highway: The Saga of a Desperate Southern Gentleman, 1955–1967 (New York: Villard, 1997).

Hunter S. Thompson created an explosive, first-person, gonzo style of reportage that brashly pushed the language and limits of American literary journalism into boldly original new directions. With weird humor and strident apocalyptic invective, his fractured, drug-crazed persona of the quintessential outlaw journalist was an actor's mask, a comic ploy he used to engage a lifelong moral and political critique of American culture and its institutions. The masterpiece of his gonzo repertoire, *Fear and Loathing in Las Vegas: A Savage Journey to the Heart of the American Dream* (1971), hailed as the "Best Book on the Dope Decade" and an "Epitaph for the Drug Culture of the Sixties," has gained the status of postmodern classic in late-twentieth-century American

Hunter S. Thompson (photograph by David Hiser, Photographers, *Aspen)*

literature. The major themes of the gonzo canon—death, doom, and failure of the American dream—are the linchpins of his distinctively Southern literary style played out with gothic black humor on the tragic stage of post-1960s America. A Southerner by birth, upbringing, and sensibility, his uncompromising moral voice mediates fear and loathing with violently avenging laughter.

Hunter Stockton Thompson was born 18 July 1939 in Louisville, Kentucky, the first son of insurance agent Jack Robert Thompson and Virginia Ray Thompson. He grew up in a two-story house at 2437 Ransdell Avenue in the quiet, middle-class Cherokee Triangle neighborhood, a suburb abandoned by the old-money elite of Louisville, and attended I. N. Bloom Elementary School where he made friends who would also attend Highland Junior High and Louisville Male High School. His writing career began at the age of ten when he contributed a one-paragraph account of childhood trench warfare, "War," to the *Southern Star,* a two-page mimeographed newsletter his friends circulated in the neighborhood at four cents a copy. The aggressively competitive Castlewood Athletic Club, a feeder into the city's high schools, initiated him in 1950, but his brief athletic career was stunted by a late growing spurt. In 1952 Thompson's fifty-seven-year-old father died after a three-month stay in the Lousville Veterans Administration Hospital. An autopsy revealed a progressive hereditary neurological disorder that affected the immune system. Virginia Thompson went to work as a secretary and a librarian to support Hunter and his two younger brothers.

The Athenaeum Literary Association, a prestigious high-school-sponsored society whose members were sons and daughters of Louisville's entrenched and wealthy social elite, provided an outlet for his emerging writing and lifestyle. "It was a very big deal," a fellow Athenaeum member recalled. "And if you got in, and if you stuck around Louisville, you were made for life. . . . The real purpose was the members presented the debutantes each year when they came out in Louisville. It was a glorified, upscale stud farm." Athenaeum members met on Saturday nights to read and to discuss literary matters. Three decades later, Thompson commented that his Athenaeum experience was "a kind of compensation" for truancy: "When you're cutting school, you're reading for power, reading for advantage." Thompson was a voracious reader, with particular fondness for William Faulkner, Ernest Hemingway, Henry Miller, and especially F. Scott Fitzgerald's *The Great Gatsby* (1925) and J. P. Donleavy's *The Ginger Man* (1961). "Hunter read everything," a childhood friend remembered. "Hunter was trying to live out *The Ginger Man.* It had a lot of influence on him. The whole bar scene, the kind of rugged, masculine, macho approach to life." Thompson contributed a humorous column to the literary annual of the Athenaeum, *Spectator,* under the name "Harried Hunto." Thompson's satiric essay "Open Letter to the Youth of Our Nation," signed "John J. Righteous-Hypocrite," won third prize in the Nettleroth Contest for the Athenaeum.

"Young people of America, awake from your slumber of indolence and harken to the call of the future," he wrote. "Do you realize you are rapidly becoming a doomed generation?" His essay "Security" (1955) decried "the tragedy of a man who has sacrificed his freedom on the altar of security."

Membership in the Athenaeum contributed to Thompson's growing anger, disaffection, and resentment. "Hunter really resented being on the outside looking in," a wealthy classmate observed. "He was an outsider not because of who he was, but because he didn't have the family money and connections behind him to allow him to do some of the things that his friends did." Athenaeum members were college-bound, many destined for the Ivy League. "Somebody asked Hunter, 'Where are you going to college?'" recalled an Athenaeum member who later attended Princeton. "And he said, 'I don't know. I don't know, but somewhere.' I overheard that, and I imagined at the time there was almost desperation or frustration in his voice. . . . So I think he saw his contemporaries carrying on, and he was unable to do so himself. And this turned from hurt and disappointment to anger and rage and frustration. I think that accounts for some of the violence and vandalism, too."

Acquaintances, classmates, and friends during his high-school years (and in adulthood, for that matter) variously described him as attention-getting and charismatic; dominating and destructive, yet polite to the point of being courtly; outspoken and witty; and most of all, confident. The self-confidence came from "an intuitive understanding that he was smarter, stronger and quicker than the kids we were running with in society," a high-school friend said. "You could pick up a lot of confidence knowing that the people who were the establishment, the power structure, were not that impressive." Thompson earned a reputation for being the "token thug" of the Athenaeum. "Hunter's idea of a good time . . . was to drive around town, find a construction site, and just destroy the place. Dump over the outhouse, let it roll down the hill, dump out all the nails. Essentially he would vandalize the place," recalled a classmate. His shenanigans took destructive turns—setting fire to sulfur poured across the top of lockers, flooding the first floor of the high school with three inches of water during an assembly, dumping a truckload of pumpkins in front of a downtown hotel. "Shock value. That was Hunter's forte," recalled an Athenaeum president. "My major job was trying to control Hunter. He was absolutely uncontrollable. . . . We—the entire legacy of the Athenaeum—were going to hell in a handbasket if we didn't do something to counteract Hunter. He was Fagin from *Oliver Twist*." His all-night carousing and drinking escapades were legendary. "A dance would end, and we would always attempt to find a party until the wee hours," another classmate said. "I remember one dance where we stayed out for the whole weekend. We came to school Monday morning in our tuxedos."

Extracurricular drinking, shoplifting, and vandalism were youthful versions of the "profoundly active Balance of Terror with local police authorities" that he described decades later living near Aspen, Colorado. In the spring of his senior year Thompson and five friends were thrown into a Danville, Kentucky, jail for vandalism. "We did so much damage in that town, and when we got in jail we did about two hundred dollars damage to the jail," a partner in the crime recalled. "To a jail! All six of us in a big cell. Hunter loved it. He led that charge." Three consecutive nights of trashing a gas station led to Thompson's being arrested and handcuffed by a Louisville policeman in the middle of the day at Male High and taken to the juvenile detention center. Eleven days before graduation he was arrested with two friends and charged with armed robbery. The well-connected father of one of his cohorts, a former president of the Kentucky Bar Association, succeeded in getting his son's charge reduced to disorderly conduct with a fifty-dollar fine. A minor player in the incident lost his admission to Yale and had to settle for Princeton. Thompson's repeated scrapes with the law had filled a social worker's file, and the juvenile court judge ordered the seventeen-year-old repeat offender to spend the next sixty days in the adult county jail without bail. Another Athenaeum member's father, an attorney and former juvenile judge, intervened, persuading the judge to release Thompson after thirty days with the expectation that he enlist in the United States Air Force.

Hunter Thompson's high-school days ended in a Louisville jail about the time Allen Ginsberg was reading "Howl" in San Francisco. He did not graduate with his Athenaeum classmates, who had excommunicated him. His academic record was lackluster, anyway. He ranked number 241 in a class of 255, and the highest grade of his senior year was a 72 from a generous teacher. National standardized tests taken a year before showed his percentile rankings in the nineties in English, math, and social studies. Sitting in jail, he wrote extensive letters to his friends. Thompson was ready to exit Louisville and its tradition-bound caste system. "I think Hunter always hated what Louisville stood for," a friend commented. "It's a boring, provincial,

Caricature of Thompson by Ralph Steadman, from Fear and Loathing in Las Vegas *(1971)*

middle-class, family-oriented town that has nothing going for it except the Derby two minutes a year. . . . And Hunter couldn't wait to get out of there!"

A week after his release from jail–time enough to heave a case of beer bottles through a high-school teacher's living room windows on three consecutive nights–Hunter Thompson arrived drunk at Randolph Air Force Base near San Antonio, Texas, for basic training. In December 1955 he was assigned to electronics school at Scott Air Force base in southern Illinois. Six months later he was sent to Eglin Air Force Base at Pensacola, Florida, where he quickly became a staff writer and sports editor for the *Command Courier,* the base newspaper. He also moonlighted as a sports columnist for the *Playground News* in nearby Fort Walton Beach, writing under the byline "Thorne Stockton." A fictitious 8 November 1957 news release on Air Proving Ground Command stationery signaled his "early out" discharge. Thompson's news release, sent to friends, described him as a "fanatical airman" and "uncontrollable iconoclast" who had thrown a wine bottle from a speeding auto into the base gatehouse upon his discharge. Thompson was "totally unclassifiable," the release said, quoting an Air Force classification officer. "I almost had a stroke yesterday when I heard he was being given an honorable discharge. It's terrifying–simply terrifying."

Thompson's first civilian writing job was a brief stint with a newspaper in the abandoned coal mining town of Jersey Shore, Pennsylvania. He soon quit after driving the newspaper feature writer's car into a river. Thompson then went to New York City where he landed an eighty-five-dollar-a-week job as a copyboy for *Time* magazine. He lived in a subterranean Greenwich Village apartment on Perry Street and took a few courses at Columbia University. He spent his leisure hours imbibing Beat culture and reading, outlining, and typing passages from *The Great Gatsby,* he later confided to an editor, to learn in his own "neurological system how it felt to write that kind of prose." Thompson met and dated a well-educated businessman's daughter, Sandra Dawn Conklin, a Goucher College graduate whose degree got her a job as a secretary-receptionist. Thompson tried to talk *Time* editors into making him a reporter or foreign correspondent. Unsuccessful, he quit to take a reporting job with the Middletown, New York, *Daily Record.* After only two months on the job he was fired for kicking the office candy machine that had refused to deliver on his nickel investment. Composing-room employees stole the candy bars from the damaged machine, Thompson recalled in *Songs of the Doomed: More Notes from the Death of the American Dream, Gonzo Papers* (1990), and "they docked my pay for all those candy bars. . . . That was when I gave up on journalism completely." Supported by unemployment checks, Thompson rented a cabin in the woods near Cuddebackville, New York, and began writing "Prince Jellyfish," a novel later excerpted in *Songs of the Doomed.* Thompson finished a first draft by April 1959 and returned to New York City where he stayed with friends long enough to land a job as a reporter for *El Sportivo* in San Juan, Puerto Rico, a start-up publication that was billing itself as "the *Sports Illustrated* of the Caribbean." When Thompson arrived in San Juan, he found himself covering the bowling boom in Puerto Rico. Conklin joined him in Puerto Rico where he survived by earning extra income as a stringer for the *New York Herald Tribune* and by writing tourist brochures. It was during this time in San Juan that his important friendship with writer William Kennedy began. He also began work on another novel, "The Rum Diary," later excerpted in *Songs of the Doomed.*

Thompson and Conklin returned to the continental United States in 1960 and after a brief stint in New York City were lured to California's Big Sur, a long-fabled artists' and writers' colony once home to Henry Miller, among others. Thompson worked as a caretaker in exchange for the rent on a dilapidated cottage on property that a few years later would become the Esalen Institute, West Coast mecca of the human potential movement. In a July 1961 article in *Rogue for Men,* "Big Sur: The Tropic of Henry Miller," Thompson wrote: "This place is a real menagerie, flavored with everything from bestiality to touch football. . . . There are two legitimate wives on the property; the other females are either mistresses, 'companions,' or hopeless losers." The owner of the property–Bunny Murphy, grandmother of best-selling novelist Dennis Murphy–was furious. "You have twenty-four hours to get out of here," she told Thompson, pointing to a copy of *Rogue.*

Now homeless and broke, his "companion," Sandy Conklin, went back to New York, and Thompson retreated to live with his mother in Louisville and to continue freelancing. He wrote a few minor assignments for the *Louisville Courier-Journal,* and the *Chicago Tribune* sent him to cover the Old Kentucky Barn Dance in Renfro, Kentucky. His story "Traveller Hears Mountain Music Where It's Sung" appeared in the *Tribune* in February 1962 when the parent company of the *Wall Street Journal* began publishing the *National Observer.* Thompson sent the fledgling newspaper clips and a letter explaining his background and willingness to cover South America. A few weeks later his dispatches describing politics and smuggling in Colombia started arriving at the *National Observer.* At $150 a story, Thompson worked and wrote his way from Colombia ("Why Anti-Gringo Winds Often Blow South of the Border") through Ecuador ("Chatty Letters During a Journey from Aruba to Rio"), Peru ("The Inca of the Andes: He Haunts the Ruins of His Once-Great Empire"), and Bolivia ("A Never-Never Land High Above the Sea") en route to Rio de Janeiro, Brazil ("Brazilian Soldiers Stage a Raid in Revenge"), where he was joined once again by Conklin. The *National Observer* paid about $2,000 for sixteen dispatches from Thompson during his year in South America and gave him a rousing reception upon his return. "I came as a man who'd been a star–off the plane all the editors met me and treated me as such," he recalled. Once again Thompson headed for California, writing his way across the country for the *National Observer.* He stopped long enough in Jeffersonville, Indiana, across the Ohio River from Louisville, to marry Conklin in May

1963 and headed for San Francisco, his base of operations for "What Lured Hemingway to Ketchum?," "Marlon Brando and the Indian Fish-In," and "When Beatniks Were Social Lions."

The emerging counterculture attracted his attention, but the *National Observer* showed little interest. "There was a great rumbling—you could feel it everywhere," he recalled. "I wanted to cover the Free Speech Movement, but they didn't want me to. Berkeley, Hell's Angels, Kesey, blacks, hippies . . . I had these connections. Rock and roll. I was a crossroads for everything and they weren't making use of it. I was withdrawn from my news position and began writing book reviews—mainly for money." He reviewed J. P. Donleavy's *A Singular Man* (1963), saying the book was "like sitting down to an evening of good whiskey and mad laughter in a rare conversation somewhere on the edge of reality" where "humor is forever at war with despair." The rejection by the *National Observer* of his "strongly positive" review of Tom Wolfe's *Kandy-Kolored Tangerine Flake Streamline Baby* (1965) so strained his relations with the newspaper that he quit after sending to Wolfe a copy of the review, the rejection, and his own letter stating that the review was killed for "bitchy, personal reasons."

In late 1964 the California attorney general issued a report on the Hell's Angels, a motorcycle gang accused of viciously raping two teenaged girls during a Labor Day weekend rally. The national press—*The New York Times, Newsweek,* and *Time*—jumped on the lurid stories of the outlaw gang. The reportage caught the attention of Carey McWilliams, editor of the *Nation,* who sent clips to Thompson with the request for a brief, fact-based, investigative article on the Hell's Angels. "The difference between the Hell's Angels in the papers and the Hell's Angels for real is enough to make a man wonder what newsprint is for," Thompson's May 1965 *Nation* article said, pointing out erroneous, misleading, and exaggerated claims in the press and the attorney general's report. The *Nation* article grabbed the attention of publishers, who sent letters with book offers. Bantam Books president Ian Ballantine saw potential for an insider account of the motorcycle gang and authorized a $6,000 advance. Random House paid Bantam $3,000—half went to Thompson—for the right to publish a hardback version before the Bantam paperback. Thompson, so broke at the time that the telephone company cut off service, jumped at the opportunity. "For fifteen hundred dollars I'd have done the definitive text on hammerhead sharks," he recalled, "and stayed in the water with them for three months!"

With the advance Thompson bought a BSA 650 motorcycle and began a yearlong investigation, hanging out and riding with the renegade gang, and finally getting stomped. In the the two-page postscript to the book Thompson wrote, "On Labor Day 1966, I pushed my luck a little too far and got badly stomped by four or five Angels who seemed to feel I was taking advantage of them. A minor disagreement suddenly became very serious. . . . The attack ended with the same inexplicable suddenness that it had begun." He drove himself, spitting blood on the dashboard, nearly fifty miles to the hospital in Santa Rosa. "I was tired, swollen, and whipped," he wrote. "My face looked like it had been jammed into the spokes of a speeding Harley." On his way back to San Francisco he tried to compose a fitting epitaph to the violent saga, but the only words that came to him were echoes of Kurtz's final words in Joseph Conrad's *Heart of Darkness* (1902): "'The horror! The horror! . . . Exterminate the brutes!'"

Hell's Angels: The Strange and Terrible Saga of the Outlaw Motorcycle Gangs was published in March 1967, selling about forty thousand copies; the paperback followed in 1968. Twenty years later the paperback edition of *Hell's Angels* had gone through twenty-nine printings with sales of more than two million copies. Reviewers praised *Hell's Angels* as having "a kind of Rimbaud delirium of spirit for nearly everybody to which, of course, only the rarest geniuses can come close." The reviews in *Newsweek, The New Yorker,* and *The New York Times* were all positive. Thompson himself said, "I'm a word freak. I like words. I've always compared writing to music. . . . When it really works, it's like music." A passage at the end of the book emerged as one of his favorite pieces of writing, he recalled in *Songs of the Doomed.* Thompson described racing his motorcycle at three in the morning:

when the strange music starts, when you stretch your luck so far that fear becomes exhilaration and vibrates along your arms. You can barely see at a hundred. . . . You watch the white line and try to lean with it . . . howling through a turn to the right, then to the left . . . letting off now, watching for cops, but only until the next dark stretch and another few seconds on the edge. . . . The Edge. . . . There is no honest way to explain it because the only people who really know where it is are the ones who have gone over. The others—the living—are those who pushed their control as far as they felt they could handle it, and then pulled back. . . . But the edge is still Out there. Or maybe it's In. The association of motorcycles with LSD is no accident of publicity. They are both a means to an end, to the place of definitions.

Abbie Hoffman, Timothy Leary, and Thompson in Seattle, 1987

His familiarity with the West Coast drug culture was a conspicuous part of *Hell's Angels,* in which he described his role as intermediary between novelist Ken Kesey's Merry Pranksters and the motorcycle gang. In July 1965 Thompson introduced Kesey to several Hell's Angels, and the author of *One Flew Over the Cuckoo's Nest* invited them to his La Honda estate for a weekend "acid trip" with music by the Grateful Dead. Psychedelic drug guru Timothy Leary ("Turn On, Tune In, Drop Out") and Beat poet Ginsberg joined Thompson for the weekend frolic. (Ginsberg and Thompson tape-recorded the event and gave the tape to Wolfe, who described the scene in *The Electric Kool-Aid Acid Test.*) Thompson took LSD for the first time that weekend. "My own acid-eating experience is limited in terms of total consumption," he wrote in *Hell's Angels,* "but widely varied as to company and circumstances . . . and if I had a choice of repeating any one of the half dozen bouts I recall, I would choose one of those Hell's Angels parties in La Honda, complete with all the mad lighting, cops on the road, Ron Boise sculpture looming out of the woods, and all the big speakers vibrating with Bob Dylan's 'Mr. Tambourine Man.'"

Hell's Angels brought the twenty-six-year-old writer a degree of notoriety—and a steady stream of writing offers. *The New York Times Magazine* in May 1967 published "The 'Hashbury' Is the Capital of the Hippies," Thompson's incisively critical account of the drug culture in the Haight-Ashbury section of San Francisco where he had lived for two years.

Thompson respected the political activism of the Berkeley Free Speech Movement but found the Haight-Ashbury dropout hippie culture, like the Merry Pranksters, a depressing failure. "Students who once were angry activists were content to lie back in their pads and smile at the world through a fog of marijuana smoke—or, worse, to dress like clowns or American Indians and stay zonked for days at a time on LSD," he wrote. He also wrote that the move from Berkeley to Haight-Ashbury, figuratively and literally, signaled a shift from "pragmatism to mysticism, from politics to dope, from the hang-ups of protest to the peaceful disengagement of love, nature and spontaneity." Yet, the Haight-Ashbury scene was "the orgiastic tip of a great psychedelic iceberg that is drifting in the sea lanes of the Great Society," he observed. A much larger and "more discreet" population of respectable, upwardly mobile, middle-class professionals participated in the drug culture in "peaceful anonymity"—and out of the view of law enforcement authorities. "The only people who can afford to advertise their drug menus are those with nothing to lose," he wrote. "And these—for the moment, at least—are the young lotus-eaters, the barefoot mystics and hairy freaks of the Haight-Ashbury—all those primitive Christians, peaceful nay-sayers and half-deluded 'flower children' who refuse to participate in a society which looks to them like a mean, calculated and soul-destroying hoax."

In "The Ultimate Free Lancer," published in the *Distant Drummer* (November 1967), Thompson leveled a frontal assault on the "cheap, mean, grinning-hippie capitalism" that had overtaken the counterculture.

> While the new wave flowered, Lenny Bruce was hounded to death by the cops. For "obscenity" . . . and the world we have to live in is controlled by a stupid thug from Texas. A vicious liar, with the ugliest family in Christendom. . . . And California, "the most progressive state," elects a governor straight out of a George Grosz painting, a political freak . . . Ronnie Reagan, the White Hope of the West. . . . And then to see a madman like Ginsberg copping out with tolerance poems . . . Kennedy with his head blown off and Nixon back from the dead. . . . And there's the chill of it . . . Leary's "drop-out generation" of the 1960's. The Head Generation . . . a loud, cannibalistic gig where the best are fucked for the worst reasons, and the worst make a pile feeding off the best . . . all selling the New Scene to *Time* magazine and the Elks Club. The handlers get rich while the animals either get busted or screwed to the floor with bad contracts.

The New Left and Free Speech Movement of the 1960s framed Hunter Thompson's politics. *Pageant* magazine sent him to the New Hampshire primary in 1968 to write about the political comeback of former vice president Richard Milhous Nixon, then a candidate for the Republican presidential nomination. In "Presenting: The Richard Nixon Doll (Overhauled 1968 Model)," published in July, Thompson described the "man behind all these masks," including an hour-long conversation with the candidate about professional football–"Nixon *knows* pro football"–during a limousine ride to the Manchester airport. Thompson unleashed the invective characteristic of his lifelong disgust for the politician who he thought symbolized the decadence of American life. Thompson thought Nixon was "a foul caricature of himself, a man with no soul, no inner convictions, with the integrity of a hyena and the style of a poison toad." Thompson concluded, "I suppose it's only fair to say that this latest model might be different and maybe even better in some ways. . . . But as a customer, I wouldn't touch it—except with a long cattle prod." He attended the Democratic National Convention in August 1968 where he was surrounded by anti–Vietnam War demonstrators, clubbed by police, and pushed through a plate glass window. The Convention "permanently altered my brain chemistry," he said. He returned as "a raving beast" to his new home.

Thompson had grown weary of Haight-Ashbury by the "Summer of Love" in 1967 when thousands of would-be hippies arrived on the scene. The "whole neighborhood had become a cop-magnet and a bad sideshow," he wrote later. "Be-tween the narcs and psychedelic hustlers, there was not much room to live." He was ready to move with Sandy and their three-year-old son, Juan Fitzgerald Thompson (born in March 1964), back to New York City where he could "whoop it up like Fitzgerald, be a famous writer." They stopped at Aspen, Colorado, a ski resort town where land values still remained affordable. He had been in Aspen a few years earlier, writing articles on the area for the *National Observer*. Thompson bought a house and approximately 120 acres for $75,000 on a lease-to-buy deal to avoid making a down payment. "Owl Farm" at Woody Creek, five miles northeast of Aspen, became the base for his freelance forays and retreat for the next thirty years. Woody Creek, Colorado, would be to Thompson what Ketchum, Idaho, was to Ernest Hemingway.

Aspen quickly became the battleground for Thompson's bizarre and comically theatrical style of political activism. In 1969 developers and politicians were proposing to capitalize on the underdeveloped potential of Aspen as a ski resort with high-priced luxury condominiums and four-lane highways to lure rich tourists. Thompson opposed them with "the old Berkeley-born notion of beating the System" on its own turf and formed the Freak Power Party with a slate of candidates for local offices in the 1970 election. He was a candidate for Pitkin County sheriff. The party faced the daunting task of getting its politically alienated constituency of "freaks, heads, fun-hogs" and "Haight-Ashbury refugees" who had settled in Aspen after the "Summer of Love" to register to vote. The Freak Power constituency was willing to risk being arrested for drug possession–"the 'crime' was worth the risk"–but felt that "voting wasn't worth the kind of bullshit that went with it." Thompson wrote, "This sense of 'reality' is a hallmark of the Drug Culture, which values the Instant Reward–a pleasant four-hour high–over anything involving a time lag between the Effort and the End."

The Freak Power program was designed to drive the real estate developers completely out of the valley, prevent construction of a four-lane highway into Aspen, and "create a town where people could live like human beings, instead of slaves to some bogus sense of Progress that is driving us all mad." The party platform called for ripping up the asphalt, sodding the streets, and changing the name of Aspen to "Fat City" to prevent exploitation of the name *Aspen*. As candidate for sheriff, Thompson promised "savagely to harass all those engaged in any form of land-rape" and to install on the courthouse lawn "a bastinado platform and a set of stocks–in order to punish dishonest dope dealers in a proper public fashion. . . . The only realistic approach is to make life in this town very ugly for all profiteers—in drugs and all other fields." The Freak Power campaign drew press coverage from the *Los Angeles Times, The New York Times,* and the *National Observer.*

Seven months before the election the Freak Power candidate for sheriff took time out from his campaign to earn money with a freelance article about the Kentucky Derby for *Scanlan's Monthly.* Warren Hinckle, editor for *Scanlan,* teamed Thompson with British illustrator Ralph Steadman, a thirty-four-year-old artist whose garish cartoons had appeared in London newspapers. "We didn't give a hoot in hell what was happening on the track," he wrote. "We had come there to watch the *real* beasts perform." Thompson's article, "The Kentucky Derby Is Decadent and Depraved" (June 1970) unleashed his pent-up rage at the bigoted, chauvinistic, and caste-bound culture of his hometown. Thompson was looking for "that special kind of face" at the Derby for Steadman to sketch as the lead drawing for the article. In his mind's eye the face was "the mask of the whiskey gentry," he wrote, a symbol of the "whole doomed atavistic culture that makes the Kentucky Derby what it is." Steadman sketched the face of an old friend from the writer's youth—"a prep school football star in the good old days with a sleek red Chevy convertible and a very quick hand . . . with the snaps of a 32 B brassiere." Steadman whispers to Thompson, "Jesus, look at the corruption in that face."

The writer and artist went to New York after the Kentucky Derby to finish the story in a hotel room *Scanlan's* had reserved with a wide-open room service account and four quarts of Johnny Walker scotch. Thompson was having difficulty putting the story together. "At first I was typing," he recalled, "then I was just ripping pages out of my notebook." Hinckle liked the notes and wanted more. Thompson edited his notes, and with a little reshuffling the story was done. "I was full of grief and shame," Thompson recalled. "This time I made it, but in what I considered to be the foulest and cheapest way." A few days after the story appeared, however, Thompson began getting phone calls and letters from around the country calling the article a journalistic breakthrough. Bill Cardoza, editor of the *Boston Globe Sunday Magazine,* wrote "this is it; this is pure Gonzo. If this is a start, keep rolling." "The Kentucky Derby Is Decadent and Depraved" proved to be the gonzo breakthrough—and a new beginning. "In a way it was an almost accidental breakthrough," Thompson recalled, "a whole new style of journalism which now passes for whatever Gonzo is . . . accident and desperation."

The term eventually found its way into the American vocabulary.

Back in Colorado, Thompson resumed the Freak Power campaign to drive the money changers out of Aspen. In the November election the Freak Power ticket went down in defeat with Thompson finishing second, 468 votes behind the winner in the three-way race for sheriff. His account of the campaign, "The Battle of Aspen," appeared on 1 October 1970, a month before election day, in the San Francisco–based rock magazine *Rolling Stone.*

Rolling Stone was only two years old when Thompson met its founder and publisher, Jann Wenner, a Berkeley dropout who later worked for Warren Hinckle's *Sunday Ramparts* until it folded in May 1966. Former *Distant Drummer* editor John Lombardi had joined *Rolling Stone* and thought the gonzo journalist might "jazz up the magazine" and broaden its scope beyond rock music to politics. Wenner was disinclined to make drastic changes in his "little rock magazine," but Lombardi talked him into a meeting. Lombardi warned Thompson that he really would have to impress the publisher. "I decided to take the unconventional approach," Thompson recalled. Lombardi said, "He was wearing his famous 'gook' Hawaiian shirt, and carrying a six-pack of beer. . . . He had a little case under his arm . . . with all kinds of things coming out of it: papers, string, very strange-looking. And he wore a Dynell wig, a cheap gray lady's wig that he kept taking off, straightening, putting back on. And his sunglasses." Thompson swilled beer and told Wenner about Aspen politics and the Freak Power ticket. When Thompson excused himself to use the restroom, Wenner told Lombardi: "I know I am supposed to be the spokesman for the counterculture and all that but what the fuck is this?" "The Battle of Aspen" was the first of more than thirty articles that would appear in *Rolling Stone* under the byline of Hunter S. Thompson.

The 29 August 1970 death of Chicano journalist Reuben Salazar in East Los Angeles provided the peg upon which the gonzo journalist based his second *Rolling Stone* piece on radical politics and set the stage for the masterpiece of his literary career. A Chicano lawyer, activist, and kindred spirit—Oscar Zeta Acosta served as Thompson's liaison with the Chicano community, which was highly distrustful of the "gobacho pig writer." Thompson took the offer of *Sports Illustrated* to cover the Mint 400 motorcycle race in Las Vegas as an opportunity for him and Acosta to "get away from the angry vortex" of the Salazar story and "sort out the evil realities." Acosta returned to a trial in Los Angeles, leaving Thompson furiously writing notes about their two-day stay in Las Vegas. Thompson fled Las Vegas, by his account leaving behind a "massive" unpaid hotel bill. *Sports Illustrated* "aggressively rejected" his twenty-five-hundred-word manuscript on the Mint 400. When he returned to Los Angeles, Thompson wrote the Salazar story, "Strange Rumblings in Aztlan" (April 1971), during the day and spent the night hours lashing together his Las Vegas notes. *Rolling Stone* saw potential for a story in the first twenty pages. Back in Woody Creek, Thompson's junk mail contained an invitation to the National District Attorneys Conference in Las Vegas. "I guess I was thinking *Vegas 2* already: 'Hmm, this story's not finished, really,'" Thompson told P. J. O'Rourke in a *Rolling Stone* interview. "So I called Oscar and I said, 'Hey, are you ready to go? We have another date in Las Vegas. . . . Don't tell anyone we're going to penetrate the deepest bowels of the enemy. This is not funny.'" Under the guise of drug-crazed journalist "Raoul Duke" (Thompson) and his "Samoan attorney" (Acosta), the 1960s-style road trip to the Mint 400 and the District Attorneys Conference in Las Vegas became the framework for Thompson's hilarious and widely acclaimed masterpiece of gonzo journalism.

Fear and Loathing in Las Vegas: A Savage Journey to the Heart of the American Dream, first published in two parts with Ralph Steadman's illustrations in *Rolling Stone* (November 1971), begins: "We were somewhere around Barstow on the edge of the desert when the drugs began to take hold. I remember saying something like 'I feel a bit lightheaded; maybe you should drive. . . . ' And suddenly there was a terrible roar all around us and the sky was full of what looked like huge bats, all swooping and screeching and diving around the car, which was going about a hundred miles an hour with the top down to Las Vegas." With the Rolling Stones' "Sympathy for the Devil" blaring from the tape player, Raoul Duke tells a young hitchhiker: "I want you to know that we're on our way to Las Vegas to find the American Dream . . . a very ominous assignment—with overtones of extreme personal danger." His comic quest ends with the realization that the "vortex" of the Amercan Dream was housed in the madness of the Circus-Circus casino. The casino's owner wanted to run away and join the circus, Thompson wrote. "Now the bastard has his own circus, and a license to steal, too. . . . It's pure Horatio Alger, all the way down to his attitude." The American dream was the surreal Circus-Circus spectacle of "the Forty Flying Carazito Brothers . . . doing a high-wire trapeze act, along with four muzzled Wolverines and the Six Nymphet Sisters" while custom-

ers in the upstairs balconies were hustled with "all kinds of funhouse-type booths."

In Thompson's gonzo imagination the American dream ended in failure for an entire generation. The 1960s began with "a fantastic universal sense that whatever we were doing was right, that we were winning . . . that sense of inevitable victory over the forces of Old and Evil," Thompson wrote, and ended in the "doomstruck era of Nixon." The Woodstock generation that mistakenly believed it could buy "Peace and Understanding for three dollars a hit" had been permanently crippled in its failure to understand "the essential old-mystic fallacy of the Acid Culture: the desperate assumption that somebody—or at least some force—is tending the Light at the end of the tunnel." Thompson wrote, reflecting on the mid 1960s, "We were riding the crest of a high and beautiful wave." From the vantage point of a hill in Las Vegas five years later, Thompson could look West toward Berkeley and Haight-Ashbury and "with the right kind of eyes" see "the high water mark—the place where the wave finally broke and rolled back." *Fear and Loathing in Las Vegas* marked the end of an era, Thompson wrote, "a vile epitaph for the Drug Culture of the Sixties."

The literary establishment greeted *Fear and Loathing in Las Vegas* with critical acclaim. Thompson has written "a scorching epochal sensation," New Journalism guru Tom Wolfe declared. "Best Book of the Dope Decade," a *New York Times* headline proclaimed. "The whole book boils down to a kind of mad, corrosive prose poetry that picks up where Mailer's 'An American Dream' left off and explores what Tom Wolfe left out," Christopher Lehman-Haupt wrote in *The New York Times*. "Besides, its—gulp—funny." More recently, on the twenty-fifth anniversary of the gonzo set piece, O'Rourke in *Rolling Stone* wrote: "*Fear and Loathing in Las Vegas* addresses the great themes of late-20th-century literature—anomie, being and nothingness, existential terror." Thompson is a "better writer" than the "common herd of modern-lit angst peddlers" such as Camus, Kafka, and Sartre, he said, and besides, Thompson takes "the darkest questions of ontology, the grimmest epistemological queries, and by his manner of posing them, sends us doubled over in fits of risibility."

In his "very unauthorized biography," *When the Going Gets Weird,* Peter O. Whitmer argues that Thompson deliberately set out to rewrite and update Fitzgerald's masterpiece, *The Great Gatsby,* in *Fear and Loathing in Las Vegas.* In an interview with another biographer, William McKeen, Thompson offered his own lofty assessment of *Fear and Loathing in Las Vegas.*

Thompson after the dismissal of the 1990 charges against him of sexual assault and possession of controlled substances and incendiary devices (University of Washington Daily*)*

"It's as good as *The Great Gatsby,*" he said, "and better than *The Sun Also Rises.*" The Modern Library edition of 1996 solidified the status of *Fear and Loathing in Las Vegas* as a contemporary classic.

A forty-year-old Thompson was less confident of his achievement in the 1970s. In a previously unpublished essay, "Jacket Copy for Fear and Loathing in Las Vegas," that appeared for the first time in *The Great Shark Hunt* nearly ninety pages after an "Author's Note" bearing Joseph Conrad's inscription, "Art is long and life is short, and success is very far off," Thompson called his book "a failed experiment in Gonzo Journalism" and "a victim of its own conceptual schizophrenia, caught & finally crippled in that vain, academic limbo between 'journalism' and 'fiction.'" Gonzo journalism was to be "a style of 'reporting' based on William Faulkner's idea that the best fiction is far more true than any kind of journalism." Fiction and journalism are different means to the same end. "My idea was to buy a fat notebook and record the whole thing, *as it happened,* then send in the notebook for publication—without editing," he said. "That way, I felt, the eye & mind of the journalist would be functioning as a camera." With *Fear and Loathing in Las Vegas* Thompson imposed a fictional framework on what began as journalism. "True Gonzo reporting needs the talents of a mas-

ter journalist, the eye of an artist/photographer and the heavy balls of an actor," he wrote. The writer must be "a participant in the scene, while he's writing it—or at least taping it, or even sketching it." The closest analogy to ideal gonzo journalism, he said, would be "a film director/producer who writes his own scripts, does his own camera work and somehow manages to film himself in action, as the protagonist or at least a main character."

The next book-length treatise of gonzo journalism, *Fear and Loathing: On the Campaign Trail '72* (1973), was born during a *Rolling Stone* editorial staff meeting at the Esalen Institute at Big Sur in December 1971. *Rolling Stone* agreed to bankroll Thompson's yearlong gonzo immersion in national presidential campaign politics. The Twenty-sixth Amendment giving eighteen-year-olds the right to vote had been ratified, and Thompson saw the gonzo political venture as a way to mobilize the youth vote into a "million pound shithammer" to prevent President Nixon's reelection. The anti–Vietnam War Democratic presidential nominee, U.S. senator George McGovern of South Dakota, took the gonzo journalist seriously. "I was told that he was an eccentric, brilliant, perceptive reporter, that he reached a wide and young audience, and that he was not to be taken lightly," McGovern said.

Thompson's participatory gonzo style offered readers political hilarity tinged with absurdity. He infiltrated a spontaneous Youth for Nixon demonstration at the Republican National Convention. They were uncomfortable with the prospect of network television cameras focusing on "a weird-looking, 35-year-old speed freak with half his hair burned off from overindulgence, wearing a big blue MCGOVERN button on his chest, carrying a tall cup of 'Old Milwaukee' and shaking his fist at John Chancellor up in the NBC booth." He laced his dispatches with slashes of "weird humor," saying NBC correspondent Chancellor put acid in his drink during the Democratic convention. CBS anchor Walter Cronkite was "heavy into the white slavery trade—sending agents to South Vietnam to adopt orphan girls, then slipping them back to his farm in Quebec to be lobotomized and sold into brothels up and down the Eastern seaboard." The gaffes of Democratic presidential aspirant Edmund Muskie of Maine were rumored to be "The Ibogaine Effect," resulting from massive doses of a West African root drug. Former vice president Hubert Humphrey, "a treacherous, gutless old ward-heeler who should be put in a goddam bottle and sent out with the Japanese drift," Thompson said, campaigned like "an eighty-year-old woman who has just discovered speed." Thompson's guerrilla-style campaign coverage made no pretense of playing by the "objective" rules of mainstream journalism. "Don't bother to look for it here—not under any byline of mine," he wrote. McGovern's campaign chief, Frank Mankiewicz, said: "We were always running a guerrilla campaign, living off the land. So we never worried about Hunter disgracing us. . . . I have always said that Hunter's writing was the most accurate and least factual account of the campaign."

Three high-profile books in six years created a pill-popping gonzo persona for the thirty-four-year-old writer and bestowed a measure of celebrity status. Cartoonist Garry Trudeau, a Yale graduate who began his syndicated cartoon "Doonesbury" in 1970, introduced Thompson's gonzo alter ego Raoul Duke as "Uncle Duke" in December 1974. A "Doonesbury" character, Zonker, introduces his Uncle Duke as a "nice but a little strange" *Rolling Stone* writer who is "incredibly reckless with drugs." Thompson was hardly flattered. "Do you have any idea what it is like to wake up, look in the mirror . . . and see a cartoon?" he asked a friend. "My God, I'm not even forty years old yet, and I've been MYTHOLOGIZED!"

The Vietnam War strained an already quixotic relationship between Thompson and *Rolling Stone* publisher Wenner. In the waning days of the conflict, shortly before the fall of Saigon in 1975, Thompson "needed to see the end of it and be a part of it somehow." He went to Vietnam in April 1975, and about that time Wenner folded Straight Arrow Books, publisher of *Fear and Loathing: On the Campaign Trail '72.* Thompson was furious, claiming that Wenner closed Straight Arrow when it owed him a $75,000 advance for his next book. He wrote Wenner a letter of complaint. According to Thompson, Wenner flew into a rage and fired him while he was in Saigon. Although Thompson continued contributing to *Rolling Stone* after the flare-up and the magazine's move from San Francisco to New York City in 1977, he no longer felt comfortable with it after it became an "establishment" magazine.

The first collection of Thompson's writing appeared in *The Great Shark Hunt: Strange Tales from a Strange Time* in 1979, a turning point in his personal life and writing career. *The Great Shark Hunt,* inscribed "To Richard Milhous Nixon, who never let me down" and "When the going gets weird, the weird turn pro-Raoul Duke," anthologized writing from the *National Observer, Playboy, Rolling Stone, Scanlan's,* and other magazines. In an "Author's Note" signed "HST #1, R.I.P." at the beginning of *The Great Shark Hunt,* Thompson contemplated figuratively leaping from his twenty-eighth-story New York City hotel room on Fifth Avenue at one o'clock in the morning. He felt that he had "already lived and finished the life I planned to live—(13 years longer, in fact)—and everything from now on will be A New Life." The book's dedication to his son without mentioning his wife of sixteen years suggests an ending. Sandra Conklin Thompson and Hunter S. Thompson filed for divorce in February 1979; the divorce became final in 1981.

Thompson's new life began with the filming in August and September 1979 of *Where the Buffalo Roam,* a Hollywood production loosely lashed together from episodes in *Fear and Loathing: On the Campaign Trail '72* and *The Great Shark Hunt.* Thompson received more than $100,000 for the movie. He was ecstatic when the movie's star, Bill Murray, was filmed reading the epilogue in the final scene. The epilogue was his ideal of gonzo journalism—a director writing his own script, managing to film himself in action as main character. *Where the Buffalo Roam* had a short theater run, however, and critics panned it, even *Rolling Stone.* For many gonzo aficionados, though, the film became a cult classic, and film posters with the slogan "I don't advocate the use of drugs, alcohol and violence—but they've always worked for me" are pricey collector's items.

Thompson's brief retirement from journalism ended in 1980 when he teamed up again with Steadman to cover the Honolulu Marathon in Hawaii for *Running* magazine. Ostensibly another installment of comic-style gonzo sports reporting, "The Charge of the Weird Brigade" (March/April 1981) actually addressed the weightier theme of physical fitness in the 1980s. "Run for your life, sport, because that's all you have left," he wrote. "The same people who burned their draft cards in the '60s and got divorced in the '70s are now into *running*." Running made sense for the failures and losers of the "doomed generation" in the 1980s when finishing—not winning—a twenty-six-mile marathon race was a victory. "The concept of victory through defeat has already taken root," he wrote. "The Honolulu Marathon was a showcase example of the New Ethic." Bantam Books offered Thompson and Steadman $45,000 each to turn "The Charge of the Weird Brigade" into *The Curse of Lono* (1983). Thompson struggled to expand the manuscript with illustrations to the length of 160 pages by inserting extensive excerpts from Richard Hough's *The Last Voyage of Captain James Cook* into the text. Bantam published *The Curse of Lono* on heavy stock to enhance Steadman's illustrations and to give the short book more weight. The book, dedicated to Thompson's mother, Virginia Ray Thompson, sold well—two-hundred thousand copies in ten years.

San Francisco Examiner publisher William Randolph Hearst III hired Thompson in 1985 to write columns at $1,200 apiece in an effort to boost circulation. *Generation of Swine: Tales of Shame and Degradation in the '80s* (1988) collects the columns published between December 1985 and March 1988. "Huge brains, small necks, weak muscles and fat wallets—these are the dominant physical characteristics of the '80s—the Generation of Swine," he wrote. Death, doom, and failure were his major themes. His epistolary-style columns resonate with apocalyptic religious motifs and quotes from the Book of Revelation. His denunciatory literary jeremiads challenged conventional morality, politics, and culture. President Ronald Reagan was a "flag-waving front man for a gang of fast-buck Southern California profit-takers"; Vice President George Bush had "the instincts of a dung beetle"; televangelists were "the scum of the earth . . . acting like a gang of baboons"; and the television industry was a "cruel and shallow money trench . . . where thieves and pimps run free and good men die like dogs, for no good reason." His satiric epithets possessed the tonality of a doomsday oracle; images of death, destruction, and dismemberment were deployed to describe the nation's capital with "blood in the water," "human remains on the sidewalk," and "the hallways of the White House basement . . . slick with human scum."

He attacked politicians for their deception and betrayal with a parody of biblical prophecy.

Another anthology, *Songs of the Doomed,* collected excerpts from his unpublished novels, "Prince Jellyfish" and "The Rum Diary," and previously published articles interspersed with autobiographical commentaries on incidents in his career. The book concludes with a twenty-five-page section, "Welcome the Nineties: Welcome to Jail," that describes his trial for "Sex, Drugs, and Rock and Roll" in the Pitkin County, Colorado, district court. The writer was arrested in February 1990 for third-degree sexual assault and, after an eleven-hour search of his Owl Farm compound, indicted in April on eight counts of sexual assault and possession of controlled substances (acid, cocaine, and marijuana) and incendiary devices (blasting caps and dynamite). The sexual-assault charges stemmed from writer and former pornographic film producer Gail Palmer-Slater's visit to Owl Farm in February, the *Aspen Times Daily* reported, when she claimed Thompson grabbed her left breast and "punched her during an argument about whether the interview should take place in a hot tub." Thompson pleaded innocent, saying she was "drunk at the time and dopey with fear and booze and bad nerves" and tried to stop him from calling a cab to take her to a local hotel; when she tried to grab the phone, he pushed her away. The case was really about the Fourth Amendment's prohibition against unreasonable searches and seizures, he told his attorney. Thompson looked forward to his day in court. His friends published an advertisement asking for donations to the Hunter S. Thompson Legal Defense Fund; he claimed his defense had cost $150,000. In an order signed 30 May 1990 the judge approved the prosecution's motion to dismiss "with prejudice" all charges on grounds that the state was "unable to establish guilt beyond a reasonable doubt."

Better Than Sex: Confessions of a Political Junkie (1994) is a postmodern pastiche of caricatures, memos, quotes, photographs, and time lines of the 1992 presidential campaign of soon-to-be president Bill Clinton. The death of former president Richard M. Nixon in April 1994 delayed the book's publication so he could add a final word on "an American Monster." Many prominent politicians memorialized Nixon, including political adversaries such as McGovern—but Thompson steadfastly refused to utter a forgiving word. According to Thompson, "Richard Nixon broke the heart of the American Dream."

In the 1990s Thompson's writing career seemed to be winding down. *Better Than Sex* was "his final book on politics," its dust-jacket copy stated.

Newsweek proclaimed him "the wise old hipster" who had become "officially respected—if not quite respectable" with the publication of a Modern Library edition of his *Fear and Loathing in Las Vegas,* which ranks among the classics of the American literary canon. In fact, he was at work preparing a collection of letters for publication, the first volume of his collected letters, *The Proud Highway: The Saga of a Desperate Southern Gentleman, 1955–1967.*

Thompson's gonzo reportage in eight books and many articles redefined the language and the limits of post-1960s literary journalism. The secularized style of his apocalyptic literary jeremiads denounced the culture, morality, and politics of a degenerate world waiting to bushwhack the pilgrims. The great themes of his gonzo imagination—death, doom, and failure of the American dream—perform behind the comic mask of linguistic bravado. Thompson is the Joker of New Journalism, his humor often obscuring the intense moral seriousness of his critique of the American dream and the absurd matrix of its madness that inevitably leads to destructive hubris, self-delusion, and defeat. Nearly three decades after publication of his postmodern gonzo masterpiece that fused Jack Kerouac (*On the Road,* 1957) and Ginsberg with the 1960s drug culture, *Fear and Loathing in Las Vegas* has become the Woodstock generation's *The Great Gatsby.* The gonzo canon resonates with the dark and brooding nightmarish iconography of violent Southern gothic defeatism. "I have always felt like a Southerner," the expelled member of Louisville's Athenaeum Literary Association said. "And I've always felt like I was born in defeat. And I may have written everything I've written just to win back a victory. My life may be pure revenge."

References:

E. Jean Carroll, *Hunter: The Strange and Savage Life of Hunter S. Thompson* (New York: Dutton, 1993);

Arthur J. Kaul, "Hunter S. Thompson," in *A Sourcebook of American Literary Journalism: Representative Writers in an Emerging Genre,* edited by Thomas B. Connery (Westport, Conn.: Greenwood Press, 1992);

Rick Marin, "The Doctor Is Still In: Hunter S. Thompson joins the ranks of the classics," *Newsweek,* (25 November 1996): 94;

William McKeen, *Hunter S. Thompson* (Boston: G. K. Hall, 1991);

P. J. O'Rourke, "Dr. Hunter S. Thompson," *Rolling Stone* (28 November 1996): 64–68, 70–72, 144–145;

Paul Perry, *Fear and Loathing: The Strange and Terrible Saga of Hunter S. Thompson* (New York: Thunder's Mouth Press, 1992);

Ralph Steadman and David Felton, "Gonzo Goes to Hollywood: The Strange and Terrible Saga of 'Where the Buffalo Roam,'" *Rolling Stone* (29 May 1980): 38–41;

Craig Vetter, "Playboy Interview: Hunter Thompson," *Playboy* (November 1974): 75–90, 245–246;

Peter O. Whitmer, *When the Going Gets Weird: The Twisted Life and Times of Hunter S. Thompson* (New York: Hyperion, 1993).

Calvin Trillin

(5 December 1935 –   )

R. Thomas Berner
Pennsylvania State University

BOOKS: *An Education in Georgia: Charlayne Hunter, Hamilton Holmes, and the Integration of the University of Georgia* (New York: Viking, 1963; London: Victor Gollancz, 1964);

Barnett Frummer Is an Unbloomed Flower; and Other Adventures of Barnett Frummer, Rosalie Mondle, Roland Magruder, and Their Friends (New York: Viking, 1969);

U.S. Journal (New York: Dutton, 1971); republished as *Killings* (New York: Ticknor & Fields, 1984);

American Fried: Adventures of a Happy Eater (New York: Doubleday, 1974);

Runestruck (Boston: Little, Brown, 1977);

Alice, Let's Eat: Further Adventures of a Happy Eater (New York: Random House, 1978);

Floater (New Haven, Conn.: Ticknor & Fields, 1980);

Uncivil Liberties (New Haven, Conn.: Ticknor & Fields, 1982);

Third Helpings (New Haven, Conn.: Ticknor & Fields, 1983);

With All Disrespect: More Uncivil Liberties (New York: Ticknor & Fields, 1985);

Travels with Alice (New York: Ticknor & Fields, 1989);

Enough's Enough (and other Rules of Life) (New York: Ticknor & Fields, 1990);

American Stories (New York: Ticknor & Fields, 1991);

Remembering Denny (New York: Farrar, Straus & Giroux, 1993);

Deadline Poet: Or, My Life as a Doggerelist (New York: Farrar, Straus, & Giroux, 1994);

The Tummy Trilogy (includes *American Fried; Alice, Let's Eat; and Third Helpings*) (New York: Farrar, Straus & Giroux, 1994);

Too Soon to Tell (New York: Farrar, Straus & Giroux, 1995);

Messages from My Father (New York: Farrar, Straus & Giroux, 1996).

PLAY PRODUCTIONS: *Calvin Trillin's Uncle Sam*, New York, American Place Theater, 26 September 1988;

Calvin Trillin (photograph by Sigrid Estrada)

Words, No Music, New York, American Place Theater, 11 October 1990.

Calvin Trillin is an important literary journalist whose most acclaimed work to date is *Remembering Denny* (1993), his rumination on the meaning of the life of a classmate at Yale who appeared destined for great things but whose life ended in suicide in 1991. Trillin is also an essayist, poet, memoirist, social historian, satirist, humorist, novelist, short-story writer, critic, and journalist. He is not, three books on food notwithstanding, a food critic or restaurant reviewer. He is, George W. Hunt has said in *America,* "one of America's finest writers." In a 1986 interview in *Editor & Publisher,* Trillin told David Astor, "I've always assumed that reporting is at the center of what I do. If I gave up the center, I thought maybe the sides would fall in." Trillin's reporting has appeared in magazines such as *Time* and *The New*

Yorker; his journalism has also been collected in books or appeared originally in book form.

Trillin was born in Kansas City, Missouri, on 5 December 1935, the son of Avram "Abe" and Edyth (née Weitzman) Trillin (originally "Trilinsky"). Trillin's father, a grocer in Kansas City, decided that his son would attend Yale, where Trillin studied English and wrote for the *Yale Daily News.* He also worked for a summer at *Time* magazine. He graduated from Yale in 1957, spent two years in the army in and around New York City, and, after his discharge, joined *Time* in 1960. He married Alice Stewart, the "Alice" in the titles of two of his books, on 13 August 1965. She produces educational films for public television. They have two daughters, Abigail and Sarah.

Trillin's first book, *An Education in Georgia: Charlayne Hunter, Hamilton Holmes, and the Integration of the University of Georgia* (1963), grew out of his experience as a reporter at *Time* magazine covering the early days of integration in the formerly all-white student body at the University of Georgia. Two students, Charlayne Hunter (later Hunter-Gault) and Hamilton Holmes, were the first African Americans admitted to the University of Georgia. When the two were near graduation, Trillin returned to the campus to report on their experience, which is the subject of the book. The book originally appeared as a three-part series for *The New Yorker* and was Trillin's first article for that magazine. Trillin combines a capsule history of race relations in Georgia with background on Hunter and Holmes and background on their initial admission to the University of Georgia with their retrospective analysis of their four years in a virtually all-white university. The article is written in the first person, which enables Trillin to recall what he witnessed and offer his observations on what he uncovered four years later.

Claude Sitton praised *An Education in Georgia* in *The New York Times Book Review* (19 January 1964) because "it comes closer to the essential social truths of the problem than do some works of greater scope," noting that the book focused on the lives of the two pioneers as students rather than on the events surrounding them. When the book was reissued in 1992 with a new foreword by Hunter-Gault, B. Kinsey Leaks, writing in *Southern Living* (May 1992), praised the book and its treatment of the experiences of Hunter-Gault and Holmes: "With an eye for detail, an ear for conversation, and unflagging fairness to all, Trillin chronicles what those two endured and surely . . . achieve[d] at Georgia." Despite the dated nature of the subject of the reissue, Leaks said the book "remains a complete example of solid journalism."

Killings (1984), originally published in 1971 under the title *U.S. Journal,* is a collection of pieces Trillin wrote for *The New Yorker.* The stories are about various murders and trials that Trillin covered in various cities and towns throughout the country, some of which are updated in the book's afterword. Trillin's introduction prepares the reader to understand that he or she is not about to read a book about violence and not even a book about death. Trillin is often more interested in the communities than the victims, or as he puts it: "These stories are meant to be more about how Americans live than about how some of them die." He also says in his introduction that "Reporters love murders," and adds, "I have always been attracted by stories of sudden death." His criterion for selecting the subjects had nothing to do with their importance or even the type of murder. Trillin chose subjects, he says, "mostly on the basis of what sounded interesting."

The stories in *Killings* are hard to characterize. One reports on the death of a filmmaker in Jeremiah, Kentucky, shot dead while filming hillbillies at their houses by the owner of the houses in which the hillbillies lived. The owner of one house felt the film crew was trespassing, although they had gotten releases from the people they filmed. The man who shot the filmmaker eventually pleaded guilty to voluntary manslaughter. In another story a long-haired motorcycle tough who shoots someone at a drug party is revealed later to be an undercover police officer and is found not guilty after a jury deliberates for just twenty-five minutes.

Several of Trillin's books, such as *American Fried: Adventures of a Happy Eater* (1974), are collections of essays published in magazines. Some of his essays, in such books as *Alice, Let's Eat: Further Adventures of a Happy Eater* (1978) and *Travels with Alice* (1989), have focused on travel and places where he has eaten, leading some readers to think of him as a food critic and restaurant reviewer. Trillin denies it. "I never wrote restaurant reviews—I always admitted that I don't cook, that I have no knowledge—but it was a way to write jokes about the country," he told Sarah Lyall in a 1994 interview for *The New York Times.* "Or should I say, a way of writing about the country in a jocular manner." Trillin claims that his wife, Alice, requires that they eat in whatever hotel they are staying in their first night in town. When they had just arrived in Barbados, he writes in "For Queen and Fritter":

It happened to be the hotel's night for a buffet. As we approached the food that had been laid out on the buffet tables, it occurred to me that if the sons of lieutenant colonels in the Coldstream Guards had bar mitzvahs, this is what the reception spread would look like. The display reflected the extraordinary care the English have always taken with the appearance of special-occasion victuals; their interest in food tends to peak just before eating. There were slices of cold salmon that had been cut into fish shapes and given eyes made out of a material that could be eaten, although like the salmon itself, not tasted. There were several ice sculptures, confirming my impression that the number of English and sculptors on the international art scene is always limited by the fact that so many of them are kept busy fashioning sea bass out of ice. There was roast beef and Yorkshire pudding and creamed cauliflower and Brussels sprouts. I stopped in front of the Brussels sprouts and stared at them for a while. "The English have a lot to answer for," I said to Alice.

Trillin continues in his whimsical manner:

It's amazing to me that with all the issues that brought colonial people out in the streets during the long hegemony of the British Empire, nobody ever rebelled against Brussels sprouts. Or maybe somebody did. Maybe in those old newsreel clips that show hordes of chanting demonstrators rushing through the streets in the days before independence, what they are actually chanting is not "British go home!" or "Down with the Raj!" but "No more Brussels sprouts!"

Trillin then mixes his observations on food and foreign affairs:

The chicken was delicious, but I still think the best fried chicken I have ever eaten was at a sort of outdoor homecoming that Cherokee County, Georgia, held for Dean Rusk, a native son, shortly after he was named Secretary of State–fried chicken so good that I still nurture a hope, against long odds, that Cherokee County will someday produce another Secretary of State and throw another homecoming.

Trillin's humor also shows up in two one-man shows he wrote and performed: *Calvin Trillin's Uncle Sam* (1988) and *Words, No Music* (1990). While both shows are original, they are also vintage Trillin as he deadpans about his family, his roots, politicians, even fellow Yale graduate George Bush, and, as *New York Times* critic Mel Gussow said on 15 October 1990 of *Words, No Music*, "This is new material only if one is unfamiliar with Mr. Trillin's articles, magazine columns and books." He praised Trillin and said: "In his hands, words in print become performance." Edith Oliver of *The New Yorker* wrote about *Calvin Trillin's Uncle Sam*: "His tone is conversational and deadpan, and there is an underpinning of true satire to his lighthearted routines and jokes, with never a dud among them. . . . The laughter is continuous." An anonymous reviewer of the second

show said in *Legit:* "It's a show that's tough not to like." Another Trillin anthology collects the poetry he published in the *Nation*. Call it rhyme on deadline, in which Trillin analyzes the news of the week in rhyming couplets. The book is titled *Deadline Poet: Or, My Life as a Doggerelist* (1994). When Madonna published a book titled *Sex,* Trillin wrote: "Madonna has unusual friends. / Her book consists of odds–and ends." In a two-verse piece titled "Thoughts on the senator from Georgia who might have been president," he opined:

He doesn't draw the minicam.
He lacks, perhaps, a touch of ham.
He's charming as an angiogram,
Is Sam.

If he had run, he might have won,
Although his manner weighs a ton,
And we'd be having not much fun
With Nunn.

In 1993 Trillin published *Remembering Denny,* his book about a classmate at Yale who eventually committed suicide in 1991. The classmate, Roger Hansen, was known in college as "Denny." According to Trillin, Hansen was a varsity swimmer, a member of Phi Beta Kappa, a Rhodes scholar, and the subject of a *Life* magazine spread when he graduated from Yale in 1957. The book begins at Hansen's memorial service, which enables Trillin to report on and reminisce about Hansen through his friends and classmates. Although it is written in the first person, Trillin does not limit himself to personal memories but also does additional research as a way of helping Trillin (and the reader) understand Hansen.

Most reviews of *Remembering Denny* were not only positive but exuberant. Many reviewers pinpointed Trillin's virtues as a reporter and a writer–virtues that appear in most of his nonfiction. Among his merits are his understated style, descriptive writing, conversational tone, and sense of humor. Walter Goodman said in the 17–31 May 1993 issue of the *New Leader:* "With a sharp and tolerant eye, a lot of old-fashioned reporting and a controlled, clear, amiable style, he opens up characters and digs into actions, telling a good tale along the way." Writing in *Gentlemen's Quarterly,* Thomas Mallon said: "The small book that results is dignified and perceptive–the story of not just one elusive character but a generation for whom 'the rules got changed in the middle of the game.'" Stefan Kanfer, noting that the book is as much about Trillin as it is about Hansen, said in *Time* (19 April 1993): "As the author acknowledges, almost all of Denny's generation have found themselves bent with expectations that will never be realized. Unpacking, Trillin provides a class act in every sense of the word." In his review in the 7 June 1993 issue of the *Nation,* C. D. B. Bryan, who graduated from Yale in 1958, used *Remembering Denny* as a way of briefly examining his own thoughts about his alma mater and life. *Remembering Denny* is social history, the nonfiction equivalent of many of John O'Hara's novels of a generation before; in fact, seeing Yale through Trillin's eyes complements and reinforces O'Hara's reputation as a social historian.

Calling *Remembering Denny* "the best of Trillin's many books," James Fallows praised Trillin's reporting. "Trillin has always seemed reluctant to draw big-picture conclusions in his writing," Fallows wrote in June 1993 in the *Washington Monthly,* "but his reporting is so careful and his descriptions so vivid and funny that the reader has plenty to work with when drawing conclusions of his own."

Michael Lind, however, in the *New Republic* (5 July 1993), criticized Trillin for playing off "the facts of Hansen's life against a variety of clichés," for having compared Hansen's life to literary and mythical patterns Hansen didn't really fit, rather than criticizing such a stereotypical approach. In running through a list of subjects Trillin covers, Lind condemned him for "using Hansen's casket as a lectern." Lind said: "In the out-of-control confessional culture of America, Trillin has broken new ground. He has pioneered a new genre of therapeutic-liberal gossip: the vicarious confession."

Critics recognize Trillin for his understatement—for writing in a style that does not call attention to itself. "He writes with such artful grace and casual simplicity that his pieces flow along," syndicated columnist James J. Kilpatrick wrote in 1985. In summing up the comments of other critics, Scott Kraft wrote in the *American Journalism Review* (December 1985) that Trillin's writing was "simple, unornamented prose that features solid reporting rather than spectacular turns of phrase." A decade later Dwight Garner wrote in the *Boston Globe Magazine* (10 April 1994) that Trillin writes "with his typical mix of fresh, economical language and abundant good humor."

Reference:

Scott Kraft, "The Chronicles of Calvin Trillin," *American Journalism Review* (December 1985): 43–47.

Richard West

(10 June 1941 -   )

William I. Sutley
University of Southern Mississippi

BOOK: *Richard West's Texas* (Austin: Texas Monthly Press, 1981).

OTHER: "The Power of '21,'" *The Literary Journalists,* edited by Norman Sims (New York: Ballantine, 1984).

SELECTED PERIODICAL PUBLICATIONS–UNCOLLECTED: West and William Broyles Jr., "Behind the Lines," *Texas Monthly,* 7 (September 1979): 5;

"The Vertical Village," *New York,* 15 (23 March 1981): 23–36;

"Super Sundays with Charles Kuralt," *New York,* 15 (1 June 1981): 24–29;

"Fighting to Save a Neighborhood," *New York,* 15 (20 July 1981): 24–35;

"Survivors: The Saga of a Harlem Family," *New York,* 16 (22 March 1982): 18–24;

"The Lost Community of Sandbranch," *D,* 15 (September 1985): 96–101, 191–192.

Fifteen years of work as a writer for magazines in Texas and New York offered Richard West a literary canvas that he painted with style, patience, and skill. He took on several time-consuming assignments that focused on the hopes and fears of Texas's poor and middle class. But his engaging reportorial style worked equally well when he quietly gauged the cachet of power at an exclusive New York City restaurant. His astute observations of people and their interactions with the places where they live, work, and wander served West well as he evolved into a freelance travel writer. West is unique among literary journalists for his unrequited love of travel literature. His personal library of five or six hundred travel-related volumes leans more toward authors such as Paul Theroux and Colin Thubron, who write as much about internal journeys as external odysseys, than toward the failed poets of tourist-oriented guidebooks.

Charles Richard West III was born on 10 June 1941 in Dallas and has called that city, or its upscale suburb of Highland Park, home for most of his life. However, his travel-oriented writing assignments have taken him far afield to more than forty states and forty nations. His father, Charles Richard West Jr., was a newspaperman from the old school–a Dallas reporter, desk editor, and editorial writer for more than a half century. One of the younger West's childhood memories was the excitement of accompanying his father on rides to crime scenes. His father also influenced his love for literature, always encouraging him to read.

As a student at the University of Texas in the early 1960s, West discovered a less traditional style of reportage; it was a cultural awakening sparked by the words of Jimmy Breslin, Gay Talese, and Tom Wolfe. He told Norman Sims, in *The Literary Journalists* (1984), an anthology edited by Sims: "It was like hearing rock 'n' roll rather than Patti Paige. It opened your eyes to new vistas if you wanted to be a non-fiction writer." West further broadened his knowledge of people during his college years by spending two summers as a Dallas city jailer. His conversations with the toughest inmates about their experiences gave him a different look at life.

West was also interested in politics then. He earned a B.A. in government at the University of Texas at Austin in 1962, following up a year later there by adding a B.A. in journalism. After two years at a traditional newspaper job, West handled media relations and wrote speeches for Ben Barnes, a political dynamo who moved from Texas legislative leader to lieutenant governor during West's six-year employ. West was impressed by the strength of Barnes's influence in the House and Senate, and by what little opposition he encountered.

West left Barnes to make the risky move of joining a group of young writers starting *Texas Monthly.* The magazine would, from the beginning, be a publication that dared to move beyond traditional journalism's straitjacket. Alternately serious and lampoonish, *Texas Monthly* cherished good writing and nurtured the young but talented cadre of a half-dozen writers who propelled it to early success.

Cover and first page of West's 23 March 1981 magazine story on high-rise tenants in New York

One of West's primary contributions was launching the popular *Texas Monthly* "Reporter" column, a collection of observations on a wide variety of matters that innately appealed to Texan readers. Most of West's observations were based on extensive first-person reporting throughout virtually every corner of the Lone Star State.

West spent nearly a decade at *Texas Monthly,* devoting most of his final years there to a series of long articles that explored the diversity of Texas. Those seven pieces, published from November 1977 to December 1980, later were compiled as his sole book, *Richard West's Texas* (1981). The articles earned West the National Magazine Award for Reporting Excellence in 1979. A year later he was awarded the Texas Institute of Letters's Stanley Walker Journalism Award for Reporting.

William Broyles Jr., editor of *Texas Monthly,* backed the idea of West's in-depth odyssey through the state. He saw it as a way to gauge whether rural Americans from deep within the heartland of the nation were suffering the crisis of confidence described by then-president Jimmy Carter. West found people with more on their minds than the national problems: "Gas lines are nothing compared to a grasshopper invasion, a drought, a hurricane," West

wrote in a September 1979 *Texas Monthly* overview of his four-thousand-mile journey. "These Texans know who they are and where they fit into the world. They each have a strong sense of place, and of being a Texan."

West's writing is strongest when he is conveying that sense of place. For him, the phrase means more than offering a series of descriptive word images. He is also blending in historical background, dialogue, narrative, and more. At the heart of it all is West's exhaustive reporting ethic. He immerses himself in a particular location, talking to people and finding out as much as he possibly can. In *Richard West's Texas* the author focuses on seven locales to discover what made each place unique. "My plan was to wrap myself around Texas by spending two months or more in each of seven dissimilar locales—three urban, three rural, one coastal—to examine these differing styles of life, to scavenge in the creases of Texas' hands and take a look at the work, play, the past and present, and by so doing, perhaps to peep into the future," he wrote in the introduction to the book.

Each chapter, or locale, offers a different narrative, often with underlying themes. "The Coast" describes the changes that commercial and tourism development have wrought on Port Aransas, Texas, and how those changes had affected local fishermen and others. In introducing his primary character he writes:

Jimmy Gates, in a favorite phrase of Port Aransans, is a "real piece of work." A native of the island, he is, at 26, one of the few young full-time charter boat skippers remaining in a town founded by boat captains and fishing guides. His blue eyes are clear, still not discolored by the sun's glare, his brown back is covered with constellations of freckles, and his face is the color, but not yet the texture, of rawhide. Gates remembers the quaint fishing village of Port A that no longer exists, where sailors just off the bauxite ships from Trinidad played in steel bands on the flats near Fisherman's Wharf, where islanders held fish fries and street dances on Alister Street, and where fishing on the edge of the breakers yielded a hundred pounds of big speckled trout. Nowadays, Gates can barely find enough fish for his customers to catch.

The account offers an example of West's talent for weaving narrative and background elements—history, physical description, foreshadowing, geography, ethnography, and dialogue—into a storytelling quilt.

This melange is repeated as West moves to San Antonio's El West Side, the nation's second-largest barrio; the old-fashioned Texas of Presidio County and Mexico-bordering Marfa; the Piney Woods of San Augustine County; the wheat fields of Perryton, reaching north to Oklahoma and Kansas; the state's toughest black ghetto, Houston's Fifth Ward; and, finally, to the "upper-middle-class aerie" of West's hometown, Highland Park. Throughout each chapter West displays his gift for framing the hopes and fears of residents who represent the uniqueness of each region. In each he offers a strong dash of history to frame the complications encountered by his characters. Rarely—never, in some chapters—does West lapse into first-person voice. Throughout most of his Texas tales he imposes a more detached, journalistic voice.

Much of West's inspiration for diving into magazine journalism had come from reading, during the early 1960s, the work of many outstanding writers contributing to *New York,* a Sunday supplement of the *New York Herald Tribune.* The supplement's editor, Clay Felker, established the magazine as an independent entity in 1968 after the *Tribune* folded. Given the opportunity, West jumped at a chance to write for the weekly *New York,* which would be known as the prototype for many city magazines established in the late 1960s. Like Texas Monthly, which takes pride in reflecting all facets of the Lone Star state, *New York* attempts to take an in-depth look at the nation's largest city.

About the time West's book was published he succumbed to the literary allure of New York City. ("I was Texas-ed out," he recalls.) There he wrote the story of a Big Apple landmark, "21," arguably the most powerful and famous restaurant in the country. "The Power of '21'" appeared first in *New York* (5 October 1981) and was reprinted in *The Literary Journalists.* The piece was quintessential West; again, it employed his immersion-reporting stamina and his gift for creating a sense of place, but it also featured a sophisticated smartness that reflected the story subject. For West "21" was also an introduction to the rules of big-city journalism—of negotiating access and setting up ground rules for what he would report and write. Common interests helped him hit it off with restaurant management when he first proposed the story idea to them. The arrangement was simple: West would be given access to any part of the restaurant, from opening until closing. In return he would respect the privacy of restaurant patrons, mostly ignoring private conversations unrelated to the restaurant. For a month he alternated between day and night shifts. His day schedule brought him to the restaurant at 6 A.M., when the food began arriving in the basement. Night shifts ran from 4 P.M. to 1 A.M. Mostly he would listen and observe. Occasionally he would interview someone and steal a few moments to organize his thoughts and write notes to himself.

Sims quoted West's recollection of those experiences in describing the immersion reporting that is a common characteristic of quality literary journalism. "You just become part of the woodwork until they open up and do things in front of you," West told Sims. "You may get the surface details right, but you won't get the kind of emotions you're after—how people operate—until you disappear. Sometimes you never get that and your story falls flat on that point. It took a while, but they came to trust me and like me." He added that genuine interest and lack of arrogance are essential for a writer to achieve this trust.

"21" also showcased West's talent for providing the historical background of a subject, plus his penchant for using statistical detail as part of that background. He usually includes numbers to help "quantify" a subject, help define its boundaries. Describing the business side of the restaurant, he writes:

. . . "21" has continued to prosper. Restaurant receipts in 1967, $4.5 million; in 1980, $10 million. The cigar-and-gift distributorship, "21" Selected Items, which

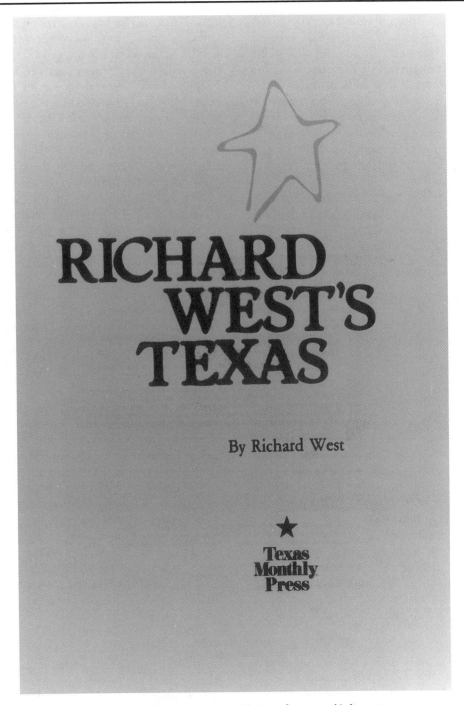

Title page for West's only book, a collection of essays on his home state

earned $750,000 in 1967, cleared $1 million last year . . . The typical top-ranked New York restaurant does $16,000 worth of business per seat annually, according to Laventhol & Horwath, an accounting firm that conducts restaurant-industry studies. A seat at "21" averages $25,000.

Such attention to detail might be considered more a mechanism of traditional, numbers-obsessed jour-

nalists, but West has also succeeded in weaving it into more-literary narratives.

One of West's first pieces for *New York,* "The Vertical Village," also capitalized on his talent for capturing a sense of place; in fact, the focal point of the article *is* a place, the thirty-six-story apartment building at 300 East Thirty-fourth Street. This building was, in fact, West's home at the time, but the writer does not mention that detail anywhere in this unique tale of a dozen or so other people who also called it home. Again, West describes in detail the story of the origin of the building—going so far as to plumb the thoughts of its architect when he was a college student. But the bulk of the piece offers a revealing look at the lives of people bound together only by the place where they live. West moves from scene to scene in such a fashion that makes the reader imagine there is a cinematographer filming through the walls and moving up and down from floor to floor.

Another early *New York* piece, "Super Sundays with Charles Kuralt," showcased West's talent for profiles—a literary endeavor that he continues to focus on in the 1990s. The subject of this profile, Kuralt, was also known for his skill at creating a sense of place. But, unlike West, the CBS correspondent-turned-anchorman also marshaled a film crew to buttress his talent for creating stunning word pictures. Much of West's profile deals with Kuralt's days as the "On the Road" correspondent, and he offers an example of Kuralt's writing talent from his first report, on fall foliage in Vermont: "As pictures of fall landscapes appeared, Kuralt's kindly voice rumpled into living rooms: 'It is death that causes this blinding show of color, but it is a fierce and flaming death. To drive along a Vermont country road in this season is to be dazzled by the shower of lemon and scarlet and gold that washes across your windshield.'" Throughout, the tone of this profile communicates that West admires Kuralt's writing skills as well as his broadcast talents.

West describes how Kuralt moved his skills to a more fixed setting for the successful *Sunday Morning* experiment. In sections on content, setting, mood, and personality West articulates precisely what factors made the show so appealing. And as always, West employs his gift for analytical detail:

> Kuralt's deep baritone, with a hint of his native North Carolina, adds to this a woodstove warmth, creating a civilized voice that also reaches the common man and gives a story not just plausibility but honesty, thoughtfulness, character. He has toned down the constantly smiling by-gum-by-cracky good guy of "On the Road," and you are seldom in danger anymore of ending up knee-deep in corn-pone homilies after he has left the screen. He has become more serious, more Sunday than Saturday afternoon.

This description, part of the personality section, captures the feel of the *Sunday Morning* program and Kuralt's role in it. It becomes clear, in this piece at least, that West enjoys doing this type of profile—particularly if the subject is something of a kindred spirit.

Hope surfaces as a recurring theme in West's works, particularly those of his *New York* days. Edward Kosner, West's former editor, calls it the "candle in the gloom" theme. In "Fighting to Save a Neighborhood" West describes an ambitious urban renewal project as viewed by the residents most affected, those calling Manhattan Valley home. Through a series of personal-experience vignettes West tells the tale of the decay of the neighborhood, largely as a result of abusive, drug-addled vagrants and negligent landlords. For the most part the storytellers are the residents of the area. West also weaves in the less-scintillating details of how federal urban renewal programs are *supposed* to work. The piece ends on an uncertain note, but overall there is hope for a better future for the neighborhood despite the fact that rehabilitation efforts are fragile: "From this symbolic resurrection, the Valley may become a reawakened world, perhaps a rebuilt province. Change will occur; it will take time. But no one expects it to be a hopeless cause."

Hope also permeates a 1982 piece, "Survivors: The Saga of a Harlem Family." West tells how most of eight children in a family have risen above the despair of the neighborhood where they grew up watching many of their friends succumb to the omnipresent lure of drugs and easy money. West paints the matriarch, Eartha Holman, as the key force in the success of the family, although he also tells of many contributions by caring educators. In one section West displays his tendency to contrast the hope that is embodied in a piece as a whole with the real and imagined fears of the principal characters. He writes: "Eartha's great fear was the junkies. She told her children she'd take the breath out of their bodies if she learned they were shooting up, that she wouldn't let them live to become the vilest, germiest beasts on earth. There would be wall-to-wall blood if she found out. They could become janitors or bank presidents but not dope fiends."

To say that hope is a favorite theme of West's early work is not to overlook the reality that can diminish hope. In a 1985 piece for the Dallas magazine *D,* West profiles "The Lost Community of Sandbranch." This narrative describes a poverty-stricken area near downtown Dallas and its struggle to obtain basic city services, including drinkable water. After describing the problems of the area and the attempts to resolve them, West basically concludes that "nothing had changed." In a sense West appears to be challenging someone, somewhere to come to the rescue of this "lost community."

West left *New York* in 1983 to work for Broyles, his former *Texas Monthly* boss, when Broyles became editor of *Newsweek.* That association was cut short when West became convinced that he should move back to Texas in 1985, partly to help care for his father, whose health was deteriorating. He produced a wide variety of pieces as a writer dividing his time between magazines in Dallas and Houston before deciding to strike out on his own as a freelancer. By the mid 1990s he was focusing most of his efforts on travel pieces.

Twentieth-century journalism standards have often clashed with the freewheeling nature of travel writing. The neutrality ethic of journalism makes some writers reticent about offering their opinions. Many journalists sincerely believe that the "truth" about a place is elusive and must be approached with stifling caution. Travel writing also defies the traditional "information model" of the modern news story, in which the audience is neutral and invisible. Travel narratives, in contrast, often seek to transport the reader, to offer a sense of escape. Interestingly, both literary and travel journalists often share the same goal: a deeper engagement with the reader. Tom Wolfe may have correctly surmised in his book *The New Journalism* (1973) that "the sort of writing that one now finds in the New Journalism probably begins with the travel literature of the late eighteenth and the early nineteenth centuries."

Although travel writing enjoyed a resurgence in the 1980s, criticism of the literature as a genre has been sporadic. At least part of the reason, suggests Michael Kowalewski in *Temperamental Journeys: Essays on the Modern Literature of Travel* (1992), is the "merchandising of adventure" trend. Skepticism of travel writing arises every time it is bastardized in some form as advertising copy that promotes a product (clothes, for example) with a string of verbose collages describing some exotic destination. In a 1996 interview West hinted at frustration that modern-day American writers, particularly travel writers, are not held in the same regard as their counterparts in countries such as Great Britain and Ireland.

Asked about other writers' influences in an unpublished interview with William I. Sutley on 7 March 1996, West immediately called to mind John McPhee, the author, academician, and literary journalist who also is known for his cerebral travel pieces. West had a chance to interview McPhee during the 1980s, and he remembers how the wall of the author's Princeton University office was covered with index cards. "He spent a lot of time working on structure," West said. "People don't realize sometimes that, first, you've got to research, then you *think,* then you outline, and *then* you write the thing. I've found that if I could map the thing out in an outline, like an architect working up a drawing, it's a lot easier to work with."

West still outlines everything he writes, although he is frequently forced to limit the reporting of his travel pieces based on time and money restraints dictated by an editor. More often than not he spends two weeks in a locale rather than the month he spent soaking up the sense of place evoked by New York's "21." Despite his move toward travel writing, West still enjoys a reputation as a meticulous reporter. He approaches assignments—whether his own idea or from an editor—with a discerning eye for scene-setting, an ear for story-propelling dialogue, and a writer's hand that can transport readers to worlds they might never have visited.

References:

Michael Kowalewski, ed., *Temperamental Journeys: Essays on the Modern Literature of Travel* (Athens: University of Georgia Press, 1992);

Tom Wolfe and E. W. Johnson, eds., *The New Journalism* (New York: Harper & Row, 1973).

Tom Wolfe
(2 March 1931 –   )

Richard A. Kallan
California State Polytechnic University, Pomona

BOOKS: *The Kandy-Kolored Tangerine-Flake Streamline Baby* (New York: Farrar, Straus & Giroux, 1965);

The Electric Kool-Aid Acid Test (New York: Farrar, Straus & Giroux, 1968);

The Pump House Gang (New York: Farrar, Straus & Giroux, 1968);

Radical Chic and Mau-Mauing the Flak Catchers (New York: Farrar, Straus & Giroux, 1970);

The New Journalism, with an anthology edited by Wolfe and E. W. Johnson (New York: Harper & Row, 1973);

The Painted Word (New York: Farrar, Straus & Giroux, 1975);

Mauve Gloves and Madmen, Clutter and Vine (New York: Farrar, Straus & Giroux, 1976);

The Right Stuff (New York: Farrar, Straus & Giroux, 1979);

In Our Time (New York: Farrar, Straus & Giroux, 1980);

From Bauhaus to Our House (New York: Farrar, Straus & Giroux, 1981);

The Purple Decades: A Reader (New York: Farrar, Straus & Giroux, 1982);

The Bonfire of the Vanities (Franklin Center, Pa.: Franklin Library, 1987; New York: Farrar, Straus & Giroux, 1987).

SELECTED PERIODICAL PUBLICATIONS– UNCOLLECTED:
"Tiny Mummies! The True Story of the Ruler of 43rd Street's Land of the Walking Dead!," *New York* (11 April 1965): 7–9, 24–27;

"Lost in the Whichy Thicket: The New Yorker–II," *New York* (18 April 1965): 16–24, 44;

"The New Journalism," *Bulletin of the American Society of Newspaper Editors* (September 1970): 1, 18–23;

"The New Journalism: A la Recherche des Whichy Thickets," *New York* (21 February 1972): 39–48;

Tom Wolfe (© 1987, Thomas Victor)

"Stalking the Billion-Footed Beast: A Literary Manifesto for the New Social Novel," *Harper's* (November 1989): 45–56.

The foremost theorist and best-known practitioner of New Journalism, Tom Wolfe has become almost synonymous with the journalistic movement he helped foster in the mid 1960s. Critics praise or reject nearly every component of Wolfe's work including his choice of subject matter; his content and perspective; his writing style; and, of course, his journalistic method. After several books and numerous articles, Wolfe's writings continue to provoke and sustain debate.

Thomas Kinnerly Wolfe Jr. was born 2 March 1931 in Richmond, Virginia, to Helen Hughes and Thomas Kinnerly Wolfe Sr., an agronomist, college professor, and editor of the *Southern Planter*. Southern raised in a traditional and stable family structure, the younger Thomas would later say: "I was lucky, I guess, in my family in that they had a very firm idea of roles: Father, Mother, Child. Nothing was ever allowed to bog down into those morass-like personal hang-ups. And there was no rebellion. The main thing about childhood was to get out of it."

Wolfe attended public school until the seventh grade when he entered Saint Christopher's (Presbyterian) School, where he achieved academic honors, coedited the campus newspaper, and chaired the student council. In 1947 he entered Washington and Lee University where he divided his extracurricular time between pitching for the baseball team and writing for the school newspaper. An English major, he graduated cum laude in 1951. That same year after a brief, unsuccessful attempt to become a professional baseball player, Wolfe enrolled at Yale University, where he earned a doctorate in American studies in 1957.

Upon leaving Yale in 1956 Wolfe was offered a college teaching position that he declined because he was tired of academic life and longed instead to become a writer. After a two-month, soul-searching stint as a bohemian/furniture mover, he began his newspaper career as a reporter for the *Springfield* (Massachusetts) *Union*. Wolfe had written inquiry letters to 120 newspapers, but his only positive response came from the *Union*, which hired him at fifty-five dollars per week.

After three years at the *Union*, in 1959 Wolfe headed to the *Washington Post*, where he reported local and foreign events and wrote humor articles. Believing his future at the *Post* to be limited, he left in 1962 to become a feature writer for the *New York Herald Tribune*. Shortly after his hiring, however, employees of the newspaper went on strike. With time on his hands, Wolfe accepted a freelance assignment from *Esquire* magazine to go to California and write about custom cars.

But after gathering his facts and returning to New York, Wolfe had trouble composing the story. Byron Dobell, managing editor of *Esquire*, told Wolfe just to submit his notes, and another writer would finish the story. The ensuing experience defined Wolfe's career and marked the beginning of his unique writing style. He later described what happened in the book *The Kandy-Kolored Tangerine-Flake Streamline Baby* (1965):

So about 8 o'clock that night I started typing the notes out in the form of a memorandum that began, "Dear Byron." I started typing away, starting right with the first time I saw any custom cars in California. I just started recording it all, and inside of a couple of hours, typing along like a madman, I could tell that something was beginning to happen. By midnight this memorandum to Byron was twenty pages long and I was still typing like a maniac. . . . I wrapped up the memorandum about 6:15 a.m., and by this time it was 49 pages long. I took it over to *Esquire* as soon as they opened up, about 9:30 a.m. About 4 p.m. I got a call from Byron Dobell. He told me they were striking out the "Dear Byron" at the top of the memorandum and running the rest of it in the magazine.

The now-famous "Kandy" memorandum represented one of the first exercises of what Wolfe would soon call the New Journalism. Quite by accident, Wolfe realized that what had otherwise been a bland and structurally rigid form—magazine journalism—could be transformed into an exciting and creative *literary* journalism that, while still factual, *sounded* like a novel. By applying the stylistic techniques usually associated with fiction writing to factual data collected from exhaustive research, Wolfe could produce an audience-involving, realistic *non*fiction.

When the *Herald Tribune* strike ended and Wolfe resumed working, his duties included writing a weekly feature story for the Sunday supplement of the *Tribune, New York* magazine (which later became an independent publication). In 1965 several articles Wolfe wrote for *New York* and other magazines were published in the anthology *The Kandy-Kolored Tangerine-Flake Streamline Baby;* also included were eighteen Wolfe drawings. (He illustrated many of his subsequent books as well, and his art was featured in New York galleries.) Reactions to the book varied. *Newsweek* called Wolfe "one of the most stylized, imaginative, discussed, and sought-after magazine writers in the country." Emile Capouya in the *Saturday Review* (31 July 1965), on the other hand, labeled Wolfe a talented, clever, "startlingly well-informed" writer who wasted his time on undeserving subjects. And Dwight Macdonald in the *New York Review of Books* (26 August 1965) predicted that Wolfe and his work would prove ephemeral ("Parajournalism, or Tom Wolfe and His Magic Writing Machine").

The first of several Wolfe books to employ the techniques of New Journalism, *The Kandy-Kolored Tangerine-Flake Streamline Baby* focuses on how people attempt to create their *own* notion of status by constructing private "statuspheres." Wolfe believes that whereas previously the orthodox symbols of prestige were the schools one attended, the land one

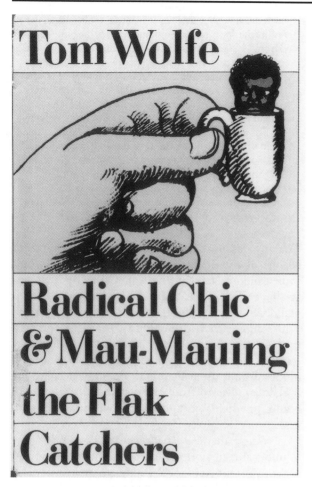

Dust jacket for Wolfe's most controversial piece of New Journalism, in which he asserts that guilt-ridden whites were being exploited and intimidated by some blacks

Of the twenty-two articles in *The Kandy-Kolored Tangerine-Flake Streamline Baby,* the *Esquire* article of the same title perhaps best illustrates Wolfe's thesis. Few people were more removed from the mainstream of conventional society than custom-car builders George Barris and Ed Roth. After World War II they sought to erect "monuments" reflecting their personalities. They set up shops in California catering to the whims of a teenage clientele. At first hardly anyone other than a few custom-car enthusiasts noticed them. Yet Barris's and Roth's followings soon grew, eventually including even Hollywood celebrities. All the while, major automobile manufacturers paid little respect to the customizers, or so it seemed; later, however, many of their revolutionary designs appeared on Detroit cars. Barris and Roth, states Wolfe, advanced the Dionysian style—which many "'serious' designers, Anglo-European-steeped designers, are just coming around to." Custom-car shows ultimately became acceptable and popular, and their creators viewed as credible artists. Once a "tainted underground," the customized-car world was assimilated into the larger culture.

Whatever their demographic background, Wolfe's subjects successfully analyze and affect their environment. *The Kandy-Kolored Tangerine-Flake Streamline Baby* thus pays homage to figures as diverse as Lawrence Mendelsohn because he shrewdly recognized a quality in the American character and responded with car demolition derbies, record producer Phil Spector because he knew how to promote rock music, and young Cassius Clay because he could draw a crowd even when not in a fight ring.

Also in 1965 Wolfe caught the attention of prominent literati in America with his blistering attack on *The New Yorker* on the occasion of the magazine's fortieth birthday. Wolfe first considered using parody to develop his thesis that the magazine had become dull, but he quickly realized that any good parody would be dull as well. So he chose a style seemingly more appropriate: *anti*-parody. "Rather than mimicking *The New Yorker* I was going to give them a voice they couldn't stand. In the anti-parody, as I thought of it, the wilder and crazier the hyperbole, the better," as Wolfe explained later in "The New Journalism: A la Recherche des Whichy Thickets."

The resulting two-part article in *New York*—"Tiny Mummies! The True Story of the Ruler of 43rd Street's Land of the Walking Dead!" and "Lost in the Whichy Thicket: The New Yorker-II" (11 and 18 April 1965)—was not an exercise in New Journalism, insists Wolfe, but simply a spoof that served as

owned, or the private clubs to which one belonged, status today is defined more personally. Conventional status systems have given way to a new orientation wherein a person can "win" status by simply setting his own standards.

While winning motivates construction of a statusphere, money provides the means. Nowadays, almost anyone can afford custom-molded status. After World War II, Wolfe writes in the introduction to the book, there were "massive infusions of money into every level of society. Suddenly classes of people whose styles of life had been practically invisible had the money to build monuments to their own styles." Moreover, even the most out-of-the-way statusphere might influence the attitudes and tastes of the larger, more established culture. Often today "high styles come from low places, from people who have no power, who slink away from it, in fact, who are marginal, who carve out worlds for themselves in the nether depths, in tainted 'undergrounds.'"

a break from the more serious writing he was doing at the time. Still, this never-anthologized article helps explain some of the enduring distrust of Wolfe and the New Journalism. *New Yorker* loyalists condemned what they perceived as Wolfe's ad hominem style and vigorously challenged the accuracy of his reporting. The best (and longest) refutations came from Macdonald ("Parajournalism II: Wolfe and The New Yorker"), and Adler and Gerald Jonas, who outlined numerous factual errors Wolfe committed. In replying to their criticisms years later, Wolfe claimed that most of his mistakes were intentional, all part of his anti-parody. Deliberate exaggerations aside, Wolfe still thought he had targeted his prey; moreover, he said, writers opposed to New Journalism had expediently chosen to criticize a nonexample of the form.

Wolfe's second collection of previously published articles, *The Pump House Gang* (1968), offers a sharper elaboration of his worldview; almost all its fifteen articles relate to pursuit of status. Among others, the reader meets The Pump House Gang, teenagers who spend all their time on the beaches of La Jolla, California. They live what Wolfe calls "The Life"–surfing, swimming, and sunning. And they segregate themselves from everyone except aficionados of the life.

Still others construct elaborate, sophisticated statuspheres. The classic case is Hugh Hefner, who like many has become a status dropout–"dropping out of conventional status competition in order to start their own league–in the privacy of the home, as it were." By renovating an old mansion into an ode to electronic gadgetry, Hefner need never leave home. "The new status dropouts," Wolfe postulates, "can pull it off precisely because twentieth-century technologies have made it possible for them to lead a full life–a *damned full life* here!–without *going out* amongst the community." Meanwhile, back in Columbus, Ohio, Tom Reiser rides 130 miles an hour on a motorcycle with a V-8 engine. He is not alone. Less daring but equally zealous, many middle-of-the-road, law-abiding citizens have made motorcycling their statusphere. In fact, expounds Wolfe: "The motorcycle life has been perfect as a statusphere. It is dangerous and therefore daring. . . . It can liberate you physically from the *communitas*."

Statuspheres are not restricted to Americans. Many enterprising English businessmen acquire notice by adopting the trappings and nuances of the "American" lifestyle. "The American," declares Wolfe,

has always gone English in order to endow himself with the mystique of the English upper classes. The English-

man today goes American, becomes a Mid-Atlantic Man, to achieve the opposite. He wants to get out from under the domination of the English upper classes by . . . going classless. And he goes classless by taking on the style of life, or part of the style of life, of a foreigner who cannot be fitted into the English class system, the modern, successful, powerful American.

For Wolfe the study of statuspheres provides a close-up of primarily the American and to a lesser degree the British character. Because statuspheres provide identity, security, and recognition, the important question for Wolfe becomes: How is status sought and achieved? That again is the issue addressed in *The Electric Kool-Aid Acid Test* (1968), his first full-length book. Wolfe concentrates on the travels of Ken Kesey and his following, the Merry Pranksters, innovative members of a then-proliferating but still underground drug statusphere. Completed in four months, the one-hundred-thousand-word tome scrutinizes the swirling force driving Kesey and his following.

A frequent characteristic of Wolfe's style is repetition of a single metaphor to synthesize his thesis. Throughout *The Electric Kool-Aid Acid Test,* for example, Wolfe notes Kesey's battle cry, "You're either on the bus or off the bus." Because Kesey and the Merry Pranksters are indeed traveling by their own bus across country, the statement has literal meaning. Yet the bus, as the reader soon realizes, symbolizes the entire trip, the quest for personal growth and self-discovery. To say one is either on the bus or off the bus is to say he is either committed to the search for identity or he is not. There is no middle ground, no partial enthusiasm–one is completely dedicated or he is off the "bus."

Wolfe's most controversial piece of New Journalism, *Radical Chic and Mau-Mauing the Flak Catchers* (1970) comprises two lengthy articles: "Radical Chic" explores how upper-class whites obtain status when they attend a society fund-raising gathering for imprisoned members of the Black Panther Party hosted by Leonard and Felicia Bernstein; "Mau-Mauing the Flak Catchers" describes the status enjoyed by blacks in San Francisco when they intimidate (mau-mau) lower-echelon bureaucrats (flak catchers) of the Office of Economic Opportunity. Of the two articles, *Radical Chic* (a term Wolfe popularized) received more attention. Wolfe, who attended the Bernstein gathering, describes how various, mostly white celebrities and socialites attempt to achieve status by socially "slumming" with black militants. In a witty, stinging analysis Wolfe captures the silliness of what he tags the radically chic rage of the time: guilt-ridden whites willingly being insulted and intimidated by their more rhetorical black beneficiaries. Wolfe unexpectedly found himself and his work politicized: conservatives applauded the truth and courage of his reporting; liberals scoffed at his inaccuracy and insensitivity.

Wolfe's first four books had produced a swell of critical commentary. Reviewers frequently judged his work brilliant, creative, insightful, and funny. Kurt Vonnegut went so far as to announce that Wolfe "knows everything." Karl Shapiro wrote of Wolfe, "He really understands his subjects, is really compassionate (when possible), really involved with what he says and clearly responsible to his judgments." Others, however, had their doubts. "Wolfe is curious about his subjects," says Neil Compton, "but has no real concern for them." Some attacked Wolfe's failure to disclose his feelings of right and wrong. Christopher Ricks contended that Wolfe was "adept at suspending his moral sense," while Jack Newfield concluded Wolfe "has the social conscience of an ant." Ricks and Newfield objected to Wolfe's merely explicating his material rather than also evaluating it and advancing a position. Many others criticized Wolfe's reportorial method and his school of journalism.

In the early 1970s Wolfe began formally answering his critics with a series of magazine essays explaining and defending his journalistic method. The gist of these writings became the introductory chapters of *The New Journalism* (1973) with an anthology edited by Wolfe and E. W. Johnson.

According to Wolfe, New Journalists are motivated by their desire to provide a fuller, more realistic prose than traditional journalism—a style that both excites and informs readers. Coupling the stylistic techniques of the novelist with the investigative method Wolfe calls "saturation reporting," the journalist can offer audiences a capacious reading experience that facilitates judgment. Theoretically, a writer can practice New Journalism "neutrally" on any topic: the form prescribes neither a subject matter nor a posture of advocacy. New Journalists, Wolfe explains, do "analyze and evaluate their material, although seldom in a moralistic fashion." Wolfe thus welcomed the charge that he was a nonpositional literary chameleon who assumed the voice of any character he described.

Wolfe isolates four literary devices integral to New Journalism: *scene-by-scene construction*—recreating rather than historically narrating important scenes; *extensive character dialogue*—letting the characters do most of the talking; *third person point of view*—telling the story through multiple viewpoints, not just the subject's or the author's; and *status life recordings*—describing those symbolic behaviors and possessions that reveal one's status or desire for status.

Additionally, the New Journalism allows for author-specific stylistic inventiveness. Wolfe, for instance, often plays with words, punctuation, and even topography to illustrate a point. Such creativity is especially apparent in Wolfe's first four books, written at a time when he was most concerned with attracting readers. Wolfe's description in *The Electric Kool-Aid Acid Test* of Ken Kesey operating the strobe lights at an LSD party is typical. By setting off key words from the rest of the text, Wolfe re-creates Kesey's stream of consciousness:

CONTROLS

Kesey looks out upon the stroboscopic whirlpool—the dancers! flung and flinging in *ecstasis!* gyrating! levitating! men in slices! in ping-pong balls! in the creamy bare essence! and it reaches a

SYNCH

he never saw before. Heads from all over the acid world out here and all whirling into the pudding. Now let a man see what

CONTROL

is. Kesey mans the strobe and twist of mercury lever

UP

and they all speed up.

Wolfe and the New Journalists were of course not the first to use literary techniques. Nevertheless, qualifies Wolfe, they differ from their predecessors by doing more reporting—and doing it differently. Saturation reporting, a field-study method of data gathering, replaces the direct interview. Rather than questioning the subject after the fact, the New Journalist "shadows" the subject, mindful of how every word, interaction, and nuance might evidence the moment and elucidate the story. "You are after not just facts," said Wolfe. "The basic units of reporting are no longer who-what-when-where-how and why but whole scenes and stretches of dialogue" ("The New Journalism"). In this respect, Wolfe answers his critics, the New Journalism *is* "new."

In subsequent works Wolfe corralled his tone and stylistic inventiveness while he continued to embrace many of the literary devices earlier championed. Moreover, he broadened his literary range. He wrote two relatively conventional critical essays—one on modern art, *The Painted Word* (1975), the other on modern architecture *From Bauhaus to*

Our House (1981). While saturation reporting informs neither work, each still sports a refined version of Wolfe's familiar style: breezy, energized, hyperbolic.

The arguments made in both books evoked sharp rebuttal, especially from the communities of art and architecture. *The Painted Word,* which originally appeared in *Harper's,* leveled criticism at the art world because a small group of prominent artists, critics, and patrons control it and determine the parameters and direction of "acceptable" art based on what they arbitrarily perceive as fashionable. As a result Wolfe sees "a whole generation of artists" who, wanting to further their careers, devote themselves "to getting the Word (and to internalizing it) and to the extraordinary task of divesting themselves of whatever there was in their imagination and technical ability that did not fit the Word." While an occasional reviewer applauded Wolfe's courage and wit in writing *The Painted Word,* most complained it was simplistic, parochial, and uninformed.

Critics reacted similarly to *From Bauhaus to Our House,* which also originally appeared in *Harper's.* As he did in *The Painted Word,* Wolfe argues that Americans have been pressured into accepting a mass aesthetic they really do not like—in this case, the austere "glass box" architecture whose sameness has become the standard for corporate and residential buildings. Enchanted by the status they bestowed on European sensibilities, American architects promulgated a sterile, culturally inappropriate style ill adapted to our national character. Again critics dismissed Wolfe as ignorant, overstated, and unoriginal. Yet, as Albert Bergesen reminds us:

> Wolfe always raises interesting questions. We may not like his answers, or even his questions, but there are things that need to be explained. Why is modern art getting more abstract, or why did the glass-box paradigm take hold in architecture, or how could a socially conscious architectural community concerned with humanitarian values generate such a cold, austere vision of modern housing? You can always tell that his questions have struck some kind of nerve by the inevitable intellectual stonewalling by his reviewers. For such a purportedly lightweight critic, who always misunderstands art, architecture, or Manhattan parties, there is certainly a lot of huffing and puffing in those reviews.

The Painted Word and *From Bauhaus to Our House* aside, Wolfe did not forsake New Journalism. He produced another collection of twelve pieces (mostly work previously published from 1967 to 1976)—*Mauve Gloves and Madmen, Clutter and Vine* (1976)—which describes how status is achieved

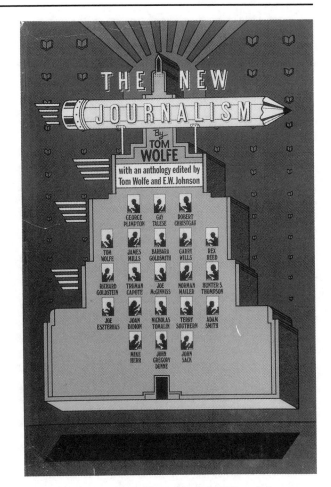

Dust jacket for Wolfe's influential 1973 anthology

through expressions of valor, attitude, and fashion. *Mauve Gloves and Madmen, Clutter and Vine* also reflects Wolfe's breadth: it includes his fictional story "The Commercial" and an illustrated-only-story, "The Man Who Always Peaked Too Soon." The book also includes the article that described the 1970s by its now famous epithet, "The Me Decade," and a piece about America's heroic aerial combat pilots during the Vietnam war, "The Truest Sport: Jousting with Sam and Charlie," presager of *The Right Stuff* (1979).

Wolfe's most critically acclaimed work, *The Right Stuff* became his best-selling nonfiction book and later was made into a successful film of the same title. Originally begun in 1973 as a four-part series for *Rolling Stone* and then substantially enlarged, *The Right Stuff* depicts the Mercury Program and the original seven astronauts. *Right stuff,* another term Wolfe helped popularize, characterized the competence and confidence that enabled fighter pilots/astronauts calmly to risk their lives almost daily.

The Right Stuff offers rich insights into the beginnings of America's space program, which Wolfe

Dust jacket for Wolfe's critically acclaimed work, an account of the Mercury Program and its astronauts

stunningly conveys through such techniques of New Journalism as third-person point of view and status life recordings. Through them he treats the reader to a full diagnostic of the essence of the Mercury Program, its key participants, and a nation mesmerized by it all. In particular Wolfe intricately explores the goals, values, and perceptions of the astronauts from a multitude of angles. What evolves is a clash between public personae and private lives as revealing as it is enlightening.

The Right Stuff, though, is not a comprehensive model of New Journalism. Wolfe does not rely heavily on the other devices of New Journalism—scene-by-scene construction and extensive character dialogue. And while the book is thoroughly researched, Wolfe wrote *after* the events it describes; hence, saturation reporting gives way to archival investigation. Still, Wolfe emerges as a writer stylistically in control of his subject because he is willing to shape and adapt his form (New Journalism) in a way that complements his analysis.

In the decade that followed Wolfe further demonstrated his versatility. His first coffee-table book, *In Our Time* (1980), contained some previously published text but mostly featured drawings about individuals pursuing fashion/status that Wolfe had done over his career, starting at the *Springfield*

Union. Finally, after years of proclaiming that the novel was dead and New Journalism was the new reigning literary form, Wolfe authored in serialized form for *Rolling Stone* his first full-length fictional work. The revised version, *The Bonfire of the Vanities* (1987), became an enormously popular, best-selling novel about social class; the motion picture that followed, however, resulted in a disappointing box office.

Interestingly, Wolfe relies on reportorial fieldwork to inform his story, which chronicles the plunge from grace of wealthy Sherman McCoy, bond trader extraordinaire. McCoy's car, driven by his mistress, is involved in a hit-and-run accident with a teenage African American who later dies. Wolfe's extensive understanding of New York, achieved by his own legwork, allows him to describe in meticulous detail the people, places, and politics of the city, all of which show how and why McCoy suffers his wretched odyssey. Not surprisingly, Wolfe's stylistically exuberant prose also adopts the four novelistic devices central to New Journalism. What results, Wolfe maintains, is the kind of realistic, relevant writing sorely missing in fiction today.

In defending *Bonfire of the Vanities,* Wolfe remains highly critical of contemporary novelists. In a lengthy essay for *Harper's,* "Stalking the Billion-

Footed Beast: A Literary Manifesto for the New Social Novel" (November 1989), he amplifies what he said earlier in *The New Journalism,* namely that American novelists since 1960 have forsaken realism in favor of "myth, fable, parable, legend." Wolfe's latest essay elaborates on the reasons for this shift, beginning with the intelligentsia's long-held disdain for the realistic novel because they viewed it as an unrefined "form that wallows so enthusiastically in the dirt of everyday life and dirty secrets of class envy and that, still worse, is so easily understood and obviously relished by the mob, i. e., the middle class."

Additionally, contends Wolfe, post-1960 novelists accepted Lionel Trilling's view that the realistic novel could no longer describe the impact of society on the individual because its source—the bourgeoisie and the old class order—were disintegrating. But, Wolfe replies, "If we substitute for *class,* in Trilling's formulation, the broader term *status,* that technique has never been more essential in portraying the innermost life of the individual. This is above all true when the subject is the modern city.... The status structure of society has changed, but it has not disappeared for a moment." Finally, Wolfe describes how futile an endeavor the realistic novel seemed to contemporary writers who viewed the world as "chaotic, fragmented, random, discontinuous; in a word, *absurd.*" He agrees with Philip Roth that the novelist could not compete creatively with the actual headlines of tomorrow, but he discounts the conclusion drawn by others that they therefore should not compete. "The answer is not to leave the rude beast, the material, also known as the life around us, to the journalists but to do what journalists do, or are supposed to do, which is to wrestle the beast and bring it to terms."

Tom Wolfe currently lives in New York with his wife, Sheila Berger, whom he married in 1978; they have two children, a daughter born in 1980 and a son born in 1985. Although in recent years Wolfe's literary output has declined, he appears too creative to fade away and too perceptive and articulate—as even his sharpest detractors must concede—to be ignored. More will likely be heard from Wolfe.

Whatever his future literary offerings, Wolfe thus far has delivered a bursting portfolio of provocative observations and thoughts. When students of American culture look back on the last third of the twentieth century, Wolfe may well be the person toward whom they turn. More than any other fiction or nonfiction writer, he has recorded in detail the popular mentality of the period. For this reason his essays seem certain to be restudied. Already,

signs of reevaluation and discussion of his work are evident: once criticism focused on Wolfe's writing style and his school of journalism, but now it looks more to the meaning and implications of his message.

Nor are the style and structure of Wolfe's journalism likely to be forgotten. The engaging, realistic journalism he helped inspire now enlists a growing legion of practitioners. While the "New Journalism" stamp has faded—replaced by "literary journalism," a conceptually broader but more precise designation—the movement continues to enjoy greater acceptance and proliferation. In "Tom Wolfe's Revenge" Chris Harvey observes that "elements of the New Journalism that Wolfe so tirelessly promoted have become as commonplace as the pie chart in many newspapers, ranging from the *New York Times* to the *Oregonian* to the weekly *Washington City Paper.*" To be sure, literary journalism enjoys perhaps its strongest readership approval and in-house, editorial support.

Wolfe's writings have produced penetrating social and cultural insights, raised intriguing journalistic questions, and suggested the vast potential of nonfictional writing when exercised by a stylistically inventive, perceptive author committed to investigative reporting. For these accomplishments Tom Wolfe ranks as one of the premier literary journalists in America.

Interview:

Dorothy Scura, ed., *Conversations with Tom Wolfe* (Jackson: University Press of Mississippi, 1990).

References:

Renata Adler and Gerald Jonas, "The Letter," in Leonard C. Lewin, "Is Fact Necessary? A Sequel to the Herald Tribune-New Yorker Dispute," *Columbia Journalism Review,* 4 (Winter 1966): 29–34;

Albert Bergesen, "From Bauhaus to Our House," *American Journal of Sociology,* 89 (November 1983): 739–741;

Sheri F. Crawford, "Tom Wolfe: Outlaw Gentleman," *Journal of American Culture,* 13 (Summer 1990): 39–50;

David L. Eason, "The New Journalism and the Image-World: Two Modes of Organizing Experience," *Critical Studies in Mass Communication,* 1 (March 1984): 51–65;

Thomas R. Edwards, "The Electric Indian," *Partisan Review,* 36, no. 3 (1969): 535–544;

Chris Harvey, "Tom Wolfe's Revenge," *American Journalism Review* (October 1994): 40–46;

John Hellmann, "Reporting the Fabulous: Representation and Response in the Work of Tom Wolfe," in his *Fables of Fact: The New Journalism as New Fiction* (Urbana: University of Illinois Press, 1981), pp. 101–125;

John Hollowell, "Life in Edge City: Wolfe's New Journalism," in *Fact and Fiction: The New Journalism and the Nonfiction Novel* (Chapel Hill: University of North Carolina Press, 1977), pp. 126–152;

Journal of American Culture, special issue on Wolfe, 14 (Fall 1991);

Journal of Popular Culture, special issue on Wolfe, 9 (Summer 1975);

Richard A. Kallan, "Style and the New Journalism: A Rhetorical Analysis of Tom Wolfe," *Communication Monographs,* 46 (1979): 52–62;

Kallan, "Tom Wolfe," in *A Sourcebook of American Literary Journalism: Representative Writers in an Emerging Genre,* edited by Thomas B. Connery (Westport, Conn.: Greenwood Press, 1992), pp. 249–259;

Barbara Lounsberry, "Tom Wolfe's American Jeremiad," in her *The Art of Fact: Contemporary Artists of Nonfiction* (Westport, Conn.: Greenwood Press, 1990), pp. 37–64;

Dwight Macdonald, "Parajournalism, or Tom Wolfe and His Magic Writing Machine," *New York Review of Books* (26 August 1965): 3–5;

Macdonald, "Parajournalism II: Wolfe and The New Yorker," *New York Review of Books* (3 February 1966): 18–24;

Jack Newfield, "Is There a 'New Journalism?,'" *Columbia Journalism Review* (July/August 1972): 45–47;

Rick Rogoway, "Profile of an Electric Journalist," in *The Magic Writing Machine: Student Probes of the New Journalism,* edited by Everette E. Dennis (Eugene: School of Journalism, University of Oregon, 1971), pp. 17–23;

Doug Shomette, ed., *The Critical Response to Tom Wolfe* (Westport, Conn.: Greenwood Press, 1992);

Robert Sommer, "Tom Wolfe on Modern Architecture: Further Comparison of New Journalism and Social Science," *Journal of Popular Culture,* 18 (Fall 1984): 111–115;

James N. Stull, "The Cultural Gamesmanship of Tom Wolfe," in *Literary Selves: Autobiography and Contemporary American Nonfiction* (Westport, Conn.: Greenwood Press, 1993), pp. 49–63;

Kurt Vonnegut Jr., "Infarcted! Tabescent!," *New York Times Book Review,* 27 June 1965, pp. 4, 38;

Ronald Weber, "Tom Wolfe's Happiness Explosion," *Journal of Popular Culture,* 8 (Summer 1974): 71–79.

Checklist of Further Readings

Adam, G. Stuart. "Notes Towards a Definition of Journalism: Understanding an Old Craft as an Art Form." Saint Petersburg, Fla.: Poynter Institute for Media Studies (The Poynter Papers: No. 2), 1993.

Allot, Miriam. "The Temporal Mode: Four Kinds of Fiction," *Essays in Criticism,* 8 (1958): 214–216.

Anderson, Chris. *Style as Argument: Contemporary American Nonfiction.* Carbondale & Edwardsville: Southern Illinois University Press, 1987.

Anderson, ed. *Literary Nonfiction: Theory, Criticism, Pedagogy.* Carbondale & Edwardsville: Southern Illinois University Press, 1989.

Anderson, Walter Truett. *Reality Isn't What It Used to Be.* New York: HarperCollins, 1990.

Arlen, Michael J. "Notes on the New Journalism," *Atlantic Monthly* (May 1972): 43–47.

Bagdikian, Ben H. *The Information Machines: Their Impact on Men and Media.* New York: Harper & Row, 1971.

Baldwin, James. "Sonny's Blues," in *The Story and Its Writers,* edited by Ann Charters. Boston: St. Martin's Press, 1991.

Balz, Daniel J. "Bad Writing and the New Journalism," *Columbia Journalism Review* (September/October 1972): 51–53.

Balz. "Want to See New Journalism in Newspapers? Well, Don't Hold Your Breath," *Quill* (September 1972): 18–21.

Baritz, Loren. *Backfire: Vietnam—The Myths That Made Us Fight the Illusions That Helped Us Lose, The Legacy That Haunts Us Today.* New York: Ballantine, 1986.

Barry, Jan. "Green Hell, Green Death," in *Unaccustomed Mercy,* edited by W. D. Ehrhart, pp. 28–29. Lubbock: Texas Tech University Press, 1989.

Baumbach, Jonathan. *The Landscape of Nightmare: Studies in the Contemporary Novel.* New York: New York University Press, 1966.

Behar, Jack. "Fiction and History," *Novel,* 3 (1970): 260–265.

Beidler, Philip. *American Literature and the Experience of Vietnam.* Athens: University of Georgia Press, 1982.

Beidler. *Re-Writing America: Vietnam Authors in Their Generation.* Athens: University of Georgia Press, 1991.

Bellamy, Joe David, ed. *Superfiction, or the American Story Transformed.* New York: Random House, 1975.

Bercovitch, Sacvan. *The American Jeremiad.* Madison: University of Wisconsin Press, 1978.

Berner, R. Thomas. "Literary Notions and Utilitarian Reality," *Style,* 16 (Fall 1982): 452–457.

Berner. *Writing Literary Features.* Hillsdale, N.J.: Lawrence Erlbaum Associates, 1988.

Berthoff, Warner. *Fictions and Events: Essays in Criticism and Literary History.* New York: Dutton, 1971.

Brown, Charles H. "New Art Journalism Revisited," *Quill* (March 1972): 18–23.

Brown. "The Rise of the New Journalism," *Current* (June 1972): 31–38.

Brown, David, and W. Richard Bruner, eds. *How I Got That Story.* New York: Dutton, 1967.

Brown, Edith Baker. "A Plea for Literary Journalism," *Harper's Weekly,* 46 (1902): 1558.

Buffum, Richard. "The New Journalism," *Los Angeles Times,* 5 October 1971, II: 1.

Chase, Dennis. "From Lippmann to Irving to New Journalism," *Quill* (August 1972): 19–21.

Chase, W. M. "New Journalism Isn't New: Fact, Fiction and Fraud in American Newspapers," *Stanford Observer* (January 1982): 2–3.

Christianson, F. Scott. "The New Muckraking," *Quill* (July 1972): 10–15.

Coffey, Michael. "Interview with Tim O'Brien," *Publishers Weekly* (16 February 1990): 60–61.

Cohen, Ted. "Metaphor and the Cultivation of Intimacy," *Critical Inquiry,* 5 (Autumn 1978): 3–12.

Compton, Neil. "Hijinks Journalism," *Commentary* (February 1969): 76–78.

Connery, Thomas B. *A Sourcebook of American Literary Journalism: Representative Writers in an Emerging Genre.* Westport, Conn.: Greenwood Press, 1992.

Corbett, Edward P. J. "The Rhetoric of the Closed Hand and the Rhetoric of the Open Fist," *College Composition and Communication,* 20 (1969): 288–296.

Cowley, Malcom, ed. *Writers at Work: The "Paris Review" Interviews.* New York: Viking, 1960.

DeMott, Benjamin. "In and Out of Universal City: Reflections on New Journalism and the Old Fiction," *Antioch Review,* 29 (1969): 7–13.

Dennis, Everette E., ed. *The Magic Writing Machine: Student Probes of the New Journalism.* Eugene: University of Oregon Press, 1971.

Dennis and William L. Rivers. *Other Voices: The New Journalism in America.* San Francisco: Canfield Press, 1974.

Dickstein, Morris. "The Working Press, the Literary Culture and the New Journalism," *Georgia Review,* 30 (1976): 856–877.

Eason, David. "The New Journalism and the Image-World: Two Modes of Organizing Experience," *Critical Studies in Mass Communication,* 1 (1984): 51–65.

Eason. "New Journalism, Metaphor and Culture," *Journal of Popular Culture,* 15 (Spring 1982): 142–149.

Fishkin, Shelly Fisher. *From Fact to Fiction: Journalism and Imaginative Writing in America.* Baltimore & London: Johns Hopkins University Press, 1985.

Fishwick, Marshall, ed. *New Journalism.* Bowling Green, Ohio: Bowling Green University Popular Press, 1975.

Fishwick, ed. "New Journalism," *Journal of Popular Culture,* 9 (1975): 95–151.

Fixx, James F. "The New Journalism," *Saturday Review* (12 February 1966): 65.

Fletcher, Angus, ed. *The Literature of Fact.* New York: Columbia University Press, 1976.

Flippen, Charles C., ed. *Liberating the Media: The New Journalism.* Washington, D.C.: Acropolis Books, 1974.

Ford, Edwin H. *A Bibliography of Literary Journalism in America.* Minneapolis: Burgess, 1937.

Frus, Phyllis. *The Politics and Poetics of Journalistic Narrative: The Timely and the Timeless.* New York: Cambridge University Press, 1994.

Goldstein, Richard. *Reporting the Counterculture.* Boston: Unwin Hyman, 1989.

Good, Howard. *The Journalist as Autobiographer.* Metuchen, N.J.: Scarecrow Press, 1993.

Grant, Gerald. "The 'New Journalism' We Need," *Columbia Journalism Review,* 9 (Spring 1970): 12–16.

Gusdorf, Georges. "Conditions and Limits of Autobiography," in *Autobiography: Essays Theoretical and Critical,* edited by James Olney. Princeton, N.J.: Princeton University Press, 1980.

Hallin, Daniel C. *The "Uncensored" War.* Oxford: Oxford University Press, 1986.

Hanley, Lynne. *Writing War.* Amherst: University of Massachusetts Press, 1991.

Hapgood, Hutchins. "A New Form of Literature," *Bookman,* 21 (1905): 424–447.

Hayes, Harold. "Editor's Notes on the New Journalism," *Esquire* (January 1972): 12.

Hayes, ed. *Smiling through the Apocalypse: Esquire's History of the Sixties.* New York: McCall, 1969.

Hellmann, John. *American Myth and the Legacy of Vietnam.* New York: Columbia University Press, 1986.

Hellmann. *Fables of Fact: The New Journalism as New Fiction.* Urbana: University of Illinois Press, 1981.

Hellmann. "The New Journalism and Vietnam: Memory as Structure in Michael Herr's *Dispatches*," *South Atlantic Quarterly,* 79 (1980): 141–151.

Hernadi, Paul. *Beyond Genre: New Directions in Literary Classification.* Ithaca, N.Y.: Cornell University Press, 1972.

Herzog, Tobey C. *Vietnam War Stories: Innocence Lost.* New York: Routledge, 1992.

Heyne, Eric. "Toward a Theory of Literary Nonfiction," *Modern Fiction Studies,* 33 (Autumn 1987): 479–490.

Hogarth, Paul. *The Artist as Reporter.* New York: Reinhold, 1967.

Hollowell, John. *Fact and Fiction: The New Journalism and the Nonfiction Novel.* Chapel Hill: University of North Carolina Press, 1977.

Horne, A. D., ed. *The Wounded Generation: America after Vietnam.* Englewood Cliffs, N.J.: Prentice-Hall, 1981.

Howe, Quincy. "The New Age of the Journalist-Historian," *Saturday Review* (20 May 1967): 25–27, 69.

Hvistendahl, J. K. "The Reporter as Activist: A Fourth Revolution in Journalism," *Quill* (February 1970): 8–11.

Jensen, Jay. "The New Journalism in Historical Perspective," *Journalism History,* 1 (Summer 1974): 37, 66.

Johnson, Michael L. *The New Journalism: The Underground Press, the Artists of Nonfiction, and Changes in Established Media.* Lawrence: University of Kansas Press, 1971.

Karl, Frederick R. *American Fictions, 1940–1950.* New York: Harper & Row, 1983.

Klinkowitz, Jerome. *Literary Disruptions: The Making of a Post-Contemporary American Fiction.* Urbana: University of Illinois Press, 1975.

Klinkowitz and John Somer, eds. *Innovative Fiction: Stories for the Seventies.* New York: Dell, 1972.

Klinkowitz and Somer, eds. *Writing under Fire: Stories of the Vietnam War.* New York: Dell, 1978.

Kramer, Mark, and Norman Sims, eds. *Literary Journalism: A New Collection of the Best American Nonfiction.* New York: Ballantine, 1995.

Lee, Gerald Stanley. "Journalism as a Basis for Literature," *Atlantic* (February 1900): 231–237.

Lomperis, Timothy J. *Reading the Wind: The Literature of the Vietnam War.* Durham, N.C.: Duke University Press, 1987.

Lounsberry, Barbara. *The Art of Fact: Contemporary Artists of Nonfiction.* Westport, Conn.: Greenwood Press, 1990.

Lounsberry and Gay Talese. *Writing Creative Nonfiction: The Literature of Reality.* New York: HarperCollins, 1996.

Many, Paul. "Toward a History of Literary Journalism," *Michigan Academician,* 24 (1992): 359–369.

Masterson, Mark. "The New Journalism," *Quill* (February 1971): 15–17.

McCord, Phyliss Frus. *News and the Novel: A Theory and a History of the Relation between Journalism and Fiction.* dissertation, New York University, 1985.

McCormick, J. "The Non-Fiction Novel," *Yale Literary Magazine* (May 1966): 22–24.

McHam, David. "The Authentic New Journalists," *Quill* (September 1971): 9–14.

McKerns, Joseph P. "The History of American Journalism: A Bibliographical Essay," *American Studies,* 15 (1976): 17–34.

Mills, Nicolaus, ed. *The New Journalism: An Historical Anthology.* New York: McGraw-Hill, 1974.

Murray, Donald M. "From *What* to *Why:* The Changing Style of Newswriting," *Style,* 16 (Fall 1982): 448–451.

Myers, Thomas. *Walking Point: American Narratives of Vietnam.* New York: Oxford University Press, 1988.

"The New Journalism," *Journal of Popular Culture,* 9 (Summer 1975): 99–249.

Newfield, Jack. "Is There a New Journalism?," *Columbia Journalism Review,* 11 (July/August 1972): 45–47.

Peer, Elizabeth. "New Journalism Now," *Newsweek* (31 March 1975): 67.

Pinkerton, W. Stewart Jr. "New Journalism: Believe It or Not," in *The Press,* edited by A. Kent MacDougall. New York: Dow Jones Books, 1972.

Ridgeway, James. "The New Journalism," *American Libraries* (June 1971): 585–592.

Robinson, L. W., Harold Hayes, Gay Talese, and Tom Wolfe. "The New Journalism: A Panel Discussion," *Writer's Digest* (January 1970): 19, 32–35.

Scanlon, Paul, ed. *Reporting: The Rolling Stone Style.* New York: Anchor/Doubleday, 1977.

Self, Charles. "The New Journalism?," *Quill and Scroll* (December/January 1973): 10–11.

Sims, Norman. "A New Generation of 'New' Journalists," *Quill* (July–August 1982): 9–14.

Sims, ed. *Literary Journalism in the Twentieth Century.* New York: Oxford University Press, 1990.

Sims, ed. *The Literary Journalists.* New York: Ballantine, 1984.

Sims and Mark Kramer, eds. *Literary Journalism: A New Collection of the Best American Nonfiction.* New York: Ballantine, 1995.

Tebbel, John W. "The 'Old' New Journalism," *Saturday Review* (13 March 1971): 96–97.

Warnock, John, ed. *Representing Reality: Readings in Literary Nonfiction.* New York: St. Martin's Press, 1989.

Webb, Joseph M. "Historical Perspective on New Journalism," *Journalism History,* 1 (Summer 1974): 38–42, 60.

Weber, Ronald. "Art-Journalism Revisited," *South Atlantic Quarterly,* 78 (1979): 275–289.

Weber. "Letting Subjects Grow: Literary Nonfiction From the *New Yorker,*" *Antioch Review,* 36 (Fall 1978): 486–499.

Weber. *The Literature of Fact: Literary Nonfiction in American Writing.* Athens: Ohio University Press, 1980.

Weber. "Moon Talk," *Journal of Popular Culture,* 9 (Summer 1975): 142–152.

Weber. *The Reporter as Artist: A Look at the New Journalism Controversy.* New York: Hastings House, 1974.

Wiegand, William. "The 'Non-Fiction Novel,'" *New Mexico Quarterly,* 3 (Autumn 1967): 243–257.

Wolfe, Tom. "The Birth of the 'New Journalism': Eyewitness Report by Tom Wolfe," *New York* (14 February 1972): 30–45.

Wolfe. "The New Journalism," *Bulletin of the American Society of Newspaper Editors* (September 1970): 1, 18–23.

Wolfe and E. W. Johnson, eds. *The New Journalism.* New York: Harper & Row, 1973.

Zavarzadeh, Mas'ud. *The Mythopoeic Reality: The Postwar American Nonfiction Novel.* Urbana: University of Illinois Press, 1976.

Zinsser, William. *Speaking of Journalism: 12 Writers and Editors Talk about Their Work.* New York: HarperCollins, 1994.

Contributors

Edd Applegate ....*Middle Tennessee State University*

Paul Ashdown ....*University of Tennessee*

David Bennett..*University of Southern Mississippi*

R. Thomas Berner ....*Pennsylvania State University*

Douglas Birkhead ....*University of Utah*

Ginger Rudeseal Carter ....*Georgia College & State University*

Lloyd Chiasson ....*Nicholls State University*

Jim Collins ....*Dartmouth College*

Thomas B. Connery ....*University of Saint Thomas*

David R. Davies ....*University of Southern Mississippi*

Michael J. Dillon ....*State University of New York at New Paltz*

Howard Good ....*State University of New York at New Paltz*

Dan R. Jones..*University of Houston*

Richard A. Kallan ....*California State Polytechnic University, Pomona*

A. J. Kaul ....*University of Southern Mississippi*

Barbara Lounsberry ....*University of Northern Iowa*

Jack Lule..*Lehigh University*

Jack A. Nelson...*Brigham Young University*

John J. Pauly ....*Saint Louis University*

Sam G. Riley...*Virginia Polytechnic Institute and State University*

Donald J. Ringnalda...*University of Saint Thomas*

James Rogers ....*University of Massachusetts*

Robert Schmuhl...*University of Notre Dame*

Norman Sims ....*University of Massachusetts*

Linda Steiner ....*Rutgers University*

James Stewart..*Nicholls State University*

William I. Sutley ....*University of Southern Mississippi*

Susan Weill..*University of Southern Mississippi*

Cumulative Index

Dictionary of Literary Biography, Volumes 1-185
Dictionary of Literary Biography Yearbook, 1980-1996
Dictionary of Literary Biography Documentary Series, Volumes 1-16

Cumulative Index

DLB before number: *Dictionary of Literary Biography*, Volumes 1-185
Y before number: *Dictionary of Literary Biography Yearbook*, 1980-1996
DS before number: *Dictionary of Literary Biography Documentary Series*, Volumes 1-16

H

K

M

Q

X